Study Guide and Practice Tests

Tina E. Stern

Georgia Perimeter College

PSYCHOLOGY

Sixth Edition

Carole Wade

Dominican College of San Rafael

Carol Tavris

PRENTICE HALL, Upper Saddle River, New Jersey 07458

©2000 by PRENTICE-HALL, INC.
Upper Saddle River, New Jersey 07458

ISBN-0-321-05956-5

Printed in the United States of America

CONTENTS

HOW TO STUDY

TIRED??

* of reading a chapter and not remembering any of the contents five minutes later?

* of fighting against drooping eyelids and losing?

* of thinking you've studied enough only to find that you can't remember anything that's on the test?

* of studying definitions and terms only to find that the test questions don't ask for definitions and terms; instead, they ask for examples that you never saw in the text?

* of test scores that don't reflect what you know?

I'd like to be able to say, "Guaranteed, 100%!!! Follow these simples guidelines and you, too, can get a 4.0! Simple! Easy! Money-back guarantee! Teachers and parents will love you, and it will change your life!!" Of course, I cannot make those claims, but I can say the following: "**YOU CAN** change the above behaviors **IF** you read **AND** attempt to use the techniques that are described in this section of the Study Guide." Changing your study habits is like going on a diet. First, you must know the details of the diet: How does it propose to help you eat healthier? **BUT** knowing how the diet works and what you are supposed to eat will **NOT** cause you to develop healthier eating habits. You must implement the diet. In other words, to receive the benefits, you must **DO IT!** It is not enough to know what you are supposed to do...you must actually do it! It is the same thing with changing your study habits. It is not enough to know the changes you need to make...you must **MAKE THE CHANGES!**

STEP 1: DIAGNOSING THE PROBLEM

Some students have developed study skills that work well for them, and they do not wish to change their habits. Some students have many study skills with which they are generally satisfied, but they have one or two areas that need improvement. Other students have difficulty with a number of their study skills. Below is a list of some study skills. Review this list and try to identify whether you are satisfied or dissatisfied with each of these abilities. The preface to this Study Guide focuses on study skills and how to use this manual. As you read the preface, focus on the areas in which you need improvement. If this chapter does not cover that particular area, identify and **USE** the resources that are available on your campus to get assistance. **DON'T** ignore study problems. It is unlikely that they will just disappear on their own or improve simply by your trying to do more of what you are already doing!

Check all of the following areas that are problems for you:

Reading the text _____
    Comprehending the material _____
    Concentrating while reading _____
    Identifying what is important _____
    Recalling what you have read _____
    Being distracted easily _____
Time Management _____
    Not planning your time _____
    Not having enough time to study _____
    Not using the time you have allotted to study _____
    Underestimating the time you need to study _____
    Difficulty saying no to other plans _____
    Not sticking to your study schedule _____
Getting the Most out of Class _____
    Trouble paying attention in class _____
    Not going to classes _____
    Not understanding what is important _____
Taking Notes _____
    Your notes aren't helpful _____
    Your notes are disorganized _____
Taking Tests _____
    Trouble recalling informatior _____
    Test anxiety _____
    Trouble on multiple choice questions _____
    Trouble on fill-in-the-blank questions _____
    Trouble on essay questions _____
    Trouble predicting what will be on the test _____
    Trouble going from definitions to examples _____

Identifying your problem areas should help you to focus on the skills that you most need to improve. Think about your problem areas as you read the preface and apply the information to your particular situation.

ON BEING A LEARNER or DON'T STOP BEFORE YOU BEGIN!

What was the last new skill you tried to learn? Were you learning to play basketball, softball, tennis, the guitar? Or were you learning a new language? Whatever you were learning to do, it is very likely that you were not very good at it at first. In fact, you were probably **BAD** at it! That is how it is supposed to be! Your ability to do something well depends on gaining experience with that activity; the more you do it, the better you become at the task. This means that it is necessary to go beyond the beginning period of learning when the new skill is difficult and awkward and you are not very good at it. This can be frustrating for students who often think they already should know how to study, and if they have to learn new study skills, they should be learned quickly and easily. During the early stages of learning a new skill, a person may be tempted to say, "This isn't working," or "This will never work" or "These techniques feel so artificial." **RESIST** those thoughts. Learning these skills may be difficult at first, but no more difficult than continuing to use skills that you already know **DO NOT WORK!!** If you want to change any long-standing behavior, you will have to tolerate the early phases of learning when the new behaviors won't yet feel like "your own." In college, graduate school and employment, you will find that persistence pays. So, **RESIST** returning to your old habits and **PERSIST** with learning the new habits. Don't stop before you begin...give it some time.

MASTERING YOUR MEMORY (OR AT LEAST GETTING THE UPPER HAND!)

A great deal of the information contained in most study skills manuals and courses is based on what is known about how human memory works. Experimental psychologists study memory and how it works; therefore, it is appropriate in this course for you to understand the findings of scientific research on memory and how they apply to **YOU**. Ignore these findings at your peril! This section will present a few general findings about memory that are particularly relevant to your studying. This information comes directly from Chapter 10, which will discuss memory in more detail. Information about memory has applicability not only to your psychology class, but to all your classes.

KEEPING INFORMATION IN SHORT-TERM MEMORY

The three-box model of memory suggests there are three types of memory: sensory memory, short-term memory (STM) and long-term memory (LTM). Sensory memory is a very brief type of memory that lasts less than a second. Sensory memory is important because if information does not get noticed in sensory memory, it cannot be transferred into either short-term or long-term memory. The limits of short-term memory are known. Short-term memory can hold seven (plus or minus two) pieces of information for about 30 seconds or less. A person can extend the amount of time information is held in STM by repeating it over and over (this is called maintenance rehearsal); however, once you stop repeating the information, it is quickly lost. Think of times that you have called information to get the number of the nearest pizza place. You repeat the number over and over and hope your roommate does not come along and ask to borrow your comb, because if your repetition is interrupted, you will forget the number. Many professors believe that most students study in ways that get information into short-term memory, but not in ways that get it into long-term memory.

GETTING INFORMATION INTO LONG-TERM MEMORY

Long-term memory can hold an infinite amount of information for an unlimited amount of time. **THAT'S** where you want to store all the information you are studying!! The important question becomes how to transfer information from short-term memory into long-term memory. The transfer of memory from STM into LTM relies upon the use of elaborative rehearsal. Elaborative rehearsal involves more than the simple repetition of information required by short-term memory; it requires that you make the information meaningful. Making information meaningful requires more than saying "This has deep meaning to me." Meaningfulness can be accomplished by interacting with the material in any **ACTIVE** way. Some examples of ways to make information meaningful include putting it into a story, putting it into a rhyme (i.e. "30 days has September"), forming visual images of the information, forming associations with people or things already familiar to you or associating information to other pieces of information, organizing it into categories, putting it into your own words, explaining it to someone else--almost anything that you do with the information that is **ACTIVE**. Being **ACTIVE** with the information and aiming for **UNDERSTANDING** and not simple repetition of the material are the keys. Almost anything you do with the material that is active will help move it into long-term memory. Passively reading the material will not help the information transfer into long-term memory, and this is the technique most students use.

CRITICAL THINKING AND LONG-TERM MEMORY

Critical thinking is emphasized throughout this textbook. Every chapter includes information on how to approach that topic critically. Critical thinking requires organizing, analyzing and evaluating information. This may sound suspiciously like elaborative rehearsal. Critical thinking is important for many reasons. In the context of study skills, critical thinking is important because it involves the same processes that promote the transfer of information into long-term memory.

GETTING MORE INFORMATION INTO SHORT-TERM AND LONG-TERM MEMORY

One last piece of information about memory has to do with expanding the amount of information contained in short-term memory. To get information into LTM, it must pass through STM, and we know that STM holds only about seven (plus or minus two) units of information. That does not seem like a practical system, since most text book chapters seem to contain hundreds of pieces of new information in each chapter! Short-term memory holds **units** or chunks of information, and your chance to increase the amount of information being held in STM is to include more information in each chunk. For example, you can change 26 separate pieces of information (which far exceeds the capacity of STM) into one piece of information (well within the capacity of STM) by chunking! Whenever you use the word "alphabet" to refer to 26 separate letters, you are chunking. If you organize the information you are studying into categories, or chunks, you will improve your chances of getting more information into LTM in two ways: 1) you will increase the information contained in the units getting into STM, and 2) you will be making the information meaningful by the act of organizing it into the chunks! You can't lose! Making outlines is a good way to chunk information. Outlines naturally organize information into categories (chunks) and subcategories. This study guide presents the information in ways that help you to organize information into chunks, which also helps make the information meaningful.

STUDYING WITH THE SQ3R OR STAYING AWAKE, STAYING ACTIVE AND OPENING THE DOOR TO LONG-TERM MEMORY

The SQ3R method was developed by Francis Robinson, a psychology professor at Ohio State University. It is a method of reading assignments that implements many techniques that promote the transfer of information into long-term memory. The letters "SQ3R" stand for survey, question, read, receive, review.

SURVEY
Before you read a chapter or reading assignment, it is important to survey what is in the chapter and how the information is organized. You can do this by simply looking over the headings or the chapter outlines at the beginning of each chapter. This Study Guide also provides more detailed preview outlines for this purpose. It is important that you survey the information before you read, because surveying turns what otherwise would seem like hundreds of independent facts (which far exceeds the capacity of STM) into a much smaller number (probably five to nine--text book authors know how memory works) of main topics identified in separate headings. Once you have seen the main headings, you have an organizational structure to begin your reading. This helps you organize the information when you begin reading (remember that organizing is one way to make information meaningful, which transfers it into LTM). Surveying a chapter in the text is like going on a trip. Before you arrive at a city you do not know, it is very helpful to look at a map. You quickly can see the location of the airport, your hotel, downtown, the river and the three important sites you want to see. This orients you to your journey. If you do not look at a map before your arrival, you are wandering around without knowing where you are going. You do not want to wander around a 40-page chapter that contains a great deal of information without knowing where you are going.

QUESTION
Assume you are taking a college entrance exam that contains a comprehension section. There are several paragraphs for you to read, and then you are to answer five questions about the reading. Would you read the questions before you read the paragraphs, or would you read the paragraphs and then begin to try to answer the questions? Most of you would read the questions first, so that as you read the paragraphs, you could keep the questions in mind and look for the answers while you read. The reasons for formulating questions before you read your text are: 1) to help you read with a purpose, and 2) to help you be more active while you read.

After you have surveyed the chapter, formulate questions by converting the headings, key terms and definitions into questions. For example, "The Major Psychological Perspectives" is a subheading in Chapter 1. "What are the names and key concepts of the major psychological perspectives?" would be an example of changing that subheading into a question. This Study Guide has listed the relevant learning objectives for each section below the preview outline for that section of text. In addition, you should try to formulate additional questions and write them on a separate piece of paper. The intention is that you will write the answers to all these questions while you read the chapter. This helps you read with a purpose: your purpose is to answer the questions. This also helps you to be active while you read. You are being active by looking for the answers to the questions **AND** by writing down the answers as you find them. You will also have answers to all the learning objectives in writing when you go to study for quizzes and exams.

READ
You are now ready to read. You have surveyed the chapter in order to know where you are going and how the chapter is organized. You have formulated your questions in order to know what you are looking for as you read. As you read, you will be organizing the information and answering the questions. These are both ways to increase the transfer of information into long-term memory. As you begin your reading, look at your first question. Open your textbook to the part of the chapter that applies to the question and read to answer that question.

RECITE
After you have surveyed the reading assignment to get the general idea of its content, have turned the first heading into a question, and have read that section to answer the question, you are now ready to recite. Reciting helps make information meaningful (did you ever notice that when you speak in class, you tend to remember the information you spoke or asked about?). Also, it is another way that you can be active (which also makes the information meaningful). Reciting requires that you put the information into your own words, and it is an excellent way to identify what you don't yet understand. There are a number of ways to recite.

Using the learning objectives and the questions that you have formulated, recite aloud the answers to the questions (without looking at the answers). You can give definitions or examples of key terms, terms that are listed in bold, or terms that are underlined as a vehicle for reciting information. You can recite responses to learning objectives. You can use the flash cards in this Study Guide to explain key concepts and terms, and then check your responses against the answers on the flash cards. Explaining information to other people, either classmates or patient friends who are willing to help, is also a good way to recite the information. Explaining the information to others also allows you to identify areas that you do not understand well. Remember, your recitation of information should be in your own words and should attempt to give examples of the concepts you are describing. If you simply try to memorize definitions given in the text and recite these definitions, you are simply camouflaging maintenance rehearsal.

Remember, getting information into long-term memory involves meaning--so make sure you understand the material and can make it "your own" to get it into long-term memory.

REVIEW

The final step in the SQ3R approach is to review the material again. Frequent reviews, even brief reviews, are among the important keys to learning. After at least one hour, review the material once more. This can be done by going over the main points of the chapter (with your book closed), going over the answers to the questions you have written (without looking at them), reviewing key terms and concepts. Limit your reviews to about five minutes. Reviews can be used in other ways too. Begin each study session with a five-minute review. Before each class, review notes from the previous class for five minutes. At the end of every class, review your notes for five minutes.

SUMMARY

The SQ3R method incorporates the information that psychologists know about how people learn and remember. The key points to remember include: ***BE ACTIVE, MAKE INFORMATION MEANINGFUL, INTERACT WITH THE INFORMATION, AIM FOR UNDERSTANDING NOT JUST REPETITION, THINK CRITICALLY.*** All this can be achieved by writing, talking, thinking, making outlines, forming associations, developing questions and examples and putting definitions in your own words. The SQ3R method suggests that these goals can be achieved if you:

1. Survey the information: Use headings and chapter summaries to orient yourself to the information you plan to read. Give the information an organizational structure.
2. Question: Turn the headings, terms, concepts into questions.
3. Read: Read each section to answer the specific questions that you asked. Write your answers on a separate sheet of paper.
4. Recite: Close your book and rehearse the information contained in the section by answering the relevant questions or giving examples of key terms or concepts.
5. Review: After at least an hour-long break, close your book, turn over your notes and list the main points of the chapter and the answers to your questions.

REMEMBER, this may feel awkward or cumbersome at first, **BUT** the more you use this method, the easier it will become.

WHEN AND WHERE TO STUDY

In many courses, several weeks can pass betweer tests. You might wonder whether it is better to study intensely the night before the test or to spread out your studying time. Memory research clearly suggests that "cramming" just doesn't work. You may know this from personal experience. Rather than studying for hours and hours just before the test, it is much more effective to study as you go along in the course.

In terms of when to study, the best time to study is immediately after class. **BEFORE** going to class, you should preview the material to be covered, form general questions and read the text. Study the subject that was covered as soon after the lecture as possible. You will find it easier to master the material and will have an opportunity to test your understanding of the lecture if you study right away. The procedure of continuously studying fairly small chunks will also help you to avoid the nightmare of the infrequent studier--the sudden realization that you don't understand any of what you have been covering for the last few weeks. If you study for a short period after each lecture, you will not have to worry about this. You will also find that tomorrow's lecture will be easier to understand if you study today's material and master the essential points covered by your teacher. Most professors structure lectures so that each one builds on earlier lectures and readings. Studying as you go along will guarantee that you are well prepared to get the most out of each new lecture. It is also a good idea to set a specific time to study. Even if it is for a short time, you should study at a regular time every day.

In terms of where to study, many students indicate that they have difficulty concentrating. Upon further examination, it seems that many students study with their T.V. or CD player on at the same time and place their roommates are having a snack or are on the phone. Some general guidelines about where to study include:
1. Limit the places that you study to one or two special locations. These could be the library, a desk or a designated study area. They are special in the sense that they should be places where the only thing you do there is study. That means you should not study in places where you regularly do something else (such as the dining room table or bed).
2. Make these places free from distractions. Distractions like the T.V., telephone or friends can cause studying to be abandoned.
3. Set a specific time to begin studying and then study in that same place every day. In that way, that place will become a cue to study.

OTHER SKILLS THAT INFLUENCE STUDYING

Many skills influence study habits. The diagnostic check list at the beginning of this section identifies some of the skills that students must possess to study effectively. Skills that affect studying include the following: time management, note-taking, test-preparation, test-taking, stress-management, using the library, dealing with professors and classroom participation. All of these abilities are important. In fact, they are so important that entire books have been devoted to helping students develop these skills. Many colleges and universities offer various types of academic assistance, from courses on study skills to individual counseling on study skills. One of the survival skills necessary for college students is to be aware of the services offered by your institution and to make use of them as needed. If you have identified problem areas that influence your performance, you have several choices: find a book on study skills in your library, look for courses at your school that deal with study skills or identify other campus resources that are available to assist you in developing these abilities.

THE BEST WAY TO USE THIS STUDY GUIDE

This Study Guide is structured to incorporate the research information on learning and memory. Each chapter is set up so that students can easily utilize the SQ3R method. The structure of the Study Guide is designed so students can be actively involved in their learning.

LEARNING OBJECTIVES

Learning Objectives begin each chapter. Knowing the main objectives for each chapter can help students to know what to look for as they read the chapter and to discern the most important aspects of each chapter. Students should read the Learning Objectives **BEFORE** they begin reading the chapter.

CONCEPT MAPS AND CHAPTER SUMMARIES

Following the Learning Objectives, each chapter has a concept map and chapter summary. Broad concepts are identified and the concept map presents a visual display of relationships that exist among the concepts. This allows students to identify the main chunks, or ideas, in the chapter along with the subdivisions that come underneath each main concept. This provides a general overview to the chapter. The chapter summary uses a narrative format to tell the student what the chapter will cover. Both the concept map and the chapter summaries give the student the overall survey (the "S" in SQ3R) to the entire chapter.

SECTION-BY-SECTION PREVIEW OUTLINES

The entire chapter is then broken down by section. Each section of the chapter is presented in a general outline format, which students are intended to examine **BEFORE** they read the chapter. Once again, students should preview or survey a section of text before they read it. The outline format is used to help students organize the section of the chapter into main topic areas. It is suggested that students use the SQ3R method for each section of the text before going on to the next section. The preview outlines have some blank spaces in them. Some key terms and concepts have been left blank so that students may look for the terms during their reading. While students read the text, they should find the terms that fit the blanks in the outline.

SECTION-BY-SECTION LEARNING OBJECTIVES

The Learning Objectives that relate to each section of the text are listed below the preview outline for each section so that students can look for the answers as they read. Students can also formulate additional questions on a separate sheet of paper by using headings, key terms and concepts. For example, empirical evidence is a highlighted term in Chapter 1. "How is empirical evidence different from other types of evidence?" is an example of using a term as the basis of a question. Students should examine all these questions before reading the text and answer them while reading that particular section of text. This represents the "Q" or question aspect of the SQ3R.

CROSSWORD PUZZLES

Each chapter has a crossword puzzle that utilizes key terms, figures or concepts from the chapter. This is another way students can attempt to make the information meaningful, interact with it actively and improve the transfer of information into long-term memory.

FLASH CARDS

Each chapter has tables with key terms. The reverse sides of the tables gives the definitions of the terms. The tables are designed so they can be cut out and used as flash cards. Students can use the flash cards to review the information and to test themselves. The key terms can be turned into questions (the "Q" in SQ3R) and they can be recited (an "R"s in SQ3R).

TABLES

Many chapters have tables that help students organize, categorize and form associations to the information in the chapters. The completed table will be a great study aid, but the act of completing the table is just as important; it is another way to make the information meaningful.

FIVE PRACTICE TESTS

Each chapter has five practice tests that represent four different testing methods. All practice tests try to tap into different types of thinking skills. Practice Tests 1 and 2 are multiple choice tests. Practice Test 1 requires that students know definitions, terms, concepts and figures. The second practice test requires students to identify, analyze, interpret, compare, contrast and synthesize information. Practice Tests 3 and 4 are new features of this study guide and they were added because they give students still another way to test their knowledge. Practice Test 3 is a short answer test and requires that students recall (rather than just recognize) information from the chapter. Practice Test 4 is a true false test. The fifth practice test requires that students apply, analyze and synthesize the information in essay or short-answer responses.

ANNOTATED ANSWER KEYS

Answer Keys for all practice tests and for the crossword puzzles are presented at the end of the Study Guide. They were separated from the chapters to encourage students to try to answer the questions before they look at the key. Annotated answer keys are included for Practice Tests 2 and 5. Answer keys for Practice Test 2 contain explanations for correct and incorrect answers. This can help students understand the material, analyze the questions, and identify problem-solving strategies. Answers for Practice Test 1 are keyed to page numbers in the text.

CONCLUSION

This Study Guide has been developed utilizing psychological research findings in the areas of learning and memory. As a beginning psychology student, you have the opportunity to apply the findings of psychological research to your lives. In essence, that is the goal of this course: for you to learn the information, think about it critically and make use of it in your life.

CHAPTER 1

What Is Psychology?

LEARNING OBJECTIVES

After studying this chapter, you should be able to do the following:

1. Define psychology.

2. Distinguish psychology from pseudoscience and "psychobabble."

3. Summarize the relationship between the discipline of psychology and public opinion.

4. Explain eight guidelines for critical-thinking.

5. Summarize the early history and development of psychology and the role of empirical evidence.

6. Describe the aims and methods of structuralism and functionalism.

7. Describe the basic ideas of psychoanalysis.

8. Describe the major principles of the biological, learning, cognitive, psychodynamic, and sociocultural perspectives in psychology.

9. Discuss humanistic psychology and feminist psychology.

10. Distinguish between applied and basic psychology.

11. Discuss and give examples of the concerns of various specialties in psychology.

12. Distinguish between a psychotherapist, a psychoanalyst, a psychiatrist, a clinical psychologist and other practicing mental health professionals.

13. Identify basic areas of agreement among psychologists.

CHAPTER CONCEPT MAP

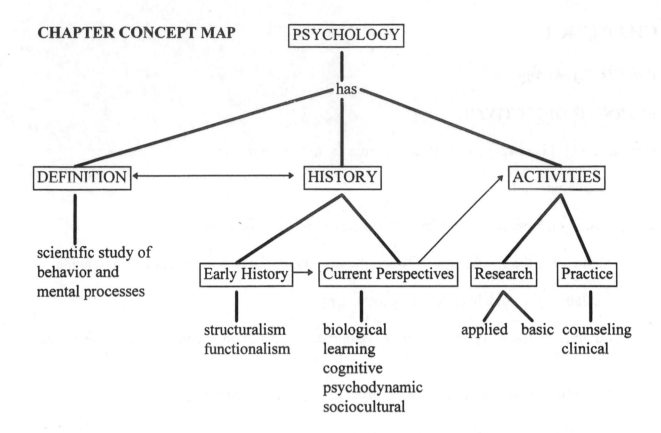

BRIEF CHAPTER SUMMARY

Chapter 1 defines psychology and follows the historical and disciplinary roots of the field to its current perspectives, specialty areas and activities. Five current perspectives and two important movements are identified. The current perspectives include the biological perspective, the learning perspective, the cognitive perspective, the psychodynamic perspective and the sociocultural perspective. Each perspective reflects a different emphasis and approach to understanding human behavior. A review of the specialty areas within the field helps students appreciate that psychology includes many diverse topics. The practice of psychology, which helps people with mental health problems, is discussed, and a description of practitioners, both within the field of psychology and outside it, is given. Critical thinking guidelines are described, and students are encouraged to understand and apply these as they read the text. The complexity of human behavior requires that psychology students resist simplistic thinking and the search for simple answers.

PREVIEW OUTLINE AND REVIEW QUESTIONS

Before you read the chapter, review the preview outline and the Learning Objectives for each section of the text. Answer all questions as you read the text.

SECTION 1 - PSYCHOLOGY, PSEUDOSCIENCE, AND POPULAR OPINION (PP. 2-4) AND SECTION 2 - THINKING CRITICALLY AND CREATIVELY ABOUT PSYCHOLOGY (PP. 5-13)

I. **PSYCHOLOGY, PSEUDOSCIENCE, AND POPULAR OPINION**
    A. **Psychology** - scientific study of *behavior* and *mental processes* and how they are affected by an organism's physical state, mental state and the external environment
    B. **Psychobabble** - pseudoscience covered by veneer of psychological language
        1. Psychology is based on *research* evidence, popular opinion is not
        2. Psychobabble confirms existing beliefs, psychology challenges them and deepens our understanding of accepted facts

II. **THINKING CRITICALLY AND CREATIVELY ABOUT PSYCHOLOGY**
    A. **Critical thinking** - ability and willingness to assess claims and make objective judgments on the basis of well-supported reasons and evidence rather than emotion and anecdote; the basis of all science
    B. **Eight critical-thinking guidelines**
        1. Ask questions; be willing to wonder
        2. Define your terms
        3. Examine the evidence
        4. Analyze assumptions and biases
        5. Avoid emotional reasoning
        6. Don't oversimplify
        7. Consider other interpretations
        8. Tolerate uncertainty

Answer these Learning Objectives while you read Sections 1 and 2.

1. Define psychology.

2. Distinguish psychology from pseudoscience and "psychobabble."

3. Summarize the relationship between the discipline of psychology and public opinion.

4. Explain eight guidelines for critical-thinking.

SECTION 3 - PSYCHOLOGY'S PAST: FROM THE ARMCHAIR TO THE LABORATORY (PP. 13-17)

III.   **PSYCHOLOGY'S PAST: FROM THE ARMCHAIR TO THE LABORATORY**
   A.   **Early history**
      1.   Not a formal discipline until the 19th century
      2.   Most great thinkers asked questions that today are called psychological
      3.   Today's psychologists describe, predict, understand, and modify behavior
      4.   Did not rely on empirical evidence; sometimes they were right, but sometimes they were wrong as in the case of _____
   B.   **The birth of modern psychology**
      1.   Some researchers started to use the scientific method
      2.   Wilhelm _____ is considered the "father of psychology"
      3.   Wundt used trained introspection, established the first psychology laboratory, and published his findings in a scholarly journal
   C.   **Three early psychologies**
      1.   Structuralism and E.B. _____
         a.   Popularized Wundt's ideas in the United States
         b.   Structuralism used introspection to analyze sensations, images and feelings into their most basic elements
      2.   Functionalism and William James
         a.   Critical of structuralism and introspection because the brain and mind are constantly changing
         b   Interested in how and why behavior occurs; causes and consequences of behavior
         c.   Influenced by Darwin and asked how certain attributes enhance survival and adapt to the environment
         d   Used a variety of methods and studied a broader range of subjects
      3.   Psychoanalysis and Sigmund Freud
         a.   Believed that patients' symptoms had mental, not bodily, causes
         b.   Unconscious part of mind has strong influence on behavior

Answer these Learning Objectives while you read Section 3.

5.   Summarize the early history and development of psychology and the role of empirical evidence.

6.   Describe the aims and methods of structuralism and functionalism.

7.   Describe the basic ideas of psychoanalysis.

IV.   PSYCHOLOGY'S PRESENT: BEHAVIOR, BODY, MIND, AND CULTURE
   A.   **The major psychological perspectives**
      1.   The biological perspective
         a.   Examines how bodily events interact with the environment to produce perceptions, memories and behavior
         c.   Related to _____ psychology, which examines how evolutionary past may explain some present behaviors and psychological traits
      2.   The learning perspective
         a.   Behaviorist focus
            (1)   Examines how the environment and experience affect a person's actions
            (2)   Does not use the mind to explain behavior: they study only what they can observe and measure directly
         b.   Social-cognitive focus
            (1)   Combines _____ with research on mental processes like thoughts, values, expectations, and intentions
            (2)   Expands behaviorism beyond the study of behavior to include learning by observation, insight, imitation
      3.   The cognitive perspective
         a.   Emphasizes what goes on in people's head; reasoning, remembering, understanding, problem-solving, explaining
         b.   Shows how thoughts and feelings affect actions
         c.   Uses new methods for studying these phenomena
         c.   One of the strongest forces in psychology today
      4.   The sociocultural perspective
         a.   Focuses on the social and cultural forces outside the individual that shape every aspect of behavior
         b.   Social psychologists focus on social rules and roles, and on the influence of groups, friends, lovers, and others
         c.   Cultural psychologists examine how cultural rules and values affect people's development, behavior, and feelings
      5.   The psychodynamic perspective
         a.   Deals with unconscious dynamics within the individual, such as inner forces, conflicts, or instinctual energy
         b.   Based on Freud's theory of _____, but other psychodynamic theories also exist
         c.   Focuses on unconscious origins of self-defeating behavior
         d.   Language, methods, standards of evidence differ from other approaches

5

B. **Two influential movements in psychology**
    1.   Humanistic psychology
        a.   Rejects _____ perspective as too pessimistic and behaviorism as too mechanistic
        b.   Rejects determinism by the unconscious (psychoanalysis) or by the environment (behaviorism); believes in free will
        c.   Goal of humanism is to help people express themselves and reach their full potential
        d.   Not a dominant movement, but it has had a strong influence in and out of the field
        e.   Greatest influence has been in the "human potential" and self-help movements
    2.   Feminist psychology
        a.   Identifies biases in research and psychotherapy
        b.   Feminist psychologists may identify with any of the major perspectives
        c.   Analyzes _____ relations and behavior of the sexes
        d.   Motivates the study of new topics such as _____, menstruation
        e.   Reminds us that research and psychotherapy are social processes, affected by all the attitudes and values that people bring to any endeavor

Answer these Learning Objectives while you read Section 4.

8.   Describe the major principles of the following perspectives:

biological

learning

cognitive

psychodynamic

sociocultural

9.   Discuss humanistic psychology and feminist psychology.

SECTION 5 - WHAT PSYCHOLOGISTS DO (PP. 22-27) AND
SECTION 6 - THE MOSAIC OF PSYCHOLOGY (P. 27)

V.   **WHAT PSYCHOLOGISTS DO**
    A.   **Overview of professional activities**
        1.   Teach and conduct research in colleges and universities
        2.   Provide health or mental health services (psychological practice)
        3.   Conduct research or apply its findings in nonacademic settings
        4.   Combination of the above
    B.   **Psychological research**
        1.   _____ psychology - research that seeks knowledge for its own sake
        2.   Applied psychology - research concerned with practical uses of knowledge
        3.   Some major nonclinical specialties in psychology
            a.   Experimental psychologists - conduct laboratory studies of learning, motivation, emotion, sensation and perception, physiology, and cognition
            b.   _____ psychologists - study principles that explain learning and look for ways to improve educational systems
            c.   Developmental psychologists - study how people change and grow over time physically, mentally and socially over the life span
            d.   Industrial/organizational psychologists - study behavior in the workplace
            e.   _____ psychologists - design and evaluate tests of mental abilities, aptitudes, interests and personality
    C.   **Psychological Practice**
        1.   Those who try to understand and improve physical and mental health
        2.   Practitioners of psychology work in mental or general hospitals, _____ , schools, counseling centers, and private practice
        3.   Proportion of psychologists who are practitioners has greatly increased
        4.   Types of psychologist practitioners
            a.   _____ psychologists deal with problems of everyday life
            b.   School psychologists try to enhance students' performance and resolve emotional difficulties
            c.   Clinical psychologists diagnose, treat and study mental or emotional problems
        5.   Degrees for practice may include Ph.D., Ed.D. (doctorate in education), and Psy.D. (doctorate in psychology)
        6.   Types of non-psychologist practitioners
            a.   _____ - anyone who practices psychotherapy; unrelated to formal education and is not legally regulated
            b.   Psychoanalyst - someone with specialized training at a recognized

7

psychoanalytic institute
- c. Psychiatrist - a medical doctor (M.D.) with a residency in psychiatry
  - (1) Some do research and do not practice
  - (2) Can write prescriptions
  - (3) May not have thorough training in current psychological theories and methods
- d. Social workers, school counselors, marriage, family, and child counselors also practice; they treat general problems in adjustment, and licensing requirements vary
- e. Current concerns are that psychotherapists may not have training in research methods or know empirical findings and may use unvalidated therapy techniques

D. Psychology in the community
1. Psychologists work in other areas within the community
2. Psychologists work with diverse groups of people and in a variety of types of settings

VI. THE MOSAIC OF PSYCHOLOGY
A. Variety in psychologists' activities, goals, perspectives creates a mosaic
B. Though there is disagreement about emphasis, psychological scientists and scientist-clinicians agree on basic guidelines
1. Most believe in importance of empirical evidence
2. Most reject supernatural explanations of events
3. Share a fascination with human behavior and mind

Answer these Learning Objectives while you read Sections 5 and 6.

10. Distinguish between applied and basic psychology.

11. Discuss and give examples of the concerns of various specialties in psychology.

12. Distinguish between a psychotherapist, a psychoanalyst, a psychiatrist, a clinical psychologist and other practicing mental health professionals.

13. Identify basic areas of agreement among most psychologists.

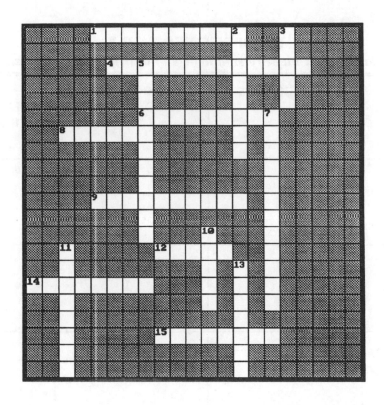

ACROSS

1. perspective of psychology that states that actions, feelings and thoughts are associated with bodily events
4. early approach that asks how and why
6. psychological perspective that studies perception, memory, problem solving and language
8. type of psychologist who works with students to enhance performance
9. the scientific study of behavior and mental processes
12. developed psychoanalysis
14. movement in psychology that studies motherhood and menopause
15. psychologists whose goal is to improve mental health engage in the _____ of psychology

DOWN

2. the perspective of psychology that states that psychology should study observable events and not mental processes
3. research that explores knowledge for its own sake
5. experimental, educational, developmental, industrial and social psychology are _____ specialty areas in psychology
7. type of psychologist who studies learning, motivation, emotion and sensation
10. the "father" of psychology
11. movement in psychology that emphasizes human potential
13. type of research that is concerned with practical uses of knowledge

PERSPECTIVES TABLE

Complete this table, then identify similarities and differences between perspectives.

PERSPECTIVE OR MOVEMENT	KEY FIGURES	KEY CONCEPTS AND TERMS	MAJOR INFLUENCES ON BEHAVIOR
BIOLOGICAL PERSPECTIVE			
LEARNING PERSPECTIVE			
COGNITIVE PERSPECTIVE			
PSYCHODYNAMIC PERSPECTIVE			
SOCIOCULTURAL PERSPECTIVE			
HUMANISTIC MOVEMENT			
FEMINIST MOVEMENT			

FLASH CARDS

Cut the following chart along the borders and test yourself with the resulting flash cards.

1.1 EMPIRICAL	1.2 PSYCHOLOGY	1.3 "PSYCHOBABBLE"
1.4 CRITICAL THINKING	1.5 WILHELM WUNDT	1.6 TRAINED INTROSPECTION
1.7 STRUCTURALISM	1.8 FUNCTIONALISM	1.9 WILLIAM JAMES
1.10 CHARLES DARWIN	1.11 PSYCHOANALYSIS	1.12 SIGMUND FREUD
1.13 BIOLOGICAL PERSPECTIVE	1.14 EVOLUTIONARY PERSPECTIVE	1.15 BEHAVIORISTS
1.16 COGNITIVE SOCIAL-LEARNING THEORISTS	1.17 COGNITIVE PERSPECTIVE	1.18 SOCIOCULTURAL PERSPECTIVE

1.3 Pseudoscience and quackery covered by a veneer of psychological language.	1.2 The scientific study of behavior and mental processes and how they are affected by an organism's physical and mental state, and external environment.	1.1 Evidence gathered by careful observation, experimentation, and measurement.
1.6 Research method in which trained people observed, analyzed, and described their own sensations, mental images, and emotional reactions.	1.5 He founded the first psychological laboratory and was the first person to announce his intention to make psychology a science.	1.4 The willingness to assess claims and make judgments based on well-supported reasons and evidence rather than emotion and anecdote.
1.9 An American philosopher, physician, and psychologist who was a proponent of functionalism.	1.8 An early approach to psychology that emphasized the function or purpose of behavior, as opposed to its analysis and description.	1.7 An early approach to psychology that hoped to analyze sensations, images, and feelings into basic elements.
1.12 A neurologist who developed the theory of personality and method of treating problems called psychoanalysis.	1.11 Personality theory and method of psychotherapy, originally formulated by Freud.	1.10 A British naturalist who developed evolutionary theories who inspired the early psychological approach of functionalism.
1.15 Part of the learning perspective, behaviorists focus on observable and measurable environmental conditions that affect specific behaviors.	1.14 A new specialty in which researchers study how our evolutionary past may explain some of our present behaviors and psychological traits.	1.13 An approach that focuses on how bodily events affect behavior, feelings, and thoughts.
1.18 An approach that focuses on the social and cultural forces outside the individual that shape every aspect of behavior.	1.17 An approach that emphasizes what goes on in people's heads - how they reason, remember, understand, solve problems, form beliefs.	1.16 Part of the learning perspective, they combine elements of behaviorism with research on thoughts, values, expectations, and intentions.

1.19 SOCIAL PSYCHOLOGISTS	**1.20 CULTURAL PSYCHOLOGISTS**	**1.21 PSYCHODYNAMIC PERSPECTIVE**
1.22 HUMANIST PSYCHOLOGY	**1.23 FEMINIST PSYCHOLOGY**	**1.24 PSYCHOLOGICAL PRACTICE**
1.25 BASIC PSYCHOLOGY	**1.26 APPLIED PSYCHOLOGY**	**1.27 EXPERIMENTAL PSYCHOLOGIST**
1.28 EDUCATIONAL PSYCHOLOGIST	**1.29 DEVELOPMENTAL PSYCHOLOGIST**	**1.30 INDUSTRIAL/ ORGANIZATIONAL PSYCHOLOGIST**
1.31 PSYCHOMETRIC PSYCHOLOGIST	**1.32 COUNSELING PSYCHOLOGIST**	**1.33 SCHOOL PSYCHOLOGIST**
1.34 CLINICAL PSYCHOLOGIST	**1.35 PSYCHOTHERAPIST**	**1.36 PSYCHIATRIST**

1.21 An approach that deals with unconscious dynamics within the individual, such as inner forces, conflicts, or instinctual energy.	1.20 Part of the sociocultural perspective, they examine how cultural rules and values affect people's development, behavior, and feelings.	1.19 Part of the sociocultural perspective, they focus on social rules and roles, the affect of groups, obedience to authority, the influence of other people.
1.24 A category of professional activities of psychologists that involves providing health or mental health services.	1.23 An influential movement that has spurred research on topics like menstruation, motherhood, dynamics of power and sexuality.	1.22 An influential movement that states that people have free will. Its goal is to help people express themselves and achieve their full potential.
1.27 Psychologist who conducts laboratory studies of learning, motivation, emotion, sensation and perception, physiology, and cognition.	1.26 A type of psychology in which psychologists are concerned with the practical uses of knowledge.	1.25 A type of psychology in which psychologists seek knowledge for its own sake and conduct "pure" research.
1.30 Studies behavior in the workplace. I/O psychologists study topics like group decision making, employee morale, work motivation, and productivity.	1.29 Studies how people change and grow over time, physically, mentally, and socially.	1.28 Studies psychological principles that explain learning and search for ways to improve educational systems.
1.33 A psychological practitioner who works with parents, teachers, and students to enhance students' performance.	1.32 A psychological practitioner who generally helps people deal with problems of everyday life, such as test anxiety, family conflicts or low motivation.	1.31 Designs and evaluates tests of mental abilities, aptitudes, interests, and personality.
1.36 A medical doctor (M.D.) who has done a residency in psychiatry and has learned to diagnose and treat mental disorders.	1.35 Anyone who does any kind of psychotherapy and who may not have any training at all.	1.34 A psychological practitioner who diagnoses, treats, and studies mental or emotional problems and is trained to do psychotherapy.

PRACTICE TEST 1 - Multiple Choice

1. Psychology is defined as
    A. the scientific study of behavior and how it is affected by an organism's physical state, mental state and the external environment.
    B. the scientific study of behavior and mental processes and how they are affected by an organism's physical state, mental state and the external environment.
    C. the scientific study of mental processes and how they are affected by an organism's physical state, mental state and the external environment.
    D. the scientific study of groups and institutions in society.

2. The main difference between psychological knowledge and popular opinion is that
    A. psychological knowledge is contained in text books, popular opinion is not.
    B. psychological knowledge is based on research evidence, popular is not.
    C. findings based on psychological knowledge are often the opposite of popular opinion.
    D. popular opinion is usually very obvious and psychological knowledge is rarely the expected result.

3. The ability and willingness to assess claims and make objective judgments on the basis of well-supported reasons and evidence rather than emotion and anecdote defines
    A. critical thinking.   B. psychobabble.
    C. common sense.   D. psychology.

4. Which of the following is one of the essential elements of critical thinking?
    A. Ask questions; be willing to wonder.
    B. Examine the evidence.
    C. Avoid emotional reasoning: "If I feel this way, it must be true."
    D. All of the above are essential elements of critical thinking.

5. _____ established the first psychology lab in 1879 and is considered the "father of psychology."
    A. E.B. Titchener   B. William James
    C. B.F. Skinner   D. Wilhelm Wundt

6. An early school of psychology, popularized by E.B. Titchener, attempted to analyze sensations, images and feelings into their most basic elements. This school was called
    A. structuralism.   B. introspection.
    C. functionalism.   D. behaviorism.

15

7. A second early school of psychology asked how and why an organism's behavior helps it to adapt to its environment. It was called
   A. structuralism.
   B. introspection.
   C. functionalism.
   D. behaviorism.

8. "To understand a person's actions, we must concentrate on the environmental conditions-the rewards and punishers-that maintain or discourage specific behaviors rather than studying the mind or mental states." This reflects the position of the _____ perspective.
   A. learning
   B. psychodynamic
   C. cognitive
   D. biological

9. Which perspective or movement has helped people eliminate unwanted habits?
   A. humanism
   B. biological
   C. learning
   D. psychodynamic

10. _____ theorists combine elements of behaviorism with research on thoughts, values, expectations, and intentions.
    A. Social-cognitive learning
    B. Psychodynamic
    C. Humanist-biological
    D. Biological

11. "Psychological distress is a result of inner forces, specifically unresolved unconscious conflicts from early childhood." This statement reflects the position of the _____ perspective.
    A. behavioral
    B. psychodynamic
    C. cognitive
    D. biological

12. Proponents of the _____ perspective believe that to understand the mind one must study the nervous system, because all actions, feelings and thoughts are associated with bodily events.
    A. behavioral
    B. psychodynamic
    C. cognitive
    D. biological

13. What goes on in people's heads, including how people reason, remember, understand language, solve problems are some of the topics emphasized by the
    A. the sociocultural perspective.
    B. humanists.
    C. social-cognitive theory.
    D. cognitive perspective.

14. "The answer to violence and cruelty doesn't reside in instincts, brain circuits or personal dispositions, but in situational, economic and cultural factors." This statement is consistent with the thinking of _____ psychologists.
    A.   sociocultural   B.   humanistic
    C.   cognitive   D.   psychodynamic

15. Developed in reaction to Freudian pessimism and behavioristic "mindlessness," _____ was based on the notion that human beings had free will.
    A.   feminist psychology   B.   social learning theory
    C.   sociocultural psychology   D.   humanistic psychology

16. Which of the following might be one of the goals of feminist psychology?
    A.   Encourage research on menstruation and motherhood.
    B.   Identify biases in psychological research and psychotherapy.
    C.   Make sure that both male and female subjects are used in research design.
    D.   All of the above.

17. Which of the following best describes the difference between applied and basic research?
    A.   Basic research examines the basic elements of sensations, images and feelings, whereas applied research studies how these processes help a person adapt to the environment.
    B.   Basic psychological research seeks knowledge for its own sake, whereas applied psychological research is concerned with the practical uses of knowledge.
    C.   Applied research seeks knowledge for its own sake, whereas basic research is concerned with the practical uses of knowledge.
    D.   Basic research is based on the psychoanalytic perspective, whereas applied research is based on the humanistic approach.

18. Psychologists who conduct laboratory studies of learning, motivation, emotion, sensation and perception, physiology, and cognition are called _____ psychologists.
    A.   experimental   B.   educational
    C.   developmental   D.   social

19. A psychometric psychologist
    A.   studies how groups, institutions and the social context influence individuals.
    B.   studies how people change and grow over time physically, mentally and socially.
    C.   designs and evaluates tests of mental abilities, aptitudes, interests and personality.
    D.   studies behavior in the workplace.

20. Psychologists who help people deal with problems of everyday life, such as test anxiety, family or marital problems, or low job motivation, are called _____ psychologists.
    A.   psychometric   B.   clinical
    C.   counseling   D.   school

21. Which of the following is a research area in psychology rather than a practice specialty?
    A.   counseling psychology
    B.   school psychology
    C.   clinical psychology
    D.   educational psychology

22. Which type of psychologist would be most likely to work with highly disturbed people?
    A.   clinical   B.   experimental
    C.   counseling   D.   school

23. Which of the following has a medical degree and can prescribe medication?
    A.   clinical psychologist   B.   psychotherapist
    C.   psychoanalyst   D.   psychiatrist

24. A psychotherapist
    A.   has specialized training at a psychoanalytic institute.
    B.   is not required to have any training at all in most states.
    C.   has a medical degree.
    D.   is a psychologist.

25. Though there are many areas of disagreement among psychologists, which of the following describes one of the guidelines on which psychological scientists and scientist-clinicians agree? Most
    A.   agree that psychiatrists are better able to help people than psychologists.
    B.   agree that the behavioral perspective is superior to all other perspectives.
    C.   believe that applied psychology is more important that basic psychology.
    D.   believe in the importance of empirical evidence.

PRACTICE TEST 2 - Multiple Choice

1.   Of the following studies, the one that meets the definition of psychology is
     A.   a study of someone who engages in self-injurious behavior.
     B.   a study examining the components of emotion.
     C.   a study of the effects of peer pressure on adolescents.
     D.   all of the above.

2.   Your friend is fond of telling you all the latest psychological tips she hears on TV, in magazines or in the latest self-help book. What would you tell her to help her determine what information is scientific and what is "psychobabble?"
     A.   If she hears something on the news, it is likely to be true.
     B.   Information she reads in the newspaper or magazines is likely to be correct.
     C.   Information from experts is usually accurate.
     D.   Information must be supported by documented research evidence in order to be considered scientific.

3.   Unhappy memories are often repressed and then later recalled accurately, most women suffer from emotional symptoms of "PMS," abstinence from alcohol reduce rates of alcoholism are all examples of
     A.   popular opinions that have been supported by research evidence.
     B.   common beliefs that have been contradicted by the evidence.
     C.   scientific research findings.
     D.   ideas that have been rejected by popular opinion.

4.   Which of the following are examples of the use of critical thinking?
     A.   To be open-minded, Hank discusses whether the Holocaust happened.
     B.   After Yolanda was refused from veterinary school, she took a job at a zoo.
     C.   Robert was taught that spanking is the best way to discipline children and he plans to parent in the same way.
     D.   Shaquille has decided not to major in psychology because there are so many contradictory research findings and there are too few clear-cut answers.

5.   Dr. Friedlander is a teacher who encourages students to disagree with her as long as they have evidence that supports their point of view. If students use arguments such as "It's my opinion," or "I know it's true because it happened to my neighbor that way," they lose points. This approach
     A.   fosters critical thinking by encouraging students to examine the evidence.
     B.   confuses students.
     C.   discourages students from having confidence in their opinions.
     D.   helps students define their terms.

6. Wilhelm Wundt is often considered the "father of psychology" because
   A. he established the first psychology laboratory.
   B. he was the first to announce that he intended to make psychology a science.
   C. he attempted to use scientific methods to study psychological phenomena.
   D. all of the above.

7. The year is 1900 and you are a participant in a research project. You are told to respond to a series of words, like triangle, by telling the researchers about the basic elements of your mental experience. Which early brand of psychology used this approach?
   A. functionalism   B. behaviorism
   C. trained introspection   D. structuralism

8. _____ is critical of the goals of the previous experiment because of the belief that the brain and the mind are constantly changing. This school is more interested in why you are participating in the study in the first place
   A. Functionalism   B. Behaviorism
   C. Trained introspection   D. Structuralism

9. Titchener is to James as
   A. trained introspection is to Wundt.
   B. functionalism is to structuralism.
   C. trained introspection is to functionalism.
   D. structuralism is to functionalism.

10. You have recently started psychotherapy with a psychologist who believes in the learning perspective. Which of the following statements would she make?
    A. "To best address your problem, we must identify the behaviors that are causing problems, the environmental conditions including the rewards and punishments that maintain the behaviors and then we must modify those behaviors."
    B. "To help you we must identify your unconscious inner conflicts, memories and emotional traumas from your early childhood."
    C. "Your problem has to do with how you are thinking about this situation. You must examine your expectations and try to understand this differently."
    D. "We must examine your problem in the context of the broader culture and how cultural expectations and beliefs are affecting your behavior."

11. The social-cognitive learning theory combines behaviorism with
    A. ideas about unconscious conflicts.
    B. an examination of the social and cultural forces that influence behavior.
    C. research on mental processes like thoughts, values, and expectations.
    D. the study of human evolution.

12.	You have started psychotherapy with a psychologist who believes in the psychodynamic perspective. Which statement is he most likely to make?
	A.	"To best address your problem, we must identify the behaviors that are causing problems and then we must modify those behaviors."
	B.	"We must examine your unconscious conflicts from your early childhood."
	C.	"Your actions are self-regulated. We must discover how they are shaped by your thoughts, values, self-reflections and intentions."
	D.	"We must examine your problem in the context of the broader culture and how cultural expectations, pressures and beliefs are affecting your behavior."

13.	Dr. Pine is conducting a research project in which she is looking for genetic and biochemical causes of depression. Which perspective is she most likely to follow?
	A.	biological			E.	humanistic
	C.	behavioral			D.	cognitive

14.	"It is not what happened at the party that is upsetting you. It is your perception of what happened and your explanation of those events that are causing problems." This statement best reflects which of the following perspectives?
	A.	biological			B.	humanistic
	C.	sociocultural			D.	cognitive

15.	"To understand the causes of the high rates of anorexia nervosa among older adolescent women, we must consider the influence of society's norms for female beauty and thinness." This statement reflects which of the following perspectives?
	A.	sociocultural			B.	humanistic
	C.	psychoanalytic			D.	cognitive

16.	A _____ psychologist would say, "The goal of psychotherapy is to help people express themselves creatively and utilize their free will to reach their full potential."
	A.	humanistic			B.	cognitive
	C.	feminist			D.	sociocultural

17.	A _____ psychologist examines research for bias in subject selection.
	A.	humanist			B.	cognitive
	C.	feminist			D.	sociocultural

18.	Most people think a psychologist is a someone who listens intently while a client pours forth his or her troubles. This description leaves out which specialty in psychology?
	A.	clinical			B.	counseling
	C.	developmental			D.	school

19. Dr. Borynko is designing a research study to answer each of the following research questions. Which study would be considered basic research?
   A. Can rats learn to press a bar for a reward?
   B. Can emotionally disturbed children learn to control aggression for a reward?
   C. Can training in moral development be used to prevent teenage violence?
   D. Can behavioral approaches be used to reduce alcohol abuse?

20. Dr. Cassales is designing a program to increase student performance in math. Other psychologists will implement his program in the schools. He is a(n) _____
   A. experimental psychologist.   B. developmental psychologist.
   C. educational psychologist.   D. school psychologist.

21. Dr. Abee is helping teachers, students and parents know how to use the Cassales Program at his school. He is a(n) _____ psychologist.
   A. experimental   B. developmental
   C. educational   D. school

22. A developmental psychologist would
   A. conduct a study on infant attachment behavior.
   B. conduct research on the role of arousal in the experience of emotions.
   C. develop a new test to measure personality.
   D. design and evaluate tests of mental abilities, aptitudes, interests, and personality.

23. Clinical and counseling psychologists, psychiatrists and psychoanalysts
   A. conduct psychotherapy and prescribe medication.
   B. conduct research and teach.
   C. are educated at the doctoral level.
   D. work in psychiatric hospitals.

24. Dr. Iriko believes that Jon's depression is biochemical and writes him a prescription for antidepressant drugs. She is most likely a
   A. counseling psychologist.   B. psychotherapist.
   C. psychiatrist.   D. social worker.

25. John is receiving psychoanalysis from Dr. Good, a well-known psychoanalyst. Dr. Good
   A. has specialized training at a psychoanalytic institute and has undergone psychoanalysis herself.
   B. has a medical degree.
   C. may have no college degree at all.
   D. may practice psychotherapy from any of the perspectives described in the text.

PRACTICE TEST 3 - Short Answer

1. Psychology is defined as the scientific study of _____ and _____ and how they are affected by an organism's physical state, mental state and the external environment.

2. Scientific psychology differs from popular psychology in that it is based on _____ evidence.

3. The ability and willingness to assess claims and make objective judgments on the basis of well-supported reasons and evidence rather than emotion and anecdote describes _____.

4. Two of the eight guidelines for critical thinking are:

   _____

   _____

5. Early psychologists, like today's psychologists, wanted to describe, _____, understand, and _____ behavior in order to add to human knowledge and increase human happiness.

6. William Wundt's favorite research method was _____.

7. Titchener named this early approach_____.

8. According to psychoanalysis, distressful symptoms are due to _____.

9. The _____ perspective is related to Freud's theory of psychoanalysis.

10. The five major current psychological perspectives are:

    _____

11. The _____ perspective is concerned with how the environment and experience affect a person's actions.

12. Unlike behaviorists and psychoanalysts, humanists believe that human beings have

    _____.

13. The _____ is one of the strongest forces in psychology today, and it has inspired an explosion of research on the workings of the mind.

14. The sociocultural perspective focuses on _____ _____.

15. Within the sociocultural perspective, social psychologists focus on _____ _____ while _____ psychologists emphasize how cultural rules and values affect people's development, behavior, and feelings.

16. Psychologists from the _____ movement have noted that many studies used only men as subjects.

17. _____ psychology is the generation of knowledge for its own sake; whereas _____ psychology is concerned with the practical uses of such knowledge.

18. _____ psychologists study behavior in the workplace, while _____ psychologists study principles that explain learning and look for ways to improved educational systems.

19. Both of the psychological specialties described in question 18 are considered _____ specialties.

20. Three examples of practice specialties in psychology are _____, _____, and _____

21. In the past, the focus of _____ psychologists was mainly on childhood, but many now study adolescence, young and middle adulthood, or old age.

22. To practice psychology, one must have a _____, and in almost all states, this requires a _____ degree.

23. People often confuse clinical psychologist with _____, _____, and _____.

24. _____ have a medical degree and may prescribe medication, while _____ are not required to have any degree at all since the term is not legally regulated.

25. Other types of professionals who engage in mental-health fields include _____, _____, and _____.

PRACTICE TEST 4 - True-False

1.   T F   Psychology is the scientific study of human behavior and how it is affected by an organism's physical state, mental state and the external environment.

2.   T F   Empirical evidence is based on conclusions from one's own experiences.

3.   T F   Primal scream therapy, rebirthing therapy, and the idea that unhappy memories may be repressed and then accurately recalled years later, as if they had been tape recorded are examples of pseudoscience and popular opinion.

4.   T F   Being open-minded is one of the eight guidelines for critical thinking.

5.   T F   Critical thinkers generate as many interpretations of the evidence as possible before settling on the most likely one.

6.   T F   Psychology did not become a formal discipline until the 19th century.

7.   T F   Researchers in Wundt's laboratory used a method called trained introspection to observe, analyze, and describe their own sensations.

8.   T F   Structuralism, popularized by E. B. Titchener, emphasized the function or purpose of behavior, as opposed to its analysis and description.

9.   T F   Structuralism, functionalism, and psychoanalysis are among the major perspectives in psychology.

10.   T F   Psychoanalysis, developed by Freud, proposes that patients' symptoms were due to conflicts and emotional traumas that occurred in early childhood and were too threatening to be remembered consciously.

11.   T F   The major psychological perspectives include the biological perspective, the learning perspective, the cognitive perspective, the sociocultural perspective, and the psychodynamic perspective.

12.   T F   The sociocultural perspective has its origins in Freud's theory of psychoanalysis.

13.   T F   The humanistic movement and the learning perspective share the belief that human beings have free will.

14.   T F   Social-cognitive theorists believe that people learn by imitating others and by thinking about the events happening around them.

15.   T F   Both the learning perspective and the sociocultural perspective focus on the environment and forces outside the individual that shape behavior.

16.   T F   Contemporary cognitive researchers rely on the structuralists' method of introspection.

17.   T F   The psychodynamic perspective deals with unconscious dynamics within the individual, such as inner forces, conflicts, or instinctual energy.

18.   T F   Feminist psychologists may identify with any of the five major perspectives.

19.   T F   The professional activities of psychologists generally fall into two categories: (1) teaching and doing research in colleges and universities; and (2) providing health or mental health services.

20.   T F   Both basic psychology and applied psychology are concerned with practical uses of knowledge.

21.   T F   The question of whether a chimpanzee or a gorilla can learn to use sign language would be asked by an applied psychologist.

22.   T F   Educational and school psychologists basically do the same kind of work.

23.   T F   Experimental psychology, educational psychology, and developmental psychology are among the nonclinical specialties in psychology.

24.   T F   Psychologists are the only people who work in the mental-health field who can practice psychotherapy.

25.   T F   Psychotherapist, psychoanalyst, and psychologists are all synonyms and are used interchangeably to refer to the same type of professional.

PRACTICE TEST 5 - Essay

1. Several activities are described below. For each activity, indicate whether it is an example of applied or basic psychology, the area of specialization most likely to be involved and whether that area of specialization is a clinical or non-clinical area. Explain the reasons for your answers.

   A. Psychologist David Wechsler designed an intelligence test expressly for use with adults.

   B. Researchers Hubel and Wiesel (1962, 1968) received a Nobel Prize for their work in the area of vision. They found that special cells in the brain are designed to visually code complex features of an object. Their research involved recording impulses from individual cells in the brains of cats and monkeys.

   C. Swiss biologist Jean Piaget observed that children understand concepts and reason differently at different stages. Based on his observations, he developed a theory of cognitive development.

   D. Several researchers have studied work motivation. They have been interested in the conditions that influence productivity and satisfaction in organizations.

   E. In 1963, Stanley Milgram conducted a classic study on obedience to authority. In subsequent variations of the original study, Milgram and his colleagues were interested in the conditions under which people might disobey.

   F. Strupp conducted research in 1982 to examine the characteristics of effective psychotherapy. He found that the relationship between the therapist and client greatly affects the success of the therapy.

   G. A national study of 3,000 children in fourth through tenth grades found that over this period of time girls' self-esteem plummeted (American Association of University Women, 1991). As a result of recommendations based on the findings of this and other research, changes in school systems have been suggested.

   H. Several psychologists have studied the process of career development and use career development theories to assist college students in selecting their careers.

27

2. Harold is 17 years old and has been abusing alcohol and marijuana for the past year. He has been missing school and his academic performance is declining. Harold was formerly a "B" student and was involved in sports. He is now getting D's and F's and has dropped out of most extracurricular activities. Answer the following questions: What influences would each of the five perspectives (learning, psychodynamic, biological, cognitive and sociocultural) and two movements in psychology (humanist and feminist) identify as central to the development of Harold's drug problem?

3. Juanita is suffering from depression and she is interested in seeking professional help for her problem. Briefly describe the general types of treatment that would most likely be utilized by a psychologist, a psychiatrist, a psychoanalyst and a psychotherapist. Indicate the types of training they are likely to have had.

CHAPTER 2

How Psychologists Do Research

LEARNING OBJECTIVES

After studying this chapter, you should be able to do the following:

1. List the reasons research methods are important to psychologists.

2. List and discuss the characteristics of scientific psychological research.

3. List and discuss the characteristics of descriptive research methods.

4. Describe and give examples of case studies, naturalistic observation, laboratory observation, tests, and surveys. Discuss the advantages and disadvantages of each.

5. List and discuss the characteristics and limitations of correlational studies and provide examples of positive and negative correlations.

6. Distinguish between independent and dependent variables and identify examples of each.

7. Distinguish between experimental and control groups and discuss the use of placebos.

8. Describe single- and double-blind studies and explain how they improve experiments.

9. Discuss the advantages and limitations of experimental research.

10. List and describe the types of descriptive statistics.

11. Describe how inferential statistics are used and explain statistical significance.

12. Compare and contrast cross-sectional and longitudinal studies.

13. Describe the technique of meta-analysis.

14. Discuss the principles of the ethical code for conducting research with human beings.

15. Discuss ethical problems in research, including the use of animals and deception.

16. Describe some of the reasons for using animals in research.

CHAPTER CONCEPT MAP

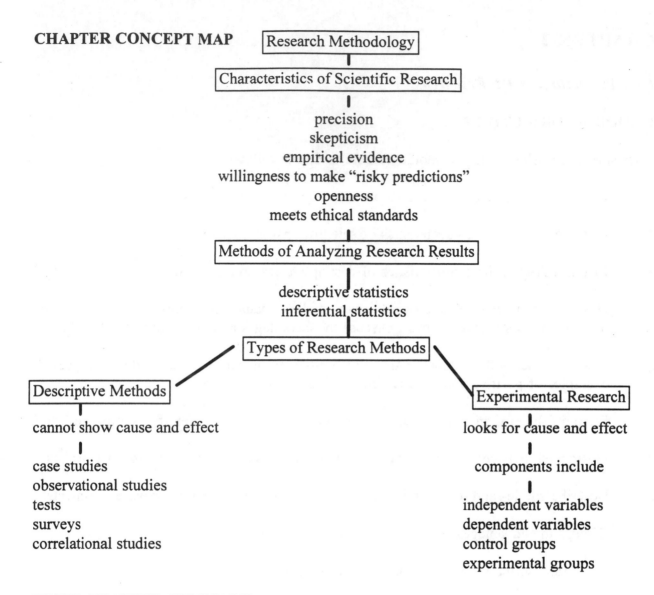

Research Methodology

Characteristics of Scientific Research

precision
skepticism
empirical evidence
willingness to make "risky predictions"
openness
meets ethical standards

Methods of Analyzing Research Results

descriptive statistics
inferential statistics

Types of Research Methods

Descriptive Methods

cannot show cause and effect

case studies
observational studies
tests
surveys
correlational studies

Experimental Research

looks for cause and effect

components include

independent variables
dependent variables
control groups
experimental groups

BRIEF CHAPTER SUMMARY

Chapter 2 discusses the importance of understanding scientific methodology to making a critical evaluation of research findings. Three major types of research studies are described: descriptive studies, correlational studies and experimental studies. Descriptive studies include case studies, observational studies, studies based on psychological tests, and studies based on surveys. Correlational studies are a special category of descriptive studies; they analyze the relationship between two variables. Experimental research is the only type that can examine cause and effect because it is conducted in a highly controlled fashion. The components of experimental research are examined, along with descriptive and inferential statistics.

PREVIEW OUTLINE AND REVIEW QUESTIONS

Before you read the chapter, review the preview outline and the Learning Objectives for each section of the text. Answer all questions as you read the text.

SECTION 1 - WHAT MAKES PSYCHOLOGICAL RESEARCH SCIENTIFIC? (PP. 34-37)

I.   **WHAT MAKES PSYCHOLOGICAL RESEARCH SCIENTIFIC?**
    A.   **Why are research methods so important to psychologists?**
        1.   Helps separate truth from unfounded belief
        2.   Helps sort out conflicting views
        3.   Helps correct false ideas that may cause people harm
    B.   **What makes research scientific?**
        1.   Precision
            a.   Scientists start an investigation with a hunch based on previous findings, observations or theory
                (1)   Characteristics of a _____
                    (a)   Organized system of assumptions and principles that purports to explain certain phenomena
                    (b)   Accepted by a large part of scientific community
            b.   From a hunch or theory, a scientist derives a hypothesis that may be general initially, but must become specific
            c.   Hypotheses leads to predictions
            d.   Terms must be defined in ways that can be observed and measured - called _____ definitions
        2.   Skepticism
            a.   Must accept conclusions with caution
            b.   Balance caution with openness to new ideas and evidence
        3.   Reliance on _____ evidence rather than on personal accounts
        4.   Willingness to make "risky predictions" and the principle of falsifiability, or an idea could be disproved if contrary evidence is discovered
        5.   Openness - scientists must discuss ideas, testing procedures and results so their findings can be replicated to reduce fraud and error

Answer these Learning Objectives while you read Section 1.

1.   List the reasons research methods are important to psychologists.

2.   List and discuss the characteristics of scientific psychological research.

SECTION 2 - DESCRIPTIVE STUDIES: ESTABLISHING THE FACTS (PP. 37-44)

II. **DESCRIPTIVE STUDIES: ESTABLISHING THE FACTS**
    A. **General characteristics of descriptive methods**
        1. Allow psychologists to describe and predict behavior
        2. Do not allow psychologists to choose an explanation for the behavior
    B. **Case Studies**
        1. General characteristics
            a. Detailed descriptions of particular individuals
            b. Based on careful observation or psychological testing
        2. Advantages
            a. Produce detailed picture of an individual
            b. Can illustrate psychological principles well
        3. Disadvantages
            a. Rely on memories, which can be inaccurate
            b. Vital information is often missing so they are difficult to interpret
            c. Cannot use to _____ about human behavior because the individual under study may not be representative of the group
            d. They are not tests of hypotheses
    C. **Observational Studies**
        1. General characteristics
            a. Researchers observe, measure, and record behavior without interfering with the people being observed
            b. Usually involves many participants
            c. Can only describe, not explain, behavior
        2. Two types of observational studies
            a. _____ observation
                (1) Describes behavior in the natural environment
                (2) Can be used to describe animals or humans
                (3) Involves counting, rating or measuring specific behaviors; specificity and measurability reduces errors and biases
            b. Laboratory observation
                (1) Subjects observed in the laboratory where the psychologist has more control
                (2) A drawback is that being observed might cause subjects to alter their behavior

D. **Tests**
1. Also called assessment instruments - procedures to measure personality traits, emotional states, aptitudes, interests, abilities and values
2. Types of tests
    a. _____ tests - measure beliefs, behavior, feelings of which person is aware
    b. Projective tests - designed to tap unconscious
3. Characteristics of a good test
    a. Standardization - uniform procedures for giving and scoring the test
    b. Norms - established standards of performance
    c. _____ - getting the same results from one time to another
        (1) Ways to measure reliability
            (a) Test-retest reliability - giving the test twice to the same people
            (b) Alternate-forms reliability - giving different versions of the same test
    d. Validity - a test measures what it set out to measure
        (1) _____ validity - test questions ask about a broad array of beliefs and behaviors relevant to what is being measured
        (2) Criterion validity - predicts other measures of the trait

E. _____
1. Gather information by asking people directly
2. Potential problems with surveys
    a. Representative sample - it is crucial that the subjects represent the larger population being described
    b. Volunteer bias - volunteers differ from non-volunteers
    c. Subjects may lie, forget or remember incorrectly
    d. Potential biases or ambiguities in wording of questions

Answer these Learning Objectives while you read Section 2.

3. List and discuss the characteristics of descriptive research methods.

4. Describe and give examples of case studies, naturalistic observation, laboratory observation, tests and surveys. Discuss the advantages and disadvantages of each.

**SECTION 3 - CORRELATIONAL STUDIES: LOOKING FOR RELATIONSHIPS
(PP. 44-47)**

III.   **CORRELATIONAL STUDIES: LOOKING FOR RELATIONSHIP**
    A.   **Purpose and definitions**
        1.   Purpose - to determine whether two or more variables are related, and if so, how strongly
        2.   Definition - Numerical measure of the strength of the relationship
        3.   _____ - anything that can be measured, rated or scored
        4.   Correlations always occur between sets of observations
    B.   **Characteristics of correlations**
        1.   Direction of a relationship between variables
            a.   Positive correlation - high values of one variable are associated with high values of the other; low values of one variable are associated with low values of the other
            b.   _____ correlation - high values of one variable are associated with low values of the other
            c.   Uncorrelated - no relationship between two variables
        2.   Strength of relationship between the two variables expressed as correlation
            a.   Correlation _____ - statistic used to express a correlation
            b.   Possible range of correlation coefficient is -1 to +1
                (1)   -1 indicates a strong negative relationship
                (2)   +1 indicates a strong positive relationship
                (3)   _____ indicates no relationship
                (4)   The closer to either +1 or - 1, the stronger the relationship
                (5)   The closer to 0, the weaker the relationship
    C.   **Benefits and limitations of correlations**
        1.   Benefit - allows someone to predict from one variable to another
        2.   Limitation - cannot show causation

Answer this Learning Objective while you read Section 3.

5.   List and discuss the characteristics and limitations of correlational studies and provide examples of positive and negative correlations.

SECTION 4 - EXPERIMENTS: HUNTING FOR CAUSES (PP. 48-52)

IV. **EXPERIMENTS: HUNTING FOR CAUSES**
- A. **Purpose of experimentation** - to look for _____ of behavior because the experiment allows the researcher to control the situation being studied
- B. **Experimental variables** - the characteristics the researcher is studying
    1. Independent variable - the characteristic manipulated by the experimenter
    2. _____ variable - the behavior the researcher tries to predict
- C. **Experimental and control conditions**
    1. Experimental condition - the condition or group in which subjects receive some amount of the independent variable
    2. Control condition - the condition or group in which subjects do not receive any amount of the independent variable
        - a. Subjects in the control condition are treated the same in all other respects and are similar to experimental condition subjects
        - b. Random assignment balances individual differences among subjects between the two groups
        - c. A fake treatment or _____, controls for the expectations of control condition subjects
- D. **Experimenter effects**
    1. To control the effects of the expectations of subjects and experimenters
        - a. Single-blind studies - subjects don't know whether they are in the experimental or control group
        - b. _____ studies - neither the experimenter nor the subjects know which subjects are in which group
- E. **Advantages and limitations of experiments**
    1. Experiments allow conclusions about cause and effect
    2. The setting is artificial and subjects' behavior may differ from real life
    3. Subjects' behavior may be a reaction to the experimental situation
    4. Because of the limitations, more _____ research, is being called for

Answer these Learning Objectives while you read Section 4.

6. Distinguish between independent and dependent variables and identify examples of each.

7. Distinguish between experimental and control groups and discuss the use of placebos.

8. Describe single-blind and double-blind studies and explain how they improve experiments.

9. Discuss the advantages and limitations of experimental research.

SECTION 5 - EVALUATING THE FINDINGS (PP. 52-58)

V.   **EVALUATING THE FINDINGS**
     A.   **General goals** - describe, assess and explain findings
     B.   **Descriptive statistics: Finding out what's so**
          1.   To use descriptive statistics, a researcher must summarize individual data into group data and then use the following statistics to analyze the scores
               a.   Arithmetic _____ - Compare group scores between two or more groups - add scores, divide by number of scores
               b.   Standard deviation - Examines how much individual scores vary
                    (1)   Standard deviation shows how clustered or spread out individual scores are around the mean
                    (2)   The more spread out the scores are, the less typical the mean is
     C.   **Inferential statistics: Asking "So What?"**
          1.   Determines the likelihood that the result of the study occurred by chance
          2.   Statistical _____ - the result is expected to occur by chance fewer than 5 times in 100; it does not necessarily indicate real-world importance
          3.   Significance tests are used to determine statistical significance
          4.   Statistically significant results allow general predictions to be made about human behavior, though not about any particular individual
     D.   **Interpreting the findings**
          1.   Researchers must choose among competing explanations for the best one
          2.   Researchers must test a hypothesis in different ways several times
               a.   Cross-sectional studies - compare groups at one time
               b.   Longitudinal studies - study subjects across the life span
          3.   Researchers must judge the result's importance with procedures like meta-analysis which combine and analyze data from many studies

Answer these Learning Objectives while you read Section 5.

10.   List and describe the types of descriptive statistics.

11.   Describe how inferential statistics are used and explain statistical significance.

12.   Compare and contrast cross-sectional and longitudinal studies.

13.   Describe the technique of meta-analysis.

VI. **KEEPING THE ENTERPRISE ETHICAL**
   A. **The ethics of studying human beings**
      1. American Psychological Association's ethical _____
         a. Dignity and welfare of subjects must be respected
         b. People must participate voluntarily
         c. People must know enough about the study to make an intelligent decision, known as informed _____
         d. Researchers must protect participants from physical and mental harm and warn subjects, in advance, of any risks
         e. Subjects must be free to withdraw from a study at any time
      2. Use of deception - misleading subjects so the results are not affected
         a. Guidelines exist that govern use of deception and they are being revised
         b. Researchers are required to show
            (1) that a study's potential value justifies the use of deception
            (2) alternative procedures have been considered
            (3) that they plan to debrief participants about the true purpose and methods of the study afterward
   B. **The ethics of studying animals**
      1. Animals are used in small percentage of psychological studies
      2. Many purposes exist for conducting research using animals
         a. To conduct basic research on a particular species
         b. To discover practical applications
         c. To study issues that cannot be studied experimentally with human beings because of ethical or practical considerations
         d. To clarify theoretical questions
         e. To improve human welfare
      3. Treatment and regulations have improved due to opposition

Answer these Learning Objectives while you read Section 6.

14. Describe the principles of the ethical code for conducting research with human beings.

15. Discuss ethical problems in research, including the use of animals and deception.

16. Describe some of the reasons for using animals in research.

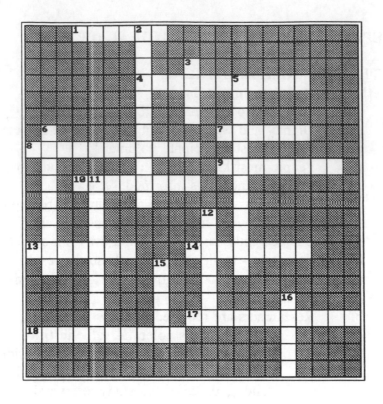

ACROSS

1. organized system of assumptions & principles that tries to explain a set of phenomena
4. the variable manipulated by the experimenter
7. type of descriptive research that gathers information by asking people directly
8. general term for scientific approach to research
9. whether a test measures what it sets out to
10. type of correlation in which high values of one variable are associated with low values of another

13. the condition or group in an experiment in which subjects do not receive any amount of the independent variable
14. spread of scores around the mean
17. measure of how strongly two variables are related to one another
18. one of the characteristics that makes research scientific

DOWN

2. getting the same test results over time
3. average
5. type of observational study that describes behavior in the natural environment
6. a controversial ethical issue
11. the only type of research able to look for causes of behavior
12. fake treatment
15. established standards of performance in testing
16. difference between the highest and lowest scores in a group of scores

FLASH CARDS
Cut the following chart along the borders and test yourself with the resulting flash cards.

2.1 THEORY	2.2 HYPOTHESIS	2.3 OPERATIONAL DEFINITION
2.4 PRINCIPLE OF FALSIFIABILITY	2.5 REPLICATE	2.6 DESCRIPTIVE METHODS
2.7 CASE STUDY	2.8 OBSERVATIONAL STUDIES	2.9 NATURALISTIC OBSERVATION
2.10 LABORATORY OBSERVATION	2.11 PSYCHOLOGICAL TESTS	2.12 STANDARDIZATION
2.13 NORMS (IN TESTING)	2.14 RELIABILITY	2.15 TEST-RETEST RELIABILITY
2.16 ALTERNATE-FORMS RELIABILITY	2.17 VALIDITY	2.18 CONTENT VALIDITY
2.19 CRITERION VALIDITY	2.20 SURVEYS	2.21 REPRESENTATIVE SAMPLE
2.22 VOLUNTEER BIAS	2.23 CORRELATIONAL STUDY	2.24 CORRELATION

2.3 A precise definition of a term in a hypothesis that specifies how the phenomena in question will be observed and	2.2 A statement that attempts to describe or explain a given behavior.	2.1 An organized system of assumptions and principles that purports to explain certain phenomena.
2.6 Research methods that allow psychologists to describe and predict behavior but not necessarily to explain it.	2.5 Scientists must tell others about their research procedures and results so others can repeat and verify their findings.	2.4 A principle that a scientist must state an idea in such a way that it can be refuted, or disproved by counterevidence.
2.9 A study that observes, measures, and records behavior in the natural social environment.	2.8 A study in which the researcher observes, measures, and records behavior without interfering with the behavior.	2.7 A detailed description of a particular individual, based on careful observation or on formal psychological testing.
2.12 In test construction, the development of uniform procedures for giving and scoring a test.	2.11 Procedures to measure and evaluate personality traits, emotional states, aptitudes, interests, abilities, and values.	2.10 A study in which researchers make observations of behavior in the laboratory rather than in the real world.
2.15 Reliability that is measured by giving the test twice to the same group of people, then comparing the sets of scores.	2.14 In test construction, the consistency, from one time and place to another, of scores derived from a test.	2.13 In test construction, established standards of performance.
2.18 A type of validity in which the test items broadly represent the trait in question.	2.17 The ability of a test to measure what it was designed to measure.	2.16 A type of reliability in which different versions of a test are given to the same group on separate occasions.
2.21 A group of subjects that accurately represents the larger population that the researcher wishes to describe.	2.20 Questionnaires and interviews that ask people directly about their experiences or attitudes.	2.19 A type of validity in which the test results predict other, independent measures of the trait in question.
2.24 A numerical measure of the strength of the relationship between two things.	2.23 A descriptive study that examines whether two or more phenomena are related, and if so, how strongly.	2.22 Samples using volunteers may be biased since those who volunteer their opinions may differ from those who do not.

2.25 VARIABLE	**2.26 POSITIVE CORRELATION**	**2.27 NEGATIVE CORRELATION**
2.28 COEFFICIENT OF CORRELATION	**2.29 EXPERIMENT**	**2.30 INDEPENDENT VARIABLE**
2.31 DEPENDENT VARIABLE	**2.32 CONTROL CONDITION**	**2.33 EXPERIMENTAL AND CONTROL GROUPS**
2.34 RANDOM ASSIGNMENT	**2.35 PLACEBO**	**2.36 SINGLE-BLIND STUDY**
2.37 EXPERIMENTER EFFECTS	**2.38 DOUBLE-BLIND STUDY**	**2.39 DESCRIPTIVE STATISTICS**
2.40 ARITHMETIC MEAN	**2.41 STANDARD DEVIATION**	**2.42 INFERENTIAL STATISTICS**
2.43 STATISTICAL SIGNIFICANCE	**2.44 CROSS-SECTIONAL STUDY**	**2.45 LONGITUDINAL STUDY**
2.46 META-ANALYSIS	**2.47 INFORMED CONSENT**	**2.48 APA ETHICAL CODE**

41

2.27 A relationship in which high (or low) values of one variable are associated with low (or high) values of the other.	2.26 Relationship in which high (or low) values of one variable are associated with high (or low) values of the other.	2.25 Events, scores, or anything else that can be recorded and tallied and can vary in quantifiable ways.
2.30 The aspect of an experimental situation manipulated or varied by the researcher.	2.29 A procedure that allows for cause and effect conclusions because the researcher controls the experimental situation.	2.28 A statistic used to express a correlation. It conveys both the size and direction of the correlation.
2.33 In an experiment, the experimental group is exposed to the independent variable and the control group is not.	2.32 In an experiment, a comparison condition in which subjects are not exposed to the independent variable.	2.31 The reaction of the subjects - the behavior that the researcher tries to predict.
2.36 An experiment in which subjects do not know whether they are in an experimental or control group.	2.35 An inactive substance or fake treatment used as a control in an experiment.	2.34 A way to assign people to groups that results in balancing individual characteristics that could affect the results.
2.39 Statistics that organize and summarize research data so comparisons can be made between groups.	2.38 A study in which neither the subjects nor the researchers know whether subjects are in an experimental or control group.	2.37 Unintended influences on subjects' behavior due to cues inadvertently given by the experimenter.
2.42 A statistic that allows researchers to draw inferences about how meaningful the findings are.	2.41 A descriptive statistic that describes how clustered or spread out individual scores are around the mean.	2.40 An average that is calculated by adding up a set of quantities and dividing the sum by the total number in the set.
2.45 A type of study in which the same people are followed over a period of time and are reassessed at regular intervals.	2.44 A type of study in which groups of subjects of different ages are compared at a given time.	2.43 Pertains to a result that would be expected to occur by chance 5 or fewer times in 100 repetitions of the study.
2.48 The American Psychological Association has a code of ethics that governs the use of research subjects.	2.47 Participants must be able to make an intelligent decision about study participation and participation must be voluntary.	2.46 A statistical procedure for combining and analyzing data from many studies.

RESEARCH METHODS TABLE

Complete this table and compare the differences among the research methods.

RESEARCH METHOD	DEFINITION AND DESCRIPTION	EXAMPLE
CASE HISTORY		
NATURALISTIC OBSERVATION		
LABORATORY OBSERVATION		
TESTS		
SURVEY		
CORRELATIONAL STUDY		
EXPERIMENT		

PRACTICE TEST 1 - Multiple Choice

1. Introductory psychology students study research methodology to
    A.   find proof for our existing beliefs so we can argue against those who disagree.
    B.   be able to critically evaluate psychological findings.
    C.   be able to manipulate statistics to our advantage.
    D.   be able to use our own experiences as scientific proofs.

2. Which of the following is NOT a characteristic of scientific research?
    A.   reliance on common sense   B.   precision
    C.   skepticism   D.   openness

3. An organized system of assumptions and principles that purports to explain a specified set of phenomena is called a(n)
    A.   hypothesis.   B.   operational definition.
    C.   theory.   D.   risky prediction.

4. Which of the following is an example of a hypothesis?
    A.   Alcohol decreases reaction time.
    B.   Studying improves grades.
    C.   Employees perform better in a supportive climate.
    D.   All of the above are examples of hypotheses.

5. Defining terms in ways that can be observed and measured employs
    A.   operational definitions.   B.   theories.
    C.   common sense.   D.   skepticism.

6. Descriptive research methods
    A.   explain behavior by identifying the causes of the behavior.
    B.   allow the researcher to describe and predict behavior.
    C.   include the experimental study.
    D.   all of the above

7. Freud based his theory on studying a small number of particular individuals in great detail. This type of research method is called a(n)
    A.   survey.   B.   experiment.
    C.   naturalistic observation.   D.   case study.

8. One disadvantage of the research method used by Freud is that
   A. it relies on memories, which can be inaccurate.
   B. it is difficult to interpret.
   C. it cannot be used to generalize about human behavior.
   D. all of the above are disadvantages

9. Naturalistic observations involve
   A. giving subjects a series of psychological tests.
   B. assigning research participants to experimental and control groups.
   C. observing subjects in the natural environment.
   D. asking people a series of questions.

10. In the area of test construction, standardization refers to
   A. the use of uniform procedures in the administration and scoring of a test.
   B. the establishment of standards of performance.
   C. getting the same results over time.
   D. the condition that a test measures what it set out to.

11. _____ validity indicates that the test questions represent the trait being measured.
   A. test-retest   B. content
   C. criterion   D. alternate forms

12. A problem with surveys is that
   A. they can by weakened by volunteer bias.
   B. respondents may lie, forget or remember incorrectly.
   C. there may be biases or ambiguities in the wording of questions.
   D. all of the above may be problems with surveys

13. Correlations
   A. determine the causes of behavior.
   B. determine whether two or more phenomena are related, and if so, how strongly.
   C. can be expressed on a numeric scale from 1 to 10.
   D. require research participants to be observed in a laboratory.

14. The more Rupert studies, the more his test scores improve. This is an example of
   A. a naturalistic observation.   B. a positive correlation.
   C. a negative correlation.   D. proof of causation.

15. Dr. Smith is studying the relationship between hair color and shoe size. He is likely to find
    A. a negative correlation.   B. a positive correlation.
    C. zero correlation.   D. it is impossible to say

16. Experimentation is
    A. a type of observational study.
    B. the only research method that looks for the causes of behavior.
    C. one of the descriptive research methods.
    D. more limited in its conclusions than the other types of methodologies.

17. The independent variable is the one that
    A. is manipulated by the researcher.
    B. the researcher tries to predict.
    C. is defined in a way that can be observed and measured.
    D. cannot be controlled.

18. Dr. Knowles is conducting research on the effects of alcohol on reaction time. She assigns students to two groups. One group receives three ounces of alcohol and the other group receives an alcohol-free beverage that looks, smells and tastes like alcohol. Following ingestion of the beverage, the reaction time of subjects in both groups is tested. Which of the variables is the dependent variable?
    A. alcohol   B. control group
    C. alcohol-free beverage   D. reaction time

19. In the above study, the group of research participants who receive the alcohol-free beverage is called
    A. the independent variable.   B. the control group.
    C. the experimental group.   D. the random group.

20. In the study described in question 18, neither Dr. Knowles nor the research participants knew whether they were in the experimental or control group. This type of study is called a
    A. single-blind study.   B. longitudinal study.
    C. double-blind study.   D. case study.

21. The arithmetic mean and standard deviation are
    A. types of descriptive statistics.   B. inferential statistics.
    C. examples of meta-analyses.   D. statistically significant.

22. Inferential statistics
    A. summarize individual data into group data.
    B. combine data from many studies.
    C. study abilities across the life span.
    D. tell the researcher the likelihood that the result of the study occurred by chance.

23. Cross-sectional studies differ from longitudinal studies in that
    A. cross-sectional studies compare different groups at one time, whereas longitudinal studies examine abilities across the life span.
    B. cross-sectional studies examine groups in the laboratory, whereas longitudinal studies examine behavior in the natural environment.
    C. cross-sectional studies examine abilities across the life span, whereas longitudinal studies compare different groups at one time.
    D. cross-sectional studies cannot establish cause and effect, whereas longitudinal studies can.

24. Meta-analyses are helpful in the interpretation of research findings because they
    A. determine which studies are accurate and which are not.
    B. combine data from many studies.
    C. establish whether the findings have any real-world importance.
    D. establish the statistical significance of studies.

25. For ethical purposes, researchers must show they have considered alternative procedures and that they plan to debrief subjects in order to use
    A. animals.
    B. more than one experimental condition.
    C. an informed consent.
    D. deception.

PRACTICE TEST 2 - Multiple Choice

1. Which of the following violates the principle of falsifiability?
    A. Lack of evidence for a phenomenon is described as predictable since destroying evidence is an alleged characteristic of the phenomenon under study.
    B. Subjects in a study do not represent the larger population being described.
    C. A study uses only volunteer subjects who differ from non-volunteers.
    D. An experimenter's expectations subtly influence the outcome of a study.

2. Frank's neighbor was abused as a child and he is now abusive with his own children. Based on this, Frank now believes that adults who were abused become child abusers themselves. Which characteristic of scientific research does this violate?
    A. precision   B. skepticism
    C. reliance on empirical evidence   D. openness

3. Scores on a depression test, changes in time spent sleeping and food intake might be
    A. hypotheses.   B. theories of depression.
    C. operational definitions of depression   D. empirical evidence.

4. Which of the following is an example of a theory?
    A. The id, ego and superego interact to shape our personalities.
    B. Child abuse is correlated with alcoholism.
    C. Children of alcoholics will become alcoholic.
    D. People who exercise will have lower rates of depression.

5. To find out whether males or females talk more, Danielle goes to a cafe and systematically records the talking time of eight male-female pairs. This is an example of a(n)
    A. experiment.   B. case study.
    C. naturalistic observation.   D. survey.

6. To conduct research on attitudes toward abortion, Dr. Kim distributes surveys to people leaving church after a service. The problem with this survey is that
    A. people are likely to lie or forget.
    B. the questions are unclear.
    C. the sample is nonrepresentative.
    D. the procedures are not uniform.

7. Validity is to reliability as
   A. consistency is to accuracy.
   B. accuracy is to consistency.
   C. criterion is to content.
   D. objective is to projective.

8. You take an intelligence test on Monday and receive a high score. You repeat it on Tuesday and receive a low score. This test lacks
   A. content validity.
   B. criterion validity.
   C. test-retest reliability.
   D. alternate forms reliability.

9. Which of the following is an example of a positive correlation?
   A. The less students study, the worse their grades will be.
   B. The more people exercise, the fewer health problems they will have.
   C. The more alcohol people consume, the slower their reaction time will be.
   D. Hair color is unrelated to shoe size.

10. In general, older employees have fewer short-term absences. This is an example of
    A. a positive correlation.
    B. a case study.
    C. a negative correlation.
    D. zero correlation.

11. Based on a correlational study showing that those who exercise regularly experience lower rates of depression, which of the following conclusions can be reached?
    A. Exercise causes a reduction in depression.
    B. People who are depressed stop exercising.
    C. There is a relationship between exercise and depression.
    D. Self-esteem influences both exercise and depression levels.

12. Dr. Redbird is studying the effect of a new teaching method on psychology test scores. Subjects come to her laboratory and she randomly assigns them to one of two groups. Though the subjects do not know this, one group gets instruction in the new teaching method while the other group receives instruction in the traditional method. The independent variable in this study is
    A. the new teaching method.
    B. psychology scores.
    C. the control group.
    D. Dr. Redbird.

13. In the study in question 12, the group that receives the new teaching method is
    A. the control group.
    B. the independent variable.
    C. the experimental group.
    D. none of the above.

14. In question 12, the subjects did not know whether they were in the experimental or control group, but Dr. Redbird did know. This is a _____ study.
    A. descriptive   B. single-blind
    C. double-blind   D. laboratory observation

15. The way that Dr. Redbird tried to make subjects equal in the experimental and control group on all characteristics except the independent variable was to
    A. randomly assign them to groups.   B. use single-blind techniques.
    C. select each subject individually.   D. use only volunteers.

16. The purpose of single and double-blind studies is to
    A. control for the effects of volunteer subjects.
    B. equate subjects in the experimental and control groups.
    C. utilize a placebo.
    D. control for the expectations of subjects in a single-blind study and the expectations of both subjects and experimenter in a double-blind study.

17. The scores of the subjects in the experimental group in Dr. Redbird's study were: 93, 85, 75, 82, 77, 84, 92, 52. The mean is
    A. 93.   B. 52.
    C. 80.   D. 75.

18. The standard deviation for a set of scores allow the researcher to know
    A. whether the results are significant.
    B. whether the mean is typical for that set of scores.
    C. the score that was most often received.
    D. the score that represents the midpoint of the scores.

19. Subjects in the control group received a mean score of 77. Before Dr. Redbird can say whether the new technique was superior in this study, she must
    A. calculate the statistical significance of the results to evaluate the probability that this result could have happened by chance.
    B. conduct a meta-analysis.
    C. calculate the statistical significance to determine the real-world importance.
    D. conduct a longitudinal study to see if the improved learning lasts.

20. To calculate the statistical significance, _____ must be used.
    A. descriptive statistics   B. meta-analysis
    C. inferential statistics   D. cross-sectional analysis

21. Assessing a group's IQ scores across the life span requires using
    A. cross-sectional research.
    B. a case study approach.
    C. longitudinal research.
    D. a naturalistic study.

22. Meta-analysis would be used to
    A. establish a relationship between two variables.
    B. examine the causes of behavior.
    C. combine data from many studies.
    D. examine abilities across the life span.

23. A situation that violates the ethical code of the American Psychological Association governing research using human subjects is
    A. providing subjects with an informed consent form that describes potential risks of participation in a study.
    B. allowing subjects to withdraw from the study at any time.
    C. requiring subjects to participate in a study for class credit.
    D. following institutional regulations governing research.

24. Psychologists use animals in research
    A. because sometimes practical or ethical considerations prevent the use of human beings as subjects.
    B. to discover practical applications.
    C. to conduct basic research on a particular species.
    D. all of the above are reasons that animals are used in research

25. Dr. Milner is conducting a study in which a co-researcher pretends to trip and fall in the presence of research subjects who are taking a reading comprehension test. The subjects have been told the study is on memory, but Dr. Milner is really studying the circumstances under which strangers provide assistance to others. According to ethical principles, Dr. Milner
    A. must demonstrate that his study's potential value justifies the use of deception.
    B. may not continue with this study no matter what he does because it is unethical to be dishonest with the subjects.
    C. never needs to disclose the true purpose of the study to the subjects.
    D. needs only show that no harm will come to the subjects.

PRACTICE TEST 3 - Short Answer

1.   Research methods are important to psychologists because they help separate truth from _____.

2.   "Students who spend more time studying perform better in college." This is an example of a _____.

3.   Dr. Smith is conducting a study on the effects of anxiety on test performance. She is using subjects' scores on a stress test as her _____ definition of anxiety.

4.   Any theory that cannot in principle be refuted violates the _____.

5.   Scientists must discuss ideas, testing procedures and results so their findings can be _____ to reduce fraud and error.

6.   Research methods that allow psychologists to describe and predict behavior but not to explain its causes are _____ methods.

7.   A detailed description of particular individuals that is based on careful observation refers to the _____ research method.

8.   Often scientists need a good description of behavior as it occurs in the natural environment before they can explain it. This is the primary purpose of _____ _____.

9.   _____ tests measure beliefs, behavior, and feelings of which the person is aware, while _____ tests are designed to tap the unconscious.

10. To be meaningful, a person's test score should be compared to established standards of performance called _____.

11. At 8:00 a.m. Hank weighs 179 pounds. He moves the scale slightly and decides to weigh himself again. Though it's only a minute later, he now weighs 177. Hank's scale lacks the test characteristic of _____.

12. A test that purports to measure personality, but, in fact, measures verbal abilities lacks _____.

13. If SAT scores are able to accurately predict students' grade point averages, the SAT is demonstrating that it has _____.

14. A survey on alcohol use among college students reported that alcohol use among students had dramatically decreased. Later the study reported that the subjects were female students from an expensive Ivy League university. This survey did not use a _____ sample.

15. Often one drawback to surveys is that those who agree to participate may differ from those who do not. A psychologist would say these surveys suffer from _____ bias.

16. A _____ is the numerical measure of the strength and direction of the relationship between two _____.

17. Height and weight are _____ correlated, however, this correlation does not show _____ between the two variables.

18. When psychologists want to look for causes of behavior, they must use a more controlled method called the _____.

19. In an experiment on caffeine on alertness, caffeine intake would be the _____ variable and alertness would be the _____ variable.

20. In the study described in question 19, the subjects who receive caffeinated coffee are in the _____ group while those who receive decaffeinated coffee are in the _____ group.

21. The decaffeinated coffee is a _____ which is used to control for the control group subjects' _____.

22. A study is called _____-blind when the subjects do not know whether they are in the experimental or control group.

23. Numbers summarizing the data we collect from subjects are called _____ statistics.

24. If the result of a study is unlikely to have happened by chance, then we say the result is statistically _____.

25. Research in which groups are all compared at the same time is called _____ _____; in _____ studies, people are followed over a period of time and reassessed at periodic intervals.

PRACTICE TEST 4 - True/False

1.   T F   A hypothesis is an organized system of assumptions and principles that purports to explain certain phenomena.

2.   T F   The principle of falsifiability refers to the reliance on empirical evidence rather than on personal accounts.

3.   T F   Although case studies can produce a detailed picture of an individual and often illustrate psychological principles well, they can be difficult to interpret and cannot be used to generalize about human behavior.

4.   T F   A laboratory observational study is the same type of research as the experimental study.

5.   T F   Observational studies are descriptive and do not allow the researcher to make any conclusions about the causes of behavior.

6.   T F   It is important that procedures for test administration remain flexible so they can be adapted to the needs of different groups of subjects.

7.   T F   A test is reliable if it measures what it set out to measure.

8.   T F   Test-retest and alternative forms are two ways to measure reliability.

9.   T F   If the Stern Test of College Success accurately predicts college performance, the test has demonstrated that it has good criterion validity.

10.   T F   Volunteer bias refers to the fact that volunteers are more likely than non-volunteers to answer survey questions dishonestly.

11.   T F   The purpose of correlational research is to determine whether two or more variables are related, and if so, how strongly.

12.   T F   If two variables are strongly correlated and I know the value of one of the variables, I should be able to predict with some accuracy the value of the other variable.

13.   T F   Correlations are a good way to identify the causes of behavior.

14.   T F   If there is a negative correlation between exercise and depression, then one can conclude that high levels of exercise are associated with low depression scores.

15.   T F   In a study on the effect of exercise on energy level, exercise is the dependent variable.

16.   T F   Random assignment of subjects to groups balances individual differences among subjects between the groups.

17.   T F   Subjects in the experimental condition do not receive any amount of the independent variable.

18.   T F   It is very important that the experimenter know which subjects are in the experimental and the control group since it increases the amount of control the researcher has over the experiment.

19.   T F   Experiments have been criticized because the research setting is artificial and that subjects' behavior may be different in real life.

20.   T F   Descriptive statistics show the likelihood that the result of the study occurred by chance.

21.   T F   Standard deviation is an inferential statistic that shows how clustered or spread out individual scores are around the mean.

22.   T F   Statistically significant results allow general predictions to be made about human behavior, though not about any particular individual.

23.   T F   Meta-analysis is a research technique that studies subjects across the life span.

24.   T F   It is ethically acceptable to require students to participate as research subjects as part of their course requirements.

25.   T F   Psychology has rejected the use of animals in research since there is always another way to find out the same information.

PRACTICE TEST 5 - Essay

1.　Determine which research method is best for each situation below and explain why.

　　A.　Determine the favorite foods of adolescents.
　　B.　Determine whether a person is introverted or extroverted.
　　C.　Determine whether or not frustration causes aggression.
　　D.　Determine whether level of education is associated with criminal behavior.
　　E.　Determine conversational patterns of men and women.
　　F.　Determine why a violinist gave up a flourishing career in business to play in the local symphony.
　　G.　Determine the parenting patterns used on a child who is having behavior problems and whose parents cannot control him.

2.　In the following experiments identify: 1) a possible hypothesis, 2) the independent and dependent variables, 3) their operational definitions, and 4) experimental and control conditions.

　　A.　A study was conducted on the effects of caffeine on studying. Experimental subjects were given 32 ounces of caffeine. Subjects in the control group were given a decaffeinated beverage that looked and tasted like the beverage consumed by the experimental group. After consuming the drinks, all subjects were provided with a chapter of a text to read and then were tested.

　　B.　A study was conducted on the effects of types of music on aggressive behavior. There were three experimental groups: one listened to classical music, the second listened to jazz, and the third listened to heavy metal music. Subjects in the control condition were exposed to a white noise machine for the same period of time. Following exposure to the 45 minute music session, all subjects were put in a situation in which they were able to engage in aggressive behavior (punch a punching bag).

　　C.　A study was conducted on the effects of exercise on relaxation. There were two experimental groups of subjects. One group engaged in supervised aerobic exercise for 45 minutes. The second experimental group engaged in sit-ups and push-ups for 45 minutes. The control group engaged in a supervised study session. Following the exposure, all subjects were told to wait in a room for the experimenter to return. During this period, they were hooked up to medical equipment monitoring their heart rate, muscle tension, respiration and blood pressure.

3. Among the following examples, identify which correlations are positive, negative or zero.

    A.   Height and weight
    B.   Smoking and health
    C.   Studying and drop-out rates
    D.   SAT score and grade point average (GPA)
    E.   Education level and height
    F.   Smoking and education level
    G.   Alcohol intake and reaction time
    H.   Alcohol intake and automobile accidents
    I.   Delinquency and education level
    J.   Weight and schizophrenia

4. After reviewing the ethical guidelines adopted by the American Psychological Association (APA), determine which of the following research practices are ethical or unethical and explain why.

    A.   Require psychology students to participate as subjects in a research study.
    B.   Tell subjects that once they begin a study as a research subject, they must continue until the research is complete.
    C.   Withhold information about the hypothesis and research purposes.
    D.   Deliberately misrepresent research purposes.
    E.   Use animals to check the side-effects of a drug thought to cure depression.
    F.   Carry out a study that causes discomfort in people after securing informed consent that includes full information about possible risks.

CHAPTER 3

Evolution, Genes, and Behavior

LEARNING OBJECTIVES

1. Describe two historical positions advanced to explain human similarities and differences.

2. Distinguish among genes, chromosomes and DNA.

3. Describe how the basic elements of DNA affect the characteristics of the organism.

4. Describe one type of research used to search for genes associated with many physical and mental conditions.

5   Explain how natural selection accounts for many similarities among humans.

6. Explain the assumption that the mind develops as independent "modules."

7. Describe the approach of evolutionary psychology.

8. Describe evidence for Chomsky's position on language acquisition as well as the evidence for the role of learning in language acquisition based on artificial neural networks.

9. Explain sociobiologists' and evolutionary psychologists' views on mating and marriage.

10. Cite evidence for and against evolutionary approaches to mating and marriage.

11. Define and discuss the characteristics of heritability and describe how it is studied.

12. Explain set-point theory and other genetic and environmental influences on weight.

13. Summarize heritability estimates for intelligence and environmental factors that influence intelligence.

14. Summarize the debate and research explaining the differences in IQ between blacks and whites, including errors in the interpretation of research findings.

15. Summarize the prevailing ideas about the role of nature and nurture in explaining similarities and differences among people.

CHAPTER CONCEPT MAP

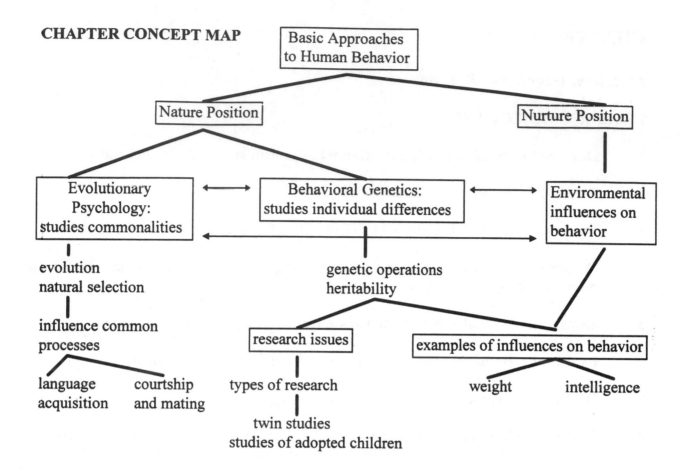

BRIEF CHAPTER SUMMARY

Chapter 3 examines the biological and evolutionary bases of behavior. Evolutionary psychology emphasizes the evolutionary mechanisms that might help explain commonalities in human behavior. Genetic operations and the principle of natural selection contribute to the understanding of commonalities among humans. Language acquisition shares similar features across cultures, suggesting that this is an innate capacity. Evolutionary psychologists (and sociobiologists) argue that certain social behaviors, such as courtship and mating, also have a biological base and serve an evolutionary function. A discussion of heritability helps explain differences among human beings. Heritability is used in an analysis of weight and intelligence, two characteristics on which human beings differ. Common misuses of heritability are discussed, along with the difficulties and complexities of behavioral-genetic research. The complexities of human behavior do not allow for simple "either-or" explanations, and the chapter demonstrates the need to be able to tolerate uncertainty in the exploration of the origins of human behavior.

PREVIEW OUTLINE AND REVIEW QUESTIONS

Before you read the chapter, review the preview outline and the Learning Objectives for each section of the text. Answer all questions as you read the text.

SECTION 1 - UNLOCKING THE SECRETS OF GENES (PP. 66-68)

I. **UNLOCKING THE SECRETS OF GENES**
- A. **Explaining human similarities and differences**
  - 1. Two main camps
    - a. Those who emphasized genes and inborn characteristics or nature
    - b. Those who focused on learning and experience or nurture
  - 2. Current position recognizes interaction of heredity and environment
- B. **Definition and characteristics of genes**
  - 1. Definition - basic units of _____
  - 2. Characteristics
    - a. Located on _____ (found in all cells in the body)
      - (1) Each sperm and egg cell contains 23 chromosomes
      - (2) At conception, the fertilized egg contains 23 chromosomes from each (sperm and egg) or 23 pairs
    - b. Chromosomes consist of strands of _____; genes consist of small segments of this DNA
    - c. Each chromosome contains thousands of genes, each with a fixed location
      - (1) Collectively, all genes are called the human _____
      - (2) Some genes are found in animals, some are uniquely human
      - (3) some genes are inherited in the same form by everyone; others vary contributing to our individuality
- C. **How elements of DNA affect characteristics of the organism**
  - 1. Each gene has four basic _____ elements of DNA (A,T,C,G)
  - 2. They are arranged in a particular order
  - 3. The order helps determine the synthesis of one of the many proteins that affect every aspect of the body
- D. **The search for genes that contribute to specific traits**
  - 1. It is very difficult to identify a single gene
  - 2. Most traits depend on more than one pair of genes, which makes tracking down the genetic contributions to a trait very difficult
  - 3. _____ studies - look at genes located close together that may be inherited together across generations
    - a. Researchers begin by looking for genetic markers, DNA segments whose locations on the chromosomes are already known

<blockquote>
b.   Then they look for patterns of inheritance of these markers in large families in which a condition is common
</blockquote>

4.   Researchers are trying to map the entire human genome which consists of 3 billion units of DNA; called The Human Genome Project

5.   Even when a gene is located, its role in physical and psychological functioning is not automatically known

6.   Genes are not the only factor involved in complex psychological traits

Answer these Learning Objectives while you read Section 1.

1.   Describe two historical positions advanced to explain human similarities and differences.

2.   Distinguish among genes, chromosomes and DNA.

3.   Describe how the basic elements of DNA affect the characteristics of the organism.

4.   Describe one type of research used to search for genes associated with many physical and mental conditions.

II. THE GENETICS OF SIMILARITY
    A. Evolutionary psychologists - apply principles of evolution to human psychological qualities and behavior
    B. Evolution and natural selection - General characteristics
        1. Definition: A change in the gene _____ within a population over many generations
        2. Why do frequencies change?
            a. Variations arise as genes spontaneously mutate and recombine
            b. Principle of natural _____ formulated by Charles Darwin
                (1) As individuals with a genetically influenced trait become more successful at surviving and reproducing in a particular environment, their genes will become more common and may spread
                (2) Those with traits not as adaptive will die before reproduction and their genes will become extinct
        3. Approach of _____-psychology
            a. Asks what challenges humans faced in prehistoric past and draws inferences about behaviors that might have evolved to solve survival problems - evaluates the inferences using research
            b. Assumes the human mind evolved as a collection of specialized _____ to handle specific survival problems
            c. They believe they can distinguish behavior that has a biological origin from behavior that does not; evidence is based on
                (1) The discovery of brain circuits
                (2) The ease with which young children acquire certain skills
    C. Innate human characteristics
        1. Common evolutionary history may explain universal abilities
        2. This includes traits such as infant reflexes, the attraction to novelty, and the motive to explore and manipulate objects, impulse to play, basic arithmetic skills

Answer these Learning Objectives while you read Section 2.

5. Explain how natural selection accounts for many similarities among humans.

6. Explain the assumption that the mind develops as independent "modules."

7. Describe the approach of evolutionary psychology.

SECTION 3 - OUR HUMAN HERITAGE: LANGUAGE (PP. 72-76)

III.   **OUR HUMAN HERITAGE: LANGUAGE**
    A.   **The nature of language**
        1.   Definition - language is a set of rules for combining elements that are in themselves meaningless into utterances that convey meaning
        2.   Humans seem to be the only species that acquires language naturally and that can combine sounds to produce original sentences
        3.   Some non-human animals can be taught aspects of language
        4.   Allows expression and comprehension of novel utterances
    B.   **The innate capacity for language**
        1.   Noam _____ - changed thinking about how language is acquired
            a.   Not learned bit by bit, but with language acquisition device, or "mental module" in the brain
            b.   Children learn surface structure - the way a sentence is spoken, and _____ structure - the meaning of a sentence
            c.   Though the rules of grammar (syntax) aren't taught to them, toddlers use it to transform surface structures into deep structures
            d.   Psycholinguists' arguments to support Chomsky's position
                (1)   Children in different cultures go through similar stages of language development - born with a universal grammar
                (2)   Children combine words and make errors called _____ that adults would not, so they are not simply imitating
                (3)   Adults do not consistently correct children's syntax yet children learn to speak correctly
                (4)   Even profoundly retarded children acquire language
                (5)   Infants as young as 7 months can derive simple linguistic rules from a string of sounds
        2.   Researchers are trying to identify brain modules and genes involved in language acquisition
    C.   **Learning and language**
        1.   Some psychologists believe experience plays a role in language acquisition
        2.   They have used computers to develop a "neural network" model
        3.   It is likely that language depends on both _____, biological readiness and _____, social experience
        4.   There is a critical period for learning language

Answer this Learning Objective while you read Section 3.

8.   Describe evidence for Chomsky's position on language acquisition as well as evidence for the role of learning in language acquisition based on artificial neural networks.

SECTION 4 - OUR HUMAN HERITAGE: COURTSHIP AND MATING (PP, 77-80)

IV.   OUR HUMAN HERITAGE: COURTSHIP AND MATING
    A.   **Agreement about the role of evolution in simple behaviors, disagreement about complex social behaviors**
    B.   **Evolution and sexual strategies**
        1.   Sociobiologists believes that gender differences in courtship and mating evolved in response to a species' survival needs
        2.   Males and females have faced different survival and mating problems, which has led to differences in behaviors according to sociobiologists
            a.   Males profit by competing for fertile females and females need to "shop" for the male with the best genes since their childbearing is limited
            b.   This explains why males are often promiscuous, and females are faithful
        3.   Evolutionary psychologists agree with these conclusions but focus more on commonalities in human behavior and less on cross-species comparisons
        4.   Cross-cultural support exists for the presence of these behaviors in humans
    C.   **Culture and the "genetic leash"**
        1.   Critics of evolutionary approach argue that
            a.   Evolutionary explanations of sexual behaviors are based on stereotypes and actual behaviors often contradict these descriptions
            b.   Among humans, sexual behavior is _____ and changeable
        2.   Critics worry that evolutionary arguments will be used to justify inequalities and violence
        3.   Debate in this area has to do with the relative power of biology and culture; sociobiologists, evolutionary psychologists, and critics all have different views

Answer these Learning Objectives while you read Section 4.

9.   Explain sociobiologists' and evolutionary psychologists' views on mating and marriage.

10.   Cite evidence for and against evolutionary approaches to mating and marriage.

SECTION 5 - THE GENETICS OF DIFFERENCE (PP. 80-83) AND
SECTION 6 - OUR HUMAN DIVERSITY: BODY WEIGHT AND SHAPE (PP. 84-89)

V. THE GENETICS OF DIFFERENCE
   A. **Behavioral** _____ - scientists who study the genetic bases of individual differences in behavior and personality
   B. **The meaning of** _____: estimates of the proportion of the total variance in a trait that is attributable to genetic variation within a group
   C. **Facts about heritability**
      1. Heritability estimates apply only to a particular group living in a particular environment, and estimates may differ for different groups
      2. Heritability estimates do <u>not</u> apply to individuals, <u>only</u> to variations within a group
      3. Even highly heritable traits can be modified by the _____
   D. **Computing heritability**
      1. Can't estimate heritability directly, must study people whose degree of genetic similarity is known
      2. Researchers study those who share either genes or environments; _____ children, _____ twins reared apart, and fraternal twins

VI. **OUR HUMAN DIVERSITY: BODY WEIGHT AND SHAPE**
   A. **Genes and weight**
      1. Formerly thought overweight was related to emotional problems - not so
      2. Heaviness not always caused by overeating
      3. Set-point theory - _____ mechanism that keeps a body at a genetically influenced set point
         a. Genetically programmed basal _____ rate interacts with fat cells and hormones to keep people at their set point
         b. Studies suggest genes contribute to size and weight differences
   B. **Tracking obesity genes**
      1. Progress has been made in identifying genes involved in obesity
      2. The gene causes fat cells to secrete _____ which travels through the blood to the hypothalamus and signals the size of fat cells; the brain then adjusts appetite and metabolism based on the leptin levels
      3. Role of leptin in human obesity is complicated; often doesn't play major role in obesity
      4. Other genes and body chemicals play important role
   C. **Environmental influences on weight**
      1. Diet and exercise
         a. Amount of food, caloric and fat levels influence weight
         b. Fat level in diets may change set points
         c. Exercise boost metabolic rate and may lower set point

            d.   Obesity has increased greatly due to changes in diet and exercise

      2.   Cultural attitudes

            a.   Cultures' standards for ideal beauty influence eating and activity

            b.   North American-European standard for white women gets thinner and thinner; may be related to expectations for women's work

D.   **Biology meets culture: The problem of eating disorders**

      1.   Many women in cultures that value thinness become obsessed with weight and continual dieting; some develop eating disorders

            a.   Bulimia involves binge eating and purges

            b.   Anorexia nervosa involves eating hardly anything

            c.   Ten times more common in _____, begin in late adolescence

            d.   Genes may play a role in the development of eating disorders

      2.   Conclusion - genes interact with cultural rules, psychological needs, and personal habits to influence weight

Answer these Learning Objectives while you read Sections 5 and 6.

11.   Define and discuss the characteristics of heritability and describe how it is studied.

12.   Explain set-point theory and other genetic and environmental influences on weight.

SECTION VII - OUR HUMAN DIVERSITY: ORIGINS OF INTELLIGENCE (PP. 89-94) AND
SECTION VIII - IN PRAISE OF HUMAN VARIATION (P. 94)

VII. **OUR HUMAN DIVERSITY: ORIGINS OF INTELLIGENCE**
    A.   **Genes and individual differences**
        1.   Intelligence is measured as an intelligence quotient, or IQ score
            a.   Compares people with others of the same age
            b.   Distribution of scores approximates a bell-shaped curve
        2.   Concept of IQ is controversial and IQ tests are criticized
        3.   Intelligence that produces high IQ scores is highly heritable
    B.   **The question of group differences**
        1.   Interpretations of group differences have been marred by prejudice
        2.   Focus has been on black-white differences in IQ scores and the research has been used for political purposes
        3.   Problems with and conclusions from between-group studies
            a.   _____ estimates based on differences within group cannot be used to compare differences between groups
            b.   Black-white IQ differences influenced by environment
            c.   Sound methodological studies do not reveal genetic differences between blacks and whites
    C.   **The environment and intelligence**
        1.   Environmental factors associated with reduced mental ability include poor prenatal care, malnutrition, exposure to toxins, large family _____, stressful family circumstances
        2.   Healthy and stimulating environment can raise mental performance
VIII. **IN PRAISE OF HUMAN VARIATION**
    A.   **Heredity and environment interact to produce most human qualities**
    B.   **The fitness of a species depends on its _____**

Answer these Learning Objectives while you read Sections 7 and 8.

13.   Summarize heritability estimates for intelligence and environmental factors influencing intelligence.

14.   Summarize the debate and research explaining black-white differences in IQ, including errors in the interpretation of research findings.

15.   Summarize the prevailing ideas about the role of nature and nurture in explaining similarities and differences among people.

FLASH CARDS

Cut the following chart along the borders and test yourself with the resulting flash cards.

3.1 GENES	3.2 CHROMOSOMES	3.3 DNA (DEOXYRIBONUCLEIC ACID)
3.4 GENOME	3.5 LINKAGE STUDIES	3.6 GENETIC MARKERS
3.7 EVOLUTIONARY PSYCHOLOGY	3.8 EVOLUTION	3.9 MUTATE
3.10 NATURAL SELECTION	3.11 CHARLES DARWIN	3.12 LANGUAGE
3.13 SYNTAX	3.14 SURFACE STRUCTURE/ DEEP STRUCTURE	3.15 LANGUAGE ACQUISITION DEVICE

3.3 The molecule in the chromosomes that transfers genetic characteristics by way of coded instructions for the structure of proteins.	3.2 Rod-shaped structures that carry the genes. They are found in the center of every cell of the body.	3.1 They are the basic units of heredity and are located on chromosomes.
3.6 DNA segments that vary considerably among individuals and whose locations on the chromosomes are already known.	3.5 Genetic studies that look for patterns of inheritance of genetic markers in large families in which a particular condition is common.	3.4 The full set of genes in each cell of the organism.
3.9 The ability of genes to spontaneously change during formation of a sperm or an egg, due to an "error" in copying the original DNA sequence.	3.8 A change in gene frequencies within a population over many generations.	3.7 A field that applies the principles of evolution to human psychological qualities and behavior to explain human similarities.
3.12 A set of rules for combining meaningless elements into utterances that convey meaning.	3.11 British naturalist who first formulated in general terms the principle of natural selection.	3.10 Evolutionary process in which individuals with genetically influenced traits that are adaptive survive and reproduce.
3.15 According to Chomsky, the human brain has a "mental module" for language that allows children to develop language.	3.14 Identified by Chomsky, surface structure is the way a sentence is actually spoken; deep structure refers to the meaning of a sentence.	3.13 The rules that make up the grammar of a language.

3.16 PSYCHOLINGUISTICS	3.17 UNIVERSAL GRAMMAR	3.18 OVERREGULARIZATIONS
3.19 CRITICAL PERIOD (FOR LANGUAGE ACQUISITION)	3.20 SOCIOBIOLOGY	3.21 BEHAVIORAL GENETICS
3.22 HERITABILITY	3.23 IDENTICAL (MONOZYGOTIC) TWINS	3.24 FRATERNAL (DIZYGOTIC) TWINS
3.25 SET POINT	3.26 LEPTIN	3.27 ANOREXIA NERVOSA
3.28 BASIL METABOLIC RATE	3.29 BULIMIA	3.30 INTELLIGENCE QUOTIENT (IQ)

3.18 Non-random errors that children make when learning language in which they overgeneralize grammatical rules.	3.17 Children everywhere seem to go through similar stages of linguistic development.	3.16 Researchers who study the psychology of language.
3.21 An interdisciplinary field of study concerned with the genetic bases of behavior and personality.	3.20 The application of biological principles to the social and sexual customs of both non-human animals and human beings.	3.19 A period, possibly from ages 1 to 5, when there is a biological readiness to learn language.
3.24 Twins who develop from two separate eggs fertilized by different sperm. They are no more alike genetically than any two siblings.	3.23 Twins born when a fertilized egg divides into two parts that develop into separate embryos.	3.22 Estimate of the proportion of the total variance in a trait within a group, attributable to genetic differences among those in the group.
3.27 An eating disorder in which the person eats hardly anything and becomes dangerously thin because of a delusional belief that she or he	3.26 A protein secreted by fat cells that signals the hypothalamus to maintain the set point by adjusting appetite and metabolism.	3.25 A theory that a genetically-influenced weight range is maintained by a homeostatic mechanism regulating intake, fat reserves,
3.30 A measure of intellectual functioning in which scores on a test are compared to others of the same age.	3.29 An eating disorder in which the person binges and then purges by inducing vomiting or using laxatives.	3.28 A genetically programmed rate at which the body burns calories for energy.

72

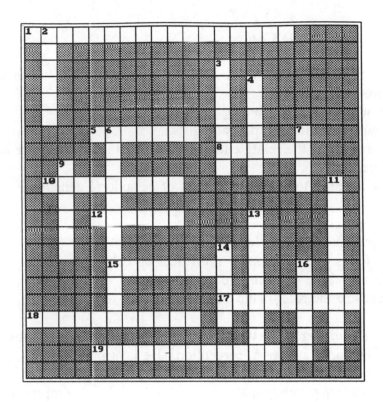

ACROSS

1. The psychology of language
5. Linguist who argued that the human brain contains a language acquisition device
8. The full set of genes in each cell of an organism
10. An environmental influence on intelligence
12. British naturalist who formulated the principle of natural selection
15. System that combines meaningless elements into utterances that convey meaning
17. A change in gene frequencies over many generations
18. Type of twins born when a fertilized egg divides into two parts that develop into separate embryos
19. A characteristic that IQ tests attempt to measure

DOWN

2. The rules that make up the grammar of a language
3. Type of study that looks for patterns of inheritance in large families
4. Influence on intelligence
6. Estimate of the proportion of the variance in a trait within a group that is attributable to genetic differences among individuals
7. Type of structure that refers to the meaning of a sentence
9. How genes change spontaneously
11. Rod-shaped structures, within every cell, that carry the genes
13. Type of twins who develop from two separate eggs
14. The functional units of heredity
16. A social behavior that may be influenced by evolution

PRACTICE TEST 1 - Multiple Choice

1. Historically, those who agree with the nature position and those who believe in the nurture approach
   A. both agree with sociobiologists.
   B. are both evolutionary psychologists.
   C. disagree about the relative importance of nature and nurture in explaining human differences.
   D. work together to develop the field of behavioral genetics.

2. Evolutionary psychology and sociobiology
   A. are branches of behavioral genetics.
   B. both focus on evolutionary influences on behaviors.
   C. have very little in common.
   D. emphasize the role of the environment.

3. Dr. Ricardo is studying how evolutionary mechanisms might help explain commonalities in language learning, attention, perception. He is a(n)
   A. behavioral geneticist.   B. sociobiologist.
   C. evolutionary psychologist.   D. empiricist.

4. Genes are
   A. rod-shaped structures found in every cell of the body.
   B. thread-like strands that make up chromosomes.
   C. one of the four basic elements of DNA.
   D. the basic units of heredity.

5. Chromosomes are
   A. rod-shaped structures found in every cell of the body.
   B. located on genes.
   C. one of the four basic elements of DNA.
   D. the basic units of heredity.

6. The full set of genes contained in each cell is the
   A. DNA.   B. chromosome.
   C. genome.   D. basis.

7. When a sperm and egg unite at conception, the fertilized egg, and all the body cells that eventually develop from it (except for sperm cells and ova) contain
   A. 46 pairs of chromosomes.
   B. 23 chromosomes.
   C. 46 chromosomes in 23 pairs.
   D. 23 pairs of genes.

8. Most human traits depend on
   A. more than one pair of genes.
   B. a single pair of genes.
   C. one gene.
   D. between 5 and 10 pairs of genes.

9. In search of a genetic marker for Huntington's disease, researchers studied large families in which this condition was common. This type of study is called a(n)
   A. case study.
   B. linkage study.
   C. evolutionary study.
   D. family research.

10. One reason new traits keep arising is because of the genes' ability to _____ spontaneously.
    A. divide
    B. multiply
    C. split
    D. mutate

11. Within each gene, elements of DNA are arranged in a particular order which forms a code that influences the synthesis of particular proteins. This affects every aspect of the body, from its structure to the chemicals that keep it running. This process describes
    A. linkage studies.
    B. how genes affect characteristics of the organism.
    C. how genes mutate.
    D. how natural selection occurs.

12. As gene frequencies change within a population over generations, certain genetically influenced characteristics become more or less common. This refers to
    A. evolution.
    B. natural selection.
    C. sociobiology.
    D. heritability.

13. A way to explain WHY gene frequencies change is the idea that individuals with traits that are adaptive in an environment will stay alive to reproduce, and over generations their genes will become more common. This describes
    A. evolution.
    B. natural selection.
    C. sociobiology.
    D. heritability.

14. Psycholinguists suggest that by applying rules that make up the grammar of language, we are able to understand and produce new sentences correctly. These rules are called
    A. surface structure.   B. overregularizations.
    C. syntax.   D. mental modules.

15. Chomsky's contribution to the understanding of language acquisition was the idea that
    A. language is learned bit by bit, as one might learn a list of U.S. presidents.
    B. there is a critical period for learning language.
    C. children go through different stages of language development.
    D. language is too complex to learn bit by bit, so there must be a "mental module" in the brain that allows young children to develop language.

16. Which of the following supports Chomsky's position on language acquisition?
    A. Children everywhere go through similar stages of linguistic development.
    B. Children combine words in ways adults never would, which rules out imitation.
    C. Even children who are profoundly retarded acquire language.
    D. All of the above support Chomsky's position on language acquisition.

17. Which of the following reflects the sociobiological view on mating and marriage?
    A. Marriage and mating behaviors have been learned through reinforcements.
    B. Males and females have faced different kinds of survival and mating problems and have evolved differently in aggressiveness and sexual strategies.
    C. Socialization accounts for differences in mating behaviors.
    D. None of the above reflect the sociobiological position.

18. "It pays for males to compete for access to fertile females and to try to inseminate as many females as possible; because females can conceive and bear only a limited number of offspring, it pays for them to be selective and look for the best mate." This reflects the position of
    A. outdated psychologists.
    B. an empiricist.
    C. sociobiology.
    D. Chomsky.

19. Critics of the evolutionary approach cite which of the following positions to support their view?
    A. Though humans and animals may engage in similar behaviors, the motives or origins of the behaviors differ.
    B. Not all animal and human behavior conforms to the sexual stereotypes.
    C. Among human beings, sexual behavior is extremely varied and changeable.
    D. All of the above are arguments used by critics of the evolutionary approach.

20. Heritability
    A. estimates the proportion of difference in a trait that is attributable to genetic variation within a group.
    B. is equivalent in meaning to the term genetic.
    C. estimates the proportion of a trait that is attributable to genes in an individual.
    D. estimates the proportion of difference in a trait that is attributable to genetic variation between groups.

21. To study the heritability of a particular trait, which groups of people are studied?
    A. adopted children and twins   B. unrelated people
    C. biological mothers and daughters   D. husbands and wives

22. Set-point theory suggests that
    A. a genetically influenced weight range is maintained by a homeostatic mechanism that regulates food intake, fat reserves and metabolism.
    B. in almost all cases, being overweight is caused by overeating.
    C. obesity is an indicator of emotional disturbance.
    D. weight is not influenced by genes but by learned behaviors.

23. Heritability estimates of intelligence for children and adolescents
    A. are very low since IQ is shaped primarily by environmental influences.
    B. vary widely but they have an average of .50.
    C. have an average of .90
    D. have an average of .10

24. Which of the following is a flaw in genetic theories of black-white differences in IQ?
    A. Blacks and whites do not grow up, on average, in the same kind of environment.
    B. Because of racial discrimination and de facto segregation, black children receive less encouragement and fewer opportunities than whites.
    C. Heritability estimates based on one group (whites) are used to estimate the role heredity plays in differences between groups.
    D. All of the above are flaws.

25. Which of the following is an environmental influence on IQ that can have a negative impact on mental ability?
    A. poor prenatal care   B. malnutrition
    C. exposure to toxins   D. all of the above

PRACTICE TEST 2 - Multiple Choice

1.   Dr. Schmidt is interested in cross-cultural similarities in language acquisition. She thinks that evolution might help explain these similarities. She is a(n)
   A.   behavior geneticist.   B.   evolutionary psychologist.
   C.   empiricist.   D.   sociobiologist.

2.   The position of behavioral geneticists and evolutionary psychologists is related to
   A.   the nature position, which focuses on learning and experience.
   B.   the nurture position, which focuses on learning and experience.
   C.   the nature position, which focuses on genes and inborn characteristics.
   D.   the nurture position, which focuses on genes and inborn characteristics.

3.   Which statement describes the relationship between genes, chromosomes and DNA?
   A.   Genes, the basic unit of heredity, are located on chromosomes, which consist of strands of DNA. Genes consist of small segments of DNA molecules.
   B.   Genes are composed of chromosomes and DNA.
   C.   Chromosomes, the basic unit of heredity, direct the genes and the DNA.
   D.   DNA houses both genes and chromosomes in its rod-shaped structures.

4.   Which of the following describes how the basic elements of DNA within each cell affect characteristics of the organism?
   A.   DNA affects characteristics of the organism directly.
   B.   The process by which DNA affects the organism is unknown.
   C.   The basic elements are arranged in a particular order, which is a chemical code that specifies the sequence of amino acids, which influences protein synthesis, which affects the characteristics of the organism.
   D.   The basic elements direct specific genes that influence particular traits.

5.   Dr. Sayeed is trying to track down the genetic contributions to eye color. Which of the following is likely to be true?
   A.   Because it is a simple trait, probably a single pair of genes is responsible.
   B.   Most human traits, even simple ones, depend on more than one pair of genes.
   C.   She can locate the gene or genes through using a high resolution microscope.
   D.   She will have to map the entire human genome.

6. Which of the following processes contribute to new genetic variations?
    A. Genes can spontaneously change, or mutate.
    B. Genes recombine during the production of sperm and eggs.
    C. Small segments of genetic material can exchange places between members of a chromosome pair.
    D. All of the above account for new genetic variations.

7. "Characteristics that increase survival, and hence the opportunity to reproduce, will become more common over many generations." This reflects the theory of
    A. natural selection.   B. evolution.
    C. dominant genes.   D. heritability.

8. To handle survival problems in the prehistoric past, the human mind evolved as a collection of specialized _____ for certain behavioral tendencies.
    A. instincts   B. modules
    C. mutations   D. intuition

9. Like attraction to novelty and the motive to explore and manipulate things, evolutionary psychologists suggest that language and mating practices
    A. reflect our common evolutionary history.
    B. are learned behaviors.
    C. are examples of social Darwinism.
    D. differ across cultures.

10. "Lee gave the ball to Lynne," and "Lynne received the ball from Lee" have
    A. the same surface structure.
    B. different deep structures.
    C. the same surface and deep structures.
    D. the same deep structure.

11. Though they are learning different languages, Lana from Morocco, Ayse from Turkey and Paulo from Italy are going through similar stages of language development and combine words in ways that adults never would. This supports the conclusion that
    A. language is learned in bits and pieces.
    B. the syntax of all languages is remarkably similar.
    C. the brain contains a language acquisition device that allows children to develop language if they are exposed to an adequate sampling of speech.
    D. language acquisition is primarily the result of imitation of speech.

12. The sexually promiscuous male and the coy and choosy female
    A. are outdated stereotypes.
    B. are learned through the socialization process.
    C. have evolutionary origins according to sociobiologists.
    D. are common behaviors among most human beings.

13. "Even if human beings and other animals seem to behave in a similar fashion, this does not mean that the origins of the behavior must be the same in both species." This statement represents
    A. the position of evolutionary psychologists.
    B. the position of sociobiologists.
    C. the position of behavior geneticists.
    D. the position of natural selection.

14. Heritability can be used to estimate
    A. IQ differences between whites and Asians.
    B. IQ differences among Harvard graduates.
    C. how much of an individual's IQ is determined by heredity.
    D. exactly which genes are responsible for intelligence.

15. Which of the following is consistent with the facts about heritability?
    A. If one knows the heritability of alcoholism, it is possible to know the extent to which a particular individual's alcoholism is inherited.
    B. Even height can be dramatically affected by diet.
    C. About fifty per cent of an individual's personality is due to heredity.
    D. Research is being conducted to locate THE math gene.

16. Dr. Wood is studying the heritability of schizophrenia. The type of study that would accomplish this best would be a study of
    A. monozygotic twins reared apart.
    B. monozygotic twins reared together.
    C. dizygotic twins reared together.
    D. siblings reared together.

17. Dr. Cane's brother weighs much more than he does although he eats much less. How can this best be explained?
    A. His brother is not honest about how much he eats.
    B. Set-point theory explains this.
    C. His brother has a faster metabolic rate.
    D. Dr. Cane has more fat cells.

18. Set point is to _____ as thermostat is to _____.
    A.   basal metabolic rate; furnace
    B.   fat cells; temperature
    C.   weight; furnace
    D.   genes; temperature

19. Pete is adopting a child whose biological parents have low IQs. Pete asks whether this child is also likely to have a low IQ. Which of the following is the best response?
    A.   The child is also quite likely to have a low IQ, since heritability of IQ is high.
    B.   The IQs of the child's biological parents are irrelevant, since environmental influences outweigh heritability.
    C.   While IQ is at least in part heritable, environmental influences can have a great impact; however, it is impossible to make predictions about any individual.
    D.   Nothing is known about the heritability of IQ.

20. Richard wants to positively influence the IQ of his daughter as much as possible. To do this, he should
    A.   provide good nutrition.
    B.   remove environmental toxins.
    C.   provide opportunities for mental stimulation.
    D.   do all of the above.

21. Children fathered by black and white American soldiers in Germany after World War II, and reared in similar German communities by similar families, did not differ significantly in IQ. This study
    A.   supports genetic theories explaining black-white IQ differences.
    B.   refutes genetic theories explaining black-white IQ differences.
    C.   has been criticized for methodological errors.
    D.   demonstrates the IQ superiority of blacks over whites.

22. Two pots of tomatoes were planted with seeds of identical quality. One pot used enriched soil and one pot used impoverished soil. A comparison of the plants from each of these pots is analogous to
    A.   comparing the IQs of two Asian-Americans from similar socioeconomic backgrounds, communities and school systems.
    B.   looking for a genetic explanation of IQ differences between blacks and whites.
    C.   comparing the IQs of two siblings.
    D.   None of the above

23. Behavior geneticists might study which of the following?
    A.   universal characteristics that all individuals share like reflexes
    B.   similarities in language learning
    C.   the genetic basis of individual differences in intelligence
    D.   all of the above

24. Although IQ is a predictor of success in schooling, schooling also has a substantial effect on IQ. This reflects the fact that
    A.   IQ test scores are not very reliable.
    B.   IQ is primarily influenced by the environment.
    C.   IQ cannot be predicted.
    D.   even highly heritable traits can be modified.

25. Which of the following statements best summarizes the prevailing ideas about the role of nature and nurture in explaining similarities and differences among people?
    A.   Heredity determines some characteristics and environment determines others.
    B.   It is likely that in time we will find genetic explanations for most behaviors.
    C.   Heredity and environment always interact to produce a unique mixture of qualities; once present, they blend and become indistinguishable.
    D.   We really know very little about the relative contributions of each on any given trait.

PRACTICE TEST 3 - Short Answer

1. _____ are the basic unit of heredity, and they are located on _____.

2. Collectively, the 100,000 or so human genes are referred to as the human _____.

3. To find the gene responsible for Huntington's disease, researchers studied large families in which this condition was common. This approach is called a _____ study.

4. _____ psychologists try to explain commonalities in language learning, perception memory, sexuality, and many other aspects of behavior.

5. As genes become more common in the population or less common, so do the characteristics they influence. This is referred to as _____.

6. Gene frequencies in a population change because they spontaneously _____.

7. The principle of _____ says that individuals with a genetically influenced trait tend to be more successful at staying alive long enough to produce offspring; their genes will become more and more common in the population.

8. Evolutionary psychologists believe that the human mind developed as a collection of specialized and independent _____ to handle specific survival problems.

9. Evolutionary psychologists believe that certain abilities, tendencies, and characteristics evolved because they were useful to our ancestors. Two of these abilities or tendencies include _____ and _____.

10. Language is a set of _____ for combining meaningless _____ into utterances that convey meaning.

11. "Mary kissed John" and "John was kissed by Mary" have the same _____ structure but a different _____ structure.

12. _____ said that language was far too complex to be learned bit by bit, therefore there must be an innate mental module for learning language called a language _____ device.

13. One piece of evidence that children have an innate mental module for language is that children in different cultures go through _____ of linguistic development.

14. The fact that children who are not exposed to language until late childhood rarely speak normally supports the idea that there is a _____ in language development during the first few years of life.

15. _____ believe that human gender differences in courtship and mating evolved in response to a species' survival needs.

16. Evolutionary psychologists differ from sociobiologists in that they tend to argue less by _____ and focus on the _____ in human mating and dating practices around the world.

17. Critics of evolutionary approaches to infidelity and monogamy argue that these explanations are based on _____ of gender differences.

18. The proportion of the total variance in a trait that is attributable to genetic variation within a group refers to _____.

19. Heritability estimates do not apply to _____.

20. To estimate heritability of a trait, researchers study _____ children and _____ twins.

21. One approach to weight holds that a biological mechanism keeps a person's body weight at a genetically influenced _____, which is the weight you stay at when you are not consciously trying to gain or lose.

22. Though there is considerable evidence that genes contribute to size and weight differences, it is also true that environmental influences such as _____ and _____ also play an important role.

23. For children and adolescents, heritability estimates of intelligence average around _____ and the estimates for adults are in the _____ range.

24. Genetic explanations for differences in intelligence between blacks and whites are flawed because they use estimates based on a white sample to estimate the role of heredity in _____ differences.

25. Environmental influences on mental ability include poor _____ care and _____.

PRACTICE TEST 4 - True/False

1.   T F   Chromosomes consist of threadlike strands of DNA molecules, and genes consist of small segments of this DNA.

2.   T F   An international collaboration of researchers has successfully completed a map of the entire human genome.

3.   T F   Once researchers locate a gene on a chromosome, they then know its role in physical or psychological functioning.

4.   T F   Evolutionary psychologists attempt to explain human similarities by applying the principles of evolution to human psychological qualities and behavior.

5.   T F   While scientists agree on the basic processes of evolution and on natural selection, they debate how gradually or abruptly such changes occur and whether competition for survival is always the primary mechanism of change.

6.   T F   Some non-human animals are able to acquire and use language.

7.   T F   Noam Chomsky introduced the idea that children learn language by imitating adults and paying attention when adults corrected their mistakes.

8.   T F   Surface structures refer to what people say while deep structure refers to the unconscious meaning of their sentences.

9.   T F   The fact that children combine words in ways that adults never would is evidence that language is not learned through simple imitation and, because their errors are not random, demonstrates that they have grasped some grammatical rules.

10.   T F   Chomsky suggested that humans have an inborn grammatical capacity and there is a critical period for learning language.

11.   T F   Social scientists disagree about whether biology and evolution can help account for complex social customs.

12.   T F   Sociobiologists study the genetic bases of individual differences in behavior and personality.

13.   T F   According to sociobiologists, there is an evolutionary basis to male interest in many different sexual partners and females' interest in stability and security.

14.   T F   Evolutionary arguments can be used to justify social and political inequalities and violent behavior.

15.   T F   Heritability refers to the extent to which a particular trait has been inherited in a particular individual.

16.   T F   Environmental influences have relatively little impact on highly heritable traits, like height.

17.   T F   The best way to estimate the heritability of a trait is to compare blood relatives within families.

18.   T F   According to set-point theory, a complex interaction of metabolism, fat cells, and hormones keeps people at the weight their bodies are designed to be.

19.   T F   For most obese people, leptin has been found to play a major role.

20.   T F   One explanation for the changes in the cultural ideal for women has to do with the equation between slimness and masculine competence.

21.   T F   High IQ scores are primarily the result of environmental influences.

22.   T F   IQ scores of adopted children are more highly correlated with those of their birth parents than with those of their biologically unrelated adoptive parents.

23.   T F   Studies that have overcome methodological problems fail to reveal any genetic differences between blacks and whites in the abilities measured on IQ tests.

24.   T F   IQ tends to decline slightly in each successive child in a family.

25.   T F   Nature loves genetic diversity, not similarity.

PRACTICE TEST 5 - Essay

1   A.   You are working in a drug treatment program. You hear many clients in this program describe their alcoholic family backgrounds and state their belief that their alcoholism is genetic. Using information about genes, chromosomes and DNA, give a general description of how this might be possible.

        B.   You attend a lecture in which an author of a self-help book on alcoholism says that alcoholism is fifty percent inherited and, therefore, if you have an alcoholic parent, you have a fifty percent chance of becoming an alcoholic. Discuss the problems with these statements using the facts about heritability.

        C.   If you wanted to search for the genes associated with alcoholism, describe the type of study you would conduct and how you would go about collecting your data.

2.   Using the approach of evolutionary psychology, expand on the idea that the following characteristics were inherited because they were useful during the history of our species (they had an evolutionary function). Explain how they might have been useful in adapting.

        A.   the feeling of disgust
        B.   intuition
        C.   self-concept
        D.   kinship
        E.   male promiscuity
        F.   female selectivity

3.   Compare Chomsky's position with an earlier position on the acquisition of language and use arguments to support this view.

4.   A.   Describe a study that you would design to evaluate the heritability of intelligence. Describe your conclusions about both hereditary and environmental influences on intelligence. What cautionary statements would you make about the heritability estimate?

        B.   Based on your findings, you are to make recommendations to a federal panel to be convened to develop a parental training program for low income families to help them promote intellectual development in their children. Discuss the recommendations you would make to the panel.

CHAPTER 4

Neurons, Hormones, and the Brain

LEARNING OBJECTIVES

1. List and describe the features and functions of the central and peripheral nervous systems.

2. Distinguish between the somatic and autonomic nervous systems.

3. Describe biofeedback.

4. Distinguish between the sympathetic and parasympathetic nervous systems.

5. Describe the structure of a neuron and explain how impulses are transmitted from one neuron to another.

6. Describe the roles of neurotransmitters and endorphins.

7. Describe the functioning of hormones, specifically those in which psychologists are especially interested.

8. List and describe techniques psychologists use to study brain functions.

9. List and describe the location and function of each of the major portions of the brain.

10. Summarize the functions of the brain's two hemispheres and explain their relationship.

11. Describe the general position taken by neuroscientists on the self, and discuss two specific approaches advanced by scientists to explain the sense of a unified self.

12. Summarize the evidence on whether there are sex differences in the brain and how any differences might affect behavior.

13. Describe the effect of experience on brain development.

CHAPTER CONCEPT MAP

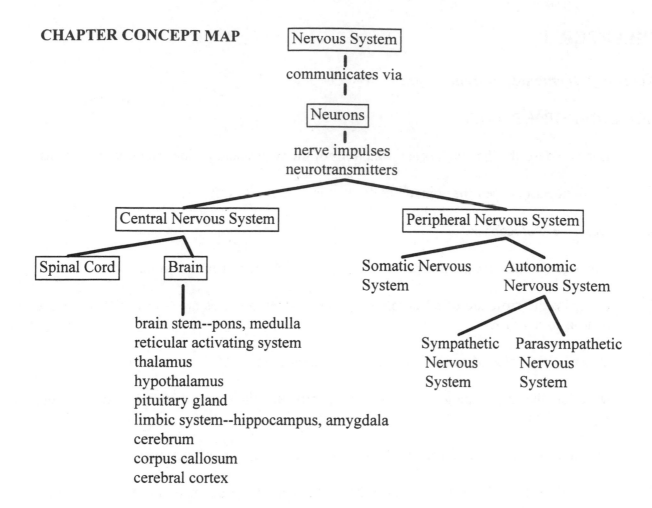

Nervous System

communicates via

Neurons

nerve impulses
neurotransmitters

Central Nervous System

Peripheral Nervous System

Spinal Cord

Brain

Somatic Nervous
System

Autonomic
Nervous System

brain stem--pons, medulla
reticular activating system
thalamus
hypothalamus
pituitary gland
limbic system--hippocampus, amygdala
cerebrum
corpus callosum
cerebral cortex

Sympathetic
Nervous
System

Parasympathetic
Nervous
System

BRIEF CHAPTER SUMMARY

Chapter 4 reviews the brain and nervous system. The central nervous system is composed of the brain and spinal cord. It receives incoming messages from the senses, processes that information, and sends output to the muscles and organs. The nerves in the rest of the body are part of the peripheral nervous system, which is composed of the somatic nervous system and the autonomic nervous system. The autonomic nervous system is made up of the sympathetic and parasympathetic nervous systems. The nervous system is made up of nerve cells--or neurons. A neuron is made up of dendrites, a cell body, and an axon, which ends in axon terminals. A neural message goes from the beginning to the end of a neuron via an electrical impulse. Neurons communicate with other neurons through chemicals called neurotransmitters. They are released by one neuron and temporarily received by another at the synapse, a tiny space between two neurons. Different brain structures and their functions are discussed, along with general issues about how the brain processes information.

PREVIEW OUTLINE AND REVIEW QUESTIONS

Before you read the chapter, review the preview outline and the Learning Objectives for each section of the text. Answer all questions as you read the text.

SECTION 1 - THE NERVOUS SYSTEM: A BASIC BLUEPRINT (PP. 100-103)

I. **THE NERVOUS SYSTEM: A BASIC BLUEPRINT**
    A.   **The central nervous system (CNS)**
        1.   Functions - receives, processes, interprets and stores incoming information; sends out messages to muscles, glands, internal organs
        2.   Parts - brain and _____ _____ (an extension of the brain which can produce automatic reflexes without the help of the brain)
    B.   **The _____ nervous system (PNS)** - nervous system outside brain and spinal cord which handles the input and output of the CNS
        1.   Functions
            a.   _____ neurons - bring input to CNS from skin, muscles, organs
            b.   Motor neurons - carry output to muscles, glands and organs
        2.   Divisions
            a.   _____ nervous system (also called skeletal nervous system)
                (1)   Nerves connected to sensory receptors
                (2)   Nerves connected to skeletal muscles - voluntary action
            b.   Autonomic nervous system - works automatically
                (1)   Functions: regulates blood vessels, glands, internal organs
                (2)   Has two parts
                      (a)   _____ nervous system - mobilizes body for action
                      (b)   Parasympathetic nervous systems - slows action
                (3)   Biofeedback - helps people control autonomic responses

Answer these Learning Objectives while you read Section 1.

1.   List and describe features and functions of the central and peripheral nervous systems.

2.   Distinguish between the somatic and autonomic nervous systems.

3.   Describe biofeedback.

4.   Distinguish between the sympathetic and parasympathetic nervous systems.

SECTION 2 - COMMUNICATION IN THE NERVOUS SYSTEM (PP. 103-112)

II.   **COMMUNICATION IN THE NERVOUS SYSTEM**
    A.   **Components of the nervous system**
        1.   Neurons - _____ cells that communicate to, from or inside the CNS
        2.   Glial cells - hold neurons in place, nourish, insulate neurons
    B.   **The structure of the neuron**
        1.   Dendrites - receive messages from other neurons, transmit to cell body
        2.   Cell body - keeps the neuron alive, determines whether to fire
        3.   _____ - transmit messages away from cell body to other neurons, muscles or gland cells
            a.   End in branches or axon terminals
            b.   Many axons insulated by fatty material or myelin sheath
        4.   Nerves - bundles of nerve fibers in the PNS
            a.   Humans have 43 pairs, most enter or leave the spinal cord
            b.   Twelve pairs, the cranial nerves, connect directly to the brain
            c.   Formerly thought injured nerves could not regrow, new research finds some can and some precursor cells can produce new neurons
    C.   **How neurons communicate**
        1.   Synapses = axon terminal + synaptic _____ (small space between one axon and next dendrite) + membrane of receiving dendrite
            a.   Axon terminals from many neurons may connect at a synapse
            b.   Axons and dendrites continue to grow throughout life, and synaptic connections get more complex, while some unused connections die
            c.   The brain's circuits continually change - plasticity
        2.   Neural impulses - how neurons communicate
            a.   When a nerve cell is stimulated, an electrical impulse, or action potential, occurs (an exchange of positive and negative charged ions), and moves down axon to end of axon terminal's tip
            b.   Synaptic vesicles (sacs in the tip of the axon terminal) open and release chemical neurotransmitters which cross the synaptic cleft and bind briefly with receiving dendrites' receptor sites
            c.   They can excite or _____ the firing of the receiving neuron; what occurs is determined by the net effect of all messages received
            d.   Neurons either fire or do not fire (all or none); the strength of firing does not alter
    D.   **Chemical messengers in the nervous system**
        1.   Neurotransmitters: Versatile couriers
            a.   _____ have been identified, more are being found
            b.   Each binds only to certain types of receptor sites

      c.   Neurotransmitters affect many behaviors and functions

      d.   Some better understood neurotransmitters and some of their effects

            (1)   Serotonin - sleep, mood, and other behaviors

            (2)   Dopamine - movement, learning, memory, emotion

            (3)   Acetylcholine - muscle action, memory, emotion, cognition

            (4)   Norepinephrine - heart rate, learning, memory, emotion

            (5)   GABA - inhibitory neurotransmitter

      e.   Harmful effects can occur when levels are too high or too low

      f.   Neurotransmitters play multiple roles and cause and effect between neurotransmitters and specific behaviors is unclear

2.   _____: The brain's natural opiates (endogenous opioid peptides)

      a.   Produce effects similar to natural opiates; reduce pain, promote pleasure as well as other behaviors

      b.   Most act as _____ which influence actions of neurotransmitters

      c.   Increase during stress response which gives evolutionary advantage

3.   Hormones: Long-distance messengers

      a.   Produced in _____ glands and released into the bloodstream, which carries them to other organs and cells

      b.   Some may also be classified as neurotransmitters

      c.   Hormones have dozens of jobs

      d.   Hormones of particular interest to psychologists

            (1)   Melatonin - regulates biological rhythm

            (2)   Adrenal hormones - involved in emotions and stress and some nonemotional conditions

            (3)   produced by the adrenal glands

                  (a)   the outer part produces cortisol

                  (b)   inner part produces epinephrine and norepinephrine which activate the sympathetic nervous system

            (4)   Sex hormones - secreted by gonads and occur in both sexes

                  (a)   Androgens (i.e. testosterone) - masculinizing

                  (b)   _____ - feminizing

                  (c)   Progesterone - maintenance of uterine lining

Answer these Learning Objectives while you read Section 2.

5.   Describe the structure of a neuron and explain how impulses are transmitted from one neuron to another.

6.   Describe the roles of neurotransmitters and endorphins.

7.   Describe the functioning of hormones in which psychologists are especially interested.

SECTION 3 - MAPPING THE BRAIN (PP. 113-115)

III.   **MAPPING THE BRAIN** - Methods for studying the brain
    A.   **Researchers study the brains of those who have experienced disease or injury**
    B.   _____ **method** - damaging or removing section of brain in animals and then observing the effects
    C.   **Electrode methods** - detect electrical activity of the neurons
        1.   Electroencephalogram (EEG)
            a.   Brain _____ recording
            b.   Computer technology is used with EEG to yield brain activity patterns associated with specific events
        2.   Needle _____
            a.   Thin wires inserted into the brain to record electrical activity and to stimulate the brain
            b.   Microelectrodes - fine wires that can be inserted into single cells
            c.   Used to record electrical activity and to stimulate the brain
    D.   **Positron-Emission Tomography - PET scan**
        1.   Records biochemical changes in the brain as they occur
        2.   Utilizes a harmless radioactive glucose-like substance that accumulates in particularly active parts of the brain and can then be used to indicate brain involvement during certain behaviors
        3.   Used to diagnose abnormalities or to learn about normal brain activity
    E.   **Magnetic Resonance Imaging (MRI)**
            a.   Allows the exploration of "inner space" without chemicals
            b.   Uses _____ fields and radio frequencies which produce vibrations that are picked up by special receivers
            c.   New "functional MRI" captures brain changes very quickly
            d.   Used for both diagnosing disease and studying normal brains
    F.   **Cautions about brain research**
        1.   Findings are difficult to interpret
        2.   Don't tell us what is happening inside the person's head
        3.   This research is an important first step

Answer this Learning Objective while you read Section 3

8.   List and describe techniques psychologists use to study brain functions.

SECTION 4 - A TOUR THROUGH THE BRAIN (PP. 116-123)

IV. **A TOUR THROUGH THE BRAIN**
- A. **Localization of function**
  1. Theories of brain function that assume that different brain parts perform different (though overlapping) tasks
  2. Generally, the more reflexive or automatic a behavior, the more likely it is to involve lower brain areas, while the more complex a behavior, the more likely it is to involve areas that are higher up
- B. **The brain stem** - rises out of spinal cord; paths from upper areas pass through the two main structures
  1. Medulla - regulates automatic functions; breathing and heart rate
  2. Pons - regulates sleeping, waking, and dreaming
  3. Reticular _____ system - network of neurons, extends upward and connects with higher brain areas; screens information, alertness
- C. **The cerebellum**
  1. Atop brain stem; regulates balance and coordination of muscle movement
  2. May play a role in analyzing sensory information, in remembering certain simple skills, solving problems, understanding words
- D. **The thalamus**
  1. Relays motor impulses out of brain, directs incoming sensory messages to higher centers
  2. Smell bypasses the thalamus and goes to the olfactory bulb
- E. **The hypothalamus and pituitary gland**
  1. Hypothalamus - associated with _____, such as hunger, thirst, emotion, sex and reproduction, body temperature and the autonomic nervous system
  2. Pituitary gland - "master gland" governed by hypothalamus
- F. **Limbic system** - loosely interconnected structures involved in emotions
  1. Amygdala - evaluates sensory information to determine its importance; also mediates depression and anxiety
  2. _____ - "gateway to memory;" allows formation and storage of new memories
- G. **Cerebrum** - site of higher forms of thinking
  1. Divided into two halves or cerebral _____ that are connected by a band of fibers called the _____ callosum
     - a. Right hemisphere in charge of left side of the body
     - b. Left hemisphere in charge of right side of the body
     - c. Each hemisphere has somewhat different tasks and talents called lateralization
  2. Cerebral cortex - layers of densely packed cells covering the cerebrum
     - a. Cells have gray appearance leading to the term gray matter,

95

whereas myelinated cells elsewhere have a white appearance
b. Contains three-fourths of all cells in the brain
c. Fissures divide the cortex into four regions or lobes
    (1) _____ lobes - contain the visual cortex
    (2) Parietal lobes - contain somatosensory cortex, which receives information about pressure, pain, touch and temperature from all over the body
    (3) Temporal lobes - involved in memory, perception and emotion, contain auditory cortex, Wernicke's area which is involved in language comprehension
    (4) Frontal lobes - contain the motor cortex; responsible for making plans, taking initiative and thinking creatively, contain Broca's area (speech production)
d. Contain _____ areas
    (1) "Silent areas" involved in higher mental processes
    (2) The prefrontal lobe contains association area of interest to psychologists
        (a) Involved personality, rational decision making, social judgment, ability to set goals, and to make and carry out plans
        (b) Damage results in flattening of emotion and feeling
        (c) Involved in helping us determine the proper order of behaviors and knowing when to stop

Answer this Learning Objective while you read Section 4.

9. List and describe the location and function of each of the major parts of the brain.

**SECTION 5 - THE TWO HEMISPHERES OF THE BRAIN (PP. 124-128) AND
SECTION 6 - TWO STUBBORN ISSUES IN BRAIN RESEARCH (PP. 129-132)**

V.   **THE TWO HEMISPHERES OF THE BRAIN**
    A.   **Split brains: A house divided**
        1.   Normal brain - the two hemispheres communicate with each other via the corpus callosum
        2.   Split brain refers to surgery in which the corpus callosum is severed
        3.   This surgery is performed in animal studies and for some human conditions
        4.   Findings of split brain surgery in humans
            a.   Already known that hemispheres are not identical; language is largely handled by the _____ hemisphere
            b.   Medical goals were generally achieved
            c.   Daily lives of split-brain patients were not much affected
            d.   Effects on perception and memory are observable under experimental conditions
    B.   **A question of dominance**
        1.   Many researchers believe the left side is dominant because cognitive skills, including language, rational and analytic abilities, originate here
        2.   Others point to abilities of the right hemisphere: superior visual-_____ abilities, facial recognition and nonverbal sounds, appreciation of art and music; some researchers claim it is holistic and intuitive
        3.   Differences are relative, in real life, the hemispheres cooperate

VI. **TWO STUBBORN ISSUES IN BRAIN RESEARCH**
    A.   **Where is the self?**
        1.   Most neuroscientists believe that the mind can be explained in physical terms as a product of the cerebral cortex
        2.   One theorist suggests the brain consists of independent parts that deal with different aspects of thought and are continually conferring and revising their drafts of reality
        3.   Another suggests that a unified self is an illusion and that the brain is independent modules working in parallel with one module interpreting the actions, moods, thoughts of the others
        4.   Subjective experiences are not well understood

B. Are there "his" and "hers" brains?
    1.   Efforts to identify male-female differences have reflected biases
    2.   Two questions must be asked:
        a.   Are male and female brains physically different?
            (1)   _____ differences have been found in animal brains
            (2)   Human sex differences more elusive
                (a)   Findings change and are often contradictory
                (b)   Many different conclusions can be drawn
                (c)   Some evidence exists for sex differences in lateralization
        b.   If there are brain differences, what do they mean for the behavior of men and women in real life?
        c.   Problems exists with conclusions drawn by popular writers about sex differences in the brain
            (1)   These supposed sex differences are stereotypes
            (2)   A biological difference does not necessarily have behavioral implications
            (3)   Sex differences in the brain could be the result rather than the cause of behavioral differences since research shows that experience can influence brain circuitry and males and females have different experiences
    3.   It is important to be aware of how results on sex differences might be exaggerated and misused

Answer these Learning Objectives while you read Sections 5 and 6.

10.   Summarize the functions of the brain's two hemispheres and explain their relationship.

11.   Describe the general position taken by neuroscientists on the self, and discuss two specific approaches advanced by scientists to explain the sense of a unified self.

12.   Summarize the evidence on whether there are sex differences in the brain and how any differences might affect behavior.

13.   Describe the effect of experience on brain development.

FLASH CARDS

Cut the following chart along the borders and test yourself with the resulting flash cards.

4.1 CENTRAL NERVOUS SYSTEM	**4.2 SPINAL CORD**	**4.3 SPINAL REFLEX**
4.4 PERIPHERAL NERVOUS SYSTEM	**4.5 SENSORY NERVES**	**4.6 MOTOR NERVES**
4.7 SOMATIC NERVOUS SYSTEM	**4.8 AUTONOMIC NERVOUS SYSTEM**	**4.9 BIOFEEDBACK**
4.10 SYMPATHETIC NERVOUS SYSTEM	**4.11 PARASYMPATHETIC NERVOUS SYSTEM**	**4.12 NEURON**
4.13 GLIAL CELLS	**4.14 DENDRITES**	**4.15 CELL BODY**
4.16 AXON	**4.17 AXON TERMINALS**	**4.18 MYELIN SHEATH**

4.3 Automatic behavior, requiring no conscious effort, produced by the spinal cord without any help from the brain.	4.2 Extension of the brain that runs from the base of the brain down the center of the back and acts as a bridge between the brain and body below the neck.	4.1 Receives and processes incoming sensory information; sends out messages to muscles, glands, organs; consists of the brain and spinal cord.
4.6 Nerves in the peripheral nervous system that carry messages from the central nervous system to muscles, glands, and internal organs.	4.5 Nerves in the peripheral nervous system that carry sensory messages toward the central nervous system.	4.4 All portions of the nervous system outside the brain and spinal cord. It handles the central nervous system's input and output.
4.9 A technique for controlling bodily functions by attending to an instrument that monitors the function and signals changes in it.	4.8 A subdivision of the peripheral nervous system that regulates blood vessels, glands, and internal organs.	4.7 Also called the skeletal nervous system, a subdivision of the peripheral nervous system that connects to sensory receptors and skeletal muscles.
4.12 Also called a nerve cell, it is the basic building block of the nervous system.	4.11 The subdivision of the autonomic nervous system that slows down the body and enables the body to conserve and store energy.	4.10 The subdivision of the autonomic nervous system that mobilizes the body for action and an output of energy.
4.15 The part of the neuron that keeps it alive and determines whether it will fire.	4.14 Branches on a neuron that receive information from other neurons and transmit it toward the cell body.	4.13 Cells that hold neurons in place, provide them with nutrients, insulate them, and remove cellular debris when they die.
4.18 A fatty material that surrounds many axons and insulates them. It also speeds up the conduction of neural impulses.	4.17 Branches at the end of the axon into which the axon divides.	4.16 Extending fiber of a neuron that conducts impulses away from the cell body and transmits them to other neurons.

4.19 NERVE	4.20 SYNAPTIC CLEFT	4.21 SYNAPSE
4.22 PLASTICITY	4.23 ACTION POTENTIAL	4.24 SYNAPTIC VESICLES
4.25 NEUROTRANSMITTER	4.26 RECEPTOR SITES	4.27 ENDORPHINS
4.28 NEUROMODULATORS	4.29 HORMONES	4.30 ENDOCRINE GLANDS
4.31 MELATONIN	4.32 ADRENAL HORMONES	4.33 ADRENAL CORTEX AND MEDULLA
4.34 CORTISOL	4.35 EPINEPHRINE	4.36 NOREPINEPHRINE

4.21 The site where transmission of a nerve impulse occurs; it includes the axon terminal, the cleft, and the receiving dendrite or cell body.	4.20 A minuscule space where the axon terminal of one neuron nearly touches a dendrite or the cell body of another.	4.19 A bundle of fibers of individual neurons (axons and sometimes dendrites) in the peripheral nervous system.
4.24 Tiny sacs in the tip of the axon terminal that open and release neurotransmitters when a neural impulse reaches the terminal's tip.	4.23 An electrical current or impulse produced by brief change in the electrical voltage of a neuron that is the result of stimulation.	4.22 Refers to the brain's ability to be flexible and to change in response to information, challenges and changes in the environment.
4.27 Neuromodulators that are similar in structure and action to opiates. They ar involved in pain reduction, pleasure, and other behaviors.	4.26 Special molecules in the membrane of the receiving neuron to which the neurotransmitter molecules bind briefly.	4.25 A chemical substance that is released by the transmitting neuron at the synapse and that alters the activity of the receiving neuron.
4.30 Internal organs that produce hormones and release them into the bloodstream.	4.29 Chemical messengers, produced primarily in endocrine glands, that affect organs and cells that may be far from their point of origin.	4.28 Chemical messengers which alter the effects of neurotransmitters--for example, by limiting or prolonging those effects.
4.33 Each adrenal gland has an outer layer called the cortex and an inner core or medulla.	4.32 Hormones produced by the adrenal glands and are involved in emotions, stress, and certain nonemotional conditions, such as heat, cold, and pain.	4.31 A hormone secreted deep within the brain which helps regulate biological rhythms and promotes sleep.
4.36 Adrenal hormone produced by the inner core of the adrenal gland. It activates the sympathetic nervous system which increases arousal.	4.35 Adrenal hormone, also known as adrenalin, produced by the inner core of the adrenal gland. It activates the sympathetic nervous system.	4.34 An adrenal hormone produced by the outer layer of the adrenal gland. It increases blood-sugar levels and enhances energy.

4.37 SEX HORMONES (ANDROGENS, ESTROGENS, PROGESTERONE)	4.38 LESION METHOD	4.39 ELECTRODES
4.40 ELECTROENCEPHALOGRAM	4.41 PET SCAN	4.42 MAGNETIC RESONANCE IMAGING (MRI)
4.43 LOCALIZATION OF FUNCTION	4.44 BRAIN STEM	4.45 MEDULLA
4.46 PONS	4.47 RETICULAR ACTIVATING SYSTEM	4.48 CEREBELLUM
4.49 THALAMUS	4.50 OLFACTORY BULB	4.51 HYPOTHALAMUS
4.52 PITUITARY GLAND	4.53 LIMBIC SYSTEM	4.54 AMYGDALA

4.39 A method for studying the brain that detects and records electrical activity.	4.38 Method for studying the brain that involves damaging or removing sections of brain in animals, then observing the effects.	4.37 Regulate the development and functioning of reproductive and sex organs and stimulate the development of sex characteristics.
4.42 A method for studying the brain that uses magnetic fields and special radio receivers.	4.41 A method for analyzing biochemical activity in the brain, using injections of a radioactive, glucose-like substance.	4.40 A brain wave recording. It is useful but not very precise because it reflects the activities of many cells at once.
4.45 A structure in the brain stem responsible for certain automatic functions, such as breathing and heart rate.	4.44 Part of the brain at the base of the skull. Pathways to and from upper brain areas pass through its two structures, the medulla and pons.	4.43 Assumption made by all modern brain theories that major brain parts perform different (though overlapping) tasks.
4.48 Stands atop the brain stem, it regulates movement and balance.	4.47 A dense network of neurons which extends above the brain stem to the brain's center: arouses the higher center and screens information.	4.46 A structure in the brain stem involved in, among other things, sleeping, waking, and dreaming.
4.51 Brain structure associated with survival; controls hunger, thirst, emotion, sex, and reproduction, temperature, and the autonomic nervous system.	4.50 The switching station for the sense of smell.	4.49 Brain structure that relays motor impulses from higher centers to the spinal cord and directs incoming sensory messages to higher centers.
4.54 A limbic structure that evaluates sensory information for its emotional importance; also mediates anxiety and depression.	4.53 A set of loosely interconnected structures involved in emotions, such as rage and fear.	4.52 Called the body's "master gland" because the hormones it secretes affect many other endocrine glands.

4.55 HIPPOCAMPUS	4.56 CEREBRUM	4.57 CEREBRAL HEMISPHERES
4.58 CORPUS CALLOSUM	4.59 LATERALIZATION	4.60 CEREBRAL CORTEX
4.61 OCCIPITAL LOBES	4.62 VISUAL CORTEX	4.63 PARIETAL LOBES
4.64 SOMATOSENSORY CORTEX	4.65 TEMPORAL LOBES	4.66 WERNICKE'S AREA
4.67 AUDITORY CORTEX	4.68 FRONTAL LOBES	4.69 MOTOR CORTEX
4.70 BROCA'S AREA	4.71 ASSOCIATION CORTEX	4.72 PREFRONTAL CORTEX
4.73 SPLIT-BRAIN SURGERY	4.74 CEREBRAL DOMINANCE	4.75 THE SELF

4.57 The two halves of the cerebrum. Each hemisphere (left and right) is in charge of the opposite side of the body.	4.56 Largest part of the brain; in charge of most sensory, motor, and cognitive processes in humans. It is divided into two cerebral hemispheres.	4.55 Limbic structure called the "gateway to memory" because, along with adjacent brain areas, it enables us to form and store new memories.
4.60 Several thin layers of densely packed cells that cover the cerebrum; largely responsible for higher functions.	4.59 Refers to the idea that the two hemispheres have somewhat different tasks and talents.	4.58 The large band of fibers connecting the two cerebral hemispheres.
4.63 Regions of the cerebral cortex located at the top of the brain that contain the somatosensory cortex.	4.62 A section of the occipital lobe where visual signals are processed. Damage to the visual cortex can cause visual impairment.	4.61 Regions of the cerebral cortex located at the back of the brain that contain the visual cortex, where visual signals are processed.
4.66 Region in the left, temporal lobe that handles language meaning and comprehension.	4.65 Regions of the cerebral cortex at the sides of the brain that are involved in memory, perception, emotion, language, and audition.	4.64 A section of the parietal lobe that receives information about pressure, pain, touch, and temperature from all over the body.
4.69 Section of the frontal lobe which issues orders to the muscles that produce voluntary movement.	4.68 Regions of the cortex located in the front part of the brain that contain the motor cortex, Broca's area, and are responsible for making plans.	4.67 Contained in the temporal lobes, the auditory cortex processes sounds.
4.72 An association area in the forwardmost part of the frontal lobe, it is involved in personality, judgment, and making and carrying out plans.	4.71 Areas of the cortex involved in higher mental processes. The association area in the prefrontal lobe involves personality.	4.70 Region in the left, frontal lobe that handles speech production.
4.75 Our conscious sense of a unified being. Refers to the mind-brain puzzle that has plagued philosophers for years.	4.74 The left side of the brain has greater cognitive talents than the right hemisphere, therefore many researchers believe it is dominant.	4.73 Surgery performed on animals for experiments and on humans in the case of illness that involves severing the corpus callosum.

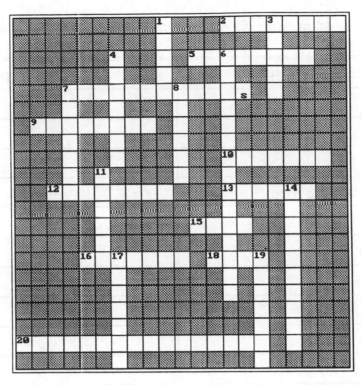

ACROSS

2. Part of limbic system involved in arousal and regulation of emotion
5. Receives information from other neurons
7. Regulates autonomic nervous system
9. Lobe that contains the somatosensory cortex
10. Site where transmission of a nerve impulse from one neuron to another occurs
12. Largest brain structure
13. Layer of cells covering the cerebrum
15. Conducts impulses away from the cell body
16. Hormone produced by the pancreas
18. Structure in the brain stem involved in waking, sleeping and dreaming
20. Chemical released by neurons at the synapse

DOWN

1. Region in left, frontal lobe that handles speech production
3. Cells that hold neurons in place
4. Region of the cortex that contains the motor cortex
6. Field concerned with the neural bases of behavior and mental processes
7. Chemicals secreted by the glands
8. System containing brain areas involved in emotions and motivated behaviors
14. Neuromodulator similar to opiates
17. Neurons that carry messages toward the central nervous system

Complete this chart by identifying the function that corresponds to the brain structure listed in the left column.

BRAIN STRUCTURE	FUNCTION
BRAIN STEM	
Medulla	
Pons	
Reticular Activating System	
CEREBELLUM	
THALAMUS	
Olfactory Bulb	
HYPOTHALAMUS	
PITUITARY GLAND	
LIMBIC SYSTEM	
Amygdala	
Hippocampus	
CEREBRUM	
Left Cerebral Hemisphere	
Right Cerebral Hemisphere	
Corpus Callosum	
Cerebral Cortex	
Occipital Lobes	
Temporal Lobes	
Parietal Lobes	
Frontal Lobes	
Association Areas	

PRACTICE TEST 1 - Multiple Choice

1. The function of the central nervous system is
    A. to receive, process and interpret incoming information.
    B. to send out messages to muscles.
    C. to send out messages to glands and organs.
    D. all of the above.

2. The peripheral nervous system
    A. is made up of the brain and spinal cord.
    B. handles the central nervous system's input and output.
    C. depends exclusively on sensory neurons.
    D. depends exclusively on motor neurons.

3. The _____ nervous system is part of the peripheral nervous system.
    A. somatic   B. sympathetic
    C. autonomic   D. all of the above

4. One function of the somatic nervous system is to
    A. carry information from the senses to the CNS and from the CNS to the skeletal muscles.
    B. carry information to the glands and organs.
    C. control the sympathetic and parasympathetic nervous systems.
    D. process information in the brain.

5. The sympathetic nervous system handles _____ responses, while the parasympathetic nervous system governs _____ responses.
    A. voluntary; involuntary   B. involuntary; voluntary
    C. arousal; relaxing   D. sensory; motor

6. Biofeedback has been used to help people
    A. control their temper.
    B. learn to speak after a stroke.
    C. learn to control involuntary autonomic responses such as blood pressure.
    D. treat depression.

7. The autonomic nervous system is involved with
    A. voluntary responses.
    B. the nerves connected to the senses and skeletal muscles.
    C. involuntary responses such as the regulation of blood vessels and glands.
    D. only sensory nerves.

8.	Neurons
	A.	are the basic units of the nervous system.
	B.	are held in place by glial cells.
	C.	transmit electrical messages throughout the nervous system.
	D.	are characterized by all of the above.

9.	The three main parts of the neuron are the
	A.	dendrites, cell body and axon.
	B.	axon, dendrites and synapse.
	C.	synapse, impulse and cleft.
	D.	myelin sheath, dendrites and synapse.

10.	The _____ receive messages from other neurons, while the _____ carry messages on to other neurons or to muscle or gland cells.
	A.	cell bodies; dendrites
	B.	dendrites; axons
	C.	axons; dendrites
	D.	myelin sheaths; cell bodies

11.	The cell body
	A.	determines whether the neuron should fire.
	B.	receives incoming impulses from other neurons.
	C.	speeds the conduction of the neural impulse.
	D.	connects with the synapse.

12.	What occurs at the synapse?
	A.	The electrical charge jumps from the synaptic end bulb across the synaptic cleft to the dendrites of the next neuron.
	B.	The axon terminals contact the dendrites of the next neuron and neurotransmitters are transferred.
	C.	Synaptic vesicles in the synaptic end bulb release neurotransmitters into the synaptic cleft, and they lock into receptor sites of receiving dendrites.
	D.	Scientists are studying the process because the exact mechanism is unknown.

13. How do neurotransmitters affect the post-synaptic neuron?
    A. They cause a change in the electrical potential, exciting the neuron and causing it to fire.
    B. They cause a change in the electrical potential, either exciting or inhibiting the next neuron.
    C. They cause a change in the electrical potential, inhibiting the neuron and stopping it from firing.
    D. They do not make contact with the next neuron; they stay in the synapse.

14. Mood, memory, well-being, Alzheimer's disease, depression, sleep, appetite, pain and temperature regulation are all influenced by
    A. dopamine.   B. neurotransmitters.
    C. endorphins.   D. all of the above.

15. _____ is a neuromodulator that influences pain and pleasure.
    A. dopamine   B. serotonin
    C. insulin   D. endorphin

16. _____ are chemicals that are released directly into the bloodstream, which then carries them to organs and cells that may be far from their point of origin.
    A. Neurotransmitters   B. Endorphins
    C. Hormones   D. Neuromodulators

17. Androgen, estrogen and progesterone are three types of
    A. sex hormones.   B. neurotransmitters.
    C. neurons.   D. neuromodulators.

18. The _____ is a method for analyzing biochemical activity in the brain that uses injections containing a harmless radioactive element.
    A. MRI (magnetic resonance imaging)
    B. PET scan (positron-emission tomography)
    C. EEG (electroencephalogram)
    D. EP (evoked potentials)

19. The limbic system includes the
    A. cortex and corpus callosum.
    B. spinal cord and brain.
    C. cerebellum and brain stem.
    D. amygdala and hippocampus.

20. The four distinct lobes of the cortex are the
     A. occipital, parietal, temporal and frontal lobes.
     B. sensory, auditory, visual and motor lobes.
     C. hind, mid, fore and association lobes.
     D. front, back, side and top lobes.

21. The _____ has deep crevasses and wrinkles that enable it to contain billions of neurons without requiring people to have the heads of giants.
     A. corpus callosum   B. cerebral cortex
     C. cerebellum   D. hypothalamus

22. Which of the following summarizes the different hemispheric functions?
     A. The left brain is more active in logic and the right brain is associated with visual-spatial abilities.
     B. The left brain is more active in artistic and intuitive tasks, and the right brain is more involved in emotional and expressive abilities.
     C. The left brain has visual-spatial abilities, while the right brain is more involved in artistic and creative activities.
     D. The right brain is more dominant and the left brain is more subordinate.

23. Localization of function refers to the fact that
     A. personality traits are reflected in different areas of the brain.
     B. information is distributed across large areas of the brain.
     C. different brain parts perform different jobs and store different sorts of information.
     D. brain processes are like holography.

24. The issue of whether there are sex differences in the brain is controversial because
     A. evidence of anatomical sex differences in humans is contradictory.
     B. findings have flip-flopped as a result of the biases of the observers.
     C. even if anatomical differences exist, we do not know what they mean.
     D. all of the above reasons.

25. Evidence for the somewhat different talents of the two cerebral hemispheres comes from studies of split brain patients who have had
     A. the lobes of the cerebral cortex separated.
     B. the corpus callosum cut.
     C. a prefrontal lobotomy.
     D. had their optical nerve severed.

PRACTICE TEST 2 - Multiple Choice

1.   The _____ receives, processes, interprets and stores incoming information from the senses and sends out messages destined for the muscles, glands, and internal organs. The _____ handles its input and output.
      A.   central nervous system; peripheral nervous system
      B.   peripheral nervous system; autonomic nervous system
      C.   sympathetic nervous system; parasympathetic nervous system
      D.   peripheral nervous system; central nervous system

2.   _____ nerves carry messages from the receptors in the sense organs to the spinal cord and brain, and _____ nerves carry orders from the central nervous system to the muscles, glands and organs.
      A.   Voluntary; involuntary
      B.   Motor; sensory
      C.   Sensory; motor
      D.   Autonomic; sympathetic

3.   As you are driving along, you hear the sound of tires screeching and then see a car hit another car. The sounds and sights are carried to your brain via the
      A.   autonomic nervous system.
      B.   somatic nervous system.
      C.   sympathetic nervous system.
      D.   central nervous system.

4.   Which of the following examples accurately describes the types of output associated with the somatic and autonomic nervous systems?
      A.   The somatic nervous system is involved when you turn off a light.
      B.   The autonomic nervous system is involved when your heart races after a scare.
      C.   The somatic nervous system is involved when you write your name.
      D.   all of the above

5.   Dr. Miller is training you to control your blood pressure by monitoring it with a device that delivers a signal to you whenever it drops. This is called
      A.   a PET scan.   B.   biofeedback.
      C.   phrenology.   D.   an EEG.

6. Sympathetic is to _____ as parasympathetic is to _____.
   A.   arousal; relaxation   B.   autonomic; somatic
   C.   voluntary; involuntary   D.   somatic; autonomic

7. The path of a neural impulse is
   A.   axon, cell body, neuron, dendrite.
   B.   dendrite, cell body, axon, axon terminals.
   C.   dendrite, axon, axon terminals, cell body.
   D.   neuron, cell body. dendrite, axon.

8. Neurons are like catchers and batters. The _____ are like catchers because they receive information; the _____ are like batters because they send on the message.
   A.   dendrites; axons   B.   cell bodies; axons
   C.   axons; dendrites   D.   dendrites; glials

9. When a neural impulse reaches the tip of the axon terminal,
   A.   the neuron fires.
   B.   synaptic vesicles in the synaptic end bulb release neurotransmitters that cross the synaptic cleft and lock into receptor sites on the post-synaptic neuron.
   C.   the synaptic end bulb sends an electrical current into the dendrites of the next neuron.
   D.   the synaptic end bulb locks into the receptor sites on the post-synaptic dendrites.

10. During Dr. Wisch's hospital rounds, he meets with patients who are suffering with Alzheimer's disease, Parkinson's disease and severe depression. To understand these disorders better, he looks to the role of
   A.   hormones.   B.   endorphins.
   C.   neurotransmitters.   D.   melatonin.

11. Serotonin, dopamine, acetylcholine and norepinephrine are
   A.   adrenal hormones.   B.   endorphins.
   C.   sex hormones.   D.   neurotransmitters.

12. During a dangerous situation, pain sensations are reduced. This reduction of pain is due to an increase in
   A.   testosterone levels.
   B.   endorphin levels.
   C.   androgen levels.
   D.   insulin levels.

13. What do insulin and melatonin have in common with androgen and estrogen?
    A. They are all neurotransmitters.
    B. They are all sex hormones.
    C. They are all adrenal hormones.
    D. They are all hormones.

14. For a recording of brain wave patterns, a(n) _____ device would be used. To find out what parts of the brain are normally active while listening to music, a(n) _____ device would be used.
    A. magnetic resonance imaging; electroencephalogram
    B. electroencephalogram; positron-emission tomography
    C. positron-emission tomography; needle electrode
    D. positron-emission tomography; magnetic resonance imaging

15. Brain stem is to _____ as cerebrum is to _____.
    A. emotions; vital functions
    B. vital functions; emotions
    C. higher forms of thinking; vital functions
    D. vital functions; higher forms of thinking

16. The condition of being "brain dead" refers to the loss of the higher functions of the _____, but the person remains alive due to the functions of the _____.
    A. cortex; medulla   B. pons; medulla
    C. thalamus; cortex   D. hypothalamus; pons

17. Shondra is sitting at her desk trying to study psychology. The stereo is on too loud and is distracting her, so she decides to turn it down. While singing along with the music, she crosses the room, reaches out to the stereo and turns it off. Which brain structure is most directly involved when Shondra reaches out to turn off the stereo?
    A. amygdala   B. thalamus
    C. cerebellum   D. pons

18. In question 17, which brain structure is most directly involved when Shondra listens to the music?
    A. cerebellum   B. limbic system
    C. hippocampus   D. auditory cortex

19. In question 17, which brain structure is most directly involved when Shondra remembers information contained in the psychology text?
    A. hypothalamus   B. hippocampus
    C. thalamus   D. parietal lobe

20. In question 17, which part of the brain is involved when Shondra sings?
    A. Broca's area   B. left brain
    C. frontal lobe   D. all of the above

21. Reed just missed being in a bad car accident. Immediately following the incident, his heart was racing, his palms were sweaty and he felt terrified. Which of the following was involved in these responses?
    A. autonomic nervous system   B. limbic system
    C. pituitary gland   D. all of the above

22. If Lucy is like most people, her _____ is most involved when she calculates a math problem and her _____ is most active when she reads a map.
    A. right brain; left brain   B. left brain; right brain
    C. corpus callosum; cerebellum   D. amygdala; thalamus

23. For modern brain scientists, the issue of the self or mind is
    A. a matter of matter, or can be understood through brain structure and function.
    B. strictly a philosophical issue and should not be addressed by psychology.
    C. a religious issue.
    D. a reflection of a soul that exists entirely apart from the brain.

24. Some of the controversy surrounding the idea of sex differences in the brain centers around
    A. the reasons that male brains are more localized.
    B. whether anatomical differences exist and if they do, what they mean.
    C. the reluctance to publicize the unpopular finding that female brains have greater capacity.
    D. all of the above.

25. Throughout life, new learning results in the establishment of new synaptic connections in the brain, with stimulating environments producing the greatest changes. Conversely, some unused synaptic connections are lost as cells or their branches die and are not replaced. This indicates that the brain
    A. is more lateralized than scientists once thought.
    B. continues to develop and change in response to the environment.
    C. develops new brain cells on a regular and ongoing basis.
    D. is more holistic than scientists once thought.

PRACTICE TEST 3 - Short Answer

1. The nervous system is divided into two main parts: the _____ nervous system, which receives, processes, interprets, and stores incoming information; and the _____ nervous system, which contains all parts of the nervous system outside the brain and spinal cord.

2. The peripheral nervous system is divided into: the _____ nervous system, which controls the skeletal muscles and permits voluntary action; and the _____ nervous system, which regulates blood vessels, glands, and internal organs and works more or less without a person's conscious control.

3. The autonomic nervous system is divided into the _____ nervous system, which mobilizes the body for action and increases energy, and the _____ nervous system, which conserves and stores energy.

4. Neurons have three main parts. The _____ contains the biochemical machinery for keeping the neuron alive.

5. The _____ of a neuron receive messages from other nerve cells and transmit them toward the cell body. The _____ transmits messages away from the cell body to other cells.

6. Most neurons are insulated by a layer of fatty tissue called the _____ that prevents signals from adjacent cells from interfering with each other and speeds up the conduction of neural impulses.

7. Individual neurons are separated by tiny gaps called the _____.

8. When an electrical impulse reaches the _____ of a neuron, chemical substances called _____ are released into the synapse. Once across the synapse, the molecules fit into sites on the receiving neuron, changing the membrane of the receiving cell.

9. What any given neuron does at any given moment depends on the net effect of all the messages being received from other neurons. The message that reaches a final destination depends on the rate at which individual neurons are firing, how many are firing, what types are firing and where they are located. It does NOT depend on how strongly neurons are firing because the firing of a neuron is an _____ event.

10. _____ are chemical messengers that reduce pain and promote pleasure. Dopamine, serotonin, and norepinephrine are examples of another type of chemical messenger called _____.

11. Hormones originate primarily in the _____ glands, which deposit them into the bloodstream where they are carried to organs and cells.

12. Neurotransmitters affect a variety of behaviors. Low levels of _____ and _____ may be implicated in severe depression; _____ affects memory and loss of cells producing this neurotransmitter may help account for some of the symptoms of Alzheimer's disease.

13. The three main types of sex hormones that occur in both sexes, though in differing amounts are _____, _____, and _____.

14. Living brains can be studied by probing them with electrodes. The procedure for obtaining brain wave recordings is called a(n) _____.

15. Other methods of investigating living brains are PET scans, which record biochemical changes in the brain as they are happening, and _____ which utilize magnetic fields and radio frequencies to explore the "inner space" of the brain.

16. This dense network of neurons, which extends above the brain stem into the center of the brain and has connections with higher areas, screens incoming information and arouses the higher centers when something happens that demands their attention. Without the _____ system, we could not be alert or perhaps even conscious.

17. The structures of the brain stem include the _____ which is responsible for sleeping, waking, and dreaming, while the _____ is responsible for bodily functions like breathing and heart rate. Standing atop the brain stem, the _____ contributes to a sense of balance and muscle coordination.

18. The _____ is a busy traffic officer and directs sensory messages from the spinal cord to higher brain centers.

19. The _____ sits beneath the thalamus and is involved with drives vital for survival, such as hunger, thirst, emotion, sex, and reproduction.

20. The _____ system is heavily involved in emotions.

21. Case histories of brain-damaged people such as H.M. indicate that the _____ enables us to store new information for future use.

22. The cerebral cortex, the layer of cells that covers the cerebrum, is divided into four distinct lobes. The _____ lobes contain the visual cortex, the _____ lobes contain the somatosensory cortex, the _____ contain the auditory cortex, and the _____ lobes contain the motor cortex.

23. A large bundle of nerve fibers called the _____ connects the two cerebral hemispheres. The left and right sides of the brain seem to have somewhat different tasks and talents, a phenomenon known as _____.

24. There are two main language areas in the brain. _____ area is involved in language comprehension and is located in the _____ lobe, while _____ area is involved in speech production and is located in the _____ lobe.

25. To examine the issue of sex differences, we need to ask two separate questions: Do physical differences actually exist in male and female brains, and if so, what do they have to do with _____?

PRACTICE TEST 4 - True/False

1.   T F   Scientists divide the nervous system into the central nervous system (CNS) and the somatic nervous system (SNS).

2.   T F   The parasympathetic nervous system is involved when we become aroused, such as when we have a close call with an auto accident.

3.   T F   The autonomic nervous system and the somatic nervous system are the subdivisions of the peripheral nervous system.

4.   T F   Contrary to old beliefs, new evidence has found that neurons in the human central nervous system can regrow after damage and new neurons can be produced if treated with certain chemicals.

5.   T F   Myelin sheath speeds up the conduction of neural impulses and prevents signals in adjacent cells from interfering with one another.

6.   T F   The route a nerve impulse travels is: cell body, dendrites, axon, axon terminals.

7.   T F   In humans, all synapses are formed at birth.

8.   T F   Thousands of messages, both excitatory and inhibitory come into a cell. Whether the neuron fires depends on the strength of the neural impulse of the previous neuron.

9.   T F   Neurotransmitters affect mood, memory, and well-being. Specifically, levels of serotonin and norepinephrine are associated with severe depression and acetylcholine levels are associated with some of the symptoms of Alzheimer's disease.

10. T F   Endorphins are neurotransmitters that affect pain and pleasure.

11. T F   Melatonin, testosterone, progesterone, and estrogens are all examples of hormones.

12. T F   Brain researchers use electroencephalograms (EEGs) to study brain activity while it occurs.

13. T F   Localization of function refers to the fact that the left and right hemisphere have separate talents and areas of specialization.

14.   T F   The thalamus and hypothalamus are part of the limbic system. They are involved in emotions and certain pathways involved in pleasure.

15.   T F   The two main structures of the brain stem are the pons and the medulla. They are involved in involuntary bodily functions such as sleeping, waking, dreaming, breathing, and heart rate.

16.   T F   The hypothalamus controls the complex operations of the autonomic nervous system, as well as the pituitary gland.

17.   T F   The amygdala, part of the limbic system, is considered the "gateway to memory."

18.   T F   The cerebrum is where higher forms of thinking take place. It is divided into two separate halves, or cerebral hemispheres, connected by a large band of fibers called the corpus callosum.

19.   T F   Each cerebral hemisphere is divided into four distinct regions: the frontal lobes which house the motor cortex, the parietal lobes which house the somatosensory cortex, the temporal lobes in which the auditory cortex is located, and the occipital lobes in which the visual cortex is located.

20.   T F   Wernicke's area and Broca's area are related to language. Wernicke's area is in the right temporal lobe, and is involved in speech comprehension, and Broca's area is in the right frontal lobe and is involved with speech production.

21.   T F   Silent areas of the brain, sometimes called the association cortex, are involved in higher mental processes such as personality, making and implementing plans.

22.   T F   Split-brain patients have great difficulty living normal lives.

23.   T F   Because the right hemisphere is superior in visual-spatial abilities, excels in facial recognition, and cognitive talents, researchers refer to the right hemisphere as dominant.

24.   T F   Research has supported certain biological sex differences in the brain. These differences have been found consistently in various different research studies and support the notion that many behaviors are based in brain differences between men and women.

25.   T F   Sex differences in the brain could be the result rather than the cause of behavioral differences.

PRACTICE TEST 5 - Essay

1. You are sitting at your desk trying to study for a test you are very nervous about, and all you can focus on is the stereo playing in the other room. You get up, go to the other room and turn down the stereo. Beginning with the external stimuli (the sound) and ending with your movement to the other room, describe what happens in terms of:
    A. from the standpoint of a single neuron
    B. the brain structures that are involved, in sequence
    C. the nervous system involvement

2. For each scenario indicate the brain structure(s) most likely to be involved in the behavior that is described.
    A. Dr. Smith inserts an electrode into a structure within the brain. As this electrode is activated, the person sweats and shivers, feels hungry and thirsty, and sometimes even seems angry and sexually aroused.
    B. A computer-enhanced image has enabled a research team to observe the flow of information within the nervous system. While watching this flow, the researchers notice that incoming sensory messages are relayed through this center before finally reaching their destination in the cerebral hemispheres.
    C. As a result of a serious automobile accident, Fred's ability to make plans and show initiative were seriously impaired.
    D. Bjorn's great grandmother has had a serious stroke. As a result, she is unable to speak, though she appears to understand and respond non-verbally to what is being said.
    E. Tiffany's elderly neighbor is showing signs of memory loss.
    F. Mary has been unable to continue as a gymnast since the lower rear area of her brain was damaged in a car accident. All tasks requiring balance or coordinated movements are beyond Mary's capacities.

3. As a result of mixing tranquilizers and alcohol, Helen has become what is called "brain dead," and though she does not respond to people, she continues to live without any life-sustaining equipment. Describe which parts of her brain have been damaged and which parts continue to function?

4. In the descriptions that follow, cortical functions are disrupted in various ways. From the descriptions identify the cortical structures and state their functions.
    A. Removing a tumor from an area just behind her forehead has dramatically altered Denise's personality. Previously outgoing and warm, she is now hostile and needs prodding to get anything done.
    B. Lately Ralph has been experiencing tingling sensations in various body parts and he sometimes "forgets" where his hands and fingers are. Tests reveal a growth near the surface of the brain just under the center of his head.
    C. Hazan has a large blind spot in his visual field and doctors have eliminated the possibility of eye and optic nerve problems.

5. In the examples below, identify whether the phenomena are primarily related to the functioning of the right hemisphere, the left hemisphere, or both.
    A. Ken is being tested for school placement. Part of the test involves putting puzzle pieces together so they form geometric shapes. Ken performs well.
    B. Another portion of the test involves reading simple sentences aloud. Ken garbles the words and says them in an improper sequence.
    C. A third portion of the test requires Ken to respond to sets of photographs, each set containing five pictures of a person posed identically except for facial expression.
    D. The last portion of the test assesses manual dexterity in the nondominant arm and hand. Because Ken is left-handed, he is required to perform all sorts of mechanical tasks with his right hand. He fails this part of the test.
    E. What overall conclusion might be reached about Ken's hemispheric functioning?

CHAPTER 5

Body Rhythms and Mental States

LEARNING OBJECTIVES

1. Define consciousness and the biological rhythms often associated with states of consciousness.

2. Describe circadian rhythms, including how they are studied and how they may be desynchronized.

3. Discuss examples of ultradian and infradian rhythms and distinguish endogenous rhythms from those caused by external factors.

4. Summarize the research evidence on "PMS" and discuss whether emotional symptoms associated with "PMS" are tied to the menstrual cycle.

5. Summarize theories about the biological functions of sleep.

6. Distinguish between rapid eye movement (REM) and non-REM periods in sleep and describe the four stages of non-REM sleep.

7. Summarize the principles of the psychoanalytic, problem-solving, mental housekeeping and activation-synthesis theories of dreaming.

8. List the types of psychoactive drugs that can alter states of consciousness and describe their physical and behavioral effects.

9. List and explain the factors that influence the effects of psychoactive drugs.

10. Define hypnosis and summarize its characteristics.

11. Describe dissociation and sociocognitive theories of hypnosis.

CHAPTER CONCEPT MAP

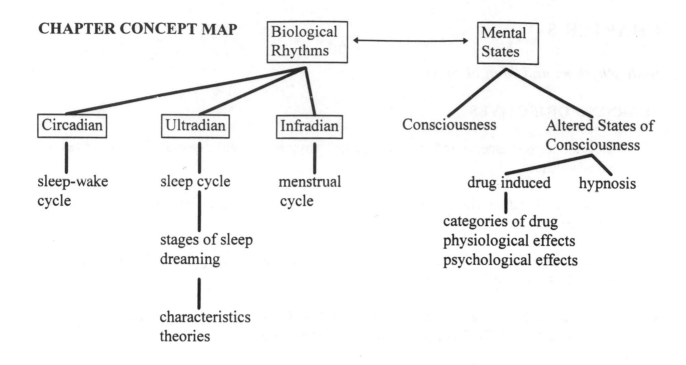

BRIEF CHAPTER SUMMARY

Chapter 5 examines biological rhythm and states of consciousness. There are three types of endogenous rhythms: circadian (occurs once a day), ultradian (occurs more than once a day) and infradian (occurs less than once a day). During the sleep cycle, four stages of non-rapid eye movement (NREM) sleep alternate with rapid eye movement sleep (REM), on average, every 90 minutes during the night. Dreaming is more likely to occur during REM sleep. Though the purpose of dreams is not really known, psychologists have proposed several explanations. The Chapter reviews four different theories of dreaming. While endogenous biological rhythms can influence our states of consciousness, drugs can also alter consciousness. Different categories of drugs are described, along with their physiological and psychological effects. There are two main theories of hypnosis. Some consider it a result of dissociative processes while others believe it is a function of normal sociocognitive processes.

PREVIEW OUTLINE AND REVIEW QUESTIONS

Before you read the chapter, review the preview outline and the Learning Objectives for each section of the text. Answer all questions as you read the text.

SECTION 1 - BIOLOGICAL RHYTHMS: THE TIDES OF EXPERIENCE (PP. 162-176)

I.   **Biological rhythms: The tides of experience**

    A.   **Definitions**

        1.   _____ - awareness of oneself and the environment

        2.   Biological rhythms - regular fluctuations in biological systems

            a.   Entrainment - synchronization of rhythms with external events

            b.   Endogenous rhythms - occur in absence of external cues - 3 types

                (1)   _____ rhythms - occur every 24 hours

                (2)   Infradian rhythms - occur less often than once a day

                (3)   Ultradian rhythms - occur more often than once a day

    B.   **Circadian rhythms** - exist in plants, animals, insects, and humans

        1.   Can be studied by isolating subjects from environmental time cues

        2.   The body's clock

            a.   Circadian rhythms controlled by a master biological clock located in the in the suprachiasmatic nucleus (SCN) in the hypothalamus

            b.   SCN regulates neurotransmitters and hormones which provide feedback to the SCN and affect its functioning

            c.   _____, a hormone regulated by the SCN, responds to light-dark

        3.   When the clock is out of sync

            a.   Change in routine may cause internal _____

            b.   Cycles are affected by environmental and individual factors

    C.   **Mood and long-term rhythms - Infradian rhythms**

        1.   Does the season affect moods?

            a.   Some people report seasonal affective disorder (SAD); evidence for a biological basis for this disorder is inconsistent

            b.   Light treatment is used though its efficacy is not clear

        2.   Does the menstrual cycle affect moods?

            a.   First half of the cycle, estrogen increases; midcycle, ovaries release egg, then progesterone increases; if conception does not occur, estrogen and progesterone levels fall

            b.   _____ syndrome introduced in 1970s yet clear support is lacking

                (1)   Physical symptoms are common, emotional symptoms are rare and are not clearly tied to the menstrual cycle

                (2)   Belief in PMS is influenced by cultural attitudes though research evidence does not support "PMS" as a syndrome

    c. Research on hormonal influences on men is lacking

    d. Conclusion - few people of either sex are likely to undergo personality shifts because of hormones

D. **The rhythms of sleep - ultradian rhythms**

  1. Why we sleep? Some theories

    a. Sleep is recuperative for body

    b. Sleep is necessary for normal mental functioning

  2. The realms of sleep - sleep is not an unbroken state of rest

    a. Ultradian cycle occurs, on average, every 90 minutes

      (1) 4 Non-REM stages, each deeper than the previous

        (a) 1 - small, irregular brain waves; light sleep

        (b) 2 - high-peaking waves called sleep spindles

        (c) 3 - _____ waves begin; slow with high peaks

        (d) 4 - mostly delta waves and deep sleep

      (2) After stage 4 the cycle reverses and Rapid Eye-Movement (REM) sleep occurs following stage 1

        (a) REM sleep is characterized by active brain waves, increased heart rate and blood pressure, limp muscles, twitching, and dreaming

        (b) Called paradoxical sleep because body is inactive but the brain is very active

      (3) REM and non-REM sleep _____ throughout the night

      (4) The purpose of REM sleep is unclear

Answer these Learning Objectives while you read Section 1.

1. Define consciousness and the biological rhythms associated with states of consciousness.

2. Describe circadian rhythms; how they are studied and how they may be desynchronized.

3. Discuss examples of ultradian and infradian rhythms and distinguish endogenous rhythms from those caused by external factors.

4. Summarize the research evidence on "PMS" and discuss whether emotional symptoms associated with "PMS" are tied to the menstrual cycle.

5. Summarize theories about the biological functions of sleep.

6. Distinguish between rapid eye movement (REM) and non-REM periods in sleep and describe the four stages of non-REM sleep.

SECTION 2 - EXPLORING THE DREAM WORLD (PP. 176-181)

II. **EXPLORING THE DREAM WORLD**
    A.   **Characteristics of dreams**
        1.   Focus of attention is inward
        2.   _____ dreams - dreams in which people know they are dreaming
    B.   **Theories of dreams** - every culture has its theories about dreams
        1.   Dreams as _____ wishes
            a.   Freud - "royal road to the unconscious;" all dreams meaningful
                (1)   Manifest content - what we experience and remember
                (2)   _____ content - hidden, symbolic; unconscious wishes
            b.   Many people disagree with Freud's interpretations
        2.   Dreams as reflections of current concerns
            a.   Reflect ongoing _____ of waking life; problem-focused approach to dreaming in which dreams convey true, not symbolic, meaning
            b.   Dreams often do contain material related to current concerns
            c.   Sex differences in dream content are no longer big
            d.   Some believe dreams provide an opportunity for resolving problems
        3.   Dreams as a by-product of mental housekeeping
            a.   Physiological information-processing approach; unnecessary neural connections are eliminated and important ones are strengthened
            b.   Dreams are the remains of the sorting, scanning and sifting process
            c.   Variations on this theme have been proposed, but these approaches have shortcomings and may tell us more about REM sleep than about dreams
        4.   Dreams as interpreted brain activity
            a.   Activation-_____ theory
                 (1)   Dreams are the result of neurons firing spontaneously in the lower brain (in the pons) that are sent to the cortex
                (2)   Signals from pons have no meaning, but the cortex tries to make sense of, or synthesize, them
            b.   Critics say sometimes dreams do make sense
    C.   **Conclusion**
        1.   No single theory explains all facets of dreaming
        2.   All approaches account for some of the evidence

Answer this Learning Objective while you read Section 2.

7.   Summarize the principles of the psychoanalytic, problem-solving, mental housekeeping and activation-synthesis theories of dreaming.

SECTION 3 - CONSCIOUSNESS-ALTERING DRUGS (PP. 181-189)

III. **CONSCIOUSNESS-ALTERING DRUGS**
- A. **Altering mood and consciousness**
    1. Efforts to alter mood and consciousness appear to be universal
    2. During the 1960s, people sought to produce altered states of consciousness
- B. **Classifying drugs**
    1. Definition - _____ drug - substance affecting perception, mood, thinking, memory or behavior by changing the body's biochemistry
    2. Reasons for taking such drugs vary
    3. Classified according to the drug's effects on central nervous system
        - a. Stimulants - speed up activity in central nervous system; include cocaine, amphetamines, nicotine, caffeine
        - b. Depressants (sedatives) - slow down activity in central nervous system; include alcohol, tranquilizers, barbiturates
        - c. Opiates - mimic endorphins; include opium, morphine, heroine, methadone
        - d. Psychedelics - alter _____; include LSD, mescaline, psilocybin
        - e. Anabolic steroids and Marijuana - don't fit other classifications
- C. **The physiology of drug effects**
    1. Effects produced by acting on _____ in a variety of ways
    2. Can produce cognitive or emotional effects
    3. Repeated use of certain drugs can cause permanent brain damage
    4. Some drugs lead to _____ (needing more over time) and withdrawal (symptoms upon removal of the drug)
- D. **The psychology of drug effects**
    1. Effects depend on a person's physical condition, experience with the drug, environmental setting, and _____ _____
    2. Alcohol can provide an excuse for violent or other behavior
- E. **The drug debate**
    1. Often people fail to distinguish between drug abuse and drug use
    2. Legality of drugs not always linked to dangerousness
    3. People have strong feelings and biases that may interfere with rational thinking about drugs

Answer these Learning Objectives while you read Section 3.

8. List the types of psychoactive drugs and describe their physical and behavioral effects.

9. List and explain the factors that influence the effects of psychoactive drugs.

SECTION 4 - THE RIDDLE OF HYPNOSIS (PP. 190-197)

IV.   **THE RIDDLE OF HYPNOSIS**
- A.   **Definition - procedure in which the practitioner suggests changes in the sensations, perceptions, thoughts, feelings, or behavior of the subject**
  - 1.   Suggestions involve performance of an action
  - 2.   Compliance with suggestions feels involuntary
- B.   **The nature of hypnosis** - researchers agree on the following
  - 1.   Hypnotic state is not sleep
  - 2.   Responsiveness depends more on person being hypnotized than hypnotist's skill
  - 3.   Participants cannot be forced to do things against their will
  - 4.   Hypnotic inductions increase suggestibility but only to a modest degree; people accept suggestions with and without hypnosis
  - 5.   Hypnosis does not increase the accuracy of memory; it can increase amount of information remembered, but it also increases errors
  - 6.   Does not produce a literal re-experiencing of long-ago events
  - 7.   Hypnosis has been effective for medical and psychological purposes
- C.   **Theories of hypnosis** - two competing theories predominate
  - 1.   _____ theories
    - a.   Like lucid dreaming and simple distractions, it involves dissociation, a split in consciousness in which one part of the mind operates independently of the rest of consciousness
    - b.   Several theories of dissociation attempt to explain the state
    - c.   These theories fit well with recent research and brain theories
  - 2.   The sociocognitive approach
    - a.   The effects are a result of the interaction between the hypnotist and the abilities, beliefs, and expectations of the subject
    - b.   People are playing the _____ of a hypnotized person without faking
    - c.   This role, like others, is so engrossing, it's done without intent
    - d.   People use imagination and fantasy to fulfill the role requirements

Answer these Learning Objectives while you read Section 4.

10.   Define hypnosis and summarize its characteristics.

11.   Describe dissociation and sociocognitive theories of hypnosis.

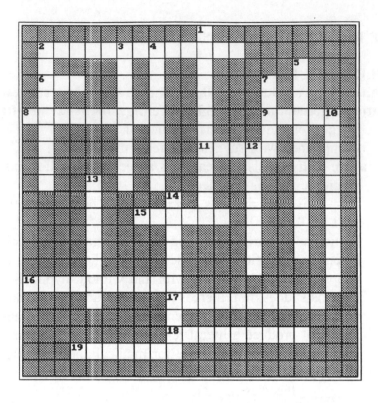

ACROSS

2. awareness of the environment and of one's own existence
6. sleep periods characterized by eye movement
8. most widely used illicit drug in the U.S.
9. dream in which the dreamer is aware of dreaming
11. large, slow brain waves, characteristic of relaxed wakefulness
15. dream content that expresses unconscious wishes symbolically
16. symptoms that occur when someone addicted to a drug stops taking it
17. activity in the lower part of the brain that causes dreams
18. increased resistance to a drug's effects with continued use
19. drugs that relieve pain and produce euphoria

DOWN

1. ebbing and flowing of hormones in females over roughly a 28-day period
2. biological rhythm of about 24 hours
3. biological rhythm exemplified by birds flying south
4. biological rhythm exemplified by the sleep cycle
5. drugs capable of influencing mood, perception, cognition, behavior
7. wave characteristic of stage 3 and stage 4 sleep
10. slows down activity in the central nervous system
12. a condition in which a person is focused and extremely responsive to suggestion
13. synthetic derivatives of testosterone
14. speeds up central nervous system activity

FLASH CARDS

Cut the following chart along the borders and test yourself with the resulting flash cards.

5.1 CONSCIOUSNESS	5.2 STATES OF CONSCIOUSNESS	5.3 BIOLOGICAL RHYTHM
5.4 ENTRAINMENT	5.5 ENDOGENOUS	5.6 CIRCADIAN RHYTHM
5.7 INFRADIAN RHYTHM	5.8 ULTRADIAN RHYTHM	5.9 SUPRACHIASMATIC NUCLEUS (SCN)
5.10 MELATONIN	5.11 INTERNAL DESYNCHRONIZATION	5.12 SEASONAL AFFECTIVE DISORDER (SAD)
5.13 MENSTRUAL CYCLE	5.14 "PREMENSTRUAL SYNDROME (PSM)"	5.15 RAPID EYE MOVEMENT (REM) SLEEP
5.16 NON-REM SLEEP	5.17 ALPHA WAVES	5.18 DELTA WAVES

5.3 A periodic, more or less regular fluctuation in a biological system; may or may not have psychological implications.	5.2 Distinctive and discrete patterns in the functioning of consciousness, characterized by particular modes of thought, perception, memory, or feeling.	5.1 Our awareness of ourselves and the environment.
5.6 A biological rhythm with a period (from peak to peak or trough to trough) of about 24 hours; from the Latin circa, "about," and dies, "a day."	5.5 Generated from within rather than as a result of external events.	5.4 The synchronization of biological rhythms with external cues, such as fluctuations in daylight.
5.9 An area of the brain containing a biological clock that governs circadian rhythms.	5.8 A biological rhythm that occurs more frequently than once a day; from the Latin for "beyond a day."	5.7 A biological rhythm that occurs less frequently than once a day; from the Latin for "below a day."
5.12 Depression that occurs in winter, when periods of daylight are short, and improves every spring, as daylight increases.	5.11 A state in which biological rhythms are not in phase (synchronized) with one another.	5.10 A hormone secreted by the pineal glad; it is involved in the regulation of circadian rhythms.
5.15 Sleep periods characterized by eye movement, loss of muscle tone, and dreaming.	5.14 A cluster of symptoms associated with the days preceding menstruation that has come to be thought of as an "illness" and given this label.	5.13 The ebbing and flowing of hormones in females over roughly a 28-day period; related to reproduction.
5.18 Slow, regular brain waves characteristic of stage 3 and stage 4 sleep.	5.17 Relatively large, slow brain waves characteristic of relaxed wakefulness.	5.16 Periods of fewer eye movements that alternate with REM sleep in an ultradian cycle; there are 4 stages of non-REM sleep.

5.19 LUCID DREAM	5.20 PSYCHOANALYTIC THEORY OF DREAMS	5.21 MANIFEST VERSUS LATENT CONTENT OF DREAMS
5.22 PROBLEM-FOCUSED APPROACH TO DREAMS	5.23 MENTAL-HOUSEKEEPING APPROACH TO DREAMS	5.24 ACTIVATION-SYNTHESIS THEORY OF DREAMS
5.25 ALTERED STATES OF CONSCIOUSNESS	5.26 PSYCHOACTIVE DRUG	5.27 STIMULANTS
5.28 DEPRESSANTS	5.29 OPIATES	5.30 PSYCHEDELIC DRUGS
5.31 ANABOLIC STEROIDS	5.32 MARIJUANA	5.33 TOLERANCE
5.34 WITHDRAWAL SYMPTOMS	5.35 "THINK-DRINK" EFFECT	5.36 HYPNOSIS
5.37 DISSOCIATION	5.38 HIDDEN OBSERVER	5.39 SOCIOCOGNITIVE EXPLANATION OF HYPNOSIS

5.21 Part of the psychoanalytic theory of dreams; manifest content is what we experience and recall, latent content is the symbolic meaning.	5.20 Freudian approach that dreams are the "royal road to the unconscious." All dreams have meaning related to our wishes and desires.	5.19 A dream in which the dreamer is aware of dreaming.
5.24 The theory that dreaming results from the cortical synthesis and interpretation of neural signals triggered by activity in the lower brain.	5.23 The theory that dreaming is an opportunity for mental housekeeping; dreams are snippets from a process of sorting, scanning, and sifting.	5.22 Theory that dreams reflect the ongoing emotional preoccupations of waking life.
5.27 Drugs that speed up activity in the central nervous system.	5.26 A drug capable of influencing perception, mood, cognition, or behavior.	5.25 A state of consciousness that differs from ordinary wakefulness or sleep.
5.30 Consciousness-altering drugs that produce hallucinations, change thought processes, or disrupt normal perceptions of time and space.	5.29 Drugs, derived from the opium poppy, that relieve pain and commonly produce euphoria.	5.28 Drugs that slow down the activity in the central nervous system.
5.33 Increased resistance to a drug's effects with continued use; larger doses are needed to produce effects once brought about by smaller ones.	5.32 Probably the most widely used illicit drug in the U.S. Tetrahydrocannabinol (THC) is the active ingredient.	5.31 Synthetic derivatives of testosterone. It is unclear whether they are psychoactive.
5.36 A procedure in which the practitioner suggests changes in the sensations, perceptions, thoughts, feelings, or behavior of the subject.	5.35 The phenomenon in which people who thought they had alcohol (even if they didn't) behaved in ways consistent with their expectations.	5.34 Physical and psychological symptoms that occur when someone addicted to a drug stops taking it.
5.39 The theory that states that the hypnotized person is playing the role of a hypnotized person; analogous to other roles we play in life.	5.38 Part of the dissociation theory of hypnosis that suggests one part of the person goes along with the suggestions while the other part observes.	5.37 A split in consciousness in which one part of the mind operates independently of others.

PRACTICE TEST 1 - Multiple Choice

1.   Being aware of one's own existence is
     A.   a psychological problem.   B.   a philosophical dilemma.
     C.   the definition of consciousness. D.   an altered state.

2.   Geraldo goes to sleep by 11:00 p.m. and awakens at 7:00 a.m. This cycle is a(n)
     A.   infradian rhythm.   B.   circadian rhythm.
     C.   nocturnal rhythm.   D.   ultradian rhythm.

3.   The seasonal migration of birds is an example of
     A.   a circadian rhythm.   B.   an infradian rhythm.
     C.   an ultradian rhythm.   D.   a diurnal rhythm.

4.   Rhythms that continue in the absence of all external time cues are called
     A.   endogenous rhythms.   B.   exogenous rhythms.
     C.   indigenous rhythms.   D.   none of the above.

5.   Periods of dreaming and nondreaming occur during the night in
     A.   a circadian rhythm.   B.   an infradian rhythm.
     C.   an ultradian rhythm.   D.   a diurnal rhythm.

6.   Which of the following can desynchronize circadian rhythms?
     A.   an overseas trip   B.   switching shifts at work
     C.   going on daylight savings time D.   all of the above

7.   Premenstrual syndrome
     A.   has been experienced by a majority of women according to scientific studies.
     B.   has been questioned, particularly its association with emotional symptoms.
     C.   has been widely documented and confirmed in scientific studies.
     D.   is a diagnosable psychological disorder.

8.   The relationship between menstruation and intellectual performance is
     A.   absent.
     B.   that women perform intellectual tasks best at the start of the cycle.
     C.   that women perform intellectual tasks best at the middle of the cycle.
     D.   that women perform intellectual tasks best near the end of the cycle.

9. Sleep is necessary
    A. because of its recuperative properties.
    B. because the brain requires sleep.
    C. to repair cells and remove waste products from the muscles.
    D. for all of the above reasons.

10. The brain waves that occur when you first go to bed and relax are called
    A. alpha waves.   B. delta waves.
    C. beta waves.   D. gamma waves.

11. REM sleep is called paradoxical sleep because
    A. dreams are often paradoxical and they occur most often in REM sleep.
    B. the brain is extremely active but the body is devoid of muscle tone.
    C. people are easily awakened, even though it is a deep sleep.
    D. the brain is very calm and inactive, but the body is quite active.

12. After the first 30 to 45 minutes of sleep, you have progressed from stage 1 sleep to stage
    4 sleep. After this, you
    A. go into a prolonged non-REM period.
    B. enter REM sleep.
    C. progress back up the ladder from stage 4 to stage 3 to stage 2 to stage 1.
    D. go back to stage 1 and continue through the four stages all night.

13. The most vivid dreams occur during
    A. the menstrual cycle.   B. REM sleep.
    C. stage 1 sleep.   D. non-REM sleep.

14. Which hypothesis suggests that dreams result from cortical attempts to interpret
    spontaneous neural activity?
    A. mental housekeeping   B. psychoanalytic
    C. activation-synthesis   D. problem-solving

15. According to the _____ hypothesis, dreams express our unconscious desires.
    A. information-processing hypothesis   B. psychoanalytic hypothesis
    C. activation-synthesis hypothesis   D. problem-solving hypothesis

16. When Ruth dreams, she is in the dream, but also observing the dream and controlling
    what happens in it. Ruth is experiencing
    A. nightmares.   B. manifest dreams.
    C. lucid dreams.   D. REM dreams.

17. Which of the following are psychoactive drugs?
    A. tobacco
    C. caffeine
    B. opium
    D. all of the above

18. Psychoactive drugs work primarily by affecting
    A. brain structures.
    C. neurotransmitters.
    B. bodily rhythms.
    D. blood flow to the brain.

19. Alcohol, tranquilizers and sedatives are examples of
    A. opiates.
    C. psychedelics.
    B. depressants.
    D. stimulants.

20. When Micky began using drugs, he used only a small amount. After six months, he required more and more to achieve the same effect. Micky experienced
    A. withdrawal.
    C. tolerance.
    B. brain damage.
    D. mental set.

21. Hank and Bill both used the same amount of cocaine, but they each had different reactions. Which of the following differences between them might account for this?
    A. physical condition
    C. prior experience with cocaine
    B. expectations for the drug
    D. all of the above

22. Which of the following statements describes the effect of hypnosis on memory?
    A. "age regression" allows one to remember childhood experiences accurately.
    B. under hypnosis, people can accurately recall events from earlier lives.
    C. memories recalled under hypnosis are often vivid but inaccurate.
    D. memory errors decrease under hypnosis.

23. Those who say hypnosis is a(n) _____ believe that hypnosis involves role-playing.
    A. altered state
    C. sociocognitive process
    B. deliberate deception
    D. none of the above

24. Those who believe that hypnotic state differs from normal consciousness believe
    A. that hypnosis involves dissociation.
    B. the powers of hypnosis are exaggerated.
    C. that suggestion alone can produce the same results.
    D. all of the above.

25. Hypnosis has been successfully used for
    A. state shows.
    C. medical and psychological treatments.
    B. legal purposes.
    D. past-lives regression.

PRACTICE TEST 2 - Multiple Choice

1. Jim likes to get drunk and smoke marijuana because this enables him to see himself and the world differently. This motive is consistent with which of the following statements about consciousness?
    A. Consciousness is awareness of one's bodily changes or rhythms.
    B. Consciousness is awareness of oneself and the environment.
    C. Consciousness is directly related to changes in brain wave patterns.
    D. Consciousness is a philosophical issue that cannot be defined.

2. What is the relationship between consciousness and bodily rhythms?
    A. Consciousness can vary with bodily rhythms.
    B. Changes in consciousness direct changes in bodily rhythms.
    C. Bodily rhythms can change but consciousness does not.
    D. Consciousness and bodily rhythms are unrelated.

3. As part of a research study, Bob is living in a comfortable room with a V.C.R. and stereo, but there are no windows, clocks or sounds coming in from outside. He is told to eat, sleep and work whenever he feels like doing so. This type of study is used to
    A. examine sensory deprivation.
    B. examine the affect of daylight on depression.
    C. explore endogenous circadian rhythms.
    D. attempt to modify infradian rhythms.

4. Ursula's job requires that she change shifts often. She is likely to experience
    A. internal desynchronization.
    B. internal synchronization.
    C. a need for less sleep.
    D. external desynchronization.

5. Which of the following is an example of an infradian rhythm?
    A. hibernation of bears   B. stages of sleep
    C. sleep-wake cycle   D. all of the above

6. Which of the following is an example of an ultradian rhythm?
    A. stomach contractions   B. hormone level fluctuations
    C. appetite for food   D. all of the above

7. Menstrual cycle research on hormones and mood shifts suggests that
    A. for most people, hormones are reliably and strongly correlated with mood.
    B. hormonal shifts cause mood shifts.
    C. mood changes cause hormonal shifts.
    D. no causal relationship has been established between hormonal shifts and moods.

8. Which of the following conclusions reflects the findings on premenstrual symptoms?
    A. The idea of mood swings as a premenstrual symptom has been questioned since men and women don't differ in the number of mood swings they experience in a month.
    B. For most women, the relationship between cycle stage and symptoms is weak.
    C. There is no reliable relationship between cycle stage and work efficiency.
    D. All of the above have been found.

9. Theories about the biological functions of sleep include; to facilitate
    A. bodily restoration and brain function.
    B. psychic healing.
    C. providing a time for dreaming.
    D. all of the above.

10. One reason why people are likely to be dreaming when the alarm goes off is because as the night progresses, REM periods _____
    A. get longer.   B. get shorter.
    C. become more intense.   D. occur at more regular intervals.

11. Joe is a subject in a sleep study. When his brain emits occasional short bursts of rapid, high-peaking waves, he is in which stage of sleep?
    A. stage 1   B. stage 3
    C. stage 2   D. stage 4

12. In what type of sleep is Joe's body totally limp, but his brain wave pattern is active?
    A. paradoxical sleep   B. dream sleep
    C. REM sleep   D. all of the above

13. Pat had an upsetting disagreement with her father before going to sleep and she dreamt about her brother. The theory of dreams as _____ suggests the latent content is about her father.
    A. problem solving theory   B. unconscious wishes
    C. information processing   D. activation-synthesis

14. Which theory suggests that neurons in Pat's brain stem are spontaneously firing and her cortex is simply trying to make sense of the neuronal activity?
    A.   dreams as problem solving theory   B.   dreams as unconscious wishes
    C.   dreams as information processing   D.   activation-synthesis theory

15. Which theory suggests that Pat's dream reflects her desire to talk to her brother?
    A.   dreams as problem solving theory   B.   dreams as unconscious wishes
    C.   dreams as information processing   D.   activation-synthesis theory

16. Drug classifications are based on
    A.   the legality of a drug.
    B.   whether a drug is addictive.
    C.   the effects of a drug on the central nervous system.
    D.   all of the above.

17. Though cocaine is a(n) _____, heroin is a(n) _____, and marijuana is a(n) _____, they can all produce euphoria.
    A.   stimulant; psychedelic; depressant
    B.   amphetamine; opiate; psychedelic
    C.   psychedelic; stimulant; unclear category
    D.   stimulant; opiate; unclear category

18. Bruno smokes four packs of cigarettes and drinks nine cups of coffee a day. He
    A.   is using drugs.   B.   is relying on stimulants.
    C.   may feel excited and confident.   D.   all of the above

19. Drugs can affect neurotransmitters by
    A.   increasing or decreasing them at the synapse.
    B.   eliminating them altogether.
    C.   mutating their chemical formula.
    D.   all of the above.

20. Half of all men arrested for assaulting their wives claim to have been drinking at the time of the assault, yet most of these men did not have enough alcohol in their bloodstreams to qualify as legally intoxicated. Of the factors that influence drug effects, which does this represent?
    A.   physical condition   B.   environmental setting
    C.   mental set   D.   experience with the drug

21. Rick and Dick had the same amount to drink, yet Rick cannot walk a straight line and Dick seems fine. Which of the following might explain this difference?
    A.   Rick was very upset about an argument he'd had with Nick before the party.
    B.   Dick drank while watching T.V. at home with a friend, while Rick was at a party.
    C.   Dick grew up drinking with meals and does not think about alcohol use as a way to get drunk, while Rick sees it as a way to blow off steam.
    D.   all of the above

22. Hypnosis and drugs can be used in a similar fashion to
    A.   justify letting go of inhibitions.
    B.   dissociate.
    C.   hallucinate.
    D.   alter neurotransmitter levels.

23. Susan, who is normally very modest, is removing her clothes under hypnosis. How might this be explained, according the theory that hypnosis is a social-cognitive process?
    A.   She is in an altered state.
    B.   She has dissociated.
    C.   She is playing the role of a hypnotized person.
    D.   She has relinquished control to the hypnotist.

24. Which of the following evidence argues against the credibility of age regression?
    A.   Subjects who were age regressed as part of a study could not accurately recall their favorite comforting object from age three.
    B.   Subjects in a study did not know basic facts about the time period in which they were supposed to have lived in a previous life.
    C.   When people are regressed to an earlier age, brain wave patterns do not resemble those of children.
    D.   all of the above

25. "Hypnotically refreshed" memories
    A.   are generally quite accurate.
    B.   should always be believed.
    C.   often contain many errors.
    D.   are always inaccurate.

PRACTICE TEST 3 - Short Answer

1. _____ is defined as the awareness of oneself and the environment.

2. The sleep cycle is an example of a(n) _____ rhythm.

3. Circadian rhythms are controlled by a biological clock called the _____ _____.

4. An example of an ultradian rhythm is _____. An example of an infradian rhythm is _____.

5. Internal _____ occurs when your normal routine changes, such as when you must take a long airplane flight over many time zones.

6. Few people of either sex are likely to undergo personality shifts solely as a result of _____.

7. The majority of vivid dreams occur during _____.

8. The short bursts of rapid, high-peaking waves that occur during Stage 2 sleep are known as sleep _____.

9. REM sleep is called paradoxical sleep because the body is _____ while the brain is _____.

10. _____ dreaming occurs when people feel they know they are dreaming.

11. Psychoanalytic theory suggests that we must distinguish the obvious, or _____, content of a dream from the hidden, or _____, content that reveals the true meaning of the dream.

12. The theory of dreaming that suggests dreams are the remains of a sorting, scanning, and sifting process is called the _____ view.

13. The _____ hypothesis suggests that dreams are the result of spontaneous neural firing.

14. _____ drugs affect perception, mood, thinking, memory or behavior.

15. Drugs are classified according to their effects on the _____.

16. Amphetamines, cocaine, caffeine, and nicotine are all examples of _____.

17. Some drugs, such as heroine and tranquilizers can lead to _____, a state in which larger and larger doses are needed to produce the same effect.

18. The effects of drugs are often the result of their influence on _____ levels.

19. Several factors influence the way a particular individual reacts to the use of a drug. Two of those factors are _____ and _____.

20. Some research shows that alcohol can provide an excuse for violent behavior. This is called the _____ phenomenon.

21. Hilgard suggests that only one part of consciousness goes along with hypnotic suggestions. The other part is like a _____, watching but not participating.

22. Some people report that hypnosis has helped them recall long-ago events. These memories are likely to be _____.

23. The _____ explanation of hypnosis suggests that during hypnosis a split in consciousness occurs.

24. Hypnosis has been used effectively for _____ purposes.

25. The _____ explanation regards hypnosis as a form of role playing.

PRACTICE TEST 4 - True/False

1. T F   States of consciousness are distinct patterns of consciousness often associated with biological rhythms.

2. T F   Entrainment refers to the fact that many biological rhythms are generated from within, or endogenous.

3. T F   Menstruation is an example of a circadian rhythm.

4. T F   Cycles that occur during sleep are examples of ultradian rhythms.

5. T F   Ultradian rhythms are governed by a biological "clock" in the suprachiasmatic nucleus.

6. T F   Recent research suggests that light treatments can be effective for seasonal affective disorder.

7. T F   Premenstrual Syndrome is a well-documented phenomenon and is experienced by many women.

8. T F   Overall, men and women do not differ in the emotional symptoms they report or in the number of mood swings they experience over the course of a month.

9. T F   During sleep, periods of rapid eye movement (REM) alternate with non-REM sleep in an ultradian rhythm.

10. T F   During REM sleep, the skeletal muscles are limp, and the brain is inactive.

11. T F   After stage 4 of NREM sleep, the cycle enters REM sleep and then begins the descent from stage 1 through stage 4 all over again.

12. T F   In dreams, according to Freud, thoughts and objects are disguised as symbolic images.

13. T F   Findings on recurrent and traumatic dreams support the approach that dreams express current concerns or help us solve current problems.

14. T F   The activation-synthesis approach suggests that dreams occur when the cortex tries to make sense of spontaneous neural firing initiated in the pons.

15. T F Alcohol and marijuana belong to the same classification of drugs.

16. T F Drugs are classified according to their effects on the central nervous system.

17. T F Nicotine and caffeine are not considered psychoactive drugs.

18. T F In moderate doses, marijuana can interfere with the transfer of information to long-term memory and, in large doses, it can cause hallucinations.

19. T F Psychoactive drugs produce their effects exclusively by increasing levels of neurotransmitters in the brain.

20. T F Reactions to a psychoactive drug involve more than the drug's chemical properties. They also depend on a person's physical condition, experience with the drug, environmental setting, and mental set.

21. T F The "think-drink" phenomenon is related to the drinkers mental set, or expectations, about the effects of alcohol.

22. T F About half the men arrested for assaulting their wives had enough alcohol in their bloodstreams to qualify as legally intoxicated.

23. T F Hypnotic responsiveness depends on the efforts and skills of the hypnotist.

24. T F The hidden observer refers to the fact that hypnotic responsiveness improves if the person being hypnotised believes that an observer will be watching the procedure.

25. T F The sociocognitive explanation regards hypnosis as a product of normal social and cognitive processes.

PRACTICE TEST 5 - Essay

1. Identify which type of rhythm each example represents and explain why.
   A. hunger
   B. mating behavior in dogs and cats
   C. fatigue
   D. sexual behavior in human beings
   E. concentration
   F. full moons

2. Dr. Irving is conducting a survey on premenstrual syndrome (PMS). Of the 100 subjects who responded to the survey, 70% indicated that they experience PMS on a regular basis. Compare these findings to the research in the text that argues against PMS and answer the following questions:
   A. How was PMS defined? What symptoms were included and why is this important?
   B. What are some of the problems with the self-reporting of PMS symptoms?
   C. Describe possible influences of expectations and attitudes toward menstruation on the results of the survey.
   D. Describe the results of research findings from studies that did not reveal their true purpose.

3. For the ninth grade science project, Megan kept a detailed diary of her sleep experiences during a one-month interval. The information obtained and her conclusions are submitted below. Using actual evidence related to sleep, comment on each of these claims.

   A. During the period of the study, I awakened myself once during each night at different times. Each time I woke myself up, I felt the same as when I wake up in the morning. This indicates that sleep actually is the same kind of thing all through the night.
   B. I was allowed to stay up all night twice. It was really hard to keep my eyes open at around 4:00 a.m., but by 6:00 a.m. I felt wide awake. This suggests that the loss of sleep is invigorating.
   C. After missing sleep two nights in a row, I felt like going to bed extra early the next day. This indicates that we need to catch up on our rest.
   D. Even though I felt O.K. after missing sleep for two nights, I got a "D" on an exam at school. This suggests that maybe sleep loss has more effects than I thought!
   E. During the time of the study, I had two dreams and my sister had five. This indicates that we only dream several times a month.

4. Gretchen had a dream that she and her husband had gone horseback riding. He was far ahead of her and, though she was riding as fast as she could, she was unable to catch up. Eventually she lost her way and was unsure where she was going. She dismounted her horse and found that she was in a beautiful valley, and she stopped there and felt very peaceful. Identify which theory would give each of the following interpretations of this dream.

    A. This dream has little significance or meaning. It represents the attempt of the cortex to make sense of random neuronal firing in the brainstem.
    B. This dream has little significance. It represents the brain's mental housekeeping. It is sorting, scanning and sifting new information into "wanted" and "unwanted" categories.
    C. The dream has great significance. It is likely to be a dream about Gretchen's unresolved relationship with her father. She has always felt abandoned by him and could never win his attention or affection, which she has always deeply desired.
    D. The dream has to do with Gretchen's concern that she cannot keep up with her husband's pace. He always has more energy than she does and although she tries, what she would most like to do is "get off the merry-go-round," relax, and take life easier.

5. For each type of drug listed below, indicate the following: 1) the type of drug, 2) the common effects of the drug, and 3) the result of abusing the drug.

    A. alcohol
    B. tranquilizers
    C. morphine
    D. amphetamines
    E. cocaine
    F. LSD
    G. marijuana

CHAPTER 6

Sensation and Perception

LEARNING OBJECTIVES

1. Distinguish between sensation and perception.

2. Distinguish between anatomical and functional codes in the nervous system.

3. Define psychophysics, absolute and difference thresholds and signal detection theory.

4. Explain sensory adaptation, sensory deprivation, sensory overload and selective attention.

5. List the characteristics of light waves and their correspondence to the visual experience.

6. Identify the parts of the eye and describe how they convert light to vision.

7. Discuss two theories of color vision and how they relate to stages of processing.

8. Explain how form, distance and depth perception occur.

9. List and explain visual constancies and distinguish them from visual illusions.

10. Describe how sound wave characteristics correspond to loudness, pitch, and timbre.

11. Identify the parts of the ear, describe how they convert sound to hearing, and discuss the role of perceptual processes in making sound meaningful.

12. List and explain the factors that affect gustation (taste) and olfaction (smell).

13. List the four skin senses.

14. Describe the gate-control theory of pain and the neuromatrix theory of pain.

15. Describe the internal senses of kinesthesis and equilibrium.

16. Summarize the evidence for innate abilities in perception and describe the psychological and cultural influences on perception.

17. Discuss the evidence on the effectiveness of "subliminal perception" tapes and ESP.

CHAPTER CONCEPT MAP

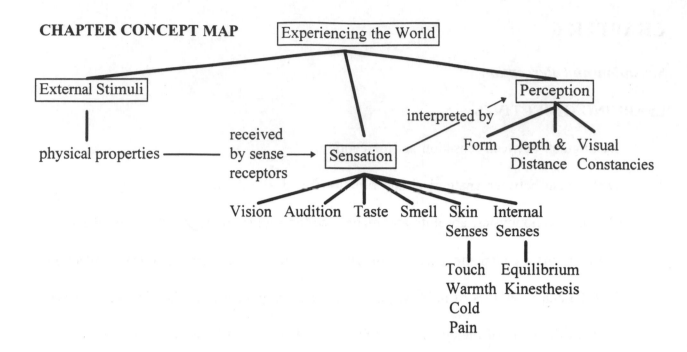

BRIEF CHAPTER SUMMARY

Chapter 6 examines the processes of sensation and perception and the relationship between them. Receptors in the senses change physical energy into neural energy. The physical characteristics of the stimuli correspond to psychological dimensions of our sensory experience. The general processes of vision, hearing, taste, smell, pain, equilibrium and kinesthesis are reviewed. Once sensation has occurred, the process of organizing and interpreting the sensory information, or perception, begins. Perceptual strategies, including depth and distance strategies, visual constancies and form perception strategies, are described. Some perceptual abilities appear to be inborn, while others are influenced by psychological, environmental and cultural factors. Two current theories of pain are reviewed. Conscious and nonconscious processes are examined. Extrasensory perception is critically evaluated.

PREVIEW OUTLINE AND REVIEW QUESTIONS

Before you read the chapter, review the preview outline and the Learning Objectives for each section of the text. Answer all questions as you read the text.

SECTION 1 - OUR SENSATIONAL SENSES (PP. 180-187)

I. OUR SENSATIONAL SENSES
   A. Definitions
      1. _____ - the detection of physical energy emitted or reflected by physical objects by cells (receptors) located in the sense organs and internal body tissues
      2. Perception - processes that organize sensory impulses into meaningful patterns
   B. **The riddle of separate sensations** - How we can explain separate sensations
      1. Introduction to the senses
         a. There are ___ widely known senses and other lesser known senses
         b. All senses evolved to help us survive
      2. Sensation begins with sense receptors, cells in the sense organs that detect appropriate stimuli
      3. Sense receptors detect a stimulus and convert the stimulus energy into electrical impulses that travel along nerves to the brain - called _____
      4. The nervous system encodes the neural messages using two kinds of codes
         a. _____ codes
            (1) Doctrine of specific _____ energies - signals received by the sense organs stimulate different nerve pathways, which terminate in different areas of the brain
            (2) Does not fully explain separate sensations because it doesn't explain sensory variations within a sense (i.e. pink vs. red)
         b. Functional codes
            (1) Particular receptors fire or are inhibited from firing in the presence of certain stimuli
            (2) Information about which cells, how many, and the rate and pattern of firing constitutes a functional code
   C. **Measuring the senses**
      1. Psychophysics - how the _____ properties of stimuli are related to our psychological experience of them
      2. Absolute _____

        a.   The smallest amount of energy a person can detect reliably (50 percent of the time)

        b.   The senses can pick up only a narrow band of physical energies

3.   _____ thresholds

        a.   The smallest difference in stimulation that a person can detect reliably (50 percent of the time); also called just noticeable difference (j.n.d.) and depends on the intensity of the stimuli

        b.   The ability to detect a difference between two stimuli, A and B, depends on the size of A; the larger A is, the greater the change must be before it can be detected

4.   Signal detection theory

        a.   Accounts for _____ bias (tendency to say yes or no to a signal)

        b.   Separates sensory processes (the intensity of the stimulus) from the _____ process (influenced by observer's response bias)

        c.   Recognizes that stimulus detection depends not only on the stimulus but also on characteristics of the observer

D.   **Sensory Adaptation**

    1.   Senses designed to respond to change and contrast in the environment

    2.   Decline in sensory _____ occurs when a stimulus is unchanging; nerve cells temporarily get "tired" and fire less frequently

    3.   Sensory deprivation studies

        a.   When sensory experiences are removed subjects became edgy, disoriented, confused, restless and had visions

        b.   Early studies overexaggerated the negative reactions

    4.   Brain requires minimum stimulation to function normally

E.   **Sensory overload**

    1.   "Cocktail party phenomenon" - blocking out unimportant sensations

    2.   Selective _____ - protects us from being overwhelmed with sensations

Answer these Learning Objectives while you read Section 1.

1.   Distinguish between sensation and perception.

2.   Distinguish between anatomical and functional codes in the nervous system.

3.   Define psychophysics, absolute and difference thresholds and signal detection theory.

4.   Explain sensory adaptation, sensory deprivation, sensory overload and selective attention.

SECTION 2 - VISION (PP. 188-199)

II. **VISION**
   A.   **What we see**
      1.   Stimulus for vision is _____, which travels in waves
      2.   Characteristics of light _____
         a.   Hue - color, which is related to wavelength
         b.   Brightness - intensity, corresponds to _____ and wavelength
         c.   Saturation - colorfulness, complexity of the range of wavelengths
      3.   _____ dimensions of visual experience - hue, brightness, saturation
      4.   Physical properties of light - wavelength, intensity, complexity
   B.   **An eye on the world - Parts of the eye**
      1.   Cornea - front part of the eye; protects the eye and bends light rays
      2.   Lens - located behind the cornea; focuses light by changing curvature
      3.   Iris - _____ that controls the amount of light that gets into the eye
      4.   Pupil - round opening surrounded by iris; dilates to let light in
      5.   Retina - in the back of the eye where the visual _____ are located
         a.   Parts of retina
            (1)   Two types of receptors
               (a)   Rods: sensitive to light, not to color
               (b)   Cones: see color, but need more light to respond
            (2)   Fovea - center of retina, sharpest vision, has only cones
         b.   Processing visual information
            (1)   Dark _____ - time it takes to adjust to dim illumination
            (2)   Rods and cones connect to _____ neurons, which connect to ganglion cells, which converge to form _____ nerve, which carries information out of the eye to the brain
   C.   **Why the visual system is not a camera**
      1.   Eyes are not a _____ recorder of external world; neurons build picture
      2.   Visual system cells have response specialties (feature detectors in animals)
      3.   Visual perception depends on many cells in far-flung parts of the brain and the rhythm of their activity
   D.   **How we see colors**
      1.   Trichromatic theory (Young-Helmholtz theory)
         a.   This approach applies to the first level of processing in the retina
         b.   The retina contains three types of _____: one responds to blue, another to green, another to red
         c.   The combined activity of the three types produces all colors
      2.   Opponent-process theory
         a.   Second stage of color processing in the _____ and ganglion cells of the retina and neurons in the thalamus (opponent process cells)

        b.   They fire in response to one wavelength in a pair and turn off in response to the other and vice versa

        c.   Result is a color code that is passed on to higher visual centers

        d.   Opponent-process cells explain afterimages

    3.   Color in context - perceived color of an object also depends on the wavelengths reflected by everything around it

E.   **Constructing the visual world**

    1.   Visual perception - the mind interprets the retinal image and constructs the world using information from the senses

    2.   Form perception - Gestalt descriptions of how we build perceptual units include: figure/ground distinction, _____, closure, similarity, continuity

    3.   Depth and distance perception - object's location inferred from estimating its distance or depth

        a.   Binocular cues - dependent on information from both _____

            (1)   Changes in angle of convergence of the image seen by each eye provide distance cues

            (2)   Retinal _____ - differing retinal images of same object enables us to infer depth and distance

        b.   _____ cues - cues that do not depend on using both eyes include: interposition and linear perspective

    4.   Visual constancies: When seeing is believing

        a.   Perceptual constancy - perception of objects as unchanging though the sensory patterns they produce are constantly shifting

        b.   Visual constancies include shape constancy, _____ constancy, brightness constancy, color constancy and size constancy

    5.   Visual illusions: When seeing is misleading

        a.   Systematic errors that provide hints about perception

        b.   Can occur from misleading information from the senses or because the brain misinterprets sensory information

Answer these Learning Objectives while you read Section 2.

5.   List the characteristics of light waves and their correspondence to the visual experience.

6.   Identify the parts of the eye and describe how they convert light to vision.

7.   Discuss two theories of color vision and how they relate to stages of processing.

8.   Explain how form, distance and depth perception occur.

9.   List and explain visual constancies and distinguish them from visual illusions.

III. **HEARING**
    A. **What we hear**
        1. Stimulus for sound is a wave of pressure created when an object vibrates, which causes molecules in a transmitting substance (usually air) to move
        2. Characteristics of sound _____
            a. Loudness - intensity (amplitude) of a wave's pressure; decibels
            b. Pitch - frequency (and intensity) of wave; measured in hertz
            c. Timbre - _____ of wave; the distinguishing quality of a sound
        3. Psychological properties of sound - loudness, pitch, timbre
        4. _____ properties of sound waves - amplitude, frequency, complexity
    B. **An ear on the world - the process of hearing**
        1. Ear has outer, middle and inner sections
        2. Sound wave passes into the outer ear through a canal to strike the eardrum
        3. Eardrum vibrates at the same _____ and amplitude as the wave
        4. The wave vibrates three small bones in the inner ear; the third bone pushes on a membrane that opens into the inner ear which contains the cochlea
        5. The cochlea contains the organ of _____, the actual organ of hearing
        6. Organ of Corti contains the receptor cells called cilia, or hair cells, which are imbedded in the _____ membrane stretching across the cochlea
        7. Pressure causes motion of the fluid in the cochlea which causes the basilar membrane to move; the hair cells initiate a signal to the auditory nerve, which carries the message to the brain
        8. The pattern of movement of the basilar membrane influences the pattern and frequency of how the neurons fire, which determines what we hear
    C. **Constructing the auditory world**
        1. Perception is used to organize patterns of sounds to construct meaning
        2. Strategies include figure/ground, proximity, _____, similarity, closure
        3. Loudness is a distance cue; using both ears helps estimate direction

Answer these Learning Objectives while you read Section 3.

10. Describe how the characteristics of sound waves correspond to loudness, pitch, timbre.

11. Identify the parts of the ear, describe how they convert sound to hearing, and discuss the role of the perceptual processes in making sound meaningful.

IV. **OTHER SENSES**
    A.   **Taste: Savory sensations**
        1.   _____ stimulate receptors on tongue, throat and roof of mouth
            a.   Papillae - bumps on tongue, contain taste buds
            b.   Replaced every 10 days - number declines with age
        2.   Four basic tastes: salty, _____, bitter, sweet
            a.   Each taste produced by a different type of chemical
            b.   Each can be perceived wherever there are receptors
            c.   Flavors are a combination of the four, but unclear how this occurs
            d.   Some taste preferences are universal, part of evolutionary heritage
            e.   Taste is heavily influenced by smell, temperature and texture of food, culture, individual differences, some of which are genetic and create sensitivities to certain tastes
    B.   **Smell: The sense of scents**
        1.   Receptors are specialized neurons (5 million) in a mucous membrane in upper part of nasal passage that respond to chemical molecules in the air
        2.   Molecules trigger responses in the receptors and there may be a _____ different receptor types
        3.   Signals travel from receptors to the brain's olfactory bulb by the olfactory nerve to the higher regions of the brain
        4.   Smell can be important to survival and contributes to sexual chemistry
            a.   _____ - chemicals released by one member of a species that affect other members
            b.   Involved in animal behavior - role is less clear in humans
        5.   The psychological impact of odors may be because olfactory centers in the brain are linked to areas that process memories and emotions
        6.   Odor preferences influenced by culture, context and experience
    C.   **Senses of the skin**
        1.   Skin protects the innards, it helps identify objects, it is involved in intimacy, and it serves as a boundary
        2.   Skin senses include: _____, warmth, cold and pain
            a.   No correspondence between four sensations and types of receptors
            b.   Skin senses are influenced by neural codes
    D.   **The mystery of pain**
        1.   Pain differs from other senses in that the removal of the stimulus doesn't always terminate the sensation
        2.   _____ theory of pain - for years, the leading explanation
            a.   To experience pain sensation, impulses must pass a "gate" of neural activity that either blocks pain messages or lets them through

        b.   Normally the gate is kept shut

        c.   Chronic pain results when fibers that close the gate are damaged and pain messages reach the brain unchecked

        d.   The theory correctly predicts that thoughts and feelings can influence pain perception

        e.   Limitations of gate-control theory - explanations are incomplete

            (1)   Pain is more complicated than once thought

            (2)   Cannot explain pain that occurs without injury or disease or phantom limb pain

   3.   _____ theory of pain

        a.   The brain not only responds to incoming pain signals, but it is also capable of generating pain on its own

        b.   An extensive network of neurons (neuromatrix) in the brain provides us with a sense of our bodies and body parts

        c.   When these neurons become hyperactive, pain results

        d.   Hyperactivity may result from peripheral nerves, but also from memories, emotions, expectations or signals from other brain centers

        e.   Therefore pain can occur without external stimulation

E.   **The environment within**

   1.   Kinesthesis - tells us about location and movement of body parts using pain and pressure receptors in muscles, joints, and tendons

   2.   Equilibrium - gives information about body as a whole

        a.   Information is from three _____ canals in the inner ear

        b.   These thin tubes are filled with fluid that moves and presses hairlike receptors whenever the head rotates

   3.   Normally, kinesthesis and equilibrium work together

Answer these Learning Objectives while you read Section 4.

12.   List and explain the factors that affect gustation (taste) and olfaction (smell).

13.   List the four skin senses.

14.   Describe the gate-control theory of pain and the neuromatrix theory of pain.

15.   Describe the internal senses of kinesthesis and equilibrium.

SECTION 5 - PERCEPTUAL POWERS: ORIGINS AND INFLUENCES (PP. 211-215)
AND SECTION 6 - PUZZLES OF PERCEPTION (PP. 215-219)

V.   **PERCEPTUAL POWERS: ORIGINS AND INFLUENCES**
    A.   **Inborn abilities and perceptual lessons**
        1.   Studies with _____ show that experience during a critical period may ensure survival and the development of skills already present at birth
        2.   Research concludes that infants are born with many perceptual abilities
            a.   Visual cliff experiment shows depth _____ by two months of age
            b.   Ability to distinguish tastes and smells and ability to localize sound are present early in life
    B.   **Psychological and _____ influences on perception**
        1.   Perceptions affected by needs, beliefs, emotions, _____ (perceptual set)
        2.   Culture and experience also influence perception

VI. **PUZZLES OF PERCEPTION**
    A.   **Subliminal perception**
        1.   Perceiving without awareness
        2.   Evidence exists that simple visual images can affect your behavior even when you are unaware that you saw it
        3.   Evidence for nonconscious processes in memory, thinking, decision making
        4.   Real world implications are small and short lived
        5.   There is no evidence for subliminal persuasion
    B.   **Extrasensory perception: Reality or illusion?**
        1.   Four categories of ESP or (Psi) experiences: telepathy, clairvoyance, precognition, _____ experiences
        2.   Evidence--or just coincidence?
            a.   Most reports come from _____ accounts
            b.   Studies under controlled conditions in field of parapsychology
                (1)   Some positive results found but there were methodological problems and results were not replicated
                (2)   Conclusion is that there is no supporting scientific evidence
    C.   **Lessons from a Magician** - we can be easily tricked by our senses

Answer these Learning Objectives while you read Sections 5 and 6.

16.   Summarize the evidence for innate abilities in perception and describe the psychological and cultural influences on perception.

17.   Discuss the evidence on the effectiveness of "subliminal perception" tapes and ESP.

FLASH CARDS

Cut the following chart along the borders and test yourself with the resulting flash cards.

6.1 SENSATION	**6.2 PERCEPTION**	**6.3 SENSE RECEPTORS**
6.4 ANATOMICAL CODES	**6.5 DOCTRINE OF SPECIFIC NERVE ENERGIES**	**6.6 FUNCTIONAL CODES**
6.7 PSYCHOPHYSICS	**6.8 ABSOLUTE THRESHOLD**	**6.9 DIFFERENCE THRESHOLD/JND**
6.10 SIGNAL-DETECTION THEORY	**6.11 SENSORY ADAPTATION**	**6.12 SENSORY DEPRIVATION**
6.13 SELECTIVE ATTENTION	**6.14 HUE**	**6.15 BRIGHTNESS**
6.16 SATURATION	**6.17 COMPLEXITY OF LIGHT**	**6.18 RETINA**

6.3 Specialized cells that convert physical energy in the environment or body to electrical energy that can be transmitted as nerve impulses.	6.2 The process by which the brain organizes and interprets sensory information.	6.1 The detection of physical energy emitted or reflected by physical objects; it occurs when energy in the environment or the body stimulates receptors.
6.6 A way the nervous system processes different sensations; certain receptors and neurons fire only in the presence of certain sorts of stimuli.	6.5 Different sensory modalities exist because signals received by sense organs stimulate different nerve pathways leading to different areas of the brain.	6.4 One way the nervous system processes different sensations; different senses stimulate different nerve pathways to different brain areas.
6.9 The smallest difference in stimulation that can be reliably detected when two stimuli are compared; also called just noticeable difference (jnd).	6.8 The smallest quantity of physical energy that can be reliably detected by an observer.	6.7 The areas of psychology concerned with the relationship between physical properties of stimuli and sensory experience.
6.12 The absence of normal levels of sensory stimulation.	6.11 The reduction or disappearance of sensory responsiveness that occurs when stimulation is unchanging or repetitious.	6.10 A psychophysical theory that divides the detection of a sensory signal into a sensory process and a decision process.
6.15 Lightness of luminance; the dimension of visual experience related to the amount of light emitted from or reflected by an object.	6.14 The dimension of visual experience specified by color names and related to the wave length of light.	6.13 The focusing of attention on selected aspects of the environment and the blocking out of others.
6.18 Natural tissue lining the back of the eyeball's interior, which contains the receptors for vision.	6.17 Refers to the number of different wavelengths contained in light from a particular source.	6.16 Vividness or purity of color; the dimension of visual experience related to the amount of light emitted from or reflected by an object.

6.19 RODS AND CONES	**6.20 DARK ADAPTATION**	**6.21 GANGLION CELL**
6.22 OPTIC NERVE	**6.23 FEATURE DETECTORS**	**6.24 TRICHROMATIC THEORY**
6.25 OPPONENT-PROCESS THEORY	**6.26 NEGATIVE AFTERIMAGE**	**6.27 GESTALT PRINCIPLES**
6.28 FIGURE AND GROUND	**6.29 BINOCULAR CUES**	**6.30 CONVERGENCE**
6.31 RETINAL DISPARITY	**6.32 MONOCULAR CUES**	**6.33 PERCEPTUAL CONSTANCY**
6.34 PERCEPTUAL ILLUSION	**6.35 AUDITION**	**6.36 LOUDNESS**

6.21 Neurons in the retina of the eye that gather information from receptor cells; their axons make up the optic nerve.	6.20 A process by which visual receptors become maximally sensitive to dim light.	6.19 Visual receptors. Rods respond to dim light but are not involved in color vision. Cones are involved in color vision.
6.24 Theory of color perception that proposes three mechanisms in the visual system, each sensitive to a certain range of wavelengths.	6.23 Cells in the visual cortex that are sensitive to specific features of the environment	6.22 Formed by a bundle of axons of ganglion cells; carries information out from the back of the eye and on to the brain.
6.27 Principles that describe the brain's organization of sensory building blocks into meaningful units and patterns.	6.26 When we stare at a particular hue, we see a different color when we look away; a sort of neural rebound effect.	6.25 A theory of color perception that assumes that the visual system treats pairs of colors as opposing or antagonistic.
6.30 The turning of the eyes inward that occurs when they focus on a nearby object.	6.29 Visual cues to depth or distance requiring two eyes.	6.28 The Gestalt idea that the visual field is organized into a figure, which stands out from the rest of the environment, and a formless background.
6.33 The accurate perception of objects as stable or unchanged despite changes in the sensory patterns they produce.	6.32 Visual cues to depth or distance, which can be used by one eye alone.	6.31 The slight difference in lateral separation between two objects as seen by the left eye and the right eye.
6.36 The dimension of auditory experience related to the intensity of a pressure wave.	6.35 The sense of hearing.	6.34 An erroneous or misleading perception of reality.

6.37 PITCH	6.38 FREQUENCY (OR A SOUND WAVE)	6.39 TIMBRE
6.40 COCHLEA	6.41 BASILAR MEMBRANE	6.42 AUDITORY NERVE
6.43 GUSTATION	6.44 PAPILLAE	6.45 TASTE BUD
6.46 OLFACTION	6.47 GATE-CONTROL THEORY OF PAIN	6.48 PHANTOM PAIN
6.49 NEUROMATRIX THEORY OF PAIN	6.50 KINESTHESIS	6.51 EQUILIBRIUM
6.52 SEMICIRCULAR CANALS	6.53 VISUAL CLIFF	6.54 PERCEPTUAL SET
6.55 SUBLIMINAL PERCEPTION	6.56 EXTRASENSORY PERCEPTION	6.57 PARAPSYCHOLOGY

6.39 The distinguishing quality of a sound; the dimension of auditory experience related to the complexity of the pressure wave.	6.38 The number of times per second that a sound wave cycles through a peak and low point.	6.37 The dimension of auditory experience related to the frequency of a pressure wave; height or depth of a tone.
6.42 The fibers that carry the signal from the auditory receptors to the brain.	6.41 The receptors (hair cells) of the cochlea are embedded in this membrane, which stretches across the interior of the cochlea.	6.40 A snail-shaped, fluid-filled organ in the inner ear, containing the receptors for hearing.
6.45 Nests of taste-receptor cells.	6.44 Knoblike elevations on the tongue, containing the taste buds.	6.43 The sense of taste.
6.48 Pain that continues to be felt that seemingly comes from an amputated limb, breast or internal organ that has been surgically removed.	6.47 The theory that the experience of pain depends on whether pain impulses get past a neurological "gate" in the spinal cord and reach the brain.	6.46 The sense of smell.
6.51 The sense of balance.	6.50 The sense of body position and movement of body parts; also called kinesthesia.	6.49 The theory that a matrix of neurons in the brain is capable of generating pain (and other sensations) in the absence of signals from sensory nerves.
6.54 A habitual way of perceiving, based on expectations.	6.53 A device used in research to ascertain if babies have depth perception; the "cliff" is a pane of glass covering a shallow and a deep surface.	6.52 Sense organs in the inner ear that contribute to equilibrium by responding to rotation of the head.
6.57 The study of purported psychic phenomena, such as ESP and mental telepathy.	6.56 The hypothesized system for sending and receiving messages about the world without relying on the usual sensory channels.	6.55 The perception of messages that are below sensory thresholds.

ACROSS

2. a skin sense and an internal sense
3. sense of body position and movement of body parts
7. detection of physical energy due to stimulation of receptors in the sense organs
9. snail-shaped, fluid-filled organ
10. the relationship between physical properties of stimuli and sensory experience
12. hearing
13. center of retina where vision is sharpest
14. contains receptors for vision
17. allows us to see objects as unchanged despite changes in the sensory patterns they produce
18. receptor for hearing imbedded in this membrane
19. cells that convert physical energy in the environment into neural energy
20. odorous chemical substances

DOWN

1. neurons in the retina that gather information from receptor cells
2. height or depth of a tone
4. process of organizing and interpreting sensory information
5. it has amplitude and frequency
6. taste
8. smell
9. visual receptors involved in color
11. dimension of vision related to wavelength of light
14. visual receptors that respond to dim light
15. the distinguishing quality of a sound
16. two ways the nervous system processes different sensations

167

Complete the following charts on vision and audition and on perceptual strategies

VISION AND AUDITION

SENSE	RECEPTORS AND THEIR LOCATIONS	PHYSICAL PROPERTIES OF THE STIMULUS	PSYCHOLOGICAL DIMENSIONS OF THE SENSORY EXPERIENCE
VISION			
AUDITION			

PERCEPTUAL STRATEGIES

PERCEPTUAL STRATEGY	DEFINITION	GIVE EXAMPLE
FORM PERCEPTION Proximity		
Closure		
Similarity		
Continuity		
DEPTH AND DISTANCE Retinal Disparity		
Interposition		
Linear Perspective		
VISUAL CONSTANCIES Shape		
Location		
Brightness		
Color		

PRACTICE TEST 1 - Multiple Choice

1. When energy in the environment stimulates receptors in the sense organs, we experience
   A. perception.
   B. sensory overload.
   C. sensation.
   D. sensory adaptation.

2. The eyes, ears, tongue, nose, skin and internal body tissues all contain
   A. anatomical codes.
   B. functional codes.
   C. sense receptors.
   D. sense organs.

3. Perception differs from sensation in that
   A. perception allows us to organize and interpret sensations.
   B. perception is the raw data coming in from the senses.
   C. sensation is an organizing and interpretive process, perception is not.
   D. perception can be measured, sensations cannot.

4. Which theory argues that light and sound produce different sensations because they stimulate different brain parts?
   A. signal detection theory
   B. trichromatic theory
   C. doctrine of specific nerve energies
   D. opponent-process theory

5. Which of the following best accounts for the fact that light and sound produce different sensations due to the specific cells that are firing, how many are firing, the rate at which they are firing and the patterning of each cell's firing?
   A. anatomical codes
   B. functional codes
   C. doctrine of specific nerve energies
   D. feature detectors

6. Signal detection theory takes into account
   A. observers' response tendencies.
   B. sensory differences among species.
   C. the role of feature detectors.
   D. which cells are firing, how many cells are firing and the rate at which they fire.

7. As a research subject, Betsy is asked to compare lights within several pairs of lights and indicate whether one is brighter than the other. Betsy is being asked to detect
   A. the absolute threshold.
   B. the j.d.n.
   C. the difference threshold.
   D. Weber's Law.

169

8. Researchers have found that sensory deprivation may
   A. lead to confusion and grouchiness.
   B. produce a restless, disoriented feeling.
   C. cause hallucinations.
   D. cause all of the above.

9. Maria enjoys the wonderful smells from the kitchen when she first arrives at her mother's house, but after a while, she no longer notices them. What accounts for this?
   A. sensory adaptation
   B. selective attention
   C. absolute thresholds
   D. difference thresholds

10. In class, Jonah is completely focused on the professor's words, though there are noises and distractions all around him. This is best accounted for by
    A. sensory adaptation.
    B. selective attention.
    C. sensory deprivation.
    D. sensory overload.

11. Humans experience the wavelength of light as
    A. hue or color.
    B. brightness.
    C. saturation or colorfulness.
    D. wave complexity.

12. The fovea contains
    A. only rods.
    B. only cones.
    C. an equal number of rods and cones.
    D. more rods than cones.

13. The visual receptors are located in the
    A. cornea.
    B. pupil.
    C. lens.
    D. retina.

14. The optic nerve connects
    A. rods and cones.
    B. the cornea with the brain.
    C. the pupil and the lens.
    D. the retina with the brain.

15. Which theory of color vision best explains negative afterimages?
    A. trichromatic theory
    B. opponent-process theory
    C. doctrine of specific nerve energies
    D. Weber's Law

16. Which Gestalt strategy would explain why you see $$$AAA### as three groups of figures instead of nine separate figures?
    A. closure
    B. figure-ground
    C. continuity
    D. similarity

17. The slight difference in sideways separation between two objects as seen by the left eye and the right eye is called
    A. a binocular cue.
    B. a depth cue.
    C. retinal disparity.
    D. all of the above.

18. As you watch a door opening, its image changes from rectangular to trapezoidal, yet you continue to think of the door as rectangular. What explains this phenomenon?
    A. perceptual constancy
    B. retinal disparity
    C. monocular depth cues
    D. selective attention

19. Pitch is the dimension of sound related to the
    A. amplitude of a pressure wave.
    B. frequency of a pressure wave.
    C. distinguishing quality of a sound.
    D. complexity of a pressure wave.

20. The part of the ear that plays the same role in hearing as the retina plays in vision is called the
    A. cochlea.
    B. eardrum.
    C. organ of Corti.
    D. auditory nerve.

21. When you bite into a piece of bread or an orange, the taste is a result of
    A. a combination of the four basic tastes: salty, sour, bitter and sweet.
    B. a combination of the four basic tastes: salty, smooth, pungent and sweet.
    C. the activation of specific taste receptors.
    D. the taste receptors located in a specific part of the tongue.

22. The skin senses are
    A. tickle, temperature, touch and pain.
    B. tickle, itch, tingle and burn.
    C. touch, warmth, cold and pain.
    D. warmth, heat, cool and cold.

23. Which theory best explains why some people experience pain even though doctors cannot find any injury or tissue damage to explain the pain.
    A. gate-control theory
    B. mind over matter theory
    C. phantom pain theory
    D. neuromatrix theory

24. Malga can touch her finger to her nose with her eyes shut. What allows her to do this?
    A. the olfactory sense   B. kinesthesis
    C. equilibrium   D. ESP

25. Which group is studied to evaluate whether perceptual abilities are inborn?
    A. cats
    B. people who first gained sensation as an adult
    C. babies and infants
    D. all of the above

PRACTICE TEST 2 - Multiple Choice

1. Sensation is to perception as neural message is to _____.
    A. encoding
    B. meaning
    C. reception
    D. transduction

2. Anatomical and functional codes
    A. explain why we see light and hear sound.
    B. explain how we experience different sensations.
    C. explain why light and sound produce different sensations.
    D. explain all of the above.

3. _____ stimulate different nerve pathways, which go to different places in the brain, while focusing on the number, rate and pattern of the firing of particular cells in response to certain stimuli describes _____.
    A. anatomical codes; functional codes
    B. neural codes; cellular codes
    C. functional codes; anatomical codes
    D. psychophysics; transduction

4. A series of barely audible tones is being played to Ethan. The researcher wants to know which is the softest tone that Ethan can reliably hear. This is called the
    A. difference threshold.
    B. absolute threshold.
    C. j.n.d.
    D. partial threshold.

5. The researcher presents Ethan with some trials in which there is no tone presented. She is interested in knowing how often Ethan thinks he hears something when no tone is presented, as compared to how often he thinks he hears something when a weak tone is presented. This type of information is used in
    A. calculating difference thresholds.
    B. determining absolute thresholds.
    C. signal detection theory.
    D. calculating just noticeable differences.

6. Which of the following describes what happens in sensory adaptation?
    A. receptors get "tired" and temporarily stop responding
    B. nerve cells high up in the sensory system temporarily switch off
    C. you no longer smell a gas leak that you noticed when you first entered the house
    D. all of the above

7. Hue is to brightness as
   A. wavelength is to amplitude.
   B. complexity is to wavelength.
   C. amplitude is to frequency.
   D. frequency is to complexity.

8. Hue, brightness and saturation are all _____ dimensions of visual experience, whereas wavelength, intensity and complexity are all _____ properties of the visual stimulus.
   A. physical; psychological
   B. temporary; permanent
   C. complex; simple
   D. psychological; physical

9. The cornea, lens, iris and pupil are part of the _____, whereas the rods and cones are the _____
   A. eye; sense organ.
   B. retina; eye ball.
   C. sense organ; receptors.
   D. receptors; retina.

10. Rods are to cones as
    A. bright light is to dim light.
    B. the iris is to the pupil.
    C. black and white vision is to color vision.
    D. none of the above.

11. In a softball game, Rocio has made it to third base. When Elena pitches she must watch the batter and Rocio out of the corner of her eye. Watching Rocio requires her to use
    A. cones.
    B. rods.
    C. both rods and cones.
    D. the optic disc.

12. Which theory of color vision suggests that one type of cone responds to blue, another to green and a third to red?
    A. doctrine of specific nerve energies
    B. opponent-process theory
    C. trichromatic theory
    D. feature detector theory

13. The fact that you see the words written on a page and pay little attention to the paper they are written on is an illustration of what aspect of our perceptual powers?
    A. figure-ground discrimination
    B. color constancy
    C. shape constancy
    D. depth perception

14. The fact that tomatoes look smaller and smaller as you look down the rows of your vegetable garden demonstrates which monocular depth cue?
    A. interposition
    B. retinal disparity
    C. relative size
    D. linear perspective

15. Pitch is to timbre as
    A. intensity is to amplitude.
    B. complexity is to intensity.
    C. frequency is to complexity.
    D. amplitude is to frequency.

16. What makes a note played on a flute sound different from the same note played on an oboe?
    A. loudness
    B. saturation
    C. timbre
    D. pitch

17. Rods and cones are to vision as the _____ is/are to hearing.
    A. cilia or hair cells
    B. eardrum
    C. basilar membrane
    D. cochlea

18. The cilia are imbedded in the _____ of the _____.
    A. cochlea; auditory nerve
    B. basilar membrane; cochlea
    C. eardrum; cochlea
    D. cochlea; basilar membrane

19. Which of the following might explain why Aiko does not like foods with a bitter taste?
    A. cultural differences
    B. supertaste for bitter substances
    C. density of tastebuds
    D. all of the above

20. How does the sense of smell differ from the sense of vision and taste?
    A. Smell does not have receptor cells.
    B. Vision and taste have limited numbers of basic cell types, smell may have as many as a thousand.
    C. Smell uses anatomical coding and not functional coding while vision and taste use both.
    D. There are fewer basic smells than basic tastes or colors.

21. Which of the following examples uses all of the skin senses?
    A. After laying in the hot sun, Kathy's skin burned as she felt the pressure of the cool shower.
    B. Herb became very warm as he ran five miles on a summer day.
    C. Carol felt her muscles ache as she felt the pressure of the massage.
    D. Mori hurt her knee when she fell off her bike.

22. Phantom pain
    A.   does not exist.
    B.   is strictly psychological.
    C.   may occur because a matrix of neurons in the brain may be generating pain.
    D.   is a result of the increase in pain fibers.

23. Calan is trying to balance on her left leg while holding her right foot with her left hand. Her ability to balance relies on the sense of _____, and her ability to grab her foot relies on the sense of _____.
    A.   equilibrium; kinesthesis
    B.   kinesthesis; equilibrium
    C.   touch; equilibrium
    D.   coordination: touch

24. Baby Huey is placed on a board in the middle of a glass covering both a shallow surface and a deep one (a visual cliff). His mother beckons to him to cross over both sides of the "cliff." This study is trying to
    A.   evaluate visual acuity in babies.
    B.   evaluate attachment in babies.
    C.   determine whether depth perception is inborn.
    D.   evaluate learned cues on distance perception.

25. There is considerable evidence that a simple visual stimulus can affect a person's responses to a task even when the person has no awareness of seeing the stimulus. What conclusions can we reach about subliminal perception?
    A.   There are dramatic implications for real world applications.
    B.   Real world implications are limited.
    C.   Subliminal persuasion has been used successfully in marketing.
    D.   Subliminal perception is an excellent learning tool.

PRACTICE TEST 3 - Short Answer

1. _____ is the process by which sensory impulses are organized and interpreted.

2. The two basic kinds of code used by the nervous system to convey sensations are _____ and _____ codes.

3. Researchers in the field of _____ study the relationships between physical properties of stimuli and our psychological experience of them.

4. The smallest amount of energy that a person can detect reliably is known as the _____ threshold.

5. The smallest difference between two stimuli that a person can reliably detect is the _____ difference.

6. Signal-detection theory holds that responses in a detection task consist of both a _____ process and a _____ process.

7. When a stimulus is unchanging or repetitious, receptors may stop firing so that we no longer notice it. This process is referred to as sensory _____.

8. The amount or intensity of light emitted or reflected by an object determines its _____.

9. Although located in the eye, the structure known as the _____ is actually part of the brain.

10. The visual receptors sensitive to low levels of light are called _____; receptors sensitive to color are called _____.

11. _____ cells are responsive to specific patterns, such as horizontal versus vertical lines.

12. Humans almost always organize the visual field into figure and _____.

13. The Gestalt principle of _____ suggests that the brain tends to fill in gaps in order to perceive complete forms.

14. Our tendency to perceive objects as stable and unchanging even when the sensory patterns they produce are changing is referred to as perceptual _____.

15. An opponent-process cell that fired in response to red would turn _____ in response to green.

16. The receptors for hearing are hair cells embedded in the _____, in the interior of the _____.

17. The physical properties that correspond to the loudness of a sound is the _____ of the pressure waves in the air.

18. The four basic tastes are _____, _____, _____, and _____.

19. People's responses to particular odors are affected by _____, and individual differences.

20. The skin senses include _____, _____, _____, _____.

21. The _____ theory of pain holds that pain depends on whether neural impulses get past a point in the spinal cord and reach the brain. The _____ is a newer theory that suggests that the brain can generate pain even in the absence of signals from sensory neurons.

22. _____ tells us where our body parts are located, and _____ tells us the orientation of the body as a whole.

23. A widely used procedure for studying depth perception in children is the _____ procedure.

24. Certain psychological influences affect perception. These include needs, beliefs, _____, and _____.

25. _____ refers to telepathy, clairvoyance, precognition, and out-of-body experiences.

PRACTICE TEST 4 - True/False

1.   T F   Sensation is the detection and direct experience of physical energy as a result of the environment and the process by which sensory impulses are organized and interpreted.

2.   T F   The doctrine of specific nerve energies refers to the fact different types of neurons go to each of the different senses.

3.   T F   Functional codes rely on the fact that sensory receptors and neurons fire, or are inhibited from firing, only in the presence of specific sorts of stimuli.

4.   T F   Psychologists study the sensitivity of human senses by examining absolute and difference thresholds.

5.   T F   Signal-detection theory explains how our senses translate physical energy from the environment to energy that can be processed by our nervous systems.

6.   T F   Sensory deprivation is not necessarily unpleasant. Many people enjoy time-limited periods of deprivation.

7.   T F   Hue is related to the intensity of light an object emits or reflects, brightness corresponds to the wavelength of light and saturation is related to the complexity of light.

8.   T F   The visual receptors, the rods and cones, are located on the transparent cornea.

9.   T F   When we are trying to find a seat in a darkened movie theater, the cones are primarily involved.

10.   T F   Specific aspects of the visual world, such as lines and angles, are detected by feature-detector cells in the visual areas of the brain.

11.   T F   The trichromatic has long been the primary theory to explain color vision. Recently, researchers have introduced the opponent-process theory and it has replaced the trichromatic theory as the favored explanation.

12.   T F   Some Gestalt principles that describe how the visual system groups sensory building blocks into perceptual units are: proximity, closure, similarity, and continuity.

13.   T F   Binocular cues for depth and distance include convergence, retinal disparity, linear perspective, interposition, and relative size.

14.   T F   Perceptual illusions occur when sensory cues are misleading or when we misinterpret cues.

15.   T F   Perceptual constancies allow us to perceive objects as stable despite changes in the sensory patterns they produce.

16.   T F   Loudness is related to the intensity of a wave's pressure, pitch is related to the frequency of the sound wave, and timbre is established by the complexity of the sound wave.

17.   T F   The eardrum is so sensitive that it can respond to the movement of a single molecule.

18.   T F   The all-important receptor cells are located on the eardrum.

19.   T F   We discriminate high-pitched sounds largely on the basis of where activity occurs along the basilar membrane; we discriminate low-pitched sounds largely on the basis of the frequency of the basilar membrane's vibration.

20.   T F   The taste buds are the receptors for taste.

21.   T F   Receptors for the four basic tastes are not located on separate areas of the tongue. Rather, they can be perceived at any spot on the tongue that has receptors.

22.   T F   One possible explanation for why odors often evoke vivid, emotionally-colored memories is that the olfactory centers in the brain are linked to areas that process memories and emotions.

23.   T F   The basic skin senses include touch, warmth, cold, pain, tickle, and itch.

24.   T F   The gate-control theory of pain best explains phantom pain.

25.   T F   The neuromatrix theory of pain proposes that when an extensive network of neurons in the brain become hyperactive, the result is pain.

PRACTICE TEST 5 - Essay

1. Explain the phenomena listed below in terms of the concept listed after it.

    A. Roberta is shopping at a flea market and has just refused to buy a scarf because the salesperson is charging $10 and she saw it at another stall for $8.00. Later that week, she is shopping for a new car and does not think anything about spending an extra $2.00 for a car. Discuss this as an analogy of Weber's Law.

    B. A nurse notices that patients perform more poorly on auditory tests - tests or auditory thresholds - when they are tired as a result of losing sleep. Analyze the effects of their performance using signal detection theory.

    C. John is looking all over for his glasses when his wife points them out at the top of his head. Explain this using principles of sensory adaptation.

    D. Malcolm is studying for a test in psychology while the T.V. is blaring and his roommate is on the phone in the same room. Discuss this in relation to sensory overload.

2. Starting with a light wave, describe what happens to that wave from the environment to the brain, including all relevant structures.

3   Assume you are developing a color-generating device that will reproduce the colors in the human color spectrum. Explain what colors you need and why, according to the two theories of color vision listed below.

    A. Trichromatic theory
    B. Opponent-process theory

4. You are watching a monitor depicting sound waves. Describe what changes in the sound would accompany the modifications indicated below.

    A. The sound waves remain constant except for their height, which is increasing.
    B. The wave frequency is changing.
    C. Waves of different types are being increasingly mixed together.

5. In each of the examples below, identify and describe the Gestalt principle involved.

    A. People scattered on a beach appear to be in clusters.
    B. A sequence of dots on a canvas appear to form a face.
    C. People crowded on a soccer field appear to be two different teams and referees.
    D. A wall seems to be continuous even though vines block sections from view.

6. Psychological factors can influence what we perceive and how we perceive it. Identify the psychological factors that could influence the following perceptions.

    A. You had an argument with your sister. As you are walking home from school, she drives past you. You saw her look at you but figured that she did not stop because she is angry with you.
    B. You think that your neighbor is an unethical character. One day you see him entering his house during the day and you are certain that he is sneaking around so no one will see him.
    C. You are expecting your best friend to come visit you and you are very excited. Every time you hear something, you run to the door, sure that there was a knock.

CHAPTER 7

Learning and Conditioning

LEARNING OBJECTIVES

1.   Identify the two types of conditioning shown by behaviorists to explain human behavior.

2.   List and explain the four components of classical conditioning.

3.   List and explain the four principles of classical conditioning.

4.   Compare the traditional and recent views of how associations are formed between unconditioned and conditioned stimuli.

5.   Describe both the impact of classical conditioning on everyday life and the therapeutic technique of counterconditioning.

6.   Compare and contrast the principles of operant and classical conditioning.

7.   List and explain the three types of consequences a response can lead to and distinguish between positive and negative reinforcement and primary and secondary reinforcement.

8.   Describe shaping, extinction, stimulus generalization and stimulus discrimination in operant conditioning.

9.   Distinguish between continuous and intermittent schedules of reinforcement and describe the four types of intermittent reinforcement schedules.

10.   Describe how superstitions might be learned according to operant conditioning.

11.   List and discuss six limitations of punishment as a way of controlling behavior and state a more effective strategy.

12.   Distinguish between intrinsic and extrinsic reinforcers, and discuss the effects of extrinsic reinforcers on motivation. Describe how extrinsic reinforcers should be used.

13.   Explain social-cognitive theories and compare them to conditioning models of learning.

14.   Compare and contrast cognitive approaches and behavioral approaches.

CHAPTER CONCEPT MAP

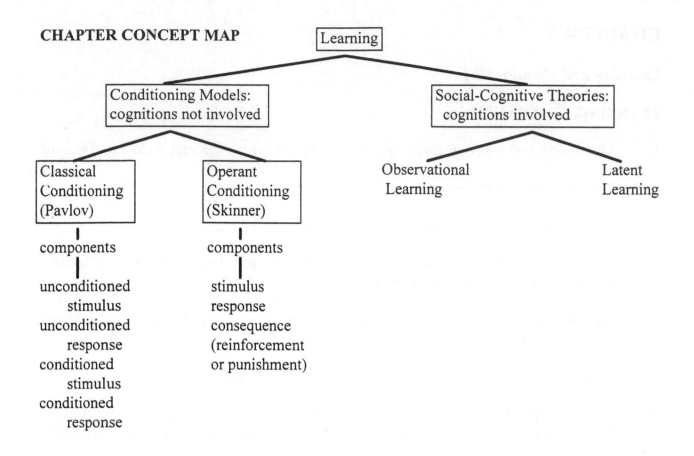

BRIEF CHAPTER SUMMARY

Chapter 7 explores how we learn to make permanent changes in our behaviors due to experience. Two broad types of learning are explored: conditioning models and social-cognitive models. Both conditioning models suggest that learning is acquired through simple stimulus-response associations without the involvement of mental processes. Classical conditioning explains how we learn involuntary behaviors, such as fears and preferences. Operant conditioning explains how we learn complex behaviors as a result of favorable or unfavorable consequences of our actions. Social-cognitive theories expand behavioral principles to recognize the role that mental processes play in the acquisition of new behaviors. Observational learning and latent learning are two social-cognitive theories of learning.

PREVIEW OUTLINE AND REVIEW QUESTIONS

Before you read the chapter, review the preview outline and the Learning Objectives for each section of the text. Answer all questions as you read the text.

SECTIONS 1 & 2 - INTRODUCTION; CLASSICAL CONDITIONING (PP. 225-231) AND SECTION 3 - CLASSICAL CONDITIONING IN REAL LIFE (PP. 231-235)

I.   **INTRODUCTION TO LEARNING**
    A.   **Definitions**
        1.   Learning - any relatively _____ change in behavior that occurs because of experience
        2.   Behaviorism - the school of psychology that accounts for behavior in terms of _____ events, without reference to mental entities like "mind" or "will"
        3.   Conditioning - a basic kind of learning that involves associations between environmental stimuli and responses
    B.   **Two types of conditioning**
        1.   Classical conditioning
        2.   _____ conditioning
    C.   **Other approaches to learning**
        1.   Social-cognitive learning theories hold that mental processes must be included in theories of human learning
        2.   Learning is not so much a change in behavior, but a change in knowledge that has the potential for affecting behavior

II.   **CLASSICAL CONDITIONING** - began with the research of Ivan Pavlov
    A.   **New Reflexes from old - terminology**
        1.   Unconditioned stimulus (US) - thing that elicits an _____ response
        2.   Unconditioned response (UR) - response that is automatically produced
        3.   Conditioned stimulus (CS) - when a _____ stimulus comes to elicit a conditioned response after being paired with a US
        4.   Conditioned response (CR) - response that is elicited by a CS
        5.   Classical conditioning - procedure by which a neutral stimulus is regularly paired with a US and the neutral stimulus becomes a CS, which elicits a CR that is similar to the original, unlearned one
    B.   **Principles of classical conditioning**
        1.   Extinction - repeating the conditioned stimulus without the _____ stimulus, and the conditioned response disappears
        2.   Spontaneous recovery - after a response has been extinguished, it may spontaneously _____ after the passage of time and with exposure to the conditioned stimulus
        3.   Higher-order conditioning - a neutral stimulus can become a conditioned

stimulus by being paired with an already established _____

    4.   Stimulus _____ - after a stimulus becomes a conditioned stimulus for some response, other, similar stimuli may produce the same reaction

    5.   Stimulus discrimination - different responses are triggered by stimuli that resemble the conditioned stimulus in some way

  C.   **What is actually learned in classical conditioning?**

    1.   The stimulus to be conditioned should precede the unconditioned stimulus because the CS serves as a signal for the US

    2.   Many psychologists say that the learner learns information which is more than an association between two stimuli; that the CS predicts the US

    3.   Rescorla introduces cognitive concepts; says organism is an information seeker and uses logical relations among events and preconceptions to form a representation of the world

III. **CLASSICAL CONDITIONING IN REAL LIFE** - recognized early by John B. Watson

  A.   Learning to like - conditioning positive emotions

    1.   Plays a big role in emotional responses to objects, symbols, events, places

    2.   Often used in advertising

  B.   Learning to fear - conditioning negative emotions

    1.   Humans biologically primed to learn some fears and tastes more easily than others

    2.   Irrational fears that interferes with normal activities, called _____, can be learned through conditioning (Watson's research with Little Albert) and unlearned through counterconditioning and systematic desensitization

  C.   Accounting for taste - conditioning likes and dislikes

  D.   Reacting to medical treatments - reactions to unpleasant treatments or to treatments that provide relief (or things associated with the treatments) may generalize to a range of other stimuli

Answer these Learning Objectives while you read Sections 1, 2 and 3.

1.   Identify the two types of conditioning shown by behaviorists to explain human behavior.

2.   List and explain the four components of classical conditioning.

3.   List and explain the four principles of classical conditioning.

4.   Compare the traditional and recent views of how associations are formed between unconditioned and conditioned stimuli.

5.   Describe both the impact of classical conditioning on everyday life, and the therapeutic technique of counterconditioning.

SECTION 4 - OPERANT CONDITIONING (PP. 236-246) AND
SECTION 5 - OPERANT CONDITIONING IN REAL LIFE (PP. 247-252)

IV.   **OPERANT CONDITIONING**
    A.   **Introduction to operant conditioning**
        1.   Idea introduced at the turn of the century
        2.   Behavior becomes more or less likely, depending on its consequences; emphasis is on environmental consequences
        3.   Responses involved differ from classical conditioning which involves reflexive responses, operant conditioning shapes complex responses
    B.   **The birth of radical behaviorism**
        1.   Thorndike's _____ box - behavior is controlled by its consequences
        2.   B.F.Skinner extended the theory, called "radical behaviorism" in which all behavior is explainable by looking outside the individual not inside
    C.   **The consequences of behavior**
        1.   A response can lead to three types of consequences: neutral consequences, _____ (makes the response it follows more likely to recur), punishment (makes the response it follows less likely to recur)
        2.   The sooner a consequence follows a response, the greater its effect
        3.   Primary and secondary reinforcers and punishers - can be very powerful
            a.   Primary reinforcers satisfy _____ needs
            b.   Primary punishers are inherently unpleasant
            c.   Secondary reinforcers (and punishers) are reinforcing (and punishing) through association with other (primary) reinforcers
        4.   Positive and negative reinforcers and punishers
            a.   Reinforcement - increases the likelihood of a response punishers
            b.   Positive reinforcement - something pleasant follows a response; negative reinforcement - something unpleasant is removed
            c.   Punishment - decreases the likelihood of a response
            d.   Positive punishment - something unpleasant occurs; negative punishment - something pleasant is removed
    D.   **Principles of operant conditioning**
        1.   Extinction - procedure that causes a previously learned response to stop because the _____ is removed
        2.   Spontaneous recovery - the return of a response that has been extinguished
        3.   Stimulus _____ - a response occurs to stimuli that resemble the stimuli present during the original learning
        4.   Stimulus discrimination - the ability to distinguish between similar stimuli and responding only to the one that results in the reinforcer
            a.   _____ stimulus signals whether a response will pay off

b. Many behaviors are controlled by discriminative stimuli since it conveys under what conditions the response will be reinforced

5. Learning on _____ - the pattern of delivery of reinforcements
   a. Continuous reinforcement - reinforcing a response each time it occurs; used most often when a new behavior is being learned
   b. Partial or _____ schedules - reinforcing only some responses which can result in learning superstitious behaviors
      (1) Ratio schedules - deliver reinforcement after a certain number of responses
         (a) Fixed-ratio schedules - reinforcement occurs after a fixed number of _____
         (b) Variable-ratio schedules - reinforcement occurs after some average number of responses, but the number varies from reinforcement to reinforcement
      (2) _____ schedules - deliver reinforcement after a certain amount of time has passed
         (a) Fixed-interval schedule - reinforcement occurs only if a fixed amount of time has passed since the previous reinforcer
         (b) Variable-interval schedule - reinforcement occurs only if a variable amount of time has passed since the previous reinforcer
   c. For a response to persist, it should be reinforced intermittently, which will make the response more difficult to _____

6. Shaping - method of getting a response in the first place
   a. Must reinforce behavioral tendencies in the right direction
   b. Then gradually reinforcing responses that are more similar to the desired response (called successive approximation)

7. Biological limits on learning
   a. All principles of operant conditioning limited by genetic dispositions and physical characteristics of the organism
   b. Reversions to instinctive behavior is called instinctive drift

E. **Skinner: The man and the myth**
   1. Often called the greatest American psychologist, also misunderstood
   2. Did not deny the existence of consciousness, he said that it cannot explain behavior, and that aspects of consciousness are learned behaviors
   3. His most controversial idea was that free will is an illusion; all people are determined by their environments

V. **OPERANT CONDITIONING IN REAL LIFE**
   A. **General problems** - if reinforcers, punishers, and discriminative stimuli in life remain the same, it is difficult to change behaviors

B. **Behavior modification** - operant conditioning programs used in real life

C. **The pros and cons of punishment**

    1. When punishment works - for behaviors that can't be ignored or rewarded, with some criminals (consistency matters more than severity)

    2. When punishment fails

        a. Punishment is often administered _____ or mindlessly

        b. The recipient often responds with anxiety, fear or rage

        c. Effects can be _____; may depend on the punisher being present

        a. Most misbehavior is hard to punish immediately

        b. Punishment conveys little information about desired behavior

        c. A punishment may be reinforcing because it brings attention

    3. Alternatives to punishment

        a. Guidelines for use - avoid abuse, give information about desirable behavior, reinforce the desirable behavior

        b. Instead, try extinction and reinforcement of alternate behaviors

D. **The problem with reward**

    1. Misuses of reward - rewards must be tied to the desired behavior

    2. Why rewards can backfire - people work for intrinsic as well as extrinsic reinforcer and extrinsic reinforcers can interfere with intrinsic motivation

    3. Conclusion - sometimes rewards are necessary; should be used sparingly

Answer these Learning Objectives while you read Sections 4 and 5.

6. Compare and contrast the principles of operant and classical conditioning.

7. List and explain the three types of consequences a response can lead to and distinguish between positive and negative reinforcement and primary and secondary reinforcement.

8. Describe shaping, extinction, stimulus generalization and stimulus discrimination in operant conditioning.

9. Distinguish between continuous and intermittent schedules of reinforcement and describe the four types of intermittent reinforcement schedules.

10. Describe how superstitions might be learned according to operant conditioning.

11. List and discuss six limitations of punishment as a way of controlling behavior and state a more effective strategy.

12. Distinguish between intrinsic and extrinsic reinforcers, and discuss the effects of extrinsic reinforcers on motivation. How should extrinsic rewards be used?

SECTION 6 - SOCIAL-COGNITIVE THEORIES (PP. 253-257)

VI.   **SOCIAL-COGNITIVE THEORIES**
- A.   **Introduction to social-cognitive theories**
  1. Conditioning theories dominated for half a century, when two social scientists introduced social-learning theory in the 1940s
  2. Added higher-level cognitive processes to the idea of how people learn
  3. Agreed that humans are subject to the laws of classical and operant conditioning, but humans also have attitudes, beliefs expectations that affect how they acquire information, make decisions, and reason
  4. Several types of social-learning theories exist, each with different names; umbrella term is social-cognitive theory
- B.   **Learning by observing** - called observational learning
  1. Vicarious conditioning occurs from observing a _____
  2. Supported by Bandura's studies with children learning social behaviors
- C.   **Behavior and the mind**
  1. Tolman and Honzik's experiment with latent learning
  2. Learning can occur even when there is no immediate response and when there is no obvious reinforcement
- D.   **What is learned?**
  1. Tolman says a mental representation, or cognitive map, is learned
  2. In observational and latent learning we learn knowledge about responses and their consequences rather than a specific response
  3. Social-cognitive theories emphasize the importance of people's _____ (of the models and of themselves) of what they learn which explains how two people can experience the same event and take different lessons from it

Answer these Learning Objectives while you read Section 6.

13.   Explain social-cognitive theories and compare them to conditioning models of learning.

14.   Describe the role of mental processes in the social-cognitive theories.

FLASH CARDS

Cut the following chart along the borders and test yourself with the resulting flash cards.

7.1 LEARNING	7.2 BEHAVIORISM	7.3 UNCONDITIONED STIMULUS (US)
7.4 UNCONDITIONED RESPONSE (UR)	7.5 CONDITIONED STIMULUS (CS)	7.6 CONDITIONED RESPONSE (CR)
7.7 CLASSICAL CONDITIONING	7.8 EXTINCTION (IN CLASSICAL CONDITIONING)	7.9 SPONTANEOUS RECOVERY
7.10 HIGHER-ORDER CONDITIONING	7.11 STIMULUS GENERALIZATION (IN CLASSICAL CONDITIONING)	7.12 STIMULUS DISCRIMINATION (IN CLASSICAL CONDITIONING)
7.13 PHOBIA	7.14 COUNTERCONDITIONING	7.15 OPERANT CONDITIONING
7.16 REINFORCEMENT/ REINFORCERS	7.17 PUNISHMENT/PUNISHERS	7.18 PRIMARY REINFORCERS/PUNISHERS
7.19 SECONDARY REINFORCERS/PUNISHERS	7.20 POSITIVE AND NEGATIVE REINFORCEMENT AND PUNISHMENT	7.21 SKINNER BOX
7.22 EXTINCTION (IN OPERANT CONDITIONING)	7.23 STIMULUS GENERALIZATION (IN OPERANT CONDITIONING)	7.24 STIMULUS DISCRIMINATION (IN OPERANT CONDITIONING)

7.3 The classical-conditioning term for a stimulus that elicits a reflexive response in the absence of learning.	7.2 An approach to psychology that studies observable behavior and the role of the environment as a determinant of behavior.	7.1 A relatively permanent change in behavior (or behavioral potential) due to experience.
7.6 The classical-conditioning term for a response that is elicited by a conditioned stimulus.	7.5 The classical-conditioning term for a stimulus that elicits a reflexive response in the absence of learning.	7.4 The classical-conditioning term for a reflexive response elicited by a stimulus in the absence of learning.
7.9 The reappearance of a learned response after its apparent extinction.	7.8 The disappearance of the learned response. In classical conditioning when the CS is no longer paired with the US.	7.7 A neutral stimulus elicits a response through association with a stimulus that already elicits a similar response.
7.12 The tendency to respond differently to two or more similar stimuli.	7.11 After conditioning, when a stimulus that resembles the conditioned stimulus elicits the conditioned response.	7.10 In classical-conditioning, a neutral stimulus becomes a CS through association with an already established CS.
7.15 The process by which a response becomes more or less likely to occur, depending on its consequences.	7.14 Pairing a CS with a stimulus that elicits a response that is incompatible with an unwanted conditioned response.	7.13 An irrational fear of an object or situation that interferes with normal activities.
7.18 A stimulus that is inherently reinforcing or punishing.	7.17 The process by which a stimulus or event weakens or reduces the probability of the response that it follows.	7.16 The process by which a stimulus strengthens or increases the probability of the response it follows.
7.21 A cage equipped with a device that delivers food into a dish when an organism makes a desired response.	7.20 The addition of (positive) or removal of (negative) a stimulus (either reinforcer or punisher) following a behavior.	7.19 A stimulus that has reinforcing or punishing properties through association with other reinforcers.
7.24 When a response occurs in the presence of one stimulus but not in the presence of similar, but different stimuli.	7.23 A response that has been reinforced in the presence of one stimulus occurs in the presence of similar stimuli.	7.22 The disappearance of a learned response. It occurs in operant conditioning when a response is not reinforced.

7.25 DISCRIMINATIVE STIMULUS	7.26 INSTINCTIVE DRIFT	7.27 CONTINUOUS REINFORCEMENT
7.28 INTERMITTENT (PARTIAL) REINFORCEMENT	7.29 FIXED-RATION (FR) SCHEDULE	7.30 VARIABLE-RATIO (VR) SCHEDULE
7.31 FIXED-INTERVAL (FI) SCHEDULE	7.32 VARIABLE-INTERVAL (VI) SCHEDULE	7.33 SHAPING
7.34 SUCCESSIVE APPROXIMATIONS	7.35 FREE WILL VS. DETERMINISM	7.36 BEHAVIOR MODIFICATION
7.37 EXTRINSIC/INTRINSIC REINFORCERS	7.38 BEHAVIORAL "ABCs"	7.39 SOCIAL-COGNITIVE THEORIES
7.40 OBSERVATIONAL LEARNING	7.41 LATENT LEARNING	7.42 VICARIOUS CONDITIONING

7.27 A reinforcement schedule in which a particular response is always reinforced.	7.26 The tendency of an organism to revert to an instinctive behavior over time; can interfere with learning.	7.25 A stimulus that signals when a particular response is likely to be followed by a certain type of consequence.
7.30 An intermittent schedule of reinforcement in which reinforcement occurs after a variable number of responses.	7.29 An intermittent schedule of reinforcement in which reinforcement occurs after a fixed number of responses.	7.28 A reinforcement schedule in which a particular response is sometimes but not always reinforced.
7.33 An operant-conditioning procedure in which successive approximations of a desired response are reinforced.	7.32 A intermittent schedule of reinforcement in which a reinforcer is delivered after a variable period of time has	7.31 An partial reinforcement schedule in which a reinforcer is delivered after a fixed period of time has elapsed since the
7.36 The application of conditioning techniques to teach new responses or to reduce or eliminate	7.35 The debate over whether humans have the power to shape their own destinies or whether we are determined by	7.34 In the procedure of shaping, behaviors that are ordered in terms of increasing similarity to the desired
7.39 Theories that emphasize how behavior is learned through observation of others, positive consequences, and	7.38 A way to analyze learning by specifying the antecedents (events preceding behavior), behavior and consequences.	7.37 Reinforcers that are not inherently related to the activity being reinforced, such as money, prizes, and praise.
7.42 Another name for observational learning, or learning by observing the behavior of another (a model).	7.41 A form of learning that is not immediately expressed in an overt response; it occurs without obvious reinforcement.	7.40 A process in which an individual learns new responses by observing the behavior of another (a model) rather than

ACROSS

2. extended principles of operant conditioning
3. Russian physiologist associated with classical conditioning
5. depending on environmental conditions
8. emphasizes the study of observable behavior and the role of the environment as a determinant of behavior
11. type of schedule of reinforcement; can be either interval or ratio
12. the pattern in which reinforcers are delivered
13. types of learning involving mental processes
15. broad category of reinforcement schedules
16. type of learning in which an individual learns new responses by oversving another's behavior

DOWN

1. not depending on environmental conditions
4. type of schedule of reinforcement
5. conditioning also known as Pavlovian
6. weakening and eventual disappearance of a learned response
7. increases the probability of a response that it follows
9. a behavior
10. an event or change in the environment that causes, elicits, or leads to a response
14. learning that is not immediately expressed

LEARNING THEORIES

Complete the following chart by providing responses under each model of learning.

	OPERANT CONDITIONING	CLASSICAL CONDITIONING	SOCIAL-COGNITIVE THEORIES
INDICATE WHAT IS LEARNED			
EXAMPLES			
IDENTIFY KEY FIGURES			
LIST KEY TERMS			
LIST PRINCIPLES			

PRACTICE TEST 1 - Multiple Choice

1. Learning is
   A. memorization of information.
   B. acquisition of practical skills.
   C. any relatively permanent change in behavior that occurs because of experience.
   D. any relatively permanent change in behavior.

2. A neutral stimulus becomes a conditioned stimulus by
   A. preceding it with an unconditioned stimulus.
   B. following it with an unconditioned stimulus.
   C. pairing it with an conditioned response.
   D. reinforcing it.

3. Once a neutral stimulus becomes a conditioned stimulus, it
   A. can elicit a conditioned response.
   B. can elicit an unconditioned response.
   C. elicits a voluntary response.
   D. elicits none of the above.

4. A loud, sudden clap behind a child causes the child to cry. The child's tears are called the
   A. conditioned stimulus.   B. unconditioned stimulus.
   C. conditioned response.   D. unconditioned response.

5. If a stimulus similar to the conditioned stimulus is repeatedly presented without being followed by the unconditioned stimulus, it will stop evoking the conditioned response. The differential responses to the conditioned stimulus and the similar stimulus demonstrate
   A. extinction.   B. stimulus discrimination.
   C. stimulus generalization.   D. higher-order conditioning.

6. If the CS is repeatedly presented without the US what will happen?
   A. extinction   B. stimulus discrimination
   C. stimulus generalization   D. higher-order conditioning

7. _____ views state that a CR is learned simply because the CS and US occur close together in time, whereas _____ views suggest that information is conveyed by one stimulus about another.
   A. Recent; traditional   B. Social learning; traditional
   C. Traditional; recent   D. Classical; operant

8. Tastes and fears are examples of behaviors learned through
   A. operant conditioning.
   B. social learning.
   C. imitation.
   D. classical conditioning.

9. Peter was afraid of rabbits. John Watson and Mary Cover Jones presented a rabbit to Peter along with milk and crackers and eventually Peter could play with the rabbit. This technique is called
   A. operant conditioning.
   B. counterconditioning.
   C. spontaneous recovery.
   D. higher-order conditioning.

10. A difference between classical and operant conditioning is that
    A. classical conditioning does not involve consequences.
    B. classical conditioning involves reflexive responses.
    C. operant conditioning involves more complex responses than classical conditioning.
    D. all of the above are differences.

11. Voluntary behavior becomes more or less likely to occur depending on its consequences. This principle is at the core of
    A. classical conditioning.
    B. Pavlovian conditioning.
    C. operant conditioning.
    D. counter-conditioning.

12. In operant conditioning, a response may lead to one of three types of consequences. One consequence strengthens or increases the probability of the response that it follows. This consequence is known as
    A. neutral.
    B. reinforcement.
    C. punishment.
    D. higher-order conditioning.

13. When a stimulus or event that follows a response weakens it or makes it less likely to recur, it is called
    A. negative reinforcement.
    B. positive reinforcement.
    C. punishment.
    D. secondary reinforcement.

14. _____ is a primary reinforcement, whereas _____ is/are a secondary reinforcement.
    A. Food; money
    B. Food; water
    C. Money; grades
    D. Applause; food

15. Cindy's teacher tells her parents, "Cindy's misbehavior is just for attention. You should just ignore her and it should stop." Cindy's teacher is using what principle?
    A. primary reinforcement
    B. extinction
    C. stimulus generalization
    D. stimulus discrimination

16. You want your roommate to be neater. Though you've told her several times, she never manages to clean up. You've made a plan that every time she does any of the five things you've asked her to do, you will reward her on what she's done and overlook what she has not done. Eventually, you plan to give her the rewards only after she has done more of the tasks you want her to do. This plan is an example of which technique?
    A. primary reinforcement
    B. extinction
    C. shaping
    D. stimulus generalization

17. Receiving your pay check every Friday represents what type of reinforcement schedule?
    A. fixed-interval
    B. fixed-ratio
    C. variable-interval
    D. variable-ratio

18. You take a quiz on every chapter in psychology. Some chapters are covered in one class and some chapters require two classes. This is a _____ reinforcement schedule?
    A. fixed-interval
    B. fixed-ratio
    C. variable-interval
    D. variable-ratio

19. You wear your "lucky sweater" whenever you have a test because you got an "A" on two tests while wearing that sweater. This is an example of
    A. a fixed-interval schedule.
    B. stimulus generalization.
    C. a learned superstition.
    D. none of the above.

20. One disadvantage of punishment is
    A. the effects of punishment are enduring.
    B. punishment conveys a great deal of information, sometimes too much to absorb.
    C. most behavior is too difficult to punish immediately.
    D. all of the above.

21. Although operant techniques have produced dramatic successes in real-world settings, some problems that can occur with behavior modification include
    A. the fact that extrinsic reinforcers may undermine intrinsic motivation.
    B. the possibility that it may crush creativity.
    C. a refusal to cooperate, since people perceive they are being manipulated.
    D. all of the above.

22. Joey has always loved to play the drums. His parents are trying to encourage this interest and they have told him that if he will take drum lessons and practice daily, they will reward him with an extra $5.00 in his allowance that he has been wanting. Since this offer, Joey's interest has decreased. One possible explanation for this is
    A. that they have put Joey on a continuous reinforcement schedule.
    B. Joey is going through a rebellious period and wants to disobey.
    C. the phenomenon that extrinsic rewards can decrease intrinsic motives.
    D. five dollars is punishing for Joey.

23. Social-cognitive theories differ from conditioning models of learning in that
    A. proponents study higher-level cognitive processes as well as environmental influences.
    B. social learning theories do not utilize discrimination and generalization.
    C. they are more scientific than conditioning models of learning.
    D. they focus almost exclusively on the use of primary reinforcers.

24. Which of the following are among the main influences on behavior identified by social-cognitive theories?
    A. reinforcers and punishers   B. observational learning
    C. perceptions and interpretations of events   D. all of the above

25. Social-cognitive models of learning believe that
    A. aspects of consciousness are learned behaviors.
    B. learning occurs as a result of reinforcers in combination with the influence of a person's attitudes, beliefs and expectations
    C. behavior can be explained in terms of "ABCs:" antecedents, behaviors and consequences.
    D. learning occurs because of the associations between stimuli and responses.

PRACTICE TEST 2 - Multiple Choice

1. Classical is to operant as
   A. learning is to instinct.
   B. voluntary is to involuntary.
   C. involuntary is to voluntary.
   D. unlearned is to instinct.

2. Every time I open any can of food, my cat Luna, comes running. The food is
   A. an unconditioned stimulus.
   B. an unconditioned response.
   C. a conditioned stimulus.
   D. a conditioned response.

3. In the example in question 2, the can opener is
   A. an unconditioned stimulus.
   B. an unconditioned response.
   C. a conditioned stimulus.
   D. a conditioned response.

4. Behra was once bitten by a collie. He is now afraid of all dogs. His fear of dogs represents
   A. extinction.
   B. stimulus generalization.
   C. stimulus discrimination.
   D. spontaneous recovery.

5. Behra was once bitten by a collie. He now has a phobia of collies but is fine with other dogs. This is an example of
   A. extinction.
   B. stimulus generalization.
   C. stimulus discrimination.
   D. spontaneous recovery.

6. When Olimpia threw tantrums, her father spent a lot of time with her to calm her down. After a while, he began to ignore this behavior and eventually it lessened. Ignoring her behavior is an example of
   A. extinction.
   B. stimulus generalization.
   C. stimulus discrimination.
   D. spontaneous recovery.

7. Which of the following was most likely learned through classical conditioning?
   A. I once got sick on Chinese food and now I hate it.
   B. Since elementary school I've learned to raise my hand in class.
   C. After losing pay once, I learned to come to work on time.
   D. all of the above

8. If, after conditioning little Albert to be afraid of rats, Watson had paired the rat with milk and cookies, he would have been using
    A. extinction.
    B. stimulus generalization.
    C. counter-conditioning.
    D. systematic desensitization.

9. Extinction, stimulus generalization and stimulus discrimination are principles of
    A. classical conditioning only.
    B. operant conditioning only.
    C. classical and operant conditioning.
    D. counter-conditioning.

10. "Since you took out the garbage, you don't have to do the dishes." Which learning principle does this represent?
    A. positive reinforcement
    B. punishment
    C. negative reinforcement
    D. primary reinforcement

11. "Since you came home after curfew, you are grounded." This represents
    A. positive reinforcement.
    B. punishment.
    C. negative reinforcement.
    D. primary reinforcement.

12. "Since you got all "A"s, you get to go on vacation." This represents
    A. positive reinforcement.
    B. punishment.
    C. negative reinforcement.
    D. primary reinforcement.

13. Not having to do the dishes and getting to take a vacation are
    A. primary reinforcers.
    B. punishers.
    C. secondary reinforcers.
    D. higher-order conditioning.

14. Liza learned to raise her hand in class when she was in first grade. She has since raised her hand in all classrooms, for all teachers and in all the schools she has attended. Which principle of operant conditioning does this represent?
    A. extinction
    B. stimulus generalization
    C. stimulus discrimination
    D. shaping

15. Liza now has Dr. Falk for a teacher and he likes a free atmosphere in which students speak when they please. He takes off points if students raise their hands. Though Liza continues to raise her hand in all her other classes, she no longer does so in Dr. Falk's class. Which principle of operant conditioning does this represent?
    A. extinction
    B. stimulus generalization
    C. stimulus discrimination
    D. shaping

16. When Jennifer throws a tantrum in the supermarket, her father tries to talk to her calmly or to ignore her behavior. Sometimes, he does not have the patience to be calm and he just gives her a cookie to quiet her down. He has put her on
    A. a partial reinforcement schedule.   B. a variable schedule.
    C. an intermittent reinforcement schedule.   D. all of the above.

17. What behavior can we expect in the future when Jennifer goes to the supermarket?
    A. She will throw tantrums.
    B. It will be difficult to get her to stop throwing tantrums.
    C. Though she might not get a cookie each time, she will keep trying.
    D. all of the above

18. One time Angus got an extra $20 from a money machine. Though it has never happened since, Angus keeps going to that machine whenever possible just in case the error is repeated. He is on a
    A. continuous reinforcement schedule.   B. variable-interval schedule.
    C. variable-ratio schedule.   D. fixed-ratio schedule.

19. A pigeon on a variable interval reinforcement schedule received food while hopping on one leg. Though hopping is not the behavior being reinforced, the pigeon continues to hop. What has occurred?
    A. The pigeon has learned a superstitious behavior.
    B. The pigeon has been negatively reinforced.
    C. The pigeon is on a continuous reinforcement schedule.
    D. none of the above

20. A prison has instituted a program to teach inmates problem-solving skills, life-coping skills and career training. This program addresses which problem related to punishment?
    A. The effects of punishment may depend on the presence of the punisher.
    B. Punishment may be reinforcing misbehavior because of the attention received.
    C. Punishment conveys little information about how to behave differently.
    D. Those who are punished often respond with anxiety, fear or rage.

21. Nick is a struggling artist who loves his work. He becomes well-known and people are now commissioning him to paint. He finds that his passion for his work has decreased. What has happened?
    A. Intrinsic reinforcers have interfered with extrinsic reinforcers.
    B. He has been put on a token economy and does not like it.
    C. Extrinsic reinforcers have interfered with intrinsic motivation.
    D. His love for his work has been extinguished through the absence of reinforcers.

22. Maggie is 16 years old and learning to drive. Though she has never driven before, she is able to put the key in the ignition, turn the starter and put the car into gear. Which of the following best explains these abilities?
     A. Maggie's intelligence
     B. observational learning
     C. cognitive maps
     D. the "ABCs" of learning

23. Mary experiences her boss as demanding, strict, and fair. Jane experiences the boss as unreasonable and overbearing. How would the social-cognitive theories account for the different learning experiences of the two women?
     A. Mary is on a variable reinforcement schedule while Jane is on a fixed schedule.
     B. Mary experienced latent learning while Jane did not.
     C. Jane had a poor relationship with her mother and the boss reminds her of her mother.
     D. Perceptions, expectations and beliefs are important parts of the learning experience and Mary and Jane have different perceptions of their experiences.

24. Tolman's experiments demonstrating latent learning showed that
     A. learning can occur even though it may not be immediately expressed.
     B. rats are capable of insight.
     C. extrinsic reinforcement can reduce intrinsic motivation.
     D. personality characteristics interact with environmental influences.

25. Bandura's study with children who watched the short film of two men playing with toys demonstrated which of the following?
     A. Children must be rewarded to imitate models.
     B. Children were likely to imitate the aggressive behaviors of adults in the film.
     C. Children will only imitate other children, not adults.
     D. Aggression cannot be learned through imitation.

PRACTICE TEST 3 - Short Answer

1. Any relatively permanent change in behavior that occurs because of experience is _____.

2. When a neutral stimulus is paired with an unconditioned stimulus that elicits some reflexive unconditioned response, the neutral stimulus comes to elicit a similar or related response. The neutral stimulus is then called a _____.

3. If a conditioned stimulus is repeatedly presented without the unconditioned stimulus, the conditioned response eventually disappears. This is called _____.

4. The process by which a neutral stimulus becomes a conditioned stimulus by being paired with an already established conditioned stimulus is known as _____ conditioning.

5. Julia developed a conditioned fear response to the cocker spaniel that bit her. She is now afraid of all dogs. This is called stimulus _____.

6. In stimulus _____, different responses are made to stimuli that resemble the conditioned stimulus in some way.

7. Many theorists believe that the conditioned stimulus (CS) elicits a conditioned response (CR) because the CS _____ the US, not simply because they are associated with one another.

8. Responses such as fear are often acquired through conditioning, and can be extinguished in the same way. One method for eliminating such fear responses is _____, which pairs a feared object with another object that elicits responses incompatible with fear.

9. In _____ conditioning, behavior becomes more or less likely to occur depending on its _____.

10. A response may be strengthened or may be more likely to occur again as a result of a stimulus known as a _____.

11. In classical conditioning, _____ responses are learned whereas in operant conditioning, more _____ responses are likely to be learned.

12. Pain, cold, and food are considered _____ reinforcers, whereas money, praise, and smiles are considered _____ reinforcers.

13. In _____ reinforcement or punishment, something is given following a desired or undesired response; in _____ reinforcement or punishment, something is taken away or withdrawn following a desired or undesired behavior.

14. Frequently, people confuse _____ reinforcement with _____ because both involve unpleasant stimuli.

15. Punishment _____ the likelihood of a response, whereas negative reinforcement _____ the likelihood of a response.

16. Responses are more resistant to extinction when they are not always followed by a reinforcer. Such schedules are called _____ schedules of reinforcement.

17. Real estate agents are paid when they sell a home, regardless of how long it takes for them to sell one. This is a _____ schedule of reinforcement.

18. In may occupations, employees are paid every two weeks. This is a _____ schedule of reinforcement.

19. In _____, you initially reinforce a tendency in the right direction, then gradually require responses that are more and more similar to the final, desired response.

20. An alternative to punishment is a combination of _____ and _____.

21. _____ reinforcers are not inherently related to the activity being reinforced but _____ are.

22. Regardless of the strength of the reinforcer, human beings cannot be taught to live underwater without a life support system. This fact demonstrates the _____ limits on learning.

23. Learning that is not immediately displayed in an overt response is called _____.

24. In _____ learning, the learner observes a model making certain responses and experiencing the consequences.

25. The _____ theories focus on the role played by beliefs, interpretations of events, and other cognitions.

PRACTICE TEST 3 - True/False

1. T F   Research on learning has been heavily influenced by behaviorism which does not consider hypothetical mental entities as "mind" or "will" in its explanations of behavior.

2. T F   The unconditioned stimulus is a previously neutral stimulus that elicits a conditioned response.

3. T F   Mostly voluntary responses are learned in classical conditioning.

4. T F   Extinction occurs in classical conditioning when the unconditioned stimulus is presented without the conditioned stimulus.

5. T F   Once a behavior has been extinguished, it is very unlikely that it will reappear again.

6. T F   In higher-order conditioning, a neutral stimulus becomes a conditioned stimulus by being paired with an already established conditioned stimulus.

7. T F   Stimulus discrimination and stimulus generalization only occur in operant conditioning.

8. T F   Theorists agree that in classical conditioning the organism learns only that there is an association between the unconditioned and conditioned stimulus.

9. T F   Classical conditioning may account for emotional responses, fear and phobias, and likes and dislikes.

10. T F   Responses in operant conditioning are generally reflexive and involuntary.

11. T F   Positive reinforcement strengthens or increases the probability of a response whereas negative reinforcement decreases the probability of a response.

12. T F   Immediate consequences usually have a greater effect on a response than do delayed consequences.

13. T F   When John misses his curfew, he is not allowed to use the phone for a week. This is an example of positive punishment.

14.   T F   Jack is very afraid of Fido since the dog bit him. He is not, however, afraid of any of the other dogs on the street. This is an example of stimulus discrimination.

15.   T F   Intermittent, or partial, schedules of reinforcement are very difficult to extinguish.

16.   T F   Pop quizzes are an example of a fixed interval schedule of reinforcement.

17.   T F   The best way to teach a human or animal a new behavior is to wait for it to occur spontaneously and then reinforce the desired response as soon after it occurred as possible.

18.   T F   It is difficult to train an animal to give a response that is contradictory to its instinctive behavior since the animal automatically returns to the more natural response. This is called instinctive drift.

19.   T F   Though it is controversial, punishment is the most effective way to change a behavior.

20.   T F   Unconditionally reinforcing children's behavior is a good way to improve a their self-esteem and increase their motivation and enjoyment in an activity.

21.   T F   Punishment can be misused and have unintended consequences like producing rage and fear.

22.   T F   Social-cognitive theories of learning reject principles of classical and operant conditioning in favor of emphasizing the role of beliefs, interpretations and other cognitions.

23.   T F   In latent learning, learning occurs without any obvious reinforcer.

24.   T F   In observational learning, also called vicarious learning, learning occurs by watching what others do and what happens to them for doing it.

25.   T F   According to social-cognitive theories, what we learn in both observational and latent learning is not a specific response, but knowledge about responses and their consequences.

PRACTICE TEST 3 - Essay

1. In the following examples, identify the unconditioned stimulus, unconditioned response, conditioned stimulus and conditioned response.

   A. When your father is angry with you, he calls you by both your first and middle names. Every time you hear him call you that way, you become anxious.

   B. You keep your dog's leash in the front closet. Every time you go to get something out of the closet, Fido comes running excitedly and waits to go out.

   C. Your true love wears a certain perfume. Every time you smell that perfume, you feel happy inside.

   D. You had a terrifying car accident at the corner of Park Place and Main Street. Now every time you approach that corner, you feel anxious.

2. In the following examples identify the principles of classical conditioning.

   A. While caring for your friend's dog, you notice that it displays a cowering posture as you roll up a newspaper. You try this several more times with magazines or stacks of notebook paper and the dog displays the same behavior. You become convinced that this dog is generally afraid of rolled-up paper.

   B. Joan, a dog breeder, has been phobic about Doberman pinschers since one attacked her. After the attack, she felt tense and apprehensive whenever she walked by a Doberman, even if the dog was in a cage or on a leash, though she was never uncomfortable with any other type of dog. Recently she has been experiencing a change in her feelings toward Dobermans. She was given four Doberman puppies to sell and since being around them for several months, she is no longer fearful of Dobermans.

   C. At a red light, Bob and Fred automatically tensed and felt chills when they heard the screech of tires behind them. Later, while watching a car race, Bob remarked that the screeching of tires was having little effect on them then.

   D. After Bill got food poisoning from roast chicken, he vowed he would never return to that restaurant nor would he ever eat chicken again. All he wanted was to go home and eat his mother's cooking. As he entered the kitchen, he became nauseated when he saw the turkey sitting on the table.

3. Using operant conditioning, identify whether the consequences in the following examples are positive or negative reinforcement, or positive or negative punishment. Indicate the probable effects of the consequences, according to operant theories of learning.

    A. A buzzer sound continues until a seat belt is fastened.
    B. Whenever Joe picks up a cigarette, his roommate complains and insults him.
    C. Whenever Warren does the dishes, his girlfriend compliments and kisses him.
    D. Whenever Fred skis down the most difficult slopes, he always has a bad fall.

4. Identify the problem or problems in the following examples and, using principles of learning theories, suggest the changes needed.

    A. Ten-year-old Sara is expected to keep her room clean. Her parents check her room weekly and in the past year, her room was clean on 20 occasions. Sara's parents praised her lavishly on 10 of those occasions that her room was clean and on the other 10 occasions, Sara received no reinforcement. This technique has not been working well since on any given day, the room is likely to be a mess.
    B. Baby Ari is not yet sleeping through the night. Every time the baby cries, one of his parents picks him up. His parents decide that after checking to make sure the baby is O.K., they will just let him cry. Ari cries and cries for five nights in a row. On the first four nights, his parents kept to their agreement, but on the fifth night, they couldn't stand it any longer and picked him up. Now Ari is crying more than ever.
    C. Sue is always in trouble in class. Her teacher has tried everything he knows to make her behave: talking to her privately, having her stay after class, and scolding her in public. Regardless of what he does, her misbehavior continues.

5. Below is a description using punishment. Identify the problems demonstrated in this example and suggest a more effective approach.

A parent discovers crayon marks and scribbling on a recently painted wall. Tommy, 18-months-old, is angrily pulled from the playpen, brought before the wall, and harshly told, "No! No! No!", and given a sharp slap on the back of his hand. He is still crying when placed in the crib for a nap. Things become quiet for a time, and then the sound of movement is heard. A quick check shows Tommy is not in his crib. A search locates Tommy in the office room. He has doodled in various places with pens and pencils from the desk.

6.   Identify the schedule of reinforcement that is being used in each example.

    A.   Pop quizzes
    B.   Quizzes after every chapter
    C.   Quizzes every Monday
    D. $10 for every A

7.   Describe similarities and differences between social-cognitive and behavioral models of learning.

CHAPTER 8

Behavior in Social and Cultural Context

LEARNING OBJECTIVES

1.   Discuss the focus of the field of social psychology and cultural psychology.

2.   Describe two controversial studies and discuss how they illustrate the influence of roles on behavior.

3.   List and explain the reasons that people obey authority and when they may disobey.

4.   Summarize the principles and components of attribution theory.

5.   Describe the relationship between attitudes and behavior.

6.   Define attitudes and identify important influences on attitudes.

7.   List and explain persuasive and manipulative techniques of attitude change.

8.   Discuss some reasons for conforming to social pressure in a group.

9.   Define diffusion of responsibility, groupthink, social loafing, and deindividuation. Discus the conditions under which each of these is most likely to occur and their consequences.

10.   Discuss the steps involved in disobedience, dissent, and altruistic action.

11.   Define ethnocentrism and explain its consequences.

12.   Describe some of the effects of competition.

13.   Describe ways that stereotypes are useful and three ways which they distort reality.

14.   Define prejudice and the psychological, social, and financial functions that perpetuate it.

15.   Discuss approaches for reducing prejudice and conflict between groups.

CHAPTER CONCEPT MAP

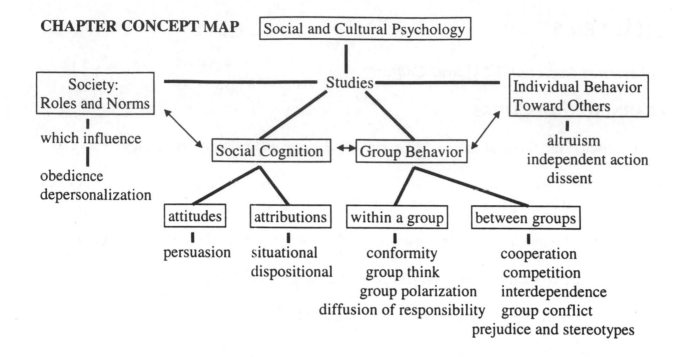

BRIEF CHAPTER SUMMARY

Chapter 8 examines some of the main topic areas in the fields of social psychology and cultural psychology, which study the individual in the social and cultural context. The influence of the social context begins with norms or rules that people are expected to follow. Each of us fills many social roles that are governed by norms about how a person in that position should behave. The roles we fill and the rules that govern those roles heavily influence our behavior, as demonstrated by two classic studies. These studies show how roles can override our own beliefs and values. The social context also influences our thought processes. Efforts to change our attitudes are ever present. To resist unwanted persuasion, one must think critically about information from all sources. Attributions--the way we explain events--influence our responses to the world. Certain types of attributional errors and tendencies can occur that may cause misinterpretations of events. Group behaviors are also examined. Certain group processes can occur as a result of the presence and influence of other group members. The chapter examines the factors that influence independent action, particularly altruism and dissent. The importance of group indentity and interactions among groups are discussed. Stereotypes help us organize new information, but they also distort reality in three ways. The origins of prejudice and efforts to reduce prejudice are discussed. Finally, the chapter raises the question of human nature and its influence on behavior. Studying individuals in a social context helps to identify the normal social influences that contribute to behaviors we often think result from individual or personality factors.

PREVIEW OUTLINE AND REVIEW QUESTIONS

Before you read the chapter, review the preview outline and the Learning Objectives for each section of the text. Answer all questions as you read.

SECTION 1 - ROLES AND RULES (PP. 264-271)

I. **ROLES AND RULES**
   A. **Definitions**
      1. Social psychology and cultural psychology - fields that examine the influence of social and cultural environment on individuals and groups
      2. Norms - _____ about how we are supposed to act
      3. Roles - positions in society that are regulated by norms about how people in those positions should behave
      4. Culture - program of shared rules for people's behavior in a society (e.g. expected gender roles, rules for conversational distance)
   B. **The obedience study by Milgram**
      1. Design and findings
         a. Question - would people obey an authority and violate their own ethical standards
         b. Subjects thought they were in an experiment about learning and were instructed to shock another subject when an error was made
         c. No one received shocks, but the subjects did not know this
         d. All participants gave some shock; two-thirds obeyed the experimenter and gave all the shocks despite cries of pain
         e. Subsequent studies found disobedience occurs when:
            (1) The experimenter left the room
            (2) The victim was right there in the room
            (3) Two experimenters issued conflicting demands
            (4) An ordinary man, not authority figure, issued commands
            (5) _____ refused to go further
            (6) They found that nothing the victim did made any difference
      2. Conclusions
         a. Obedience is a function of the _____, not of personalities
         b. The nature of the relationship to authority influences obedience
      3. Evaluating the obedience study
         a. Criticisms - unethical because subjects felt great distress afterwards
         b. The conclusions have been questioned - some personality traits do increase obedience, invalid parallel with Naziism
         c. It increased awareness of the dangers of uncritical obedience

C.   **The prison study by Zimbardo**
    1.   Design and findings
        a.   College students randomly assigned to be prisoners or guards
        b.   Given no further instructions on how to behave
        c.   "Prisoners" quickly became _____, helpless and panicky and begged to be let out of the study
        d.   Guards acted like guards; one-third became tyrannical
        e.   Researchers terminated the study early
    2.   Evaluating the prison study
        a.   Critics said students knew how to behave from the media
        b.   Researchers say that is their point - people's behavior depends, in part, on their roles which can overrule personality and values
D.   **The power of roles**
    1.   These studies demonstrate the power of social roles to influence behavior
    2.   People obey because they believe in the authority's legitimacy and to avoid negative outcomes and gain positive ones
    3.   Why people obey when it's not in their interest or violates their values
        a.   Investing the authority, not themselves, with responsibility
        b.   Routinization - defining the activity as routine; normalizing it
        c.   Rules of good manners - people lack the words to disobey
        d.   Entrapment - commitment to course of action is escalated

Answer these Learning Objectives while you read Section 1

1.   Discuss the focus of the field of social psychology and cultural psychology.

2.   Describe two controversial studies and discuss how they illustrate the influence of roles on behavior.

3.   List and explain the reasons that people obey authority and when they may disobey.

SECTION 2 - SOCIAL INFLUENCES ON BELIEFS (PP. 272-278)

II. **SOCIAL INFLUENCES ON BELIEFS**
    A.   **Social cognition**
        1.   How the social environment influences thoughts, beliefs, and memories
        2.   How people's perceptions of themselves and others affect their relationships
    B.   **Attributions**
        1.   Attribution theory - the explanations we make of our behavior and the behavior of others
        2.   Two types of attributions
            a.   _____ attributions - identify the cause of an action as something in the environment or situation
           b.   Dispositional attributions - identify the cause of an action as something in the _____, such as a trait or motive
           c.   Fundamental attribution error
               (1)   Tendency to overestimate _____ factors and underestimate the influence of the situation when explaining someone else's behavior
               (2)   More prevalent in Western nations related to notions of individual responsibility
           d.   Self-serving bias
               (1)   When explaining one's own behavior, people take credit for _____ actions and attribute the bad ones to the situation
               (2)   Also affected by culture
           e.   Just-world hypothesis
               (1)   The need to believe the world is fair and that good people are _____ and bad people are punished
               (2)   This can lead to blaming the victim
        3.   Attributions, whether accurate or not, influence emotions, actions, decisions
    C.   **Attitudes**
        1.   Relatively stable opinions containing a _____ element and an emotional element
        2.   Not always based on reason; can be based on conformity, habit, rationalization, economic self-interest, generational events
        3.   Attitudes and behavior influence each other
            a.   Often attitudes dispose people to behave in certain ways
           b.   Attitudes can change to achieve consistency; to reduce cognitive _____ (when two attitudes or an attitude and a behavior conflict)

4.   Attitudes are also influenced by other people trying to persuade us
    a.   Friendly persuasion - what works and what doesn't
        (1)   Repetition increases positive feelings about a subject and the likelihood that a statement will be believed (the validity effect)
        (2)   Exposure to an argument from someone admired
        (3)   Linking message to good feelings (for example presenting a message while offering food)
        (4)   Fear, in contrast, often causes people to _____ arguments that are in their own best interest (e.g. campaigns against drugs)
    b.   Coercive persuasion (brainwashing)
        (1)   Coercive techniques suppress ability to reason, to think critically, and to make good choices
        (2)   Key processes of coercive persuasion
            (a)   The person is put under physical or emotional _____
            (b)   The person's problems are reduced to one simple explanation, which is repeatedly emphasized
            (c)   The leader offers unconditional love, acceptance, attention
            (d)   A new _____ based on the group is created
            (e)   The person is subjected to entrapment
            (f)   The person's access to information is severely controlled

Answer these Learning Objectives while you read Section 2.

4.   Summarize the principles and components of attribution theory.

5.   Describe the relationship between attitudes and behavior.

6.   Define attitudes and identify important influences on attitudes.

7.   List and explain persuasive and manipulative techniques of attitude change.

III. **INDIVIDUALS IN GROUPS**
    A. **Conformity**
        1. Asch's conformity study - replications of this study have found that:
            a. Conformity has declined since the 1950s
            b. People in individual-oriented cultures conform less than people in group-oriented cultures
            c. Regardless of culture, conformity increases under certain conditions
        2. People conform for a variety of reasons including identification with group members, popularity, self-interest, and to avoid punishment
        3. Conformity has good and bad sides, but it can suppress critical thinking
    B. **Groupthink**
        1. Definition - the tendency for all members of the group to think alike and suppress _____
        2. Occurs when a group's need for total agreement overwhelms its need to make the wisest decision
        3. Symptoms of groupthink
            a. The group has an illusion of invulnerability
            b. The group self-censors
            c. The group pressures dissenters to conform
            d. The group creates an illusion of unanimity
        4. Groupthink can result in faulty, even disastrous, decisions
        5. Historically, bad decisions have occurred when members feel they are a tightly connected team, they are isolated from other views, and they have a strong leader
        6. Can be counteracted if doubt and dissent is encouraged and if decisions are made by a majority rather than by unanimity
        7. Easy to see retrospectively, harder to see prospectively
    C. **The anonymous crowd**
        1. Diffusion of responsibility
            a. The more people who are around when a problem occurs, the less likely one of them will offer assistance
            b. Individuals fail to act because they believe someone else will do so
            c. May explain why crowds of people fail to respond to an emergency which is often interpreted as bystander apathy
        2. Social _____ - diffusion of responsibility in work groups
            a. Individuals slow down and let others work harder
            b. More likely to occur under the following conditions
                (1) When members are not accountable for their work
                (2) When working harder duplicates efforts

        (3)   When workers feel others are getting a "free ride"
        (4)   When the work itself is uninteresting
    c. Social loafing declines under the following conditions
        (1)   When the challenge of a job is increased
        (2)   When each member has a different job
3. _____ - losing all awareness of individuality and sense of self; long considered a prime reason for mob violence
    a. Increases a person's willingness to do harm, to cheat, break the law
    b. Eliminates gender differences in aggressiveness
    c. Can also increase friendliness and self-disclosure
    d. Current explanation - people are more likely to conform to the norms of the specific situation
4. Anonymity and responsibility
    a. Deindividuation has psychological and legal implications
    b. Are individuals be responsible for "deindividuated" crowd behavior

D. Disobedience and dissent
1. Altruism - the willingness to take _____ or dangerous action for others
2. Reasons for altruistic action include a combination of conscience and conviction and situational influences
3. Steps involved in disobedience, dissent, and altruism
    a. The individual perceives the need for intervention or help; this is influenced by attentional demands, community needs, cultural rules
    b. The individual decides to take responsibility; depends on risks
    c. The individual decides that the costs of doing nothing outweigh the costs of getting involved
    d. The individual has an _____; the presence of another dissenter increases the likelihood of protest
    e. The individual becomes _____; once initial steps have been taken, most people will increase their commitment

Answer these Learning Objectives while you read Section 3.

8. Discuss some reasons for conforming to social pressure in a group.

9. Define diffusion of responsibility, groupthink, social loafing, and deindividuation. Discuss the conditions under which each of these is most likely to occur.

10. Discuss the steps involved in disobedience, dissent and altruistic action.

SECTION 4 - GROUP CONFLICT AND PREJUDICE (PP. 288-298) AND
SECTION 5 - THE QUESTION OF HUMAN NATURE (PP. 298-299)

IV. **GROUP CONFLICT AND PREJUDICE**
    A. **Group identity: Us versus them**
        1. Ethnocentrism - the belief that one's own culture is _____
        2. We all have personal identity based on particular traits and unique history and a social identity based on the groups we belong to
        3. Influence of social identities
            a. Social identities give us a place and position in the world
            b. They also create "us" or ingroup, versus "them" categories
            c. Us-them identities are strengthened when the groups compete
            d. Competition can have positive and negative results
                (1) Can lead to better services, products, inventions
                (2) Can decrease motivation, increase insecurity and anxiety, anger and frustration, jealousy and hostility
                (3) Interdependence in reaching mutual goals (cooperation) can reduce competitiveness and hostility

    B. **Stereotypes**
        1. Summary impression of a group in which all members of that group are viewed as sharing common traits that may be positive, negative, or neutral
        2. They help us process new information, retrieve memories, organize experience, make sense of differences, and predict how people will behave
        3. Stereotypes can distort reality in three ways
            a. Exaggerate differences between groups
            b. Produce selective perception
            c. Underestimate differences within other groups
         4. Can stem from cultural values and influence how an action is evaluated

    C. **Prejudice**
        1. Definition - a negative stereotype and a strong, unreasonable dislike or hatred of a group or its individual members
        2. Resists rational argument and evidence; resistant to change
        3. The origins of prejudice
            a. Scapegoating - the projection of fears and problems onto one group
            b. Some acquired through groupthink and pressures to conform
            c. Economic _____ that justify the majority group's dominance
            d. Serves cultural purposes - bonds people to their ethnic or national groups and may have an evolutionary purpose
        4. The varieties of prejudice
            a. Studies show prejudice in North America is decreasing but there is disagreement about how to get an accurate measure

          b.   Some say current prejudice lurks behind a mask of symbols, codes
          c.   Not all people are prejudiced in the same way; some are unapologetic, some are patronizing but not explicitly hostile, others feel guilty for having negative feelings

5.   Efforts to reduce prejudice

          a.   No one solution fits all kinds - must consider all variations
          b.   Some say those trying to break the "prejudice habit" should not be lumped with bigots
          c.   "Cycle of distrust" can result from unfamiliarity - both groups must be part of the solution
          d.   Sociocultural approach - change people's circumstances
          e.   Conditions necessary to reduce prejudice - to work all must exist
               (1)   Both sides must have equal _____ status, economic opportunities, and power
               (2)   The larger culture must endorse egalitarian norms and provide moral support and legitimacy for both sides
               (3)   Both sides must have opportunities to work and socialize together, formally and informally
               (4)   Both sides must cooperate; work together for common goal

V.   THE QUESTION OF HUMAN NATURE

A.   What is human nature and its role in behavior?

1.   History is full of both heroism and atrocities
2.   From standpoint of social and cultural psychology, all humans have the potential for good and bad

B.   Banality of evil

1.   Often behavior depends more on social organization than human nature
2.   No culture is wholly virtuous or villainous

Answer these Learning Objectives while you read Sections 4 and 5.

11.   Define ethnocentrism and explain its consequences.

12.   Describe some of the effects of competition.

13.   Describe ways that stereotypes are useful and three ways they distort reality.

14.   Define prejudice and the psychological, social and financial functions that perpetuate it.

15.   Discuss approaches for reducing prejudice and conflict between groups.

FLASH CARDS
Cut the following chart along the borders and test yourself with the resulting flash cards.

8.1 SOCIAL PSYCHOLOGY	8.2 CULTURAL PSYCHOLOGY	8.3 NORMS (SOCIAL)
8.4 ROLE	8.5 CULTURE	8.6 CONVERSATIONAL DISTANCE
8.7 ROUTINIZATION	8.8 ENTRAPMENT	8.9 SOCIAL COGNITION
8.10 ATTRIBUTION THEORY	8.11 SITUATIONAL ATTRIBUTIONS	8.12 DISPOSITIONAL ATTRIBUTIONS
8.13 FUNDAMENTAL ATTRIBUTION ERROR	8.14 SELF-SERVING BIAS	8.15 JUST-WORLD HYPOTHESIS
8.16 BLAMING THE VICTIM	8.17 ATTITUDE	8.18 VALIDITY EFFECT

8.3 Social conventions that regulate human life, including explicit laws and implicit cultural standards.	8.2 An area in psychology which examines the powerful influence of the cultural environment on the actions of individuals and groups.	8.1 Social psychology is the study of people in social context, including the influence of norms, roles, and groups on behavior and cognition.
8.6 How close people normally stand to one another when they are speaking; influenced by culture.	8.5 A program of shared rules that govern the behavior of members of a society, and a set of shared values, beliefs, and attitudes.	8.4 A given social position that is governed by a set of norms for proper behavior.
8.9 An area in social psychology concerned with social influences on thought, memory, perception, and other cognitive processes.	8.8 A gradual process in which individuals escalate their commitment to a course of action to justify their investment of time, money, or effort.	8.7 Defining an activity in terms of routine duties so that one's behavior becomes normalized and there is little chance to doubt or question.
8.12 Identifying the cause of an action as something in the person, such as a trait or motive.	8.11 Identifying the cause of an action as something in the environment.	8.10 The theory that people are motivated to explain behavior by attributing causes of that behavior to a situation or disposition.
8.15 The belief that the world is fair and that justice is served; that bad people are punished and good people rewarded.	8.14 The tendency, in explaining one's own behavior, to take credit for one's good actions and rationalize one's mistakes.	8.13 The tendency to overestimate personality factors and underestimate the influence of the situation when explaining other people's behavior.
8.18 The tendency of people to believe that a statement is true or valid simply because it has been repeated many times.	8.17 A relatively stable opinion containing a cognitive element and an emotional element.	8.16 An outcome of the just world hypothesis; the argument that the victim of an event deserved, provoked or wanted the situation to occur.

8.19 COGNITIVE DISSONANCE	**8.20 COERCIVE PERSUASION**	**8.21 GROUPTHINK**
8.22 DIFFUSION OF RESPONSIBILITY	**8.23 BYSTANDER APATHY**	**8.24 SOCIAL LOAFING**
8.25 DEINDIVIDUATION	**8.26 ALTRUISM**	**8.27 SOCIAL IDENTITY**
8.28 US-THEM THINKING	**8.29 ETHNOCENTRISM**	**8.30 STEREOTYPE**
8.31 PREJUDICE	**8.32 SYMBOLIC RACISM**	**8.33 "CYCLE OF DISTRUST"**
8.34 CONTACT HYPOTHESIS	**8.35 COOPERATIVE LEARNING**	**8.36 BANALITY OF EVIL**

8.21 The tendency for all members in close-knit groups to think alike for the sake of harmony and to suppress disagreement.	8.20 Severe tactics used to force someone to change his or her attitudes.	8.19 Tension that occurs when a person holds two cognitions that are psychologically inconsistent, or when a belief is incongruent with behavior.
8.24 Diffusion of responsibility in work groups. Each member of a team slows down, letting others work harder.	8.23 The belief that bystanders do not intervene in an event because they do not care or are indifferent to what is occurring.	8.22 In groups, the tendency of members to avoid taking responsibility for actions or decisions, assuming others will do so.
8.27 The part of a person's self-concept that is based on his or her identification with a nation, culture, or ethnic group or with gender or other roles in society.	8.26 The willingness to take selfless or dangerous action on behalf of others.	8.25 In groups or crowds, the loss of awareness of one's own individuality.
8.30 A summary impression of a group, in which a person believes that all members of the group share a common trait or traits.	8.29 The belief that one's own ethnic group, nation, or religion is superior to all others.	8.28 A type of thinking that occurs when any two groups perceive themselves to be in competition.
8.33 A cycle that can occur when people are unfamiliar or uncomfortable with another group;both groups misinterpret the other's behavior.	8.32 The focus of dislike is not on individuals but on racial symbols and issues like "welfare abuse."	8.31 A negative stereotype and a strong unreasonable dislike or hatred of a group or its individual members.
8.36 Under certain circumstances, good people can do bad things.	8.35 An educational technique in which the success of any individual child rests on the success of the whole group.	8.34 An approach to reducing prejudice that advocates bringing members of both sides together to let them get acquainted.

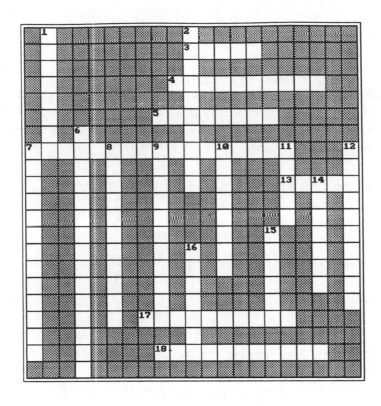

ACROSS

2. a given social position governed by norms
4. hypothesis that the world is fair
5. the willingness to take selfless action on behalf of another
7. treating another without regard for his or her individuality
13. social conventions that regulate human life
17. gradual process by which individuals escalate their commitment to a course of action
18. the opposite of cooperation

DOWN

1. forceful type of persuasion
2. the tendency for all group members to think alike
6. loss of awareness of one's own individuality
7. type of attribution that sees something within the person as the cause of an action
8. type of attribution that sees something external as the cause of an action
9. an explanation for behavior
10. a relatively stable opinion
11. social conventions
12. cognitive _____
14. when each member of a team slows down, letting others work harder
15. classic study in which college students were placed in one of two roles
16. conducted the obedience study

227

PRACTICE TEST 1 - Multiple choice

1. Culture is
    A. a program of shared rules that govern the behavior of community members.
    B. a set of values, beliefs and attitudes shared by most community members.
    C. a system of rules that is passed from one generation to another.
    D. defined by all of the above.

2. The belief that one's own culture or ethnic group is superior to all others is called
    A. ethnic separatism.   B. prejudice.
    B. social norms.   D. ethnocentrism.

3. Rules that regulate "correct" behaviors for a manager or an employee are called
    A. norms.   B. occupational roles.
    C. social rules.   D. depersonalization.

4. The major point of the prison study was
    A. to demonstrate that certain personality types should not be in positions of authority.
    B. that people's behavior depends largely on the roles they are asked to play.
    C. that students are very suggestible and are not good research subjects.
    D. how quickly people are corrupted by power.

5. In the obedience experiments, Milgram found that people were more likely to disobey the experimenter and refuse to administer shock when
    A. the experimenter stayed in the room.
    B. the subject administered shocks directly to the victim in the same room.
    C. authority figures, rather than "ordinary" people, ordered subjects to continue.
    D. the subject worked with a peer who also administered shocks.

6. In the obedience experiments, what percentage of the subjects administered the maximum amount of shock to the victim?
    A. only 1 to 2 percent   B. approximately two-thirds
    C. 30 percent   D. all of the subjects

7. Which of the following causes people to obey when they really would rather not?
    A. entrapment   B. good manners
    C. routinization   D. all of the above

8. In attributing causes to other people's behaviors, the tendency to overestimate the effects of personality factors and underestimate the effects of situational factors is called
    A. a dispositional attribution.   B. the just-world hypothesis.
    C. the fundamental attribution error.   D. the self-serving bias.

9. "Sally rides her bike to school because she is athletic" is an example of
    A. a dispositional attribution.   B. the self-serving bias.
    C. the fundamental attribution error.   D. situational attribution.

10. "Jennifer rides her bike to school because she can't get a ride" is an example of
    A. a dispositional attribution.   B. the self-serving bias.
    C. the fundamental attribution error.   D. situational attribution.

11. "People get what they deserve" is an example of
    A. the just-world hypothesis.   B. situational attribution.
    C. the fundamental attribution error.   D. the self-serving bias.

12. Attitudes are affected by
    A. thinking.   B. conformity.
    C. habit.   D. all of the above.

13. That repetition increases the perception that familiar statements are true demonstrates
    A. cognitive dissonance.   B. generational identity.
    C. the validity effect.   D. coercive persuasion.

14. One of the techniques that facilitates coercive persuasion is
    A. repeating a piece of information over and over.
    B. exposing people to arguments from someone they admire.
    C. defining a person's problems in simplistic terms, and offering simple answers.
    D. offering people food while listening to an argument.

15. People are likely to conform
    A. in order to keep their jobs, win promotions or win votes.
    B. if they wish to be liked.
    C. if they want to avoid being unpopular.
    D. for all the reasons listed above.

16. A woman was stabbed and none of the numerous onlookers called for help. What accounts for this?
    A. social loafing   B. conformity
    C. diffusion of responsibility   D. deindividuation

17. In close-knit groups, members tend to think alike and suppress dissent. This is called
    A. group polarization.   B. risky shift.
    C. diffusion of responsibility.   D. groupthink.

18. Before a bystander will behave altruistically, he or she must first
    A. have a "helpful" personality.   B. have had a similar experience.
    C. perceive the need for help.   D. experience all of the above.

19. The willingness to take selfless or dangerous action on behalf of others is called
    A. interdependence.   B. individuation.
    C. altruism.   D. all of the above.

20. Which of the following is <u>NOT</u> one of the factors that predicts altruism?
    A. an altruistic personality   B. an ally
    C. perceiving the need for help   D. entrapment

21. A stereotype
    A. may be positive.   B. may be negative or neutral.
    C. helps us to organize the world.   D. includes all of the above.

22. Stereotypes can be helpful because they help us
    A. increase the accuracy of our opinions about particular individuals.
    B. see the differences between groups.
    C. rapidly process new information and organize experience.
    D. do all of the above.

23. Stereotypes distort reality by
    A. accentuating differences between groups.
    B. producing selective perceptions.
    C. underestimating differences within other groups.
    D. propagating all of the above.

24. An unreasonable negative feeling toward a category of people is called
    A. ethnocentrism.   B. a stereotype.
    B. a prejudice.   D. social identity.

25. Which characteristic is most likely to lead to evil actions?
    A. adherence to roles, obedience to authority, conformity, entrapment
    B. lack of developed conscience
    C. mental illness
    D. an evil nature

PRACTICE TEST 2 - Multiple Choice

1. Being on time, not jay-walking and shaking hands when meeting a new person are all examples of
    A. stereotypes.
    B. shared rules that govern the behavior of members of a community.
    C. gender roles.
    D. body language.

2. People from some cultures tend to stand closer to one another during conversation than those from other cultures because
    A. those who stand closer are from friendlier cultures.
    B. those who stand closer are from cultures with looser sexual values.
    C. of differences in rules governing conversational distance.
    D. of differences in gender roles.

3. In the obedience study, the person most likely to disobey would be a subject who
    A. felt very upset about administering shocks to another person.
    B. worked with peers who refused to go further.
    C. had strong moral and religious principles.
    D. had a very passive personality.

4. The conclusion of the obedience study was that
    A. obedience was more a function of the situation than of the particular personalities of the participants.
    B. obedience was more a function of the particular personality types of the participants.
    C. participants with a past history of problems with authority were more likely to obey.
    D. obedience was a function of how much the victim complained.

5. In the prison study, subjects
    A. exhibited both the behaviors and emotions of the roles of guard and prisoner.
    B. who played prisoners developed emotions associated with their roles, but the guards did not.
    C. who were guards became very distressed that the prisoners played their part so well.
    D. guards played their role but did not enjoy it.

6. Which conclusion is shared by the prison study and the obedience study?
   A. The roles people played influenced their behavior more than their personalities.
   B. What people did depended on the role they were assigned.
   C. Social roles and obligations have a powerful influence on behavior.
   D. all of the above

7. You take Mike out for a drink to console him about his dissolving marriage. Next, you occasionally babysit his two-year-old. Then, you find yourself taking care of the child every weekend. This sequence is an example of
   A. good manners.   B. routinization.
   C. lacking a language of protest.   D. entrapment.

8. When Ashley's husband forgot to run an errand, she attributed his forgetting to his selfishness. When Andy's wife forgot to run an errand, he attributed her forgetting to her being preoccupied with problems at work. Ashley made a(n) _____ attribution, while Andy made a(n) _____ attribution.
   A. dispositional; situational   B. situational; dispositional
   C. self-serving; external   D. internal; dispositional

9. I believe that I got an A in geometry because I'm a hard worker, but I got a "D" in biology because the teacher doesn't like me. This demonstrates
   A. the just-world hypothesis.   B. the self-serving bias.
   C. the fundamental attribution error. D. blaming the victim.

10. I'm trying to understand why Jamie snubbed me today. Based on the fundamental attribution error, which explanation am I most likely to choose?
    A. Jamie is a moody person.   B. Jamie had a bad day.
    C. It had to do with the fight we had. D. I've done something wrong.

11. When Hortense was diagnosed with cancer, she believed that she must have done something wrong to have deserved such an illness. Her belief is an example of
    A. a situational attribution.   B. guilt.
    C. the just-world hypothesis.   D. an internal attribution.

12. "It's no wonder Jane was attacked. It's her own fault; she never should have been out alone." This is an example of
    A. the fundamental attribution error. B. blaming the victim.
    C. self-serving bias.   D. none of the above.

13. The Vietnam war shaped the values and attitudes of many people who were college students during that era. This is an example of a(n)
    A. social attitude.
    B. dispositional attribution.
    C. generational identity.
    D. individual identity.

14. Students were asked to publicly advocate the importance of safe sex, and then list the reasons for their own past failure to use condoms. Afterwards, they experienced
    A. friendly persuasion.
    B. cognitive dissonance.
    C. coercive persuasion.
    D. insight.

15. Following their confrontation with the discrepancy between their attitudes and their behaviors, what would the students in question 14 be most likely to do?
    A. increase their use of condoms
    B. make no change in their behavior
    C. decrease their use of condoms
    D. none of the above

16. Dr. Wyatt wants to persuade his colleagues about a particular point. He should
    A. utilize the validity effect.
    B. use the emotion of fear.
    C. appeal to their generational identity.
    D. use all of the above techniques.

17. Several years ago, Maxine became part of a cult. Looking back, she describes what happened. Which of the following probably happened to Maxine?
    A. She was not allowed to eat, sleep or exercise.
    B. She was offered unconditional love, acceptance and attention by the leader.
    C. She was given a new last name that was shared by all other members.
    D. all of the above

18. Dr. Patel is assigning a group project in her psychology class. She has structured the assignment so that to successfully complete the project each student must rely on the work of all the other students in the group. Patel has designed this project in these ways in order to promote
    A. deindividuation.
    B. social loafing.
    C. cooperation.
    D. generational identity.

19. According to the diffusion of responsibility theory, you would be more likely to receive assistance with a car problem
    A. on a small road with almost no other traffic.
    B. on a crowded highway with many other automobiles.
    C. on a city street with numerous other cars.
    D. anywhere that a lot of people could see that you needed help.

20. Geraldo's boss always likes to be right and to be the "expert" on any topic. Whenever their work team meets, he becomes irritated with whomever disagrees with him. If anyone tries to speak up to him, others in the group quickly change the subject to be sure no one challenges him. What is occurring in this situation?
   A. groupthink
   B. diffusion of responsibility
   C. social loafing
   D. deindividuation

21. Rachel and her daughter spend every Christmas working at the shelter.
   A. They are volunteering because they have deeply held moral values.
   B. They work at the shelter because they have personal feelings for the victims.
   C. They help at the shelter because they have become entrapped.
   D. Any of the above reasons could explain their altruistic behavior.

22. Healthy competition
   A. occurs in situations in which the rules are clear.
   B. occurs in situations in which both sides are equally capable.
   C. is considered by some to be a contradiction in terms because, in general, competition results in many negative outcomes.
   D. encourages good will between groups.

23. Students are shown a slide of a white male committing a crime against a black male. Later, when they are asked what they saw, most reported seeing a black male committing a crime against a white male. This error is a result of the fact that stereotypes
   A. produce selective perception.
   B. accentuate differences between groups.
   C. underestimate differences within other groups.
   D. help us process new information.

24. Jane denies being prejudice. She expresses strong feelings about reverse discrimination, welfare abuse, and hard-core criminals. Some psychologists would say that Jane
   A. is engaging in symbolic racism.
   B. has strong political views that have nothing to do with race.
   C. holds views that are atypical and not very common.
   D. has probably been discriminated herself or has been a crime victim.

25. Who among the following is most likely to commit an evil act according to the idea of the banality of evil?
   A. a person with a disturbed personality
   B. an immoral person
   C. an ordinary person
   D. an evil person

PRACTICE TEST 3 - Short Answer

1. _____ are positions in society that are regulated by norms that describe how people in those positions should behave.

2. In the obedience study by Milgram, psychologists were surprised to find that _____ gave all the shocks.

3. In the prison study, the "prisoners" became panicky and helpless and some of the guards became tyrannical and cruel. Their behavior probably depended on the _____ they were asked to play.

4. The obedience and the prison study demonstrate the power of social roles to influence behavior. Some of the reasons that people obey authority, even when it's not in their own interest or may violate their own values are the rules of good _____ and _____, which occurs when commitment to a course of action is escalated.

5. How the social environment influences thoughts, beliefs, and memories and how people's perceptions of themselves and others affect their relationships is the subject matter of social _____.

6. A _____ attribution identifies the cause of an action as something in the environment.

7. The tendency to overestimate _____ factors and underestimate the influence of the _____ when explaining someone else's behavior describes the _____ attribution error.

8. The _____ occurs when people take credit for positive actions and attribute the bad ones to the situation.

9. The need to believe the world is fair and that good people are rewarded and bad people are punished. This is called the _____.

10. A relatively stable opinion that contains an emotional element and a cognitive element is a(n) _____.

11. The more a statement is repeated, the more people will believe that it is true. This is the _____ effect.

12. _____ persuasion techniques suppress people's ability to reason, to think critically, and to make good choices.

13. _____ refers to a behavior performed when carrying out an order from someone in authority; whereas, _____ refers to behavior or attitudes that occur as a result of real or imagined group pressure.

14. Certain historical decisions have been made by strong leaders who discouraged disagreement, did not get opinions from people outside the group, and where unanimous decisions were preferred. These decisions were a result of _____.

15. Rather than bystander apathy, _____ may account for why crowds of people fail to respond to an emergency.

16. One reason for social loafing in a work group may be that the work is _____.

17. _____ increases a person's willingness to do harm to someone else, to cheat and to break the law. It may also be a primary reason for mob violence.

18. _____, or the willingness to take risks or dangerous action for others, may be a result of a combination of conscience and situational influences.

19. People have a(n) _____ identity based on their nationality, ethnic heritage, occupation, and social roles.

20. "We" are good, noble, and humane; "they" are bad, stupid, and cruel. Such beliefs reflect _____.

21. Believing that all "Wispians" are good in math, is a(n) _____. Disliking and refusing to live next to a Wispian is an example of _____.

22. One way stereotypes distort reality is that they _____ differences between groups and _____ differences within groups.

23. "Welfare abuse" and "reverse discrimination" are thought to be _____.

24. The "cycle of _____" can result from unfamiliarity or discomfort with a group.

25. Social and cultural psychologists suggest that human behavior depends more on _____ organization than on human nature.

PRACTICE TEST 4 - True/False

1. T F Norms are social conventions that regulate human life, including explicit laws and implicit cultural standards.

2. T F In Milgram's obedience study, if the confederates who were supposed to be receiving shocks asked subjects to discontinue the shocks in a calm manner a majority of the subjects agreed.

3. T F Although some of the students in the prison study who were assigned to be guards became tyrannical and aggressive, most of the other "guards" protected the prisoners and reported any cruel treatment to the researchers.

4. T F Researchers concluded that one reason people obey, even when it is not in their interest or when it conflicts with their values, is that people don't have the words to be rude and disobey.

5. T F Social cognition is an area in social psychology concerned with the social influences on thought, memory, perception, and other cognitive processes.

6. T F A relatively stable opinion containing a cognitive element and an emotional element is an attribution.

7. T F Situational and dispositional are two types of attributions. We are more likely to overestimate situational factors and underestimate dispositional factors when explaining someone else's behavior.

8. T F Attitudes can change to reduce cognitive dissonance.

9. T F Fear tactics, such as those used in drug and AIDS prevention campaigns, are very effective at changing behavior.

10. T F The more a statement is repeated, the more people will believe that it is true.

11. T F Although research has found that conformity has declined since the 1950s, under certain conditions conformity will increase.

12. T F Groupthink refers to an increase in group effectiveness that occurs when group members have the opportunity to engage in open and honest discussions.

13. T F Social loafing is an example of diffusion of responsibility in groups.

14.   T F   Deindividuation occurs when a person loses all awareness of his or her individuality and sense of self. It is considered a prime reason for mob violence.

15.   T F   The presence of an ally increases the likelihood that a person will disobey an authority.

16.   T F   One reason people may dissent or disobey is because they have become entrapped.

17.   T F   Social identity is the belief that one's own culture is superior.

18   T F   Competition tends to increase motivation and a sense of security while it decreases frustration and hostility.

19.   T F   Stereotypes, like prejudices, are generally negative.

20.   T F   Stereotypes play an important role in human thinking. They help us process new information, allow us to organize experience, make sense of differences among individuals and groups, and predict how people will behave.

21.   T F   Stereotypes distort thinking in three ways. One way is that they make the stereotyped group seem odd, unfamiliar, or dangerous, not like "us."

22.   T F   Most researchers agree that prejudice in North America is decreasing.

23.   T F   One condition that is necessary for reducing prejudice is that both sides must have equal legal status, economic opportunities, and power.

24.   T F   When any two groups are in direct competition for jobs, prejudice between them increases.

25.   T F   Harm to others is done by people who are psychologically disturbed or are "evil."

PRACTICE TEST 5 - Essay

1. Identify the influences and effects of roles and norms in the prison study and the obedience study.

2. A group of students were asked to explain the source of a person's grades. They provided the explanations below. Examine each explanation and identify the explanatory device it relies upon.

    A. Grades result from a person's intelligence and self-discipline. When these are high, grades are good and vice versa.

    B. Grades depend on doing the right things. A person should earn good grades for reading instructions, meeting deadlines, turning in assignments. If a person does not do these things, he or she should receive bad grades.

    C. Grades depend on quality teaching and educational materials. If the teacher is good, students should be motivated and do well.

    D. Grades depend on luck. Sometimes it doesn't matter whether a person has studied or not if the test is tricky.

3. You need to get a "B" in all of your classes to get the scholarship you need. You are right on the border between a "B" and a "C" in your Spanish class. Using information on persuasion, discuss how you might approach your Spanish teacher to attempt to persuade him to give you the benefit of the doubt.

4. Dr. Wong requires a group project in her sociology class. She wants each group to design a federally funded project to reduce the number of homeless and provide appropriate services for those who remain homeless. She is aware of all the principles of group behavior and she wants to reduce the likelihood of social loafing, diffusion of responsibility, groupthink, deindividuation, group polarization and competition. She wants to increase cooperation and independent action. Develop a set of instructions she should use to meet all of her goals for this assignment.

5. Jan and her sister are having a debate about the Agyflops, people from a country located in the Pacific Ocean. Jan's sister does not like the Agyflops and is explaining why to Jan. Most of her reasons are based on stereotypes. For each statement Jan's sister makes, indicate which problem with stereotypes it exemplifies.

    A.   "When I visited Agyflopia, everyone was so unfriendly. No one smiled."

    B.   "They are so different from us. Americans are so direct, but you never what the Agyflops are thinking."

    C.   "I guess that there are many Agyflops in school with us, but they never seem to speak correctly and they always seem so stupid."

    D.   "Once I saw two Agyflops being stopped by the police. I think they are basically dishonest people."

6. Why is prejudice so hard to eliminate? You are the principal of a school with students from many different backgrounds. Design a program that attempts to improve relationships and reduce prejudice.

CHAPTER 9

Thinking and Intelligence

LEARNING OBJECTIVES

1.   Define thinking.

2.   Define and distinguish among concepts (including basic concepts and prototypes), propositions and cognitive schemas.

3.   Distinguish among subconscious processes, nonconscious processes and mindless conscious processing.

4.   Distinguish between an algorithm and a heuristic.

5.   Distinguish among reflective judgment, inductive, deductive and dialectical reasoning, and between informal and formal reasoning.

6.   List and describe the stages of reflective judgment, according to studies by King and Kitchener.

7.   Discuss six types of cognitive bias that can influence reasoning.

8.   Describe the conditions under which people are most likely to try to reduce dissonance.

9.   Define and explain the g factor in intelligence.

10. Distinguish between the psychometric approach and cognitive approaches to intelligence.

11. Discuss the objectives, uses and criticisms of IQ tests.

12. Describe the components of Sternberg's theory of intelligence and discuss whether these components are measured on most intelligence tests.

13. Describe Gardner's theory of multiple intelligences.

14. Describe factors other than intelligence that contribute to achievement.

15. Discuss the cognitive abilities found in nonhuman animals.

CHAPTER CONCEPT MAP

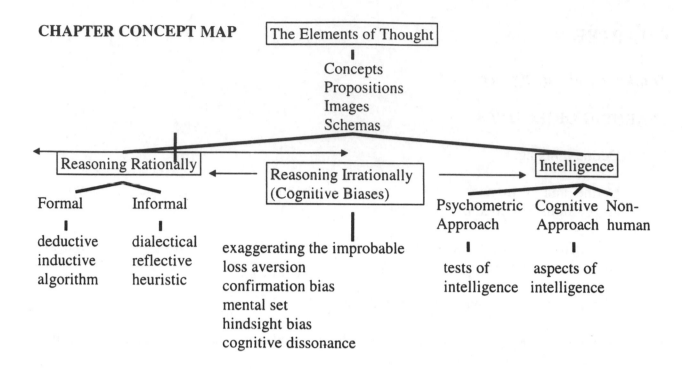

The Elements of Thought

Concepts
Propositions
Images
Schemas

Reasoning Rationally

Formal   Informal

deductive   dialectical
inductive   reflective
algorithm   heuristic

Reasoning Irrationally
(Cognitive Biases)

exaggerating the improbable
loss aversion
confirmation bias
mental set
hindsight bias
cognitive dissonance

Intelligence

Psychometric   Cognitive   Non-
Approach   Approach   human

tests of   aspects of
intelligence   intelligence

BRIEF CHAPTER SUMMARY

Chapter 9 examines the elements and processes of thinking. Concepts, propositions, schemas and images are all elements of thought. Deductive and inductive reasoning are types of formal reasoning that are useful for well-specified problems that have a single right answer. Dialectical reasoning and reflective judgment are types of informal reasoning that are useful for more complex problems that require critical thinking. Several cognitive biases affect rational thinking and cause cognitive errors and distortions. Intelligence is a characteristic that is difficult to define but is related to one's ability to think. Theorists examine intelligence from two approaches: the psychometric approach, which attempts to measure intelligence through tests, and the cognitive approach, which examines the aspects or domains of intelligence. Gardner's and Sternberg's theories are described. Intellectual achievement as measured by test scores is heavily influenced by such factors as motivation and attitude. Finally, psychologists have been interested in the cognitive abilities of nonhumans. Whether animals have language has been studied and debated; both sides of this issue are discussed.

PREVIEW OUTLINE AND REVIEW QUESTIONS

Before you read the chapter, review the preview outline and the Learning Objectives for each section of the text. Answer all questions as you read the text.

SECTION 1 - THOUGHT: USING WHAT WE KNOW (PP. 306-309)

I. THOUGHT: USING WHAT WE KNOW
   A. **The elements of** _____
      1. Thinking - mental _____ of internal representations of objects, activities and situations
      2. Concepts - a mental _____ that groups objects, relations, activities, abstractions or qualities having common properties
         a. _____ concepts - those with a moderate number of instances
         b. Prototype - most representative example of a concept
      3. _____ - units of meaning made up of concepts that express a unitary idea
      4. Cognitive schemas - _____ that are linked together in networks of knowledge, associations, beliefs and expectations
      5. Mental images - mental representations, often visual but can be in any sense
   B. **How conscious is thought?**
      1. Subconscious processes - _____ of awareness but can be made conscious; include many automatic routines
      2. _____ processes - outside of awareness but affect behavior; intuition
      3. Mindlessness - acting, speaking, making decisions out of habit

Answer these Learning Objectives while you read Section 1.

1. Define thinking.

2. Define and distinguish among concepts (including basic concepts and prototypes), propositions and cognitive schemas.

3. Distinguish among subconscious processes, nonconscious processes and mindless conscious processing.

SECTION 2 - REASONING RATIONALLY (PP. 310-316)

II. **REASONING RATIONALLY**
    A.   **Reasoning** - _purposeful_ mental activity that involves operating on information in order to reach conclusions; drawing inferences from observations or facts

    B.   **Formal reasoning: Algorithms and logic** - the information that is needed is specified and there is a right answer
        1. _Algorithms_ - procedures guaranteed to produce a solution (a recipe)
        2. _Deductive_ reasoning - if the premises are true, the conclusion must be true; it is easy to reverse the premises and reach an incorrect conclusion
        3. Inductive reasoning - the conclusion probably follows from the premises, but could conceivably be false; used in science, but new information can always prove the conclusion wrong

    C.   **Informal reasoning: Heuristics and dialectical thinking** - may be incomplete information, no clear answer, many approaches, views, or solutions may compete
        1. _Heuristics_ - rules of thumb that suggest a course of action without guaranteeing an optimal solution
        2. Dialectical reasoning - process of comparing and evaluating opposing points of view to resolve differences (used by juries to reach a verdict)

    D.   **Reflective judgment**
        1. _____ judgment - critical thinking; the ability to evaluate and integrate evidence, relate evidence to theory or opinion, and reach conclusions
        2. Research of King and Kitchener identified seven cognitive stages of reflective judgment
            a. _____ stages - assume a knowable and correct answer exists; no distinction between knowledge and belief, or belief and evidence
            b. Middle or quasi-_____ stages - recognize that some things can't be known with certainty, but unsure how to deal with this
            c. Last stages of reflective judgment - understand that some things can not be known with certainty; some judgments are more valid than others

Answer these Learning Objectives while you read Section 2.

4.   Distinguish between an algorithm and a heuristic.

5.   Distinguish among reflective judgment, inductive, deductive and dialectical reasoning, and between informal and formal reasoning.

6.   List and describe the stages of reflective judgment, according to studies by King and Kitchener.

SECTION 3 - BARRIERS TO REASONING RATIONALLY (PP. 316-324)

III. **BARRIERS TO REASONING RATIONALLY**
   A. **Human thought processes are subject to predictable biases**
   B. **Exaggerating the** _____; influenced by the availability _____ (the tendency to judge the probability of an event by how easy it is to think of examples)
   C. **Avoiding loss** - making decisions based on avoiding loss
   D. _____ **bias** - paying attention to information that confirms what we believe while ignoring information that opposes our beliefs (disconfirmation bias)
   E. **Biases due to mental sets** - trying to solve problems by using the same heuristics, strategies, and rules that worked in the past on similar problems
   F. **The hindsight bias** - believing that an outcome was known all along
   G. **The need for cognitive consistency** - motivation to reduce a state of tension (cognitive dissonance) that occurs when a person simultaneously holds two cognitions that are psychologically inconsistent or holds a belief that is inconsistent with the person's behavior
      1. Conditions under which people are most likely to try to reduce dissonance
         a. When people feel they have _____ made a decision
         b. When actions violate self-concept
         c. When people put a lot of _____ into a decision and the results are less than they hoped for; justification of effort
      2. Cognitive-dissonance theory has limitations
      3. The motive for consistency can lead to irrational decisions in some cases
   H. **Overcoming our cognitive biases** - cognitive biases are less likely under certain conditions
      1. When people have some _____ in an area
      2. When decisions have serious consequences
      3. When people understand the bias

Answer these Learning Objectives while you read Section 3.

7. Discuss six types of cognitive bias that can influence reasoning.

8. Describe the conditions under which people are most likely to try to reduce dissonance.

	N	E	S	W
Daisy²	O	O	O	X
Patsy	X	O	O	O
Jake	O	X	O	O
Fritz	O	O	X	O

SECTION 4 - MEASURING INTELLIGENCE: THE PSYCHOMETRIC APPROACH (PP. 324-330)
SECTION 5 - DISSECTING INTELLIGENCE: THE COGNITIVE APPROACH (PP. 330-335) AND SECTION 6 - ANIMAL MINDS (PP. 336-340)

IV. **MEASURING INTELLIGENCE: THE PSYCHOMETRIC APPROACH**
   A.   **Disagreements exist on the nature of intelligence**
      1.   Factor _____ is a procedure used to identify which abilities that underlie performance on the various tasks on an intelligence test
      2.   Many believe in a general ability, or g factor, underlying all other abilities
   B.   **The psychometric approach** - traditional approach that focuses on how well people perform on standardized mental tests
      1.   Types of tests
         a.   _Achievement tests_ - measure skills and knowledge that have been taught
         b.   _Aptitude_ test - measures ability to acquire skills and knowledge
      2.   The invention of IQ tests
         a.   Binet's brainstorm: a test to identify slow learners
            (1)   Measured a child's _mental_ age (MA) [_maturity_] - intellectual development relative to other children's
            (2)   The scoring system which compared mental age to _chron._ age (CA) to yield intelligence quotient (IQ) was flawed
         b.   Today, individual scores are compared to established norms and distributions of scores approximate a normal curve
      3.   The IQ test comes to America
         a.   Terman established norms for American children
         b.   _Wechsler_ developed test for adults (Wechsler Adult Intelligence Scale or WAIS) and children (Wechsler Intelligence Scale for Children or WISC) - both have been revised
         c.   Produced general IQ and scores on verbal and performance subtests
         d.   Binet said tests sample intelligence, they are not intelligence itself
         e.   In the U.S. tests were used to categorize people, not help slow learners and the diversity of the U.S. population was overlooked
      4.   Can IQ tests be culture- _free_
         a.   IQ tests from mid-1900s favored middle-class, white, city children
         b.   Development of culture-free tests (non-verbal tests) and culture-fair tests (used items common to many cultures) tried to eliminate bias
         c.   These were not very successful since culture's effects are pervasive
      5.   Expectations, stereotypes, and IQ scores
         a.   Scores are influenced by expectations which shape stereotypes, which can affect scores by creating doubt called stereotype threat
         b.   Positive stereotypes can improve performance

[handwritten margin note, left side:] attempts to write c-f are extremely difficult b/c everything we do is affected by culture, including taking the test

[handwritten note at bottom:] performance depends on expectations of themselves, for themselves & others are affected on stereotypes

6. The dilemma of differences - how can educators eliminate bias from the tests, while preserving the purpose of the tests (recognize mastery)

7. Beyond the IQ test
   a. Tests have value (to predict school performance, to recognize the retarded and gifted)
   b. Some say we should address problems that group differences show, others say they do more harm than good
   c. Educators must recognize the limits of the tests and use them better

V. DISSECTING INTELLIGENCE: THE COGNITIVE APPROACH

A. Cognitive approaches emphasize problem-solving strategies

B. The Triarchi theory of intelligence - Robert Sternberg identifies three aspects
   1. _____ intelligence - internal information-processing strategies including problem recognition, identification, implementation and evaluation of problem-solving strategies; requires metacognition
   2. Experiential intelligence - ability to transfer skills to new situations
   3. _____ intelligence - practical application of intelligence (tacit intelligence); knowing when to adapt to, change or modify an environment

C. The theory of multiple intelligences
   1. Gardner's theory of multiple intelligences
      a. Seven domains: linguistic, logical-mathematical, spatial, musical, bodily-kinesthetic, intrapersonal, and interpersonal
      b. The last two are considered emotional intelligence; there may be a biological basis for emotional intelligence
      c. Each "intelligence" is independent - may have own neural structure

D. Thinking critically about intelligence(s)
   1. There is disagreement about the idea of new intelligences
   2. Some say some of Gardner's domains are personality traits or talents
   3. These theories have caused new thinking about intelligence, like dynamic testing and teaching other types of skills to children

E. Motivation and intellectual success
   1. Terman study showed that _____ was determining factor in life success
   2. Cultural attitudes and motivation
      a. Stevenson study found that Asian students far outperformed American children on math tests and the gap is increasing
      b. Differences could not be accounted for by educational resources or intellectual abilities
      c. Results explained by differences in attitudes, expectations, efforts
         (1) Beliefs about intelligence - American parents are more likely than Asian parents to believe math ability was innate
         (2) Standards - American parents had _____ standards for their children's performance

        (3)   Conflicts - Americans had more conflicting demands

        (4)   Values - American students did not value education as much as Asian students

VI. ANIMAL MINDS

   A.   **Animal intelligence** - subject of study in cognitive ethology
      1.   Cognitive ethologists say animals anticipate future events, make plans, coordinate their activities with others of their species
      2.   Even complex actions may involve prewired behavior, not cognition
      3.   Some behaviors do demonstrate cognitive abilities
   B.   **Animals and language**
      1.   Primary ingredient in human cognition is language
      2.   Criteria for language
         a.   Meaningfulness - adequate ability to refer to things, ideas, feelings
         b.   _____ - permits communication about objects not present
         c.   Productivity - ability to produce and comprehend new utterances
      3.   By these criteria, animals communicate but do not have language
      4.   Early efforts to teach language had success which was followed by skepticism and recognition of methodological problems in the research
      5.   Newer research better controlled; has found that with training animals can use symbols, signs, understand some words, learn without formal training
      6.   Some evidence nonprimates can acquire aspects of language
   C.   **Thinking about the thinking of animals**
      1.   Scientists divided on the meaning of the studies questioned
      2.   Concerns about anthropomorphism and anthropocentrism

Answer these Learning Objectives while you read Section 4, 5 and 6.

9.   Define and explain the g factor in intelligence.

10.   Distinguish between the psychometric and cognitive approaches to intelligence.

11.   Discuss the objectives, uses and criticisms of IQ tests.

12.   Describe the components of Sternberg's theory of intelligence and discuss whether these components are measured on most intelligence tests.

13.   Describe Gardner's theory of multiple intelligences.

14.   Describe factors other than intelligence that contribute to achievement.

15.   Discuss the cognitive abilities found in nonhuman animals.

FLASH CARDS

Cut the following chart along the borders and test yourself with the resulting flash cards.

9.1 THINKING	9.2 CONCEPT	9.3 BASIC CONCEPT
9.4 PROTOTYPE	9.5 PROPOSITION	9.6 COGNITIVE SCHEMA
9.7 MENTAL IMAGE	9.8 SUBCONSCIOUS PROCESSES	9.9 NONCONSCIOUS PROCESSES
9.10 MINDLESSNESS	9.11 REASONING	9.12 ALGORITHM
9.13 HEURISTICS	9.14 PREMISE	9.15 DEDUCTIVE REASONING
9.16 INDUCTIVE REASONING	9.17 INFORMAL VERSUS FORMAL REASONING	9.18 DIALECTICAL REASONING

9.3 A concept that has a moderate number of instances and that is easier to acquire than those having few or many instances.	9.2 A mental category that groups objects, relations, activities, abstractions, or qualities having common properties.	9.1 The mental manipulation of information stored in the form of concepts, images or propositions.
9.6 An integrated mental network of knowledge, beliefs, and expectations concerning a particular topic or aspect of the world.	9.5 A unit of meaning that is made up of concepts and expresses a single idea.	9.4 An especially representative example of a concept.
9.9 Mental processes occurring outside of and not available to conscious awareness.	9.8 Mental processes occurring outside of conscious awareness but accessible to consciousness when necessary.	9.7 A mental representation that mirrors or resembles the thing it represents; mental images can occur in many and perhaps all sensory modalities.
9.12 A problem-solving strategy guaranteed to produce a solution even if the user does not know how it works.	9.11 The drawing of conclusions or inferences from observations, facts or assumptions.	9.10 Mental inertia; conscious thinking but not hard thinking; making decisions out of habit rather than consideration of the information.
9.15 A form of reasoning in which a conclusion follows necessarily from certain premises; if the premises are true, the conclusion must be.	9.14 A series of observations or propositions.	9.13 A rule of thumb that suggests a course of action or guides problem solving but does not guarantee an optimal solution.
9.18 A process in which opposing facts or ideas are weighed and compared, with a view to determining the best solution. senses.	9.17 Formal reasoning gives the needed information and there is a correct answer; Informal reasoning may lack complete information or a clear solution.	9.16 A form of reasoning in which the premises provide support for a conclusion, but it is still possible for the conclusion to be false.

9.19 REFLECTIVE JUDGMENT	**9.20 PREREFLECTIVE STAGES**	**9.21 QUASI-REFLECTIVE STAGES**
9.22 REFLECTIVE STAGES	**9.23 AVAILABILITY HEURISTIC**	**9.24 AVOIDANCE OF LOSS**
9.25 CONFIRMATION BIAS	**9.26 MENTAL SET**	**9.27 HINDSIGHT BIAS**
9.28 COGNITIVE DISSONANCE	**9.29 POSTDECISION DISSONANCE**	**9.30 JUSTIFICATION OF EFFORT**
9.31 INTELLIGENCE	**9.32 FACTOR ANALYSIS**	**9.33 G FACTOR**
9.34 PSYCHOMETRIC APPROACH TO INTELLIGENCE	**9.35 ACHIEVEMENT VERSUS APTITUDE TESTS**	**9.36 MENTAL AGE (MA)**

9.21 The middle stages of reflective thought. Those in this stage recognize that some things cannot be known with certainty.	**9.20** The early stages of reflective thought. Those in this stage assume that a correct answer exists and it can be obtained through the senses.	**9.19** Critical thinking; the ability to evaluate and integrate evidence, relate it to a theory or opinion and reach a conclusion.
9.24 A cognitive bias. The tendency to make decisions to try and avoid or minimize risks and losses.	**9.23** The tendency to judge the probability of a type of event by how easy it is to think of examples or instances.	**9.22** The last stages in the development of reflective thought in which a person becomes capable of reflective judgment.
9.27 The tendency to overestimate one's ability to have predicted an event once the outcome is known; the "I knew it all along" belief.	**9.26** A tendency to solve problems using procedures that worked before on similar problems.	**9.25** The tendency to look for or pay attention only to information that confirms one's own belief.
9.30 The tendency of individuals to increase their liking for something that they have worked hard to attain; a form of dissonance reduction.	**9.29** "Buyers regret." Following a purchase, the concern that you made the wrong decision. Cognitive dissonance theory predicts you'll try to resolve it.	**9.28** A state of tension that occurs when a person holds two inconsistent cognitions, or when a person's belief is incongruent with his or her behavior.
9.33 A general intellectual ability assumed by some theorists to underlie specific mental abilities and talents.	**9.32** A statistical method for analyzing test scores. Clusters of highly correlated scores are assumed to measure the same underlying trait or ability.	**9.31** An inferred characteristic usually defined as the ability to profit from experience, acquire knowledge, think abstractly, act purposefully, adapt to changes.
9.36 A measure of mental development expressed in terms of the average mental ability at a given age.	**9.35** Achievement tests measure skills and knowledge that have been taught. Aptitude tests measure the ability to acquire future skills or knowledge.	**9.34** The traditional approach to intelligence that focuses on how well people perform on standardized mental tests.

9.37 INTELLIGENCE QUOTIENT	9.38 STANFORD-BINET INTELLIGENCE SCALE	9.39 WECHSLER ADULT INTELLIGENCE SCALE (WAIS)
9.40 WECHSLER INTELLIGENCE SCALE FOR CHILDREN (WISC)	9.41 CULTURE-FREE TESTS	9.42 CULTURE-FAIR TESTS
9.43 COGNITIVE APPROACHES TO INTELLIGENCE	9.44 TRIARCHIC THEORY OF INTELLIGENCE	9.45 COMPONENTIAL INTELLIGENCE
9.46 EXPERIENTIAL INTELLIGENCE	9.47 CONTEXTUAL INTELLIGENCE	9.48 PRACTICAL INTELLIGENCE
9.49 TACIT KNOWLEDGE	9.50 METACOGNITION	9.51 THEORY OF MULTIPLE INTELLIGENCES
9.52 EMOTIONAL INTELLIGENCE	9.53 COGNITIVE ETHOLOGY	9.54 ANTHROPOMORPHISM
9.55 ANTHROPOCENTRISM	9.56 CONVERGENT VERSUS DIVERGENT THINKING	9.57 CRITERIA FOR LANGUAGE

9.39 An intelligence test designed by David Wechsler expressly for adults; developed two decades after the Stanford-Binet.	9.38 The adaptation of Binet's intelligence test for American children. The test was revised by Stanford psychologist, Lewis Terman.	9.37 A measure of intelligence originally computed by dividing mental age by chronological age and multiplying by 100. Now derived from norms.
9.42 Tests designed to eliminate culture bias in intelligence tests. They aimed to include knowledge and skills common to many cultures.	9.41 Tests designed to eliminate culture bias in testing by eliminating the influence of culture. The tests were usually non-verbal.	9.40 An intelligent test designed by David Wechsler for children. It yields a general IQ score and specific scores for different abilities.
9.45 An aspect of intelligence in the triarchic theory; includes information-processing strategies involved in intelligent thinking.	9.44 A theory of intelligence developed by Sternberg that identifies three aspects of intelligence: componential, experiential and contextual.	9.43 Emphasize the strategies people use when think about problems and arriving at solutions.
9.48 The ability to behave intelligently in real life; reveals itself in ordinary behavior.	9.47 An aspect of intelligence in the triarchic theory; refers to the application of intelligence and the ability to take different contexts into account.	9.46 An aspect of intelligence in the triarchic theory; includes the ability to transfer skills to new situations and to cope well with novelty.
9.51 Gardner's theory that suggests that there are actually seven relatively independent domains of talent.	9.50 The knowledge or awareness of one's own cognitive processes.	9.49 Strategies for success that are not explicitly taught but that must be inferred instead.
9.54 The tendency to falsely attribute human qualities to nonhuman beings.	9.53 The study of cognitive processes in nonhuman animals.	9.52 The ability to identify your own and other people's emotions accurately, express your emotions clearly, and regulate emotions in yourself.
9.57 The criteria for language include meaningfulness, displacement, productivity.	9.56 Convergent thinking follows a particular set of steps that are expected to converge on a solution. Divergent thinking explores multiple solutions.	9.55 The tendency to think that human beings have nothing in common with other animals.

254

ACROSS

1. cognitive bias in which one only looks for information that agrees with one's beliefs
2. solving new problems using the same heuristics that have worked in the past
4. mental manipulation of information
7. units of meaning made up of concepts
13. tension from holding two inconsistent beliefs
15. drawing conclusions from observations, facts, assumptions
16. type of reasoning in which a conclusion follows necessarily from certain premises
17. type of intelligence in Sternberg's theory

DOWN

1. mental category that groups things by common properties
3. aspect of intelligence that includes the ability to transfer skills to new situations
5. rules of thumb suggesting a course of action
6. an inferred characteristic
8. instances that are most representative of a concept
9. integrated mental networks
10. reasoning in which premises provide support for a certain conclusion, but the conclusion may still be false
11. mental processes occurring outside of and not available to conscious awareness
12. the knowledge or awareness of one's own cognitive processes
14. theory of intelligence identifying three aspects of intelligence

PRACTICE TEST 1 - Multiple Choice

1. The ability to think
   A. is defined as the physical manipulation of the environment.
   B. confines us to the immediate present.
   C. allows for the mental manipulation of internal representations of objects, activities and situations.
   D. incorporates all of the above.

2. A mental category that groups things that have common properties is called a
   A. concept.   B. symbol.
   C. proposition.   D. schema.

3. Relationships between concepts are expressed by
   A. super concepts.   B. symbols.
   C. propositions.   D. schemas.

4. What are propositions linked together in complex networks?
   A. basic concepts   B. mental images
   C. prototypes   D. cognitive schemas

5. Knitting, typing and driving a car are performed by using
   A. subconscious processes.   B. mindlessness.
   C. nonconscious processes.   D. none of the above.

6. Nonconscious processes refer to
   A. processes that can be brought into consciousness when necessary.
   B. decisions that are made without thinking very hard.
   C. processes that are outside awareness but affect behavior.
   D. the practice of operating on information in order to reach conclusions.

7. "All cats have fur. This animal is a cat. Therefore, it has fur." This is an example of
   A. deductive reasoning.   B. dialectical reasoning.
   C. inductive reasoning.   D. divergent thinking.

8. Inductive reasoning
   A. is used when the premises provide support for the conclusion, but the conclusion still could be false.
   B. is often used in scientific thinking.
   C. allows for a specific conclusion.
   D. incorporates all of the above.

9. When information is incomplete or many viewpoints compete, it is necessary to use
   A. informal reasoning.
   B. formal reasoning.
   C. inductive reasoning.
   D. deductive reasoning.

10. For complicated problems in real life, it is best to use
   A. dialectical reasoning.
   B. informal reasoning.
   C. reflective judgment.
   D. all of the above.

11. When asked about his views on abortion, Carl responds, "That's what I was brought up to believe." According to Kitchener and King, he is in the _____ stage of reflective thought.
   A. quasi-reflective
   B. prereflective
   C. reflective judgment
   D. none of the above

12. People are more likely to take risks
   A. for a potentially more rewarding solution than for a smaller sure gain.
   B. if the risks are perceived as a way to avoid loss.
   C. when the results are explained in terms of lives saved not lives lost.
   D. none of the above.

13. Which of the following helps to explain the popularity of lotteries and why people buy earthquake insurance?
   A. confirmation bias
   B. loss aversion
   C. exaggerating the improbable
   D. hindsight bias

14. Unless your coursework is totally determined for you, you probably use _____ to decide what courses to take.
   A. an algorithm
   B. a heuristic
   C. deductive reasoning
   D. hindsight

15. The g factor refers to
   A. a general ability that underlies all specific abilities.
   B. a technique using factor analysis.
   C. the psychometric approach to intelligence.
   D. all of the above.

16. The psychometric approach to intelligence focuses on
   A. culture-free and culture-fair tests.
   B. how well people perform on standardized mental tests.
   C. those with learning disabilities.
   D. strategies people use when problem solving.

257

17. Dr. Bell is more interested in how students arrive at their answers on IQ tests than in their scores. This represents
   A. the psychometric approach to intelligence. B.   the triarchic theory.
   C. the cognitive approach to intelligence.   D.   practical intelligence.

18. Which of the following is one of the criticisms of IQ tests?
   A. Tests are used to "track" people rather than identify strengths and weaknesses.
   B. Tests favor some children over others.
   C. Test-users have thought that tests reveal a person's natural ability.
   D. all of the above

19. Componential, experiential, and contextual refer to
   A. Gardner's domains of intelligence.   B.   aspects of metacognition.
   C. the triarchic theory of intelligence.   D.   divergent thinking.

20. Which of the following are measured on most intelligence tests?
   A. experiential intelligence   B.   componential intelligence
   C. contextual intelligence   D.   all of the above

21. Gardner's theory best explains which of the following?
   A. savant syndrome   B.   gifted people
   C. retarded people   D.   people of average intelligence

22. Gardner's theory suggests that there is/are
   A. three types of intelligence.
   B. seven, relatively independent, intelligences.
   C. seven, highly overlapping, intelligences.
   D. a single, overall intelligence called a g factor

23. Based on the studies comparing Asian and American school children, which of the following contributes to achievement?
   A. whether skills are seen as innate or learned
   B. standards for performance
   C. expectation for involvement in outside activities
   D. all of the above

24. Cognitive ethology refers to the study of cognitive processes in
   A. humans.
   B. children.
   C. the elderly.
   D. nonhumans.

25. Which of the following summarizes the current thinking on language ability in nonhumans?
    A.   Nonhumans are able to use the basics of language.
    B.   Though animals have greater cognitive abilities than is often thought, scientists are divided on this issue.
    C.   Animals do not demonstrate any of the aspects of human language.
    D.   Only primates (chimpanzees and gorillas) have shown any type of language abilities.

PRACTICE TEST 2 - Multiple Choice

1. Which of the following represents some type of thinking?
    A. looking over your transcript to see what courses you still need
    B. knitting a sweater
    C. having a solution "pop into your mind"
    D. all of the above

2. Which concept is most basic?
    A. footwear   B. high heels
    C. shoes   D. clothing

3. Propositions are
    A. complicated networks of knowledge.   B. prototypes.
    C. units of meaning made up of concepts. D. composed of cognitive schemas.

4. "Professors are intelligent." This represents a
    A. concept.   B. proposition.
    C. cognitive schema.   D. mental image.

5. Intuition is an example of
    A. a subconscious process.   B. a nonconscious process.
    C. mindlessness.   D. a conscious process.

6. Processes that are automated, such as typing or driving, are called _____, whereas making decisions without stopping to analyze what we are doing makes use of
    _____.
    A. subconscious processes; nonconscious processes
    B. mindlessness; subconscious processes
    C. nonconscious processes; mindlessness
    D. subconscious processes; mindlessness

7. Dr. Rey does not give "A"s. You are taking Dr. Rey's class. You probably will not get an "A". This is an example of
    A. formal reasoning.   B. inductive reasoning
    C. logic.   D. all of the above.

8. Dialectical is to deductive as
    A. deductive is to inductive.   B. formal is to informal.
    C. informal is to formal.   D. dialectic is to reflective.

260

9. What type of reasoning should Raoul use to decide what to do about his failing marriage?
    A. inductive   B. reflective judgment
    C. deductive   D. all of the above

10. The problem in Raoul's marriage is that his wife is unhappy with their traditional roles. Despite the fact that his marriage might fail, Raoul is unwilling to try anything different. He says "This is the way I was brought up to believe marriages should be." He is in the _____ stage of reasoning, according to King and Kitchener's model.
    A. prereflective   B. quasi-reflective
    C. reflective   D. oral

11. During a financial consultation, Ms. Brandt suggests investment strategies for the Washingtons' retirement plan. The strategy is based on
    A. formal logic.   B. inductive reasoning.
    C. a heuristic.   D. none of the above.

12. Though Allison lives comfortably in a city with a high crime rate, she is afraid to visit California because of a potential earthquake. Which cognitive bias does this represent?
    A. loss aversion   B. availability heuristic
    C. cognitive dissonance   D. confirmation bias

13. Harry and Larry are in a very boring class. It is a required course for Harry, but Larry chose to take this course and it is too late to withdraw. What is likely to happen?
    A. Harry is likely to try to reduce dissonance by saying he likes the class.
    B. Larry is likely to try to reduce dissonance by saying he likes the class.
    C. Larry is not likely to experience any dissonance.
    D. Both are likely to experience dissonance.

14. Gardner's theory takes the opposite point of view of which approach to intelligence?
    A. factor analysis   B. triarchic approach
    C. componential approach   D. g factor

15. The Stanford-Binet and the Wechsler tests represent which approach to intelligence?
    A. psychometric approach   B. triarchic approach
    C. cognitive approach   D. all of the above

16. The psychometric approach to intelligence is to the cognitive approach as
    A. problem solving is to test scores.
    B. test scores are to problem solving.
    C. the triarchic theory is to the theory of multiple intelligences.
    D. the g factor is to triarchic theory.

17. Stephanie is strong in componential intelligence. She should do well on
   A. conventional mental tests.   B. recognizing a problem.
   C. selecting good problem-solving strategies. D. all of the above.

18. Though Emily has never travelled overseas before, she is coping well with and adapting well to new situations on her trip to Europe. Which type of intelligence is involved?
   A. componential   B. contextual
   C. experiential   D. metacognitive

19. How did the use of Binet's test change when it was brought to America?
   A. The advantages of individualized testing were lost.
   B. The test was no longer used to bring slow learners up to average.
   C. The tests were used to "track" people according to their presumed "natural" ability.
   D. All of the above occurred.

20. As an item on an intelligence test, asking whether the "Emperor" concerto was written by Beethoven, Mozart, Bach, Brahms or Mahler represents which problem with this kind of test?
   A. IQ tests are seen as revealing the limits of a child's potential.
   B. Low scoring children do not get the attention or encouragement they need.
   C. The tests favor children from certain backgrounds.
   D. The tests are sex biased.

21. The fact that people with brain damage often lose one of several mental abilities without losing their competence in others supports
   A. Sternberg's theory.   B. Gardner's theory.
   C. Terman's theory.   D. none of the above

22. According to Gardner, actors, athletes, and dancers use _____, whereas having insight into oneself and others requires the use of _____.
   A. logical-mathematical intelligence; spatial intelligence
   B. spatial intelligence; emotional intelligence
   C. bodily-kinesthetic intelligence; emotional intelligence
   D. interpersonal intelligence; logical intelligence

23. Jacob's IQ score is in the upper one percent of the distribution, yet he continues to get "C"s in school. What might explain this?
   A. low contextual intelligence   B. poor practical intelligence
   C. low motivation   D. mild brain damage

24. Based on Stevenson and his colleagues' study comparing the performances of Asian and American students in school, what kinds of recommendations would you make to the school board for improving student achievement?

A. Change the attitudes of teachers, students and parents regarding the roles of hard work versus innate talent in math achievement.

B. Help parents to increase their standards and expectations for students.

C. Reduce outside activities and help students to focus more on school.

D. all of the above

25. Kanzi can use a sign to represent food that is not present in the room. This represents which feature of language?

A. meaningfulness
B. productivity
C. displacement
D. creativity

PRACTICE TEST 3 - Short Answer

1. Thinking can be defined most simply as the _mental_ manipulation of information.

2. One unit of thought is the _concept_, a mental category grouping objects, relations, activities, abstractions, or qualities that share certain properties.

3. Horse, shoe, chair are all examples of _basic_ concepts which have a moderate number of instances.

4. "Psychology is interesting" is an example of a(n) _proposition_, while "Psychology is an interesting subject and it is one of the most popular majors. Psychologists work with people, but they also conduct research and engage in consultation" is an example of a(n) _cog. schema_.

5. While nonconscious processes remain outside of awareness, _subconscious_ processes can be brought into consciousness when necessary.

6. "Intuition" and "insight" are thought to be a result of _nonconscious_ processes.

7. In deductive reasoning, if the premises are true, the conclusion _must_ be true, in inductive reasoning, if the premises are true, the conclusion _is probably_ be true.

8. Inductive reasoning and deductive reasoning are types of _formal_ reasoning. Problems requiring this type of reasoning can be solved by applying an _algorithm_, a set of procedures guaranteed to produce a solution.

9. Juries must weigh opposing viewpoints. They would be most likely to use _____ to reach a verdict in a case.

10. Critical thinking requires that people ask questions, analyze assumptions, tolerate uncertainty and resist oversimplification. These abilities require _____ judgment.

11. The idea that any judgment is as good as any other and is purely subjective would be most likely to occur in the _____ stage of reflective judgment.

12. One kind of rigidity that can hamper problem solving is biases due to _____, a tendency to approach problems in a particular way due to prior experience with similar problems.

13. That a person might be more afraid of an airplane crash than something much more likely to occur, like a car accident, may be a result of the _____.

14. Cognitive _____ occurs when a person simultaneously holds two cognitions that are psychologically inconsistent or holds a belief that is inconsistent with the person's behavior.

15. _____ tests measure skills and knowledge that have been taught; whereas, _____ tests measure ability to acquire skills and knowledge.

16. The _____ focuses on how well people perform on standardized mental tests while the _____ emphasizes the strategies people use to solve problems.

17. IQ tests have been criticized for being _____ in favor of certain groups. In an attempt to address this problem, psychologists developed tests that were intended to be _____ free and fair.

18. Some people believe that a _____ ability underlies the many specific abilities tapped by intelligence tests, whereas others believe that there are _____ and independent intelligences.

19. According to Sternberg's _____ theory, a person who easily adapts to the demands of new environments exhibits _____ intelligence.

20. Sternberg has identified three facets of intelligence: _____, _____, and _____.

21. Gardner's theory of _____ intelligences holds that there are actually _____ separate and independent "intelligences."

22. Intellectual achievement also depends on _____ and _____.

23. The cross-cultural study by Stevenson found that American parents had _____ standards for their children's performance and for schools than Asian parents.

24. The three criteria for language are: meaningfulness, _____, and _____.

25. Attributing human emotions to certain animal behavior is an example of _____.

PRACTICE TEST 3 - True/False

1.   T F   A concept is an integrated mental network of knowledge, beliefs, and expectations.

2.   T F   Basic concepts have a moderate number of instances and are easier to acquire than those that have few or many instances.

3.   T F   A robin is a prototype of the concept "bird," and an apple is a prototype of the concept "fruit." They are also examples of basic concepts.

4.   T F   Subconscious processes remain outside awareness but nonetheless affect behavior.

5.   T F   Formal reasoning is required to solve complex problems such as questions about abortion or gun control.

6.   T F   Following a recipe is an example of using a heuristic.

7.   T F   Formal reasoning problems can often be solved by applying an algorithm, a set of procedures guaranteed to produce a solution, or by using deductive or inductive reasoning.

8.   T F   "I've enjoyed every class that I've taken from Dr. Watson. Dr. Watson is teaching the class I need to take next semester. Therefore, I'm likely to enjoy that class." This is an example of deductive reasoning.

9.   T F   People in the prereflective state of reflective judgment think that because knowledge is sometimes uncertain, any judgment about the evidence is purely subjective.

10.   T F   The ability to reason clearly and rationally is affected by the need to be right, mental laziness, and cognitive biases.

11.   T F   John's belief that all women are bad drivers is reinforced when he notices the woman who cuts him off, but he does not notice the numerous women drivers around him who are driving well. This cognitive error is an example of the confirmation bias.

12.   T F   People are more likely to try to reduce cognitive dissonance when they feel they have made a decision freely and when they have put a lot of effort into the decision.

13.   T F   Although intelligence is hard to define, most psychologists agree on what it is and how to define it.

14.   T F   Most theorists believe that a general ability underlies the many specific abilities tapped by intelligence tests.

15.   T F   Alfred Binet originally designed intelligence tests to reveal children's natural ability and to put them in the correct categories at school. Psychologists in the U.S. used the tests to identify children who could benefit from remedial work.

16.   T F   The effectiveness of culture-free and culture-fair tests was disappointing because culture affects nearly everything to do with taking a test, including attitudes, expectations, problem-solving strategies, and comfort level.

17.   T F   Stereotype threat refers to the risk that a test administrator's stereotypes may affect his or her expectations of a test taker's ability. In turn, the expectations of the test administrator could influence the performance of the test taker.

18.   T F   IQ tests are a poor predictor of academic performance.

19.   T F   Sternberg's theory of multiple intelligences proposes that there are actually eight "intelligences."

20.   T F   The triarchic theory of identifies three aspects of intelligence: componential, exponential and contextual.

21.   T F   Most intelligence tests primarily measure a person's tacit knowledge and fail to test componential intelligence.

22.   T F   Two intelligences identified by Gardner overlap with what some psychologists call emotional intelligence.

23.   T F   Cross-cultural research shows that beliefs, parental standards, and attitudes toward education can help account for differences in academic performance.

24.   T F   The field of cognitive ethology studies the development of thought processes in humans throughout the lifespan.

25.   T F   Psychologists agree that some nonhuman animals engage in behavior that meets all the criteria for language.

PRACTICE TEST 3 - Essay

1. List a prototype for each of the concepts listed below.
    A. clothing
    B. animal
    C. pet
    D. relative

2. In each of the following examples, indicate what type of reasoning is most suitable for each problem and explain why.

    A. A navigator must determine the ship's position from the knowledge of a standard formula and the position of the North Star.
    B. A psychologist must determine if nonconformity facilitates creativity.
    C. A scientist must decide whether to pursue a career in teaching or research.
    D. A couple must decide if they are going to have a child.

3. Identify the cognitive biases in each of the following situations.
    A. Richard would rather drive 1,000 miles than fly because it is safer.
    B. Not only did you choose to go to this party 45 minutes away, but you convinced three other friends to go along. Even though no one is enjoying the party, you say you are having a good time.
    C. Jane doesn't want to get married and John does. When discussing the issue, Jane brings up only troubled relationships she knows of and cannot think of any of the happy relationships.

4. In the following examples identify what type of intelligence is being described, according to Sternberg's theory and according to Gardner's theory.
    A. Dr. Morris can go into a big organization and quickly identify the problem and select effective strategies for its solution.
    B. Dr. Mira works with people in psychotherapy and knows which strategies are working and when she needs to try something different.
    C. Regardless of what group of people Nicholas finds himself with, he is able to quickly adjust to the situation, handle himself appropriately and feel comfortable with himself.

5. Do animals have cognitive abilities? Make a case for and against this question.

CHAPTER 10

Memory

LEARNING OBJECTIVES

1. Discuss the reconstructive nature of memory and the implications for legal cases.

2. Compare recognition, recall, priming, relearning, and explicit and implicit memory.

3. Describe the information-processing approach to memory and explain its components.

4. Describe the "three-box model" of memory and explain its components.

5. Describe the parallel distributed processing model of memory.

6. Discuss the role of sensory memory.

7. Describe the processes and limitations of short-term memory (STM).

8. Describe the characteristics of long-term memory (LTM), and explain how information is organized.

9. Distinguish among procedural, declarative, semantic, and episodic memories.

10. Explain the limitations of the three-box model in accounting for the serial position effect.

11. Describe techniques for keeping information in short-term memory and for transferring information to long-term memory.

12. Summarize current findings about the physiological processes involved in memory.

13. List and discuss theories of why forgetting occurs, including childhood amnesia.

14. Describe the relationship between a person's "life story" and actual memories, including which memories are most likely to be trustworthy.

CHAPTER CONCEPT MAP

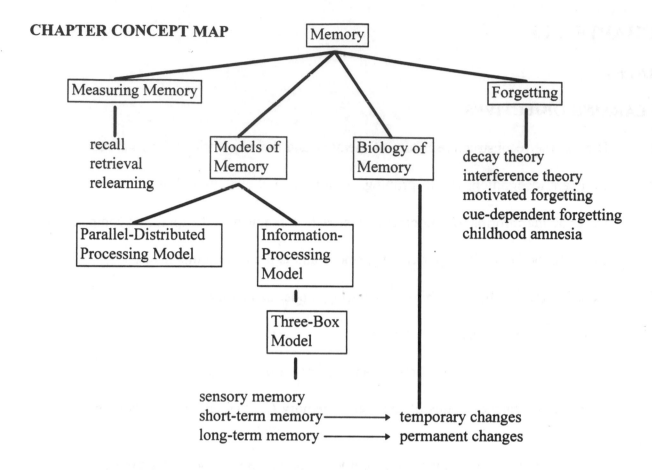

BRIEF CHAPTER SUMMARY

Chapter 10 examines the nature of memory. Memory does not record events like a video camera to be replayed at a later time. Rather, our memories incorporate outside information into our recollections so that what we recall is a reconstruction of events and not necessarily a memory of them. Memory is tested using the recall, retrieval and relearning methods. There are two prominent models of memory: the information-processing model, which compares memory processes to computer processes, and the parallel-distributed processing model, which states that knowledge is represented as connections among thousands of processing units operating in parallel. The three-box model, an information-processing model, suggests that there are three types of memory: sensory memory, short-term memory and long-term memory. Psychologists are interested in knowing what kinds of brain changes take place when we store information. Research examines memory and its relationship to neurons, brain structures and hormones. There are several different theories to explain why we forget. They include the decay theory, interference theory, the theory of motivated forgetting, cue-dependent forgetting and theories about childhood amnesia.

PREVIEW OUTLINES AND REVIEW QUESTIONS

Before you read the chapter, review the preview outline and the Learning Objectives for each section of the text. Answer all questions as you read the text.

SECTION 1 - RECONSTRUCTING THE PAST (PP. 350-357)

I. **RECONSTRUCTING THE PAST**
   A. **Definition** - memory is the capacity to retain and _____ information; it also conveys identity, both individual and collective
   B. **Reconstructing the past** - memory is a _____ process (confabulation)
      1. Reconstruction occurs in cases in which the inability to form lasting new memories resulted from surgical removal of parts of the brain
      2. Other information (e.g. stories) is integrated into memories and can't be distinguished from original experience - source amnesia or misattribution
   C. **The conditions of confabulation**
      1. The person has thought about the imagined event many times
      2. The image of the event contains a lot of details
      3. The event is easy to imagine
      4. The person focuses on his or her emotional reactions to the event rather than on what actually happened
      5. False memories can be as stable as true memories
      6. Hypnosis or electrical brain stimulation can result in false memories
   D. **The fading flashbulb** - memories of dramatic (even positive) events can be inaccurate over time; memory is best within two years of the event
   E. **The eyewitness on trial**
      1. People fill in missing pieces from memories, so eyewitness testimony can be incorrect; conviction based mainly on it are risky
      2. Errors especially likely when ethnicity of suspect differs from witness
      3. The power of suggestion
         a. The way a question is asked can influence what is recalled
         b. The more often the story is told, the more details are recalled
      4. Children's testimony - children are most suggestible when they are preschool age, when there is pressure to conform to expectations, and when they want to please the interviewer

Answer this Learning Objective while you read Section 1.

1. Discuss the reconstructive nature of memory and the implications for legal cases.

SECTION 2 - IN PURSUIT OF MEMORY (PP.357-361)

II.   **IN PURSUIT OF MEMORY**
    A.   **Measuring memory**
        1.   Conscious recollection - _____ memory
        2.   Two ways of measuring explicit memory
            a.   Recall - the ability to retrieve information encountered earlier
            b.   _____ - the ability to identify previously encountered information
        3.   Recognition is generally easier than recall
        4.   _____ memory
            a.   Previously encountered material that affects us without our awareness
            b.   Priming and relearning (savings) are methods to measure it
    B.   **Models of memory**
        1.   Information processing models are based on computers
        2.   Remembering begins with _____ information the brain can process
        3.   After encoding, next step is storage (maintenance of memory over time)
        4.   After storage, then retrieval (recovery of stored memory)
    C.   **Three-box model** - the dominant model since the 1960s; it says there are three interacting systems required for information-processing
        1.   _____ memory - retains incoming information for a second or two
        2.   Short-term memory (STM) - holds limited amount for about 30 seconds
        3.   Long-term memory (LTM) - accounts for longer storage
    D.   **Parallel _____ processing (connectionist) model** - rejects information-processing models
        1.   Maintains that memory is different than a computer; processes information simultaneously, or in parallel
        2.   Considers knowledge to be connections among thousands of units

Answer these Learning Objectives while you read Section 2.

2.   Compare recognition, recall, priming, relearning, and explicit and implicit memory.

3.   Describe the information-processing approach to memory and explain its components.

4.   Describe the "three-box model" of memory and explain its components.

5.   Describe the parallel distributed processing model of memory.

III.   **THE THREE BOX MODEL**
   A.   **Sensory memory: Fleeting impressions** (entryway of memory)
       1.   Includes separate memory subsystems for each of the senses
       2.   Acts as a holding bin until we select items for attention
       3.   Pattern recognition compares a stimulus to information already contained in long-term memory; it then goes to short-term-memory or it vanishes
       4.   Sensory memories are fairly complete
   B.   **Short-term memory: Memory's scratch pad**
       1.   Holds information up to about 30 seconds as an encoded representation
       2.   Transfers information to LTM or information decays and is lost
       3.   Working memory - holds information retrieved from _____ for temporary use
       4.   The leaky bucket - holds seven (plus or minus two) chunks of information
   C.   **Long-term memory: Final destination** - capacity is unlimited
       1.   Organization in long-term memory
           a.   Information is organized by _____ categories, sound, form, familiarity, relevance, association with other information
           b.   Network models - contents is a network of interrelated concepts
       2.   The contents of long-term memory
           a.   _____ memories - knowing how
           b.   Declarative memories - knowing that
               (1)   Semantic memories - internal representations of the world
               (2)   _____ memories - representations of experienced events
       3.   From short-term to long-term memory
           a.   Three-box model has been used to explain the serial position effect
           b.   The model explains _____ effects better than recency effects

Answer these Learning Objectives while you read Section 3.

6.   Discuss the role of sensory memory.

7.   Describe the processes and limitations of short-term memory (STM).

8.   Describe the characteristics of long-term memory (LTM), and explain how information is organized.

9.   Distinguish among procedural, declarative, semantic and episodic memories.

10.   Explain the limitations of the three-box model in accounting for the serial position effect.

SECTION 4 - HOW WE REMEMBER (PP. 361-371) AND
SECTION 5 - THE BIOLOGY OF MEMORY (PP. 372-376)

IV.   **HOW WE REMEMBER**
    A.   **Effective encoding**
        1.   Some encoding is effortless (location in space), others is effortful
        2.   Rehearsal - review or practice of material while you are learning it
            a. maintenance rehearsal - maintains information in STM only; no LTM
            b. elaborative rehearsal (elaboration of encoding) - interacting with items
        3.   Deep processing - processing of meaning
    B.   **Mnemonics** - strategies for encoding, storing and retaining information
V.   **THE BIOLOGY OF MEMORY**
    A.   **Changes in _____ and synapses**
        1.   In STM, changes within neurons temporarily alter neurotransmitter release
        2.   LTM changes involve permanent structural changes in the brain
            a.   Long-term _____ occurs - increases synaptic responsiveness
            b.   Two main and several other physical changes occur as a result
            c.   _____ is the time required for physical changes to occur in LTM; memories in LTM are vulnerable to disruption until then
    B.   **Locating memories** - researchers are learning about the location of memories
        1.   False and true memories trigger different patterns of brain activity
        2.   Brain-scan technology to study memory is an important development
        3.   Particular brain structures are responsible for certain types of memories
            a.   Areas in frontal lobes very active during short-term memory tasks
            b.   Formation of declarative memories involve _____ and parts of the temporal lobe cortex; hippocampus is especially important
            c.   Procedural memories involve the cerebellum
            d.   Different brain involvement for _____ and explicit memory tasks, and for formation and storage of long-term memories
        4.   A memory is a cluster of information processed and stored at different locations distributed across wide areas of the brain
    C.   **Hormones and memory**
        1.   The adrenalin connection - hormones released during stress enhance memory, but high levels interfere with ordinary learning
        2.   Sweet memories - the effect of these hormones may be due to glucose

Answer these Learning Objectives while you read Sections 4 and 5.

11.   Describe techniques used to keep information in STM and to transfer it to LTM.

12.   Summarize current findings about the physiological processes involved in memory

SECTION 6 - WHY WE FORGET (PP. 376-381) AND
SECTION 7 - AUTOBIOGRAPHICAL MEMORIES (PP. 381-385) AND
SECTION 8 - MEMORIES AND MYTHS (PP. 386-387)

VI. **WHY WE FORGET** - five mechanisms to account for forgetting
   A. **The decay theory** - memories _____ with time; doesn't apply well to LTM
   B. **New memories for old** - new information wipes out old information
   C. **Interference**
      1. Retroactive interference - new information interferes with old
      2. _____ interference - old information interferes with new
   D. **Motivated forgetting** - Freud said painful memories are blocked from consciousness (also called repression which is a more controversial concept)
   E. **Cue-dependent forgetting** - forgetting due to lack of retrieval cues
      1. Retrieval cues important for remembering in long-term memory
      2. Context, mental/physical states can be retrieval cues (state-dependent memory)

VII. **AUTOBIOGRAPHICAL MEMORIES: THE WAY WE WERE**
   A. **Childhood amnesia: The missing years** - the inability to remember things from the first years of life
      1. May occur because brain areas involved in formation or storage of events are not well developed until a few years after birth
      2. Cognitive explanations have also been offered: lack of a sense of self, differences between early and later cognitive schemas, impoverished encoding, a focus on routine
   B. **Memory and narrative: The stories of our lives**
      1. Narratives are a unifying theme to organize the events of our lives
      2. Narratives rely on memory, which is constructed
      3. Themes serve as a cognitive schema that guides what we remember
      4. Reminiscence bump - tendency to recall certain periods and not others

VIII. **MEMORIES AND MYTHS**
   A. Unreliable memories are those from the first years of life, those that become increasingly unlikely, and those that result from suggestive techniques
   B. Memories are considered most reliable when is corroborating evidence, other signs of trauma, and they are recalled without pressure from others

Answer these Learning Objectives while you read Sections 6, 7 and 8.

13. List and discuss theories of why forgetting occurs, including childhood amnesia.

14. Describe the relationship between a person's "life story" and actual memories, including which memories are most likely to be trustworthy.

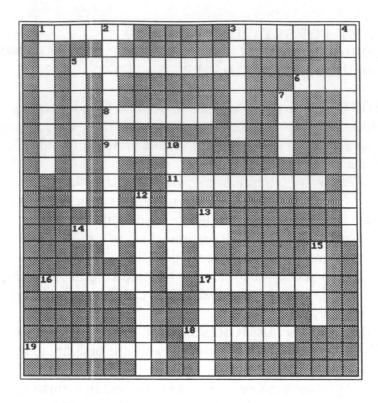

ACROSS

1. capacity to retain and retrieve information
3. type of memory that includes general knowledge, facts, rules
5. ability to identify previously encountered material
6. items that help us find specific information
8. maintenance of material over time
9. ability to retrieve and reproduce from memory previously encountered material
11. stories people live by
14. system of memory involved in the retention of information for brief periods
16. loss of ability to remember
17. memories for personally experienced events
18. the effect of improved ability to recall items at the beginning of a list
19. type of interference

DOWN

1. strategies and tricks for improving memory
2. the addition, deletion and changing of elements in ways that help make sense of information
3. memory system that momentarily preserves extremely accurate sensory images
4. memory becomes durable; the process by which long-term memory becomes stable
5. the recovery of stored material
7. level of processing of information
10. memory system with a theoretically unlimited capacity
12. type of amnesia
13. type of memory for the performance of actions
15. forgetting over time

FLASH CARDS

Cut the following chart along the borders and test yourself with the resulting flash cards.

10.1 MEMORY	10.2 RECONSTRUCTION IN MEMORY	10.3 SOURCE AMNESIA
10.4 FLASHBULB MEMORIES	10.5 LEADING QUESTIONS	10.6 EXPLICIT MEMORY
10.7 RECALL	10.8 RECOGNITION	10.9 IMPLICIT MEMORY
10.10 PRIMING	10.11 RELEARNING METHOD	10.12 INFORMATION-PROCESSING MODELS
10.13 "THREE-BOX MODEL"	10.14 ENCODING, STORAGE, AND RETRIEVAL	10.15 PARALLEL DISTRIBUTED PROCESSES (PDP) MODELS
10.16 SENSORY MEMORY	10.17 PATTERN RECOGNITION	10.18 SHORT-TERM MEMORY

10.3 The inability to distinguish what you originally experienced from what you heard or were told about an event later.	10.2 The addition, deletion and changing of elements in ways that help make sense of information and events.	10.1 The capacity to retain and retrieve information, the mental structures that account for this capacity and the material that is retained.
10.6 Conscious, intentional recollection of an event or an item of information.	10.5 Questions posed in a manner that directs the response in a particular way which can influence what is remembered.	10.4 Vivid, detailed recollections of emotional events that include surprise, illumination, and photographic detail.
10.9 Unconscious retention in memory, as evidenced by the effect of a previous experience or information on current thoughts or actions.	10.8 The ability to identify previously encountered material.	10.7 The ability to retrieve and reproduce from memory previously encountered material.
10.12 Models for understanding memory that liken the mind to and information processor or computer.	10.11 A method for measuring retention that compares the time required to relearn material with the time used in the initial learning of the material.	10.10 A method for measuring implicit memory; a person reads information and is later tested to see if performance on another task has been affected.
10.15 A memory model in which knowledge is represented as connections among thousands of networking units working in parallel.	10.14 In information-processing models, we encode information (convert it to a form that the brain can use), store it (retain it over time), and retrieve it	10.13 An information-processing model of memory that proposes three separate systems: sensory, short- and long-term memory.
10.18 In the three-box model of memory, a limited-capacity memory system that can retain information for brief periods or for temporary use.	10.17 The preliminary identification of a stimulus on the basis of information already contained in long-term memory.	10.16 A memory system that momentarily preserves extremely accurate images of sensory information.

10.19 WORKING MEMORY	10.20 CHUNKS	10.21 LONG-TERM MEMORY
10.22 SEMANTIC CATEGORIES	10.23 NETWORK MODELS	10.24 TIP-OF-THE-TONGUE STATE
10.25 PROCEDURAL MEMORIES	10.26 DECLARATIVE MEMORIES	10.27 SEMANTIC MEMORIES
10.28 EPISODIC MEMORIES	10.29 SERIAL-POSITION EFFECT	10.30 PRIMACY EFFECT
10.31 RECENCY EFFECTS	10.32 EFFORTFUL VERSUS AUTOMATIC ENCODING	10.33 MAINTENANCE REHEARSAL
10.34 ELABORATIVE REHEARSAL	10.35 DEEP PROCESSING	10.36 SHALLOW PROCESSING

10.21 In the three-box memory model, the memory system involved in the long-term storage of information.	10.20 Meaningful units of information; they may be composed of smaller units.	10.19 Short-term memory; called this because it also is used to retrieve information from long-term memory for temporary use.
10.24 Condition in which an item is near recall; aspects of the item can often be recalled, such as words similar in meaning or sound.	10.23 Models of long-term memory that represent its contents as a vast network of interrelated concepts and propositions.	10.22 Words or concepts are thought to be organized in LTM according to the word category to which they belong.
10.27 Memories of general knowledge, including facts, rules, concepts, and propositions.	10.26 Memories of facts, rules, concepts, and events ("knowing that"); they include semantic and episodic memories.	10.25 Memories for the performance of actions or skills ("knowing how").
10.30 The tendency for items at the end of a list to be recalled best.	10.29 The tendency for recall of the first and last items on a list to surpass recall of items in the middle of the list.	10.28 Memories of personally experienced events and the contexts in which they occurred.
10.33 Rote repetition of material in order to maintain its availability in memory.	10.32 The way we convert information to a form the brain can use; sometimes the conversion is automatic and sometimes it requires effort.	10.31 The tendency for items at the end of a list to be recalled best.
10.36 In the encoding of information, the processing of the physical (sound of words) or sensory features (pattern of rhythm) of a stimulus.	10.35 In the encoding of information, the processing of meaning rather than simply the physical or sensory features of a stimulus.	10.34 Association of new information with already stored knowledge and analysis of the new information to make it memorable.

10.37 MNEMONICS	10.38 LONG-TERM POTENTIATION	10.39 CONSOLIDATION
10.40 DECAY THEORY	10.41 RETROACTIVE INTERFERENCE	10.42 PROACTIVE INTERFERENCE
10.43 MOTIVATED FORGETTING OR REPRESSION	10.44 RETROGRADE AMNESIA	10.45 CUE-DEPENDENT FORGETTING
10.46 RETRIEVAL CUES	10.47 STATE-DEPENDENT MEMORY	10.48 AUTOBIOGRAPHICAL MEMORY
10.49 CHILDHOOD (INFANTILE) AMNESIA	10.50 NARRATIVES	10.51 REMINISCENCE BUMP

10.39 The process by which a long-term memory becomes durable and stable.	10.38 A long-lasting increase in the strength of synaptic responsiveness, thought to be a biological mechanism of long-term memory.	10.37 Strategies and tricks for improving memory, such as the use of a verse or a formula.
10.42 Forgetting that occurs when previously stored material interferes with the ability to remember similar, more recently learned material.	10.41 Forgetting that occurs when recently learned material interferes with the ability to remember similar material stored previously.	10.40 The theory that information in memory eventually disappears if it is not accessed; it applies more to STM than to LTM.
10.45 The inability to retrieve information stored in memory because of insufficient cues for recall.	10.44 Loss of ability to remember events or experiences that occurred before some particular point in time.	10.43 Forgetting that occurs because of a desire to eliminate awareness of painful, embarrassing, or otherwise unpleasant experiences.
10.48 The memories we have of our own lives.	10.47 The tendency to remember something when the person is in the same physical or mental state as during the original learning experience.	10.46 Items of information that can help us find the specific information we're looking for.
10.51 As we age, certain periods of our lives stand out; old people remember more from adolescence and early adulthood than from midlife.	10.50 Stories people compose to make sense of their lives; they organize the events of people's lives and give them meaning.	10.49 The inability to remember events and experiences that occurred during the first two or three years of life.

282

PRACTICE TEST 1 - Multiple Choice

1. The reconstructive nature of memory refers to
   A. the alteration of remembered information to help make sense of it.
   B. the capacity to retain and retrieve information.
   C. the ability to retrieve from memory previously encountered material.
   D. vivid, detailed recollections of circumstances.

2. Eyewitness testimony is influenced by
   A. the fact that the details of events are often inferred rather than observed.
   B. memory errors that increase when the races of the suspect and witness differ.
   C. the wording of questions.
   D. all of the above.

3. What type of memory is measured by multiple-choice tests?
   A. recall
   B. relearning
   C. recognition
   D. procedural

4. Unconsciously remembered material that continues to have an effect on actions is
   A. semantic memory.
   B. implicit memory.
   C. explicit memory.
   D. declarative memory.

5. Comparing the mind to a computer and speaking in terms of inputs and outputs reflects the
   A. parallel distributed processing model of memory.
   B. cognitive model of memory.
   C. information-processing model of memory.
   D. connectionist model of memory.

6. According to information-processing models of memory, we
   A. process information like neurons in the brain.
   B. develop a system of neural networks.
   C. encode information and then integrate it into existing cognitive schema.
   D. demonstrate all of the above.

7. According to the "three-box" model, which is the first step in memory?
   A. short-term memory
   B. retrieval
   C. storage
   D. sensory memory

8. Which of the following is not a basic memory process?
    A. encoding
    B. retrieval
    C. storage
    D. perception

9. Which model maintains that knowledge is represented in the brain as connections among thousands of interacting processing units that are distributed in a vast network and operate in parallel?
    A. "three box" model
    B. information-processing model
    C. parallel distributed processing model
    D. all of the above

10. In what way does the parallel distributed processing (PDP) model differ from the information-processing model?
    A. The PDP model suggests there are only two systems of memory rather than three.
    B. The PDP model rejects the notion that the brain can be modeled after a computer.
    C. The PDP model suggests that information is processed bit by bit, sequentially.
    D. The PDP model suggests that the brain can be likened to a computer.

11. Sensory memory contains information from
    A. any of the senses.
    B. the eyes only.
    C. the ears and eyes only.
    D. the ears only.

12. Which of the following describes the function of sensory memory?
    A. It holds information that has been retrieved from LTM for temporary use.
    B. It acts as a holding bin until we select items for attention.
    C. It retains information for up to 30 seconds.
    D. It aids in the retrieval of information from short-term memory.

13. By most estimates, information can be kept in STM for _____ without rehearsal?
    A. one half to two seconds
    B. up to 10 seconds
    C. up to 30 seconds
    D. up to 5 minutes

14. One way to increase the amount of information held in STM is to
    A. group information into chunks.
    B. form echoes and icons.
    C. reduce interference.
    D. use all of the above methods.

15. Which of the following best describes the limits of the capacity of long-term memory?
    A. It can hold from five to nine pieces of information.
    B. It can hold up to 100 pieces of information.
    C. There are no limits to what it can hold.
    D. Its capacity is not yet known.

16. How is information organized in long-term memory?
    A. by semantic category only
    B. by the way words look or sound
    C. by semantic category and by the way words look or sound
    D. none of the above

17. Learning to type, swim or drive is a function of which type of memory?
    A. semantic   B. episodic
    C. procedural   D. declarative

18. Your recollection of specific information for this test is an example of
    A. procedural memory.   B. episodic memory.
    C. semantic memory.   D. implicit memory.

19. Which of the following represents the limitations of the "three-box" model in accounting for the serial position effect?
    A. The primacy effect occurs under conditions when, theoretically, it should not.
    B. The recency effect persists even beyond the time STM should have been emptied.
    C. The primacy effect does not occur in animals.
    D. There is no serial position effect in animals.

20. Which method is the least likely to transfer information from STM to LTM?
    A. maintenance rehearsal   B. deep processing
    C. elaborative rehearsal   D. elaboration of encoding

21. Which of the following describes brain changes in long-term memory?
    A. Some permanent structural changes in the brain occur.
    B. Long-term potentiation occurs.
    C. Dendrites grow and branch out.
    D. all of the above

22. Decay theory does not seem to explain forgetting in long-term memory as evidenced by the fact that
    A. it is not uncommon to forget an event from years ago while remembering what happened yesterday.
    B. it is not uncommon to forget an event from yesterday while remembering what happened years ago.
    C. people who took Spanish in high school did not do well on Spanish tests 30 years later.
    D. people generally don't remember high school algebra by the time they go to college.

23. Which of the following is NOT an explanation advanced to explain forgetting?
    A. interference
    B. motivated forgetting
    C. the idea that new memories can wipe out old information
    D. explicit forgetting

24. Why is it difficult to remember events earlier than the third or fourth year of life?
    A. The brain systems involved in memory take up to three or four years to develop.
    B. Adults use different schema than children.
    C. Children use different encoding methods than adults.
    D. all of the above

25. Which of the following best describes the relationship between a person's "life story" and actual memories?
    A. Both are quite accurate.   B. Only memories are accurate.
    C. Both involve some reconstruction. D. Only life stories are accurate.

PRACTICE TEST 2 - Multiple Choice

1. Why does the tendency to reconstruct memories present a particularly serious problem in the courtrooms?
    A. Witnesses will lie to cover their memory errors.
    B. Reconstructed memories are almost always wrong.
    C. Witnesses who have reconstructed testimony will fail lie detector tests.
    D. Witnesses sometimes can't distinguish between what they actually saw and what they have reconstructed.

2. Memories are unintentionally reconstructed in order to
    A. fit into existing cognitive schemas.
    B. make a story more believable or interesting.
    C. achieve a specific goal.
    D. cover memory deficits.

3. Multiple choice is to essay as
    A. recall is to relearning.
    B. recall is to recognition.
    C. priming is to recall.
    D. recognition is to recall.

4. As a subject in a memory study, you are shown a list of words. Later, you are asked to complete word stems with the first word that comes to mind. You are being tested for
    A. relearning.
    B. implicit memory.
    C. explicit memory.
    D. priming.

5. "When we are exposed to information, we convert it so the brain can process and store it. As we process it, the information is integrated with what we already know." This statement reflects the
    A. parallel distributed processing model.
    B. connectionist model.
    C. information-processing model.
    D. implicit model.

6. Which of the following best represents the parallel distributed processing model?
    A. The human brain does not operate like your average computer.
    B. The human brain performs many operations simultaneously, not sequentially.
    C. Knowledge is not propositions; it is connections among thousands of interacting units distributed in a vast network and all acting in parallel.
    D. all of the above

7. Why does the parallel distributed processing model reject the computer metaphor?
   A. Unlike computers, the brain does not process information sequentially.
   B. The brain is not as complex as a computer.
   C. Unlike the brain, computers process information in a parallel manner.
   D. The brain recognizes bits of information, rather than patterns all at once.

8. Pattern recognition occurs
   A. during the storage of information in short-term memory.
   B. during the transfer of information from short-term memory to long-term memory.
   C. during the transfer of information from sensory memory to short-term memory.
   D. while in long-term memory.

9. You call information and ask the number of your favorite restaurant. How long do you have to dial the number before you forget?
   A. 10 seconds   B. up to 10 minutes
   C. up to 30 seconds   D. 3 to 5 minutes

10. What could you do to extend the time that you remember this information?
    A. maintenance rehearsal   B. deep processing
    C. elaborative rehearsal   D. all of the above

11. Short-term memory is to long-term memory as
    A. an oven is to a kitchen.
    B. episodic memory is to declarative memory.
    C. a loading dock is to a warehouse.
    D. an echo is to an icon.

12. Which of the following helps transfer information from short-term memory to long-term memory?
    A. deep processing   B. chunking
    C. elaborative rehearsal   D. all of the above

13. Information is stored by subject, category and associations in
    A. the sensory register.   B. short-term memory.
    C. the sensory memory.   D. long-term memory.

14. You recall from the chapter on learning that B.F. Skinner was involved in the development of operant conditioning. Your ability to remember this information demonstrates which type of memory?
    A. declarative   B. semantic
    C. explicit   D. all of the above

15. Semantic and episodic memories
    A.   are types of declarative memories.   B.   are types of implicit memories.
    C.   are examples of procedural memories.   D.   exhibit the primacy effect.

16. How does the "three-box" model account for the recency effect?
    A.   Recent items are recalled because they have the best chance of getting into LTM.
    B.   Short-term memory is empty when recent items are entered.
    C.   At the time of recall, recent items are still in short-term memory and have not been dumped yet.
    D.   all of the above

17. A list of words has been read to you. You are retested on them one hour later and find that you recall more words at the end of the list. This demonstrates
    A.   the primacy effect.
    B.   a problem with the explanation provided by the "three-box" model of the recency effect.
    C.   ways to extend the length of time information can remain in short-term memory.
    D.   the effects of sensory memory.

18. The best way to get information into long-term memory is by using
    A.   maintenance rehearsal.   B.   elaborative rehearsal.
    C.   repetition.   D.   all of the above.

19. Physiologically, short-term memory involves changes in _____, whereas long-term memory involves _____
    A.   the neuron's ability to release neurotransmitters; permanent structural changes in the brain.
    B.   permanent structural changes in the brain; changes in the neurons
    C.   the hippocampus; the cortex
    D.   long-term potentiation; changes in the neuron's ability to release neurotransmitters

20. Synaptic responsiveness
    A.   is influenced by long-term memory.
    B.   increases are known as long-term potentiation.
    C.   increases during the formation of long-term memories.
    D.   has all of the above characteristics.

21. Pat learned to speak Italian at home as a child. Now when she studies Spanish, she can recall only the Italian words. This is an example of
    A.   retroactive interference.   B.   motivated forgetting.
    C.   proactive interference.   D.   decay.

22. The idea that you will remember better if you study for a test in the same environment in which you will be tested is an example of
    A.   state-dependent memory.   B.   elaborated rehearsal.
    C.   cue-dependent memory.   D.   deja-vu.

23. Jocelyn is convinced that she remembers an event that occurred when she was six months old. This is impossible because
    A.   parts of the brain are not well developed for some years after birth.
    B.   cognitive processes are not in place at that age.
    C.   at that age encoding is much less elaborate.
    D.   all of the above are reasons.

24. What might explain Jocelyn's early memory?
    A.   She has incorporated into her memories stories she has heard from that time.
    B.   She is lying.
    C.   Certain people have early memory capacity and she may be someone with that ability.
    D.   She has intentionally constructed a memory.

25. What is meant by Gerbner's observation that "our species is unique because we tell stories and live by the stories we tell?"
    A.   Human beings are creative and imaginative.
    B.   Human beings compose stories to make sense of their lives and these narratives then have a profound influence on how they live their lives.
    C.   Human beings are basically self-deceptive.
    D.   Human beings are natural story-tellers.

PRACTICE TEST 3 - Short Answer

1. Research in which volunteers often eliminated or changed details of a story that did not make sense to them, and then added other details to make the story coherent, demonstrates that memory is a _____ process.

2. In reconstructing their memories, people often draw on many sources. They may incorporate information from family stories, photographs, videos in a new integrated account. Later they may not be able to separate the original experience from what they added after the fact. This phenomenon is called _____ amnesia.

3. False memories can be as _____ over time as true ones.

4. Eyewitness accounts of events are heavily influenced by _____ comments made during an interrogation.

5. Short answer questions, such as these, rely on _____ method of measuring memory; whereas multiple choice questions depend on _____.

6. Conscious recollection of an event or an item of information is called _____ memory.

7. Suppose you had read a list of words, some of which began with the letters "def." Later you are asked to complete word stems with the first word that comes to mind. You would be more likely to complete the word fragments with words from the list than you would be if you had not seen the list. This technique for measuring _____ memory is called _____.

8. Models of memory that borrow heavily from the language of computer programming are referred to as _____ models.

9. We _____ information when we convert it to a form that the brain can process and use. To use it in the future we must _____ the information and be able to recover it for use, or _____ it.

10. _____ memory holds information for a second or two, while _____ holds information for about 30 seconds.

11. The model of memory that says the human brain does not operate like a computer is called the _____, or connectionist, model.

12. We overcome the limits of short-term memory by grouping small bits of information into larger units, or _____.

13. One way words are organized in long-term memory is by the _____ categories to which they belong.

14. Many models of long-term memory represent its contents as a vast network of interrelated concepts and propositions. These conceptualizations of memory are called _____ models.

15. _____ memories are internal representations of the world, independent of any particular context, whereas _____ memories are internal representations of personally experienced events. Both are types of _____ memories.

16. The fact that recall is best for items at the beginning and end of a list is called the _____ effect.

17. _____ rehearsal will keep information in short-term memory, but to remember things for the long haul, it is better to use _____ rehearsal which involves associating new items of information with material that has already been stored.

18. "Every good boy does fine" is an example of a _____ device, a formal strategy for encoding, storing, and retaining information.

19. In long-term _____, some synaptic pathways become more excitable. This and other physical changes associated with long-term memories take time to develop. Therefore, memories undergo a gradual period of _____, or stabilization, before they "solidify" and become stable.

20. The hormones released by the adrenal glads during stress and emotional arousal, including _____, enhance memory.

21. The _____ theory of forgetting holds that memory traces fade with time if they are not "accessed" now and then.

22. A type of interference in which new information interferes with the ability to remember old information is called _____ interference. _____ interference is when old information interferes with the ability to remember new information.

23. Often, when we need to remember, we rely on _____ cues, items of information that can help us find the specific information we're looking for. The type of memory failure that occurs when we lack these cues is called _____forgetting.

24. If your emotional arousal is especially high at the time of an event, you may remember that event best when you are in the same emotional state. This is referred to as _____ memory.

25. Memories from before the age of two are not likely to be real memories because of childhood _____.

PRACTICE TEST 4 - True/False

1. T F The recovered-memory school believes that false memories are rare and that traumatic memories are commonly blocked from consciousness.

2. T F Memory is similar to a tape recorder or a movie camera, recording each moment of our lives.

3. T F Misremembering of events is especially likely to occur when the event is easy to imagine and it contains a lot of details.

4. T F Flashbulb memories tend to be more accurate than other memories.

5. T F The more certain a person is about a memory, the more likely the memory is an accurate recollection of events.

6. T F Errors by eyewitnesses are especially likely to occur when the suspect's ethnicity differs from that of the witness.

7. T F Researchers have induced people to recall events from early in life that never actually happened at all, such as getting lost in a shopping mall or being hospitalized for a high fever.

8. T F Children are more easily influenced than adults by leading questions, therefore, the use of leading questions with children is considered unacceptable.

9. T F Of the methods used for measuring implicit memory, recognition is, under most circumstances, easier than recall.

10. T F The relearning method, another way of measuring implicit memory, requires you to relearn information that you learned earlier. If you master it more quickly the second time, you must be remembering something from the first experience.

11. T F The three-box model of memory is an information-processing model.

12. T F The parallel distributed processing (PDP) model is also an information-processing model.

13. T F Information that is not transferred from sensory memory to short-term memory vanishes forever.

14. T F Working memory is a term that is often used to refer to long-term memory since that is where we use the memories that we have stored the long-term.

15. T F We organize information in long-term memory not only by semantic groupings but also in terms of the way words sound or look.

16. T F Maintenance rehearsal is the best way to keep information in short-term memory and to get it into long-term memory.

17. T F Both short-term and long-term memories cause lasting changes in the brain.

18. T F In short-term memory, some synaptic pathways become more excitable, a phenomenon known as potentiation.

19. T F The time it takes for memories to undergo consolidation explains why long-term memories are vulnerable to disruption for a while after they are stored.

20. T F The formation of declarative and procedural memories occur in different brain areas. The brain circuits that take part in the formation of long-term memories are not the same as those involved in long-term storage of those memories.

21. T F Hormones released by the adrenal glands during stress and emotional arousal enhance memory of the event and of ordinary learning.

22. T F Decay theory is the best explanation for forgetting in both short and long-term memory.

23. T F The spanish vocabulary that you learned in high school keeps coming up when you are trying to think of a French word for your college French exam. Proactive interference could account for this phenomenon.

24. T F Empirically based research studies have found repression to be a distinct phenomenon that accounts for certain types of forgetting.

25. T F If you are in a bad mood when you study for a test, being in a bad mood when you take the test should increase your ability to remember information.

PRACTICE TEST 5 - Essay

1. Identify and describe the three basic processes involved in the capacity to remember.

2. Imagine that you watched a baseball game yesterday and presently retain many details about the game. According to the "three-box" theory, what kind of sequence have such details followed?

3. The home team brings in a new pitcher in the fifth inning. In each situation below, suggest the type of memory most likely to be the prime determinant.

    A. Her warm-up style indicates the fluid and coordinated movements of an experienced athlete.
    B. After several batters are walked, she tells the umpire that the calls are no better this week than last week.
    C. As the third batter steps up, the pitcher indicates to the umpire that improper attire is being worn.

4. Written descriptions of a fight on a school bus have been collected from several students. Explain below how memory processes are likely to influence the various descriptions.

5. While searching the attic, Henry discovers his senior-year diary, written over 30 years ago and not seen since.
    A. According to decay theory, what will have been forgotten and why?
    B. The first page contains the title "Happy Times as a Senior." He tries hard to remember but is not successful until he begins reading a description of his homeroom. This triggers a flood of memories. What variable related to forgetting best explains this experience.
    C. Henry finds another section entitled "Worst Times as a Senior." He is sure there were very few but begins to change his mind as he reads. This time there is no flood of memories, but many descriptions of unhappy moments. Henry wonders whether he was overly imaginative or whether senior year was pretty awful. What variables that influence memory best explain this?

6. For finals week, you had to be prepared for exams in English, math, Spanish, Italian, and history. How should the sequence of study be arranged to minimize the possibility of interference?

CHAPTER 11

Emotion

LEARNING OBJECTIVES

1. Describe the components involved in the experience of emotion.

2. Describe the role of facial expressions in emotional experience. Discuss the role of social contexts.

3. Using research evidence, discuss the involvement of the right and left hemispheres, the amygdala, and the cerebral cortex in the experience and expression of emotion.

4. Identify the hormones involved in emotions and describe their effects on the body.

5. Explain why most researchers do not believe the polygraph test is a valid way to ascertain whether a person is lying.

6. Define and discuss the two-factor theory of emotion.

7. Explain through the use of examples how cognitive processes can affect emotions.

8. Summarize the conclusions of research related to the historic mind-body conflict.

9. Distinguish between primary and secondary emotions and describe contradictory views on primary emotions.

10. Discuss how culture can influence the experience and expression of emotion.

11. Compare and contrast emotional experience and expression in men and women.

CHAPTER CONCEPT MAP

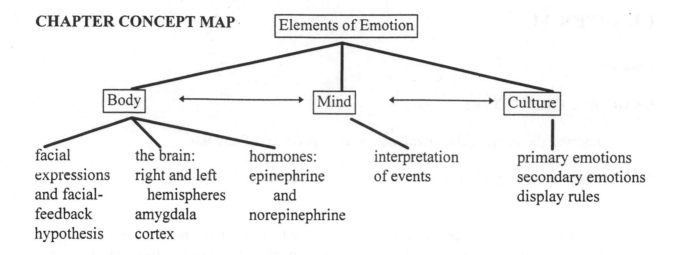

BRIEF CHAPTER SUMMARY

Chapter 11 explores the elements of emotions. Emotions have a physical component that involves facial expressions, brain involvement and hormonal activity. The physiological component does not result directly in the experience of emotion. Events are interpreted, and our perception of events influences our emotional experience. The final element that influences our emotions and their expression is culture. Cultural rules govern how and when emotions may be expressed. Researchers have searched for primary, or universal, emotions. The search for primary emotions is controversial among those who feel that culture influences even biologically based emotions. The research on gender differences in emotions suggests that men and women experience similar emotions though they differ somewhat in their physiological responses and their perceptions and expectations about emotional experiences.

PREVIEW OUTLINE AND REVIEW QUESTIONS

Before you read the chapter, review the preview outline and the Learning Objectives for each section of the text. Answer all questions as you read the text.

SECTION 1 - ELEMENTS OF EMOTION 1: THE BODY (PP. 385-392)

I. **ELEMENTS OF EMOTION 1: THE BODY**
   A. **There are three influences on emotion:** physiological changes, cognitive processes, and cultural influences
   B. **Historical approaches** - Early philosophers believed in four basic body _____
   C. **The face of emotion**
      1. Universal expressions of emotion
         a. Darwin said facial expressions of emotion had survival function
         b. Ekman's work supports this idea and found _____ universal facial expressions of emotion; called it neuro-cultural theory because it involves face muscle physiology and cultural variations
         c. Face can also mask emotions; Ekman developed way to detect faked emotions
      2. The functions of facial expressions - a way to communicate
         a. Research with babies shows they use emotions to communicate
         b. Facial-_____ hypothesis - face muscles send message to brain about emotion being expressed which then effects emotional state
      3. Facial expressions in social context - produced mainly in social contexts and may have different meanings depending on the context
      4. Scientists disagree about universality of the meaning of facial expressions
   D. **The brain and emotion**
      1. The two hemispheres
         a. The right hemisphere is particularly important in emotional experience and expression
         b. The hemispheres play different roles in regard to emotions
         c. The left is involved in positive emotions and the tendency to approach people, the right involved in negative emotions and the tendency to withdraw
      2. The amygdala and the cortex
         a. Amygdala - in the limbic system, gives initial, quick appraisal of incoming sensory information
         b. Cerebral cortex - more accurate appraisal of sensory information
   E. **Hormones and emotion** - produce the energy to respond to alarm signals
      1. Epinephrine and norepinephrine activate _____ nervous system
      2. These hormones produced in response to many environmental events

3.   Emotions differ from one another biochemically

F.   **Summary** - Emotions involve facial expressions, parts of the brain (the amygdala and parts of the cerebral hemispheres, and sympathetic nervous system activity

G.   **Detecting emotions: Does the body lie?**
1.   The polygraph machine and lie detection - based on idea that lying associated with increased autonomic nervous system activity (increased heart rate, respiration)
2.   Most researchers see polygraph tests as invalid because
      a.   There is no pattern of response specific to lying
      b.   They are unreliable
3.   Banned from use by employers and most courts, but they are still used by police

Answer these Learning Objectives while you read Section 1.

1.   Describe the components involved in the experience of emotion.

2.   Describe the role of facial expressions in emotional experience. Discuss the role of social contexts.

3.   Using research evidence, discuss the involvement of the right and left hemispheres, the amygdala, and the cerebral cortex in the experience and expression of emotion.

4.   Identify the hormones involved in emotions and describe their effects on the body.

5.   Explain why most researchers do not believe the polygraph test is a valid way to ascertain whether a person is lying.

SECTION 2 - ELEMENTS OF EMOTION 2: THE MIND (PP. 393-400)

II.   **ELEMENTS OF EMOTION 2: THE MIND**
    A.   **How thoughts create emotions** - the meaning people give to bodily changes and events
        1.   ___2 factor___ theory of emotion
            a.   Emotion depends on physiological arousal and cognitive interpretation of events
            b.   Research supporting this theory has not been replicated
        2.   Attributions and emotion - how perceptions and explanations of events (attributions) affect emotions
            a.   Appraising events for their personal implications affects emotions
            b.   Cognitions involved range from immediate perceptions of an event to general philosophy of life
        3.   The case of shame and guilt
            a.   Both are related to doing something wrong
            b.   Different cognitions provoke them and they motivate different behavior
        4.   Studies suggest people can learn how their thinking affects their emotions and then they can learn to change their thinking
    B.   **Reason and emotion: opposites or allies?**
        1.   No longer think that emotion and cognition are unrelated processes
        2.   Though some emotions don't involve cognitive appraisals, others do
        3.   Cognitions affect emotions, but emotions also influence cognitions
        4.   The distinction between reason and emotion is dissolved

Answer these Learning Objectives while you read Section 2.

6.   Define and discuss the two-factor theory of emotion.

7.   Explain through the use of examples how cognitive processes can affect emotions.

8.   Summarize the conclusions of research related to the historic mind-body conflict.

SECTION 3 - ELEMENTS OF EMOTION 3: THE CULTURE (PP. 400-406)

III.   **ELEMENTS OF EMOTION 3: THE CULTURE**
    A.   **Cultural influences on emotion** - are all emotions universal or are some specific to culture?
        1.   Language and emotion - words for certain emotional states exist in some languages and not in others
        2.   What this means is unclear
    B.   **The search for primary emotions**
        a.   Some believe it is possible to identify _____ emotions (those experienced universally)
        b.   Lists of primary emotions vary but they usually include: fear, anger, sadness, joy, surprise, disgust, contempt
        c.   Four lines of evidence support the idea that some emotions are universal
            (1)   Brain and nervous system research
            (2)   Universally recognizable facial expressions
            (3)   Existence of emotion prototypes in most languages
            (4)   Certain emotions evoked by the same situations everywhere
        1.   Secondary emotions are more _culture_-specific
        2.   Many think searching for primary emotions is hopeless and that every aspect of emotional experience is influenced by culture
    C.   **The communication of emotion**
        1.   _Display_ rules - the cultural rules that govern how and when emotions may be expressed
        a.   They tell us how and when we should show an emotion
        b.   They are learned effortlessly and not knowing the rules of another culture can cause misunderstandings, hostilities, and war
        2.   Body language - nonverbal signals; body movement, posture, gesture, gaze
        a.   Some are universal, most are culture-specific
        b.   Emotional contagion - picking up another person's emotion
        c.   Emotion _work_ - how, when to show an emotion we don't feel

Answer these Learning Objectives while you read Section 3.

9.   Distinguish between primary and secondary emotions and describe contradictory views on primary emotions.

10.   Discuss how culture can influence the experience and expression of emotion.

IV.   **PUTTING THE ELEMENTS TOGETHER: EMOTION AND GENDER**
    A.   **The experience of emotion**
        1.   No evidence for gender differences in experience of emotion
        2.   Both sexes likely to experience similar feelings in particular situations
    B.   **Physiology**
        1.   Men are _more_ physiologically reactive than women, which might explain their greater discomfort with conflict in marriages
        2.   May be due to more sensitive and reactive _autonomic_ nervous systems
        3.   Men more likely than women to rehearse negative thoughts
    C.   **Cognitions**
        1.   Men and women differ in perceptions and interpretations that create emotions
        2.   They differ in the kinds of everyday events that provoke their anger
    D.   **Sensitivity to other people's emotions** - depends more on <u>context</u> than <u>gender</u>
        1.   The ability to "read" emotional signals depends on:
            a.   The _sex_ of the sender and the receiver
            b.   How well the two people know each other
            c.   How expressive the sender is
            d.   Who has the _power_ - people with less power can read people with more power better
        2.   Expressiveness
            a.   <u>Women willing to</u> and permitted to express more emotions while <u>men expected to control them</u>
            b.   Makes it hard to know when men are really unhappy or depressed
            c.   Three factors affect emotional expressiveness; gender roles, family and cultural norms, the specific situation
        3.   Emotion work - role expectations for men and women are different

Answer this Learning Objective while you read Section 4.

11.   Compare and contrast emotional experience and expression in men and women.

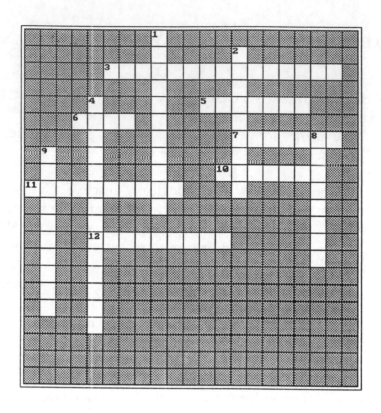

ACROSS

3. hypothesis that facial muscles send messages to the brain
5. state of arousal involving physiological changes, cognitive processes, and cultural influences
6. type of "language" that involves nonverbal signals including body movement, posture, gesture, and gaze
7. social and cultural rules that regulate when, how, and where a person may express emotions
10. emotions considered universal
11. beliefs that can influence emotions
12. machine that detects autonomic nervous system activity

DOWN

1. activates the sympathetic nervous system; provides the feeling of emotion
2. emotions that are specific to certain cultures
4. activates the sympathetic nervous system
8. structure that provides the initial appraisal of incoming sensory information
9. theory that emotions depend on both physiological arousal and a cognitive interpretation

FLASH CARDS

Cut the following chart along the borders and test yourself with the resulting flash cards.

11.1 EMOTION	11.2 NEURO-CULTURAL THEORY	11.3 FACIAL FEEDBACK
11.4 AMYGDALA	11.5 CEREBRAL CORTEX	11.6 EPINEPHRINE
11.7 NOREPINEPHRINE	11.8 POLYGRAPH ("LIE DETECTOR")	11.9 TWO-FACTOR THEORY OF EMOTION
11.10 ATTRIBUTIONS	11.11 COGNITIVE APPRAISAL	11.12 PRIMARY EMOTIONS
11.13 SECONDARY EMOTIONS	11.14 PROTOTYPES OF EMOTION	11.15 DISPLAY RULES
11.16 BODY LANGUAGE	11.17 EMOTIONAL CONTAGION	11.18 EMOTION WORK

11.3 The process by which the facial muscles send messages to the brain about the basic emotion being expressed.	11.2 Ekman's theory that there are two factors involved in facial expression of emotions: neurophysiology of facial muscles and cultural variations.	11.1 A state of arousal involving facial and bodily changes, brain activation, cognitive appraisals, subjective feelings, tendencies to action.
11.6 A hormone that activates the sympathetic nervous system to produce a state of arousal that allows the body to respond quickly.	11.5 The part of the brain that provides a more accurate analysis of incoming information following the amygdala's rapid evaluation.	11.4 Structure in the limbic system that evaluates incoming sensory information for its emotional importance.
11.9 The theory that emotions depend on both physiological arousal and a cognitive interpretation of that arousal.	11.8 A machine that detects nervous system arousal (increased heart rate, respiration, GSR) that may be associated with lying.	11.7 Along with epinephrine, activates the sympathetic nervous system to produce a state of arousal that allows the body to respond quickly.
11.12 Emotions considered to be universal and biologically based; they generally include fear, anger, sadness, contempt surprise, disgust, and joy.	11.11 The perception, interpretation, evaluation, and explanations of behaviors and events.	11.10 A person's explanations of behavior and events. Different explanations of the same event can generate different emotions.
11.15 Social and cultural rules that regulate when, how and where a person may express (or must suppress) emotions.	11.14 Emotions that people everywhere consider core examples of the category "emotion."	11.13 Emotions that some cultures recognize or emphasize and others apparently do not, including blends or variations of feeling.
11.18 Expression of an emotion, often because of a role requirement, that the person does not really feel.	11.17 The synchronization of moods between two people, as expressed through body language.	11.16 The nonverbal signals of body movement, posture, gesture, and gaze that people constantly express.

PRACTICE TEST 1 - Multiple Choice

1. The elements of emotion include
   A. the face and body.   B. the mind.
   C. the culture.   D. all of the above.

2. Which of the following is <u>NOT</u> one of the bodily aspects of emotion?
   A. the mind   B. the face
   C. the brain   D. hormones

3. Ekman suggested there two components involved in the facial expression of emotions.
   He called this theory the
   A. two-factor theory.   B. survival of the fittest.
   C. neuro-cultural theory.   D. facial-feedback hypothesis.

4. Ekman's studies found that
   A. there are 15 universal facial expressions of emotion.
   B. there are really no universal facial expressions of emotion because of the different meaning each culture attaches to the expressions.
   C. there are seven basic facial expressions of emotion.
   D. all facial expressions are learned.

5. That certain emotions are registered on the face
   A. evolved to help us communicate with others and ourselves.
   B. helps teach young children which emotions are appropriate.
   C. can cause problems for those who do not wish their emotions to be known.
   D. is a direct result of display rules and emotion work.

6. "When I clenched my jaw and knitted my brows, I suddenly felt angry." This reflects the
   A. two-factor theory.   B. prototype theory.
   C. facial-feedback hypothesis. D. neuro-cultural theory.

7. Research with infants demonstrates that facial expression help us
   A. express internal states.
   B. communicate to others.
   C. evoke a response from others.
   D. to achieve all of the above.

8. A limitation of the role of facial expressions in the experience of emotion includes
    A. the fact that facial expressions can have different meanings depending on the context.
    B. the fact that there is emotion without facial expression and facial expression without emotion.
    C. the fact that there is no way to "peek under the mask" of what people choose to display.
    D. all of the above.

9. The part of the brain that is able to process immediate perceptions of danger or threat is the
    A. left cerebral hemisphere.   B. frontal lobe.
    C. amygdala.   D. cerebellum.

10. The _____ can override the response described in question 9 with a more accurate appraisal of the situation.
    A. limbic system   B. cortex
    C. temporal lobe   D. corpus callosum

11. Left-hemisphere activation is associated with tendencies to _____, while right-hemisphere activation is associated with tendencies to _____
    A. withdraw; approach   B. approach; withdraw
    C. withdraw; withdraw   D. approach; approach

12. Your grandfather had a stroke and he is more angry, fearful and depressed than he was before the stroke. What might explain this personality change?
    A. He may have experienced damage to the right cerebral hemisphere.
    B. He may have experienced damage to the left cerebral hemisphere.
    C. He may have experienced damage to the medulla.
    D. He may have experienced damage to norepinephrine-producing neurons.

13. You are terrified and are experiencing a state of arousal. Which of the following is the involved?
    A. sympathetic nervous system   B. parasympathetic nervous system
    C. voluntary nervous system   D. all of the above

14. Which of the following is one of the hormones that provides the energy of an emotion.
    A. Epinephrine   B. Dopamine
    C. insulin   D. Serotonin

15. One function of arousal appears to be that it
    A. prepares the body to cope with danger or threat.
    B. exhausts and calms the body.
    C. responds to all emotional states with the same pattern.
    D. makes one feel nauseated and seek protection.

16. Which is(are) involved in the physiological experience of emotion?
    A. amygdala   B. cerebral hemispheres
    C. autonomic nervous system   D. all of the above

17. The two-factor theory suggests that both
    A. facial features and the limbic system are necessary to experience emotion.
    B. physiological arousal and cognitive interpretation are involved in emotion.
    C. primary and secondary emotions are necessary to experience emotion.
    D. display rules and emotion work are involved in emotional experiencing.

18. Chris and Joan pass their friend Joel, who hardly acknowledges them. Chris feels hurt
    while Joan feels worried about Joel. This demonstrates the role of
    A. the physiology of emotion.   B. the interpretation of events.
    C. the importance of facial features.   D. all of the above.

19. A study of Olympic athletes found that sometimes the third place winners were happier
    than the second place winners. Their emotional response depended on their
    A. ability to rationalize.   B. desire to win.
    C. interpretations of their award.   D. country of origin.

20. Which of the following reflects a research finding about the relationship between thinking
    and feeling?
    A. Both emotion and cognition can be "rational" or "irrational."
    B. Some emotions do not have a cognitive component, while others do.
    C. As cognitions affect emotions, so too do emotions affect cognitions.
    D. all of the above

21. Primary emotions
    A. indicate that in all cultures certain behaviors are considered acceptable.
    B. include emotions that are morally superior.
    C. are thought to be experienced universally.
    D. incorporate all of the above.

22. Which of the following represents the position of those who disagree with the search for primary emotions?
   A.   There is little agreement in what most people think of as primary.
   B.   There is a cultural influence on every aspect of emotional experience.
   C.   Some emotions may be "basic" in some cultures and not in others.
   D.   all of the above

23. Primary emotions are _____, whereas secondary emotions are _____.
   A.   universal; culture-specific   B.   desirable; undesirable
   C.   culture specific; subculture-specific   D.   agreed upon; controversial

24. In terms of gender differences in the experiencing of emotion, research suggests that
   A.   women experience more emotions more often.
   B.   women and men experience similar emotions equally often.
   C.   men experience more emotions more often.
   D.   the evidence is very contradictory.

25. Where are gender differences in emotion found?
   A.   There are some physiological difference in response to conflict.
   B.   There are differences in the perceptions and expectations that generate certain emotions.
   C.   There are different display rules.
   D.   all of the above

PRACTICE TEST 2 - Multiple Choice

1. Though Terri's heart is racing, she tries to act appropriately as she goes to the stage to receive the award she feels she has earned. As she smiles, she notices she feels better. What elements of emotion are represented in this example?
    A. face and body, mind, culture
    B. physiological arousal and interpretation
    C. brain, nervous system and hormones
    D. emotion work, display rules and nonverbal behavior

2. The ability of our forbears to tell at a glance the difference between a friendly stranger and a hostile one have survival value and serve a(n) _____ function.
    A. primary   B. evolutionary
    C. biological   D. cultural

3. Ekman's cross-cultural studies on facial expressions suggest
    A. certain facial expressions are universal in their emotional meaning.
    B. people from different cultures can recognize the emotions in pictures of people who are entirely foreign to them.
    C. that in the cultures they studied most people recognized the emotional expressions portrayed by people in other cultures.
    D. all of the above.

4. Dr. Varga is smiling. Based on the research, what can you conclude about what she feels?
    A. She is feeling happy.
    B. She is experiencing a primary emotion.
    C. You cannot be sure what she is feeling since facial expressions can communicate states besides emotions.
    D. She is experiencing something positive, though you cannot be sure what.

5. The longer Dr. Varga smiles, the more her mood improves. What best accounts for this?
    A. two-factor theory   B. neuro-cultural theory
    C. theory of primary emotions   D. facial-feedback hypothesis

311

6.	As a result of an accident Hank experienced brain damage. Since his injury, he is unable to understand jokes or the emotions portrayed in films and stories. The damage has most likely occurred in his
	A.	corpus callosum.
	B.	left hemisphere.
	C.	amygdala.
	D.	right hemisphere.

7.	You feel a tap on your shoulder outside the dorm at night. What brain structure helps you to evaluate whether this is a dangerous situation?
	A.	limbic system			B.	cortex
	C.	amygdala			D.	all of the above

8.	Left hemisphere is to _____ as right hemisphere is to _____.
	A.	anger; laughing			B.	laughing; joking
	C.	laughing; anger			D.	anger; tears

9.	My heart is beating, I'm hyperventilating and my pupils are dilated. Which of the following is involved in this response?
	A.	epinephrine			B.	adrenal glands
	C.	norepinephrine			D.	all of the above

10.	Benjamin was angry that his friends forgot his 21st birthday until he was surprised by a large party. His feelings of anger and surprise
	A.	corresponded to the same pattern of autonomic activity.
	B.	corresponded to somewhat different patterns of autonomic activity.
	C.	were different levels of the same emotion.
	D.	involved different nervous systems.

11.	According to the two-factor theory of emotion, if you are physiologically aroused and don't know why,
	A.	you will not feel a need to explain the changes in your body.
	B.	your interpretations of events will not produce a true emotion.
	C.	you will try to label your feeling, using interpretation of events around you.
	D.	you will become irritable and angry.

12. In a series of experiments, students reported occasions in which they had succeeded or failed on an exam. Researchers found that the students' emotions were most closely associated with
   A. whether they had passed or failed the exam.
   B. their explanations for their success or failure.
   C. other peoples' perceptions of their performance.
   D. past experiences with success or failure.

13. Many researchers argue against the use of polygraphs because
   A. they break often and it is not always easy to get an accurate reading.
   B. no physiological patterns of responses are specific to lying.
   C. they often let the guilty go free.
   D. of the corruption associated with their use.

14. People do not become angry or sad because of actual events, but because of their _____ those events.
   A. explanations of   B. participation in
   C. lack of control over   D. disagreement with

15. Jack was caught cheating on a test. He storms out of the room and is furious with the teacher who caught him. Jack's anger is most likely a result of the fact that he is feeling
   A. guilt.   B. regret.
   C. shame.   D. scared.

16. People who experience _____ often blame and resent the person who causes them to feel that way.
   A. guilt   B. shame
   C. either guilt or shame   D. any negative emotion

17. What have studies shown about whether people can learn about the effects of their thinking on their emotions?
   A. People have shown little success at being able to change their thinking.
   B. There is little evidence that changing thinking affects emotions.
   C. People can learn how their thinking affects their emotions and change their thinking accordingly.
   D. People can learn how their thinking affects their emotions, but people's emotions are very irrational and do not respond to reason.

18. Schadenfreude and hagaii are examples of
    A. primary emotions.
    C. secondary emotions.
    B. emotion work.
    D. prototypes.

19. Primary emotions are thought to
    A. differ in each culture.
    B. be experienced universally.
    C. result in similar behaviors in different cultures.
    D. be blends of secondary emotions.

20. Culture can affect
    A. what people feel emotional about.
    B. how particular emotions might be expressed.
    C. the meaning of expressions of emotion.
    D. all of the above.

21. "Being emotional" refers to
    A. an internal emotional state.
    C. how an emotion is displayed.
    B. nonverbal expressiveness.
    D. all of the above.

22. Dr. White objects to the notion that it is useful to search for primary emotions. Why?
    A. Different emotions are more fundamental in different cultures.
    B. Culture influences all emotional responding, even emotions that are biologically based.
    C. Most people don't agree on which emotions are really primary.
    D. all of the above

23. Which of the following is an example of emotion work?
    A. A flight attendant gets angry at a passenger when he is rude.
    B. A bill collector expresses sympathy for a person in debt.
    C. An employee conveys cheerfulness, though his boss is demanding unreasonable deadlines.
    D. For political reasons, a scientist refuses to go onstage to receive an award.

24. Which of the following statements is true?
    A. Women feel emotions more often and more intensely than men.
    B. Men are more likely than women to reveal negative emotions, such as sadness and fear.
    C. Men and women are fairly similar in how often they experience normal, everyday emotions.
    D. Powerful people are more sensitive to subordinates' nonverbal signals than vice versa.

25. Riessman questioned the assumption that men suffer less than women when relationships end, because she found that many divorced men
    A. admitted to being depressed a lot of the time.
    B. claimed they felt very sad for quite a long time.
    C. were expressing grief in acceptably "masculine" ways, such as frantic work and heavy drinking.
    D. expressed their unhappiness by staying in bed or talking about their unhappiness with friends and family.

PRACTICE TEST 3 - Short Answer

1. The most obvious place to look for emotion is on the _____, where the expression of emotion can be most visible.

2. Ekman's research found seven _____ facial expressions.

3. Ekman's theory is called the _____ theory because face muscle physiology and cultural variations affect facial expressions of emotion.

4. The _____ hypothesis would predict that the longer you smiled, the happier you would begin to feel.

5. The _____, a small structure in the limbic system, appears to be responsible for evaluating sensory information and quickly determining its emotional importance. The _____ subsequently provides a more accurate appraisal of incoming information.

6. Certain regions of the _____ cerebral hemisphere appear to be specialized for the processing of positive emotions, such as happiness; regions of the _____ hemisphere are involved in processing negative emotions, such as disgust.

7. When you are in a situation requiring the body to respond, the _____ nervous system sends out two hormones, _____ and _____, that produce a state of arousal.

8. Each emotion may be associated with a somewhat different _____ of autonomic activity that produces differences in the way we experience emotions.

9. Schachter and Singer's two-factor theory of emotion proposed that emotion depends on _____ arousal and the _____ interpretation of such arousal.

10. _____, or how we explain events or behavior, affect our emotional responses.

11. Cognitive _____ refer to the meanings that people attribute to events, including their thoughts, perceptions, interpretations and explanations.

12. In _____ the focus is on the bad self and the person can feel small, worthless, and powerless. In _____ the focus is on the bad behavior that does not affect the overall worthiness of the self.

13. An understanding of the reciprocal interaction between thoughts and feelings helps us to see that just as _____ affect emotions, so do _____ affect cognitions.

14. Most psychologists believe that it is possible to identify a number of _____ emotions that seem to be universal and _____ emotions that are more culture-specific.

15. Some evidence for the existence of primary emotions comes from the fact that most languages have emotion _____, or agreed upon core examples of the concept emotion.

16. Whatever the emotion, every society has _____ governing how and when emotions may be expressed.

17. Acting out an emotion we don't really feel is called emotion _____.

18. Emotions are expressed by body language, the countless _____ signals of body movement, posture, gesture, and gaze.

19. Although some basic signals of body language seem to be universal, most aspects of body language are specific to particular languages and _____.

20. Emotional states of can be synchronized between people. If your mood changes from cheerful to depressed after meeting with a depressed friend, this is an example of emotional _____.

21. There is _____ evidence that men and women differ in whether or how often they feel the everyday emotions of life.

22. If we define being "more emotional" in terms of physiological reactivity to _____, then men are more emotional than women. One possible explanation for this is that the male's autonomic nervous system is, on the average, more _____ than the female's.

23. From a cognitive standpoint, men and women often differ in their _____ of the same event.

24. Sensitivity to other people's emotional states depends on the sex of the sender and receiver, how well the two people know each other, and who has the _____.

25. The one gender difference that undoubtedly contributes most to the stereotype that women are "more emotional" than men is women's greater willingness to _____ their feelings, nonverbally and verbally.

PRACTICE TEST 4 - True/False

1.   T F   There are three main influences on emotion: physiological changes, cognitive processes, and personality type.

2.   T F   Early philosophers believed that our personalities derived from blends of four basic body fluids, or "humors."

3.   T F   The ability to recognize basic facial expressions are not present in early infancy; this ability develops along with language.

4.   T F   Facial expressions probably evolved to foster communication and help us survive.

5.   T F   The facial feedback hypothesis states that our facial expressions generate feedback from other people which then helps us recognize what we are feeling.

6.   T F   Many aspects of emotion are associated with specific parts of the brain. For example, regions of the right hemisphere specialize in recognizing facial expressions and expressing emotions.

7.   T F   The amygdala signals the body to release epinephrine and norepinephrine, which produce the energy to respond to alarm signals.

8.   T F   Different emotions are associated with similar biochemical responses and autonomic nervous system activity. When we experience emotions our body responds with a general state of activation.

9.   T F   The cerebral cortex is responsible for higher, or complex emotional states.

10.   T F   Physiologically, emotions involve facial expressions, parts of the brain (the amygdala and parts of the cerebral hemispheres), and sympathetic nervous system activity.

11.   T F   The polygraph machine is based on the idea that lying is associated with increased autonomic nervous system activity. While the machine is able to measure autonomic arousal, it is not a reliable indicator of lying.

12.   T F   The two-factor theory of emotion holds that emotions result from facial expressions and physiological arousal.

13.   T F   Shame and guilt can be distinguished by different patterns of brain activity and autonomic arousal.

14.   T F   Some primitive emotions can occur without cognition, but many emotions depend on higher cognitive processes.

15.   T F   Emotion and cognition are considered separate, independent processes.

16.   T F   Shame and guilt, along with four other emotions are considered primary, or universal emotions.

17.   T F   Evidence supporting the existence of primary emotions comes from findings on brain physiology, facial expressions, emotion prototypes, and the fact that similar situations, the world over evoke certain emotions.

18.   T F   Psychologists agree on the existence of primary emotions and about which emotions are primary.

19.   T F   Display rules, how and when emotions may be expressed, are universal.

20.   T F   When a language does not have a word for a particular emotion, evidence suggests that people from that country do not experience that emotion.

21.   T F   Some signals of body language seem to be "spoken" universally. However, most aspects of body language are specific to particular spoken languages and cultures.

22.   T F   People who live together are especially vulnerable to emotional contagion.

23.   T F   Emotion work refers to the effort that is required for people to deal with their emotions, both controlling and expressing them.

24.   T F   Research supports the fact that women are more emotional than men; women feel the everyday emotions of life more often and more intensely.

25.   T F   Sensitivity to another person's emotions depends far more on the context in which two people are interacting than on their gender.

PRACTICE TEST 5 - Essay

1. A. While enacting a role, performers sometimes report being lost in the feelings they are depicting. How might this be explained by the facial-feedback hypothesis?

   B. Successful negotiators and gamblers are often described as having poker faces. What does such a phenomenon indicate about the outward expression of emotion?

   C. Emotion work is the acting out of emotions the person does not truly feel. From the standpoint of facial expression and body language, how might this concept be defined?

   D. Body language is specific to cultures and is not good as a universal indicator of emotions. However, when facial expression is the clue, the ability to identify emotions universally rises dramatically. How might Charles Darwin explain this?

2. A. A nurse looks in on a patient shortly before surgery. The patient's heart rate and blood pressure are elevated, breathing is rapid, the pupils are dilated and the patient appears flushed. The nurse concludes that the patient is fearfully anticipating the surgery. What physiological mechanism produces the pattern observed by the nurse?

   B. The nurse tries to reassure the patient but he laughs and denies feeling nervous. In fact, the patient is not very cooperative and the nurse begins to feel irritated but continues to attempt to be comforting and pleasant. Explain the patient's and the nurse's behavior in terms of emotion work and display rules.

   C. What areas of the brain enable the nurse and patient to recognize and interpret the nature of their feelings?

3. Larry, Curly and Moe all got a grade of 75 on a test, yet they each had different reactions to the grade. Larry felt disappointed and depressed. Curly felt relieved that he passed, though he didn't feel particularly happy or sad about the grade. Moe felt extremely happy. Using information about the influence of interpretations on feelings, identify expectations, surrounding events and interpretations of each student's emotional responses.

4.   Mary was given a surprise party for her 40th birthday. As each gift was being opened, Mary felt the following: shocked, then touched, by the pet caterpillar from her young daughter; delighted at the earrings from her sister; warmly amused at the cane, laxatives and contributions for a facelift that came from neighbors; insulted and angry over the "girdle for burgeoning hips" from her cousin; and irritated by the insensitivity of her husband's gift of a vacuum cleaner. Regardless of her true feelings, Mary warmly expressed gratitude and appreciation after each gift, and no one except her younger sister sensed Mary's true feelings. When the guests departed, Mary's husband began to assemble the vacuum cleaner. One look at Mary's face made it clear that she was angry. After prodding, Mary heatedly revealed that her own husband might have been more thoughtful. To her surprise, another package was produced. It contained 40 beautifully arranged exotic flowers from all over the world. Mary's husband had sent out for the flowers and arranged them himself, but confessed that he was too embarrassed to give this gift in front of the guests. Mary confessed that she really wanted to punch her cousin. The next day Mary's younger sister called and was virtually perfect in guessing Mary's true feeling about each gift.

A.   Why did Mary find it important to express gratitude for each gift?
B.   What type of performance is illustrated when Mary feigns gratitude for gifts that disturb her?
C.   Mary's husband easily sees anger on her face. Why isn't this surprising?
D.   Mary privately displays aggressive feelings toward her cousin. Her husband privately displays sensitivity and tenderness. What cultural mechanisms contribute to such behavior?
E.   What advantages does Mary's younger sister have over the other guests when reading Mary's feelings?
F.   Examine Mary's reactions to each gift and think about why she felt as she did. Which reactions tend to result from a process of interpretation that involves culturally determined meanings?

322

CHAPTER 12

Motivation

LEARNING OBJECTIVES

1. Define motivation and distinguish between drives based on physiological needs and those that are psychological and social in nature.

2. Describe the importance of contact comfort in early life and the research findings on attachment.

3. List and explain three theories describing varieties or styles of love.

4. Discuss the impact of social, economic and cultural influences on gender differences in love.

5. Summarize the findings from biological research on sexual responses and behavior.

6. List and explain the cognitive, interpersonal and cultural factors that influence the sexual motives and behaviors of men and women.

7. Discuss the motivational factors involved in rape and coercive sexual behavior.

8. Describe the various explanations advanced to explain sexual orientation. Discuss the limitations of these hypotheses.

9. Explain the internal and external forces that motivate people to work and to succeed.

10. Distinguish between the need for achievement and the need for power.

11. List and discuss four types of motivational conflicts.

12. Summarize Maslow's hierarchy of needs and discuss whether motives can be ranked.

CHAPTER CONCEPT MAP

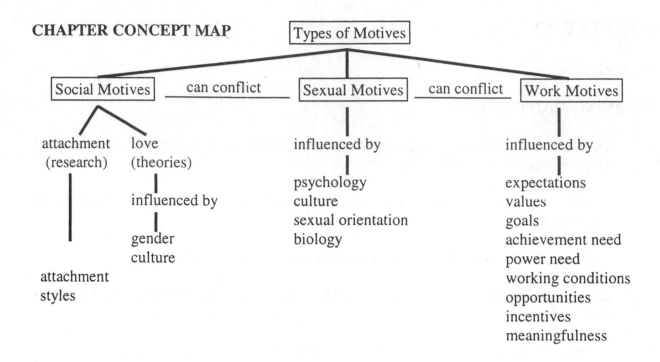

BRIEF CHAPTER SUMMARY

Chapter 12 describes three categories of motives: social motives, sexual motives and work motives. Attachment can develop between children and caregivers and between adults. Four approaches to studying love are described. Attachment theory of love is based on Ainsworth's studies of attachment styles in infants. Attachment theory suggests that early attachment experiences can affect adult relationships. The chapter discusses gender differences in love and reports that no gender differences have been found in the desire for attachment, but some other differences have been found by researchers. The biological, psychological and cultural influences on the sexual motive are discussed. Kinsey introduced the scientific study of sex, which was continued by Masters and Johnson. Coercive sex, or rape, is considered an act of dominance or aggression rather than an act motivated by sexual desire. Different theories that attempt to explain sexual orientation are reviewed. These theories lead to the conclusion that sexual orientation is a result of the interaction of biology, culture, learning and circumstances. The motive to work is influenced by internal factors, such as one's expectations, values, needs for achievement and power, and by external factors, such as working conditions.

PREVIEW OUTLINE AND REVIEW QUESTIONS

Before you read the chapter, review the preview outline and the Learning Objectives for each section of the text. Answer all questions as you read the text.

SECTION 1 - THE SOCIAL ANIMAL: MOTIVES FOR LOVE (PP. 422-431)

I. **THE SOCIAL ANIMAL: MOTIVES FOR LOVE**
    A. **Definition** - motivation is any process that causes a person or animal to move toward a goal or away from an unpleasant situation
    B. **Approaches to motivation**
        1. Drive theory - early approach which was later rejected
        2. Current approach emphasizes conscious thinking and planning
    C. **Attachment**
        1. Need for _affiliation_ - deep emotional tie to a loved one
        2. Contact comfort - pleasure of being touched and held
            a. Emotional attachment begins with early physical touching
            b. Harlow studies - showed need for _contact_ comfort
        3. Separation and security
            a. _separation_ anxiety develops between seven and nine months and last until middle of second year; experienced by all children
            b. Ainsworth - studied attachment using the "strange situation" method
                (1) Mother leaves baby in a room with stranger and the baby's reaction is observed with mother, with stranger and alone
                (2) Identified two main _attachment_ categories
                    (a) securely attached - cry when she leaves, happy upon return
                    (b) insecurely attached - takes two forms
                        i)   avoidant - not caring what the mother does
                        ii) anxious/ _ambivalent_ baby protests if mother leaves, resists when she returns
            c. What causes insecure attachment?
                (1) Ainsworth says that mother's treatment of infant in first year establishes attachment style but now believe mothers are not the only influence on attachment style
                (2) Differences in normal child-rearing practices don't affect
                (3) Daycare does not affect stability or kind of attachment
                (4) Factors related to the development of insecure attachment
                    (a) Child's temperament and genetic disposition
                    (b) Child's family circumstances
                    (c) Later stressful events in childhood

325

D.   **The varieties of love** - different theories
1.   Passionate and _compassionate_ love
2.   Lee's six styles of loving: eros (romantic); ludus (game-playing); storge (affectionate); pragma (logical); mania (possessive); and agape (unselfish)
3.   _Triangle_ theory of love (Sternberg) - consummate love has passion, intimacy, commitment; varieties of love result from combinations of these
4.   The attachment theory of love (Shaver and Hazan)
    a.   Adult attachment styles originate in infant-parent relationship; people develop "working models" of relationships
    b.   Ainsworth's attachment styles in adults: secure, _avoidance_, ambivalent
    c.   There is research support for this model
5.   Gender, culture and love
    a.   Gender differences - stereotypes oversimplify
    b.   No evidence that one sex loves more than the other, both become equally attached and suffer when a love relationship ends
    c.   Many gender differences found in how men and women express love are related to male and female role expectations
    d.   Cultural origins of gender differences
        (1)   Depend on social, economic and cultural factors
        (2)   As women entered the workforce gender differences in romantic love waned; now both sexes marry for love

E.   **Love stories and their consequences**
1.   Our beliefs about love affect our satisfaction with relationships
2.   It is important to think critically about love

Answer these Learning Objectives while you read Section 1.

1.   Define motivation and distinguish between drives based on physiological needs and those that are psychological and social in nature.

2.   Describe the importance of contact comfort in early life and the research findings on attachment.

3.   List and explain three theories describing varieties or styles of love.

4.   Discuss the impact of social, economic and cultural influences on gender differences in love.

**SECTION 2 - THE EROTIC ANIMAL: MOTIVES FOR SEX (PP. 431-440) AND
SECTION 3 - THE COMPETENT ANIMAL: MOTIVES FOR WORK (PP. 441-446)**

II.   **THE EROTIC ANIMAL: MOTIVES FOR SEX**
   A.   **The biology of desire**
      1.   Hormones and sexual response
         a.   The hormone _testosterone_ promotes sexual desire in both sexes but it doesn't "cause" sexual behavior in a direct way
         b.   Testosterone increases sexual arousal AND sexual activity increases testosterone levels; the influence goes in both directions
      2.   Arousal and orgasm
         a.   Scientific sex research began by _Kinsey_, furthered by Masters and Johnson; this research has limitations
         b.   Sex research can remove superstitions but it doesn't fully explain sexual behavior which can't be reduced to physiological responses of the body

   B.   **The psychology of desire**
      1.   Values, expectations, fantasies, beliefs affect sexual responsiveness
      2.   The many motives for sex - motives for having sex include enhancement, intimacy, coping, self-affirmation, partner approval, peer approval
      3.   Sexual coercion and rape - men and women have different experiences
         a.   Gender differences exist in perception of coercion
         b.   Motives for rape vary - primarily an act of _hostility_
         c.   Characteristics of sexually aggressive males: insecurity, hostility toward women, defensiveness, preference for promiscuous, impersonal sex; convicted rapists' motives are more disturbed

   C.   **The culture of desire** - sexual motivation and behavior occur in a context
      1.   Cultural variations in sexuality - sexual practices vary across cultures
      2.   _Sexual_ scripts - culture's requirements for proper sexual behavior; they are based on gender roles which result in different scripts
      3.   The origins of sexual attitudes
         a.   Evolutionary psychologists look to evolutionary processes
         b.   Cultural psychologists look to gender roles, economic, social arrangements

   D.   **The riddle of sexual orientation**
      1.   Psychological versus biological explanations
         a.   Biological explanations for sexual orientation are inconclusive
         b.   Psychological theories have not been supported
      2.   Sexual identity and behavior take many forms
      3.   Interaction of biology, _cultural norms_, experiences
      4.   Homosexuality and politics - sex research can have political goals

327

III. **THE COMPETENT ANIMAL: MOTIVES TO WORK**
    A.   **The effects of motivation on work**
        1.   Expectations and values - how they influence work
            a.   Work harder if success expected; creates a self-fulfilling prophecy
            b.   Work harder if you want something more which depends on values (a central motivating belief reflecting fundamental goals and ideals)
            c.   Values themselves have psychological consequences
        2.   Needs for achievement and power - use of Thematic Apperception Test
            a.   Those with high or low achievement motive differ
            b.   Power motive of leaders may be a psychological cause of war
    B.   **The effects of work on motivation**
        1.   Working conditions that influence work motivation and satisfaction
            a.   Meaningfulness, ability to control aspects of work, varied tasks, clear and consistent rules, supportive relationships, useful feedback, opportunities for growth and development
            b.   Motivation is not increased by high pay but by how and when money is paid - incentive pay in particular
        2.   Opportunities to achieve - some groups may lack opportunity (glass ceiling, segregation by gender, racism)

Answer these Learning Objectives while you read Sections 2 and 3.

5.   Summarize the findings from biological research on sexual responses and behavior.

6.   List and explain the cognitive, interpersonal and cultural factors that influence the sexual motives and behaviors of men and women.

7.   Discuss the motivational factors involved in rape and coercive sexual behavior.

8.   Describe various explanations advanced to explain sexual orientation. Discuss the limitations of these hypotheses.

9.   Explain the internal and external forces that motivate people to work and to succeed.

10.   Distinguish between the need for achievement and the need for power.

SECTION 4 - MOTIVES, GOALS, AND WELL-BEING (PP. 447-451)

IV. **MOTIVES, GOALS, AND WELL-BEING**
    A. **The importance of goals**
        1. Goals are likely to improve performance when the goal is specific, challenging but achievable, and is defined as getting what you want (approach goals) versus avoiding what you don't want (avoidance goals)
        2. Performance versus _mastery_ goals
            a. Performance goals - want to do well, failure is discouraging
            b. Mastery (learning) goals - want to improve skills, failure not discouraging; feel greater intrinsic pleasure in the task
            c. Children praised for ability and intelligence rather than effort are more likely to develop performance goals
        3. Choice, duty, and satisfaction
            a. Westerners are motivated best by goals that are freely chosen
            b. Culture influences which goals one selects and whether it matters how they are chosen

    B. **When motives conflict**
        1. Kinds of motivational conflicts
            a. Approach-_approach_ equal attraction to two or more goals
            b. Avoidance-avoidance - when you dislike two alternatives
            c. Approach-_avoidance_ one activity has a positive and negative aspect
                (1) Attraction and repulsion strongest when nearest the goal
                (2) Makes this type difficult to resolve
            d. Multiple approach-avoidance - several possible choices each containing advantages and disadvantages
        2. Consequences of high levels of conflict and ambivalence
            a. Some internal conflict inevitable
            b. Associated with anxiety, depression, headaches and other symptoms
        3. Can motives be ranked?
            a. Maslow's theory - hierarchy of needs
            b. Survival needs at the bottom, self-actualization needs at the top; lower need must be met before higher needs can be addressed
        4. Popular theory but unsupported by _research_

depends on culture, motivation

Answer these Learning Objectives while you read Section 4.

11. List and discuss four types of motivational conflicts.

12. Summarize Maslow's hierarchy of needs and discuss whether motives can be ranked.

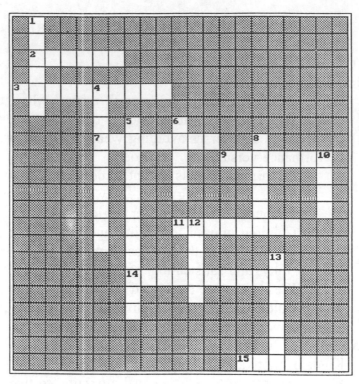

ACROSS

2. attachment style in which babies cry when mothers leave and are happy upon mother's return
3. any process that causes a person or animal to move toward a goal or away from an unpleasant situation
7. attachment style in which babies seem indifferent to the mother
9. testosterone is an example of one
11. half of an internal conflict in which one is attracted to one aspect of a choice
14. this need is measured by the TAT
15. type of goal in which people are motivated to improve their skills and failure is not discouraging

DOWN

1. theorist who proposed the idea that needs fall on a hierarchy
4. deep emotional tie to a loved one
5. a kind of love characterized by affection and trust
6. central motivating belief that reflects important goals and ideals
8. logical love according to Lee's theory
10. romantic love according to Lee's theory
13. attachment style in which babies protest when mother leaves but resist contact upon her return

330

FLASH CARDS

Cut the following chart along the borders and test yourself with the resulting flash cards.

12.1 MOTIVATION	12.2 DRIVES	12.3 NEED FOR AFFILIATION
12.4 CONTACT COMFORT	12.5 SEPARATION ANXIETY	12.6 THE STRANGE SITUATION
12.7 SECURE ATTACHMENT STYLE	12.8 AVOIDANT ATTACHMENT STYLE	12.9 ANXIOUS/AMBIVALENT ATTACHMENT STYLE
12.10 PASSIONATE AND COMPANIONATE LOVE	12.11 THE SIX "MEANINGS OF LOVE"	12.12 THE TRIANGLE THEORY OF LOVE
12.13 THE ATTACHMENT THEORY OF LOVE	12.14 GENDER ROLES	12.15 SEXUAL SCRIPTS
12.16 VALUES	12.17 NEED FOR ACHIEVEMENT (nACH)	12.18 THEMATIC APPERCEPTION TEST (TAT)
12.19 NEED FOR POWER	12.20 THE "GLASS CEILING"	12.21 INCENTIVE PAY
12.22 PERFORMANCE VS. MASTER (LEARNING) GOALS	12.23 APPROACH AND AVOIDANCE CONFLICTS	12.24 MASLOW'S HIERARCHY OF NEEDS

12.3 The motive to associate with other people, as by seeking friends, moral support, companionship, or love.	12.2 Biological states of tension resulting from deprivation of physical needs. Once thought to account for most motivation.	12.1 A process within a person that causes movement toward a goal or away from an unpleasant situation.
12.6 An experimental method used by Ainsworth to study the nature of attachment between mothers and babies.	12.5 Distress most children develop, at about 7 to 9 months of age, when their primary caretakers temporarily leave.	12.4 The need for touching; the Harlows first demonstrated this need in primates with their classic experiment.
12.9 An attachment style in which babies protest when a parent leaves the room and resist when he or she returns.	12.8 Attachment style in which babies do not seem to care if the mother leaves them and who seek little contact with her.	12.7 Attachment style in which babies protest if a parent leaves and welcomes the parent when he or she returns.
12.12 Sternberg's theory that the variations of love are a combination of passion, intimacy, and commitment.	12.11 Lee's theory that says there are six distinct kinds of love: eros, ludus, storge, pragma, mania, and agape.	12.10 Passionate love is characterized by intense emotions; companionate love by affection and trust.
12.15 Descriptions of proper sexual behavior for a person in a given situation, varying with age, culture, gender.	12.14 Collection of rules that determine the proper attitudes and behavior for men and women, sexual and otherwise.	12.13 Theory that adult styles of love originate in infant-parent attachment and can be secure, avoidant, anxious.
12.18 Personality test usually scored for various motives such as the needs for affiliation, power, and achievement.	12.17 A learned motive to meet personal standards of success and excellence in a chosen area (abbreviated nAch).	12.16 A central motivating belief that reflects fundamental goals and ideas that are important to the person.
12.21 The strongest monetary motivator; bonuses given upon completion of a goal and not as an automatic part of salary.	12.20 A barrier to promotion that is so subtle as to be transparent, yet strong enough to prevent advancement.	12.19 A learned motive to dominate or influence others.
12.24 A theory that places motives on a pyramid. At the bottom are survival needs, self-actualization at the top.	12.23 In approach conflicts, one is equally attracted to two or more goals; both goals are disliked in avoidance conflicts.	12.22 Performance goals focus on doing well and avoiding criticism; mastery goals focus on increased competence.

PRACTICE TEST 1 - Multiple Choice

1. A process within a person or animal that causes that organism to move toward a goal or away from and unpleasant situation is called
    A. energy.
    B. incentive.
    C. motivation.
    D. the need for achievement.

2. Hunger and thirst are _____ motives, while achievement and affiliation are _____ motives.
    A. drives; needs
    B. primary; social
    C. learned; unlearned
    D. learned; primary

3. Social motives are
    A. biological.
    B. unlearned.
    C. learned.
    D. primary.

4. The motive to be with others, make friends, cooperate, and love is the need for
    A. achievement.
    B. contact comfort.
    C. attachment.
    D. affiliation.

5. The deep emotional tie that babies and children develop for their primary caregivers, and their distress at being separated from them, is called
    A. attachment.
    B. affiliation.
    C. contact comfort.
    D. security.

6. Harry and Margaret Harlow's studies, in which infant rhesus monkeys ran to soft, terry cloth "mothers" when they were frightened or startled, demonstrated the need for
    A. affiliation.
    B. food.
    C. contact comfort.
    D. love.

7. Babies who are well fed and sheltered but who are not touched and held develop
    A. abnormally and have emotional problems.
    B. moodiness.
    C. no problems as long as they are not mistreated.
    D. anger.

8. "I try to keep my lover a little uncertain about my commitment to him/her" is a statement that represents which type of love?
    A. passionate love
    B. insecure
    C. ludus
    D. eros

9. Which of the following is NOT one of the theories of love discussed in the text?
   A. passionate love and companionate love
   B. friendship love, parent-child love, romantic love
   C. ludus, eros, storge, mania, pragma, agape
   D. secure, avoidant, anxious/ambivalent

10. Adult love styles originate in a person's first and most important "love relationship," the infant-parent attachment. Which approach to love does this describe?
    A. affiliation theory   B. Lee's theory
    C. attachment theory of love   D. narrative theory of love

11. Kinsey made which of the following observations about biological differences in sexual behavior between men and women?
    A. Males and females are alike in their basic anatomy and physiology.
    B. Males and females differ in frequency of masturbation and orgasm.
    C. Females have a lesser "sexual capacity."
    D. all of the above

12. Which of the following was a finding of Masters and Johnson?
    A. Male and female arousal and orgasms are remarkably similar.
    B. Orgasms are physiologically the same, regardless of the source of stimulation.
    C. Women's capacity for sexual response infinitely surpasses that of men.
    D. all of the above

13. Which of the following is true about gender differences in motives for sex?
    A. Motives for sex are generally quite similar.
    B. People rarely have sex when they don't want to.
    C. Women engage in sex when they don't want to but men do not.
    D. none of the above

14. Which characteristics were found more often in sexually aggressive males?
    A. a history of violence and psychological problems
    B. poor communication and feelings of insecurity
    C. hostile attitudes and sexual promiscuity
    D. a history of being abused and family problems

15. Motivation for rape includes which of the following?
    A. sexual outlet   B. power and anger at women
    C. crossed signals   D. psychological disturbance

16. Kissing, sexual arousal and orgasm are
    A. natural behaviors.   B. biologically based behaviors.
    C. highly influenced by culture and learning. D. normal behaviors.

17. The fact that boys are motivated to impress other males with their sexual experiences and
    girls are taught not to indulge in sexual pleasure demonstrates the effects of
    A. hormones.   B. sexual scripts.
    C. game-playing.   D. sexual orientation.

18. Which of the following best describes current thinking about the origins of sexual
    orientation?
    A. Most research supports a genetic basis.
    B. Dominant mothers and absent/passive fathers contribute to male homosexuality.
    C. Brain differences between heterosexuals and homosexuals explains sexual
       orientation.
    D. Sexual identity and behavior involve an interaction of biology, culture, and
       experiences.

19. Which of the following represents an argument against biological explanations of sexual
    orientation?
    A. The flexible sexual history of most lesbians.
    B. Most gay men and lesbians do not have a close gay relative.
    C. Studies on brain differences have not been reliable or replicated.
    D. all of the above

20. Which of the following motivations influences peoples' work habits?
    A. their expectation and values   B. how competent they feel
    C. the type of goals they have   D. all of the above

21. Stacey is studying to be a master violin maker. When she makes a mistake she feels she
    has learned useful information about what to do next time. She knows that this process
    will take time and that she must be patient. She is motivated by
    A. performance goals.   B. learning and mastery goals.
    C. self-efficacy.   D. all of the above.

22. People who dream about becoming rich and famous probably have a high need for
    _____, while those who dream about being a leader and influencing others are
    probably high in the need for _____.
    A. power; manipulation.   B. achievement; power.
    C. power; achievement.   D. none of the above

23. The motive for power in great leaders
    A. may be a psychological cause of war.
    B. has caused their personal ambition to be used for the greater good.
    C. been associated with the need for affiliation.
    D. has been associated with greater criminal activity.

24. You want to have Chinese food for dinner but you also have a craving for Italian food. This represents a(n)
    A. approach-approach conflict.   B. avoidance-avoidance conflict.
    C. approach-avoidance conflict.   D. no lose situation.

25. Research on Maslow's hierarchy of needs
    A. has supported the idea that motives are met in a hierarchy.
    B. has not supported this theory.
    C. has found that it is true that lower needs must be met first but that once these needs are met, all people do not necessarily go on to meet the higher needs.
    D. has found that very few people go on to meet the higher needs.

PRACTICE TEST 2 - Multiple Choice

1. Susan has no energy for studying. Whenever she tries, she falls asleep. She does, however, feel very energetic when asked to go to a movie. Which aspect of motivation does this demonstrate?
    A. reducing a state of physical deprivation   B. satisfying of a biological need
    C. moving toward a goal   D. fulfilling a drive

2. Affiliation, attachment, love and work are examples of
    A. unlearned motives.   B. social motives.
    C. primary motives.   D. all of the above.

3. Jerry needs a lot of solitude and "space," while Harry needs friends and family around as much as possible. They differ on
    A. the need for affiliation.   B. attachment needs.
    C. the need for contact comfort.   D. love style.

4. Lucia's mom is not very comfortable with physical affection. Although she loves Lucia and takes good care of her, she does not hold or cuddle her. In contrast, her dad likes to hug and cuddle. Based on Harlow's experiments, to which parent would Lucia be most likely to go to when she is upset?
    A. her mom   B. her dad
    C. either   D. impossible to say

5. Which of the following is consistent with the findings of the Harlow studies?
    A. Babies who are adequately fed and sheltered but deprived of touch show abnormal development and emotional problems.
    B. Emotional and physical symptoms occur in adults who are "undertouched."
    C. Patients find even mild touching by nurses comforting and reassuring.
    D. all of the above

6. Baby Huey cries for his mother to pick him up, yet when she does, he wants to be put back down. According to Ainsworth's studies, Huey exhibits a(n)
    A. avoidant attachment style.   B. ambivalent attachment style.
    C. secure attachment style   D. psychological problem.

337

7. Ainsworth identified mother's treatment of their babies as the primary determinant of attachment styles. What are other influences on attachment?
    A. Some babies are insecurely attached because they are temperamentally difficult.
    B. Stressful events.
    C. Family circumstances.
    D. All of the above.

8. Which type of love does the following personal ad represent? "Passionate male seeking companion who likes to have romantic dinners by candlelight, take moonlit walks on the beach and read poetry together."
    A. pragma   B. eros
    C. ludus   D. storge

9. Victoria knows what she wants in a man. He must be good looking, have a good job, want to have at least two children and have a college education. This represents which type of love?
    A. ludus   B. storge
    C. agape   D. pragma

10. Which types of love styles would be most likely to make the best match?
    A. avoidant-avoidant   B. ludic-ludic
    C. pragma-storge   D. avoidant female-anxious male

11. Studies of men who have been chemically castrated, women who are taking androgens, and women who kept diaries of their sexual activity while having their hormone levels measured support
    A. the role of cognitive interpretations on sexual motivation.
    B. the role of cultural scripts on sexual motivation.
    C. the role of testosterone on sexual motivation.
    D. all of the above.

12. Biological researchers have made important contributions to our understanding of the sexual behavior of men and women, including
    A. confirming that women can have two types of orgasms.
    B. identifying the similarities between men and women in their basic anatomy and in their arousal responses and orgasms.
    C. identifying how sexual responses vary among individuals according to age, experience, and culture.
    D. identifying that peoples' physiological responses are good indicators of their subjective experience of desire and arousal.

13. Jason may have sex when he doesn't want to because _____, whereas Jennifer may be sexual when she doesn't want to because _____
    A. he feels obligated: of peer pressure.
    B. of peer pressure; she feels guilty.
    C. he feels guilty; of inexperience.
    D. it is easier than having an argument; of peer pressure.

14. In a large-scale sex survey, one fourth of the women said they had been forced to do something sexually that they did not want to do, but only about 3 percent of the men said that they ever had forced a woman into a sexual act. How might this be explained?
    A. Men are in denial about their sexual behavior.
    B. What many women experience as coercion is not seen as such by many men.
    C. Women tend to overexaggerate these experiences.
    D. Women say "no," but they mean "yes."

15. Of the following men, the one who is most likely to be sexually aggressive is
    A. a man with a psychiatric disorder.
    B. a man who has not had a sexual encounter in many months.
    C. a man who had is insecure, defensive and has had many partners.
    D. a man who adores women.

16. Talking about sexual responses and motivations in a college class is embarrassing for Maia, who is from Morocco. She feels she should not be listening to this kind of information, particularly in a public place with males present. This is an example of
    A. interpersonal scripts.   B. intrapsychic scripts.
    C. cultural scripts.   D. social scripts.

17. Two students from different parts of the world met in College in the U.S. They fell in love and are beginning a sexual relationship. Because of their different cultural backgrounds, they
    A. would agree that kissing is enjoyable.
    B. would both enjoy kissing, but might disagree about whether it is appropriate.
    C. might disagree about whether kissing is erotic or deviant.
    D. would agree that they should not kiss until they have dated for a long time.

18. Felicia was a heterosexual for many years and has recently fallen in love with another woman. Felicia's situation argues against
    A. psychological explanations of sexual orientation.
    B. biological explanations of sexual orientation.
    C. cultural explanations of sexual orientation.
    D. the idea that sexual orientation is a choice.

19. Which of the following explanations for homosexuality has been supported by research?
    A. bad mothering, absent fathering
    B. parental role models
    C. homosexuals have a mental disorder
    D. none of the above

20. The person who is more likely to work hard is
    A. someone who expects to succeed.
    B. someone with a high salary.
    C. someone who has performance goals.
    D. none of the above.

21. Expectations, values, goals and the need for achievement show the effects of _____, whereas working conditions and opportunity show the effects of _____.
    A. motivation on work; work on motivation
    B. work on motivation; motivation on work
    C. external forces; internal forces
    D. none of the above

22. Julie has been passed over for a promotion several times and each time a male has been hired. What phenomenon does this describe?
    A. Her managing style is different from the approach taken by men.
    B. The "glass ceiling" limits her opportunities.
    C. She has less commitment to the job than a man would.
    D. She has poorer self-esteem and feelings of competence than men.

23. When people with a high nAch take the TAT, their stories are about
    A. pleasing other people who are important to them.
    B. pursing social goals.
    C. becoming rich and famous.
    D. taking on a great adventure, like traveling to the South Seas.

24. Going to the dentist or having one's teeth fall out is an example of a(n) _____ conflict; wanting to go out with Dan while continuing to date Stan is an example of a(n) _____ conflict; wanting to travel this summer but knowing if you do you will miss the summer with your friends is an example of a(n) _____ conflict.
    A. avoidance-avoidance; approach-approach; approach-avoidance
    B. approach-avoidance; approach-approach; avoidance-avoidance
    C. approach-approach; avoidance-avoidance; approach-avoidance
    D. approach-avoidance; approach-approach; approach-approach

25. People like Mahatma Ghandi and Martin Luther King, Jr. show that people
    A. can choose higher needs over lower ones.
    B. make their own hierarchies.
    C. may have many needs simultaneously.
    D. may do all of the above.

PRACTICE TEST 3 - Short Answer

1. Motivation refers to any process that causes a person or animal to move _____ a goal or _____ from an unpleasant situation.

2. _____ refer to states of tension resulting from the deprivation of physical needs, such as those for food and water.

3. One of the deepest and most universal of human motives is the need for _____, the need to be with others, make friends, cooperate, love.

4. In the Harlow experiments, the baby monkeys ran to the _____ "mother" when they were frightened or startled. This reaction demonstrated the need for _____.

5. A mother brings her baby into an unfamiliar room containing lots of toys. After a while a stranger comes in and attempts to play with the child. The mother leaves the baby with the stranger. She then returns, plays with the child, and the stranger leaves. Finally, the mother leaves the baby alone for three minutes and returns. This describes the research method used by _____ and it is called the _____.

6. In the research situation described in question 5, babies who did not care if their mothers left the room and made little effort to seek contact with the mothers when they returned demonstrated one of the insecure types of attachment, called _____ attachment. style.

7. Ainsworth believed that attachment styles were based on the way _____ treated their babies in the first year. Subsequent research has found that other factors contribute to insecure attachment. These other factors include family circumstances, later stressful events in childhood and the child's _____.

8. Lee's six types of love include: _____, _____, _____, pragma, mania, and eros.

9. The type of love called mania is a love that is _____ and dependent.

10. Sternberg's _____ theory of love says that the three ingredients of love are intimacy, _____, and _____.

11. Companionate love is intimacy plus _____.

12.	_____ theory of love says that the kind of relationships that people have as adults is strongly related to their reports of how their parents treated them.

13.	Men and women do differ, on average, in how they _____ love.

14.	Gender differences in ways of expressing love and intimacy do not just pop up from nowhere; they reflect social, _____, and cultural forces.

15.	The hormone _____ seems to promote sexual desire in both sexes, though it does not "cause" sexual behavior, or any other behavior, in a simple, direct way.

16.	Kinsey was the first to introduce the idea that men and women are sexually _____ though he did think that women had lesser sexual capacity.

17.	A large scale study found that there were six factors underlying the many reasons that people give for having sex. The reasons are enhancement, intimacy, coping, self-affirmation, _____ and _____.

18.	Men who coerce women into having sex have _____ that justify their behavior.

19.	The argument that rape is primarily an act of _____ and aggression is supported by the widespread evidence of soldiers who rape captive women during war, and then often kill them.

20.	A person following a gender role needs a _____ script that teaches men and women how to behave in sexual matters.

21.	The most reasonable conclusions about sexual identity and behavior is that they involve an interaction of biology, _____, and experience.

22.	Those in the field of _____ psychology study work motivation in the laboratory and in organizations, where they study the conditions that influence productivity and satisfaction.

23.	A _____ is a central motivating belief, reflecting a person's fundamental goals and ideals.

24.	The Thematic Apperception Test is used to measure the strength of two motives: _____ and _____.

25.	Sometimes minority groups and women lack the _____ to achieve.

PRACTICE TEST 4 - True/False

1.   T F   Today, motivation researchers emphasize biological drives as the primary source of human motivation.

2.   T F   Only children from certain cultures experience separation anxiety.

3.   T F   Ainsworth identified three categories of attachment; secure, avoidant, and anxious or ambivalent.

4.   T F   Research has supported Ainsworth's theory that babies need the right kind of mothering to become securely attached, and daycare can retard or impede this development.

5.   T F   Longitudinal studies have found that childhood attachment styles carry over into adulthood and remain quite stable.

6.   T F   Research has found that women love more than men in terms of "love at first sight" and over the long haul.

7.   T F   Sex is a biological drive and sexual behavior is a matter of doing what comes naturally.

8.   T F   For most women psychological factors influence sexual desire far more than hormone levels do.

9.   T F   Freud believed that women could have two types of orgasms: "childish," clitoral orgasms and "mature," vaginal orgasms.

10.   T F   Masters and Johnson confirmed that male and female arousal and orgasms are remarkably similar and that all orgasms are physiologically the same, regardless of the source of stimulation.

11.   T F   Only a very small number of male and female college students report that they are having sex not for pleasure or intimacy, but because of feelings of inadequacy or peer pressure.

12.   T F   In one survey, two-thirds of the men reported having had unwanted intercourse.

13.   T F   In most cases of rape, the rapist is known to the victim.

14. T F Sexual scripts are outdated and do not have a strong impact on behavior.

15. T F Industrialization and modernization are causing an increase in differences between sexual behaviors of men and women.

16. T F Most psychologists agree that homosexuality is a result of psychological causes including poor role models, weak or absent fathers or domineering mothers.

17. T F The children of gay parents are much more likely to become gay than children of heterosexual parents.

18. T F Generally, people who are primarily motivated to get rich have poorer psychological adjustment and lower well-being than do people whose primary values are self-acceptance, affiliation with others, or wanting to make the world a better place.

19. T F Money is one of the top five contributors to work motivation and satisfaction.

20. T F The "glass ceiling," or barriers to promotion that often affect women and members of minority groups, is a thing of the past.

21. T F Goals are likely to improve performance when they are specific, realistic, and defined in terms of getting what you want rather than avoiding what you do not want.

22. T F People who are motivated by performance goals are concerned with doing well, being judged favorably, and avoiding criticism.

23. T F It is more likely that children who are praised for effort, rather than for ability or intelligence, will be less likely to give up after a mistake and will enjoy their challenges more.

24. T F Being able to choose your own goals is a key contributor to motivation and satisfaction, across all cultures.

25. T F In approach-avoidance conflicts, both attraction and repulsion are typically strongest when you are nearest the goal.

PRACTICE TEST 5 - Essay

1.   Donna is a college student. Her work and her household responsibilities are completed and she finds herself with free time. She decides to do the following: call her friend, visit her boyfriend, do an extra credit assignment and work on an extra project for her job. Describe the influence of motives on her behaviors.

2.   Write a personal ad for each of the six types of love styles described by Lee.

3.   You are at a party and there is a debate about what "causes" homosexuality. On the one side, Jose says it is a choice that people freely make. Amy says that it is clearly biological. Describe the information that supports and refutes each of their positions. Also discuss the political implications of each point of view.

4.   Identify the type of conflict associated with each example below.
    A.   Sarah couldn't decide whether to purchase a van or a sports car. Each had desirable qualities, but neither provided everything she wanted.
    B.   Hank promised the counselor that this third switch between chemistry and physics would be the last. He dreaded both courses but had to take one to fulfill requirements.
    C.   When the networks put her favorite shows on at the same time, Lucy bought a VCR so she could watch one program and record the other for later viewing.
    D.   David, an avid fisherman, just met new neighbors who made his day. The neighbors agreed to clean his fish and split the catch. David loved landing the fish but couldn't do the cleaning because it made him nauseous.

CHAPTER 13

Theories of Personality

LEARNING OBJECTIVES

1. Define personality.

2. Describe characteristics of the Minnesota Multiphasic Personality Inventory (MMPI) and the 16 Personality Factor (PF) and how they were developed.

3. List and discuss the major trait theories of personality, including the Big Five.

4. Discuss the issue of heritability of personality, temperament, and traits including cautionary considerations.

5. Describe and evaluate the social-cognitive approach. Include reciprocal determinism, self-efficacy, and locus of control in your discussion.

6. Discuss how culture influences how we define our selves and our approach to time.

7. Explain the basic principles of Freud's psychoanalytic approach to the study of personality and list the emphases shared by modern psychodynamic theories.

8. Discuss and evaluate how projective tests attempt to measure personality.

9. Describe the structure of the personality, according to Freud, and defense mechanisms.

10. Describe the five psychosexual stages of personality development identified by Freud.

11. Discuss the challenges to psychoanalytic theory made by Horney, Jung, and the object-relations school.

12. Summarize the criticisms and contributions of psychodynamic theories.

13. Summarize the principles of humanistic psychology proposed by Maslow, Rogers, and May.

14. Discuss how each theoretical approach to personality helps to explain our public and private personalities.

CHAPTER CONCEPT MAP

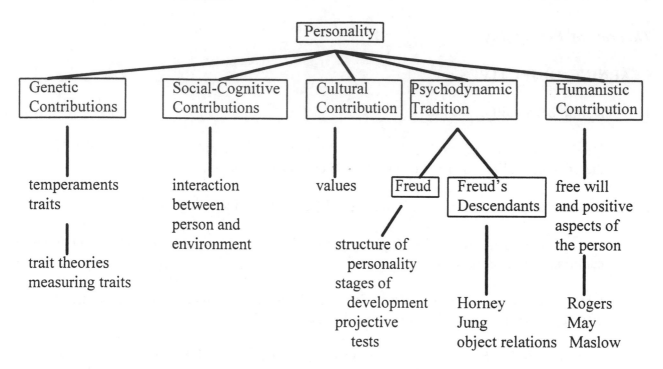

BRIEF CHAPTER SUMMARY

Chapter 13 defines personality and reviews the major theoretical approaches that have been advanced to explain its development. The biological approach looks to the heritability of traits and to the idea that there is a genetic basis to certain temperaments. The social-cognitive approach emphasizes the reciprocal interactions between specific stiuations and a person's cognitions and behaviors. Locus of control and self-efficacy are characteristics that have an important influence on how we perceive and respond to particular situations. Cognitions and behaviors are also influenced by culture. The chapter looks at some influences culture can have on personality. The psychodynamic approaches focus on the role of unconscious processes and the development of the id, ego and superego. Freud originally developed this approach, and then other theorists made modifications to his work. The humanist and existential approaches reject the negative and deterministic views of the psychoanalytic and behavioral approaches. These approaches focus on the positive aspects of humanity and the idea that human beings have free will and can shape their own destinies.

PREVIEW OUTLINE AND REVIEW QUESTIONS

Before you read the chapter, review the preview outline and the Learning Objectives for each section of the text. Answer all questions as you read the text.

SECTION 1 - MEASURING PERSONALITY (PP. 458-461)

I. **MEASURING PERSONALITY**
   - A. **Definitions** - distinctive pattern of behavior, thoughts, motives and emotions that characterizes an individual over time
     1. This pattern consists of specific _____, or habitual ways of behaving, thinking, and feeling
     2. Psychologists disagree about which traits are central and about the origin and stability of traits
   - B. **Testing for traits**
     1. Psychologists rely on two kinds of personality tests
        - a. Projective tests - psychodynamic approach measuring _____
        - b. Objective tests or inventories - standardized questionnaires
     2. Minnesota Multiphasic Personality Inventory (MMPI) - most widely used personality test; developed to screen for psychological disorders
        - a. Ten clinical scales distinguish people with mental disorders from those with no disorder; four validity scales check for lying
        - b. Test is criticized for cultural and other types of bias; often misused
   - C. **Identifying central traits**
     1. Allport's trait theory - not all traits are equally important
        - a. Central traits - characteristic ways of behaving
        - b. Secondary traits - the more _____ aspects of personality
     2. Cattell theory - studied traits using factor analysis; found 16 factors and developed the 16 Personality Factors (PF) Questionnaire
     3. The "Big Five" traits - there is evidence for fundamental personality traits
        - a. Introversion versus extroversion, neuroticism, agreeableness, conscientiousness, openness to experience
        - b. Stable over a lifetime though some maturational changes exist

Answer these Learning Objectives while you read Section 1.

1. Define personality.

2. Describe characteristics of the MMPI and the 16PF and how they were developed.

3. List and discuss the major trait theories of personality, including the Big Five.

SECTION 2 - THE GENETIC CONTRIBUTION (PP. 462-466)

II.   THE GENETIC CONTRIBUTION
    A.   **Heredity and temperament**
        1.   _____ - physiological dispositions to respond to the environment in relatively stable ways that may later form the basis of personality traits
        2.   Kagan's inhibited and uninhibited temperamental styles
            a.   Inhibited infants are excitable, nervous, overreactive
            b.   Uninhibited infants lie there, don't cry, and are happy
            c.   Both types have distinctive physiological patterns
            d.   Influence later personality traits, but aren't unchangeable; depends on how extreme the trait is in infancy and the parents' reactions
        3.   Heredity and traits
            a.   Heritability estimates based on studies of adopted children and identical twins reared together and apart
            b.   For an enormous range of traits, heritability is between .40 and .60
            c.   Some have reported high heritability estimates for specific behaviors
            d.   The only environmental effects on personality come from nonshared experiences - _____ environment, family experiences, seem to have no effect on personality
    B.   **Evaluating genetic theories**
        1.   Environment accounts for about half of the explanation for differences
        2.   Evidence that supports the influence of environment includes the following
            a.   Not all traits are equally heritable or unaffected by shared environment
            b.   Even highly heritable traits are not rigidly fixed
            c.   The relative influence of genes versus environment can change over a lifetime
        3.   Genetic predisposition does not imply genetic inevitability
        4.   Biology and experience, genetics and culture are intertwined

Answer this Learning Objective while you read Section 2.

4.   Discuss the issue of heritability of personality, temperament, and traits including cautionary considerations.

III. **THE SOCIAL-COGNITIVE CONTRIBUTION**
   A. **Focus of social-cognitive theories** - situations that affect behavior and personality
      1. Helps explains why a person may behave differently in different situations
      2. Doesn't make assumptions about internal traits, rather it looks to
         a. Influential aspects of the situation
         b. How a person perceives or interprets the situation
         c. How reinforcement history and cognitions influence both responses and situations and vice versa - reciprocal determinism
   B. **Self-efficacy** - a characteristic of interest to social-cognitive theorists
      1. The belief that you can accomplish what you set out to do
      2. It is acquired from four sources
         a. Experiencing mastery of new skills and overcoming obstacles
         b. Having successful and competent role models
         c. Getting feedback and encouragement from others
         d. Learning how to read and manage your own physiological state
      3. Sources of self-efficacy lie in the situation and in perceptions
   C. **Perceptions of** _____ (Rotter) - another example of reciprocal determinism
      1. Extent to which people believe they have control of their lives
      2. People develop _____ expectancies about which situations and acts will be rewarding which then create self-fulfilling prophecies
      3. Feelings or beliefs are as important as reinforcers - locus of control refers to beliefs about whether results of action are under a person's control
         a. _____ locus of control - people believe they are responsible for what happens to them
         b. External locus of control - people feel their lives are controlled by luck, fate or other people
      4. A scale exists that measures locus of control (Internal/External Scale)
      5. Locus of control emerges at an early age but it can change
   D. **Evaluating social-cognitive approaches - criticisms**
      1. Draws on principles of learning and cognition; shows how personality traits are acquired and how they can change
      2. Relationship between person and situation or biology and belief is unclear
      3. Which possible environmental influence is the one at work is unclear

Answer this Learning Objective while you read Section 3.

5. Describe and evaluate the social-cognitive approach. Include reciprocal determinism, self-efficacy, and locus of control in your description.

SECTION 4 - THE CULTURAL CONTRIBUTION (PP. 472-475)

IV. **THE CULTURAL CONTRIBUTION**
    A.   **Definitions**
        1.   Culture - program of shared _____ that govern the behavior of people in a community or society, and a set of values and beliefs shared by most members of that community and passed from one generation to another
        2.   Values can influence behavior
    B.   **Culture and personality**
        1.   Individualistic cultures - independence of the individual takes precedence over the needs of the group; the self is a collection of traits
        2.   Collectivist cultures - group harmony takes precedence over the individual; the self is defined in the context of relationships and community
        3.   Culture affects basic ideas about the nature and stability of personality
        4.   Culture affects attitudes about many aspects of life, including time
            a.   Monochronic cultures - time is organized into linear segments
            b.   _____ cultures - time is organized on parallel lines
    C.   **Evaluating cultural influences** - it is difficult to describe cultural influences without stereotyping

Answer this Learning Objective while you read Section 4.

6.   Discuss how culture influences how we define our selves and our approach to time.

SECTION 5 - THE PSYCHODYNAMIC TRADITION (PP. 475-486)

V. **THE PSYCHODYNAMIC TRADITION**
- E. **The elements shared by all psychodynamic theories**
  1. Emphasize _____ intrapsychic dynamics
  2. Adult behavior determined primarily by early childhood experiences
  3. Psychological development occurs in fixed _____
  4. Unconscious fantasies and symbols are main influences on behavior
  5. Reliance on subjective methods of getting at the truth of a person's life
- F. **Freud and psychoanalysis - Freud's theory of personality**
  1. The structure of personality - made up of three systems that must balance
     - a. The id - unconscious energies motivated to avoid pain and obtain pleasure, contains the life or sexual (libido) instinct and death (aggressive) instincts
     - b. The ego - referee between demands of id and society; reason
     - c. The _____ - morality and rules of parents and society; includes conscience (inner voice), source of pride and guilt
  2. Defense _____ - Reduces anxiety from conflict between id and society
     - a. They're unconscious, deny or distort _____, protect from conflict
     - b. Some defense mechanisms are: repression, _____, displacement, reaction formation, regression, denial
  3. The development of personality occurs in five psychosexual stages; if demands of a stage too great, a child may get fixated, or stuck at a stage
     - a. The oral stage - babies take the world in through their mouths
     - b. The anal stage - may become over controlled (anal retentive) or under controlled (anal expulsive)
     - c. The Oedipal stage - desire for opposite-sex parent, then identification with the same-sex parent; by the end of this stage, personality is formed and superego emerges
     - d. The latency stage - supposedly nonsexual stage
     - e. The genital stage - beginning of mature adult sexuality
  4. Psychologists disagree about the value of Freud's theory
- G. **Freud's descendants**
  1. Karen Horney - challenged the notion of _____ and female inferiority
     - a. Looked to women's status to explain feelings of inferiority
     - b. Introduced idea of "womb envy" - envy of female ability to reproduce
  2. Jungian theory - biggest difference was the nature of the _____
     - a. Collective unconscious contains the universal memory and history
     - b. Concerned with _____ - themes that appear in myths
     - c. Perceived humans as more positively motivated than did Freud

3. The object-relations school - emphasizes need for human _____
   a. Object - a representation of the mother that the child introjects
   b. Central tension is balance between _____ and connection; this requires adjustment to large and small separations and losses
   c. Emphasis on children's need for mother, which in early years is only a representation of her
   d. The maternal representation affects personality and relationships
   e. Males and females both identify first with mother, then boys must separate which can result in more rigid boundaries with others

H. **Psychodynamic measures of personality**
   1. Projective tests - measure unconscious motives, feelings, conflicts
   2. Reliability and validity too low to assess personality - Rorschach Inkblot Test is example of projective test with reliability and validity problems

I. **Evaluating psychodynamic theories**
   1. All psychodynamic theories believe that unconscious dynamics are key to personality
   2. Problems with psychodynamic theories
      a. Principle of falsifiability violated - can't confirm or disprove ideas
      b. Universal principles drawn from the experiences of patients
      c. Theories based on the patients' fallible memories and retrospective accounts which creates an illusion of causality between events
   3. In response to criticisms, some are using empirical methods and research
   4. Contributions of psychodynamic ideas
      a. Several concepts have found empirical support
      b. Theories encourage tackling large questions

Answer these Learning Objectives while you read Section 5.

7. Explain the basic principles of Freud's psychoanalytic approach to the study of personality and list the emphases shared by modern psychodynamic theories.

8. Discuss and evaluate how projective tests attempt to measure personality.

9. Describe the structure of the personality, according to Freud, and defense mechanisms.

10. Describe the five psychosexual stages of personality development identified by Freud.

11. Discuss the challenges to psychoanalytic theory made by Jung, Horney, and the object-relations school.

12. Summarize the criticisms and contributions of psychodynamic theories.

SECTION 6 - THE HUMANIST CONTRIBUTION (PP. 487-489) AND
SECTION 7 - THE PUBLIC AND PRIVATE PERSONALITY (PP. 489-490)

VI. **THE HUMANIST CONTRIBUTION**
    J.   **The inner experience**
        1.   Focus on a person's own view of the world and our free will
        2.   Developed as a reaction against psychoanalysis and _____
        3.   Main theorists were Maslow, May and _____
    K.   **Abraham Maslow**
        1.   Said psychology has forgotten the positive aspects of human nature
        2.   The traits of the self-actualized person are the most important - meaning, challenge, productivity
        3.   Personality development is a progression toward self-actualization
    L.   **Carl Roger's approach**
        1.   Interested in the fully _____ person - based on the congruence between the image a person projects to others and a person's true feelings
        2.   Becoming fully functional requires _____ positive regard
        3.   Conditional love results in unhappiness and the suppression of feelings
    M.   **Rollo May** - brought elements of _____ to American psychology which says free will is accompanied by responsibility for our actions which causes anxiety
    N.   **Evaluating humanistic and existential theories**
        1.   Many assumptions cannot be _____
        2.   Concepts are hard to define operationally
        3.   Adds balance to psychology's view of personality

VII. **THE PUBLIC AND PRIVATE PERSONALITY** - personality has two dimensions that we all weave together
    O.   **Public personality** - what we present to the world which includes our characteristic habits, temperaments and our basic traits and are addressed by biological, learning, and cultural theories
    P.   **Private personality** - our inner sense of self which consists of subjective experiences that psychodynamic and humanist theories address

Answer these Learning Objectives while you read Sections 6 and 7.

13.   Summarize the principles of humanistic psychology proposed by Maslow, Rogers, May.

14.   Discuss how each theoretical approach to personality help to explain our public and private personalities.

ACROSS

1. relatively stable pattern of behavior, thoughts, motives and emotions
7. a trait theorist who identified 16 factors he thought were necessary to describe personality
9. part of personality representing reason, good sense and self-control
10. psychological tests based on unconscious dynamics
11. founder of psychoanalysis
13. part of personality representing the conscience
14. locus of control in which one expects the results of one's actions to be under one's own control
16. complex that occurs in the stage that follows the anal stage
17. the process by which the superego emerges
18. refusal to admit to oneself that something unpleasant is happening

DOWN

1. Freud's theory of personality and a method of psychotherapy
2. a way to block a threatening emotion from consciousness
3. universal, symbolic images
4. a descriptive characteristic of an individual
5. a movement within psychology that emphasized free will and the positive aspects of human nature
6. type of unconscious proposed by Jung
8. characteristic styles of responding present in infancy
12. within the mind or self
15. introduced the idea of womb envy

FLASH CARDS

Cut the following chart along the borders and test yourself with the resulting flash cards.

13.1 PERSONALITY	13.2 TRAIT	13.3 OBJECTIVE TESTS (INVENTORIES)
13.4 MINNESOTA MULTIPHASIC PERSONALITY INVENTORY (MMPI)	13.5 GORDON ALLPORT	13.6 CENTRAL AND SECONDARY TRAITS
13.7 RAYMOND CATTELL	13.8 FACTOR ANALYSIS	13.9 THE "BIG FIVE" PERSONALITY TRAITS
13.10 TEMPERAMENT	13.11 HERITABILITY	13.12 BEHAVIORAL GENETICS
13.13 SOCIAL-COGNITIVE THEORIES	13.14 RECIPROCAL DETERMINISM	13.15 SELF-EFFICACY
13.16 GENERALIZED EXPECTANCIES	13.17 SELF-FULFILLING PROPHECY	13.18 LOCUS OF CONTROL (INTERNAL VERSUS EXTERNAL)

13.3 Personality tests that are standardized questionnaires that require written responses, typically to multiple-choice or true-false items.	13.2 A characteristic of an individual, describing a habitual way of behaving, thinking, and feeling.	13.1 A distinctive and relatively stable pattern of behavior, thoughts, motives, and emotions that characterizes an individual throughout life.
13.6 Types of traits identified by Allport. Central traits are characteristic ways of behaving and reacting; secondary traits are more changeable.	13.5 Influential personality theorist who said that not all traits have equal weight for a person. He said people have central and secondary traits.	13.4 A widely used objective personality test.
13.9 Five factors that are believed by many researchers to be able to describe personality.	13.8 A statistical method for analyzing the intercorrelations among various scores. Highly correlated scores are assumed to measure the same thing.	13.7 A trait theorist who used factor analysis to identify separate traits. He identified 16 factors necessary to describe personality.
13.12 An interdisciplinary field concerned with the genetic bases of behavior and personality.	13.11 Estimate of the proportion of the total variance in a trait within a group attributable to genetic differences among individuals within the group.	13.10 Physiological dispositions to respond to the environment in certain ways; they are present in infancy and are assumed innate.
13.15 A person's belief that he or she is capable of producing desired results, such as mastering new skills and reaching goals.	13.14 In social-cognitive theories, the two-way interaction between the environment and the individual in determining and shaping personality factors.	13.13 Theories that emphasize how personality traits are learned depending on specific situations and individual's cognitive processes.
13.18 An expectation about whether the results of your actions are under your control (internal locus) or beyond your control (external locus).	13.17 An expectation that comes true because of the tendency of the person holding it to act in ways to bring it about.	13.16 People learn that some situations and acts will be rewarding. These expectations can create self-fulfilling prophesies.

13.19 CULTURE	13.20 INDIVIDUALIST VERSUS COLLECTIVIST CULTURES	13.21 MONOCHRONIC VERSUS POLYCHRONIC CULTURES
13.22 SIGMUND FREUD	13.23 PSYCHOANALYSIS	13.24 PSYCHODYNAMIC THEORIES
13.25 INTRAPSYCHIC DYNAMICS	13.26 FREE ASSOCIATION	13.27 ID
13.28 LIBIDO	13.29 EGO	13.30 SUPEREGO
13.31 DEFENSE MECHANISMS	13.32 REPRESSION	13.33 PROJECTION
13.34 DISPLACEMENT AND SUBLIMATION	13.35 REACTION FORMATION	13.36 REGRESSION

13.21 Cultural attitude to time; whether time is organized into linear (monochronic) segments or along parallel (polychronic) lines.	13.20 Cultural attitude to the self and whether the self is regarded as autonomous (individualistic) or as embedded in relationships (collectivist).	13.19 Program of shared rules and a set of values and beliefs shared by most members of the community and passed from one generation to another.
13.24 Theories that explain behavior and personality in terms of unconscious energy dynamics within the individual.	13.23 A theory of personality and a method of psychotherapy developed by Freud; it emphasizes unconscious motives and conflicts.	13.22 Originator of the theory of psychoanalysis, the first psychodynamic theory based on movement of psychological energy within the person.
13.27 In psychoanalysis, the part of personality containing inherited psychic energy, particularly sexual and aggressive instincts.	13.26 In psychoanalysis, a method of uncovering unconscious conflicts by saying freely whatever comes to mind.	13.25 Theories that focus on what goes on within the mind (psyche) or self.
13.30 In psychoanalysis, the part of personality that represents conscience, morality, and social standards.	13.29 In psychoanalysis, the part of personality that represents reason, good sense, and rational self-control.	13.28 In psychoanalysis, the part of personality that represents reason, good sense, and rational self-control.
13.33 A defense mechanism in which one's own unacceptable feelings are attributed to someone else.	13.32 A defense mechanism in which a threatening idea, memory, or emotion is blocked from becoming conscious.	13.31 Methods used by the ego to prevent unconscious anxiety or threatening thoughts from entering consciousness.
13.36 A defense mechanism in which a person returns to an earlier stage of development after a traumatic experience.	13.35 A defense mechanism in which the feeling that causes unconscious anxiety is transformed into its opposite in consciousness.	13.34 Defense mechanisms in which feelings are redirected; to other people or things (displacement) or to higher social purposes (sublimation).

13.37 DENIAL	13.38 PSYCHOSEXUAL STAGES	13.39 OEDIPAL STAGE AND OEDIPUS COMPLEX
13.40 CLARA THOMPSON AND KAREN HORNEY	13.41 CARL JUNG	13.42 COLLECTIVE UNCONSCIOUS
13.43 ARCHETYPES	13.44 OBJECT-RELATIONS SCHOOL	13.45 PROJECTIVE TESTS
13.46 RORSCHACH INKBLOT TEST	13.47 HUMANIST PSYCHOLOGY	13.48 ABRAHAM MASLOW
13.49 PEAK EXPERIENCES	13.50 SELF-ACTUALIZATION	13.51 CARL ROGERS
13.52 UNCONDITIONAL POSITIVE REGARD	13.53 ROLLO MAY	13.54 EXISTENTIALISM

13.39 In psychoanalysis, a stage characterized by the Oedipus complex in which a child desires the other-sex parent and rivals the same-sex parent.	13.38 The stages of personality development hypothesized by Freud; they include the oral, anal, Oedipal, latency, and genital stages.	13.37 A defense mechanism in which a person refuses to admit that something unpleasant is happening or that he or she is feeling forbidden emotions.
13.42 To Carl Jung, the universal memories and experiences of humankind, seen in the unconscious images and symbols of all people.	13.41 Left Freud's circle because of disagreement about the nature of the unconscious. Jung proposed the collective unconscious and archetypes.	13.40 Early dissenters from Freud's school; challenged Freud's notion of innate female inferiority and penis envy.
13.45 Tests used to infer a person's motives, conflicts, and unconscious dynamics basis on the person's interpretations of ambiguous stimuli.	13.44 Psychodynamic approach that emphasizes the importance of the infant's first two years of life and the baby's relationships, especially with the mother.	13.43 Universal, symbolic images that appear in myths, art, stories, and dreams; to Carl Jung, they reflect the collective unconscious.
13.48 One of the leaders of humanistic psychology who said people strive for a life that has meaning, challenge, and is productive.	13.47 A psychological approach that emphasizes free will, personal growth and the achievement of human potential.	13.46 A projective personality test that asks respondents to interpret abstract, symmetrical inkblots.
13.51 A humanist who said that humans need unconditional positive regard to become fully functioning and congruent.	13.50 The culmination of personality development according to Maslow. The self-actualized person has meaning, challenge and is productive.	13.49 Described by Maslow as rare moments of rapture caused by the attainment of excellence or the drive toward higher values.
13.54 An approach based on European philosophy that holds that human beings have freedom of choice, but the freedom can cause anxiety.	13.53 Humanist theorist who emphasized some of the difficult aspects of the human condition, including loneliness, anxiety and alienation.	13.52 To Carol Rogers, love or support given to another person with no conditions attached.

PRACTICE TEST 1 - Multiple Choice

1. A distinctive and stable pattern of behavior, thoughts, motives and emotions that characterizes an individual over time is the definition of
   A. traits.
   B. temperament.
   C. personality.
   D. locus of control.

2. Allport's trait theory suggests there are
   A. central and secondary traits.
   B. surface and source traits.
   C. sixteen factors.
   D. the "Big Five" traits.

3. The "Big Five" refers to
   A. the five main trait theories.
   B. five types of traits, including cardinal, central, secondary, surface and source.
   C. robust factors that are thought to be able to describe personality.
   D. five stages of personality development.

4. Jenny is always suspicious of others and thinks they are out to hurt her. This is an example of a
   A. genetic trait.
   B. central trait.
   C. secondary trait.
   D. meaningful trait.

5. Woody is a complainer and a defeatist. He always sees the sour side of life. This demonstrates which of the following of the Big Five traits?
   A. introversion
   B. depressiveness
   C. neuroticism
   D. disagreeableness

6. In behavioral-genetic studies, the heritability of selfishness and aggression is
   A. 70%-80%
   B. 90%-100%
   C. 10%-20%
   D. 40%-60%

7. The most controversial finding to come from the heritability studies on twins is the idea that
   A. the only environmental effects on personality come from nonshared experiences.
   B. environmental effects on personality come from only shared experiences.
   C. most personality traits are highly heritable.
   D. most personality traits are primarily a result of environmental influences.

8. Which of the following suggests caution about the heritability of personality?
   A. Not all traits are equally heritable or unaffected by shared environment.
   B. Even highly heritable traits are not rigidly fixed.
   C. The relative influence of genes versus environment can change over time.
   D. all of the above

9. The social-cognitive theory can explain how a person can be friendly at work and hostile at home. The explanation is
   A. based on whether the person has internal or external locus of control.
   B. the difference between a person's public and private personalities.
   C. that personality traits can change depending on the situation and on how people perceive and interpret those situations.
   D. an interaction of the id, ego and superego.

10. The extent to which people feel they have control of their lives refers to
    A. locus of control.   B. defense mechanisms.
    C. reciprocal determinism.   D. conscientiousness.

11. According to the social-cognitive theory which two of the following traits are important to a person's personality?
    A. neuroticism and openness to experience   B. expectancies and competence
    C. locus of control and self-efficacy   D. self-efficacy and extroversion

12. Which of the following is a criticism of the social-cognitive theories of personality?
    A. They are not testable.
    B. They are too heavily focused on genetics.
    C. They are not falsifiable.
    D. Exactly which environmental factor is influencing a particular behavior.

13. Which of the following is NOT one of the shared elements among psychodynamic theories?
    A. an emphasis on environmental influences
    B. the assumption that adult behavior is determined primarily by childhood experiences
    C. the emphasis on the unconscious mind
    D. the belief that psychological development occurs in fixed stages

14. Which part of the personality would be likely to want to go for a pizza rather than study for a test?
    A. id   B. superego
    C. ego   D. ego ideal

15. The function of defense mechanisms is
    A.   to make us look good in the eyes of other people.
    B.   to protect ourselves from negative environmental consequences.
    C.   to protect us from the conflict and stress of reality.
    D.   all of the above.

16. When the Ahern's brought home baby John, four-year-old Andy began acting like a baby himself by crawling around and wanting to drink out of a bottle. This is an example of
    A.   regression.   B.   identification.
    C.   reaction formation.   D.   projection.

17. The psychosexual stages of personality development identified by Freud are (in order)
    A.   oral, anal, latency, phallic, genital.
    B.   oral, phallic, anal, genital, latency.
    C.   oral, anal, phallic, latency, genital.
    D.   anal, phallic, genital, oral, latency.

18. According to Freud, the resolution of the _____ marks the emergence of the superego.
    A.   anal stage   B.   unconscious conflict
    C.   Oedipus complex   D.   latency stage

19. Horney disagreed with Freud about
    A.   the nature of the unconscious.
    B.   the notion of the inferiority complex.
    C.   the notion that personality development continues into adult life.
    D.   penis envy and female inferiority.

20. The idea that the human psyche contains the universal memories and history of mankind was contributed by
    A.   Freud.   B.   Jung.
    C.   Erikson.   D.   Horney.

21. The idea that men are less secure than women is suggested by
    A.   Erikson.   B.   Jung.
    C.   the object-relations school.   D.   Adler.

22. Which of the following is <u>NOT</u> one of the criticisms of psychodynamic theories?
    A. It violates the principle of falsifiability.
    B. It is based on retrospective memories.
    C. It is overly comprehensive; it tries to explain too much.
    D. It draws universal principles from studying selected patients.

23. Congruence and unconditional positive regard are part of
    A. Roger's theory.
    B. Maslow's theory.
    C. May's theory.
    D. existential philosophy.

24. Humanism focuses on
    A. full human potential.
    B. measurable traits.
    C. environmental influences.
    D. unconscious dynamics.

25. One way to integrate the different perspectives on personality is to recognize that "personality" has two dimensions. Each of us has a(n) _____ and _____ personality.
    A. conscious; unconscious.
    B. public; private
    C. real; fake
    D. optimistic; pessimistic

PRACTICE TEST 2 - Multiple Choice

1. Which of the following examples demonstrates the definition of personality?
    A. Rick's bad mood must account for his outburst.
    B. Ruth is always considerate and warm.
    C. Ron is shy with strangers, but talkative among friends.
    D. Rene was very funny today.

2. Rudolph is a very suspicious person. He doesn't trust most people and generally double checks whatever someone tells him. Otherwise, he functions well at his job and has friends. This is an example of which kind of trait?
    A. cardinal   B. secondary
    C. central   D. introversion

3. As part of a reference letter, Joe is described as a very positive person who is sociable, good-natured, responsible and imaginative. This description matches
    A. traits cited by Cattell's theory.
    B. the "Big Five" personality traits.
    C. cardinal traits as described by Allport.
    D. the traits identified by factor analysis.

4. As a child, Petra was anxious and negative. She complained frequently about health problems even though she was not sick. As an adult, Petra will probably
    A. outgrow these characteristics.
    B. be equally likely to keep these characteristics or to change.
    C. continue to have the same characteristics.
    D. become even more negative and disturbed.

5. Your grandmother tells you that from the time you were born, you were a content infant and have continued to be content throughout your childhood, but your sister has been difficult right from the start. She is describing your
    A. personalities.   B. traits.
    C. motives.   D. temperaments.

6. Studies of twins have found that heritability for most traits is around .50. This means that
    A. if one twin has a trait, there is a 50 percent chance the other twin will have the same trait.
    B. most people have a 50 percent chance of having a given trait.
    C. within a group about 50 percent of the variance in a trait is attributable to genes.
    D. the differences between two groups of people can be explained.

367

7. Based on studies of twins, which of the following environmental factors would be expected to have the greatest influence on the personality of two siblings?
   A. having the same parents
   B. going to the same schools
   C. having different extracurricular activities
   D. having the same religious training

8. A study of Finnish twins, ages 18 to 59, found that the heritability of extroversion decreased from the late teens to the late twenties. What does this suggest?
   A. Heritability of traits diminishes over time.
   B. The influence of the environment increases over time.
   C. For some traits, experiences at certain periods in life become more important.
   D. all of the above

9. Christian has been told that his personality is aggressive, extroverted and conscientious. A social-cognitive theorist would say
   A. this is a description of his central traits.
   B. that Chris could behave differently in another situation or if his beliefs or expectations changed.
   C. these characteristics have a genetic basis.
   D. none of the above.

10. Dr. Story tells Christian that his behavior is influenced by his locus of control and feelings of self-efficacy in a given situation. Which approach does this represent?
    A. behavioral   B. trait
    C. social-cognitive   D. humanistic

11. "It seems the more I study, the worse I do. There's really no point to working hard in college because it doesn't seem to matter." This statement reflects
    A. an internal locus of control.   B. observational learning.
    C. an external locus of control.   D. self-handicapping.

12. Mr. Picks is conducting research on the effect of a teacher's reactions on students' self-efficacy. Which criticism of the social-cognitive approach applies to this research topic?
    A. It is not testable.
    B. It is not falsifiable.
    C. Because there are many influences on self-efficacy, it is difficult to evaluate the effect of just one environmental influence at a time.
    D. It is based on the retrospective memories of subjects.

13. Priscilla is having relationship problems. Which of the following approaches to her difficulties represents one of the shared elements of psychodynamic theories?
    A. The problems are a result of her interpretation of what is going on.
    B. The problems are a result of her previous relationship history.
    C. The problems result from the lack of unconditional positive regard.
    D. The problems are determined by experiences in her early childhood.

14. Jeff is very bossy and rigid. He is always watching the clock to see who is late and who leaves early. According to Freudian theory, Jeff
    A. overuses the defense of displacement.
    B. is too controlled by his superego.
    C. has too strong an ego.
    D. displays all of the above.

15. "I don't want to study; let's go get pizza." "If you go get pizza, you'll fail the test." "You owe it to your parents to get good grades." Which parts of the personality would make each of these statements, according to Freudian theory?
    A. id; ego; superego   B. id; superego; ego
    C. ego; id; superego   D. superego; id; ego

16. Les crusades against pornography because he feels that people have dirty minds and are oversexed. According to Freudian theory, Les is using the defense mechanism of
    A. displacement.   B. projection.
    C. reaction formation.   D. denial.

17. Johnny was aggressive as a child. He now plays professional football. This is an example of
    A. regression.   B. sublimation.
    C. reaction formation.   D. projection.

18. Max has just had his sixth birthday. Freud would expect that
    A. he has resolved the Oedipal complex.
    B. his personality pattern is basically formed.
    C. his superego has emerged.
    D. all of the above have occurred.

19. Horney is to Jung as
    A. womb envy is to penis envy.   B. archetype is to womb envy.
    C. anima is to animus.   D. womb envy is to archetype.

20. The fact that several basic archetypes appear in virtually every society supports which Jungian idea?
    A.   penis envy   B.   the strength of the ego
    C.   psychosocial stages   D.   the collective unconscious

21. Julia disagrees with Dr. Sigmund's interpretation that she is very angry at her mother. Dr. Sigmund says that Julia's disagreement is denial and, therefore, confirms that she is angry at her mother. This is an example of which criticism of psychodynamic theories?
    A.   They draw universal principles from a few atypical patients.
    B.   They base theories of development on retrospective accounts of patients.
    C.   They violate the principle of falsifiability.
    D.   They are based on the illusion of causality.

22. The object-relations school predicts that adult males will have problems permitting close attachments because
    A.   their identities are based on <u>not</u> being like women, so they develop more rigid ego boundaries.
    B.   their superegos are too strong.
    C.   they have great difficulty resolving the anal stage.
    D.   all of the above.

23. Dr. West is studying depression. He has interviewed 50 subjects about their early lives and childhoods and he has identified common threads that fit an overall theory. This example represents which of the criticisms of psychodynamic theories?
    A.   It violates the principle of falsifiability.
    B.   It is a prospective study.
    C.   It is based on the retrospective memories of subjects.
    D.   People are seen as too malleable, like jellyfish.

24. How do the humanistic approaches differ from the behavioral and psychodynamic approaches?
    A.   They focus on a person's own sense of self and experience.
    B.   They focus on the positive aspects of human nature.
    C.   They believe that human beings have free will.
    D.   all of the above

25. According to Rogers, to become a fully-functioning person,
    A.   the self and organism must be congruent.
    B.   a person must be raised with unconditional positive regard.
    C.   a person must accept his or her feelings.
    D.   a person must have all of the above.

PRACTICE TEST 3 - Short Answer

1.   Personality refers to a distinctive pattern of _____, _____, motives and emotions that characterize an individual over time.

2.   Personality tests fall into two categories. _____ tests are standardized questionnaires that require written responses, and _____ tests attempt to reveal the test-takers unconscious conflicts and motivations.

3.   The most famous and widely used objective test of personality is the _____.

4.   _____ has identified two types of traits; _____ traits that reflect a characteristic way of behavior and reacting, while secondary traits are more _____ aspects of personality, such as music preferences.

5.   The Big Five personality traits include introversion versus extroversion, neuroticism, _____, _____, and openness to experience.

6.   The fact that Joey was excitable, nervous, and overreacted to every little thing suggest that he falls into Kagan's category of _____ temperamental style.

7.   In behavioral genetics, the _____ of an enormous range of personality traits is typically between .40 and.60.

8.   In numerous behavioral genetic studies, the only environmental contribution to personality differences comes from having unique experiences not _____ with other family members.

9.   _____ theories can account for why a person may be cheerful and friendly at work but hostile and obnoxious at home because they take the specific situation into account, as well as a person's _____.

10.   People who have a strong sense of _____, or the conviction that you can accomplish what you set out to do, are quick to cope with problems, spend effort striving for their goals, and sustain effort in the face of setbacks.

11.   Over time, people learn that some acts will be rewarded and others punished, and thus they develop generalized _____ about which situations and acts will be rewarding. Once acquired, they often create a _____ prophecy.

12. Geraldo believes that if he studies hard he will pass his most difficult class. In this situation, he is demonstrating a(n) _____ locus of control.

13. _____ suggests that a person's beliefs (self-efficacy, locus of control) affect their behaviors and responses to situations which influences the outcome. In turn, specific situations activate certain beliefs and behaviors.

14. In _____ cultures, group harmony takes precedence over the wishes of the individual.

15. In _____ cultures, the needs of friends and family supersede appointments and time is organized along parallel lines.

16. _____ theories, which are based on the work of Freud, emphasize the movement of psychological energy within the person, in the form of attachments, conflicts, and motivations.

17. According to Freud, the _____ contains two competing basic instincts, the ego bows to the _____ of life, while the _____ represents morality.

18. In psychodynamic theory, the ego has weapons, called _____, that deny or distort reality and operate unconsciously. These weapons protect us from conflict and the stresses of reality.

19. Johnny was always very aggressive as a child. Now that he is in high school, he has become the top football player. From the psychodynamic perspective, Johnny's athletic success might be attributable to the defense mechanism of _____.

20. _____ and _____ argued some of Freud's ideas about women. They suggested that when women feel inferior to men, we should look for explanations in the disadvantages that women live with and their second-class status.

21. Jung introduced the idea of the _____ unconscious which contains _____, universal memories, symbols, and images that are the legacy of human history.

22. Object-relations theory states that a child creates a(n) _____ of the mother and this unconsciously affects personality throughout life.

23. Projective tests, such as the _____ Inkblot Test are not _____ enough to be used for assessing personality traits or diagnosing disorders.

24.	One of the criticisms of psychodynamic theories is that they violate the principle of _____.

25.	Abraham Maslow said that people who strive for a life that is meaningful, challenging, and productive are considered _____. Carl Rogers believed that to become a fully _____ person you must receive _____ regard.

PRACTICE TEST 4 - True/False

1.   T F   The Beck Depression Inventory is the most famous and widely used objective test of personality.

2.   T F   A criticism of the Minnesota Multiphasic Personality Inventory is that the norms for the test were based on samples in which minorities, the elderly, the poor, and the poorly educated were underrepresented.

3.   T F   Research on the Myers Briggs Test has confirmed that knowledge of a person's type on the Myers-Briggs Test can reliably predict actual behavior.

4.   T F   The 16 Personality Factors (PF) Questionnaire is based on Allport's trait theory.

5.   T F   The Big Five traits are not very stable over a lifetime.

6.   T F   While biologically based temperaments influence later personality traits, they do not provide an unchangeable blueprint for personality.

7.   T F   Behavior genetic studies have found that the heritability of an enormous range of personality traits is typically between .40 and .60.

8.   T F   Highly heritable traits are relatively unaffected by environmental experiences.

9.   T F   Self-efficacy is developed in early childhood and depends on whether parents were nurturant and consistent.

10.   T F   According to Rotter, generalized expectancies can lead to self-fulfilling prophecies.

11.   T F   The social-cognitive theorists show that many personality traits are largely acquired, and can change, depending on the demands of the situation and on how we are interpreting it.

12.   T F   Culture is as powerful an influence on personality and behavior as any biological process.

13.   T F   Monochronic cultures are relationship oriented and focus on group harmony.

14.   T F   Contemporary psychologists agree that Freud's theory is outdated, irrelevant and it has little impact on modern society.

15. T F Defense mechanisms are unhealthy and they are used primarily by those with mental disorders.

16. T F According to Freud, little girls recognize the superiority of the boy's penis and always have a lingering sense of "penis envy."

17. T F The object-relations school modified the Freudian idea of the unconscious by introducing the concept of the collective unconscious which contains archetypes.

18. T F The object-relations school provides an explanation for why women often need to assert autonomy and their own needs in relationships while men need to work on developing close attachments.

19. T F Projective tests are very useful for assessing personality traits and diagnosing disorders.

20. T F Freudian theory was developed using retrospective analysis which creates an illusion of causality between events.

21. T F Humanistic approaches were based on principles of psychoanalysis but differed in their emphasis on free-will.

22. T F Maslow introduced the idea that for a person to become fully functioning there should be harmony between the person's public image and inner self.

23. T F May brought to American psychology elements of the European philosophy of existentialism.

24. T F The major criticism of humanist psychology is that it violates the principle of falsifiability.

25. T F Biological, learning, and cultural theories help explain the public personality while the psychodynamic and humanist theories address our private personality.

PRACTICE TEST 5 - Essay

1. Lynne is having aggressive fantasies about her husband. Over a long period, he has gotten drunk on a regular basis. Lynne well remembers her alcoholic father, who was never there when she needed him. She also remembers her mother, who suffered silently for years. Lynne swears this will not happen to her, but she can't seem to make anything change. She is hostile toward the children and her neighbors. Her husband is always repentant the next day, but his sorrow never lasts more than a week. Yet, Lynne can't make the final step of leaving.

    Identify which approach to personality each of the following set of comments represents.

    A. The perseverance of Lynne's mother is the significant determinant in this case. This taught Lynne that marriage was for better or for worse, but also that silence produces suffering. Lynne's pattern was acquired from an important role model.
    B. Aggressiveness is Lynne's outstanding characteristic and it dominates her actions and relationships with most people.
    C. Lynne's marriage to and anger with an alcoholic suggests many unresolved feelings toward her father. Her marriage to an alcoholic suggests her ongoing attachment to her father and the effort to resolve her issues with him. Her anger most likely is unresolved anger at her father. Her reluctance to leave reflects her desire to stay united with her father.
    D. Lynne is struggling with her choices. While marriage is important to her, she realizes that her husband's alcoholism is a source of despair. She is struggling with her values, principles, desires for growth and fulfillment and how they should influence her choices.

2. Bernard had studied for his psychology test, but before he was finished studying, he agreed to go partying with his friends and stayed out late. The test was very difficult and he found he did not know many of the answers. The class was crowded and a good student was sitting very close to him. It would have been very easy to look over at her paper. He was worried because this test grade would make a big difference on his final grade. He struggled with whether or not he should cheat. He decided not to cheat because he felt that he would have let his parents down if he did. Instead, he decided that this grade really didn't matter so much. He felt guilty about not having studied enough and about having considered cheating.

376

Indicate whether the id, ego or superego is involved in each of the following examples and explain the basis for your answer.

A. Bernard's studying for his test
B. Going out partying with his friends rather than studying
C. Wanting a good grade under any circumstance
D. Evaluating whether or not to cheat
E. Deciding not to cheat
F. Deciding that the grade did not matter so much
G. Feeling guilty about his behavior

3. Identify which defense mechanism each example represents.

A. A mother shows exaggerated concern and love for her children, even though she unconsciously feels trapped and frustrated by motherhood.
B. Bob often feels that other people don't like him and are talking behind his back.
C. Jack is unconsciously attracted to his sister-in-law and, though he seems to have no awareness of it, his sister-in-law senses these feelings.
D. Even after finding his lighter in the jacket worn the other day, Tony swears he never misplaces anything and someone must be playing a trick on him.
E. Whenever he is frustrated, Jack has a tantrum and destroys anything he can get his hands on.
F. The football coach loves to insult John and make him angry. Whenever he does this, the opposing team really suffers because then John begins to hit extra hard.

4. Suggest the most likely stage of fixation demonstrated in the descriptions provided below.

A. A husband has had long-term marital problems due to a continuing lack of interest in sex.
B. A chain smoker begins to eat whenever he becomes the least bit upset.
C. A young man is strongly attracted to much older women because of their protective, caring ways.
D. A young woman has all her CDs, tapes and the food in her cabinets organized alphabetically and the clothes in her closets are organized by color. The pencils on her desk all must be sharpened and her desk cleared off before she can work.

5. Below are criticisms of Freudian psychoanalysis. Identify which theorist would have been most likely to make each comment.

   A. Freud saw the importance of the individual's past but failed to see the contribution of humanity's past. People have universal memories owing to the ancestry they share.

   B. Freud misunderstood women. He believed they were motivated by envy for men when the true determining forces were social injustice and second-class treatment.

   C. Freud emphasized a child's fear of the powerful father, but ignored the child's need for a powerful mother, especially during the baby's early years. He emphasized the dynamics of inner drives and impulses, but paid little attention to the child's relationship with others.

6. Explain how the social-cognitive approach would view the role of parents in personality formation.

7. Based on the three humanistic theorists, indicate how each thinker might account for a person's failure to reach his or her full potential.

8. Using the "Big Five" trait approach, indicate which set of traits would be most useful for describing each of the individuals described below.

   A. Bob is stable, happy to meet people and well-liked. He has many friends and few worries.

   B. Mary is neat, timely and dependable. She has relatively few interests or hobbies, but she is a good listener and is liked by her co-workers.

   C. John complains constantly and worries about his health and his life in general. He reads widely and loves going to movies and to museums, but he always goes alone.

378

CHAPTER 14

Development Over the Life Span

LEARNING OBJECTIVES

1. List and discuss the stages of prenatal development and describe some harmful influences.

2. List and discuss the motor and sensory capacities of newborns and infants.

3. Describe the stages of language development.

4. Describe the principles and the stages of Piaget's theory of cognitive development.

5. Evaluate Piaget's theory of cognitive development.

6. Describe and evaluate Kohlberg's theory of moral development.

7. Distinguish between gender typing and gender identity and describe the explanations that have been given for gender development. Explain how gender typing changes over the lifespan.

8. List the various styles of child-rearing and discuss the effects of each, including the limitations of parents' influence on children.

9. Describe the events that signal the onset of puberty in males and females and the relationship between age of onset of puberty and later adjustment.

10. Summarize the evidence on the relationship between adolescence and emotional turmoil.

11. Describe the four approaches to balancing ethnic identity and acculturation.

12. List and discuss the stages of Erikson's theory of psychosocial development.

13. Summarize the biological and emotional changes associated with midlife.

14. Compare and contrast older and more recent notions about aging.

15. Discuss the effects of aging on intelligence and memory.

16. Discuss the impact of childhood experience on adulthood.

CHAPTER CONCEPT MAP

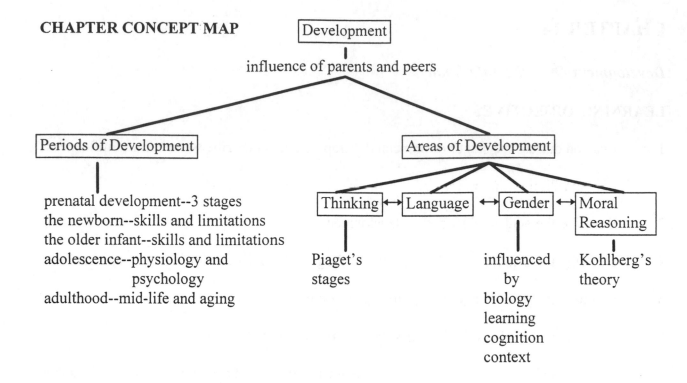

BRIEF CHAPTER SUMMARY

Chapter 14 describes the stages of prenatal development, which include the germinal stage, the embryonic stage and the fetal stage. The newborn is capable of processing information immediately, though there are many limitations to the newborn's abilities. According to Piaget's theory of cognitive development, thinking develops in four stages: the sensory-motor stage, the pre-operational stage, the concrete operations stage and the formal operations stage. While parts of Piaget's theory have been refuted, other parts have been confirmed. Language, another aspect of cognitive development, is an evolutionary adaptation of the human species. Children are responsive to aspects of language in the first months of life and by about two-years of age, they are using 2 to 3 word combinations. Moral reasoning is another aspect of cognitive development. Kohlberg's theory of moral reasoning is described. Development of gender identity is complex, and many theories attempt to explain this phenomenon. Language, thinking, gender identity and moral reasoning are all areas of development that influence one another. Myths and realities of adolescent development are discussed. The physiology of puberty is described for males and females, along with the psychological issues of this period of development. Aspects of adulthood are examined including mid-life and aging. Erikson's theory identifies eight stages of psychological development that occur throughout the life span.

PREVIEW OUTLINE AND REVIEW QUESTIONS

Before you read the chapter, review the preview outline and the Learning Objectives for each section of the text. Answer all questions as you read the text.

SECTION 1 - FROM CONCEPTION TO THE FIRST YEAR (PP. 498-503)

I. **FROM CONCEPTION TO THE FIRST YEAR**
    A. **Developmental psychologists** study universal aspects of life-span development as well as cultural and individual variations; many study socialization
    B. **Prenatal development** - all development is the result of maturation, the sequential unfolding of genetically influenced behavior and physical characteristics
        1. Three stages
            a. _____ stage - fertilized egg (zygote) divides and attaches to the uterine wall; outside becomes placenta, inner part becomes embryo
            b. Embryonic stage - after implantation (about 2 weeks) to eighth week; embryo develops; _____ is secreted in males
            c. Fetal stage - after eighth week; organs and systems
        2. Harmful influences, like German measles, x-rays, sexually transmitted diseases, cigarette smoking, alcohol, drugs can cross the placental barrier
    C. **The infant's world**
        1. Physical abilities - newborns have a series of reflexes, perceptual abilities, sensations that are not fully developed, social interest, and synchrony
        2. Culture and maturation - Infants everywhere go through the same maturational sequence, but many aspects of development depend on culture
        3. How critical are the early years?
            a. Early environment does not necessarily have permanent effects
            b. With normal stimulation, attention, nourishment babies develop normally

Answer these Learning Objectives while you read Section 1.

1. List and discuss the stages of prenatal development and describe some harmful influences.

2. List and discuss the motor and sensory capacities of newborns and infants.

SECTION 2 - COGNITIVE DEVELOPMENT (PP. 503-512)

II.   **COGNITIVE DEVELOPMENT**
    A.   **Language** - An evolutionary adaptation of the human species
        1.   In first months, babies responsive to pitch, intensity and sound of language; people talk with more varied pitch and intonation (_____)
        2.   By 4 to 6 months, babies have learned many basic sounds of their language and lose ability to perceive speech sounds in another language
        3.   Between 6 months to one year, infants become more familiar with the sound structure of their native language
        4.   At 11 months, babies develop symbolic gestures
        5.   Between 18 months and 2 years, two- and three-word telegraphic combinations are produced; then new words are acquired at a rapid rate
    B.   **Thinking**
        1.   Piaget's theory - children's errors are not random
        2.   Children make two mental adaptations to new experiences
            a.   Assimilation - fitting new information into present system of knowledge, beliefs, and mental _____ (networks of beliefs)
            b.   _____ - must change or modify existing schemas to accommodate new information that doesn't fit
        3.   Piaget proposed children go through four stages of cognitive development
            a.   Sensory-motor stage - (birth to 2 years old)
                (1)   Infants learn through concrete actions
                (2)   Accomplish _____ permanence at around six months
                (3)   Object permanence begins child's capacity to use mental imagery and other symbolic systems
            b.   Preoperational stage - (ages 2 to 7)
                (1)   Abilities - use of symbols accelerates, able to pretend
                (2)   Limitations - cannot _____ or use abstract principles (called operations), engage in egocentric thinking, lack conservation and ability to reverse operations
            c.   _____ operations stage (ages 7 to 12)
                (1)   Accomplishments - understand conservation, reversibility, cause and effect, identity, math operations, serial ordering
                (2)   Thinking is still concrete, not abstract
            d.   Formal operations stage (ages 12 to adulthood)
                (1)   Beginning of _____ reasoning
                (2)   Can reason deductively, think about future, problem-solve
        4.   Evaluating Piaget
            a.   Challenges to aspects of Piagetian theory
                (1)   Changes from stage to stage not sweeping or clear cut

(2)   Children understand more than Piaget gave them credit for
        (3)   Preschoolers are not as egocentric as Piaget thought, nor as
               fooled by appearances and they are capable of logic
               (a)   They begin taking other perspectives
               (b)   A theory of _____ has developed by age 4 or 5
        (4)   Cognitive development depends on social/cultural context
        (5)   As Piaget underestimated the cognitive skills of young
               children, he overestimated those of many adults
    b.   Researchers agree that new abilities depend on previous abilities
          and that children are not passive vessels, but they actively interpret
          their worlds and develop schemas to assimilate new information

C.   **Moral reasoning**
    1.   Piaget pioneered the study of moral reasoning in children
    2.   Kohlberg developed a theory with three levels of moral development
        a.   Level 1 - preconventional morality - children fear _____ for
              disobedience and think it is in their best interest to obey
        b.   Level 2 - conventional morality (ages 10 or 11), morality is based
              on conformity and shifts to a "law-and-order" orientation
        c.   Level 3 - postconventional ("principled") some adults realize that
              some laws can be immoral; they develop a moral standard based on
              _____ human rights
    3.   Limitations of the theory
        a.   Overlooks educational and cultural influences
        b.   Moral reasoning is often inconsistent across situations
        c.   Moral reasoning is often unrelated to moral behavior
    4.   Gilligan countered Kohlberg's theory, she said males base moral reasoning
          on justice and females base moral reasoning on _____
    5.   Research finds that moral reasoning
        a.   Depends more on what people are reasoning about, on their
              conscience and moral emotions than on age and gender
        b.   Both genders use justice and compassion in their reasoning

Answer these Learning Objectives while you read Section 2.

3.   Describe the stages of language development.

4.   Describe the principles and stages of Piaget's theory of cognitive development.

5.   Evaluate Piaget's theory of cognitive development.

6.   Describe and evaluate Kohlberg's theory of moral development.

SECTION 3 - GENDER DEVELOPMENT (PP. 512-517)

III.   **GENDER DEVELOPMENT**
    A.   **Terms**
        1.   Sex - _____ and physiological attributes
        2.   Gender - cultural and _____ attributes that children learn are appropriate for the sexes
        3.   Gender _____ - fundamental sense of maleness or femaleness regardless of what one wears or does
        4.   Gender typing - society's ideas about which abilities, traits behaviors are appropriately masculine or feminine
    B.   **Influences on gender development**
        1.   Biological factors
            a.   Some researchers think certain gender differences (toy and play preferences) are found universally and are inborn
            b.   But biological explanations are elusive; some gender differences may be a result of situations (e.g. group play) and not a cause
        2.   Gender schemas - focus on cognitive abilities
            a.   As children mature, they develop gender schemas about what it means to be male and female; the schemas then expand
            b.   Once gender schemas are learned, children fit their behavior to the schemas
            c.   All over the world, boys' schemas are more rigid than girls'; schemas can change and get more flexible over time
        3.   Learning influences on gender development
            a.   Emphasizes the process of gender socialization; there is lots of evidence that adults treat children differently based on gender
            b.   Studies show parental attitudes and expectations about gender influence children
    C.   **Gender over the lifespan**
        1.   Certain _____ and role requirements evoke gender-typed behavior
        2.   Gender typing evolves as a result of experiences at work or at home
        3.   Gender differences are greatest in childhood and adolescence, decline in young adulthood and disappear in older people

Answer this Learning Objective while you read Section 3.

7.   Distinguish between gender typing and gender identity and describe the explanations that have been given for gender development. Explain how gender typing changes over the lifespan.

SECTION 4 - PARENTS AND PEERS (PP. 518-523)

IV. **PARENTS AND PEERS**

    A. **The influence of parents**

        1. Parental methods of enforcing moral standards have effects

            a. Power _____

                (1) Threats, physical punishment, denial of privileges

                (2) Associated with a lack of moral feelings and behavior, poor self-control, and aggressiveness

            b. Induction

                (1) More successful at teaching moral feelings and behavior

                (2) The parent appeals to the child's own _____, affection for others, and sense of responsibility

        2. Baumrind's study finds three overall child-rearing styles and their results

            a. Authoritarian parents - too much power, too little _____; children have poorer social skills, self-esteem, school performance

            b. _____ parents - nurturant but too little control and too few demands for mature behavior; children are likely to be impulsive, immature, irresponsible and academically unmotivated

            c. Authoritative parents - set high reasonable _____, teach children how to meet them, give emotional support, foster communication; children have good self-control, self-esteem, are independent, mature, cheerful, helpful and do better in school

        3. Difficulty associating specific parental practices with outcomes because parents rarely use a single child-rearing style over time

        4. Not a direct connection between parenting styles and children's adjustment

    B. **How much do parents matter?**

        1. Three factors limit a parent's power to shape a child

            a. The child's temperament and perceptions - the influence of genes on personality traits is very strong

            b. The child's peer group and outside experiences - behavior depends on the situation; some say attachment to peers is essential

            c. The child's larger cultural environment - the influence of cultural obligations and the expectations of others

        2. Do parents matter? Parents influence: how children cope with inherited dispositions, peer group choices, and their relationships with their children

Answer this Learning Objective while you read Section 4.

8. List the various styles of child-rearing and discuss the effects of each, including the limitations of parents' influence on children.

SECTION 5 - ADOLESCENCE (PP. 523-529)

V. **ADOLESCENCE**
    A.   **Definition** - period of development between _____, the age at which a person becomes capable of sexual reproduction, and adulthood
    B.   **The physiology of adolescence**: Puberty and the onset of reproductive capacity
        1.   Males
            a.   Reproductive glands stimulated to produce sperm from the testes
            b.   Produce higher levels of androgens than females
            c.   Nocturnal emissions, growth of testes, scrotum and penis
        2.   Females
            a.   Reproductive glands stimulated to produce eggs from the ovaries
            b.   Produce higher levels of estrogens than males
            c.   Menstruation begins (called _____) and breasts develop
        3.   _____ responsible for secondary sex characteristics in both sexes
        4.   Timing of puberty depends on genes and environment; is occurring earlier
        5.   Early and late puberty - age of onset of puberty varies and there are different adjustment issues related to early and late maturers
    C.   **The psychology of adolescence**
        1.   Turmoil and adjustment - only a minority are seriously troubled; extreme turmoil and unhappiness are the exception
            a.   Peer group and group acceptance becomes especially important
            b.   Adolescents express unhappiness in gender typed ways; boys externalize while girls internalize
        2.   Separation and connection - adults must recognize adolescents' need for autonomy and realize that individuation does not mean lack of affection
    D.   **Ethnic identity and acculturation**
        1.   Adolescents need to find a balance between their ethnic identity (identification with one's religious or ethnic group) and acculturation (identification with the dominant culture)
        2.   Four approaches: bicultural, assimilation, ethnic separatism, marginal

Answer these Learning Objectives while you read Section 5.

9.   Describe the events that signal the onset of puberty in males and females and the relationship between age of onset of puberty and later adjustment.

10.   Summarize the evidence on the relationship between adolescence and emotional turmoil.

11.   Describe the four approaches to balancing ethnic identity and acculturation.

SECTION 6 - ADULTHOOD (PP. 529-537) AND
SECTION 7 - ARE ADULTS PRISONERS OF CHILDHOOD? (PP. 537-538)

VI. ADULTHOOD

  A. **Stages and ages** - Erikson identifies eight psychosocial stages throughout life and said that each stage revolves around an inevitable "crisis"
   1. Erikson's stages
      a. Trust versus mistrust
      b. Autonomy versus shame and doubt
      c. Initiative versus _____
      d. Competence versus inferiority
      e. Identity versus role confusion
      f. Intimacy versus isolation
      g. Generativity versus stagnation
      h. Ego integrity versus despair
   2. Evaluating Erikson
      a. He saw that cultural and economic factors affect development
      b. Erikson showed that development is an ongoing process
      c. The stages are not universal and issues do not occur at only one stage; stages do not occur in the same sequence for everyone

  B. **The transitions of life** - theories of adult development emphasize transitions and milestones rather than a rigid sequence
   1. Starting out: The social _____
      a. The "right" time to engage in certain activities is heavily influenced by culture; it's reassuring to do things at the same time as age mates
      b. Adjusting to anticipated transitions is relatively easy
   2. People are now experiencing more unanticipated transitions and "nonevent transitions" (expected changes that don't happen)

  C. **The middle years** - for most people, this is the prime of life
   1. It is a time of psychological well-being, good health, productivity
   2. Menopause - midlife cessation of _____ brought on when ovaries stop producing estrogen and progesterone
      a. Only 10% of women have severe physical symptoms
      b. Research finds most women view it positively and are not depressed
      c. No effect on most women's mental and emotional health
      d. Males lack a biological equivalent to menopause
      e. Biological changes do not predict how people feel about aging or how they will respond to it

387

D. **Old age** - gerontologists have challenged stereotypes
1. The number of older people is increasing
2. First, the bad news
    a. Some aspects of intelligence and mental functioning decline
        (1) Crystallized intelligence (knowledge and skills built over a lifetime) remains stable over the life span
        (2) Fluid intelligence (independent of education and experience) declines in later years
    b. Some aspects of memory decline; semantic memory is stable while episodic memory declines
3. Now the good news
    a. Gerontologists have separated out conditions thought to be inevitable from those that are preventable or treatable
    b. Only about 30% of decline is genetic; 70% related to behavioral and psychological factors
    c. Best predictors of healthy old age include: intellectual activity, exercise, psychological resilience
    d. In healthy brains, brain cell loss is quite modest
    e. Aging associated with improved well-being and increased happiness

VII. **ARE ADULTS PRISONERS OF CHILDHOOD?**
A. Events of childhood do not necessarily have permanent effects
B. Evidence comes from studies of children who recovered from wars, from abusive or alcoholic parents, and sexual abuse
C. Psychologists are looking to the role of resilience
1. May have to do with personality traits or temperaments
2. May have to do with love and attention from others
3. May have to do with positive experiences in other environments like school

Answer these Learning Objectives while you read Sections 6 and 7.

12. List and discuss the stages of Erikson's theory of psychosocial development.

13. Summarize the biological and emotional changes associated with midlife.

14. Compare and contrast older and more recent notions about aging.

15. Discuss the effects of aging on intelligence and memory.

16. Discuss the impact of childhood experience on adulthood.

FLASH CARDS

Cut the following chart along the borders and test yourself with the resulting flash cards.

14.1 SOCIALIZATION	14.2 MATURATION	14.3 GERMINAL STAGE
14.4 EMBRYONIC STAGE	14.5 FETAL STAGE	14.6 ZYGOTE
14.7 FETUS	14.8 FETAL ALCOHOL SYNDROME	14.9 MOTOR REFLEXES
14.10 SYNCHRONY	14.11 "PARENTESE"	14.12 TELEGRAPHIC SPEECH
14.13 JEAN PIAGET	14.14 ASSIMILATION	14.15 ACCOMMODATION
14.16 SENSORIMOTOR STAGE	14.17 OBJECT PERMANENCE	14.18 REPRESENTATIONAL THOUGHT

14.3 The first stage of prenatal development; the male sperm unites with the female egg, the zygote divides and attaches to the uterine wall.	14.2 The sequential unfolding of genetically influenced behavior and physical characteristics.	14.1 The processes by which children learn the behaviors, attitudes, and expectations required of them by their society or culture.
14.6 A fertilized egg.	14.5 The third and final stage of prenatal development; from 8 weeks until birth; organs and systems further develop.	14.4 The second stage of prenatal development; it occurs after implantation of the zygote is complete until the eighth week after conception.
14.9 Automatic behaviors that are necessary for survival.	14.8 A pattern of physical and intellectual abnormalities in infants whose mothers drank too much alcohol during pregnancy.	14.7 After eight weeks of prenatal development, the embryo is now called a fetus, and the fetal stage begins.
14.12 A child's first word combinations, which omit (as a telegraph does) unnecessary words.	14.11 A manner in which most people speak to babies; their pitch is higher and more varied and the intonation is more exaggerated than usual.	14.10 The adjustment of one person's nonverbal behavior to coordinate with another's.
14.15 In Piaget's theory, the process of modifying existing cognitive structures in response to experience and new information.	14.14 In Piaget's theory, the process of modifying existing cognitive structures in response to experience and new information.	14.13 Swiss psychologist who, in the 1920s, proposed a theory of cognitive development. His theory has had a great influence.
14.18 The capacity for using mental images and other symbolic systems (like language).	14.17 The understanding that an object continues to exist even when you cannot see it or touch it.	14.16 The first stage in Piaget's theory of cognitive development. Thinking consists of coordinating sensory input and body movements.

14.19 PREOPERATIONAL STAGE	14.20 OPERATIONS	14.21 EGOCENTRIC THINKING
14.22 CONSERVATION	14.23 CONCRETE OPERATIONS STAGE	14.24 FORMAL OPERATIONS STAGE
14.25 THEORY OF MIND	14.26 PRECONVENTIONAL LEVEL OF MORAL REASONING	14.27 CONVENTIONAL LEVEL OF MORAL REASONING
14.28 POSTCONVENTIONAL LEVEL OF MORAL REASONING	14.29 CARE-BASED VERSUS JUSTICE-BASED TYPES OF MORAL REASONING (GILLIGAN)	14.30 GENDER IDENTITY
14.31 GENDER TYPING	14.32 GENDER SCHEMA	14.33 POWER ASSERTION
14.34 INDUCTION	14.35 AUTHORITARIAN PARENTING STYLES	14.36 PERMISSIVE PARENTING STYLE

14.21 Seeing the world from only your own point of view; the inability to take another person's perspective.	14.20 In Piaget's theory, mental actions that are cognitively reversible.	14.19 The second stage in Piaget's theory of cognitive development; the use of symbols and language increases but, children lack operations.
14.24 The final stage of Piaget's theory of cognitive development. In this stage, people are capable of abstract reasoning.	14.23 The third stage in Piaget's theory of cognitive development in which children's thinking is still grounded in concrete experiences and concepts.	14.22 The understanding that the physical properties of objects can remain the same even when their form or appearance changes.
14.27 The second stage of Kohlberg's theory of moral reasoning characterized by reasoning based on trust, loyalty or "law and order."	14.26 In Kohlberg's theory, the first stage of moral reasoning characterized by obedience based on fear of punishment or self-interest.	14.25 A system of beliefs about the way your own mind and other people's minds work, and of how people are affected by their beliefs and feelings.
14.30 The fundamental sense of being male or female; it is independent of whether the person conforms to the social and cultural rules of gender.	14.29 Gilligan's approach to moral reasoning holds that men make justice-based moral choices and women make care-based moral choices.	14.28 The third stage of Kohlberg's theory of moral reasoning in which reasoning in based on universal human rights.
14.33 A method of child rearing in which the parent uses punishment and authority to correct the child's misbehavior.	14.32 A mental network of knowledge, beliefs, metaphors, and expectations about what it means to be male or female.	14.31 The process by which children learn the abilities, interests, traits, and behaviors associated with being masculine or feminine in their culture.
14.36 One of Baumrind's three child-rearing styles. This style is used by parents who are nurturant but exercise too little control and clear discipline.	14.35 One of Baumrind's three styles of child-rearing. This parenting style is related to the exercise of too much power and too little nurturance.	14.34 A method of child rearing in which the parent appeals to the child's resources, sense of responsibility, and empathy in correcting the child's behavior.

14.37 AUTHORITATIVE PARENTING STYLE	14.38 PUBERTY	14.39 MENARCHE
14.40 SECONDARY SEX CHARACTERISTICS	14.41 ETHNIC IDENTITY	14.42 ACCULTURATION
14.43 ERIK ERIKSON	14.44 IDENTITY CRISIS	14.45 THE SOCIAL CLOCK
14.46 ANTICIPATED TRANSITIONS	14.47 UNANTICIPATED TRANSITIONS	14.48 NONEVENT TRANSITIONS
14.49 MENOPAUSE	14.50 GERONTOLOGY	14.51 FLUID INTELLIGENCE
14.52 CRYSTALLIZED INTELLIGENCE	14.53 RESILIENCE	14.54 ADOLESCENCE

14.39 The onset of menstruation.	14.38 The age at which a person becomes capable of sexual reproduction.	14.37 One of Baumrind's three child-rearing styles. This style is used by parents who know how and when to discipline their children.
14.42 The process by which members of minority groups come to identify with and feel part of the mainstream culture.	14.41 Having a close identification with one's own race, religion or ethnic group.	14.40 Characteristics driven by the hormones associated with puberty; deepened voice and facial and chest hair in boys and pubic hair in both sexes.
14.45 A culture's determination of the "right" time to engage in certain behaviors like when to marry, to begin working, and to have children.	14.44 Describes what Erik Erikson considered to be the primary conflict of adolescence; when teenagers must decide what they are going to be.	14.43 The first modern theorist to propose a lifespan approach to psychological development. Just as children progress through stages, so do adults.
14.48 The changes that people expect to happen that do not. For example, not getting married at the age a person expected to.	14.47 Events that happen without warning, such as being fired from a job. They can be significant in adult development.	14.46 Experiences that nearly everyone is a group goes through at the same time; driving, voting, going to school, marrying, having a baby.
14.51 The capacity for deductive reasoning and the ability to use new information to solve problems; it tends to decline in old age.	14.50 Researchers who study aging and the old.	14.49 The cessation of menstruation which occurs when the ovaries stop producing estrogen and progesterone.
14.54 The period of development between puberty and adulthood.	14.53 A characteristic of children who, as adults, do not experience specific and inevitable effects from painful or traumatic backgrounds.	14.52 Cognitive skills and specific knowledge of information acquired over a lifetime; it tends to remain stable over the lifetime.

394

ACROSS

1. processes by which an organism grows from a fetus to an adult
6. first stage of prenatal development
10. the adjustment of one person's nonverbal behavior to coordinate with another's
11. Piagetian process of modifying existing cognitive structures
13. developed a theory of cognitive development in children
14. type of thought involving the capacity for using mental images
15. understanding that physical properties of objects can remain the same even when their appearances change
16. child-rearing style that relies on the use of power

DOWN

2. seeing the world from only one's own point of view
3. sequential unfolding of genetically governed behavior and physical characteristics
4. the third stage of prenatal development
5. the age at which a person becomes capable of sexual reproduction
7. child-rearing method in which parents appeal to child's own
8. the process of absorbing new information into existing cognitive structures
9. onset of menstruation
12. mental actions that are cognitively reversible

STAGES OF COGNITIVE DEVELOPMENT ACCORDING TO PIAGET

Complete the following chart by describing the characteristics, limitations and achievements of each stage of Piaget's theory of cognitive development.

STAGE OF DEVELOPMENT	CHARACTERISTICS	LIMITATIONS	ACHIEVEMENTS
SENSORY-MOTOR STAGE			
PREOPERATIONAL STAGE			
CONCRETE OPERATIONS STAGE			
FORMAL OPERATIONS STAGE			

PRACTICE TEST 1 - Multiple Choice

1. The order of the three stages of prenatal development is
    A. embryonic, germinal, fetal.   B. germinal, fetal, embryonic.
    C. germinal, embryonic, fetal.   D. fetal, germinal, embryonic.

2. During which stage of prenatal development do the eyes, ears, nose and mouth first develop?
    A. embryonic   B. germinal
    C. fetal   D. conception

3. Which of the following could be a problem during pregnancy?
    A. coffee   B. alcohol
    C. cigarettes   D. all of the above

4. An infant touched on the cheek or corner of the mouth will turn in the direction from which he or she was touched and search for something to suck on. This is called the
    A. sucking reflex.   B. rooting reflex.
    C. sneeze reflex.   D. grasping reflex.

5. During the first six to eight weeks, babies
    A. can distinguish contrasts, shadows and edges.
    B. show a distinct preference for curved lines over straight lines.
    C. can focus on parts of pictures.
    D. can track someone's location and movement.

6. Which of the following statements is true?
    A. Synchrony refers to the coordination of one person's behavior to another's.
    B. Newborns synchronize their behavior to adult speech, street noise, and tapping.
    C. Synchrony occurs in four stages.
    D. Synchrony is critical during the first year of life but unimportant later on.

7. The order of Piaget's stages of cognitive development is
    A. preoperational, sensory-motor, concrete operations, formal operations.
    B. concrete operations, preoperational, sensory-motor, formal operations.
    C. sensory-motor, preoperational, formal operations, concrete operations.
    D. sensory-motor, preoperational, concrete operations, formal operations.

8. Fitting new information into your present system of knowledge and beliefs is called
    A. assimilation.   B. organization.
    C. accommodation.   D. sensory-motor development.

397

9. According to Piaget, during the concrete operations stage the child
   A. thinks egocentrically.
   B. develops object permanence.
   C. grasps conservation.
   D. can reason abstractly.

10. Which of the following represents a challenge to Piaget's theory?
    A. Changes from one stage to another are not as clear-cut nor as sweeping as Piaget implied.
    B. Infants as young as 2-1/2 to 3-1/2 months are aware that objects continue to exist when masked by other objects.
    C. Most 3- and 4-year-olds can take another person's perspective.
    D. all of the above

11. During the first months, babies are highly responsive to
    A. normal adult talk.
    B. the basic sounds of their native language.
    C. the pitch, intensity and sound of language.
    D. all of the above.

12. "Mama here," "go 'way bug," and "my toy" are examples of
    A. baby talk.
    B. telegraphic speech.
    C. babbling.
    D. parentese.

13. A child's fundamental sense of maleness or femaleness that exists regardless of what one wears or does is called
    A. gender schema.
    B. gender socialization.
    C. gender identity.
    D. sex-typing.

14. According to gender schema theory
    A. gender-typed behavior increases once a gender schema is developed.
    B. gender schemas do not develop until a child is about four years old.
    C. gender schemas are formed early and basically do not change throughout life
    D. gender schemas disappear during adolescence.

15. Which of the following is evidence for the influence of learning on gender development?
    A. Adults treat boys and girls equally.
    B. Parents do not stereotype infants.
    C. Twelve- to sixteen-month old boys and girls differed significantly in the frequency of assertive acts.
    D. Adults respond to boys and girls differently even when the children are behaving in the same way.

16. Kohlberg's theory describes
    A. moral emotions.
    C. moral reasoning.
    B. moral behavior.
    D. moral actions.

17. According to Kohlberg's theory, moral reasoning is based on conformity and loyalty to others in the _____ stage.
    A. preconventional
    C. conventional
    B. postconventional
    D. egocentric

18. Critics of Kohlberg's theory of moral development argue that
    A. the hierarchy of stages actually reflects verbal, not moral, development.
    B. adults and children use the same moral reasoning in all ethical situations.
    C. Kohlberg's work implies that women are more moral than men.
    D. the stages are too similar to be meaningful.

19. In a large cross-cultural study of altruistic behavior in children, researchers found
    A. American children were the least altruistic and the most egoistic.
    B. the most altruistic children came from societies in which children were assigned many tasks.
    C. altruistic children knew that their work made a genuine contribution to the family.
    D. that all of the above were true.

20. Which of the following is a limitation on parents' influence on their children's behavior?
    A. the child's temperament
    C. grandparents
    B. siblings
    D. teachers

21. Parents who rely on power assertion for discipline produce children who
    A. lack moral feelings and behavior.
    B. accept responsibility for their misbehavior.
    C. have a sense of internal control.
    D. feel guilty if they hurt others and, thus, are considerate of other children.

22. Which of the following reflects the influence of culture on children.
    A. the choice of behaviors that are valued in public figures
    B. that children are oriented to their peers
    C. a child's temperament
    D. all of the above

23. The major sign of puberty for females is
    A. the development of pubic hair.
    C. menarche.
    B. the growth spurt.
    D. acne.

24. Which of the following is true about the idea that adolescence is inevitably a time of great turmoil?
    A. Research has supported that adolescence is a time of anguish and rebellion.
    B. The vast majority of adolescents experience turmoil, but a minority do not.
    C. In studies, only a minority of adolescents were seriously troubled.
    D. The emotional turbulence of adolescence has to do with hormonal changes.

25. The effect of childhood experiences on adulthood is
    A. not inevitable; early traumas do not necessarily have life-long consequences.
    B. irreversible.
    C. a straight and inflexible line to the future.
    D. unknown.

PRACTICE TEST 2 - Multiple Choice

1. Embryos that are genetically male will begin to secrete _____ during the
    _____ stage of prenatal development.
    A.   adrenalin; embryonic   B.   testosterone; embryonic
    C.   hormones; fetal   D.   estrogen; germinal

2. Jane has smoked heavily during her pregnancy. What are the risks?
    A.   increased chance of miscarriage   B.   premature birth
    C.   her child may be hyperactive   D.   all of the above

3. Which of the following should Jane avoid during her pregnancy?
    A.   prescription drugs   B.   over-the-counter drugs
    C.   alcohol   D.   all of the above

4. Doris and Morris just had their first child. What behaviors can they expect?
    A.   The newborn will be passive and inert.
    B.   The newborn can see, hear, touch, smell and taste.
    C.   The newborn will not be able to identify the primary caregiver.
    D.   The newborn can only see light and dark.

5. Doris and her baby seem to understand one another. The adjustment of Doris to her baby
    and the baby's adjustment to her
    A.   is called synchrony.
    B.   is related to the infant's visual development.
    C.   occurs when the baby synchronizes his or her behavior to other noises.
    D.   happens when the baby is about six months old.

6. While on a walk with his father, Butch points to a cardinal and his father says, "Birdie."
    A little bit later, Butch sees a blue jay and says, "Birdie." This is an example of
    A.   assimilation.   B.   conservation.
    C.   accommodation.   D.   an operation.

7. The next day while walking with his dad, Butch points to a butterfly and says, "Birdie."
    His dad says, "That's a butterfly." Butch says, "Butterfly." This is an example of
    A.   assimilation.   B.   a schema.
    C.   accommodation.   D.   an operation.

8. Butch's ability to say "birdie" and "butterfly" are indicators that he
    A.   can use representational thought.   B.   can use formal operations.
    C.   is still egocentric.   D.   can use concrete operations.

9. Which of the following is an example of a challenge to Piaget's theory?
   A. Babies look longer at a ball if it seems to roll through a solid barrier.
   B. When four-year-olds play with two-year-olds, they modify and simplify their speech so the younger child will understand.
   C. By the time children are four or five years old, they have developed a theory of mind.
   D. all of the above

10. Based on the stages of language development, which of the following would a four- to six-month-old baby be able to do?
    A. have a repertoire of symbolic gestures
    B. use telegraphic speech
    C. recognize "mommy" and "daddy"
    D. all of the above

11. In the first months of life, a baby is most likely to respond to
    A. his or her name.
    B. the words "mommy" and "daddy."
    C. the basic sounds of his or her native language.
    D. speech in which the pitch is higher and more varied and spoken with exaggerated intonation.

12. Both Fran and Dan know that girls play with dolls and become nurses and boys play with trucks and become doctors. This demonstrates
    A. gender socialization.   B. fixations in the oral stage.
    C. gender identity.   D. all of the above.

13. When Jill grows up she says she is going to be a boy and marry Jane. This demonstrates that Jill
    A. has a psychological problem.
    B. is going to be a homosexual.
    C. has not established her gender identity.
    D. has not yet experienced gender socialization.

14. The belief by children that bears, fire, anger, dogs, and the color black are "masculine" and butterflies, hearts, the color pink, and flowers are feminine indicates that
    A. children have accurate gender identity.
    B. children have been reinforced for these types of distinctions.
    C. children are learning gender schemas.
    D. there is a biological basis for these distinctions.

15. Adults will respond to the same baby differently depending on
    A. whether the child is dressed like a boy or girl.
    B. whether the child has long or short hair.
    C. the aggressiveness of the baby.
    D. how much the baby cries.

16. In Kohlberg's theory of moral development, your moral stage is determined by
    A. your answers to questions such as "Do you think it is morally acceptable to steal?"
    B. your answers to hypothetical moral dilemmas.
    C. your actions.
    D. your performance on tests of moral feelings.

17. Which of the following is consistent with current ideas about the extent to which parents can shape the behavior of their children.
    A. Parents can help a child become more extroverted and less shy.
    B. Parents can influence how children cope with inherited dispositions.
    C. Parents' approval is more important than peer approval.
    D. All of the above are influences parents have on their children's behavior.

18. _____ parents have children who have lower self-esteem and do more poorly in school, whereas _____ parents have children with high self-esteem and self-efficacy.
    A. Authoritarian; permissive   B. Authoritarian; authoritative
    C. Authoritative; authoritarian   D. Permissive; authoritative

19. Early-maturing boys
    A. generally have a negative body image compared to late-developing boys.
    B. are more likely to smoke, drink, use drugs and break the law than later-maturing boys.
    C. feel worse about themselves than do late-developing boys at first, but they end up the healthiest group.
    D. have more self-control and emotional stability than late-developing boys.

20. Which of the following is true for Gary, who just reached puberty?
    A. He has roughly the same amount of androgens and estrogens as a female.
    B. He has higher levels of androgens and estrogens than females.
    C. He has higher levels of androgens and lower levels of estrogens than females.
    D. He is likely to experience a growth spurt, which will begin, on average, at age 10, will peak at age 12 or 13, and will stop at about age 16.

21. Noriko is going through menopause. If she is like most women, she will
   A. experience depression and other emotional reactions.
   B. will not experience unusually severe symptoms.
   C. will regret reaching menopause.
   D. will experience severe physical discomfort.

22. The findings of gerontologists have changed our understanding of old age by
   A. reevaluating when "old age" begins.
   B. separating aging from illness.
   C. recognizing some of the benefits of aging.
   D. doing all of the above.

23. Fluid intelligence
   A. tends to remain stable or even improve over the life span.
   B. is influenced by an inherited predisposition, and it parallels other biological capacities in its growth and, in later years, decline.
   C. is the knowledge and skills that are built up over a lifetime.
   D. gives us the ability to solve math problems, define words, or summarize a president's policy.

24. According to Erikson, Heather, who is 21 years old, will
   A. experience an identity crisis.
   B. fight against stagnation.
   C. learn to share herself with another person and make a commitment.
   D. deal with her feelings of competence versus inferiority.

25. Wanda is an adult who was abused in childhood by a parent. What is most likely true for her?
   A. Most likely she will not be an abusive parent herself, because 70 percent of adults who were abused in childhood do not repeat the abuse.
   B. There is a very good chance she will become abusive with her own children.
   C. If she receives counseling she may be able to avoid becoming an abusive parent.
   D. Whether she becomes an abusive parents depends on how resilient she is.

PRACTICE TEST 3 - Short Answer

1.   The psychological and social processes by which children learn the rules and behavior expected of them by their society is called _____.

2.   Prenatal development is divided into three stages: the _____ begins at conception, the _____ begins once the implantation of the _____ into the wall of the uterus is completed.

3.   The _____, connected to the embryo by the umbilical cord, serves to screen out some, but not all, harmful substances. Some harmful influences, such as _____ and _____ can cross the barrier.

4.   Babies have rudimentary "conversations" with those who tend them. The rhythmic dialogue is called _____.

5.   When Hank speaks to his baby, his voice has a higher pitch and is more varied than usual and his intonation is exaggerated. He is using _____.

6.   Jennifer is _____ months old and she has started to smack her lips when she is hungry, to blow on something to show that it is hot, and to shrug her shoulders to indicate that she doesn't know an answer to a question. Jennifer is demonstrating her developing repertoire of _____ gestures.

7.   The Swiss psychologist, _____, proposed a theory of cognitive development.

8.   When Leah learns a _____ for birdies, she is able to identify Robins, cardinals, and pet parakeets, as birdies. This demonstrates Piaget's concept of _____, or fitting new information into existing categories.

9.   Jean-Paul is 12 months old. When his mother puts his favorite toy out-of-sight at meal time, he still cries for it. Jean-Paul has developed _____.

10.   Hillary's dad asks her advice about a birthday present for her mom. Five-year-old Hillary suggests that they buy mom one of Hillary's favorite toys. Piaget's theory proposes that Hillary is demonstrating _____. Hillary is in Piaget's _____ stage of cognitive development.

11. Jack understands the principles of conservation and cause and effect, yet he cannot think in abstractions or use logical deductions. He is in the _____ stage of cognitive development.

12. Modern research has challenged aspects of Piaget's view of cognitive development. This research suggests that Piaget _____ the cognitive skills of young children and _____ those of many adults.

13. Bill will not jay walk even when he is on a small road and there is no traffic in sight. He says "It is the law, and it is important that we obey the laws we have chosen because society is based on them." Based on this reasoning, Bill would be in the _____ stage of Kohlberg's theory of moral development.

14. Barbie knows that girls are "supposed" to behave in ways that are unassertive and boys are "supposed" to behave in ways that are aggressive and dominant. This is an example of gender _____.

15. Rough, spiky, black, mechanical things are "male" and soft, pink, fuzzy, flowery things are "female." This is an example of gender _____.

16. Learning theorists point to the role of _____, or the reinforcers and societal messages children get about what "girls" and "boys" do.

17. Longitudinal studies show how power _____ by parents can lead to _____ and poor impulse control in children.

18. _____ parents exercise too much power and give too little nurturance while _____ parents know when and how to discipline their children.

19. Three factors set limits on a parent's power to shape a child's personality, behavior, and future life. They are _____, _____, and _____.

20. Until puberty, boys and girls produce roughly the same levels of "male" hormones, or _____ and "female" hormones, _____.

21. The onset of menstruation is called _____. The cessation of menstruation is called _____.

22. When teenagers have conflicts with their parents over autonomy, they are usually trying to _____, to develop their own opinions, values, and style of dress and look.

23.   Ethnic _____ have a strong sense of ethnic identity but weak feelings of _____.

24.   Erik Erikson wrote that all individuals go through _____ stages in their lives, resolving an inevitable _____ at each one.

25.   _____ intelligence is relatively independent of education and experience and in later years it _____. _____ intelligence depends heavily on culture, education, and experience, and it tends to remain _____ over the life span.

PRACTICE TEST 4 - True/False

1.   T F   Without the secretion of the male hormone, testosterone, the embryo will develop to be anatomically female.

2.   T F   It is considered safe to have up to three alcoholic drinks a day during pregnancy.

3.   T F   Cigarette smoking is more dangerous to the fetus than cocaine use.

4.   T F   Perceptual abilities do not seem to be inborn, rather they are a result of experience with the environment.

5.   T F   Cultural customs influence the rate of physical development in infants.

6.   T F   Infants who start off with illnesses or other biological vulnerabilities are unlikely to overcome their difficult beginning.

7.   T F   By 4 to 6 weeks, babies know many of the key consonant and vowel sounds of their native language, and can distinguish such sounds from those of other languages.

8.   T F   Assimilation and accommodation are achieved during the preoperational stage of cognitive development.

9.   T F   Object permanence represents the beginning of the child's capacity to use mental imagery and other symbolic systems.

10.   T F   Piaget described the preoperational stage in terms of what the child cannot do. Piaget called the missing abilities operations.

11.   T F   Modern research has found that by the age of 4 or 5, children are developing a theory of mind, which is the ability to develop an abstract understanding of mind versus body.

12.   T F   According to Kohlberg's theory, in the conventional morality level of moral development, children begin with a "law-and-order" orientation to moral thinking. In the later stage of conventional morality, they realize that certain laws are themselves immoral.

13.   T F   People's moral reasoning is often inconsistent across situations. In one situation, a person might reveal postconventional reasoning while in another, he or she might make decisions based on conventional level reasoning.

14.   T F   Moral reasoning is a good predictor of moral behavior.

15.   T F   A person can have a strong gender identity and not be gender typed. Therefore, males who may engage in "feminine" behaviors are still likely to have a fundamental sense of themselves as male.

16.   T F   Boys do not have a greater activity level nor are they more physically active than girls when children are playing on their own.

17.   T F   If parents do not want their children to engage in society's gender-typed behaviors, they can decrease these behaviors by providing their children with "non-sexist" toys.

18.   T F   Gender differences in personality traits and motivations often cross over by middle age.

19.   T F   The power assertion style of child-rearing leads to children who are shy, submissive, and an over emphasis of moral values.

20.   T F   Child-rearing techniques seem to have little impact on children's basic temperaments and traits.

21.   T F   The age of first sexual attraction for homosexuals precedes puberty; for heterosexuals, it follows the onset of puberty.

22   T F   Though some teenagers have a positive experience during adolescence, a majority find adolescence a time of turmoil and unhappiness.

23.   T F   Of the four ways of balancing ethnic identity and acculturation, acculturation is associated with the strong ties to one's ethnicity and to the larger culture.

24.   T F   Midlife is typically a time of psychological well-being. Most women do not have a negative reaction to menopause.

25.   T F   Gerontologists estimate that only about 30 percent of the physical losses of old age are genetically based; the other 70 percent have to do with behavioral and psychological factors.

PRACTICE TEST 5 - Essay

1. Prenatal development is associated with several dangers. Identify the dangers associated with:
   A.   X-rays
   B.   cigarettes
   C.   alcohol
   D.   drugs

2. A.   You are part of a pediatric medical team and you are conducting an evaluation of a newborn infant. Discuss all the behaviors and sensory abilities that a normal newborn should have.
   B.   Many people think newborn attachment is instinctive. Discuss behaviors that contribute to attachment between the newborn and the caregiver.

3. A.   A four-year-old girl insists small people must live in the TV because they are right there behind the glass. Identify her stage of cognitive development and the phenomenon being displayed by this child.
   B.   A child adept at roller skating goes ice skating for the first time. She keeps trying to stand and move just as she would on roller skates but she falls again and again. According to Piaget, what is necessary for mastery of this new skill?
   C.   A child threatened to tell his parents when his older brother gave him only one of the three candy bars they were supposed to share. The older child then broke his brother's bar in half and gave him two pieces. This satisfied both children because they each had two pieces. Identify the cognitive stages of these children and the disadvantage that allows the younger child to be cheated.
   D.   Previously, whenever Johnny banged with a spoon, his mother would put it in a drawer and Johnny would quickly move on to something else. Now that he's eight months old, this isn't working. The child continues to demand the spoon even though he can't see it. Identify the cognitive stage of this child and the change that has taken place.

4. Harold has been babysitting for Jennie since she was an infant. She is now 23 months old. Harold has always tried to get Jennie to speak. He is now trying to get her to say, "The apple is on the table." Describe what Jennie's response might have been at 4 months old, 10 months old, 14 months old and at 23 months old.

410

5. Based on the description of the child, indicate what child-rearing styles each child's parents most likely used.

    A. Rosie feels good about herself and she sets high standards for her own performance. She is well-liked, helpful, independent and cooperative.
    B. Walter is quite timid and appears to have low self-esteem. He does not seem to know how to interact with other children.
    C. Henrietta is impulsive, immature, irresponsible and not particularly motivated.

6. Five people have been asked to explain why stealing is wrong. From the explanations provided, identify the most likely level of moral reasoning.

    A. Jim believes stealing is wrong because it hurts the feelings of others.
    B. Jane believes stealing is wrong because it is against the law.
    C. Joshua believes stealing is wrong because it violates the principle that everyone should work hard to acquire his or her own things.
    D. Jennifer believes most stealing is wrong, but in some cases, like saving someone's life, it can be justified.
    E. Joe believes stealing is wrong because you could be caught and punished.

7. Ron and Rita are going through adolescence.

    A. Describe the biological changes each is experiencing.
    B. Describe the psychological and social changes each is experiencing.

CHAPTER 15

Health, Stress, and Coping

LEARNING OBJECTIVES

1. Describe Selye's stages of stress response and compare his theory to current theories.

2. Describe the functioning of the immune system.

3. Summarize the aims of psychoneuroimmunology and health psychology.

4. Compare the three approaches to studying individual vulnerability to stress.

5. List and discuss the major sources of stress.

6. Discuss the relationship between negative emotions and illness and between emotional inhibition and illness.

7. Compare optimistic and pessimistic explanatory styles and describe their relationship to illness and coping with stress.

8. Define locus of control and explain its relationship with health and well-being.

9. Distinguish between primary and secondary control and explain how culture influences their use.

10. List and explain the major methods of coping with stress.

11. Discuss the relationship between social networks and health and well-being.

12. List and explain the factors that influence whether support is helpful.

13. Discuss the various factors that have an impact on the relationship between stress and illness.

14. Describe psychological factors that can influence illness and the reasons to avoid either-or thinking about the relationship between illness and psychological factors.

CHAPTER CONCEPT MAP

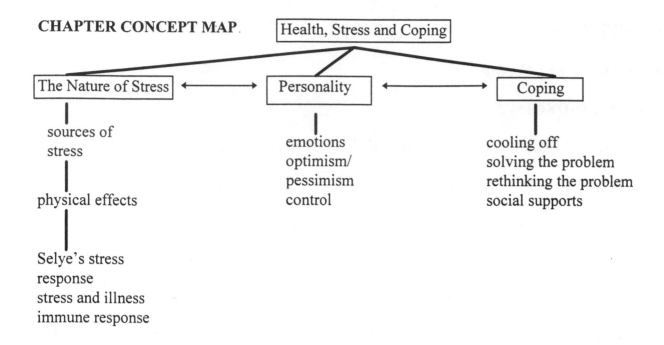

BRIEF CHAPTER SUMMARY

Chapter 15 examines the effects of stress on our lives. Hans Selye began the modern era of stress research and identified a stress response cycle. This cycle includes an alarm phase, a resistance phase and an exhaustion phase. Health psychologists study the relationship between psychological factors and health. Stress is no longer considered a purely biological condition that leads directly to illness, but rather an interaction between aspects of the individual and aspects of the environment. Current research is in the area of psychoneuroimmunology, which is an interdisciplinary field that looks at the relationship among psychological processes, the nervous and endocrine systems and the immune system. The current view of the relationship between stress and illness considers apsects of the external stressor, the individual's characteristics, a person's emotional style, and perceived coping abilities. Several coping methods are reviewed including reducing bodily arousal, solving the problem, thinking about the problem differently and drawing on social supports. Finally, the chapter examines the extent to which we can control our health.

PREVIEW OUTLINE AND REVIEW QUESTIONS

Before you read the chapter, review the preview outline and Learning Objectives for each section of the text. Answer all questions as you read the text.

SECTION 1 - THE NATURE OF STRESS (PP. 546-551)

I. **THE NATURE OF STRESS**
    A. **Definitions**
        1. Stress - refers to recurring conflicts, traumatic experience, continuing pressures that seem uncontrollable, and small irritations
        2. Health psychology
            a. Looks at the psychological factors that influence health
            b. Studies the sources of wellness and illness to learn why some people succumb to stress and disease and others do not
    B. **The physiology of stress**
        1. Hans _____ began modern era of stress research
        2. Stressors
            a. Environmental factors that throw the body out of balance
            b. The body responds by mobilizing its resources to fight or flee
        3. Selye identified three phases of the bodies response to stress
            a. Alarm phase - the body mobilizes to meet threat
            b. resistance phase - resists or copes with a stressor which makes the body more susceptible to other stressors
            c. Exhaustion phase - occurs if the stressor persists; body's resources are depleted and vulnerability to illness increases
        4. Selye said some stress is positive; but it is important to minimize its negative effects
        5. Some factors can soften the impact of a stressor
    C. **Common sources of stress**
        1. Daily hassles; don't pose threat to illness unless the stressors are uncontrollable, disruptive, or chronic
        2. Bereavement and loss
            a. The widowed and divorced have higher rates of illness than others
            b. Vulnerability to illness is related to unhappiness, poor diet and sleep, drug and cigarette use
            c. Loss has a direct effect on the body at a cellular level
        3. Work-related problems
            a. Effects can be severe because work is central to people's lives
            b. They increase vulnerability to severe and minor illnesses
        4. Poverty and powerlessness

        a.   Poverty associated with worse health and higher mortality rates

        b.   Related to health care, diet, continuous environmental stressor related to poverty (crime, discrimination, fewer services, housing)

D.   **The Stress-illness mystery**

    1.   Why people differ in their vulnerability to stress and disease

    2.   Two views - physiological and psychological

        a.   Psychoanalysts thought some illnesses related to unconscious conflicts, these were seen as "psychosomatic" illnesses

        b.   Now researchers study mechanisms that link mind and body, researchers created an interdisciplinary specialty called psychoneuroimmunology (PNI)

            (1)   PNI researchers study the white blood cells of the immune system which recognize foreign substances (_____) and destroy or deactivate them

            (2)   When an antigen invades, the immune system deploys different kinds of white blood cells that produce chemicals; the chemicals are sent to the brain which sends signals to stimulate or restrain the immune system

            (3)   Disruptions of this path can suppress the immune system

    3.   PNI researchers have focused on three areas of investigation

        a.   Individual variations in the body's cardiovascular, digestive, endocrine, and immune systems

        b.   Psychological factors like personality traits, perceptions, emotions

        c.   How people behave under stress and how they manage it

    4.   Current view of stress and illness examines the interaction between external stressors, individual qualities, a person's emotional state, and perceived coping abilities

Answer these Learning Objectives while you read Section 1.

1.   Describe Selye's stages of stress response and compare his theory to current theories.

2.   Describe the functioning of the immune system.

3.   Summarize the aims of psychoneuroimmunology and health psychology.

4.   Compare the three approaches to studying individual vulnerability to stress.

5.   List and discuss the major sources of stress.

SECTION 2 - PERSONALITY AND HEALTH (PP. 552-560)

II.   **PERSONALITY AND HEALTH** - three aspects of personality affect how people respond to stressors

overachievers always on the go + hostile

    A.   **Emotions and illness**

       1.   Evidence that negative emotions affect the course of illness once a person has a medical condition; unclear whether negative emotions cause illness

       2.   Hostility and depression

          a.   Early research focused on the Type A behavior pattern as risk factor for heart disease - it is no longer believed to be a risk factor

          b.   Cynical or antagonistic _____ found to be related to heart disease for men - the relationship is less clear for women

          c.   Depression may be a risk factor for heart disease and other diseases; the evidence is contradictory

       3.   Emotional inhibition

          a.   Trying to avoid bothersome thoughts has the opposite effect

          b.   Suppressors, those who deny feelings of anxiety, anger, or fear, have the trait of emotional _____

             (1)   Those with this trait are at greater risk of becoming ill than those who acknowledge their fears

             (2)   Those who suppress feelings tend to have decreased levels of circulating white blood cells that fight disease

       4.   Emotion and health: A two-way street

          a.   Researchers disagree about the importance of emotions to illness

          b.   Disease may cause the emotion rather than the opposite

    B.   **Optimism and pessimism**

       1.   Explanatory styles associated with characteristic responses to bad events

          a.   Pessimistic style

             (1)   Associated lower achievement, more illness and slower recovery from trauma

             (2)   More likely to engage in self-destructive behavior

          b.   Optimistic style

             (1)   Have "positive _____" (not denial), engage in active problem solving, and do not give up

             (2)   May have better health than pessimists; take better care of themselves and have better immune function

    C.   **The sense of control**

       1.   Locus of control - your expectation of whether you can control the things that happen to you

          a.   Internal locus of control - those who believe they are responsible for what happens to them

2. ~~External~~ locus of control - those who believe they are victims of circumstances

3. The benefits of control

colds

health & wellbeing

fewer illnesses & stress symptoms

↓ disease

hypertension

a. Difficult events more tolerable if more predictable or controllable

b. Feeling in control reduces chronic pain, improves adjustment to surgery and illness, speeds up recovery from diseases

c. Sense of control affects *situations* and immune systems

d. Culture affects beliefs about control and may have health effects

4. The limits of control

a. Trying to control the uncontrollable or blaming control are problems

b. Ideas about control are influenced by *culture*

(1) Westerners emphasize *primary* control - modify the situation

(2) Easterners emphasize *secondary* control - accommodate to reality by changing aspirations or desires

(3) Combining both types of control works best

c. Goal is to avoid guilt and self-blame while retaining self-efficacy

Answer these Learning Objectives while you read Section 2.

6. Discuss the relationship between negative emotions and illness and between emotional inhibition and illness.

7. Compare optimistic and pessimistic explanatory styles and describe their relationship to illness and coping with stress.

8. Define locus of control and explain its relationship with health and well-being.

9. Distinguish between primary and secondary control and explain how culture influences their use.

SECTION 3 - COPING WITH STRESS (PP. 560-568)

III. **COPING WITH STRESS**
    A.   **Coping**
        1.   The things people do to control, tolerate, or reduce the effects of stressors
        2.   Not a single strategy; people cope differently with different stressors
    B.   **Cooling off** - techniques that reduce bodily arousal have a variety of benefits
        1.   Relaxation - some people use relaxation training techniques
        2.   Massage and "contact comfort"
        3.   Exercise - not beneficial when used to avoid problems or done in excess
    C.   **Solving the problem**
        1.   Emotion-focused coping - fine initially but a person should move to problem-focused coping
        2.   Problem-focused coping - over time associated with better adjustment
               a.   The specific steps depend on the nature of the problem
               b.   Must define the problem correctly then learn all about it
               c.   Benefits - increases self-esteem, control and effectiveness
    D.   **Rethinking the problem**
        1.   Reappraising the situation - thinking about a problem differently which changes a person's emotional response
        2.   Learning from experience - finding benefit from a bad experience
        3.   Making social comparisons - comparing self to others less fortunate
        4.   Cultivating a sense of humor - buffers depression, anger, tension; reduces distress, improves immune functioning, hastens recovery
    E.   **Drawing on social support**
        1.   When friends help you cope...
               a.   Studies show positive effects of friends on health and longevity
               b.   May be beneficial effects on _____ system
        2.   ... And coping with friends
               a.   Friends and family can also be a source of stress
               b.   Support can be source of stress when there is arguing and hostility
               c.   Friends can be unhelpful in a variety of ways
    F.   **Healing through helping** - there are benefits associated with giving support

Answer these Learning Objective while you read Section 3.

10.   List and explain the major methods of coping with stress.

11.   Discuss the relationship between social networks and health and well-being.

12.   List and explain the factors that influence whether support is helpful.

SECTION 4 - HOW MUCH CONTROL DO WE HAVE OVER OUR HEALTH?
(PP. 568-571)

IV. **HOW MUCH CONTROL DO WE HAVE OVER OUR HEALTH?**
    A. **Relationship between stress and illness**
        1. Not direct, many factors, like personality traits, biological vulnerabilities, emotional inhibition, explanatory styles, coping strategies, social networks, influence outcome
        2. People's behavior (smoking, diet, exercise) has a strong influence on health
        3. Debate continues over the extent to which psychological factors are involved
        4. Certain factors play a role: long-lasting depression, hostile anger, suppression of negative thoughts and feelings, pessimism, feelings of powerlessness, lack of social support
        5. Doesn't mean that all illnesses have psychological causes
            a. Many diseases once thought to be psychological are now found to have a biological basis
            b. Health professionals worried that the "pop-health" field promotes the idea that people are always to blame if they get sick
            c. Can lead to either/or thinking about treatment options; traditional versus alternative psychological approaches
        6. Can benefit unscrupulous marketers
    B. **Avoid oversimplification, either-or thinking, or emotional reasoning about health**

Answer these Learning Objective while you read Section 4.

13. Discuss the various factors that have an impact on the relationship between stress and illness.

14. Describe psychological factors that can influence illness and the reasons to avoid either-or thinking about the relationship between illness and psychological factors.

FLASH CARDS

Cut the following chart along the borders and test yourself with the resulting flash cards.

15.1 HEALTH PSYCHOLOGY	15.2 ALARM PHASE OF STRESS	15.3 RESISTANCE PHASE OF STRESS
15.4 EXHAUSTION PHASE OF STRESS	15.5 PSYCHONEUROIMMUNOLOGY	15.6 PSYCHOLOGICAL STRESS
15.7 TYPE A PERSONALITY	15.8 CYNICAL HOSTILITY	15.9 OPTIMISTIC EXPLANATORY STYLE
15.10 PESSIMISTIC EXPLANATORY STYLE	15.11 LOCUS OF CONTROL (INTERNAL VERSUS EXTERNAL)	15.12 PRIMARY CONTROL
15.13 SECONDARY CONTROL	15.14 COPING	15.15 EMOTION-FOCUSED COPING
15.16 PROBLEM-FOCUSED COPING	15.17 REAPPRAISAL	15.18 SOCIAL COMPARISONS

15.3 The third phase of the stress response cycle identified by Selye in which the body's resources become overwhelmed.	15.2 The first phase in the stress response cycle identified by Selye in which the organism mobilizes to meet a threat with basic biological responses.	15.1 A field within psychology that addresses psychological factors that influence how people stay healthy and why they become ill.
15.6 Recurring conflicts, traumatic experiences, continuing pressures that seem uncontrollable, or small irritations.	15.5 The study of the relationships among psychology, the nervous and endocrine systems, and the immune system.	15.4 The third phase of the stress response cycle identified by Selye in which the body's resources become overwhelmed.
15.9 A type of characteristic response in which a person explains bad events by external and changing conditions.	15.8 They type of hostility felt by people who are mistrustful of others and quick to have mean, furious arguments. It is linked to heart disease for men.	15.7 A personal who wants to achieve, is irritable, impatient, has a sense of time urgency. At one time thought to be related to heart disease
15.12 An effort to modify reality by changing other people, the situation, or events; a "fighting back" philosophy.	15.11 A general expectation that one's actions are beyond one's control.	15.10 A type of characteristic response in which a person explains bad events as a permanent failing in himself or herself.
15.15 A coping style in which a person concentrates on the emotions the problem caused, whether anger, anxiety, or grief.	15.14 Cognitive and behavioral efforts to manage demands in the environment or oneself that one feels to be stressful.	15.13 An effort to accept reality by changing your own attitudes, goals, or emotions; a "learn to live with it" philosophy.
15.18 One way to rethink a problem is to compare oneself to others who are less fortunate.	15.17 Reassessing the meaning of a problem. This is one way to think about a problem in a new way.	15.16 A coping style in which a person defines the problem, learns about it, and considers possible actions.

ACROSS

1. a common source of stress that is associated with worse health and high mortality rates
3. explanatory style associated with lower achievement and more illness
6. characteristic thought to be the risk factor for heart disease in men with Type A behavior patterns
8. second stage of Selye's stress
10. researcher who began the modern era of stress research
12. everyday irritations
13. friends and family
14. can buffer depression and anger

DOWN

1. type of control in which people try to modify the situation
2. a coping technique that reduces bodily arousal
4. primary and secondary _____
5. thinking about a problem differently
7. type of psychologist who studies the sources of wellness and illness his or her desires or aspirations
9. type of control in which the person accommodates reality by changing his or her desires or aspirations
11. third phase of Selye's stress response model

423

PRACTICE TEST 1 - Multiple Choice

1. According to Selye, the body mobilizes to meet a threat during which stage?
    A. alarm
    B. resistance
    C. activation
    D. exhaustion

2. One of life's most powerful stressors is
    A. daily hassles.
    B. loud noise.
    C. crowds.
    D. loss of a loved one.

3. The immune system
    A. keeps us stress free.
    B. prepares our bodies for the fight or flight response.
    C. recognizes and defends the body against foreign substances.
    D. is designed to do all of the above.

4. White blood cells of the immune system are designed to recognize
    A. foreign substances.
    B. flu viruses and bacteria.
    C. antigens.
    D. all of the above.

5. PNI researchers have focused on three areas of investigation. Which of the following is NOT one of them?
    A. individual variations in people's bodies
    B. the number of recent stressors a person has experienced
    C. psychological factors
    D. how people behave under stress and how they manage it

6. Ideas about "psychosomatic illnesses" were based on the
    A. ideas of Freud.
    B. idea that physical symptoms are a result of unconscious conflict.
    C. idea that such disorders were all in a person's mind.
    D. all of the above beliefs.

7. Scientists interested in exploring the links between psychological processes and the immune system created an interdisciplinary field called
    A. health psychology.
    B. psychosomatic medicine.
    C. psychoneuroimmunology.
    D. behavioral medicine.

8. Negative emotions
    A. are influential in affecting the course of the illness, once a person is already ill.
    B. are influential is causing an illness.
    C. have an impact on a person's psychological, not physical, well being.
    D. are directly related to heart disease and cancer.

9. The stressfulness of noise depends on _____.
    A. whether the noise is your choice of noise.
    B. whether it is unpleasant.
    C. the type of noise it is.
    D. how loud it is.

10. Which of the following is true about the relationship between depression and disease?
    A. Depression is unrelated to physical health.
    B. Different research studies agree that depressed people of all ages are far more likely to get heart disease.
    C. The researcher findings are conflicting.
    D. Depression has been found to be one of the causal factors for heart disease and cancer.

11. The part of the Type A personality pattern that seems to be hazardous to health is
    A. a fast work pace.   B. intensity.
    C. an achievement orientation.   D. hostility.

12. Which of the following is NOT one of the hypothesized relationships between emotion and illness?
    A. Emotions may contribute to illness, but illness also influences emotions.
    B. Specific emotions are known to cause certain diseases.
    C. Researchers disagree about the strength of the link between emotion and illness.
    D. The mind and body interact.

13. A person _____ is at greater risk of becoming ill.
    A. who expresses his or her emotions
    B. with a problem-focused coping style
    C. who is emotionally inhibited
    D. who has an optimistic explanatory style

14. Optimists
    A. are the best judges of reality.   B. have positive illusions.
    C. deny that problems exist.   D. don't take care of themselves.

15. Which of the following is related to an internal locus of control?
    A. astrology   B. playing the lottery
    C. wearing seat belts   D. emotion-focused coping

16. Scheduled exams should be less stressful than pop quizzes because
    A. students can vent their emotions.   B. students are more optimistic.
    C. students have more control.   D. students can get more rest.

17. Compared to Western cultures, Eastern cultures, such as Japan's, emphasize
    A. primary control.   B. internal control.
    C. secondary control.   D. external control.

18. Which of the following demonstrates a problem that can result from the belief that an event is controllable?
    A. People could be unrealistically confident and try to control the uncontrollable.
    B. People could blame themselves for a problem they could not control.
    C. For some people, the realities of their lives are less controllable than for others.
    D. all of the above

19. Identifying the problem and learning as much as possible about it is part of
    A. emotion-focused coping.   B. rethinking the problem.
    C. problem-focused coping.   D. cooling off.

20. _____ tends to increase self-efficacy, reduce anger, anxiety, and psychological stress.
    A. problem-focused coping.   B. avoidance.
    C. external locus of control.   D. looking outward.

21. Which of the following is NOT one of the three ways of coping with stress?
    A. solving the problem   B. resisting the problem
    C. reappraising the problem   D. reducing bodily arousal

22. Which of the following quotes demonstrates strategies for reappraising the problem?
    A. "It's not so bad."
    B. "I'm better off than some people, and I can learn from those who are doing better than I am."
    C. "I've discovered that I am a much stronger person than I ever realized."
    D. All of the above are strategies for reappraising the situation.

23. Social support
    A.   helps heart rate return to normal more quickly after a stressful episode.
    B.   can extend the survival time of people with serious illnesses, in some cases.
    C.   can contribute to longer life.
    D.   all of the above.

24. Social support can actually be harmful if
    A.   the two parties frequently argue.
    B.   friends resist positive changes.
    C.   friends try to stem grief prematurely.
    D.   all of the above conditions exist.

25. Which of the following is a conclusion from findings related to health psychology?
    A.   Good coping skills are important.
    B.   The presence of social supports can mediate some of the negative effects of stress.
    C.   Stress cannot be completely eliminated.
    D.   All of the above are conclusions related to health psychology.

PRACTICE TEST 2 - Multiple Choice

1. Ellen is in finals week and she has been getting by on very little sleep. She is managing to prepare for her tests, but she is more irritable than usual and feels like she might be getting the flu. This would be compatible with the _____ of Selye's model.
    A. alarm stage
    B. exhaustion stage
    C. resistance stage
    D. activation stage

2. What would current models of stress predict about other students' reactions to finals week?
    A. An individual's reaction will depend on qualities such as personality traits, perceptions and his or her coping style.
    B. All students will find finals week stressful.
    C. A student's reaction will depend on how hard he or she has studied.
    D. The stress will result in physiological arousal (the alarm phase), which will be followed by the resistance phase.

3. You have the flu. The _____ are designed to recognize this foreign substance and _____ it.
    A. white blood cells; destroy
    B. brain chemicals; transform
    C. antigens; heal
    D. red blood cells; stimulate

4. Jerry has been under stress for a long period of time. He is very lonely at college, he is under pressure to do well, and he is in the middle of finals. Which of the following is true?
    A. He is at higher risk for getting sick.
    B. Persistent stress depletes the body of energy.
    C. How he responds will depend on his coping skills.
    D. All of the above are true.

5. Dr. Weller is conducting research on the health behaviors of people who become ill and those who do not. What field of study does this represent?
    A. health psychology
    B. psychoneuroimmunology
    C. psychosomatic medicine
    D. any of the above

6. Hank is stuck in a traffic jam and he is already late for his important appointment. This type of stressor
    A. does not pose much threat to health.
    B. increases the risk of illness.
    C. is related to heart disease.
    D. decreases the risk of illness.

7. Health psychologists now define stress as
    A. the body's response to any environmental threat.
    B. being determined by an individual's psychological makeup.
    C. including qualities of the individual and whether the individual feels able to cope
        with the stressor.
    D. a collapse of the resistance phase.

8. Jennifer goes to school very near a major airport. All day long children hear the sound
    of jets taking off and landing. Jennifer is more likely than children attending schools in
    quieter areas to have
    A. higher blood pressure.   B. poorer long-term memory.
    C. difficulty reading.   D. all of the above.

9. Crowding is most stressful
    A. in a small room.   B. on a hot day.
    C. in a crowd of strangers.   D. when you feel crowded.

10. Which of the following would most stress researchers believe to be the most serious threat
    to health?
    A. being chronically unemployed   B. crowding
    C. traffic jams   D. the demands of a deadline

11. After learning that Lucinda has cancer, Sally said, "She was so depressed, it's no wonder
    she got cancer." What is the evidence that there is a relationship between depression and
    cancer?
    A. There is evidence that cancer causes depression.
    B. There is evidence that being depressed causes poor health habits.
    C. The long-term health implications of chronic depression are still unknown.
    D. There is evidence that depression causes cancer.

12. Who among the following men has a higher risk for coronary heart disease?
    A. John is intense, ambitious, hard-driving and successful.
    B. Ron is complaining and irritable.
    C. Don is aggressive, confrontational, rude, cynical and uncooperative.
    D. Lon is easy-going and calm.

13. Which personality style may be at greater risk of serious illness and, once he or she has contracted a disease, which person may die sooner than the others?
    A. Phil has been diagnosed with clinical depression.
    B. Bill is a classic Type A personality.
    C. Lil is never angry, fearful, or anxious.
    D. Will is a true Type B personality.

14. Which of the following is likely to have been said by someone with a pessimistic explanatory style?
    A. "This problem is all my fault and it's going to ruin my life."
    B. "I couldn't do anything about this."
    C. "I have had terrible luck today."
    D. "Everything will be fine."

15. Maria has been diagnosed with cancer. She believes that if she controls her diet, exercise, and stress levels, she can have some influence over the outcome of her illness. She is exhibiting
    A. internal locus of control.   B. optimism.
    C. self-efficacy.   D. all of the above.

16. "To lose is to win" and "The true tolerance is to tolerate the intolerable" are statements hat reflect
    A. primary control.   B. secondary control.
    C. locus of control.   D. external locus of control.

17. Which of the following statements reflects a healthy internal locus of control?
    A. "I am basically in charge of my own life and well-being."
    B. "Whatever goes wrong with my health is my fault."
    C. "If I eat right, I can avoid becoming ill."
    D. "If I become sick, it was meant to be."

18. Which of the following examples reflects the best strategy for solving a problem?
    A. "I must make a plan of action."
    B. "I must deal with my feelings about what happened."
    C. "It is best not to think about this, since there is very little I can do."
    D. "I must deal with my feelings and make a plan of action."

19. Shelley's mother recently died at age 68. Thinking about her friend Sara, whose mother died at age 49, makes her feel better about her situation. This is an example of
    A. social comparisons.
    B. vigilance.
    C. humor.
    D. avoidance.

20. The strategy used by Shelley in the previous question is an example of which category of coping techniques?
    A. solving the problem
    B. living with the problem
    C. rethinking the problem
    D. vigilance

21. When is it best to use emotion-focused coping and when should one use problem-focused coping?
    A. Problem-focused coping should be used at all times; it is never desirable to use emotion-focused coping.
    B. Emotion-focused coping is useful following a trauma but a shift should be made to problem-focused coping.
    C. Emotion-focused coping is called for when stressors are continuous or can be prepared for; problem-focused coping should be used when the stressor is sudden.
    D. Emotion-focused coping should be used by people with Type A personalities, and problem-focused coping is appropriate for those with emotional inhibition.

22. Amanda has experienced high levels of stress lately. She is coping by meditating regularly and exercising daily. Which category of coping techniques is she using?
    A. solving the problem
    B. reappraising of the problem
    C. reducing bodily arousal
    D. making social comparisons

23. The positive effects of social supports may be a result of
    A. providing attachment.
    B. improved immune function.
    C. help evaluating problems.
    D. all of the above.

24. Anne has quit drinking. Her friend, Carl, continually asks her to join their group for drinks after work. This is an example of
    A. a situation in which a friend might contribute to stress.
    B. a way that friends can help reduce the effects of stress.
    C. an example of healing through helping.
    D. external locus of control.

25. Which of the following is a psychological factor that is thought to be important to good health?
    A. social support
    B. ability to relax
    C. feelings of control
    D. all of the above

PRACTICE TEST 3 - Short Answer

1. _____ psychology is concerned with the psychological factors that influence how people stay healthy, why they become ill, and how they respond when they do get ill.

2. _____ introduced the modern era of stress research. He concluded that "stress" consists of a series of physiological reactions that occur in three phases: the _____ phase, the _____ phase, and the _____ phase.

3. Divorced and _____ people are more vulnerable to illness, perhaps because they feel unhappy, don't sleep or eat well, and they consume more drugs and cigarettes.

4. People who live in poverty or have little power in their lives have _____ health and _____ mortality rates for almost every disease and medical condition than do those at the higher end of the socioeconomic scale.

5. The public thinks of _____ illness as one that is due entirely to personality problems and thus is "all in your head."

6. When an _____ invades the body, the _____ system deploys white blood cells that produce chemicals that go to the brain.

7. The interdisciplinary specialty that investigates the exact mechanisms that link mind and body, and studies how stress causes problems is called _____.

8. Negative emotions, like loneliness and worry, can suppress the _____ system.

9. The factor that can be dangerous for health in the behavior of some Type A personalities is _____.

10. People who tend to deny feelings of anxiety, anger, or fear and pretend that everything is fine exhibit a personality trait called _____.

11. People with an _____ explanatory style tend to live longer and may engage in unrealistic, but healthy, positive _____.

12. People can tolerate all kinds of stressors if they feel able to _____ them. For example, the crowd you choose to join for a football game is not as stressful as being trapped in a crowd on a busy street.

13. If you do not like a situation, you are supposed to change it or fight it. This represents _____ control, whereas if you try to accommodate to reality by changing your own desires, you are demonstrating _____ control.

14. All the things people do to control, tolerate, or reduce the effects of life's stressors is called _____.

15. Techniques that reduce bodily arousal can help people cope not only with everyday stresses but also with serious, even terminal illnesses. These techniques include: relaxation, massage and _____, and _____.

16. _____ coping in which a person focuses on the anger, anxiety, or grief the problem has caused is normal after a tragedy or trauma. However, over time _____ coping strategies are associated with better adjustment.

17. _____ the situation can help a person to think about the problem differently.

18. In a difficult situation, successful copers often _____ themselves to others who are less fortunate.

19. Friends and social supports can both _____ and _____ stress.

20. Debate continues to rage over the extent to which _____ factors are involved in the onset or course of some illnesses.

21. Many factors are links in the chain that connects stressors and illness, including personality traits, biological _____ to diseases, emotional _____, explanatory styles, _____ strategies, and social networks.

22. A study done at Harvard School of Public Health found that _____ percent of all deaths from cancer were caused by smoking, diet, and lack of exercise.

23. Health professionals worry about the _____ industry that oversimplifies findings from health research.

24. It is important to avoid _____ thinking when a person is deciding about treatments for health problems.

25. Many diseases, such as tuberculosis and ulcers, were once thought to be caused exclusively by _____ factors, until the _____ that actually do cause them were identified.

433

PRACTICE TEST 4 - True/False

1.   T F   During the alarm phase of the stress response identified by Selye, your body attempts to cope with a stressor that cannot be avoided.

2.   T F   Selye did not believe that people should aim for a stress-free life. Some stress is positive and productive.

3.   T F   Research shows that the daily "hassles" of life are associated with increased risk of illness.

4.   T F   Work-related problems do not pose much threat to health and the effects of a chronically stressful work environment is generally less stressful than other kinds of stressors.

5.   T F   One of life's most powerful stressors is the loss of a loved one or close relationship.

6.   T F   Though conditions of poverty and powerlessness affect urban African Americans disproportionately, these conditions do not seem to be responsible for their relatively high incidence of hypertension.

7.   T F   Current thinking suggests that unconscious conflicts and neurotic personality patterns contribute to rheumatoid arthritis, hypertension, asthma, ulcers, and migraine headaches.

8.   T F   Psychoneuroimmunology is the study of psychosomatic illnesses.

9.   T F   PNI researchers have focused on three areas of investigation: individual variations in the body's various physical systems, psychological factors, and coping skills.

10.   T F   There is good evidence that once a person has a virus or medical condition, negative emotions are influential in affecting the course of the illness.

11.   T F   People with a Type A behavior pattern have an increased risk for heart disease.

12.   T F   Many Type A people cope better than Type B people who have a lighter work load.

13.   T F   Men who are chronically angry and resentful and who have a hostile attitude are five times as likely as nonhostile men to get heart disease.

14.   T F   Divulging private thoughts and feelings that make you ashamed or depressed may be helpful, both psychologically and physically.

15.   T F   An optimistic explanatory style has psychological benefits over a pessimistic explanatory style, but research has not found any consistent benefits related to health and illness.

16.   T F   Positive illusions are perceptions of events that are unrealistic and therefore, unhelpful. They are similar to the defense mechanism of denial.

17.   T F   Low-income people who have a strong sense of control and mastery over their lives are as healthy, and have as high levels of well being, as people from higher-income groups.

18.   T F   Westerners tend to engage in primary control, in which people try to change a situation that they don't like. The Eastern approach emphasizes secondary control, in which people change their goals to accommodate reality.

18.   T F   Techniques that reduce bodily arousal can help people cope not only with everyday stresses but also with serious, even terminal illnesses.

19.   T F   Problem-focused coping strategies are associated with better adjustment than are emotion-focused ones.

20.   T F   Emotion-focused coping tends to increase self-efficacy and reduce anger, anxiety, and physiological stress.

21.   T F   Thinking about a stressful situation differently can change a person's emotional response.

22.   T F   In people with serious illnesses, humor reduces distress, improves immune functioning, and hastens recover from surgery.

23.   T F   People who live in a network of close connections actually live longer than those who do not.

24.   T F   Constant fights, whether people argue in a positive fashion or not, can elevate stress hormones and impair immune function.

25.   T F   People who are empathic and cooperative are healthier and happier than those who are self-involved.

PRACTICE TEST 5 - Essay

1. Indicate which member of each pair is likely to experience greater stress. Explain why.

    A. Air traffic controllers versus fishermen
    B. Type A personalities versus Type B personalities
    C. Subjects with an external locus of control versus subjects with an internal locus of control
    D. Subjects with a large social network versus single subjects
    E. Subjects with an optimistic versus pessimistic explanatory style

2. Apply Hans Selye's phases of stress response to people being held hostage. Describe what they would experience in the alarm, resistance and exhaustion phases.

3. Over a period of years, David has been under treatment for a variety of disorders, including depression and ulcers. Visits to the doctor and prescriptions have been fairly regular because symptoms recur or new ones break out whenever medication is stopped. The doctor is now beginning to suggest that the origin of the problems must be related to stress or his depression.

    A. How could stress make recurring symptoms possible?
    B. What are some possible relationships that might exist between David's depression and his illnesses?
    C. What must David examine about himself and his life?

4. Assume that a group of hostages has been held by terrorists for several years. For each description, indicate whether stress has been reduced through attempts to solve, reappraise or live with the problem, and identify the specific coping strategy being used.

    A. Margaret has decided her captors have no bad intentions and are just trying to make an important philosophical point.
    B. Frank believes escape would be difficult but not impossible. He keeps formulating escape plans and explaining them to others.
    C. Joe believes this disaster has a bright side. Had another terrorist group taken them, there might have been torture as well as captivity.
    D. Like Frank, Tony believes escape is possible, but only if the terrorists unexpectedly slip-up. His goal is to remain as calm as possible and look for an opportunity. He refuses to waste energy and lose hope by developing or considering unrealistic escape plans.
    E. Joan believes the group will remain in captivity virtually forever. Her goal is to eat as regularly as possible and combat inactivity through exercise.

CHAPTER 16

Psychological Disorders

LEARNING OBJECTIVES

1.   Describe three perspectives on mental disorders and distinguish mental disorder from abnormal behavior and from the legal definition of insanity.

2.   Describe the five axes of the *Diagnostic and Statistical Manual of Mental Disorders* (DSM) on which clinicians can evaluate a person.

3.   Summarize the positions supporting and criticizing the DSM.

4.   List and describe the principle characteristics of the anxiety disorders.

5.   Distinguish between major depression and bipolar disorder.

6.   Explain the various theories that attempt to account for depression.

7.   List the general features of personality disorders and three specific personality disorders.

8.   Describe the features of antisocial personality disorder and theories explaining the causes.

9.   List and discuss the characteristics of the three types of dissociative disorders.

10.   Describe the current controversy about the validity and nature of dissociative identity disorder (multiple personality disorder).

11.   List the signs of substance abuse.

12.   Distinguish between the biological and the learning models of addiction.

13.   List the components that interact to influence addiction and abuse.

14.   Describe the symptoms of schizophrenia.

15.   Discuss the four areas that researchers are investigating to understand schizophrenia.

CHAPTER CONCEPT MAP

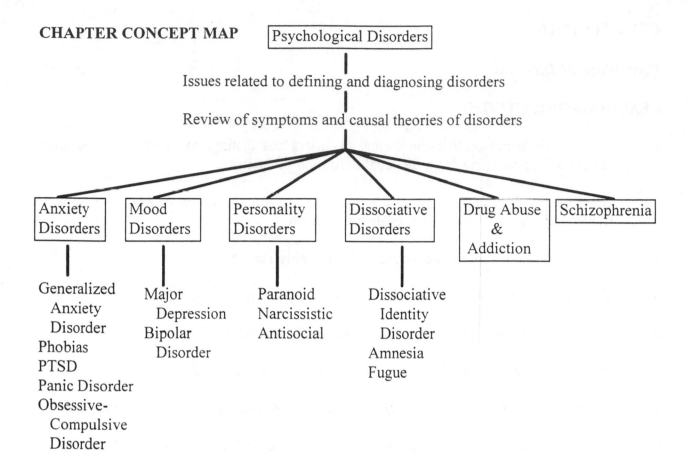

Psychological Disorders

Issues related to defining and diagnosing disorders

Review of symptoms and causal theories of disorders

Anxiety Disorders

Mood Disorders

Personality Disorders

Dissociative Disorders

Drug Abuse & Addiction

Schizophrenia

Generalized Anxiety Disorder
Phobias
PTSD
Panic Disorder
Obsessive-Compulsive Disorder

Major Depression
Bipolar Disorder

Paranoid
Narcissistic
Antisocial

Dissociative Identity Disorder
Amnesia
Fugue

BRIEF CHAPTER SUMMARY

Chapter 16 defines mental disorder and distinguishes abnormal behavior from mental disorders. The issues and difficulties involved in developing a reliable and valid diagnostic system are also discussed. The *Diagnostic and Statistical Manual of Mental Disorders* (DSM), which is the manual that contains descriptions of all diagnostic categories of mental disorders, is reviewed. Some of the problems with the diagnostic system are described. Six general categories of disorders are reviewed. The text describes symptoms, predisposing factors and theories of causation for specific mental disorders under each category of disorder.

PREVIEW OUTLINE AND REVIEW QUESTIONS

Before you read the chapter, review the preview outline and the Learning Objectives for each section of the text. Answer all questions as you read the text.

SECTION 1 - DILEMMAS OF DIAGNOSIS (PP. 576-581)

I. **DILEMMAS OF DIAGNOSIS**
    A. **Defining mental disorders** - abnormal behavior is not the same as mental disorder
        1. Legal definition is based on whether a person is aware of the consequences of his or her actions and can control his or her behavior
        2. Violation of cultural _____ - depends on the culture and time
        3. Maladaptive or harmful behavior
        4. Emotional *distress*
    B. **Definition used by text** - any behavior or emotional state that causes an individual great _____ or worry; is self-defeating or self-destructive; or is maladaptive and disrupts the person's relationships or the larger community
    C. **Diagnosis: Art or science?**
        1. Classifying disorders: The *Diagnostic and Statistical Manual of Mental Disorders* ("DSM")
            a. Standard reference used to diagnose all disorders
            b. DSM-IV is current issue; contains 300 disorders and is much larger than the original which came out in 1952 and contained nine categories of disorders
            c. Primary aim - _____; to provide criteria of diagnostic categories
            d. Lists symptoms and associated information for each disorder
            e. Classifies each disorder according to five _____ or dimensions
            f. The axes are:
                (1) Primary clinical problem
                (2) Ingrained aspects of the individual's _____
                (3) Medical conditions relevant to the disorder
                (4) Social and environmental problems that can make the disorder worse
                (5) Global assessment of the patient's overall functioning
            g. DSM has enormous medical, economic, and legal impact
        2. Problems with the DSM
            a. The danger of overdiagnosis
            b. The power of diagnostic labels - can create self-fulfilling prophecy as in Rosenhan's famous hospital study
            c. Confusion of serious mental disorders with _____ problems
            d. The illusion of objectivity

439

        (1)   As times change, so does beliefs about what is "normal"
        (2)   Inclusion and exclusion of disorders is not always based on
                empirical evidence but on pressures and cultural standards
    3.   Benefits of the DSM
        a.   New studies are improving empirical support for its categories
        b.   Advocates say when used correctly, it improves the accuracy of
                diagnosis
        c.   Biases in certain diagnosis can be corrected with awareness and
                better research
        d.   Not all diagnoses reflect society's biases, some disorders exist in all
                cultures

Answer these Learning Objectives while you read Sections 1.

1.   Describe three perspectives on mental disorders and distinguish mental disorder from
        abnormal behavior and from the legal definition of insanity.

2.   Describe the five axes of the Diagnostic and Statistical Manual of Mental Disorders
        (DSM) on which clinicians can evaluate a person.

3.   Summarize the positions supporting and criticizing the DSM.

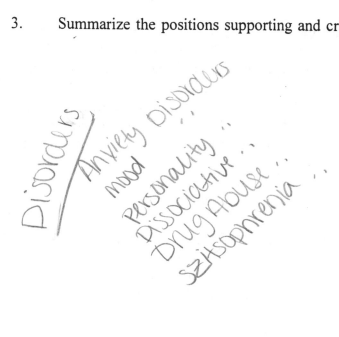

SECTION 2 - ANXIETY DISORDERS (PP. 581-585)

II. **ANXIETY DISORDERS**
    A.   **Anxiety states**
        1.   When anxiety is associated with danger, it is adaptive; when it is not, it can be maladaptive
        2.   Generalized anxiety disorder
            a.   Chief characteristics
                (1)   Continuous, _____ anxiety or worry
                (2)   Feelings of foreboding and dread
                (3)   Symptoms include restlessness, difficulty concentrating, irritability, muscle tension, jitteriness, sleep disturbance, and disturbing, unwanted, intrusive worries
            b.   May occur without specific anxiety-producing event, but may be related to physiological tendency to experience anxiety, history of uncontrollable or unpredictable life events
        3.   Posttraumatic stress disorder (PTSD)
            a.   When anxiety results from uncontrollable and unpredictable danger such as rape, war, torture, or natural disasters
            b.   Symptoms include
                (1)   Reliving the trauma in thoughts or dreams
                (2)   "Psychic numbing"
                (3)   _____ from others
                (4)   Inability to feel happy or loving
                (5)   Increased physiological arousal
            c.   Symptoms may occur immediately after a trauma or after a delay of weeks or months; episodes may recur long after for some - may be related to hippocampus
        4.   Panic disorder
            a.   This disorder most likely to develop in people who are hypersensitive to anxiety symptoms
            b.   Recurring attacks of intense fear or panic, with feelings of impending doom or death
            c.   Attacks may be brief or long
            d.   Symptoms include trembling, shaking, dizziness, chest pain, heart palpitations, feelings of unreality, hot and cold flashes, sweating, fear of dying, going crazy, or losing control
            e.   They usually follow stress, but seem to occur out of nowhere
            f.   Difference between those who develop panic disorder and those who don't is how they interpret bodily reactions
        5.   Fears and Phobias

        a.   Exaggerated fear of a specific situation, activity or thing

        b.   Some may have evolutionary basis, some may be acquired through classical conditioning, some related to culture

        c.   Social phobia - fear of situations in which a person will be _____ by others

        d.   Agoraphobia - fear of being alone in a public place from which _____ might be difficult or help unavailable

            (1)   Underlying fear is being away from safe place or person

            (2)   Usually begins with a _____ attack which sets off pattern of avoidance of the situation in which the attack occurred

6.   Obsessions and compulsions

        a.   Obsessive-compulsive disorder

            (1)   _____ - recurrent, persistent, unwished for thoughts that are frightening or repugnant and reflect maladaptive reasoning and information processing

            (2)   Compulsions - repetitive, ritualized behaviors over which people feel a lack of control; if they try to resist, they feel anxiety that is reduced only by the compulsion

            (3)   Many people have trivial compulsions, a disorder exists when this interferes with a person's life

        b.   Most common compulsions are hand washing, counting, touching, checking

        c.   Most sufferers know the behavior is senseless and don't enjoy it

        d.   PET scans find parts of the brain are hyperactive in people with OCD

Answer this Learning Objective while you read Section 2.

4.   List and describe the principle characteristics of the anxiety disorders.

SECTION 3 - MOOD DISORDERS (PP. 586-590)

III. MOOD DISORDERS
- **A. Varieties of depression**
  1. Major depression - disrupts ordinary functioning
     - a. Symptoms - emotional, behavioral, cognitive, physical changes
     - b. Rates among the young have increased rapidly recently
  2. Mania is the opposite pole - abnormally high state of exhilaration
     - a. Symptoms - opposite of those in depression; person is full of energy, feels powerful, full of ambition, inflated self-esteem
     - b. Bipolar disorder - depression alternates with mania
  3. Depression occurs two or three times as often among women
- **B. Theories of depression**
  1. Biological explanations emphasize genetics and brain chemistry
     - a. Possible deficiencies in neurotransmitters _____ and/or serotonin
     - b. Possible genetic component to bipolar disorder and depression
     - c. Less activity level in left frontal lobes of brain which are involved in positive emotions - can't make causal inferences
  2. Social explanations emphasize stressful circumstances of people's lives; may explain gender differences in depression rates
     - a. Marriage and _____ associated with lower rates of depression
     - b. Being a mother associated with higher rates of depression
     - c. Women have lower status, higher rates of poverty, and are more likely to have experienced violence
  3. Attachment explanations emphasize problems with close relationships
     - a. Related to disturbed relationships; separations and losses; and history of insecure attachments
     - b. Primary relationship disruption often triggers depressive episode
     - c. Cause and effect is not clear; may differ for husbands and wives
  4. Cognitive explanations emphasize habits of thinking and interpreting events
     - a. Involves negative habits of thinking; internality, stability, and control - depressed people have a pessimistic explanatory style
     - b. Brooding, more common to women, is associated with depression
  5. "Vulnerability-stress" explanations draw on all four previous explanations as an interaction between individual vulnerability and environmental stress

Answer these Learning Objectives while you read Section 3.

5. Distinguish between major depression and bipolar disorder.

6. Explain the various theories that attempt to account for depression.

SECTION 4 - PERSONALITY DISORDERS (PP. 591-594)

IV. **PERSONALITY DISORDERS**
    A.   **Definition** - _____, maladaptive traits that cause great distress or inability to get along with others
    B.   **Problem personalities**
        1.   Paranoid personality disorder - pervasive, unfounded _____ and mistrust
        2.   Narcissistic personality disorder - exaggerated sense of self-importance
    C.   **Antisocial personality disorder**
        1.   Individuals who lack _____ to anyone so they can cheat, con, and kill without any problem; used to be called psychopaths or sociopaths
        2.   Symptoms include: repeated law breaking, using deception, using aliases and lies to con others, acting impulsively, fighting, disregarding safety, irresponsibility, lacking remorse; some are sadistic
        3.   Antisocial personalities begin with problem behaviors in childhood
        4.   More common in males
        5.   Causes of APD
            a.   Don't respond to punishments so they may be unable to feel the anxiety necessary for learning about negative consequences
            b.   Inability to feel emotional arousal - empathy, guilt, fear of punishment, anxiety- suggests brain and central nervous system abnormality
            c.   One theory centers around behavioral _____ - an inherited characteristic shared by those who are antisocial, hyperactive, addicted or impulsive
            d.   May have suffered brain damage from physical abuse
            e.   Vulnerability-stress model - biological vulnerability (genes) is combined with environmental _____ (abuse, neglect)
            f.   One study found a combination of birth complications and maternal rejection accounted for disproportionately high number of cases
        6.   Not all those with APD are violent, not all violent criminals have APD
        7.   Can be encouraged or discouraged by the values of the culture

Answer these Learning Objectives while you read Section 4.

7.   List the general features of personality disorders and three specific personality disorders.

8.   Describe the features of antisocial personality disorder and theories explaining the causes.

SECTION 5 - DISSOCIATIVE DISORDERS (PP. 595-598)

V. DISSOCIATIVE DISORDERS

A. **Definition** - disorders in which consciousness, behavior and identity are split off
1. Dissociative states are intense and seem out of one's control
2. Often are in response to _____ events

B. **Amnesia and fugue**
1. Amnesia - inability to remember important personal information, usually of a traumatic nature, that cannot be explained by ordinary forgetfulness
2. When organic condition not responsible, called dissociative or psychogenic
3. Dissociative _____ - person forgets identity entirely and wanders far away and often takes on new identity and life
4. These disorders are controversial among psychologists who disagree about the mind's ability to "cut off" or "repress" traumatic memories

C. **Dissociative identity disorder ("Multiple personality")**
1. The appearance of two or more identities within one person
2. The MPD controversy - two views among mental health professionals
   a. A real disorder, common but often underdiagnosed or misdiagnosed which develops in childhood as a response to _____
   b. A creation of mental health clinicians who believe in it
3. Research on MPD - evidence in support of the diagnosis is questionable
   a. The research that says MPD patients show different physiological responses for different personalities is flawed
   b. Pressure and suggestion by clinicians may be creating multiple personalities
   c. The media played a major role in fostering the MPD diagnosis
4. The sociocognitive explanation
   a. Seen as an extreme form of a normal ability to present different aspects of our personalities to others
   b. May be a way for troubled people to understand their problems or to account for regretted behavior which is then rewarded by therapists
   c. Other personalities are rewarded by clinicians with attention

Answer these Learning Objectives while you read Section 5.

9. List and discuss the characteristics of the three types of dissociative disorders.

10. Describe the current controversy about the validity and nature of dissociative identity disorder (multiple personality disorder).

SECTION 6 - DRUG ABUSE AND ADDICTION (PP. 599-605)

VI. **DRUG ABUSE AND ADDICTION**
    A.   **DSM definition of substance abuse** - maladaptive pattern of substance use leading to clinically significant impairment or distress
    B.   **Biology and addiction** - addiction is a biochemical process influenced by genes
        1.   Disease model of alcoholism, early model that promotes abstinence
        2.   Beliefs associated with the biological model - accepted by researchers and the public
            a.   Addiction is due to biochemistry, metabolism and genetics
            b.   Genes are involved in ethnic group sensitivities, alcoholism that begins in adolescence, and may be related to traits that predispose a person to become an alcoholic, or may affect biochemical processes in the brain that make people more susceptible to alcohol
            c.   Research on specific genes has been contradictory
        3.   Some researchers suggest that the biological differences found in alcoholics are a result of alcohol abuse
    C.   **Learning, culture, and addiction** - challenges the biological model with four arguments
        1.   Addiction patterns vary with cultural practices and social environment
        2.   Policies of total abstinence tend to increase rates of addiction
        3.   Not all addicts go through withdrawal symptoms when they stop the drug
        4.   Addiction depends on the drug AND the reason the person is taking it
    D.   **Debating the causes of addiction**
        1.   Both approaches contribute to our understanding
        2.   Theoretical differences have treatment implications
        3.   Most heated disagreement is about controlled drinking; research finds that many people can switch to moderate drinking under certain conditions
        4.   Evidence suggests that drug abuse and addiction are an interaction of person and culture, physiology and psychology

Answer these Learning Objectives while you read Section 6.

11.   List the signs of substance abuse.

12.   Distinguish between the biological and the learning models of addiction.

13.   List the components that interact to influence addiction and abuse.

SECTION 7 - SCHIZOPHRENIA (PP. 605-610) AND
SECTION 8 - MENTAL DISORDER AND PERSONAL RESPONSIBILITY (P. 611)

VII. **SCHIZOPHRENIA**
   A. **Schizophrenia** - a psychosis or condition involving distorted perceptions of
      _____ and an inability to function in most aspects of life
   B. **Symptoms of schizophrenia**
      1. Active or _____ symptoms - distortions of normal thinking processes and
         behavior
         a. Bizarre _____ - false beliefs
         b. Hallucinations and heightened sensory awareness - usually auditory,
            but can be tactile and visual; seem intensely real
         c. Disorganized, incoherent speech - illogical jumble of ideas
         d. Grossly _____ and inappropriate behavior like catatonia
      2. Negative symptoms - loss of former abilities; often persist after active ones
         are in remission
         a. Loss of _____ - inability to pursue goals
         b. Poverty of speech - empty replies reflecting diminished thought
         c. Emotional flatness - general unresponsiveness
      3. Severity and duration of symptoms vary; onset can be abrupt (better
         prognosis) or gradual (prognosis is more uncertain)
   C. **Unraveling the mysteries of schizophrenia** - many variations and symptoms
      1. Same core signs appear in cultures around the world
      2. Biological findings
         a. Genetic predispositions exist though no specific genes identified
         b. Structural brain abnormalities - some found, but meaning is unclear
            because antipsychotic medications can affect the brain
         c. Neurotransmitter abnormalities in several neurotransmitters
         d. Prenatal abnormalities possibly related to malnutrition or a virus
         e. Vulnerability-stress model - physiology and environment interact
      3. Different factors may predominate in different kinds of schizophrenia

VIII. **MENTAL DISORDER AND PERSONAL RESPONSIBILITY**
   A. **Using mental disorders to decrease personal responsibility** is now common
   B. **Must find a balance** - criminals must face consequences, mentally ill must have
      compassionate support and help

Answer these Learning Objectives while you read Sections 7 and 8.

14. Describe the symptoms of schizophrenia.

15. Discuss the areas that researchers are investigating to understand schizophrenia.

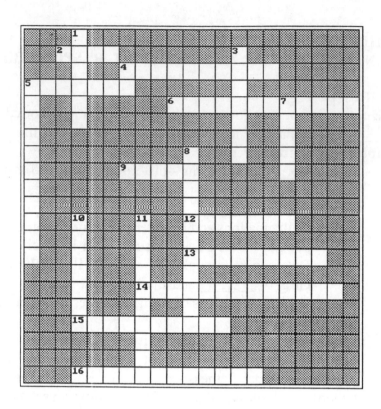

ACROSS

2. category of disorders that includes depression
4. mood disorder involving disturbances in emotion, behavior, cognition and body function
5. category of disorders that includes phobias and PTSD
6. category of disorders that includes amnesia and fugue
9. the opposite of depression
12. one model of addiction
13. general term that refers to disorders involving distorted perceptions of reality - includes schizophrenia
14. a psychotic disorder
15. one theory of depression involving early relationships between infant and caregiver
16. the learned _____ theory of depression

DOWN

1. type of phobia involving irrational fear of being observed by others
3. mood disorder in which mania and depression alternate
5. "fear of fear"
7. maladaptive pattern of substance use
8. type of behavior that is part of the definition of mental disorder
10. partial or complete loss of memory for threatening information
11. personality disorder characterized by lying, stealing and manipulating others

FLASH CARDS

Cut the following chart along the borders and test yourself with the resulting flash cards.

16.1 INSANITY	16.2 MENTAL DISORDER	16.3 DIAGNOSTIC AND STATISTICAL MANUAL OF MENTAL DISORDERS (DSM)
16.4 GENERALIZED ANXIETY DISORDER	16.5 POSTTRAUMATIC STRESS DISORDER (PTSD)	16.6 PANIC DISORDER (PANIC ATTACK)
16.7 PHOBIA	16.8 SOCIAL PHOBIA	16.9 AGORAPHOBIA
16.10 OBSESSIVE-COMPULSIVE DISORDER (OCD)	16.11 MAJOR DEPRESSION	16.12 MANIA
16.13 BIPOLAR DISORDER	16.14 LEARNED HELPLESSNESS	16.15 VULNERABILITY-STRESS MODEL OF DEPRESSION
16.16 PERSONALITY DISORDERS	16.17 PARANOID PERSONALITY DISORDER	16.18 NARCISSISTIC PERSONALITY DISORDER

16.3 Standard reference used to diagnose all mental disorders. It contains descriptions and diagnostic criteria of over 300 disorders.	16.2 Any behavior or emotional state that causes great suffering; is self-destructive; is maladaptive; and disrupts the community or relationships.	16.1 A legal term used to indicate that someone is incompetent to stand trial. The term is not used in relation to mental disorders.
16.6 An anxiety disorder in which a person experiences recurring panic attacks, periods of feelings of doom, and physical symptoms.	16.5 An anxiety disorder in which a person who has experienced a traumatic event has symptoms such as psychic numbing or reliving the trauma.	16.4 A continuous state of anxiety marked by feelings of worry and dread, apprehension, difficulties in concentration, and signs of motor tension.
16.9 A set of phobias, often set off by a panic attack, involving the basic fear of being away from a safe place or person.	16.8 Persistent, irrational fear of situations in which people know they will be observed by others. They fear doing or saying something embarrassing.	16.7 An exaggerated, unrealistic fear of a specific situation, activity, or object.
16.12 A mood state that is the opposite of depression; an abnormally high state of exhilaration.	16.11 A mood disorder involving disturbances in emotion (sadness), behavior (loss of interest), cognition (hopeless thoughts), and body function.	16.10 An anxiety disorder in which a person feels trapped in repetitive, persistent thoughts (obsessions) and repetitive behaviors (compulsions).
16.15 A model that holds that depression results from an interaction between individual vulnerabilities and sad events or environmental stress.	16.14 A theory that holds that people become depressed when their efforts to avoid pain or to control the environment consistently fail.	16.13 A mood disorder in which episodes of both depression and mania (excessive euphoria) occur.
16.18 A disorder characterized by an exaggerated sense of self-importance and self-absorption.	16.17 A disorder characterized by habitually unreasonable and excessive suspiciousness, jealousy, or mistrust.	16.16 Rigid, maladaptive personality patterns that cause personal distress or an inability to get along with others.

16.19 ANTISOCIAL PERSONALITY DISORDER (APD)	16.20 VULNERABILITY-STRESS MODEL OF APD	16.21 DISSOCIATIVE DISORDERS
16.22 AMNESIA (PSYCHOGENIC)	16.23 FUGUE	16.24 DISSOCIATIVE IDENTITY DISORDER (MULTIPLE PERSONALITY DISORDER)
16.25 SOCIOCOGNITIVE EXPLANATION OF MPD	16.26 SUBSTANCE ABUSE	16.27 BIOLOGICAL OR DISEASE MODEL OF ADDICTION
16.28 LEARNING MODEL OF ADDICTION	16.29 SCHIZOPHRENIA	16.30 PSYCHOSIS
16.31 POSITIVE SYMPTOMS	16.32 NEGATIVE SYMPTOMS	16.33 WORD SALADS
16.34 DELUSIONS AND HALLUCINATIONS	16.35 CATATONIC STUPOR	16.36 VULNERABILITY-STRESS MODEL OF SCHIZOPHRENIA

16.21 Conditions in which consciousness or identity is split or altered.	16.20 A theory that biological vulnerability to APD interacts with environmental risk factors (abuse, neglect, lack of love) to produce APD.	16.19 A disorder characterized by antisocial behavior such as lying, stealing, manipulating others, sometimes violence; a lack of guilt, shame, empathy.
16.24 A controversial disorder marked by the appearance within one person of two or more distinct personalities, each with its own traits.	16.23 A dissociative disorder in which a person flees home and forgets his or her identity.	16.22 In the absence of organic causes, a dissociative disorder involving partial or complete loss of memory for threatening information or trauma.
16.27 A model that holds that addiction is due primarily to a person's biochemistry, metabolism, and genetic predisposition.	16.26 According to the DSM-IV, it is "a maladaptive pattern of substance us leading to clinically significant impairment or distress."	16.25 An explanation for multiple personality disorder that suggests it is an extreme form of a normal human process.
16.30 An extreme mental disturbance involving distorted perceptions and irrational behavior; it may have organic or psychological causes.	16.29 A psychotic disorder or group of disorders marked by positive symptoms (delusions, hallucinations) and negative symptoms (emotional flatness).	16.28 This position argues that alcoholism is a result of physical, personal and social factors. It is a "central activity of an individual's way of life."
16.33 The illogical jumble of ideas and symbols, linked by meaningless rhyming words or remote associations, sometimes used by schizophrenics.	16.32 Symptoms of schizophrenia that include emotional flatness, loss of motivation, and poverty of speech.	16.31 Active symptoms that involve delusions, hallucinations, disorganized or incoherent speech and behavior.
16.36 A theory of schizophrenia that holds that biological vulnerability and stress interact to produce schizophrenia.	13.35 Symptoms of schizophrenia that include completely withdrawing into a private world and sitting for hours without moving.	16.34 Delusions are false beliefs and hallucinations are sensory experiences, usually hearing voices, which feel intensely real to the sufferer.

PSYCHOLOGICAL DISORDERS

Complete the following chart indicating the major symptoms, predisposing factors and explanatory theories for each of the disorders described in the left-hand column

TYPE OF DISORDER	MAJOR SYMPTOMS	PREDISPOSING FACTORS	EXPLANATORY THEORIES
ANXIETY DISORDERS Generalized Anxiety Disorder			
Social Phobia			
Agoraphobia			
Panic Attack			
Obsessive-Compulsive Disorder			
MOOD DISORDERS Major Depression			
Bipolar Disorder			
PERSONALITY DISORDERS Paranoid			
Narcissistic			
Antisocial			
DISSOCIATIVE DISORDERS Dissociative Identity Disorder			
Amnesia			
Fugue			
SUBSTANCE ABUSE			
SCHIZOPHRENIA			

PRACTICE TEST 1 - Multiple Choice

1. According to the _____ definition of mental disorder, a person who shows a total lack of sexual interest exhibits abnormal behavior.
    A. maladaptive behavior   B. violation of cultural standards
    C. emotional distress   D. impaired judgment

2. Which of the following is NOT one of the definitions of mental disorder?
    A. statistical deviation   B. lack of self-control
    C. violation of cultural standards   D. emotional distress

3. Whether a person is aware of the consequences of his or her actions and can control his or her behavior is at the heart of the legal term,
    A. mental disorder.   B. insanity.
    C. neurotic.   D. psychotic.

4. The primary aim of the *Diagnostic and Statistical Manual of Mental Disorders* ("DSM") is
    A. to provide clear criteria of diagnostic categories.
    B. to describe the causes of particular disorders.
    C. to describe the best course of treatment for a particular disorder.
    D. all of the above.

5. Which of the following is NOT one of the criticisms of the DSM?
    A. It confounds serious "mental disorders" with normal problems in living.
    B. Its heavy emphasis on theory may alienate clinicians from different perspectives.
    C. It gives the illusion of objectivity.
    D. It fosters overdiagnosis and self-fulfilling prophecies.

6. Generalized anxiety disorder is marked by
    A. unrealistic fears of specific things or situations.
    B. continuous, uncontrollable anxiety or worry.
    C. the sudden onset of intense fear or terror.
    D. unwished-for thoughts and repetitive behaviors.

7. The most disabling fear disorder that accounts for more than half of the phobia cases for which people seek treatment is called
    A. panic disorder.   B. social phobia.
    C. claustrophobia.   D. agoraphobia.

8. Checking the furnace repeatedly before one can sleep and washing one's hands many times in a hour are examples of
   A. obsessions.
   B. phobias.
   C. compulsions.
   D. superstitions.

9. Mania is an abnormally
   A. chronic state of depression.
   B. apathetic state.
   C. intense feeling of despair.
   D. high state of exhilaration.

10. Unlike normal sadness or grief, major depression involves
    A. panic attacks.
    B. low self-esteem.
    C. a lack of interest in outside activities.
    D. a negative mood.

11. Most manic episodes alternate with
    A. episodes of depression.
    B. panic attacks.
    C. obsessive-compulsive episodes.
    D. periods of elation.

12. Social theories of depression suggest that women are more likely to be depressed than men because they are more likely to lack
    A. endorphins and key neurotransmitters.
    B. positive self-images.
    C. fulfilling work and family relations.
    D. a stable network of friends.

13. Individuals with _____ personality disorder are unreasonably and excessively suspicious, jealous and mistrusting.
    A. narcissistic
    B. paranoid
    C. antisocial
    D. phobic

14. Individuals suffering from antisocial personality disorder are often charming and can be highly successful
    A. psychotherapists.
    B. con men.
    C. actors.
    D. business executives.

15. Hypothesized causes of antisocial personality disorder include
    A. problems in behavioral inhibition.
    B. neurological impairments.
    C. social deprivation.
    D. all of the above.

16. A sudden inability to remember certain important personal information describes
    A. psychogenic amnesia.
    B. a fugue state.
    C. dissociative identity disorder.
    D. post-traumatic stress disorder.

17. The controversy among mental health professionals about dissociative identity disorder has to do with
    A. whether it is a common and underdiagnosed disorder or whether it is concocted by mental health professionals and suggestible patients.
    B. whether it should be treated with traditional techniques or whether special treatments should be utilized.
    C. whether it is a biologically-based disorder or whether it results from psychosocial factors.
    D. whether the alternate personalities should be "seen" in treatment or whether they should be ignored by the therapist.

18. According to the DSM-IV, the key feature of substance abuse is
    A. the length of time a person has been using the drug.
    B. the inability to stop using the drug or to cut down on use.
    C. a maladaptive pattern of use leading to significant impairment or distress.
    D. all of the above.

19. The disease model of addiction
    A. requires abstinence.
    B. maintains that people have an inherited predisposition for alcoholism.
    C. holds that addiction is related to biochemistry, metabolism, and genetics.
    D. incorporates all of the above.

20. At the heart of the debate between the disease and learning models of addiction is the question of whether
    A. moderate drinking is possible for former alcoholics.
    B. alcoholics should be blamed for their alcoholism.
    C. there is an alcoholic personality.
    D. alcoholics are "bad" or "sick".

21. Bizarre delusions, hallucinations, incoherent speech, disorganized and inappropriate behavior are _____ symptoms of schizophrenia.
    A. positive or active   B. negative
    C. catatonic   D. maladaptive

22. Negative symptoms of schizophrenia
    A. may begin before and continue after positive symptoms.
    B. include loss of motivation.
    C. include diminished thought and emotional flatness.
    D. include all of the above.

23. Support for the idea of an infectious virus during prenatal development as a cause of schizophrenia comes from the fact that
   A. there is a significant association between a mother's exposure to the flu during the second trimester of prenatal development.
   B. most schizophrenics have very low immune functioning.
   C. most schizophrenics show abnormalities on chromosome 5.
   D. most schizophrenics have extra dopamine receptors.

24. Which of the following has been advanced as one of the biological explanations of schizophrenia?
   A. brain abnormalities
   B. extra dopamine receptors
   C. genes
   D. all of the above

25. The idea that genetic or brain abnormalities combine with family or other pressures to trigger schizophrenia reflects the
   A. interactionist model
   B. learning theory model
   C. vulnerability-stress model
   D. biology-pressure model

PRACTICE TEST 2 - Multiple Choice

1. Jody is very fearful of being far from a hospital or in a situation in which she could not get help quickly. She won't go out in traffic or crowds and refuses to travel. This behavior is beginning to affect her job. It meets which definition of mental disorder?
    A. maladaptive behavior   B. impaired judgment
    C. violation of cultural standards   D. lack of self-control

2. Clinicians are encouraged to evaluate each client according to five axes, or dimensions, in the DSM. The third dimension is
    A. the primary clinical problem.
    B. ingrained aspects of the client's personality.
    C. medical conditions that are relevant to the disorder.
    D. social and environmental problems that can make the disorder worse.

3. Rosenhan's classic study demonstrates which of the criticisms of the DSM?
    A. Confusion of serious mental disorders with normal problems.
    B. The power of diagnostic labels to become self-fulfilling prophecies.
    C. The danger of overdiagnosis.
    D. The illusion of objectivity.

4. The diagnoses of Disorder of Written Expression and Caffeine-Induced Sleep Disorder represent which criticism of the DSM?
    A. the idea that diagnosis can be made objectively scientific
    B. misusing diagnoses for social and political purposes
    C. confounding serious "mental disorders" with normal problems in living
    D. the fostering of overdiagnosis and self-fulfilling prophecies

5. Advocates of the DSM argue that
    A. when the manual is used correctly, diagnoses are more accurate and bias is reduced.
    B. correct labeling of a disorder leads people to the proper treatment.
    C. while some diagnoses reflect society's biases, some mental disorders occur in all societies.
    D. all of the above are valid.

6. Whenever Linda has to speak in public, she feels intensely anxious and uncomfortable. She fears she will humiliate herself. The only reason she agrees to do so is to keep her job. Linda has
    A. an antisocial personality disorder.   B. a generalized anxiety disorder.
    C. a social phobia.   D. agoraphobia.

7. Teresa has experienced panic attacks. She is now afraid to go to the place where she experienced the panic in case it happens again. Teresa is at risk of developing
   A. social phobia.
   B. agoraphobia.
   C. obsessive-compulsive disorder.
   D. acute stress disorder.

8. Josephine is trying to stop herself from checking the oven for the 21st time before she leaves the house. Not checking the oven results in
   A. feelings of depression.
   B. a phobia.
   C. mounting anxiety.
   D. none of the above.

9. Recently John has been overeating, having difficulty sleeping through the night, experiencing a lack of energy and interest and having trouble concentrating. These physical changes can be signs of
   A. a phobia.
   B. mania.
   C. depression.
   D. panic disorder.

10. Ricardo is full of energy and has grand plans for himself. He thinks he can do just about anything. As he is telling you his plans, you notice he is speaking very dramatically, and rapidly. Which diagnosis fits Ricardo's symptoms?
    A. mania
    B. bipolar disorder
    C. mood disorder
    D. all of the above could fit

11. Duane is taking antidepressants. How do they alleviate symptoms of depression?
    A. They decrease levels of dopamine.
    B. They increase levels of serotonin and norepinephrine.
    C. They decrease levels of serotonin and norepinephrine.
    D. They increase levels of dopamine.

12. More women receive a diagnosis of depression than men. Which of the following is a possible explanation for this gender difference in depression?
    A. Women are more likely to have a history of sexual abuse.
    B. Women are more likely to lack fulfilling jobs.
    C. Mothers are vulnerable to depression.
    D. all of the above

13. "I believe that nothing good will ever happen for me and there is nothing I can do about this." This statement is an example of the _____ explanation of depression.
    A. cognitive
    B. social
    C. attachment
    D. biological

14. Bob and Babs have been diagnosed with personality disorders. The central feature of Bob's personality disorder is that he doesn't trust anyone. The main characteristic of Babs' problem is that she is totally self-absorbed. Which personality disorder best fits Bob and which best fits Babs?
    A. paranoid; antisocial
    B. antisocial; narcissistic
    C. paranoid; narcissistic
    D. narcissistic; narcissistic

15. Fred has a diagnosis of antisocial personality disorder. He has just been found with a stolen car. What reaction will Fred be most likely to display?
    A. He will be quite nervous and will be unlikely to repeat the offense.
    B. He will act very sorry but, in fact, he will feel little regret.
    C. He will act very angry and get himself into more trouble.
    D. He will be extremely upset about being caught.

16. What do people who are antisocial, hyperactive, addicted and impulsive share?
    A. a personality disorder
    B. the same behaviors
    C. an explanatory style
    D. behavioral inhibition

17. Having a genetic disposition toward impulsivity, addiction, hyperactivity; being neglected or rejected by parents; having a history of physical abuse or birth complications are all
    A. contributors to mood disorders.
    B. risk factors for antisocial personality disorder.
    C. foundations for any mental disorder.
    D. paths to dissociative disorders.

18. People with psychogenic amnesia forget _____, whereas those experiencing a psychogenic fugue state forget _____.
    A. certain (threatening) information; their identities and habits
    B. a trauma; entire periods of time before and sometimes after the trauma
    C. their names; specific incidents
    D. an hour or less; more than an hour

19. Which of the following has been used to support the veracity of dissociative identity disorder?
    A. differential physiological responses by different personalities
    B. the media
    C. suggestions by clinicians
    D. all of the above

20. As a result of his drinking, Michael cannot make it to his classes or complete his assignments. He drinks even when he is the designated driver, and Susan has told him that unless he stops drinking, she will not continue to date him. Michael shows signs of
    A. substance abuse.   B. problem drinking.
    C. tolerance.   D. a disease.

21. Which of the following supports the biological model of alcoholism?
    A. There is strong evidence for a genetic contribution to alcoholism.
    B. Addiction patterns vary according to cultural practices.
    C. Not all drug users go through physiological withdrawal.
    D. There is not a lot of research that supports this model.

22. Elizabeth thinks she is Madonna. When she speaks she often does not make any sense at all and at times she appears to be talking to herself. She is experiencing
    A. positive symptoms of schizophrenia.
    B. negative symptoms of schizophrenia.
    C. catatonic symptoms of schizophrenia.
    D. emotional flatness.

23. Which of the following is NOT considered to be a factor that increases the likelihood of schizophrenia?
    A. parents who give children mixed messages
    B. the existence of schizophrenia in the family
    C. exposure to an infectious virus during prenatal development
    D. unstable, stressful environments in adulthood

24. According to the vulnerability-stress model of schizophrenia, who among the following would be most likely to develop schizophrenia?
    A. Harry has schizophrenia in his family, but he lives in a very stable, loving environment.
    B. Jerry has no biological risks for schizophrenia, but he lives in a stressful environment with emotionally disturbed parents.
    C. Gary was exposed prenatally to the flu and, as an adult, he lives in a very stressful environment.
    D. It is impossible to say.

25. Brain abnormalities that have been found to be associated with schizophrenia include
    A. decreased brain weight.
    B. reduced numbers of neurons in specific layers of the prefrontal cortex.
    C. enlarged ventricles.
    D. all of the above.

PRACTICE TEST 3 - Short Answer

1. One perspective on the definition of mental disorder is of mental disorder as a violation of _____ standards.

2. The official manual describing the major categories of mental disorder is the
    _____.

3. The fact that Attention Deficit/Hyperactivity Disorder is the fastest-growing disorder in America, where it is diagnosed at least ten times as often as it is in Europe supports the criticism of the DSM that it fosters _____.

4. _____ anxiety disorder is continuous, uncontrollable anxiety or worry.

5. Typical anxiety symptoms in _____ include reliving the trauma in recurrent, intrusive thoughts or dreams.

6. The essential difference between people who develop panic disorder and those who do not lies in how they _____ their bodily reactions.

7. John will not take a class if there a class presentation is one of the requirements. He is terrified of speaking in class because he worries that he will do or say something that will humiliate or embarrass himself. The most likely diagnosis for John is
    _____.

8. The most disabling fear disorder which accounts for more than half of the phobia cases for which people seek treatment is _____.

9. _____ are recurrent, persistent, unwished-for thoughts or images; whereas, _____ are repetitive, ritualized, stereotyped behaviors that the person feels must be carried out to avoid disaster. If the person does not carry out the behaviors, he or she will experience high levels of _____.

10. People who suffer from major depression experience emotional, _____, and _____ changes severe enough to disrupt their ordinary functioning.

11. _____ occurs two or three times as often among women as among men, all over the world.

12. _____ explanations of depression emphasize problems with close relationships.

13. Cognitive explanations of depression focus on three typically negative habits of thinking. They are internality, _____, and _____.

14. The DSM-IV describes _____ disorders as "an enduring pattern of inner experience and behavior that deviates markedly from the expectations of the individual's culture [and] is pervasive and inflexible."

15. People with antisocial personality disorder may have problems in behavioral _____, the ability to control responses to frustration and provocation.

16. The _____ model of APD says that disorder is more likely to develop when biological predispositions are combined with physical abuse, parental neglect, lack of love, or other environmental _____.

17. In psychogenic _____, a person is unable to remember important personal information, usually of a traumatic nature. In a related disorder called dissociative _____, a person forgets his or her identity entirely and wanders far from home.

18. On one side of the MPD controversy, there are those who think MPD is _____, but often misdiagnosed. On the other side are those who believe that most cases of MPD are generated by _____ themselves, knowingly or unknowingly.

19. The _____ explanation of MPD holds that it is simply an extreme form of the ability we all have to present different aspects of our personalities to others.

20. The biological model holds that addiction, whether to alcohol or any other drug, is due primarily to a person's _____, metabolism, and genetic predisposition.

21. The fact that within a particular country, addiction rates can rise or fall rapidly in response to cultural changes supports the _____ model of addiction.

22. Schizophrenia is an example of a _____, a mental condition that involves distorted perceptions of reality and an inability to function in most aspects of life.

23. Two active or positive symptoms of schizophrenia include bizarre _____ or false beliefs, and _____.

24. There is good evidence for the existence of a _____ contribution to schizophrenia. In addition, _____ abnormalities are also associated with it.

25. An infectious _____ during prenatal development may affect schizophrenia.

PRACTICE TEST 4 - True/False

1.   T F   Abnormal behavior has the same meaning as mental disorder.

2.   T F   The three approaches to defining mental disorder described in the text include: violation of cultural standards, maladaptive or harmful behavior, criminal behavior.

3.   T F   The Diagnostic and Statistical Manual of Mental Disorders (DSM) has five axes, or dimensions on which a clinician can evaluate a client.

4.   T F   The proliferation of the diagnosis of Attention Deficit/Hyperactivity Disorder (ADHD) demonstrates the criticism that the DSM confuses normal problems with serious mental disorders.

5.   T F   The changes in DSM diagnostic categories underscores that as times change, so does the cultural consensus about what is normal, and thus what is abnormal.

6.   T F   Some people suffer from generalized anxiety disorder without having lived through any specific anxiety-producing event.

7.   T F   One possible explanation for why some veterans suffer from Post Traumatic Stress Disorder (PTSD) when most do not is that the stress hormones of those who suffer continue to be released after the danger is passed.

8.   T F   Panic attacks generally occur out of nowhere.

9.   T F   The most disabling and by far the most common type of phobia is social phobia.

10.   T F   Most sufferers of Obsessive-compulsive disorder (OCD) do not realize that their compulsion is senseless.

11.   T F   Depression is accompanied by physical changes including changes in eating, sleeping, concentrating, and energy level.

12.   T F   Bipolar disorder occurs equally in both sexes, major depression occurs two or three times as often among women as among men, all over the world.

13.   T F   Violence has many negative psychological effects, but it has not been identified as a risk factor for depression.

14. T F The thought "I'm ugly and awkward; no wonder I'm not making friends." is an example of the negative thinking habit of internality which can be associated with depression.

15. T F Learned helplessness refers to a parenting style that is associated with depression. Parents who are very controlling and do everything for their children do not give children opportunities to achieve and the children learn that they are helpless.

16. T F Antisocial personality disorder (APD) refers to people who experience great fear and discomfort with other people. They tend to be very shy and to be loners.

17. T F Antisocial individuals do not respond to punishments that would make most people anxious.

18. T F Now that understanding of Dissociative Identity Disorder (Multiple Personality Disorder) has improved, psychologists agree that there are many more people with this disorder that was previously thought.

19. T F Healthy people can alter physiological measures such as brain wave activity by changing their moods, energy levels, and concentration, so these measures are not a valid way to verify Multiple Personality Disorder.

20. T F For alcoholics who begin heavy drinking in adulthood, genetic factors seem to be involved.

21. T F Policies of total abstinence tend to increase rates of addiction rather than reduce them.

22. T F Research has supported the fact that alcoholics cannot become controlled drinkers.

23. T F Schizophrenia is the same thing as "split personality."

24. T F Schizophrenics sometimes have both positive symptoms (symptoms that are additions to normal behavior) and negative symptoms (symptoms that involve the loss or absence of normal traits and abilities).

25. T F Some people with schizophrenia are almost completely impaired in all spheres; others do extremely well in certain areas.

PRACTICE TEST 5 - Essay

1. Jason spends all day at the shopping mall. Every day he stops people who look in his direction and literally begs for their forgiveness. What makes Jason so noticeable are his boldly colored sweatshirts. These are worn every day, over his coat when it's cold, and each one has exactly the same inscription: "Jason is not a thief." Discuss the aspect of Jason's behavior that conforms with each of the definitions of mental disorder.

   A. Violation of cultural standards
   B. Maladaptive behavior
   C. Emotional distress
   D. Impaired judgment and self-control

2. In the formulation of Jason's diagnosis according to the DSM-IV, indicate whether the types of information identified below would be included. Explain your answers.

   A. A diagnostic label for Jason's condition
   B. The suspected cause(s) for Jason's symptoms
   C. An estimate of potential treatment effects
   D. How well Jason is functioning
   E. Any medical condition that Jason might have

3. For each description below, indicate whether the anxiety that is present is normal or abnormal. When it is abnormal, suggest the most likely diagnostic category.

   A. Carl loves the racetrack but he will not go there again. The last time he was there he suddenly felt his heart racing, he was gasping for breath, his hands began to tremble and he broke out into a cold sweat.
   B. Sandy is very clean! She feels contaminated unless she bathes and changes her clothes at least four times a day, and she is meticulous about the house as well. Every room is scrubbed at least twice a week and the bathroom is cleaned daily.
   C. A college student becomes anxious whenever assigned a project that requires speaking in front of class. The anxiety motivates meticulous preparation and the student rehearses material again and again.
   D. Marsha was stranded in a building for over two hours. The stairway was blocked by men moving large cartons, and the only path downward was the elevators. Elevators cause Marsha to sweat, tremble and suffer from images of being crushed. She decided to wait rather than take the elevator.
   E. Harry has had problems since returning from Vietnam. He is listless and quarrelsome, and has fitful sleeps, reliving his past in nightmarish dreams.

4. Decide whether each of the statements below is correct or incorrect. When it is incorrect, rewrite it in a more factual form.

   A. Mood disorders consist primarily of emotional symptoms and have little impact on behavioral, cognitive or physical functioning.
   B. In bipolar disorder, periods of sluggishness alternate with active attempts to commit suicide.
   C. Antidepressant drugs work by altering the activity level of the limbic system.
   D. Lack of fulfilling work and family relationships are a good predictor of depression.
   E. Negatively distorted thinking is the result, not the cause, of depression.
   F. Repeated failure is an unlikely source of major depressive episodes.

5. Josephine is highly mistrustful of airline personnel. She believes that airplanes dirty the streets and sidewalks by dripping oil and that pilots have a power called "telectic penetration." On hearing a plane, Josephine becomes introspective and claims she is being used as a radar. She feels the pilots are tuning in to her latitude and longitude and asking her questions about her location. She is unable to speak until they are through.

   A. Does Josephine have delusions? If so, what?
   B. Is Josephine hallucinating? If so, describe her hallucinations.
   C. Is Josephine having any disorganized or incoherent speech? If so, describe.
   D. Is Josephine demonstrating any disorganized or inappropriate behavior? If so, what?
   E. Is Josephine demonstrating emotional flatness? If so, describe.

CHAPTER 17

Approaches to Treatment and Therapy

LEARNING OBJECTIVES

1. Discuss the uses of antipsychotic drugs, antidepressants, tranquilizers and lithium in treating emotional disorders.

2. Summarize the problems inherent in treating psychological disorders with drugs.

3. Describe the procedures used in attempts to alter brain function directly.

4. List and explain the goals and principles of the four major schools of psychotherapy.

5. Explain the scientist-practitioner gap and why it has developed.

6. Describe the results of efforts to evaluate the effectiveness of psychotherapy.

7. Discuss the factors most likely to lead to successful therapy and discuss the role of the therapeutic alliance.

8. Discuss which therapies work best for specific problems.

9. Discuss the circumstances in which therapy can be harmful.

10. Discuss the goals and methods of various alternatives to psychotherapy, including community programs and self-help groups.

11. Explain the limitations of psychotherapy.

CHAPTER CONCEPT MAP

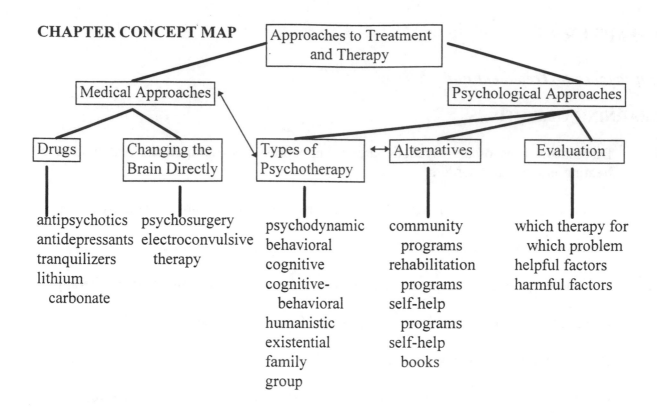

BRIEF CHAPTER SUMMARY

Chapter 17 describes various approaches to the treatment of mental disorders. Three general types of approaches are reviewed. Medical approaches include drug treatments, psychosurgery and electroconvulsive therapy. Drug treatments include medications that treat psychoses (antipsychotic medications), depression (antidepressants), anxiety (tranquilizers) and bipolar disorder (lithium carbonate). While drugs have contributed to significant advances in the treatment of mental disorders, they require great caution in their use. Psychosurgery, which was used more commonly in the 1950s, is rarely used any longer because of its serious and irreversible side effects. Electroconvulsive therapy is still used for serious cases of depression that do not respond to other treatments. Types of psychotherapy exist based on each of the major perspectives. The general principles and techniques of each of these approaches are reviewed along with research on their effectiveness. While there are certain commonalities among all the different types of psychotherapy, research indicates that some approaches are more effective for particular problems. Alternative treatment approaches include community and self-help programs. These approaches can be helpful in certain circumstances.

PREVIEW OUTLINE AND REVIEW QUESTIONS

Before you read the chapter, review the preview outline and the Learning Objectives for each section of the text. Answer all questions as you read the text.

SECTION 1 - BIOLOGICAL TREATMENTS (PP. 617-623)

I. **BIOLOGICAL TREATMENTS**
    A.   **The question of drugs**
        1.   Biological treatments are enjoying a resurgence because of evidence that some disorders have a biological component and because of the limitations of psychotherapy for chronic sufferers
        2.   Drugs commonly prescribed for mental disorders
            a.   Antipsychotic drugs, or neuroleptics; used in the treatment of psychoses and schizophrenia (not effective for everyone)
                (1)   Reduce receptivity to dopamine, some increase serotonin
                (2)   Reduce agitation, delusions, hallucinations; little relief from other symptoms of schizophrenia
                (3)   Can have dangerous side effects, including tardive _____ and neuroleptic malignant syndrome
            b.   Antidepressant drugs - used to treat depression, anxiety, phobias, and obsessive-compulsive disorder
                (1)   Monoamine oxidase (MAO) inhibitors - elevate levels of norepinephrine and _____ by blocking inhibitors
                (2)   Tricyclic antidepressants - boosts norepinephrine and serotonin by preventing their reabsorption
                (3)   Selective serotonin reuptake inhibitors (SSRIs) - work like tricyclics but specifically on serotonin
                (4)   Nonaddictive but can have unpleasant side effects
            c.   Tranquilizers - increase activity of neurotransmitter, GABA
                (1)   Prescribed for depressed mood, panic, and anxiety though they're not effective for depression or panic; antidepressants are preferable
                (2)   Not considered treatment of choice because they can be overused and result in tolerance and withdrawal
            d.   _____ carbonate - prescribed for bipolar disorder; must be administered in the correct dose or can be dangerous
            e.   Currently only psychiatrists can prescribe medication, but psychologists are trying to be allowed to do so
        3.   Cautions about drugs
            a.   Placebo effect - effectiveness is influenced by a belief in a drug;

> new antidepressants have strong placebo effect
>
> b. Relapse and drop-out rates - high drop-out rates from side effects
>
> c. Dosage problems - race, gender and age all influence dosage
>
> d. Long-term risks - some are known and some unknown
>
> e. Overprescription of drugs is partly due to pressure from managed-care companies and drug companies
>
> f. Because a disorder has biological origins doesn't mean only medical treatments can help; behavioral changes can affect biology
>
> g. Concern about the prescription of medications without therapy

B. **Surgery and electroshock**

1. Psychosurgery - surgery to destroy selected areas of the brain thought to be responsible for emotional disorders

   a. Most famous modern psychosurgery was prefrontal _____ which was never assessed scientifically and resulted in personality changes

   b. Rarely used today

2. Electroconvulsive therapy (ECT) or "_____ treatments"

   a. Treatment procedure modified so trauma is minimized

   b. Unclear how or why ECT works

   c. Most effective with the suicidally depressed, who cannot wait for antidepressants to take effect; not effective with other disorders

   d. Its use is controversial

Answer these Learning Objectives while you read Section 1.

1. Discuss the types and uses of antipsychotic drugs, antidepressants, tranquilizers and lithium in treating mental disorders.

2. Summarize the problems inherent in treating psychological disorders with drugs.

3. Describe the procedures used in attempts to alter brain function directly.

II. **KINDS OF PSYCHOTHERAPY**
- A. **Commonalities among psychotherapies** - help clients think about their lives in new ways and find solutions to their problems
- B. **Psychodynamic therapy**
    1. Probes the past and the unconscious to produce _____ and emotional release to eliminate symptoms
    2. Psychoanalysis evolved into psychodynamic therapies
    3. Considered "depth" therapies because they explore the unconscious by using techniques such as _____ association and transference (displacement of unconscious feelings onto the analyst)
    4. They do not aim to solve an individual's immediate problem - symptoms are seen as the tip of the iceberg
    5. Many psychodynamic therapists use Freudian principles but not methods
    6. Brief psychodynamic therapy does not go into whole history, but focuses on main issue or dynamic focus as well as self-defeating habits
- C. **Behavioral and cognitive therapy** - focus is behavior change not insight
    1. Behavioral techniques - derived from classical and operant conditioning
        - a. Systematic _____ - a step by step process of "desensitizing" a client to a feared object or experience; uses counterconditioning
        - b. Aversive conditioning - substitutes _____ for a reinforcement that has perpetuated a bad habit
        - c. Exposure treatment (or flooding) - therapist accompanies client into the feared situation (called "in vivo" exposure)
        - d. Behavioral records and contracts identify _____ that are keeping unwanted behaviors going; used with behavioral goals
        - e. Skills training - practice in behaviors necessary for achieving goals
    2. Cognitive techniques
        - a. Aim is to identify thoughts, beliefs and expectations that might be prolonging a person's problems
        - b. Requires clients to examine evidence for their beliefs and consider other interpretations
        - c. Albert Ellis and _____ emotive behavior therapy - therapist challenges unrealistic beliefs directly with rational arguments
        - d. Beck's approach uses other, less direct, techniques
    3. Cognitive-behavior therapy - combines the above two approaches; most common treatment
- D. **Humanistic and existential therapy**
    1. Humanistic therapies - assume that people seek self-_____ and self-fulfillment

2. Do not delve into the past, help people to feel better about themselves
3. Client-centered or nondirective therapy by Carl _____
    a. Therapist offers unconditional positive regard to build self-esteem
    b. No specific techniques, but therapists must be warm, genuine and empathic; client adopts these views and becomes self-_____
4. Existential therapy - helps client explore meaning of existence, choose a destiny and accept self-responsibility

E. Therapy in social context
1. Family Therapy - believes that the problem developed and is maintained in the social _____, and that is where change must occur
2. The family kaleidoscope - the family as a changing pattern in which all parts affect each other and efforts to treat a single member doomed to fail
    (1) Observing the family together reveals family tensions and imbalances in power and communication
    (2) Some use _____ - family tree of psychologically significant events to reveal origins of problems
    a. Family systems approach - if one member in the family changes, the others must change too
3. Group therapy - people with same or different problems work together
    a. Used in institutional settings
    b. Useful for those with social difficulties like shyness

F. Psychotherapy in practice - eclecticism
1. Most psychotherapists use techniques from different approaches
2. A common element in all therapies is to replace self-defeating narratives or life stories with ones that are more hopeful and attainable

Answer this Learning Objective while you read Section 2.

4. List and explain the goals and principles of the four major schools of psychotherapy.

SECTION 3 - EVALUATING PSYCHOTHERAPY (PP. 633-642)

III. **EVALUATING PSYCHOTHERAPY**
    A.   **The scientist-practitioner gap**
        1.   Conflict between scientists and practitioners about the relevance of research findings to clinical practice
            a.   Scientists want therapists to keep up with empirical findings in the field on topics relevant to their practice
            b.   Practitioners believe it is difficult to empirically study psychotherapy
        2.   Breach between scientists and therapists has widened, partly related to professional schools of psychology that are unconnected to academic psychology departments and because of many untested new therapies
        3.   Consumers should know how well a treatment works
    B.   **Assessing therapy's effectiveness**
        1.   Managed-care programs require research-based therapy guidelines
        2.   Overall conclusions from research on the effectiveness of therapy
            a.   Psychotherapy is better than doing nothing at all
            b.   People who have less serious problems and are _____ to improve do best in psychotherapy
            c.   For the common emotional problems of life, short-term treatment is usually sufficient
            d.   In some cases, psychotherapy is harmful because of the therapist's incompetence, biases, unethical behavior, or lack of knowledge
    C.   **When therapy helps**
        1.   Successful clients and therapists - clients and therapists are most likely to be successful in therapy under the following conditions
            a.   When there is a good fit between client and therapist
            b.   When clients have a strong sense of self and enough distress to motivate them to change
            c.   Hostile, negative clients are less likely to benefit
            d.   When therapists are _____, warm, genuine, respectful and clients feel accepted and understood
            e.   When client and therapist establish a bond, or therapeutic alliance
        2.   Cultural and group differences
            a.   Cultural differences can cause misunderstandings from ignorance and prejudice
            b.   Some minority group members stay in therapy longer with therapists of the same ethnicity
            c.   American Psychiatric Association recommends consideration of a

person's cultural background when making a diagnosis or for treatment
- d.   Must be aware of cultural differences without stereotyping
3.   Which therapy for which problem? - Empirically validated treatment include the following findings:
- a.   Behavior and cognitive therapies are the method of choice for:
  - (1)   Depression - can also be useful for prevention
  - (2)   Anxiety disorders including panic attacks, phobias and obsessive-compulsive disorder
  - (3)   Anger and impulsive violence
  - (4)   Health problems
  - (5)   Childhood and adolescent behavior problems
- b.   Cognitive-behavior therapies help schizophrenics by teaching their families skills for dealing with the schizophrenic children
- c.   These approaches help best for clearly defined problems and may not be appropriate for everyone seeking therapy
- d.   They are not successful for those with personality disorders and psychoses
- e.   Some problems and some clients need combined methods and approaches

D.   When therapy harms
1.   Coercion by the therapist to accept the therapist's advice, sexual intimacies, or other unethical behavior
2.   Bias on the part of a therapist who doesn't understand the client because of the client's gender, culture, religion, or sexual orientation
3.   Therapist-_____ disorders resulting from inadvertent suggestions or influence - might explain increase in MPD diagnoses and pseudomemories

Answer these Learning Objectives while you read Section 3.

5.   Explain the scientist-practitioner gap and why it has developed.

6.   Describe the results of efforts to evaluate the effectiveness of psychotherapy.

7.   Discuss the factors most likely to lead to successful therapy and discuss the role of the therapeutic alliance.

8.   Discuss which therapies work best for specific problems.

9.   Discuss the circumstances in which therapy can be harmful.

**SECTION 4 - ALTERNATIVES TO PSYCHOTHERAPY (PP. 642-645) AND
SECTION 5 - THE VALUE AND VALUES OF PSYCHOTHERAPY (P. 646)**

IV.   **ALTERNATIVES TO PSYCHOTHERAPY**
    A.   **The community and rehabilitation psychology**
        1.   Majority of people with mental illness live in the community
        2.   _____ psychologists help the mentally ill in their own communities rather than hospitals; nature of support depends on the problem
        3.   Types of community support
            a.   _____-way houses, clubhouse models
            b.   Other community approaches include family therapy, foster care, family home alternatives and family support groups
        4.   Rehabilitation psychologists - concerned with assessment and treatment of people who are physically disabled
    B.   **The self-help movement** - for problems that don't require a professional
        1.   Self-help groups organized around a common concern
        2.   Support groups offer understanding, empathy, solutions to shared problems
        3.   Doesn't provide psychotherapy; not for those with serious difficulties
        4.   Not regulated by law or professional standards; approaches vary widely
        5.   Self-help books
            a.   Some are based on solid psychological principles, some are not
            b.   APA guidelines for evaluating a self-help book
                (1)   Authors should be qualified - contain research support
                (2)   Should include evidence of the program's effectiveness
                (3)   Advice should be organized in a step-by-step program
                (4)   Should not promise the impossible
V.   **THE VALUE AND VALUES OF PSYCHOTHERAPY**
    A.   **Zilbergeld says psychotherapy promotes three myths**
        1.   People should always.be happy, and if they are not happy they need fixing
        2.   Almost any change is possible
        3.   Change is relatively easy
    B.   **What psychotherapy can do**: it can teach new skills and new ways of thinking
    C.   **What psychotherapy can't do**: it can't transform you into another person, cure a disorder overnight, or provide a life without problems

Answer this Learning Objective while you read Sections 4 and 5.

10.   Discuss the goals and methods of various alternatives to psychotherapy, including community programs and self-help groups.

11.   Explain the limitations of psychotherapy.

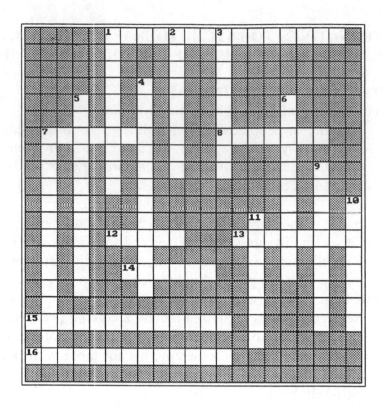

ACROSS

1. behavioral technique; step by step process intended to reduce fear
7. fake treatment used as a control in an experiment
8. a salt used to treat bipolar disorder
12. type of therapy with several people at once
13. the bond that develops between the therapist and the client
14. type of therapy in which the problem is not seen as within the individual but within the social context
15. operation designed to destroy selected areas of the brain
16. general term for treatment that helps people through talking

DOWN

1. late-appearing neurological effects of drugs taken over many years
2. life story
3. kind of drug that prevents reabsorption of norepinephrine and serotonin
4. type of regard discussed in Rogerian psychotherapy
5. patient projects emotional feelings for his or her parents onto the therapist
6. type of psychotherapy that helps the client explore the meaning of life
7. Freud's original method of psychotherapy
9. approach that centers on the idea that human beings have free will
10. behavioral technique in which punishment is substituted for reinforcement
11. technique in which the therapist takes the client right into the feared situation

FLASH CARDS

Cut the following chart along the borders and test yourself with the resulting flash cards.

17.1 ANTIPSYCHOTIC DRUGS (NEUROLEPTICS)	17.2 ANTIDEPRESSANT DRUGS	17.3 MONOAMINE OXIDASE (MAO) INHIBITORS
17.4 TRICYCLIC ANTIDEPRESSANTS	17.5 SELECTIVE SEROTONIN REUPTAKE INHIBITORS (SSRIs)	17.6 TRANQUILIZERS
17.7 LITHIUM CARBONATE	17.8 PLACEBO EFFECT	17.9 PSYCHOSURGERY
17.10 PREFRONTAL LOBOTOMY	17.11 ELECTROCONVULSIVE THERAPY (ECT)	17.12 PSYCHOANALYSIS
17.13 PSYCHODYNAMIC ("DEPTH") THERAPIES	17.14 FREE ASSOCIATION	17.15 TRANSFERENCE
17.16 BRIEF PSYCHODYNAMIC THERAPY	17.17 BEHAVIOR THERAPIES	17.18 BEHAVIORAL RECORDS AND CONTRACTS
17.19 BEHAVIORAL GOALS	17.20 SYSTEMATIC DESENSITIZATION	17.21 AVERSIVE CONDITIONING

17.3 Antidepressant drugs that elevates levels of norepinephrine and serotonin in the brain by blocking an enzyme that deactivates them.	17.2 Drugs used primarily in the treatment of mood disorders, especially depression and anxiety.	17.1 Drugs used primarily in the treatment of schizophrenia and other psychotic disorders.
17.6 Medications, such as Valium and Xanax, that increase the activity of the neurotransmitter GABA.	17.5 Antidepressant drugs such as Prozac that boost serotonin levels by preventing the normal reabsorption, or "reuptake."	17.4 Antidepressant drugs used primarily in the treatment of depression, anxiety, phobias, and obsessive-compulsive disorders.
17.9 Any surgical procedure that destroys selected areas of the brain believed to be involved in emotional disorders or violent, impulsive behavior.	17.8 The apparent success of a medication or treatment that is due to the patient's expectations or hopes rather than to the drug or treatment itself.	17.7 A drug frequently given to people suffering from bipolar disorder.
17.12 Freud's original method of treatment in which unconscious dynamics of personality are explored using techniques like free association.	17.11 A procedure used in cases of prolonged and severe major depression, in which a brief brain seizure is induced.	17.10 Psychosurgery done in the mid-1900s to reduce patients' emotional symptoms without impairing intellectual ability. It resulted in serious
17.15 In psychodynamic therapies, a step in which the client transfers unconscious emotions onto the therapist.	17.14 In psychoanalysis, a method of recovering unconscious conflicts by saying freely whatever comes to mind.	17.13 Different forms of therapy that evolved from Freudian psychoanalysis, which share the goal of exploring unconscious dynamics.
17.18 A behavior therapy technique in which clients keep track of certain specific behaviors.	17.17 Types of therapeutic approaches derived from principles of operant and classical conditioning.	17.16 A form of psychodynamic therapy that is time-limited. It usually consists of 15 to 25 sessions.
17.21 In behavior therapy, a method in which punishment is substituted for the reinforcement that is perpetuating a bad habit.	17.20 In behavior therapy, a step-by-step process of desensitizing a client to a feared object or experience; it is based on counterconditioning.	17.19 A technique used in behavior therapies in which a client sets small step-by-step goals that he or she can work toward.

17.22 FLOODING (EXPOSURE)	17.23 SKILLS TRAINING	17.24 COGNITIVE THERAPIES
17.25 RATIONAL EMOTIVE BEHAVIOR THERAPY	17.26 HUMANIST THERAPIES	17.27 CLIENT-CENTERED THERAPY
17.28 UNCONDITIONAL POSITIVE REGARD	17.29 EXISTENTIAL THERAPY	17.30 FAMILY THERAPY
17.31 GENOGRAM	17.32 FAMILY SYSTEMS APPROACH	17.33 GROUP THERAPY
17.34 COMMUNITY PSYCHOLOGISTS	17.35 CLUB-HOUSE MODEL	17.36 REHABILITATION PSYCHOLOGISTS
17.37 SELF-HELP GROUPS	17.38 SCIENTIST-PRACTITIONER GAP	17.39 CONTROLLED CLINICAL TRIALS
17.40 THERAPEUTIC ALLIANCE	17.41 EMPIRICALLY VALIDATED TREATMENT	17.42 SELF-HELP BOOKS

17.24 Therapies in which the aim is to help clients identify the thoughts, beliefs, and expectations that might be prolonging their problems.	17.23 A behavioral technique that provides practice in behaviors necessary for achieving the person' goals.	17.22 In behavior therapy, a method in which a person with an anxiety disorder is taken into the feared situation until the anxiety subsides.
17.27 A type of humanistic therapy developed by Carl Rogers. The therapist's role is to listen and offer unconditional positive regard.	17.26 Therapies based on the assumption that people seek self-actualization, self-fulfillment and have free will.	17.25 A type of cognitive therapy in which the therapist challenges the client's illogical beliefs directly with rational arguments.
17.30 A type of therapy that conceptualizes and treats individual problems in terms of the social context of family.	17.29 A type of therapy that helps clients explore the meaning of existence and deal with the great questions of life.	17.28 A humanistic technique developed by Rogers in which a client is helped to feel that he or she is loved and respected no matter what.
17.33 A form of therapy in which people with the same or different problems are put together to find solutions.	17.32 A perspective within the family therapy approach that recognizes that if one family member changes, the other must change too.	17.31 A technique used by family therapists that involves drawing a family tree of psychologically significant events across generations.
17.36 Type of psychologist who is concerned with the assessment and treatment of people who are physically disabled.	17.35 A community based program for mentally ill people that provides rehabilitation counseling, job and skills training, and a support	17.34 A psychologist who sets up programs within the community, rather than in hospitals, to help people who are mentally ill.
17.39 Research procedure used to establish therapy guidelines; people with a given disorder were randomly assigned to a treatment or a control group.	17.38 The gap created by the disagreement between scientists and therapists about the relevance of research findings to clinical practice.	17.37 Groups for people who do not need professional help or who have serious problems. The groups are organized around a common concern.
17.42 Books that give advice on personal or relationship problems. Some books can be effective, others are not based on psychological principles.	17.41 Treatments that have been tested repeatedly against a placebo or other treatment and had their efficacy demonstrated by different investigators.	17.40 The bond of confidence and mutual understanding established between therapist and client, which allows them to work together.

482

APPROACHES TO PSYCHOTHERAPY

Complete the following chart by listing specific techniques and general goals of therapy for each of the approaches in the left-hand column.

THERAPY APPROACH	SPECIFIC TECHNIQUES	GENERAL GOALS OF THERAPY
PSYCHODYNAMIC APPROACHES		
BEHAVIORAL APPROACH		
COGNITIVE APPROACHES		
HUMANISTIC APPROACHES		
GROUP THERAPY		
FAMILY THERAPY		

PRACTICE TEST 1 - Multiple Choice

1. The most widespread biological treatment is
   A. medication.
   B. psychosurgery.
   C. ECT.
   D. psychotherapy.

2. Antipsychotic drugs do <u>NOT</u>
   A. restore normal thought patterns.
   B. lessen hallucinations.
   C. reduce dramatic symptoms.
   D. have side effects.

3. Lithium carbonate is often effective in treating people who
   A. have schizrenia.
   B. have tardive dyskinesia.
   C. complain of unhappiness or anxiety.
   D. have bipolar disorder.

4. The drugs that are most effective in treating mood disorders are
   A. antipsychotic drugs.
   B. minor tranquilizers.
   C. antidepressant drugs.
   D. major tranquilizers.

5. A problem with using drugs in treating psychological disorders is that
   A. there are high drop-out rates.
   B. tests of drug effects in long-term usage are often missing.
   C. there is a strong placebo effect in evaluating their effectiveness.
   D. all of the above are potential problems.

6. The original intention of prefrontal lobotomy was to
   A. reduce the patient's emotional discomfort without impairing intellectual capacity.
   B. "ventilate" evil impulses or mental pressures.
   C. remove an abnormal organic condition, such as a tumor.
   D. replace drugs and electroconvulsive therapy, which were considered dangerous.

7. Critics of ECT say that it
   A. only helps people with minor psychological problems.
   B. is too often used improperly, and it can damage the brain.
   C. requires high voltages that could be fatal.
   D. causes epileptic seizures.

8. The placebo effect
   A. declines after a while and many drugs turn out to be less effective than promised.
   B. seems to be responsible for a considerable amount of the effectiveness reported on drugs like Prozac.
   C. ensures that some people will respond positively to new drugs because of their own expectations.
   D. all of the above.

9. In psychodynamic therapies, the patient's displacement of emotional elements in his or her inner life onto the therapist is called
   A. free association.
   B. transference.
   C. insight.
   D. dynamic focus.

10. The factor considered to be most helpful in psychodynamic therapies is
    A. insight.
    B. behavior change.
    C. changing conscious beliefs.
    D. the reduction of symptoms.

11. A type of therapy that takes the individual right into the most feared situation is called
    A. systematic desensitization.
    B. aversive conditioning.
    C. flooding or exposure treatment.
    D. brief psychodynamic therapy.

12. Systematic desensitization, aversive conditioning, flooding and skills training are all
    A. techniques used in cognitive therapies.
    B. psychodynamic techniques.
    C. methods employed by humanists.
    D. behavioral techniques.

13. Which two therapies often borrow each other's methods, so that a combination of the two is more common than either method alone?
    A. psychoanalysis; behavior therapy
    B. family therapy; group therapy
    C. cognitive therapy; behavior therapy
    D. support groups; group therapy

14. In which approach does the therapist challenge the client's illogical beliefs?
    A. cognitive therapy
    B. humanistic therapy
    C. psychodynamic therapy
    D. existential therapy

15. What type of therapist would try to provide unconditional positive regard?
    A. cognitive
    B. humanistic
    C. psychodynamic
    D. existential

16. Which type of therapist might make use of insight, transference, and free association?
    A.   a humanistic therapist   B.   a behaviorist therapist
    C.   an psychodynamic therapist   D.   a cognitive therapist

17. Professionals who help those who are physically disabled to work and live independently are called
    A.   behavioral psychologists.   B.   family therapists.
    C.   rehabilitation psychologists.   D.   group therapists.

18. Based on controlled clinical trials, which of the following is true about the effectiveness of therapy?
    A.   Psychotherapy is better than doing nothing at all.
    B.   People who do best in psychotherapy are those who have less serious problems and are motivated to improve.
    C.   For the common emotional problems of life, short-term treatment is usually sufficient.
    D.   all of the above

19. Good therapeutic candidates are those who
    A.   are introspective and want to talk about their childhoods.
    B.   want a chance to talk about their feelings without any limits.
    C.   recognize the expertise of the therapist.
    D.   are unhappy and motivated enough to want to work on their problems.

20. A therapeutic alliance is
    A.   an organization of therapists who advocate for the benefits of therapy.
    B.   a group of consumers who were harmed because of a therapist's incompetence or unethical methods.
    C.   a bond between the client and therapist that depends on their ability to understand each other.
    D.   a support group in which people share common problems.

21. Depth therapies work best for
    A.   anxiety disorders.
    B.   people who are introspective and want to explore their pasts and examine their current lives.
    C.   people with sex problems.
    D.   people who are drug abusers.

22. Research suggests that cognitive and behavioral approaches are very successful with many types of problems, however, they are <u>NOT</u> thought to work well for
   A. personality disorders and psychoses.
   B. phobias and panic disorder.
   C. moderate depression.
   D. agoraphobia and anxiety disorders.

23. Which factors can cause psychotherapy to be harmful?
   A. coercion
   B. bias
   C. therapist-induced disorders
   D. all of the above

24. One explanation for the growing number of patients diagnosed with multiple personalities is that the diagnosis is a result of
   A. bias.
   B. therapist inducement.
   C. incompetence.
   D. coercion.

25. A realistic expectation for the outcome of psychotherapy is
   A. to learn that any change is possible.
   B. to help make decisions and clarify values and goals.
   C. to be happy all, or almost all, of the time.
   D. to help eliminate the problems from one's life.

PRACTICE TEST 2 - Multiple Choice

1. Herbert has been diagnosed with major depression. Pete has been diagnosed with an anxiety disorder. Both of them are dealing with their problem with psychotherapy and medication. Which medication(s) should be prescribed for treating these problems?
    A. Tranquilizers should be prescribed for both types of disorders.
    B. Herbert should be on antidepressants while Pete should be on tranquilizers.
    C. Antidepressant drugs are used for both types of disorders.
    D. Herbert should be on lithium and Pete should be on Prozac.

2. Randolf is taking antipsychotic medication. Which of the following should concern him?
    A. the possibility of tardive dyskinesia
    B. the fact that while the more dramatic symptoms may be helped, normal thinking may not
    C. though he may be well enough to be released from a hospital, he may not be able to care for himself
    D. All of the above are concerns.

3. Jay is taking a medication that elevates the levels of norepinephrine and serotonin in his brain. What is his most probable diagnosis?
    A. depression   B. an anxiety disorder
    C. bipolar disorder   D. a psychosis

4. Felicia has been prescribed an antidepressant. Which of the following might she be taking?
    A. a neuroleptic   B. a tricyclic
    C. lithium   D. a tranquilizer

5. Based on the cautions about drug treatment, Felicia should probably have concerns about
    A. whether the drug is more effective than a placebo.
    B. whether the drug has been tested for long-term use.
    C. whether the right dosage has been identified.
    D. all of the above.

6. Among the following patients, who would be a likely candidate for electroconvulsive therapy (ECT)?
    A. Fran is suicidally depressed.
    B. Dan is anxious.
    C. Stan is moderately depressed.
    D. ECT should not be used on any of them, since it is outdated and barbaric.

488

7. Stan is taking an antidepressant but he is not receiving any help with learning how to cope with his problems. Which of the following is true?
   A. Medication alone is sufficient.
   B. If he is feeling better, medication is sufficient. If not, he needs psychotherapy.
   C. People who take antidepressants without learning how to cope with their problems are more likely to relapse in the future than those who receive such help.
   D. He does not need medication, he only needs psychotherapy.

8. During her first visit to Dr. Bhoutos, Patrece is told to say whatever comes to mind. Dr. Bhoutos is using _____ as part of _____ psychotherapy.
   A. transference; behavioral
   B. flooding; behavioral
   C. free association; psychodynamic
   D. transference; psychodynamic

9. After several months of therapy, during one session Patrece had a momentous awareness about how her relationship with her father had been affecting her for years. This realization
   A. is called insight.
   B. along with emotional release, should cause her symptoms to disappear, according to psychodynamic principles.
   C. is the key to therapeutic gains in psychodynamic approaches.
   D. incorporates all of the above.

10. To help Bob with his fear of flying, Dr. Rose teaches Bob to relax while they proceed through a series of steps that go from reading a story about an airplane, to visiting an airport, to boarding a plane, to taking a short flight. This _____ technique is called

    _____.
    A. cognitive; rational emotive therapy
    B. humanistic; flooding
    C. behavioral; systematic desensitization
    D. behavioral; flooding

11. Cognitive therapies focus on changing _____, whereas humanistic therapies focus on _____.
    A. beliefs; self-acceptance
    B. behaviors; changing families
    C. behaviors; insight into the past
    D. thoughts; skills

12. A cognitive therapist would treat a procrastination problem by
    A. helping the client gain insight through free association and transference.
    B. having the client keep a diary of how time is actually spent and then establishing specific goals.
    C. asking the client to write down negative thoughts about work, to read the thoughts as if someone else had said them, and then to write a rational response to each.
    D. building self-esteem and putting the client in touch with his or her real feelings.

489

13. Dr. Smith is treating procrastination by having Stuart keep a diary of how much time he spends working, establishing goals, identifying his negative thoughts about his abilities, gaining insight into his fears of succeeding and the origins of the negative thoughts, changing these thought patterns, and helping him to feel better about himself. Dr. Smith is what type of therapist?

  A. behavioral
  B. cognitive
  C. eclectic
  D. humanistic

14. The clubhouse model provides
  A. self-help groups for the mentally ill.
  B. behavioral training for families of schizophrenics.
  C. rehabilitation counseling, job and skills training, and a support network for the mentally ill.
  D. ongoing depth psychotherapy for the mentally ill.

15. Frank participates in a self-help group because he gets many things out of it, including
  A. help that focuses on specific problems.
  B. help that focuses on his underlying issues and problems.
  C. the fact that others have been there and know what he is going through.
  D. none of the above.

16. _____ maintain that effectiveness of therapy must be demonstrated, whereas _____ wish that academic psychologists would pay more attention to clinical evidence.
  A. Scientists; paraprofessionals
  B. Scientists; practitioners
  C. Practitioners; clinicians
  D. Researchers; scientists

17. Sandra is trying to decide whether to seek psychotherapy. She has done some reading on its effectiveness and has found that
  A. people in almost any professional treatment improve more than people who do not get help.
  B. people who do best in psychotherapy are those who have the most serious problems to begin with.
  C. unfortunately, psychotherapy is harmful in about 30 percent of all cases.
  D. psychotherapy helps in all types of psychological problems.

18. Sandra decides she is going to start psychotherapy. She should look for a psychotherapist
  A. of the same race and gender.
  B. whom she respects and whom she feels respects and understands her.
  C. who is detached and objective.
  D. who gives her a lot of information.

19. Sandra will be most successful in therapy if she
    A. challenges the therapist whenever she disagrees.
    B. is aware of any mistakes the therapist makes and is willing to point them out.
    C. goes along with whatever the therapist says or suggests.
    D. has a personal style of dealing actively with problems instead of avoiding them.

20. Based on research on the effectiveness of psychotherapy, which of the following clients should benefit most from cognitive therapies?
    A. Hank has a major depression.
    B. Frank is schizophrenic.
    C. Mary who wishes to explore moral issues and learn more about herself.
    D. They would all benefit most from cognitive therapies.

21. Helen is suffering from agoraphobia. Which type of therapy would be most helpful?
    A. exposure treatments   B. flooding
    C. behavioral approaches   D. all of the above

22. Cassandra wants to understand herself better; she wants to know why she does some of the things she does and to know what she is feeling. She believes that her past has a big impact on her present. Which type of therapy would best meet these goals?
    A. cognitive therapy   B. behavioral therapy
    C. psychodynamic and existential approaches D. solution-oriented therapy

23. In which of the following cases is Melina most likely to find the therapeutic experience harmful?
    A. Her therapist firmly believes that Melina was sexually abused in childhood, though she has no memories of this and does not believe it is so.
    B. Her therapist disagrees with her about several issues.
    C. Her therapist does not always give her an immediate appointment when she calls.
    D. All of the above may be harmful.

24. It is considered acceptable for a therapist to engage in sexual relations or other intimate behaviors with a client
    A. when it is necessary to learn about close and loving relationships.
    B. to help him or her overcome sexual difficulties.
    C. when the client invites it or asks for it.
    D. under no circumstances.

25. Ophelia says that all of her friends are in therapy and she wants to be in therapy also. Which of the following is a reasonable expectation for her to have of therapy?
    A. It may help her to make decisions.
    B. It may help her get through bad times.
    C. It may teach her new skills.
    D. all of the above

PRACTICE TEST 3 - Short Answer

1. Neuroleptics, or antipsychotic drugs, are used in the treatment of _____ and other _____.

2. One of the side effects of the antipsychotic drugs is a neurological disorder called _____, which is characterized by hand tremors and other involuntary muscle movements.

3. Monoamine oxidase inhibitors, tricyclics, and selective serotonin reuptake inhibitors are all examples of _____ drugs.

4. _____ is a special category of drug which often helps people who suffer from bipolar disorder.

5. People who take antidepressant drugs without also learning how to cope with their problems are more likely to _____ in the future.

6. An form of psychosurgery that was supposed to reduce the patient's emotional symptoms without impairing intellectual ability, called a _____, left many patients apathetic, withdrawn, and unable to care for themselves.

7. _____ is used as a treatment for severe depression, for patients who are at risk of committing suicide and cannot wait for antidepressants or psychotherapy to take effect.

8. To bring unconscious conflicts to awareness, _____ therapists often ask the client to say whatever comes to mind. This technique is called _____.

9. Bob has been seeing Dr. Sigmund. He has always felt that his mother rejected him and now he finds that he is furious at Dr. Sigmund for planning a vacation. This major element of psychodynamic therapy is called _____.

10. _____ is one of the _____ techniques that involves a step-by-step process of desensitizing a client to a feared object or experience.

11. The technique of _____ has clients who are suffering from specific anxieties confront the feared situation or memory directly.

12. Cognitive therapists require clients to examine the _____ for their beliefs and to consider other _____ of events that might result in less disturbing emotions.

13. One of the best known schools of cognitive therapy was developed by Albert Ellis and is now called rational _____ therapy.

14. _____ therapy, developed by Carl Rogers, the therapist listens to the client in an accepting, nonjudgmental way and offers _____ positive regard.

15. _____ therapists maintain that problems develop in a social context, and that any changes a person makes in therapy will affect that context.

16. The scientist-practitioner gap refers to the breach between scientists and therapists about the importance of _____ methods and findings on the practice of psychotherapy.

17. In some cases, psychotherapy has been found to be harmful because the therapist may be _____ or unethical behavior.

18. The personality of the therapist is also critical to the success of any therapy, particularly the qualities that Carl Rogers praised: _____, expressiveness, warmth, and _____ .

19. A task force from the American Psychological Association found that _____ treatment is particularly effective for depression and _____ disorders.

20. The APA task force also found that young adults with schizophrenia are greatly helped by family therapies that teach parents _____ skills in dealing with their troubled children.

21. _____ to accept the therapist's advice, sexual intimacies, or other unethical behavior can result in harm to the client.

22. Therapist influence is a likely reason for the growing number of people diagnosed with _____ disorder in the 1980s and 1990s.

23. _____ groups are designed for people who have problems that do not require professional help.

24. _____ psychologists set up programs to help people who are mentally ill in their own communities rather than in hospitals. _____ psychologists are concerned with the assessment and treatment of people who ar physically disabled.

25. Self-help books should include _____ of the program's effectiveness.

PRACTICE TEST 3 - True/False

1.   T F   Medication is used primarily for common psychological problems like anxiety and depression rather than for more severe disorders.

2.   T F   Antipsychotic drugs, such as MAO inhibitors and SSRIs, can have serious side effects like tardive dyskinesia.

3.   T F   Tranquilizers, like Valium and Xanax, are often prescribed by general physicians for depressed mood and panic even though they are not effective for these disorders.

4.   T F   Many psychologists are now lobbying for the right to prescribe medication.

5.   T F   African-Americans suffering from depression or bipolar disorder seem to need lower dosages of tricyclic antidepressants and lithium than other ethnic groups do.

6.   T F   New drugs are often tested on only a few hundred people for only a few weeks or months, even when the drug is one that patients might take for years.

7.   T F   Electric convulsive therapy (ECT), or "shock treatment," is no longer used.

8.   T F   Transference refers to whether the client is able to use, or transfer, what he or she has learned in the therapy setting to his or her life.

9.   T F   In psychoanalysis, the analyst uses free association and dreams to try to cure the problem that brought the client into therapy.

10.   T F   Counterconditioning, a classical conditioning procedure, is the basis of systematic desensitization.

11.   T F   Teaching people new skills is an educational approach to behavior change and is not actually part of any psychotherapy approach.

12.   T F   Rational emotive behavior therapy uses rational arguments to directly challenge a client's unrealistic beliefs. Beck's cognitive approach encourages clients to test their beliefs against the evidence and to stop "catastrophizing."

13.   T F   Strict behaviorists consider thoughts to be "behaviors" but they do not regard thoughts as the causes of behavior.

14.　T F　Humanists explore the past instead of what is going on in the "here and now."

15.　T F　Existential therapists, like humanist therapists, believe that our lives are not inevitably determined by our pasts or our circumstances.

16.　T F　Family therapists believe that if clients learn to change their behavior, even for the better, their families may protest or send subtle messages for them to return to their old ways of behaving.

17.　T F　The four approaches discussed in the text are quite different and, in practice, most psychotherapists select one approach that they use almost exclusively.

18.　T F　The scientist-practitioner gap refers to the fact that scientific psychologists have little experience with and therefore understand little about the practice of psychology.

19.　T F　For all types of problems, it is important that clients have access to long-term psychotherapy.

20.　T F　Clients do better, both in the short-term and long-term, if they are in psychotherapy with therapists who match their own ethnicity.

21.　T F　Anxiety disorders are best treated by cognitive-behavioral approaches, but depression responds best to depth therapies.

22.　T F　Some therapists so zealously believe in the prevalence of certain problems that they induce the client to produce the symptoms they are looking for.

23.　T F　A therapeutic alliance only forms in unhealthy client-therapist relationships. When this occurs the client and therapist can unite against the client's family.

24.　T F　Today, the majority of those with severe mental disorders spend most of their lives in boarding houses, hotel rooms, hostels, jails, hallways, abandoned buildings, halfway houses, or on the streets.

25.　T F　Self-help groups provide psychotherapy for specific problems.

PRACTICE TEST 3 - Essay

1. Identify the three major categories of approaches to psychological problems and briefly describe the help they offer. Indicate under what circumstances each would be desirable.

2. Identify the drugs typically prescribed for each of the disorders listed below and then briefly explain why drugs alone may not be sufficient treatment.

   A. Anxiety disorders
   B. Mood disorders
   C. Psychotic disorders

3. Summarize the major features of each of the five major approaches to psychotherapy. Specify the goals and common techniques of each.

4. Identify the features of the client, the therapist, and their relationship that are associated with therapeutic success.

5. Identify and briefly describe the factors that contribute to therapeutic harm.

APPENDIX A

Statistical Methods

LEARNING OBJECTIVES

1. Describe a frequency distribution and explain how one is constructed.

2. Describe the different types of graphs and explain how graphs can mask or exaggerate differences.

3. Describe the three measures of central tendency and how each is calculated.

4. Define standard deviation and describe how it is calculated.

5. Compare and contrast percentile scores and z-scores.

6. Describe a normal distribution and the two types of skewed distributions.

7. Describe the characteristics of a normal curve.

8. Distinguish between the null and the alternative hypothesis.

9. Explain what is meant by statistical significance, and discuss the relationship between statistical significance and psychological importance.

10. Define sampling distribution.

SECTION BY SECTION PREVIEW OUTLINE AND REVIEW QUESTIONS

Before you read the Appendix, review the preview outline and the questions for each section of the. Answer all the questions as you read.

SECTION 1 - ORGANIZING DATA (PP. A-1 TO A-3)

I. **ORGANIZING DATA**
   A. **Constructing a frequency distribution** - often the first step in organizing data
      1. Shows how often each possible score actually occurred
      2. To construct one, order all possible scores from _____ to lowest
      3. Then tally how often each score is obtained
      4. Grouped frequency distributions
         a. Groups adjacent scores into equal-sized classes or intervals
         b. Grouped frequencies are used when there are _____ scores
         c. Frequencies within each interval are tallied
   B. **Graphing the data**
      1. A graph is a picture that depicts numerical relationships
      2. Types of graphs
         a. _____ or bar graph - draw rectangles or bars above each score indicating the number of times it occurred from the bar's height
         b. Frequency polygon, or line graph - each score is indicated by a dot placed directly over the score on the horizontal axis, at the appropriate height on the vertical axis
      3. Caution about graphs - they can mask or _____ differences

Answer these Learning Objectives while you read Section 1.

1. Describe a frequency distribution and explain how one is constructed.

2. Describe the different types of graphs and explain how graphs can mask or exaggerate differences.

II. **DESCRIBING DATA**
    A.   **Measuring Central Tendency** - characterizes an entire set of data in terms of a single representative number
        1.   The mean
            a.   To calculate the mean, add up a set of scores and _____ the total by the number of scores in the set
            b.   Means can be misleading because very high or very low scores can dramatically raise or lower the mean
        2.   The median
            a.   The median is the _____ in a set of scores ordered from highest to lowest
            b.   The same number of scores falls above the median as below it
            c.   A more representative measure when extreme scores occur
        3.   The mode
            a.   The score that occurs _____ often
            b.   Used less often than other measures of central tendency
    B.   **Measuring variability**
        1.   Tells whether the scores are clustered closely around the mean or widely scattered
        2.   The _____
            a.   The simplest measure of variability
            b.   Found by subtracting the lowest score from the highest one
        3.   The standard deviation
            a.   Tells how much, on the average, scores in a distribution differ from the _____
            b.   To compute the standard deviation
                (1)   Subtract the mean from each score yielding deviation scores
                (2)   Square deviation scores
                (3)   Average the squared deviation scores
                (4)   Take the square root of the result
            c.   Large standard deviations signify that scores are _____ scattered and the mean is probably not very representative; small standard deviations signify that scores cluster near the mean and that the mean is representative
    C.   **Transforming scores** - used when researchers don't want to work directly with raw scores
        1.   Percentile scores
            a.   Percentage of people scoring at or below a given raw score

    b.   A drawback to percentiles is that they do not tell how far apart people are in terms of raw scores
2.   Z-scores or _____ scores
    a.   Tell how far a given raw score is above or below the mean, using the standard deviation as the unit of measurement
    b.   To calculate, subtract the mean of the distribution from the raw score and divide by the standard deviation
    c.   They preserve the relative spacing of the original raw scores
    d.   Z-scores comparisons must be done with caution

D.   **Curves,** or the _____ of the distribution
1.   A normal distribution has a symmetrical, bell-shaped form when plotted in a frequency polygon - called a normal curve
2.   Characteristics of a normal curve
    a.   Right side is the mirror image of the left side
    b.   Mean, median and mode have the _____ value and are at the center of the curve
    c.   The percentage of scores falling between the mean and any given point on the horizontal axis is always the same when standard deviations are used on that axis
3.   Not all types of observations are distributed normally, some are lopsided or skewed
    a.   When the tail goes to the left, it is a negative skew
    b.   When the tail goes to the right, it is a _____ skew

Answer these Learning Objectives while you read Section 2.

3.   Describe the three measures of central tendency and how each is calculated.

4.   Define standard deviation and describe how it is calculated.

5.   Compare and contrast percentile scores and z-scores.

6.   Describe a normal distribution and the two types of skewed distributions.

7.   Describe the characteristics of a normal curve.

SECTION 3 - DRAWING INFERENCES (PP. A-7 TOA-9)

III. **DRAWING INFERENCES** with inferential statistics
   A. **The null versus the _____ hypothesis**
      1. The null hypothesis states the possibility that the experimental manipulations will have no effect on the subjects' behavior
      2. The alternative hypothesis states that the average experimental group score will differ from the average control group score
      3. The goal is to _____ the null hypothesis
   B. **Testing hypotheses**
      1. Goal - to be reasonably certain the difference did not occur by _____
      2. Sampling distribution is used - the theoretical distribution of differences between means
      3. When the null hypothesis is true, there is no difference between groups
      4. If there is a difference, how likely is it to occur by chance?
      5. If it is highly improbable that a result occurs by chance, it is said to be _____ significant
      6. If more than chance was operating, it is safe to assume the independent variable had some influence
      7. Characteristics of statistical significance
         a. Psychologists accept a finding as statistically significant if the likelihood of its occurring by chance is five percent or less
         b. Statistically significant results are not always psychologically interesting or important
         c. Statistical significance is related to sample _____ - results from a large sample are likely to be found statistically significant

Answer these Learning Objectives while you read Section 3.

8. Distinguish between the null and the alternative hypothesis.

9. Explain what is meant by statistical significance, and discuss the relationship between statistical significance and psychological importance.

10. Define sampling distribution.

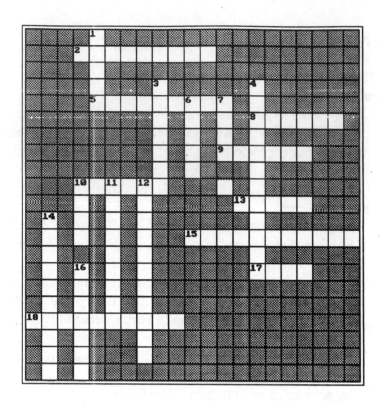

ACROSS

2. _____ distribution
5. bar graph
8. a lopsided curve
9. a symmetrical, bell-shaped curve
10. the midpoint of a distribution of scores
13. the pattern of distribution of scores
15. when a result is extremely unlikely to have occurred by chance, it is considered statistically _____
17. type of hypothesis that asserts that the independent variable in a study will have no effect on the dependent variable
18. type of score that indicates the percentage of people who scored at or below a given raw score

DOWN

1. a drawing that depicts numerical relationships
3. a line graph
4. frequency _____
6. calculated by subtracting the lowest score in a distribution from the highest score
7. the most common measure of central tendency
10. the most frequently occurring score in a distribution
11. standard _____
12. type of hypothesis, sometimes called the research hypothesis
14. the null or alternative _____
16. standard score

FLASH CARDS

Cut the following chart along the borders and test yourself with the resulting flash cards.

APP.1 FREQUENCY DISTRIBUTION	APP.2 MODE	APP.3 NORMAL CURVE
APP.4 GRAPH	APP.5 RANGE	APP.6 RIGHT-SKEWED DISTRIBUTION
APP.7 HISTOGRAM/BAR GRAPH	APP.8 STANDARD DEVIATION	APP.9 LEFT-SKEWED DISTRIBUTION
APP.10 FREQUENCY POLYGON/LINE GRAPH	APP.11 DEVIATION SCORE	APP.12 NULL HYPOTHESIS
APP.13 MEASURE OF CENTRAL TENDENCY	APP.14 PERCENTILE SCORE	APP.15 ALTERNATIVE HYPOTHESIS
APP.16 MEAN	APP.17 Z-SCORE (STANDARD SCORE)	APP.18 SAMPLING DISTRIBUTION
APP.19 MEDIAN	APP.20 NORMAL DISTRIBUTION	APP.21 STATISTICALLY SIGNIFICANT

APP.3 A symmetrical, bell-shaped frequency polygon representing a normal distribution.	APP.2 A measure of central tendency; the most frequently occurring score in a distribution.	APP.1 A summary of how frequently each score in a set occurred.
APP.6 A non-normal distribution of observations in which the "tail" of the curve is longer on the right; it is said to be positively skewed.	APP.5 A simple measure of variability, calculated by subtracting the lowest score in a distribution from the highest score.	APP.4 A drawing that depicts numerical relationships.
APP.9 A non-normal distribution of observations in which the "tail" of the curve is longer on the left; it is said to be negatively skewed.	APP.8 A commonly used measure of variability that indicates the average difference between scores in a distribution from their mean.	APP.7 A graph in which the heights (or lengths) of bars are proportional to the frequencies of individual scores or classes of scores in a distribution.
APP.12 An assertion that the independent variable in a study will have no effect on the dependent variable.	APP.11 The difference between each individual score in a distribution and the mean of that distribution.	APP.10 A graph showing a set of points obtained by plotting score values against score frequencies. Adjacent points are joined by straight lines.
APP.15 An assertion that the independent variable in a study will have a certain predictable effect on the dependent variable.	APP.14 A number that indicates the percentage of people who scored at or below a given raw score.	APP.13 A number intended to characterize an entire set of data.
APP.18 The theoretical distribution of an entire population that would occur if only chance were operating.	APP.17 A number that indicates how far a given raw score is above or below the mean, using the standard deviation of the distribution.	APP.16 A measure of central tendency; an average calculated by adding up all the scores in a set and dividing the sum by the number of quantities in the set.
APP.21 The term used to refer to a result that is extremely unlikely to have occurred by chance.	APP.20 A theoretical frequency distribution having certain special characteristics.	APP.19 A measure of central tendency; the value at the midpoint of a distribution of scores when the scores are ordered from highest to lowest.

PRACTICE TEST 1 - Multiple Choice

1. The first step in organizing raw data is to
   A. get a measure of the central tendency.
   B. establish the range.
   C. construct a frequency distribution.
   D. identify the standard deviation.

2. A "histogram" is the technical term that describes a
   A. bar graph.
   B. polygon.
   C. mean.
   D. line graph.

3. The most frequently occurring score in a distribution is called the
   A. mean.
   B. median.
   C. standard deviation.
   D. mode.

4. The mean, median and mode are
   A. measures of central tendency.
   B. measures of variability.
   C. characteristics of a normal distribution, but not a skewed distribution.
   D. characteristics of a skewed distribution, but not a normal distribution.

5. A measure of variability that indicates the average difference between scores in a distribution and their mean is called the
   A. range.
   B. standard deviation.
   C. mode.
   D. z-score.

6. A score that indicates how far a given score is from the mean is called a
   A. range.
   B. mode.
   C. standard deviation.
   D. z-score.

7. A lopsided distribution in which scores cluster at the high or low end of the distribution is referred to as
   A. normal.
   B. bimodal.
   C. skewed.
   D. standard.

8. What asserts that experimental manipulations have no effect?
   A. null hypothesis
   B. sampling distribution
   C. alternative hypothesis
   D. statistical significance

9. Results that are not attributable to chance are referred to as
   A. non-chance fluctuations.
   B. skewed.
   C. statistically significant.
   D. all of the above.

10. The theoretical distribution of the results of the entire population is called the
    A.   null hypothesis.   B.   sampling distribution.
    C.   statistical significance.   D.   random error.

PRACTICE TEST 2 - Multiple Choice

1. Dr. Starr gives 10-question quizzes in her psychology class. When she returns quizzes, she puts on the board how many people scored a 10, 9, 8, 7, 6, 5, 4, 3, 2 and 1. This is called a
   A. normal curve.
   B. frequency distribution.
   C. frequency polygon.
   D. histogram.

2. A histogram is to a polygon as
   A. a line is to a bar.
   B. null is to alternative.
   C. a bar is to a line.
   D. normal is to skewed.

3. Students in Dr. Friedlander's class got the following scores on their first test: 75, 77, 87, 63, 93, 77, 72, 80, 57, 68, 76. What is the mode?
   A. 77
   B. 75
   C. 36
   D. 76

4. What is the median in the distribution of scores in question 3?
   A. 77
   B. 75
   C. 36
   D. 76

5. What is the range in the distribution of scores in question 3?
   A. 77
   B. 36
   C. 30
   D. 76

6. Because the sum of the deviation scores is always zero, the standard deviation is based on
   A. the squared deviation scores.
   B. the mean of the deviation scores.
   C. the square root of the deviation scores.
   D. none of the above.

7. If the mean is 10, and the standard deviation is 2, a person with a raw score of 8 has a z-score of
   A. 8.
   B. -1.
   C. 1.
   D. 2.

8. A distribution in which there are many low scores and a small number of very high scores is referred to as
   A. normal.
   B. positively skewed.
   C. bimodal.
   D. negatively skewed.

509

9. If the null hypothesis is true, differences between experimental and control groups are due to
   A. standard deviations.
   B. skew.
   C. chance fluctuations.
   D. true differences.

10. Statistical significance
    A. suggests that a result would be highly improbable by chance alone.
    B. does not necessarily have anything to do with psychological importance.
    C. is a likely outcome with a large sample.
    D. incorporates all of the above

PRACTICE TEST 3 - Short Answer

1.   A _____ distribution shows how often each possible score occurs.

2.   In a frequency _____, each score is indicated by a dot placed on a horizontal axis at the appropriate height on the verticle axis.

3.   The _____ is calculated by adding up a set of scores and dividing by the number of scores in the set. The _____ is the score that occurs most often.

4.   The above terms are ways of characterizing an entire set of data in terms of a representative number. They are measures of _____ tendency.

5.   The _____ is the simplest measure of variability, while the standard _____ tells how much, on average, scores in a distribution differ from the _____ .

6.   When researchers don't want to work directly with raw scores, they can convert the scores to either _____ or to _____ .

7.   A _____ distribution has a symmetrical, bell-shaped form when plotted on a frequency polygon.

8.   When a distribution of scores is lopsided and the tail goes to the left, it is a _____ skew.

9.   The _____ hypothesis states the possibility that the experimental manipulations will have no effect on the subjects' behavior.

10.   If it is highly improbable that a result occurs by chance, it is said to be _____ significant.

PRACTICE TEST 4 - True/False

1. Frequency distributions are only used if there is a question about the data.

2. While graphs can be helpful, they can also be deceiving by masking or exaggerating differences.

3. Means are considered a very accurate way of characterizing a set of scores.

4. The median score is a more representative measure of central tendency in cases where extreme scores occur.

5. The range and standard deviation are measures of central tendency.

6. Small standard deviations signify that scores cluster near the mean and therefore the mean is representative.

7. A drawback to percentiles is that they do not tell how far apart people are in terms of raw scores. Z-scores preserve the relative spacing of the original raw scores.

8. A normal curve can be bell-shaped, or it can have a negative or positive skew.

9. The null hypothesis states that the average experimental group score will differ from the average control group score.

10. Psychologists accept a finding as statistically significant if the likelihood of its occurring by change is ten percent or less.

PRACTICE TEST 3 - Essay

1. Researchers organize and describe data in a variety of ways. Below, different statistical devices have been grouped together. Examine each grouping and describe the common purpose of the statistics within each.

    A.   Mean, median, mode
    B.   Range and standard deviation
    C.   Frequency distributions, bar graphs (histograms) and line graphs (frequency polygons)
    D.   Percentile scores and z-scores

2. Assume that the height of the male population is normally distributed with a mean of 70 inches and a standard deviation of 3 inches. Given such information, examine each of the statements below and decide whether it is justified or unjustified. Explain the basis for your answer.

    A.   The most frequently occurring male height is 70 inches.
    B.   The percentage of men above 70 inches is much higher than the percentage below this height.
    C.   If the height requirement for entering the police academy were set at 73 inches, less than half the male population would qualify.
    D.   A curve depicting the height of players in professional basketball would also be normally distributed.

3. Below are two inaccurate statements about hypothesis testing and statistical significance. Revise each statement so that it is accurate.

    A.   The null hypothesis is accepted whenever results are statistically significant.
    B.   Statistical significance is a measure of the relative strengths of experimental and control treatments.

ANSWER KEYS FOR ALL CHAPTERS

ANSWER KEYS FOR CHAPTER 1

ANSWER KEY - PRACTICE TEST 1 - MULTIPLE CHOICE

1. B (pp. 1-2)	2. B (p. 1)	3. A (p. 4)	4. D (pp. 6-11)
5. D (p. 14)	6. A (p. 15)	7. C (p. 16)	8. A (p. 18)
9. C (p. 18)	10. A (p. 18)	11. B (p. 19)	12. D (p. 18)
13. D (p. 18)	14. A (pp. 18-19)	15. D (pp. 19-20)	16. D (pp. 20-21)
17. B (p. 23)	18. A (p. 23)	19. C (p. 23)	20. C (p. 24)
21. D (p. 24)	22. A (p. 24)	23. D (p. 25)	24. B (p. 24)
25. D (p. 27)			

ANSWER KEY - PRACTICE TEST 2 - MULTIPLE CHOICE

1. D	2. D	3. B	4. B
5. A	6. D	7. D	8. A
9. D	10. A	11. C	12. B
13. A	14. D	15. A	16. A
17. C	18. C	19. A	20. C
21. D	22. A	23. C	24. C
25. A			

ANNOTATED ANSWER KEY - PRACTICE TEST 2

1. Answer D in correct. Psychology is defined as the scientific study of behavior and mental processes and how they are affected by an organism's physical state, mental state and the external environment. Answer A meets the definition of psychology because it is the scientific study of behavior. Answer B also meets the definition because it is the scientific study of emotions which is a mental process. Answer C meets the definition because it is the scientific study of behavior and environmental influences. Therefore answer D is correct answer since all of the above meet the definition of psychology.

2. Answer D is correct. Psychology is based on research evidence. Answer A is not correct because hearing something on T.V., regardless of how often, does not necessarily mean it is based on research evidence. Reading information in print (Answer B) does not necessarily mean the information is based on research evidence either. Calling oneself an expert does not make it so. Unless the information presented by the "expert" in Answer C is based on verifiable research evidence, the position may not represent psychological knowledge. Answer D is correct because only when information is supported by documented research, is it considered psychological knowledge.

3. Answer B is correct because the statements in the question are examples of popular ideas that have filtered into public consciousness, the media, and education even though they are not based on research evidence. In fact, the statements contained in answers A and C have been contradicted by research.

4. Answer B is an example of creative and constructive thinking which is an aspect of critical thinking. Answer A is a misinterpretation of critical thinking. Absurd claims that go against solid evidence is not evidence of critical thinking. Answer C is an example of unquestioning acceptance of assumptions. A willingness to question one's assumptions is considered one aspect of critical thinking. Being willing to tolerate uncertainty (Answer D) is another characteristic of critical thinking. An insistence for clear cut answers and an inability to tolerate uncertainty inhibits critical thinking.

5. Answer A is correct because beliefs must be supported by evidence to be taken seriously. Answers B and C are incorrect because students must learn to distinguish between personal preferences which need not be supported and positions that reflect more than opinion. Answer D is incorrect because providing evidence for an opinion is a difference process than defining terms.

6. Answer D is correct. Wundt established the first psychological laboratory. He was also the first person to announce that he intended to make psychology a science. He attempted to use objective and scientific methods to study psychological phenomenon.

7. Answer D is correct. Structuralism was an early brand of psychology that hoped to analyze sensations, images, and feelings into their most basic elements. Since that is what is being done in this study, Answer D is correct. Functionalism (Answer A) was an early school of thought that emphasized the function of behavior which was not emphasized in the study described in this question. Trained introspection (Answer C) was a research METHOD involving careful observation and analysis by specially trained people of their own mental experiences. While this study uses the method of introspection, that method is not one of the early schools of psychology. Behaviorism (Answer B) is a modern school that rejects the subject of this study: mental experiences.

516

8.	Answer A is correct because functionalism is interested in the causes and consequences of behavior, in this example your reason for participating in the study. Trained introspection (Answer C) was a research METHOD involving careful observation and analysis by specially trained people of their own mental experiences. The method of trained introspection is not one of the early schools of psychology. Behaviorism (Answer B) is a modern school and is interested only in observable and measurable events rather than the mind and consciousness. Structuralism (Answer D) was an early brand of psychology that hoped to analyze sensations, images, and feelings into their most basic elements.

9.	The correct answer is D which compares structuralism, which was the brand of psychology developed by Titchener to functionalism, the brand of psychology developed by James. Answer A compares an early research method to the founder of the method. Answer B is the opposite of the correct answer. Answer C compares a research method to functionalism, an early school of psychology.

10.	Answer A is the correct answer because the problem is discussed in terms of behaviors and environmental conditions that cause and maintain behaviors. Behaviorists study behaviors rather than mental processes and are interested in the effects of the environment. Unconscious inner conflicts, memories, and emotional traumas from early childhood (Answer B) reflect the psychoanalytic perspective. Social-cognitive learning theory, which is related to behaviorism, is reflected in Answer C. Social learning theory examines the role of mental processes in our behavior. This theory emphasizes thoughts, values, self-reflection and intentions. Answer D reflects the position of the sociocultural perspective which sees behavior within the broader social and cultural context.

11.	Answer C is correct. Social-cognitive learning theory combines the behavioral perspective with aspects of the cognitive perspective, not with aspects of the psychodymanic perspective (Answer A), the sociocultural perspective (Answer B), or evolutionary psychology (Answer D).

12. Answer B is correct because unconscious inner conflicts, memories, and emotional traumas from early childhood reflect the psychoanalytic perspective. Answer A is incorrect because the problem is discussed in terms of behaviors and environmental conditions that cause and maintain behaviors. Behaviorists focus on behaviors rather than mental processes and unconscious inner conflicts and memories are mental processes. Answer C reflects the social learning theory position, which is related to behaviorism. Social learning theory emphasizes thoughts, values, self-reflection and intentions as well as the notion of self-regulation. Answer D reflects the position of the sociocultural perspective which sees behavior within the broader social and cultural context.

13. Answer A is the correct answer because biological psychologists believe that all actions, feelings, and thoughts are associated with bodily events such as genes or biochemicals. Answer B is incorrect because to a humanist, depression would be explained by a failure to achieve one's full potential. Answer C is incorrect because behaviorists look to environmental conditions to understand depression. Answer D is incorrect because cognitive psychology looks to people's thoughts, perceptions, interpretations, beliefs, and problem solving abilities to understand depression.

14. Answer D is correct because cognitive psychology looks to people's thoughts, perceptions, interpretations, beliefs, and problem solving abilities to understand behavior. The statement suggests that it is not what happened at the party but rather the perception of those events that is significant. Answer A is incorrect because biological psychologists believe that all actions, feelings, and thoughts are associated with bodily events such as genes or biochemicals not perceptions of events. Answer B is incorrect because a humanist would not focus on an individual's interpretation of events but rather whether they are expressing themselves creatively and reaching their full potential. Answer C is incorrect because a sociocultural psychologist would not look to an individual's interpretations of events but rather to how the historical and social context shapes behaviors.

15. Answer C is correct because the approach taken in this quote to anorexia is not an individual approach but rather looks at the influence of the social context, in this case, society's attitudes about female beauty. Answer A is incorrect because humanism focuses on achievement of full potential and expression of creativity rather than on the social context of behavior. Answer B is incorrect because psychodynamic approaches focus on unconscious inner conflicts, memories, and emotional traumas from early childhood. Answer D is incorrect because the cognitive approach focuses on an individual's thoughts, perceptions, interpretations, beliefs, and problem solving abilities.

16. Answer A is correct because a humanist focuses on creative expression and the realization of full human potential. Answer B is incorrect because cognitive psychologists focus on an individual's thoughts, perceptions, interpretations, beliefs and problems solving abilities. Answer C could be correct because a feminist psychologist can also share beliefs with the other perspectives. Their focus, however, is on how social, economic, and political inequities affect gender relations and the behavior of the sexes. Since no mention is made of gender inequities, answer A is the better answer. Answer D is incorrect because creative expression and human potential are not the focus of the sociocultural perspective. The influence of the social and historical context on behavior is the focus of the sociocultural perspective.

17. Answer C is correct because feminist psychology focuses on gender bias in research. Answer A is incorrect because the focus of the humanist perspective is creative expression and human potential. Answer B is incorrect because cognitive psychology emphasizes thoughts, perceptions, interpretations, beliefs, and problem solving. Answer D is incorrect because sociocultural psychology studies the influence of social and historical context on behavior.

18. Answer C is correct because this is the only non-practice specialty listed among the answer options. Clinical (Answer A), counseling (Answer B), and school (Answer D) psychology all could fit the description in the question since they are all practice specialties.

19. Answer A is correct because basic psychology seeks knowledge for its own sake and whether rats can learn to press a bar for a reward has no direct application to life. Answers B, C and D are all examples of applied psychology which is concerned with the practical uses of knowledge.

20.   Answer C is correct because educational psychology studies principles that explain learning and searches for ways to improve learning in educational systems. Dr. Cassales is developing such a program. Answer A is incorrect because experimental psychologists conduct laboratory studies in learning, motivation, emotion, sensation and perception, physiology, human performance, and cognition. Dr. Cassales is developing a program and not conducting a study in a laboratory. Answer B is incorrect because developmental psychologists study how people change and grow over time, physically, mentally, and socially. Answer D is incorrect because school psychologists work in schools directly with parents, teachers, or students.

21.   Answer D is correct. Dr. Abee is a school psychologist because he is working directly with teachers, students and parents to enhance student's performance. Answer A is incorrect because experimental psychologists conduct laboratory studies in learning, motivation, emotion, sensation and perception, physiology, human performance, and cognition. Developmental psychologists (Answer B) study how people change and grow over time. Answer C is incorrect because educational psychologists study the principles that explain learning and search for ways to improve learning in educational systems rather than working directly with people.

22.   Answer A is correct because developmental psychologists study how people grow and change over time. Experimental psychologists (Answer B) study emotion, and psychometric psychologists design tests of mental abilities, aptitudes, interests (Answer D) and personality (Answer C).

23.   Answer C is correct. Clinical and counseling psychologists, psychiatrists, and psychoanalysts all have doctoral degrees. Only psychiatrists prescribe medication (Answer A). While all four professionals can conduct research and teach (Answer C) or work in psychiatric hospitals (Answer D), they do not necessarily do so.

24.   Answer C is correct. A psychiatrist is the only practitioner among the four answer options who currently may write a prescription for medication.

25.   Answer A is correct because specialized training and a period of psychoanalysis is required to be a psychoanalyst. Answers B and C are not correct because people with Ph.D. and master's degrees may become psychoanalysts, but not those with no college education. Psychoanalysts practice from the psychoanalytic perspective only which makes Answer D incorrect.

ANSWER KEY - PRACTICE TEST 3 - SHORT ANSWER

1. behavior and mental processes
2. empirical
3. critical thinking
4. any two of the following: ask questions, define your terms, examine the evidence, analyze assumptions and biases, avoid emotional reasoning, don't oversimplify, consider other interpretations, tolerate uncertainty
5. predict, modify
6. trained introspection
7. structuralism
8. conflicts and traumas from early childhood
9. psychodynamic
10. biological, learning, cognitive, sociocultural, psychodynamic
11. learning
12. free will
13. cognitive
14. social and cultural forces
15. social rules and roles, groups, authority and how each of us is affected by other people; cultural
16. feminist
17. basic; applied
18. industrial/occupational; educational
19. nonclinical
20. clinical psychology, counseling psychology, school psychology
21. developmental
22. license; doctorate
23. psychotherapist, psychoanalyst, psychiatrist
24. psychiatrists; psychotherapists
25. social workers, school counselors, marriage, family and child counselors

ANSWER KEY - PRACTICE TEST 4 - TRUE/FALSE

1. F	2. F	3. T	4. T	5. T
6. T	7. T	8. F	9. F	10. T
11. T	12. F	13. F	14. T	15. T
16. F	17. T	18. T	19. F	20. F
21. F	22. F	23. T	24. F	25. F

ANSWER KEY - PRACTICE TEST 5 - ESSAY

1   A.   This activity is an area of basic psychology because this research is not applying the measurement of intelligence for a particular use. This falls in the area of psychometrics, which is a nonclinical specialty.

        B.   The study of vision falls in the area of basic research, since the findings are not concerned with the practical uses of its findings. This research is conducted by experimental psychologists because they conduct laboratory studies of sensation as well as other areas. Experimental psychology is a nonclinical specialty.

        C.   Piaget's work is an example of basic psychology because the theory does not address practical uses of the knowledge. This activity falls in the area of developmental psychology because Piaget studied how people change and grow over time. It is a nonclinical area.

        D.   Studying work motivations falls in the basic psychology area because this project does not involve direct use or application of the findings. This type of research falls into the specialty area of industrial or organizational psychology, which studies behavior in the workplace. It is a nonclinical specialty.

        E.   Milgram's study represents basic psychology because there is no direct application of the findings. It falls under the nonclinical specialty area, social psychology. The study examines how the social context influences individuals.

        F.   Strupp's study is basic research because direct application for these findings is not part of the purpose of the study. It falls under the specialty of clinical psychology, which is interested in treating mental or emotional problems and is a clinical specialty area.

        G.   The study of children's self-esteem is applied research, since it was used to make changes in the school systems. This type of research falls under the specialty area of developmental psychology, since it deals with how people change and grow over time. Developmental psychology is a nonclinical specialty.

        H.   Using findings from career development research to assist students is an example of applied psychology. This activity falls into the specialty of counseling psychology, a clinical area, because it is dealing with problems of everyday life rather than with mental disorders.

2.   Learning theory or behaviorism would explore how Harold learned his behavior and how his environmental conditions encouraged his drug abuse. Specifically, behaviorists would be interested in the payoffs or rewards that result from the drug use. Social learning theorists might wonder if Harold had learned this behavior from observing or imitating others, such as peers or parents.

Psychologists from a psychodynamic perspective would understand Harold's drug abuse as a result of unconscious conflicts that remain unresolved from his early childhood. Harold is unaware of his true motivations because they are unconscious.

The biological perspective understands Harold's drug abuse as a direct result of addictive processes by which the body comes to crave and depend on drugs. If Harold were to attempt to discontinue his drug use, he would experience unpleasant bodily sensations related to withdrawal. Therefore, to avoid bodily withdrawal symptoms, his drug use is continued. Biological predispositions may be operating that may have made Harold more sensitive to drug exposure.

Cognitive psychologists would be interested in Harold's perception and reasoning about drug use. Are his ideas about drugs irrational or unreasonable? What does he tell himself about drug use or nonuse? For example, does he believe that he must use drugs to be accepted by his peers? Cognitive psychologists would be interested in whether Harold believes he has control of himself or whether he sees his drug use as a problem. Sociocultural psychologists would look to the attitude in the culture toward alcohol use. They would understand the role alcohol plays for people and how it is expected to be used. For example, attitudes and expectations for alcohol use are different in other countries where alcohol is used as a beverage at meals and is consumed at meal times by adolescents and sometimes children.

According to humanists, Harold's drug abuse represents a choice. He is freely choosing to use drugs and is equally free to choose not to do so. Humanists may inquire whether he believes it assists him in dealing with questions about reaching his full potential.

Feminist psychologists would be interested in gender differences in drug abuse. They would see Harold's drug use as a way of dealing with emotions that are compatible with the male gender role in this society. Since the expression of certain emotions is not considered masculine, they might speculate that drug use would be a way of dealing with "unmasculine" emotions.

3. A psychologist would use psychotherapy based on psychological theories to treat Juanita's depression. The psychologist would have formal training and would hold either a Ph.D., an Ed.D., or a Psy.D. A psychiatrist would be likely to prescribe medication for Juanita's depression. A psychiatrist is a medical doctor (M.D.) with a residency in psychiatry. A psychoanalyst would use psychoanalysis, which is a type of psychotherapy based on the work of Sigmund Freud. To practice psychoanalysis, specialized training at a recognized psychoanalytic institute is required. A psychotherapist would use psychotherapy. A psychotherapist may or may not have formal education in psychology or a related field.

CROSSWORD PUZZLE ANSWER KEY

ACROSS		DOWN	
1.	biological	2.	learning
4.	functionalism	3.	basic
6.	cognitive	5.	nonclinical
8.	school	7.	experimental
9.	psychology	10.	Wundt
12.	Freud	11.	humanist
14.	feminist	13.	applied
15.	practice		

ANSWER KEYS FOR CHAPTER 2

ANSWER KEY - PRACTICE TEST 1 - MULTIPLE CHOICE

1. B (p. 34)	2. A (pp. 34-36)	3. C (p. 34)	4. D (p. 34)
5. A (p. 35)	6. B (p. 38)	7. D (pp. 38-39)	8. D (pp. 38-39)
9. C (pp. 39-40)	10. A (p. 41)	11. B (p. 42)	12. D (p. 43)
13. B (p. 44-46)	14. B (p. 45)	15. C (p. 45)	16. B (p. 48)
17. A (p. 48)	18. D (p. 48)	19. B (p. 50)	20. C (p. 51)
21. A (pp. 54)	22. D (pp. 54-55)	23. A (p. 57)	24. B (pp. 57-58)
25. D (p. 59)			

ANSWER KEY - PRACTICE TEST 2 - MULTIPLE CHOICE

1. A	2. C	3. C	4. A
5. C	6. C	7. B	8. C
9. A	10. C	11. C	12. A
13. C	14. B	15. A	16. D
17. C	18. B	19. A	20. C
21. C	22. C	23. C	24. D
25. A			

ANNOTATED ANSWER KEY - PRACTICE TEST 2

1. Answer A is correct. The principle of falsifiability requires that a scientist must state an idea in such a way that it can be refuted, or disproved by counterevidence. Answer A describes a situation in which lack of evidence for a phenomenon is said to be predictable and therefore, does not disprove it. Answer B is an example of a nonrepresentative sample. Answer C describes volunteer bias and Answer D demonstrates the problem of experimenter effects.

2. Answer C is correct since Frank is basing his beliefs on personal accounts and not empirical evidence. Answers A, B, and D refer to other aspects of research.

3. Answer C is correct. Operational definitions involve defining terminology in a way that can be observed and measured. Depression test scores, time spent sleeping and food intake can all be objectively observed and measured and therefore, could be used as operational definitions of depression. They are not statements of hypotheses or theories, nor are they independent variables in a study.

4. Answer A is correct because it describes an organized system of assumptions and principles to explain personality so it fits the definition of a theory. Answers B, C, and D are all examples of hypotheses, statements that attempt to predict a set of phenomena.

5. Answer C is correct. Danielle conducted this study by making observations of behavior as it occurs in the natural environment, which is the description of a naturalistic observation. The study does not follow the procedures of an experiment, case study or survey.

6. Answer C is the correct answer to this question. While answers A, B and D are all potential problems with surveys, they are not the problem with this survey. The problem in this study is that the subjects who attend church services may not represent the general population.

7. Answer B is correct. Validity refers to whether a test measures what it was designed to measure, or how accurately it measures a particular characteristic. Reliability refers to consistency of scores from one time to another. Answer A is backwards, Answer C refers to two different types of validity and Answer D refers to types of tests.

8. Answer C is correct. Repeating the same test on two separate occasions is the definition of test-retest reliability. Answer D would involve taking a different form of the same test and Answers A and B refer to the validity of a test or whether it measures what it was designed to measure.

9. Answer A is an example of a positive correlation since decreases (in this case) in one variable are associated with decreases in the other or increases in one variable are associated with increases in the other. Answers B and C are examples of a negative correlation. Answer D is an example of a zero correlation.

10. Answer C is correct. This is an example of a negative correlation because increases in one variable (age) are associated with decreases in the other (absences). Answer A is incorrect because positive correlations describe a relationship in which increases (or decreases) in one variable are associated with increases (or decreases) in the other. Answer D occurs when there is no relationship between the variables. Answer B is another type of research method.

11. Answer C is correct because correlations cannot establish causation so we can only say that we know that exercise and depression are related. This makes Answers A and B incorrect answers. Answer D implies that a third variable causes both.

12. Answer A is correct. The independent variable is the variable which is manipulated by the experimenter and in this example, the experimenter assigns the teaching method for each group of subjects. Answer B is an operational definition of the dependent variable. Answer D is the experimenter. Answer C refers to groups not variables.

13. Answer C is correct because the group that receives some amount of the independent variable (the new teaching method) is the experimental group. The group being taught by the old method is the control group (Answer A). The independent variable is the teaching method.

14. Answer B is correct because a single-blind study is one in which the subjects do not know if they are in an experimental or control group. Answer A refers to a category of studies. A double-blind study is one in which neither subjects nor the experimenter are aware of whether subjects are in the experimental or control group. Answer D is a type of descriptive study.

15. Answer A is correct because random assignment to groups balances individual differences among subjects in the two groups. Selecting each subject individually (Answer C) could lead to possible biases in selection and difficulty obtaining subjects. Answer D does not insure that subjects are equal between the two groups and, in fact, can lead to volunteer bias. Answer B would not effect subject characteristics.

16. Answer D is correct. Single and double blind studies control for the effects of subject and experimenter expectations on outcomes. It is not the purpose of these procedures to control the effect of volunteer subjects (Answer A), to use a placebo (Answer C), nor to match subjects in the experimental and control groups (Answer B).

17. The correct answer is Answer C. To find the mean, add all scores and divide by 8. The result is 80.

18. Answer B is correct. A standard deviation tells us how clustered or spread out the individual scores are around the mean. The more spread out the individual scores are, the less "typical" the mean is. Answer A is incorrect because inferential statistics are used to tell us whether the results are statistically significant and standard deviation is a descriptive statistic. Answers C and D are incorrect because they refer to other descriptive statistics that are not discussed in this chapter.

19. The correct answer is Answer A. The mean score of the experimental teaching method is 3 points higher than the mean score of the control group. It is necessary to determine how likely it is that a difference of 3 points might have happened by chance alone which is done by calculating statistical significance (Answer A). Meta-analysis (Answer B) combines the results of different studies and would not apply to this example. Statistical significance may not be related to real-world importance (Answer C) and longitudinal studies (Answer D) are studies conducted over the life span.

20. Answer C is correct because statistical significance is calculated using inferential statistics. Descriptive statistics (mean, range, and variance) do not apply to statistical significance. Meta-analyses (Answer B) combine the results of different studies and cross-sectional analyses (Answer D) compare different age groups at a given time.

21. Answer C is correct because longitudinal research follows subjects over time and periodically assesses them. Cross-sectional research (Answer A) compares different age groups at a given time. Case studies (Answer B) examine one individual in great detail and naturalistic studies (Answer D) examine behavior in the natural environment.

22. Answer C is correct. Meta-analyses combine data from many different studies. Answer A refers to a correlation. Answer B refers to experimentation and Answer D refers to longitudinal research.

23. Answer C is correct because it violates the APA Code of Ethics which says subjects must participate voluntarily. All the other answers meet the Code of Ethics.

24. Answer D is correct. All answers are possible reasons for using animals in research.

25. Answer A is correct because the APA's ethical guidelines require researchers to show that any deceptive procedures are justified by a study's potential value, to consider alternative procedures, and to thoroughly debrief participants about the true purpose of the study (which makes Answer C incorrect). The existence of ethical guidelines for the use of deception makes Answer B incorrect. Answer D is incorrect because researchers must do more than simply show that no harm will come to subjects in order to use deception.

ANSWER KEY - PRACTICE TEST 3 - SHORT ANSWER

1. unfounded belief
2. hypothesis
3. operational
4. principle of falsifiability
5. replicated
6. descriptive
7. case study
8. naturalistic observational studies
9. objective; projective
10. norms
11. reliability
12. validity
13. criterion validity
14. representative
15. volunteer
16. correlation; variables
17. positively; a causal relationship
18. experimental method
19. independent; dependent
20. experimental; control
21. placebo; expectations
22. single
23. descriptive
24. significant
25. cross-sectional; longitudinal

ANSWER KEY - PRACTICE TEST 4 - TRUE/FALSE

1. F	2. F	3. T	4. F	5. T
6. F	7. F	8. T	9. T	10. F
11. T	12. T	13. F	14. T	15. F
16. T	17. F	18. F	19. T	20. F
21. F	22. F	23. F	24. F	25. F

ANSWER KEY - PRACTICE TEST 5 - ESSAY

1   A.   Survey. Adolescents constitute a large population and the information sought should be accessible through questionnaires or interviews. Care is needed to construct a sample that is representative of the population under consideration.

        B.   Psychological tests. The goal is to measure psychological qualities within an individual. Other methods (e.g., case history, naturalistic observation) might be employed, but they are more time-consuming and do not offer the degree of standardization, reliability and validity found in a well-constructed test.

        C.   Experiment. Cause-and-effect information is being sought. In science this information is obtained through experiments in which the proposed causal variable is manipulated under controlled conditions.

        D.   Correlation. This technique is used to determine if and how strongly two variables are related. Establishing that a correlation exists, however, does not address the problem of why two things are related.

        E.   Naturalistic observation. A description of behavior as it occurs in a real-life situation is being sought. Making the observations without arousing suspicion in subjects could be problematic.

        F.   Case study. Making this determination requires in-depth information about the way a variety of psychological factors - expectation, values, motives, past experiences, and so forth - blend together within the person. This kind of information is unique to the person under consideration and could not be assessed through standardized tests.

        G.   Laboratory observation. The goal is to identify what the parents are doing that may be contributing to the child's problems and help them to parent differently. To ascertain what is currently going on in the family, observing them interact in the laboratory would be the best way to actually see what is occurring. Information could be collected with an interview or questionnaire, but parents may not be aware of what they are doing.

2   A.   Hypothesis: Caffeine improves studying
Independent variable and its operational definition: caffeine; ounces
Dependent variable and its operational definition: studying; test score
Experimental condition: group receiving caffeine
Control group: group receiving decaffeinated beverage

B. Hypothesis: Heavy metal music increases aggression
Independent variable and its operational definition: music; jazz, classical, heavy metal
Dependent variable and its operational definition: aggression; amount of time spent punching bag
Experimental condition: groups exposed to jazz, classical and heavy metal music
Control group: group exposed to white noise machine

C. Hypothesis: Exercise increases relaxation
Independent variable and its operational definition: exercise; aerobics, number of sit-ups and push-ups
Dependent variable and its operational definition: relaxation; heart rate, muscle tension, respiration, blood pressure
Experimental condition: groups engaging in aerobics, sit-ups and push-ups
Control group: group having supervised study session

3   A. Positive   B. Negative
     C. Negative   D. Positive
     E. Zero   F. Negative
     G. Negative   H. Positive
     I. Negative   J. Zero

4   A. Unethical. Requiring research participation for a course, without providing an alternate way of satisfying the course requirement, violates the principle of voluntary consent.
     B. Unethical. Not only should subjects be free to withdraw at any time, but they should also be informed of this right before they begin to participate.
     C. Ethical. Although it is controversial, outright deception has not been ruled out by the American Psychological Association's guidelines.
     D. Ethical. Under the American Psychological Association's guidelines, the use of animals is acceptable in research that reduces human suffering and promotes human welfare.
     E. Ethical. The investigator is obligated to protect subjects from physical and mental discomfort by using both voluntary and informed consent.

CROSSWORD PUZZLE ANSWER KEY

ACROSS		DOWN	
1.	theory	2.	reliability
4.	independent	3.	mean
7.	survey	5.	naturalistic
8.	methodology	6.	deception
9.	validity	11.	experiment
10.	negative	12.	placebo
13.	control	15.	norms
14.	variance	16.	range
17.	correlation		
18.	skepticism		

ANSWER KEYS FOR CHAPTER 3

ANSWER KEY - PRACTICE TEST 1 - MULTIPLE CHOICE

1. C (p. 65)	2. B (pp. 68;77)	3. C (p. 68)	4. D (p. 66)
5. A (p. 66)	6. C (p. 66)	7. C (p. 66)	8. A (p. 66)
9. B (pp. 66-67)	10. D (p. 68)	11. B (p. 66)	12. A (p. 68)
13. B (p. 68)	14. C (p. 73)	15. D (p. 73)	16. D (p. 74)
17. B (p. 77)	18. C (p. 77)	19. D (p. 79)	20. A (p. 81)
21. A (pp. 82-83)	22. A (pp. 84-85)	23. B (p. 90)	24. D (pp. 90-92)
25. D (pp. 92-93)			

ANSWER KEY - PRACTICE TEST 2 - MULTIPLE CHOICE

1. B	2. C	3. A	4. C
5. B	6. D	7. A	8. B
9. A	10. D	11. C	12. C
13. A	14. B	15. B	16. A
17. B	18. A	19. C	20. D
21. B	22. B	23. C	24. D
25. C			

ANNOTATED ANSWER KEY - PRACTICE TEST 2

1. Answer B is correct. Behavior geneticists (Answer A) study the contribution of heredity to individual differences, while evolutionary psychologists emphasize the evolutionary mechanisms in common behaviors like language. Sociobiologists (Answer D) examine the role of evolution in social behaviors like mating and empiricists (Answer C) look to the role of learning and experience in the acquisition of behaviors.

2. Answer C is correct and Answers A and B are incorrect because like behavioral geneticists and evolutionary psychologists, the nature position focuses on genes and inborn characteristics. The nurture position focuses on learning and experience.

3. Answer A is correct. Answer B is incorrect because genes are located on chromosomes, they are not composed of them. Answer C is incorrect because chromosomes are not the basic unit of heredity and Answer D is incorrect because genes and chromosomes are not housed in DNA.

4. Answer C correctly describes that DNA affects characteristics of the organism indirectly by affecting the synthesis of proteins. Therefore, Answers A, B and D are incorrect.

5. Answer B is correct. Though the simplest type of inheritance is the result of a single pair of genes, most human traits depend on more than one pair of genes. This makes Answer A incorrect and Answer B correct. Genes cannot be located directly through a microscope (Answer C) nor is it necessary or possible the map the entire human genome (Answer D).

6. Answer D is correct since all of the processes described in the other answers contribute to genetic variations.

7. Answer A is correct because the question is the definition of natural selection. Answer C, dominant genes, refers to the status of an individual gene in a gene pair and not to a change in the gene frequency in a population over generations. Evolution (Answer B) refers to the fact that gene frequencies change in populations over generations but, unlike the question, it does not explain why such changes occur. Heritability (Answer D) is an estimate of the proportion of the variance of a trait within a group.

8. Answer B is correct. The guiding assumption of evolutionary psychology is that the human mind evolved as a collection of specialized "modules" to handle specific survival problems. Instincts (Answer A) refer to simple reflexive behaviors. Answer C refers to spontaneous changes in a gene and Answer D refers to a mental process for which there might be a mental module according to evolutionary psychologists.

9. Answer A is correct because the characteristics described in the question reflect behaviors common to humans and therefore, evolutionary psychologists believe they reflect our evolutionary history. Evolutionary psychologists do not believe that these behaviors are learned (Answer B). Social Darwinism (Answer C) suggests that the social order is influenced by evolution. Evolutionary psychologists believe that evolution helps explain behavioral similarities, therefore Answer D is incorrect.

10. Answer D is correct because deep structure refers to the meaning of a sentence. Since both sentences have the same meaning, they have the same deep structure. Surface structure refers to the way a sentence is actually spoken or written. These sentences have different surface structures. This makes all other answers incorrect.

11. Answer C is correct. That children in different cultures learning different languages go through similar stages of language development is one of the arguments that supports the position that the brain contains a language acquisition device. This fact argues against Answer A which is that language is learned (Answer A). That children all make errors adults would not make argues against Answer D, the idea that language is a result of imitation. Different languages do not have similar syntax making Answer B incorrect.

12. Answer C is correct because according to sociobiologists, male promiscuity and female selectivity are adaptive and have evolutionary origins. While they conform to stereotypes, sociobiology has suggested that the stereotypes have an evolutionary basis (Answer A). Sociobiologists reject the idea that these behaviors are learned and believe that they are inborn (Answer B). There is disagreement about whether these behaviors are not common to all humans (Answer D).

13. Answer A is correct. Attributing the same motives to animal behavior and human behavior is one of the criticisms of the evolutionary approach to sex differences. The evolutionary approach does look to animal behavior for evidence of an evolutionary basis to a behavior, so Answer B incorrect. Answer C is incorrect because behavior geneticists are interested in individual differences not similarities in human behavior. The quote counters an position that attempts to explain human similarities. Answer D is incorrect because natural selection refers to the process by which traits become more common in a population and that is not what the quote is addressing.

14. Answer B is correct because heritability accounts for a proportion of the variance in a trait within a group. Answer A is incorrect because it compares two groups. Answer C is incorrect because it attempts to explain an individual's inheritance which heritability cannot do. Answer D is incorrect because heritability does not look for specific genes.

15. Answer B is correct because even highly heritable traits can be influenced by the environment. Height, which is highly heritable, can be influenced by diet, an environmental factor. Answers A and C are incorrect because heritability cannot make statements about an individual and finally Answer D is incorrect because most human abilities are affected by more than one pair of genes.

16. Answer A is correct because monozygotic (identical) twins reared apart share genes but not an environment. The studies described in Answers B, C and D would not be able to separate the influence of environment from heredity because all these twins share environments as well as genes.

17. Answer B is correct. Set point theory can partially account for the relationship between food intake and weight. According to set point theory, Dr. Cannon, not his brother, would have a faster metabolic rate and fewer fat cells (Answers C and D).

18. Answer A is correct. A set point, like a thermostat, sets a level that the organism tries to maintain by controlling the rate of release of energy. The set point influences the basal metabolic rate, which is the rate at which the body burns calories for energy. A thermostat is a set temperature that influences the rate at which a furnace generates energy to maintain a temperature. The terms in Answers B, C, and D all have relationships to one another but they are not analogous to the relationships of the terms in the root of the question.

19. Answer C is correct and Answer A is incorrect because although intelligence is, in part, heritable, environmental factors can affect intelligence. Although this is true, heritability provides information about the characteristic in a group, not an individual. Answer B is incorrect since intelligence is partly heritable. Answer D is incorrect because some things are known about the heritability of intelligence.

20. Answer D is correct because all of the above environmental influences can affect IQ.

21. Answer B is correct. This study refutes genetic theories explaining black-white IQ differences because when the environmental circumstances were similar, IQ differences were absent. This eliminates Answer A. Answer C is incorrect because there have not been methodological criticisms of this study. Answer D is also incorrect because no differences were found between black and white subjects.

22. Answer B is correct because the comparison of two groups in different environments is analogous to the comparison of IQ's of blacks and whites, two groups who, on average, live in different environments. Answers A and C compare people within the same group.

23. Answer C is correct because behavior geneticists study the genetic bases of individual differences in behavior and personality such as those described in this answer. Answers A and B, and therefore D, are incorrect because they are studying similarities among people.

24. Answer D is correct. This statement demonstrates that even highly heritable traits can be modified by the environment. IQ scores are fairly reliable so Answer A is incorrect. This does not demonstrate that IQ is primarily influenced by the environment nor does it address whether IQ can be predicted.

25. Answer C is correct. Current thinking about nature and nurture is that they interact to produce a mixture of qualities. It is not thought that some characteristics are shaped only by heredity and others by the environment (Answer A). It is not known that we will find genetic explanations for most behaviors (Answer B). We do have some ideas about the relative contributions of environment and heredity on certain traits which makes Answer D incorrect.

ANSWER KEY - PRACTICE TEST 3 - SHORT ANSWER

1. Genes; chromosomes
2. genome
3. linkage
4. evolutionary
5. evolution
6. mutate
7. natural selection
8. modules
9. language; mating
10. rules; elements
11. surface; deep
12. Chomsky; acquisition
13. similar stages
14. critical period
15. sociobiologists
16. analogy; commonalities
17. stereotypes
18. heritability
19. individuals
20. identical (monozygotic); fraternal (dizygotic)
21. setpoint
22. diet; exercise
23. .50; .60 -.80
24. group
25. prenatal care; malnutrition or exposure to toxins or large family size or stressful family circumstances

ANSWER KEY - PRACTICE TEST 4 - TRUE/FALSE

1. T	2. F	3. F	4. T	5. T
6. F	7. F	8. F	9. T	10. T
11. T	12. F	13. T	14. T	15. F
16. F	17. F	18. T	19. F	20. T
21. F	22. T	23. T	24. T	25. T

ANSWER KEY - PRACTICE TEST 5 - ESSAY

1   A.   The basic elements of DNA within the genes influence protein synthesis in the body by specifying the sequence of amino acids, which are the building blocks of the proteins. The sequence of amino acids are affected by the arrangement of the basic elements, which comprises a chemical code. Proteins then go on to affect virtually all structural and biochemical characteristics of the organism. Genes for alcoholism might influence the basic elements of DNA or their arrangement, which then go on to influence the amino acids, the proteins and the structures or biochemistry of the body.

        B.   This statement misinterprets heritability estimates. Heritability estimates do <u>NOT</u> apply to individuals, only to variations within a group. No one can determine the impact of heredity on any particular individual's trait. For one person, genes may make a tremendous difference; for another, the environment may be more important. This statement ignores the fact that even highly heritable traits can be modified by the environment. This statement ignores environmental influences.

        C.   One might use a linkage study, which would examine large families in which alcoholism is common.

2   A.   The feeling of disgust may have been useful in warding off contamination from disease and contagion.

        B.   Intuition may have allowed people to anticipate others' behaviors based on their beliefs and desires and thereby prepare for problems.

        C.   Self-concept may have been useful in knowing one's value to others.

        D.   Feelings of kinship may have promoted protection and help to one's kin, thereby insuring their survival.

        E.   Male promiscuity has the effect of increasing the offspring of any individual male, thereby continuing his genes.

        F.   Female selectivity increases the chances of conceiving with the best genes.

3. Until the middle of this century, views about language acquisition suggested that language is learned (not inborn) bit by bit and that children learn to speak by imitating adults and paying attention when adults correct their mistakes. Chomsky stated that language was too complex to learn in this way. He said that children learn not only which sounds form words, but can apply the rules of syntax and discern underlying meaning. He said that the capacity for language is inborn and that the brain has a language acquisition device, or a "mental module" that allows children to develop language if they are exposed to an adequate sampling of speech. According to Chomsky, human beings are designed to use language. The following support his position:
   1. Children everywhere seem to go through similar stages of linguistic development.
   2. Children combine words in ways that adults never would, and so could not simply be imitating.
   3. Adults do not consistently correct their children's syntax.
   4. Even children who are profoundly retarded acquire language.

4 A. The study would use pairs of identical twins reared apart. IQ tests would be given to both members of the pairs and the following comparisons would be made:
      1. Scores of both members of the pairs of identical twins
      2. Scores of identical twins reared together
      3. Scores of siblings reared apart
      4. Scores of siblings reared together
      5. Scores of unrelated people

   The conclusions would depend on the results of these comparisons. Similarity of IQ scores based on genetic similarity, regardless of shared environment, would be supportive evidence for heritability estimates. Cautionary statements would include:
      1. Heritable does not mean the same thing as genetic.
      2. Heritability applies only to a particular group living in a particular environment, and estimates may differ for different groups.
      3. Heritability estimates do not apply to individuals, only to variations within a group.
      4. Even highly heritable traits can be modified by the environment.

B. The following recommendations would be made:
1. Develop a prenatal care program for mothers-to-be that involves education about drug use, nutrition, health, environmental pollutants
2. Nutrition program for young children
3. Assistance related to exposure to toxins
4. Information on the importance of mental stimulation
5. Family therapy and support to reduce stressful family circumstances
6. Training in parent-child interactions

CROSSWORD PUZZLE KEY

ACROSS

1. psycholinguistics
5. Chomsky
8. genome
10. nutrition
12. Darwin
15. language
17. evolution
18. monozygotic
19. intelligence

DOWN

2. syntax
3. linkage
4. toxins
6. heritability
7. deep
9. mutate
11. chromosomes
13. dizygotic
14. genes
16. mating

ANSWER KEYS FOR CHAPTER 4

ANSWER KEY - PRACTICE TEST 1 - MULTIPLE CHOICE

1. D (p. 100)   2. B (p. 101)   3. D (pp. 101-102)   4. A (p. 101)
5. C (p. 102)   6. C (p. 101)   7. C (p. 102)   8. D (pp.103-104)
9. A (p. 105)   10. B (p. 105)   11. A (p. 105)   12. C (pp. 107-108)
13. B (pp. 107-108) 14. B (pp. 108-109) 15. D (p. 110)   16. C (p. 111)
17. A (p. 111)   18. B (p. 114)   19. D (p. 119)   20. A (pp. 120-121)
21. B (p. 120)   22. A (p. 127)   23. C (p. 116)   24. D (p. 132)
25. B (pp. 124-127)

ANSWER KEY - PRACTICE TEST 2 - MULTIPLE CHOICE

1. A   2. C   3. B   4. D
5. B   6. A   7. B   8. A
9. B   10. C   11. D   12. B
13. D   14. B   15. D   16. A
17. C   18. D   19. B   20. D
21. D   22. B   23. A   24. B
25. B

ANNOTATED ANSWER KEY - PRACTICE TEST 2

1. Answer A is correct. Information from the senses comes into the brain and spinal cord (central nervous system) to be received, processed, interpreted, and stored. Once processed and interpreted the brain and spinal cord send messages to the muscles, glands, and internal organs. The peripheral nervous system carries the input from the rest of the body to and from the brain and spinal cord. Answer D is incorrect because it is backwards. The autonomic nervous system (Answer B), the sympathetic and parasympathetic nervous systems (Answer C) are all involved primarily with the organs.

2. Answer C is correct. Nerves carrying messages to and from the sense organs are called sensory nerves while nerves carrying messages to the muscles, glands, and organs are called motor nerves. Answer A is incorrect because nerves are not voluntary and involuntary. Answer B is backwards and Answer D refers to nervous systems.

3. Answer B is correct since the somatic nervous system carries information from the senses (sights and sounds) to the central nervous system. Answers A and C are incorrect because they do not carry sensory messages to the brain, but rather they carry messages from the brain to the muscles, glands, and organs. Answer D is incorrect because it does not carry messages to the brain since the brain is part of that nervous system.

4. Answer D is correct. Answers A and C describe voluntary movements which are a function of the somatic nervous system. Answer B involves activation of the organs which is a function of the autonomic nervous system.

5. Answer B is correct. Biofeedback uses monitoring devices to track bodily processes and deliver a signal whenever a person makes the desired response. PET scans (Answer A) and EEGs (Answer D) are both methods for studying the brain. Phrenology (Answer C) was an early theory about how personality is encoded on the brain.

6. Answer A is correct. The sympathetic nervous system is involved with arousal responses and the parasympathetic nervous system is active during relaxation. The relationship between autonomic and somatic nervous systems (Answers B and D) is not analogous. Answer C is incorrect because the activities of both the sympathetic and parasympathetic nervous systems are involuntary.

7. Answer B is correct. A neural impulse begins with the dendrites, which receive information from the previous neuron. The neural information then goes to the cell body which passes it along to the axon which ends in the axon terminals. All other answers include incorrect information about the sequence or structures involved.

8. Answer A is correct. Dendrites receive information, therefore they are like catchers. Since axons send information, they are like batters. Cell bodies (Answer B) pass the information along within the neuron to the axon and glial cells (Answer D) are cells which hold neurons in place. Answer C is backwards.

9. Answer B is correct. An action potential is a neural impulse which occurs when a wave of electrical voltage travels along the axon. This means the neuron has fired before it reaches the tip of the axon terminal, therefore Answer A incorrect. Answer B is correct because when the action potential reaches the tip, neurotransmitters are released into the synapse from the vesicles held in the end bulb. They then cross the cleft and lock into receptor sites on post-synaptic neurons. Answer C is incorrect because the electrical current occurs only within a neuron and ends with the release of neurotransmitters into the synapse. Answer D is incorrect because synaptic end bulbs do not lock into post-synaptic dendrites, neurotransmitters do.

10. Answer C is correct. Neurotransmitters are involved in all the conditions described. Hormones (Answer A and D) have dozens of jobs, from promoting growth to aiding digestion and regulating metabolism. Endorphins (Answer B) are involved in pain and pleasure.

11. Answer D is correct because all of the chemicals listed are neurotransmitters. Adrenal hormones (Answer A) include cortisol, epinephrine, and norepinephrine. Sex hormones (Answer C) include androgens, estrogen, and progesterone. Endorphins (Answer B) are neuromodulators.

12. Answer B is correct. Endorphins decrease pain and increase pleasure. Testosterone (Answer A) and androgen (Answer C) are masculinizing sex hormones and insulin (Answer D) is a hormone affecting appetite and the body's use of glucose.

13. Answer D is correct because all the chemicals listed are hormones. None are neurotransmitters (Answer A), only androgen and estrogen are sex hormones (Answer B), and only melatonin is an adrenal hormone (Answer C).

14. Answer B is correct. Electroencephalograms (EEG) record brain wave patterns and positron-emission tomography (PET scans) allow us to find out which parts of the brain are active during specific activities. Magnetic resonance imaging utilizes magnetic fields and radio frequencies. It is used for studying the brain and diagnosing disease (Answer A and D). Needle electrodes can be used to record and stimulate electrical activity (Answer C).

15. Answer D is correct. The brain stem is responsible for vital functions while the cerebrum is involved in higher forms of thinking. Answer C is incorrect because it is backwards. Answers A and B are incorrect because the limbic system, not the brain stem nor the cerebrum are involved in emotions and the brain stem and not the cerebrum is involved in vital functions.

16. Answer A is correct. Being "brain dead" refers to the loss of the higher functions of the cortex. The person is able to remain alive because the medulla, responsible for breathing and heart rate, must be undamaged. The thalamus receives and directs sensory input (Answer C), the pons (Answer B) is involved in sleeping, waking, and dreaming and the hypothalamus (Answer D) is involved in drives like hunger and thirst.

17. Answer B is correct. The cerebellum is involved in balance and muscle coordination making movement smooth and precise. The thalamus (Answer B) receives and directs sensory messages, the amygdala (Answer A) evaluates sensory information and the pons (Answer D) is involved in sleeping, waking, and dreaming.

18.   Answer D is correct. The auditory cortex is involved in hearing. The cerebellum (Answer A) is involved in balance and muscle coordination. The hippocampus (Answer C) is involved in memory and the limbic system (Answer B) has many structures that are involved in emotions.

19.   Answer B is correct. The hippocampus has been called "the gateway to memory". The thalamus (Answer C) receives and directs sensory messages, the hypothalamus (Answer A) is involved in drives like hunger and thirst and the parietal lobe (Answer D) of the cortex contains the somatosensory cortex which receives information about pressure, pain, touch, and temperature from all over the body.

20.   Answer D is correct. Broca's area (Answer A) is involved in speech production. It is located in the frontal lobe (Answer C) in the left hemisphere (Answer B).

21.   Answer D is correct. Fight or flight responses are controlled by the autonomic nervous system (Answer A). In any arousal response the pituitary gland is also involved (Answer C) as is the limbic system (Answer B) which deals with emotions like fear.

22.   Answer B is correct. The left hemisphere is more active in logical, symbolic, and sequential tasks like math problems. The right hemisphere is more active in visual-spatial tasks like map reading. Answer A is backwards. Answers C and D list parts of the brain less directly involved in these activities.

23.   Answer A is correct because modern brain scientists believe that what we call "mind" can be explained in physical terms as a product of the cerebral cortex. They do not take the positions described in Answers B, C, and D.

24.   Answer B is correct. The central controversy about sex differences in the brain is whether there are anatomical differences and, if there are, what do they mean. There have been no suggestions that males brains are more localized (Answer A) or that female brains have greater capacity (Answer C).

25.   Answer B is correct. If stimulation causes new synaptic connections to be formed then the brain continues to change in response to the environment. It suggests no changes in the thinking about lateralization (Answer A), nor whether brain functions are localized or distributed (Answer D). This information does not provide evidence for the idea that new brain cells are continually being developed (Answer C).

ANSWER KEY - PRACTICE TEST 3 - SHORT ANSWER

1.   central; peripheral
2.   somatic; autonomic
3.   sympathetic; parasympathetic
4.   cell body
5.   dendrites; axon
6.   myelin sheath
7.   synapse
8.   axon terminal; neurotransmitters
9.   all or none
10. Endorphins; neurotransmitters
11. endocrine
12. norepinephrine and serotonin; acetylcholine
13. androgens; estrogen; progesterone
14. electroencephalogram
15. magnetic resonance imaging
16. reticular activating
17. pons; medulla; cerebellum
18. thalamus
19. hypothalamus
20. limbic
21. hippocampus
22. occipital; parietal; temporal; frontal
23. corpus callosum
24. Wernicke's; temporal; Broca's; frontal
25. behavior

ANSWER KEY - PRACTICE TEST 4 - TRUE/FALSE

1. F	2. F	3. T	4. T	5. T
6. F	7. F	8. F	9. T	10. F
11. T	12. F	13. F	14. F	15. T
16. T	17. F	18. T	19. T	20. F
21. T	22. F	23. F	24. F	25. T

ANSWER KEY - PRACTICE TEST 5 - ESSAY

1   A.   The dendrites of neurons in the ear are stimulated and the message is sent to the cell body, which causes an inflow of sodium ions and an outflow of potassium ions that result in a wave of electrical voltage travelling down the axon. At the end of the axon, synaptic vesicles held in the synaptic end bulb release neurotransmitters, which cross the synaptic cleft and lock into receptor sites on the next neuron.

        B.   The sound causes neurons in the ear to fire, going via sensory neurons to the thalamus, which directs the message to the auditory cortex in the temporal lobes, to the prefrontal lobes to figure out what to do and make a plan, to the motor cortex in the frontal lobe, out of the brain via motor neurons to the skeletal muscles to get up and move.

        C.   Information from the ears goes to the brain via the somatic nervous system of the peripheral nervous system. Once at the thalamus, it is in the central nervous system. As information exits the brain from the motor cortex, the somatic nervous system gets involved again as messages go to the muscles that allow you to cross the room. Your feeling nervous involves the autonomic nervous system, which carries messages from the central nervous system about your preparedness for the test to the glands and organs.

2   A.   Hypothalamus
        B.   Thalamus
        C.   Prefrontal lobe
        D.   Broca's area
        E.   Hippocampus
        F.   Cerebellum

3.   It is difficult to say exactly, but the cerebrum, which is responsible for higher functioning, has been damaged. Parts of the brain stem, specifically the medulla, which is responsible for heart rate and respiration, are still in tact, but because Helen is not conscious, it is possible that the pons, which is responsible for sleeping and waking, may be damaged.

4   A.   Frontal lobes; personality, planning, initiative
        B.   Parietal lobes; body senses and location
        C.   Occipital lobes; vision

5   A.   Right
       B.   Left
       C.   Right
       D.   Left
       E.   There are problems with functions controlled by the left hemisphere, but not with the right hemisphere.

CROSSWORD PUZZLE KEY

ACROSS

2.	amygdala
5.	dendrite
7.	hypothalamus
9.	parietal
10.	synapse
12.	cerebrum
13.	cortex
15.	axon
16.	insulin
18.	pons
20.	neurotransmitter

DOWN

1.	Broca
3.	glial
4.	frontal
6.	neuropsychology
7.	hormone
8.	limbic
14.	endorphins
17.	sensory

ANSWER KEY - PRACTICE TEST 1 - MULTIPLE CHOICE

1. C (p. 139)	2. B (p. 140)	3. B (p. 140)	4. A (p. 140)
5. C (p. 140)	6. D (pp. 141-143)	7. B (pp. 145-148)	8. A (p. 147)
9. D (pp. 149-150)	10. A (p. 151)	11. B (p. 152)	12. C (pp. 151-152)
13. B (p. 152)	14. C (pp. 157-158)	15. B (p. 154)	16. C (p. 153)
17. D (p. 161)	18. C (pp. 163-164)	19. B (p. 162)	20. C (p. 165)
21. D (pp. 165-167)	22. C (p. 170)	23. C (pp. 171-173)	24. A (pp. 179-171)
25. C (p. 170)			

ANSWER KEY - PRACTICE TEST 2 - MULTIPLE CHOICE

1. B	2. A	3. C	4. A
5. A	6. D	7. D	8. D
9. A	10. A	11. C	12. D
13. B	14. D	15. A	16. C
17. D	18. D	19. A	20. C
21. D	22. A	23. C	24. D
25. C			

ANNOTATED ANSWER KEY - PRACTICE TEST 2

1. Answer B is correct because consciousness is defined as the awareness of oneself and the environment. Answer A is incorrect because consciousness is awareness of more that bodily changes and it is not always related to changes in brain wave patterns (Answer C). Answer D is incorrect because consciousness has been defined.

2. Answer A is correct. States of consciousness are often associated with bodily rhythms, such as dreaming which is associated with a 90-minute cycle of brain activity. There is no evidence that changes in consciousness direct bodily changes (Answer B). Answers C and D are incorrect because changes in consciousness are often associated with changes in bodily rhythms.

3. Answer C is correct. To identify endogenous circadian rhythms, scientists must isolate people from artificial and natural time cues. The studied described in Answer A is an example of this research. Answer A is incorrect because the subjects are not deprived of all sensory stimulation, only those that provide time cues. Answer B is incorrect because this study is not examining depression. Answer D is incorrect because the researchers are not attempting to modify infradian rhythms.

4. Answer A is correct because when a person's normal routine changes, circadian rhythms may be thrown out of phase with one another and this is called internal desynchronization. Internal synchronization (Answer B) implies that internal rhythms become synchronized which is not what occurs when workers must adjust to a new shift. Changes in one's normal routine are not accompanied by a need for less sleep (Answer C) and the term external desynchronization (Answer D) is not used in the text.

5. Answer A is correct because infradian rhythms refer to rhythms that occur less often than once a day, like the hibernation of bears. Answer B is an ultradian rhythms and Answer C is a circadian rhythm. Therefore, Answers B, C, and D are all incorrect.

6. Answer D is correct. Stomach contractions (Answer A), hormone level fluctuations (Answer B), and appetite for food (Answer D) all occur more than once a day and are therefore all ultradian rhythms.

7. Answer D is correct and Answers A, B, and C are incorrect because evidence that mood swings are tied to the menstrual cycle has not been reliably demonstrated and some evidence indicates that hormone changes are not be responsible for reported symptoms.

8. Answer D is correct because Answers A, B, and C are descriptions of research findings about "PMS" that are described in the text. Research evidence has found that men and women do not differ in the number of mood swings they experience in a month, the relationship between cycle stage and symptoms is weak and there is no reliable relationship between cycle stage and work efficiency.

9. Answer A is correct. One likely function of sleep is so that the body can restore itself. Since loss of sleep affects mental functioning, sleep must have to do with brain functioning as well. Answers B (psychic healing) and C (to provide a time for dreaming) do not represent theories about the biological function of sleep and therefore, Answer D is also incorrect.

10. Answer A is correct. As the night progresses, REM periods get longer and closer together. Therefore, Answer B is incorrect, REM periods do not get shorter. There is no evidence that REM periods get more intense (Answer C) nor that they occur at more regular intervals (Answer D).

11. Answer C is correct because stage 2 sleep is characterized by occasional short bursts of rapid, high-peaking brain waves called sleep spindles. Stage 1 (Answer A) is characterized by small and irregular brain waves. Stage 3 sleep (Answer B) is characterized by the brain waves that occurred in stage 2 along with very slow, high-peaked brain waves called delta waves. Stage 4 (Answer D) is characterized by the presence of predominantly delta waves.

12. Answer D is correct because REM sleep (Answer C) is called paradoxical sleep (Answer A) because the brain is extremely active while the body is almost devoid of muscle tone. Answer B is also correct because it is during these periods that people are most likely to dream.

13. Answer B is correct. According to Freud, if a dream's message arouses anxiety, the rational part of the mind must disguise and distort it therefore, Pat dreamt about her brother instead of her father. Also the term "latent content" refers to Freud's idea that the unconscious wishes are expressed symbolically and are different from the manifest content, or the aspects of a dream one remembers upon awakening. Problem-solving theory (Answer A), information processing theory (Answer C), and the activation-synthesis theory (Answer D) of dreaming do not include the concept that dreams have a latent content.

14. Answer D is correct since the activation-synthesis theory explains dreams as a result of neurons firing spontaneously in the lower part of the brain and the cortex tries to make sense of them by synthesizing them with existing knowledge or memories. Answers A, B, and C, refer to other theories of dreaming. Answer A suggests that dreams reflect not unconscious wishes but current preoccupations of waking life. Answer B is based on Freudian theory and suggests that dreams reflect deep-seated unconscious problems that originate in early life. Answer D refers to the idea that dreams are a result of spontaneous firing of neurons in the brain stem that the cortex tries to synthesize.

15. Answer A is correct because problem-solving theory suggests that dreams are not symbols designed to convey the dream's true meaning, but rather that they are about current problems and their subject is not disguised. Answers B, C, and D refer to other theories of dreaming.

16. Answer C is correct because drugs are classified depending on their effects on the central nervous system. Drugs may be classified as stimulants, depressants, opiates, or psychedelics and this does not have to do with the legality (Answer A) or the addictive potential (Answer B) of a drug. Since only Answer A is correct, Answer D is incorrect.

17.   Answer D is correct. Cocaine is a stimulant, not an amphetamine (Answer B) nor a psychedelic (Answer C). Heroine is an opiate, not a psychedelic (Answer A) nor a stimulant (Answer C) and the classification of marijuana is unclear.

18.   Answer D is correct. Nicotine and coffee are drugs classified as stimulants which may make the user feel excited and confident.

19.   Answer A is correct. Drugs produce their effects by increasing or decreasing the release of neurotransmitters at the synapse, by preventing the reabsorption of a neurotransmitter after its release, by blocking the effects of a neurotransmitter on a receiving nerve cell or by binding to receptors that would ordinarily be triggered by a neurotransmitter. Drugs do not eliminate neurotransmitters altogether (Answer B) nor do they mutate their chemical formulas (Answer C). Therefore Answers B, C, and D are incorrect.

20.   Answer C is correct. Mental set refers to expectations about a drug's effects, the reasons for taking the drug, and whether a person wants to justify some behavior by being "under the influence." Physical condition (Answer A) refers to the extent to which drug use may interact with variables like a person's body weight, metabolism, initial state of arousal, and individual tolerance for the drug. Answer B (environmental setting) refers to the influence of place and context on the individual's response to a drug. Experience with the drug (Answer D) refers to the number of times the drug has been used and the levels of past usage.

21.   Answer D is correct because Answers A, B, and C refer to the environmental setting, mental set, and experience with the drug, all of which can affect an individual's response to a drug.

22.   Answer A is correct that both hypnosis and drugs can be used to justify letting go of inhibitions. Some theorists believe that hypnosis involves dissociation (Answer B). Some drugs produce hallucinations (Answer C) and drugs may alter neurotransmitter levels (Answer D), only Answer A describes characteristics shared by both hypnosis and drug use.

23.   Answer C is correct. The sociocultural explanation of hypnosis is that the hypnotized person is playing the part of a hypnotized person. The person is not faking, however; the role of hypnotized person, like many other social roles, is so engrossing that actions required by the role may occur without conscious intent. Answer A, that hypnosis is an altered state, was the leading explanation for hypnosis. While some theorists believe that hypnosis is both an altered state and involves dissociation (Answer B), these are not the views of the sociocognitive perspective. Researchers agree that participants are able to control their behavior during hypnosis which makes answer D false.

24.   Answer D is correct because Answers A, B, and C cite evidence from research studies. The results of these studies argue against the credibility of age regression.

25.   Answer C is correct. The American Psychological Association opposes the use of "hypnotically refreshed" testimony in courts of law because pseudomemories and errors are so common. This fact makes Answers A and B incorrect. While they contain many errors, they are not always inaccurate (Answer D).

ANSWER KEY - PRACTICE TEST 3 - SHORT ANSWER

1. consciousness
2. circadian
3. suprachiasmatic nucleus
4. hormone levels; the menstrual cycle
5. desynchronization
6. hormones
7. REM sleep
8. spindles
9. inactive; active
10. lucid
11. manifest; latent
12. mental housekeeping
13. interpreted brain activity
14. Psychoactive
15. central nervous system
16. stimulants
17. tolerance
18. neurotransmitter
19. physical factors, experience with the drug, environmental setting, or mental set
20. "think-drink" effect
21. hidden observer
22. pseudomemories
23. dissociation
24. medical and psychological
25. sociocognitive

ANSWER KEY - PRACTICE TEST 4 - TRUE/FALSE

1. F	2. F	3. F	4. T	5. F
6. T	7. F	8. T	9. T	10. F
11. F	12. T	13. T	14. T	15. F
16. T	17. F	18. T	19. F	20. T
21. T	22. F	23. F	24. F	25. T

ANSWER KEY - PRACTICE TEST 5 - ESSAY

1.
   A. Ultradian, because the cycle repeats several times a day
   B. Infradian, because the cycle repeats less than once a day
   C. Ultradian, because the cycle repeats several times a day
   D. Could be Circadian if cycle repeats daily; could be ultradian if cycle repeats more than once a day; could be infradian if cycle repeats less than once a day
   E. Ultradian, because the cycle repeats several times a day
   F. Infradian, because the cycle repeats less than once a day

2.
   A. The definition of PMS is important because physical and emotional symptoms often appear on the same questionnaire. Because many women may experience physical symptoms, they are likely to have a higher score than if these two categories of symptoms were presented separately.

   B. Negative moods are likely to be attributed to PMS when they occur just prior to the onset of menstruation, whereas negative moods that occur at different stages of the menstrual cycle are likely to be attributed to other factors. Another problem related to the self reporting of PMS symptoms is the tendency to notice negative moods that occur before menstruation, and to ignore the absence of negative moods before menstruation.

   C. Expectations can influence perceptions. The very title of a widely used questionnaire, the Menstrual Distress Questionnaire, can bias responders to look for and find certain symptoms, while ignoring other, more positive, symptoms.

   D. Research findings include:
      1. Women and men do not differ in the emotional symptoms or number of mood swings they experience over the course of a month.
      2. For most women, the relationship between cycle stage and symptoms is weak or nonexistent.
      3. There is no reliable relationship between cycle stage and behaviors that matter in real life.
      4. Women do not consistently report negative psychological changes from one cycle to the next.

3. A. Sleep consists of REM and four distinct non-REM periods.
   B. The extra alertness results from the fact that the body is synchronized to wake itself up as the morning approaches. Loss of sleep is not invigorating.
   C. Although theorists do not agree on the exact functions of sleep, rest is one of its presumed functions. We can "catch up" on several nights of sleep deprivation in just one night.
   D. Though people can function pretty well after losing a single night's sleep, mental flexibility, originality and other aspects of creative thinking may suffer.
   E. We display four to five REM periods each night, and laboratory research indicates that we dream every night.

4. A. Activation-synthesis theory or dreams as interpreted brain activity
   B. Dreams as information processing
   C. Dreams as unconscious wishes or psychoanalytic theory
   D. Dreams as problem-solving

5. A1. Depressant
   A2. Disinhibition, anxiety reduction, slower reaction times, memory loss, poor coordination
   A3. Death, psychosis, organic damage, blackouts

   B1. Depressant
   B2. Sedation, anxiety and guilt reduction, release of tension
   B3. Tolerance and addiction, sensory and motor impairment, coma, death

   C1. Opiate
   C2. Pain reduction, euphoria
   C3. Addiction, convulsions, nausea, death

   D1. Stimulant
   D2. Elevated metabolism and mood, increased wakefulness
   D3. Nervousness, delusions, psychosis, death

   E1. Stimulant
   E2. Appetite suppression, excitability, euphoria
   E3. Sleeplessness, sweating, paranoia, depression

   F1. Psychedelic
   F2. Hallucinations and visions, feelings of insight, exhilaration
   F3. Psychosis, panic, paranoia

G1. Classification unclear, some say mild psychedelic
G2. Relaxation, increased appetite, culturally determined effects
G3. Controversial abusive effects

CROSSWORD PUZZLE KEY

ACROSS		DOWN	
2.	consciousness	1.	menstruation
6.	REM	2.	circadian
8.	marijuana	3.	infradian
9.	lucid	4.	ultradian
11.	alpha	5.	psychoactive
15.	latent	7.	delta
16.	withdrawal	10.	depressants
17.	activation	12.	hypnosis
18.	tolerance	13.	steroids
19.	opiates	14.	stimulants

ANSWER KEYS FOR CHAPTER 6

ANSWER KEY - PRACTICE TEST 1 - MULTIPLE CHOICE

1. C (p. 180)	2. C (p. 179)	3. A (p. 179)	4. C (p. 181)
5. B (p. 182)	6. A (p. 184)	7. C (p. 183)	8. D (p. 186)
9. A (p. 185)	10. B (p. 187)	11. A (p. 188)	12. B (p. 189)
13. D (p. 189)	14. D (p. 190)	15. B (p. 193)	16. D (p. 195)
17. D (pp. 196)	18. A (p. 197)	19. B (p. 201)	20. C (p. 202)
21. A (p. 205)	22. C (p.208)	23. D (p. 209)	24. B (p. 210)
25. D (pp. 212-213)			

ANSWER KEY - PRACTICE TEST 2 - MULTIPLE CHOICE

1. B	2. D	3. A	4. B
5. C	6. D	7. A	8. D
9. C	10. C	11. B	12. C
13. A	14. C	15. C	16. C
17. A	18. B	19. D	20. B
21. A	22. C	23. A	24. C
25. B			

ANNOTATED ANSWER KEY - PRACTICE TEST 2

1. Answer B is correct. Sensation is the detection of physical energy emitted or reflected by physical objects while perception is the set of processes that organize and interpret sensory impulses so they have meaning. Neural messages, like sensation, provide the raw data, but perception is required to give the neural messages meaning. Answer A, encoding, is the way the nervous system registers neural messages. Reception, Answer C, is the way sense receptors detect the physical energy reflected by physical objects. Transduction, Answer D, is the conversion of one form of energy into another and is related to reception.

2. Answer D is correct because anatomical and functional codes explain how we experience different sensations (Answer B). Answers A and C are examples of how we experience different sensations and therefore, they are also correct.

3.   Answer A is correct. The nervous system encodes messages using two basic kinds of code. When signals received by the sense organs are coded anatomically (anatomical code), different nerve pathways are stimulated and they terminate in different areas of the brain. Functional codes register sensory signals based on which cells are firing, how many cells are firing, the patterning and rate at which cells are firing. Answer B refers to neural codes, which is a general term and cellular codes which is not a term in the text. Answer C gives the correct terms but in the incorrect order. Answer D lists psychophysics, which is a general term for the study of how the physical properties of stimuli are related to our psychological experience of them and transduction which refers to the conversion of one form of energy to another.

4.   The correct answer is B. The absolute threshold refers to the smallest amount of energy that a person can detect reliably and that is what the researcher is asking Ethan. Answers A and C refer to the same thing; the smallest different in stimulation that a person can detect reliably. These terms would be correct if the researcher played two tones for Ethan and asked him whether the tones were the same or different. Answer D is not a term used in the text.

5.   Answer C is correct. Signal detection theory suggests that an observer's response is affected not only by sensory processes, but by decision processes that are influences by an observer's response bias. To separate these two components, researchers include some trials in which no stimulus is presented and others in which a weak stimulus is presented (the strategy described in the question). Difference thresholds (Answer A) and just noticeable differences (Answer D) are calculated by comparing two stimuli. Determining absolute thresholds (Answer B) is accomplished by identifying the weakest stimuli that can be detected.

6.   Answer D is correct because all answers describe what happens in sensory adaptation.

7.   Answer A is correct. Hue (the visual experience specified by color names) is related to the wavelength of light while brightness (the visual experience related to the intensity of light) corresponds to the amplitude of the wave. This question is comparing the psychological characteristics of the visual experience to the physical properties of the visual stimulus. Answer B is incorrect because the complexity of the lightwave relates to saturation or colorfulness. Answers C and D are incorrect because frequency is not discussed in regard to light.

8. Answer D is correct because hue, brightness, and saturation are psychological dimensions of the visual experience. whereas wavelength, intensity, and complexity are physical properties of the visual stimulus, light. Answer A contains the correct terms, but lists them backwards. Answers B and C are incorrect because hue, brightness and saturation are not discussed in terms of whether they are temporary or complex and wavelength, intensity and complexity are not identified as permanent or simple.

9. Answer C is correct. The cornea, lens, iris, and pupil are part of the sense organ while the rods and cones are the receptors. While Answer A could be considered correct, Answer C is the better answer since it is more specific. Answer B is incorrect since the cornea, lens, iris, and pupil are not part of the retina. Answer D is incorrect since the cornea, lens, iris, and pupil are not receptors and while the rods and cones are on the retina, they are not the same thing as the retina.

10. Answer C is correct because rods cannot distinguish different wavelengths of light and therefore are not sensitive to color whereas, cones are differentially sensitive to specific wavelengths of light and allow us to see colors. Answer A is incorrect because it is reversed; rods enable us to see in dim light and at night and cones are involved in bright light. Answer B is incorrect because the iris and the pupil control the amount of light that gets into the eye.

11. Answer B is correct (and Answers A and C are incorrect) because from the center to the periphery of the retina, the ratio of rods to cones increases, and the outer edges contain virtually no cones. The center of the retina contains only cones, clustered densely together. Answer D is incorrect because the optic disc is where the optic nerve leaves the eye and there are no rods or cones.

12. Answer C is correct because the trichromatic theory of color vision assumes that the retina contains three types of cones; one type responds to blue, another to green, and a third to red. Answers A and D are incorrect because they do not refer to theories of color vision. Answer B is incorrect though it does describe a second theory of color vision. The opponent-process theory assumes that the visual system treated particular pairs of colors (blue/yellow and red/green) as opposing or antagonistic.

13. Answer A is correct. People always organize the visual field into figure and ground. The figure (words) stands out from the rest of the environment (paper), which provides a formless background. Answers B, C, and D refer to other perceptual abilities.

14. Answer C is correct because the smaller the retinal image of an object, the farther away the object appears to be. Interposition (Answer A) occurs when an object is between the viewer and a second object, partly blocking the view of the second object, the first object is perceived as being closer. Retinal disparity (Answer B) is a binocular cue that occurs because of the slight difference in lateral separation between two objects as seen by the left eye and the right eye. Linear perspective (Answer D) occurs when two lines known to be parallel appear to be coming together, they imply the existence of depth.

15. Answer C is correct. Pitch and timbre are both psychological dimensions of the auditory experience. Pitch is related to the frequency of the sound wave and timbre is related to the complexity of the wave. Answer A is incorrect because while pitch is, to some extent, related to a sound wave's intensity, amplitude corresponds to intensity or loudness. Answer B is incorrect because complexity corresponds to timbre and intensity to amplitude. Answer D is incorrect because amplitude corresponds to loudness while frequency corresponds to pitch.

16. Answer C is correct. Timbre is the distinguishing quality of sound. While both a flute and an oboe can vary in loudness (Answer A), that does not account for the different sound each produces. Saturation (Answer B) refers to a dimension of the visual experience (colorfulness). Answer D (pitch) refers to the frequency of a sound wave and does not account for differences in the quality of sound.

17. Answer A is correct because, like rods and cones, the cilia or hair cells are the receptor cells. The eardrum (Answer B) is an oval shaped membrane that responds to the movement of sound waves and stimulates bones in the middle ear. The basilar membrane (Answer C) is a rubbery membrane that stretches across the interior of the cochlea and contains the hair cells of the cochlea. Answer D (the cochlea) contains the actual organ of hearing, the organ of Corti.

18. Answer B is correct. The cilia are imbedded in the basilar membrane which stretches across the interior of the cochlea. Answer A is incorrect because the cochlea is not in the auditory nerve. The auditory nerve carries the message out of the ear and to the brain. Answer C is incorrect because the cilia are not imbedded in the eardrum. Answer D is incorrect because the terms are presented in the reverse order.

19. Answer D is correct because cultural differences (Answer A), supertaste for bitter substances (Answer B), and the density of tastebuds (Answer C) can all contribute to individual tastes.

20. Answer B is correct. Vision has only three basic receptor cell types, taste has only four basic types, but smell may have as many as a thousand receptor cell types. Answer A is incorrect because smell does have receptor cells. The types of codes used by the three senses is not discussed directly (Answer C). The text does not discuss basic smells (Answer D).

21. Answer A is correct because the skin senses include touch (or pressure), warmth, cold, and pain. Kathy felt the warmth of the sun, the coolness of the shower, the pressure of the shower, and the pain of the sunburn. Herb (Answer B) experienced only warmth. Carol (Answer C) felt the pain of her aching muscles and the pressure of the massage, but she felt no warmth or cold. Mori (Answer D) felt only pain.

22. Answer C is correct. According to the neuromatrix theory of pain, the brain not only responds to incoming signals from sensory nerves, but it is also capable of generating pain on its own. Pain can be generated when an extensive network of neurons in the brain produce abnormal patterns of activity. This is thought to account for phantom pain. Answers A, B, or D are not considered explanations for phantom pain.

23. Answer A is correct. Equilibrium is the sense of balance and provides information about our bodies as a whole. Kinesthesis tells us where our body parts are located and lets us know when they move. Answer B reverses the terms. Answer C refers to one of the skin senses (touch) and incorrectly uses equilibrium. Coordination (Answer D) is not one of the senses and touch is not the sense that is used when Calan grabs her foot.

24. Answer C is correct. The visual cliff experiment tests an infant's perception of depth and supports the idea that depth perception occurs early and may be present from the beginning. This study is not examining visual acuity (Answer A), attachment (Answer B), nor the effect of learned cues on distance perception (Answer D).

25. Answer B is correct. While, in the laboratory, simple visual subliminal messages can influence behavior, at least briefly, there is no evidence that complex behaviors can be manipulated by "subliminal-perception" tapes. Therefore, there are no dramatic implications for real world applications (Answer A), nor it is an excellent tool for learning (Answer D). Subliminal persuasion has not been used successfully in marketing (Answer C).

ANSWER KEY - PRACTICE TEST 3 - SHORT ANSWER.

1.   Perception
2.   anatomical; functional
3.   psychophysics
4.   absolute
5.   just noticeable difference (jnd)
6.   sensory; decision
7.   adaptation
8.   brightness
9.   retina
10. rods; cones
11. Feature-detector
12. ground
13. closure
14. constancies
15. off
16. basilar membrane; cochlea
17. intensity or amplitude
18. salty, sour, bitter, sweet
19. culture
20. touch (or pressure), warmth, cold, pain
21. gate-control; neuromatrix theory
22. kinesthesis; equilibrium
23. visual cliff
24. emotions, expectations
25. Extrasensory perception

ANSWER KEY - TEST 4 - TRUE/FALSE

1. F	2. F	3. T	4. T	5. F
6. T	7. F	8. F	9. F	10. T
11. F	12. T	13. F	14. T	15. T
16. T	17. T	18. F	19. T	20. F
21. T	22. T	23. F	24. F	25. T

ANSWER KEY - PRACTICE TEST 5 - ESSAY

1.   A.   When a person compares two stimuli (the scarf and the car), the size of the change necessary to produce a just noticeable difference is a constant proportion of the original stimulus. In this case, $2.00 is a much larger proportion of $10 than it is of $10,000. Therefore, $2.00 on the price of a car would not produce a just noticeable difference. Two dollars represents 1/5 of the price of the scarf. One-fifth of the price of the car would be $2,000 and would produce a j.n.d.

        B.   Signal detection theory indicates that active decision making is involved in determining an absolute threshold. The fatigue, as well as attention, of subjects may be interfering with decision making.

        C.   A reduction in sensitivity results from unchanging, repetitious stimulation or sensory adaptation. John may be having trouble feeling the glasses on his head because they have been there for a while.

        D.   When people find themselves in a state of sensory overload, they often cope by blocking out unimportant sights and sounds and focusing only on those they find useful. Unimportant sounds are not fully processed by the brain. This capacity for selective attention protects us from being overwhelmed by all the sensory signals impinging on our receptors.

2.   Light, the stimulus for vision, travels in the form of waves. Waves have certain physical properties: length, which corresponds to hue or color; amplitude, which corresponds to brightness; complexity, which corresponds to saturation or colorfulness. The light enters the cornea and is bent by the lens to focus. The amount of light getting into the eye is controlled by muscles in the iris, which surrounds the pupil. The pupil widens or dilates to influence the amount of light let in. The light goes to the retina located in the back of the eye. The retina contains rods and cones, which are the visual receptors. The cones are responsible for color vision and the rods for black-and-white vision and seeing things in dim light. The fovea, where vision is sharpest, is in the center of the retina and contains only cones. Rods and cones are connected to bipolar neurons that communicate with ganglion cells. The axons of the ganglion cells converge to form the optic nerve, which carries information out through the back of the eye and on to the brain.

3. A. Three colors will be needed - blue, red and green - corresponding to three types of cones. Combining such colors produces the human color spectrum.
   B. Four colors will be needed - blue, yellow, red and green. They must be paired in a way that allows them to function as opposites.

4. A. Loudness is increasing as indicated by changes in the amplitude of the waves.
   B. Pitch changes are related to changes in wave frequency.
   C. The quality of sound, called timbre, is being altered by mixing various waves.

5. A. Proximity is the tendency to perceive objects that are close together as a group.
   B. Closure is the tendency to fill in gaps to perceive complete forms.
   C. Similarity is the tendency to see things that are alike as belonging together.
   D. Continuity is the tendency for lines and patterns to be perceived as continuous.

6. A. Your expectation could influence your interpretation of what you saw and what happened.
   B. Your belief about your neighbor's character could influence your perception that he was sneaking around.
   C. Your emotions could influence your perception that someone was at the door.

CROSSWORD PUZZLE ANSWERS

ACROSS
2. pain
3. kinesthesis
7. sensation
9. cochlea
10. psychophysics
12. audition
13. fovea
14. retina
17. constancies
18. basilar
19. receptors
20. pheromones

DOWN
1. ganglion
2. pitch
4. perception
5. wave
6. gustation
8. olfaction
9. cones
11. hue
14. rods
15. timbre
16. codes

ANSWER KEYS FOR CHAPTER 7

ANSWER KEY - PRACTICE TEST 1 - MULTIPLE CHOICE

1. C (p. 225)	2. B (p. 228)	3. A (p. 228)	4. D (p. 233)
5. B (pp. 229-230)	6. A (pp. 228-229)	7. C (p. 230)	8. D (pp. 231-235)
9. B (pp. 233-234)	10. D (p. 236)	11. C (p. 236)	12. B (p. 237)
13. C (p. 237)	14. A (p. 238)	15. B (p. 241)	16. C (pp. 243-244)
17. A (p. 243)	18. B (p. 242)	19. C (pp. 241-242)	20. C (pp. 248-249)
21. D (pp. 251-252)	22. C (p. 251)	23. A (pp. 253-254)	24. D (pp. 253-257)
25. B (p. 257)			

ANSWER KEY - PRACTICE TEST 2 - MULTIPLE CHOICE

1. C	2. A	3. C	4. B
5. C	6. A	7. A	8. C
9. C	10. C	11. B	12. A
13. C	14. B	15. C	16. D
17. D	18. C	19. A	20. C
21. C	22. B	23. D	24. A
25. B			

ANNOTATED ANSWER KEY - PRACTICE TEST 2

1. Answer C is correct because involuntary behaviors are likely to be learned through classical conditioning while voluntary behaviors are learned through operant conditioning. Learning is to instinct (Answer A) represents the relationship between nurture and nature which is not the relationship between classical and operant conditioning. Answer B contains the correct terms but in the reverse order. Answer D is incorrect because an instinct is a type of unlearned behavior and this is a different relationship that which exists between classical and operant conditioning.

2. Answer A is correct. An unconditioned stimulus is an event or thing that elicits a response automatically or reflexively, which describes food. An unconditioned response (Answer B) is the response (In this case, the cat running to the food) that is automatically produced by the unconditioned stimulus. Answer C is incorrect because a conditioned stimulus (the sound of a can being opened in this example) is a neutral stimulus that is regularly paired with an unconditioned stimulus. The conditioned response (Answer D) is the learned response to the conditioned stimulus (the cat running to the sound of the can being opened).

3.	Answer C is correct. See the explanations in the annotated answers for question 2.

4.	Answer B is correct. Stimulus generalization is a phenomenon that occurs after a stimulus becomes a conditioned stimulus for some response, other, similar stimuli may produce a similar reaction. In this case other dogs (the stimuli that are similar to the conditioned stimuli, the original collie) produced a similar reaction to the conditioned stimulus. Extinction (Answer A) refers to the disappearance of the conditioned response if the conditioned stimulus is repeatedly presented without the unconditioned stimulus. Answer C (stimulus discrimination) is the mirror image of stimulus generalization; different responses are made to stimuli that resemble the conditioned stimulus in some way. Spontaneous recovery (Answer D) refers to the reappearance of a response after it has been extinguished.

5.	Answer C is correct. See the explanations in the annotated answers for question 4.

6.	Answer A is correct. In operant conditioning, extinction takes place when the reinforcer that maintained the response (attention from Olimpia's father) is removed. Answer B is incorrect because stimulus generalization in operant conditioning occurs when a response may generalize to stimuli not present during the original learning situation. Answer C is incorrect because stimulus discrimination occurs in operant conditioning when a response is given only to the stimulus that results in a reinforcer and not to other similar stimuli. As in classical conditioning, spontaneous recovery (Answer D) occurs in operant conditioning when a response returns after it has been extinguished.

7.	Answer A is correct. Getting sick from Chinese food is the UR and that particular Chinese meal is the US. As a result of stimulus generalization, the negative response (the CR) to all Chinese food (the CS) is learned through classical conditioning. Answers B and C are both examples of voluntary behaviors learned through operant conditioning. This makes Answer D also incorrect.

8.	Answer C is correct. Counter-conditioning is a procedure in which a stimulus that produces pleasant feelings incompatible with fear is paired with a stimulus that has been conditioned to produce fear. Answer A is incorrect because extinction is the disappearance of the CR after the CS is repeatedly presented without the US. Stimulus generalization (Answer B) occurs when a stimulus becomes a conditioned stimulus for some response and other, similar stimuli may produce a similar reaction. Systematic desensitization (Answer D) is a variation of this procedure that was later devised for treating phobias in adults.

9. Answer C is correct since extinction, stimulus generalization and discrimination are principles of both classical and operant conditioning. This makes Answers A and B incorrect. Answer D is incorrect because counterconditioning is a procedure that involves pairing a stimulus that produces pleasant feelings and is incompatible with fear with another stimulus that has been conditioned to produce fear.

10. Answer C is correct because negative reinforcement involves the removal of something unpleasant (doing the dishes). Positive reinforcement (Answer A) occurs when something pleasant follows a response. Answer B is incorrect because punishment decreases the likelihood of a response and being relieved of dish-washing duties is likely to increase the desired response (garbage removal). Primary reinforcement (Answer D) refers to reinforcers that satisfy biological needs.

11. Answer B is correct since punishment decreases the likelihood of a response. Being grounded is intended to decrease the likelihood that the person will come home after curfew again! Answers A, C and D are incorrect. See the explanations in the annotated answers for question 10.

12. Answer A is correct. See the explanations in the annotated answers for question 10.

13. Answer C is correct. Secondary reinforcers are reinforcers that are learned like money, praise, applause, and good grades. Primary reinforcers (Answer A) satisfy biological needs. Examples would be food and water. Answer B is incorrect because punishments decrease the likelihood of a response. Higher-order conditioning (Answer D) is not discussed in the text.

14. Answer B is correct. Stimulus generalization in operant conditioning refers to responses that are generalized to stimuli not present during the original learning situation that resemble the original stimuli. Classrooms, teachers, and schools other than those from first grade still produce the response of hand raising. Answer A is incorrect because extinction refers to a procedure that causes a previously learned response to stop. Stimulus discrimination (Answer C) occurs when different responses are made to stimuli that resemble the original stimuli. Shaping (Answer D) refers to the reinforcement of responses that are similar to the final desired response.

15. Answer C is correct. See the explanations in the annotated answers for question 14.

16. Answer D is correct. This example describes a partial reinforcement schedule which involves reinforcing only some responses, not all of them (he only gives her cookies when he runs out of patience). Intermittent (Answer C) is another term for a partial schedule and variable (Answer B) is a type of intermittent schedule, therefore all answers are correct (Answer D).

17. Answer D is correct. Answer A is correct because throwing tantrums has been positively reinforced with cookies so we can expect tantrums to continue. Answer B is correct because behaviors that are on a partial reinforcement schedule are resistant to extinction. Answer C is correct because partial reinforcement schedules are based on intermittent delivery of reinforcement.

18. Answer C is correct because variable ratio schedules deliver a reinforcer after a variable number of responses have occurred and not, like interval schedules (Answer B), based on the passage of time since the last reinforcer. Because the number of responses until the next reinforcer is unclear, Answer D (fixed-ratio schedule) is incorrect. This question does not describe a continuous reinforcement schedule (Answer A) because Angus does not receive extra money after every response.

19. Answer A is correct. This describes a phenomenon first demonstrated by Skinner; how superstitious behaviors are learned. Skinner found that behaviors are repeated even if they are reinforced by chance and have no effect on the deliver of the reinforcer. Negative reinforcement (Answer B) involves the removal of something unpleasant which does not apply. Continuous reinforcement (Answer C) refers to the reinforcement of a response each time it occurs. Answer D is incorrect because a correct answer is given.

20. Answer C is correct. Though all answer options describe problems related to the use of punishment, in this example, new behaviors are being taught through this program. Therefore, undesirable behavior is being punished, while appropriate behaviors are being taught.

21. Answer C is correct. Psychologists have found that sometimes extrinsic reinforcements can kill the pleasure of doing something for its own sake. Answer A is incorrect because it reverses the relationship between extrinsic and intrinsic reinforcers. Answer B is incorrect because token economies use secondary reinforcers (tokens) that are exchangeable for primary or other secondary reinforcers and a token economy is not described in this question. Answer D is incorrect because Nick has received reinforcers for his work (success).

22.   Answer B is correct. Observational learning is learning by watching what others do and what happens to them for doing it. Maggie has learned to perform the behaviors described in the question by having watched others. While Maggie might be intelligent (Answer A), had she not observed others performing these tasks, she would not know what to do. Cognitive maps (Answer C) refers to the work of Tolman, in which he argued that a people develop cognitive maps, or mental representations of the spatial layout of environments. The "ABCs" of learning (Answer D) refer to explanations of learning held by theories that preceded social-learning theories. This question gives an example best explained by one of the social-learning theories.

23.   Answer D is correct. Social-cognitive theories emphasize the influence of perceptions, expectations, and beliefs on learning. Answer A is incorrect because nothing is said about schedules of reinforcement. Answer B is incorrect because evidence for latent learning is absent. Answer C is incorrect because this type of consideration of early relationships is consistent with psychodynamic theories, not social-cognitive theories.

24.   Answer A is correct. Tolman demonstrated in his experiments with rats that learning can occur even though it may not be immediately expressed. Answer B is incorrect because the research on insight was not conducted by Tolman, nor was it conducted with rats. Answer C is incorrect because latent learning is not concerned with the relationship between extrinsic reinforcement and intrinsic motivation. Answer D is incorrect because latent learning does not examine the interaction between personality characteristics and environmental influences.

25.   Answer B is correct because it correctly describes the outcome of Bandura's study. Answer A is incorrect because the children did not receive a reward, yet they imitated the models. Answer C is incorrect because the children did imitate adults, and Answer D is incorrect because the children in the study did imitate aggressive behavior.

ANSWER KEY - PRACTICE TEST 3 - SHORT ANSWER

1.   learning
2.   conditioned stimulus
3.   extinction
4.   higher-order
5.   generalization
6.   discrimination
7.   predicts
8.   counterconditioning
9.   operant; consequences
10.   reinforcement

11. reflexive; complex
12. primary; secondary
13. positive; negative
14. negative; punishment
15. reduces; increases
16. intermittent (or partial)
17. fixed-ratio
18. fixed-interval
19. shaping
20. extinction; reinforcement
21. extrinsic; intrinsic
22. biological
23. latent
24. observational
25. social-cognitive

ANSWER KEY - PRACTICE TEST 4 - TRUE/FALSE

1. T	2. F	3. F	4. F	5. F
6. T	7. F	8. F	9. T	10. F
11. F	12. T	13. F	14. T	15. T
16. F	17. F	18. T	19. F	20. F
21. T	22. F	23. T	24. T	25. T

ANSWER KEY - PRACTICE TEST 5 - ESSAY

1. A. CS = first and middle name; US = father's anger; UR = anxiety; CR = anxiety
   B. CS = closet and leash; US = walk; UR = excitement; CR = excitement
   C. CS = perfume; US = true love; UR = happy; CR = happy
   D. CS = Park Place and Main Street; US = accident; UR = fear; CR = anxiety

2. A. Dogs are often disciplined by being swatted (US) with rolled-up newspapers (CS). Fear is a natural response (UR) to being hit and a learned response to such objects (CR). Furthermore, stimulus generalization is demonstrated in that the dog gives the CR to other types of rolled-up papers.
   B. When attacked (US) by a Doberman (CS) in the past, Joan experienced fear (US). Since that time, she has been nervous about all Dobermans (stimulus generalization), though not around other dogs (stimulus discrimination). Her reduction of fear toward Dobermans represents extinction.
   C. The sudden noise of screeching tires (CS) often causes people to tense up and flinch (CR). The lack of response during a car race is stimulus discrimination.

D. Getting sick (UR) from spoiled chicken (US) caused Bill to experience stimulus generalization to turkey (CS), which is similar to the chicken on which he originally became ill, and to experience a CR to the turkey.

3. A. The tendency to buckle-up is strengthened through negative reinforcement (the desire to eliminate the sound of the buzzer).

   B. Punishment is weakening the tendency to smoke around the roommate. This becomes more complicated because of the addictive process, which negatively reinforces smoking by removing uncomfortable withdrawal symptoms.

   C. Reinforcement is strengthening Warren's dishwashing behavior.

   D. Punishment is weakening Fred's tendency to go down the most difficult slopes.

4. A. Sara is on a partial reinforcement schedule. While this may be enough to maintain a behavior once it is well established, when a response is weak it should be reinforced each time it occurs (continuous reinforcement).

   B. By picking him up sometimes in response to his cries, Ari's parents have put him on a partial reinforcement schedule, which causes behaviors to be very persistent and difficult to extinguish. To change this pattern, they must consistently respond by not picking him up when he cries and eventually the behavior will extinguish. It will take longer to do so now that he is on this intermittent schedule.

   C. It appears that all the things the teacher is trying to use as punishment are reinforcing Sue's behavior. They all involve extra attention, so by finding a consequence that is unpleasant and does not involve attention, this behavior might be decreased by using punishment. She might also try teaching her and then reinforcing her for other types of attention.

5. The initial punishment occurs long after the marks are made and therefore may not be associated with the behavior that is being punished. The parent is also scolding the child when he or she is feeling angry and therefore he or she may be harsher than usual. The child may also be aroused because of the punishment. Ideally, the behavior should be directed to an appropriate medium, such as paper or coloring books, and then that behavior should be reinforced.

6. A. Variable-interval
   B. Fixed-ratio
   C. Fixed-interval
   D. Fixed-ratio

7. Similarities:
    1. Agree about the importance of laws of operant and classical conditioning
    2. Recognize the importance of reinforcers and the environment

    Differences:
    1. In addition to behaviors, study attitudes, beliefs, and expectations
    2. Emphasize interaction between individuals and their environment

CROSSWORD PUZZLE ANSWER KEY

ACROSS

2. Skinner
3. Pavlov
5. conditioned
8. behaviorism
11. fixed
12. schedule
13. cognitive
15. intermittent
16. observational

DOWN

1. unconditioned
4. variable
5. classical
6. extinction
7. reinforcement
9. response
10. stimulus
14. latent

ANSWER KEYS FOR CHAPTER 8

ANSWER KEY - PRACTICE TEST 1 - MULTIPLE CHOICE

1. A (p. 265)	2. D (p. 288)	3. A (p. 264)	4. B (p. 269)
5. B (p. 268)	6. B (p. 267)	7. D (pp. 270-271)	8. C (p. 272)
9. A (p. 272)	10. D (p. 272)	11. A (p. 274)	12. D (p. 274)
13. C (p. 276)	14. C (p. 277)	15. D (p. 280)	16. C (p. 282)
17. D (p. 281)	18. C (pp. 285-287)	19. C (p. 285)	20. A (pp. 285-287)
21. A (p. 290)	22. C (p. 290)	23. D (p. 290)	24. B (p. 290)
25. A (pp. 299)			

ANSWER KEY - PRACTICE TEST 2 - MULTIPLE CHOICE

1. B	2. C	3. B	4. A
5. A	6. D	7. D	8. A
9. B	10. A	11. C	12. B
13. C	14. B	15. A	16. A
17. D	18. C	19. A	20. A
21. D	22. C	23. A	24. A
25. C			

ANNOTATED ANSWER KEY - PRACTICE TEST 2

1.   Answer B is correct. According to most researchers, culture is defined as a program of shared rules that govern the behavior or members of a community and a set of values, beliefs, and attitudes shared by most members of that community. The examples given in this questions are part of the system of shared rules. Stereotypes (Answer A) are a summary impression of a group of people in which a person believes that all members of that group share a common trait or traits. The reification of culture (Answer C) refers to the tendency to regard "culture" an explanation without identifying the specific mechanisms or aspects of culture that influence behavior. Body language (Answer D) refers to the nonverbal signals of body movement, posture, gesture, and gaze that people constantly express.

2.   Answer C is correct. Distance between speakers has to do with cultural rules not with the friendliness of the culture (Answer A), the sexual values of the culture (Answer B) or the way each type of culture organizes time (Answer D).

3. Answer B is correct. In variations of Milgram's study, they found that people might disobey the experimenter under several conditions. One condition was when the subject worked with peers who refused to go further. While many subjects felt upset about administering the shocks (Answer A), they obeyed even when they themselves were anguished about the pain they believed they were causing. They obeyed even as they wept. Answers C and D are incorrect because Milgram found that obedience was more of a function of the situation than of the particular personalities of the participants. "The key to the behavior of subjects," Milgram (1974) summarized, "lies not in pent-up anger or aggression but in the nature of their relationship to authority."

4. Answer A is correct. Milgram found that obedience was more of a function of the situation than of the particular personalities of the participants. "The key to the behavior of subjects," Milgram (1974) summarized, "lies not in pent-up anger or aggression but in the nature of their relationship to authority." Therefore Answers B and C are incorrect. Answer D is incorrect because Milgram also found that virtually nothing the victim did or said changed the likelihood of the person's compliance--even when the victim said he had a heart condition, screamed in agony, or stopped responding entirely as if he had collapsed.

5. Answer A is correct. In the prison study, within a very short time, the prisoners became distressed, helpless, and panicky. Within an equally short time, the guards adjusted to their new power. Some were nice, some were tough, and some became tyrannical. Since both the prisoners and guards played their roles, Answer B is incorrect. The guards did not become distressed but, instead, many were willing to work overtime without additional pay. When the researchers ended the experiment early, the prisoners were relieved, but most of the guards were disappointed which makes Answer D incorrect. They had enjoyed their short-lived authority. Answer C is incorrect since researchers made no correlation between those research participants who obeyed and past history of problems.

6. Answer D is correct. The two studies demonstrate the power of social roles and obligations to influence the behavior of individuals. Answers A, B, and C are all correct.

7. Answer D is correct. In entrapment, individuals escalate their commitment to a course of action in order to justify their investment in it. The first steps of entrapment pose no difficult choices. But one step leads to another, and before the person realizes it, he or she has become committed to a course of action that does pose problems. Good manners (Answer A) is one reason people obey when they would rather not. Once people are caught in what they perceive to be legitimate roles and obeying a legitimate authority, good manners further ensnare them into obedience. Because of good manners, many people lack a language of protest (Answer C). Routinization is the process of defining the activity in terms of routine duties and roles so that one's behavior becomes normalized and there is little opportunity to raise doubts or ethical questions.

8. Answer A is correct. Dispositional attributions are explanations of behaviors in which the cause of an action is identified as something in the person, such as a trait or a motive. Ashley decided that her husband forgot because of something inside him--his selfishness. A situational attribution is an explanation of behavior that identifies the cause of an action as something in the environment. Andy decided that it was his wife's work problems-- something external, that caused her to forget rather than something about her. Answer B contains the correct terms but in the wrong order. Answer C contains two terms that do not describe types of attributions. Answer D contains one term that is not a type of attribution and uses the term dispositional attribution incorrectly.

9. Answer B is correct. The self-serving bias involves choosing attributions that are favorable to oneself, taking credit for good actions and letting the situation account for bad actions. The good grade is a result of effort while the bad grade is a result of unfairness. The just-world hypothesis (Answer A) refers to attributions that are consistent with the belief that the world is fair; that good people are rewarded and villains punished. The fundamental attribution error (Answer C) refers to attributions in which personality factors are overestimated and situations factors are underestimated when people try to find reasons for someone else's behavior. Blaming the victim (Answer D) can be a result of the just-world hypothesis. When everyone agrees that A did something to harm B, A can argue that B deserved the treatment.

10. Answer A is correct because the fundamental attribution error refers to attributions in which personality factors are overestimated and situations factors are underestimated when people try to find reasons for someone else's behavior. In this example, I am attributing her behavior to personality factors and underestimating the role that situational factors might have. Answers B, C and D are examples of possible situational attributions that are not even considered.

11. Answer C is correct. The just-world hypothesis refers to attributions that are consistent with the belief that the world is fair; that good people are rewarded and villains punished. Hortense sees her illness as a punishment and her belief that the world is just causes her to think she did something to deserve the illness. She is not identifying the cause of her illness as something in the environment, like exposure to carcinogens, therefore this is not an example of a situational attribution (Answer A). Guilt (Answer B) is not discussed in the context of attributions. There is no attributional type called internal attributions (Answer D).

12. Answer B is correct. Blaming the victim can be a result of the just-world hypothesis. If the world is just and something bad happens to someone, then they must have deserved it. In this example, the fact that Jane was attacked was seen as her own fault. The fundamental attribution error (Answer A) refers to attributions in which personality factors are overestimated and situations factors are underestimated when people try to find reasons for someone else's behavior. The self-serving bias (Answer C) involves choosing attributions that are favorable to oneself, taking credit for good actions and letting the situation account for bad actions. Since there is a correct answer, Answer D is incorrect.

13. Answer C is correct. Each generation has its own experiences and economic concerns, and therefore its own characteristic attitudes. The ages of 16 to 24 appear to be critical for the formation of a generational identity that lasts throughout adulthood. While social attitudes (Answer A) were influenced by the war, the question is not an example of a specific attitude. A dispositional attribution (Answer B) refers to attribution theory, specifically, when a person identifies the cause of an action as something in the person, such as a trait or a motive. The question is not an example of a dispositional attribution. Since the question refers to the attitudes of many people, it is not an example of individual identity (Answer D).

14. Answer B is correct. Because of a need for consistency, when two attitudes, or when an attitude and behavior, are in conflict, people experience cognitive dissonance. When this occurs, people are often motivated to resolve the conflict by changing an attitude or their behavior. This question describes a situation in which an attitude and behavior are inconsistent. Friendly persuasion (Answer A) describes the efforts of advertisers, politicians, and friends to try to get you to change your attitudes. It involves exposing people to a new idea and persuading them to accept it. Coercive persuasion (Answer C) refers to efforts to change attitudes that go beyond friendly persuasion. The manipulator uses harsh tactics, attempting to force people to change their minds. Insight (Answer D) refers to a new understanding of a situation. Based on the material in this chapter, the students are most likely to experience cognitive dissonance.

15. Answer A is correct. When people experience cognitive dissonance, they are often motivated to resolve the conflict between two attitudes or between an attitude and behavior by changing an attitude or their behavior. Therefore, since they have already stated an attitude publicly, it is unlikely that they would not change their behavior (Answer B) or decrease their use of condoms (Answer C). Since there is a correct answer, Answer D is incorrect.

16. Answer A is correct. The validity effect is a weapon of friendly persuasion and it involves repeatedly exposing people to the desired position and it is very effective. Using fear (Answer B) can cause people to resist arguments that are in their own best interest. Appealing to generational identity (Answer C) is not described as one of the persuasion techniques. Since Answers B and C are incorrect, Answer D is also incorrect.

17. Answer D is correct. All the techniques described in Answers A, B, and C are those associated with brainwashing or coercive persuasion. Studies of religious, political, and other cults have identified some of the processes by which individuals, whether singly or in groups, can be coerced.

18. Answer C is correct. In one study, interdependence in reaching mutual goals was highly successful in reducing competitiveness and hostility. When adults work together in a cooperative group in which teamwork is rewarded, they often like each other better and are less hostile than when they are competing for individual success. Deindividuation (Answer A) refers to a state in which people lose all awareness of their individuality and sense of self. Social loafing (Answer B) refers to a form of diffusion of responsibility in which each member of a team slows down, letting others work harder. This occurs primarily when individual group members are not accountable for work they do; when people feel that working harder would only duplicate their colleagues' efforts; when workers feel exploited; or when the work itself is uninteresting. Generational identity (Answer D) refers to the influence of experiences and economic concerns that affect a generation.

19. Answer A is correct. Diffusion of responsibility occurs when individuals fail to take action because they believe that someone else will do so. Therefore, the more bystanders, the more likely they will spread the responsibility among many people. The fewer bystanders, the more likely the individual will feel responsible. Answers B, C, and D describe situations in which there are many bystanders.

20. Answer A is correct. Groupthink is the tendency for all members of the group to think alike and to suppress dissent. Groups are susceptible to groupthink when they are highly cohesive, when they are isolated from other viewpoints, when they feel under pressure from outside forces, and when they have a strong, directive leader as described in this question. Diffusion of responsibility (Answer B) refers to the tendency of group members to avoid taking action because they believe others will do so. Social loafing (Answer C) refers to diffusion of responsibility in work groups. Deindividuation (Answer D) refers to a loss of awareness of one's own individuality.

21. Answer D is correct. There are many reasons, both moral values and social and situational reasons for altruism. According to evidence from field and laboratory research, several factors predict independent action: The individual perceives the need for help, the individual decides to take responsibility, the individual decides that the costs of doing nothing outweigh the costs of getting involved, the individual has an ally, the individual feels competent to help, the individual becomes entrapped. Any of the reasons given in Answers A, B, and C could be the reasons that Rachel and her daughter spend Christmas working at the shelter.

22. Answer C is correct. After reviewing a huge number of studies on the effects of competition, Alfie Kohn (1992) concluded that "the phrase healthy competition is a contradiction in terms." Competition, research shows, often decreases work motivation and makes people feel insecure and anxious; it fosters jealousy and hostility and can stifle achievement. Therefore Answers A, B, and D are incorrect.

23. Answer A is correct. One of the distortions of reality that stereotyping can lead to is selective perception. Selective perception occurs when people tend to see only what fits the stereotype and to reject any perceptions that do not fit. While stereotypes do result from accentuating differences between groups (Answer B) and underestimating the differences within groups (Answer C), that is not the cause of the students' error in this question. While stereotypes can help us process new information (Answer D), in this example the stereotype is not being helpful but causing an error in perception.

24. Answer A is correct. Some social scientists believe that racism and sexism are undiminished and certain issues, such as those mentioned in this question, have become code words for racism. These issues are seen as symbolic racism and as expressing the continuing animosity of some whites towards blacks. Therefore, Answer B is incorrect. These issues have become codes and are not unusual, therefore Answer C is incorrect. There is no evidence that those who express the beliefs that are described in this question have a history of victimization therefore Answer D is incorrect.

25. Answer C is correct. People want to believe that a person who does monstrous deeds must be a monster--someone sick and evil. But otherwise good people can and do behave in monstrous ways. Hannah Arendt used the phrase "the banality of evil" to describe this phenomenon. This concept rejects the idea that only a person with a disturbed personality (Answer A), or who is immoral (Answer B) or evil (Answer D) will commit evil acts.

ANSWER KEY - PRACTICE TEST 3 - SHORT ANSWER

1. Roles
2. two-thirds
3. roles
4. manners; entrapment
5. cognition
6. situational
7. dispositional; situational; fundamental
8. self-serving bias
9. just-world hypothesis
10. attitude
11. validity
12. coercive
13. obedience; conformity
14. groupthink
15. diffusion of responsibility
16. uninteresting
17. Deindividuation
18. Altrusim
19. social
20. ethnocentrism
21. stereotype; prejudice
22. emphasize; underestimate
23. symbolic racism
24. distrust
25. social

ANSWER KEY - PRACTICE TEST 4 - TRUE/FALSE

1. F	2. F	3. F	4. T	5. T
6. F	7. F	8. T	9. F	10. T
11. T	12. F	13. T	14. T	15. T
16. T	17. F	18. F	19. F	20. T
21. F	22. F	23. T	24. T	25. F

ANSWER KEY - PRACTICE TEST 5 - ESSAY

1. The prison study: The students were either playing the roles of prison guards or prisoners. These roles were governed by norms of how prisoners and guards should behave. The students knew the roles and the norms that governed them and played the parts.

    The obedience study: The role of the research subject and authority figure was known to the study participants, who then played that role. Knowing the norms for both sets of roles made it difficult for subjects to violate their roles and the roles of the authority.

2. A.   Dispositional attribution
    B.   Just-world hypothesis
    C.   Situational attribution - self-serving bias
    D.   Situational attribution

3. You might want to use some techniques of friendly persuasion. You could use the validity effect by repeating that you have worked very hard in this class. Repeatedly referring to your effort may make it seem more believable to the faculty member. You also might want to make a reference to a class you have taken by a well-respected colleague in which you did very well. This is attempting to influence your teacher's attitude by using the respected colleague's opinion. You might try to link your message with a good feeling by telling your professor how much you enjoyed the class.

4. To reduce social loafing, Dr. Wong should make sure each student is responsible for a different part of the project that is essential to the whole project. She might make part of the grade an individual grade and part of the grade a group grade. To reduce groupthink she might want to make grades dependent on the presentation of multiple points of view and different positions and approaches. She will want to structure the project so that success depends on the cooperation and interdependence of all students. Finally, to promote altruism and independent action, she might want students to volunteer at a homeless shelter to get to know some homeless people personally.

4. A.   Underestimating differences within other groups
    B.   Accentuating differences between groups
    C.   Producing selective perceptions
    D.   Illusory correlations

5.   Factors that contribute to the persistence of prejudice include:
   1.   Socialization - children learn prejudices from their parents.
   2.   Social benefits - prejudices bring support from others who share them and the threat of losing support when one abandons the prejudice.
   3.   Economic benefits and justification of discrimination - when economic or social times are difficult, prejudice increases.

Reducing prejudice: efforts that have not been particularly successful include: the contact hypothesis, efforts aimed at individuals, such as education, and the legal approach.

A program to reduce prejudice must include: multiple efforts, the cooperation of both sides, equal status and economic standing of both sides, comprehensive support from authorities and the opportunity to work and socialize together, formally and informally.

CROSSWORD PUZZLE KEY

ACROSS

3.	roles
4.	just-world
5.	altruism
7.	depersonalization
13.	rules
17.	entrapment
18.	competition

DOWN

1.	coercive	2.	groupthink
6.	deindividuation	7.	dispositional
8.	situational	9.	attribution
10.	attitude	11.	norms
12.	dissonance	14.	loafing
15.	prison	16.	Milgram

ANSWER KEY - PRACTICE TEST 1 - MULTIPLE CHOICE

1. C (p. 306)	2. A (p. 306)	3. C (p. 306)	4. D (p. 307)
5. A (pp. 308-309)	6. C (p. 308)	7. A (p. 310)	8. D (p. 311)
9. A (pp. 311-312)	10. D (pp. 311-316)	11. B (p. 314)	12. B (p. 317)
13. C (p. 317)	14. B (pp. 311-312)	15. A (p. 324)	16. B (p. 324)
17. C (p. 330)	18. D (p. 327)	19. C (pp. 330-331)	20. B (p. 330)
21. A (p. 332)	22. B (p. 331)	23. D (p. 335)	24. D (p. 337)
25. B (p. 340)			

ANSWER KEY - PRACTICE TEST 2 - MULTIPLE CHOICE

1. D	2. C	3. C	4. B
5. B	6. D	7. D	8. C
9. B	10. A	11. C	12. B
13. B	14. D	15. A	16. B
17. D	18. C	19. D	20. C
21. B	22. C	23. C	24. D
25. C			

ANNOTATED ANSWER KEY - PRACTICE TEST 2

1.   Answer D is correct. Answer A is an example of reasoning which is purposeful mental activity that involves operating on information in order to reach conclusions. Answer B is an example of subconscious thought processes which lie outside of awareness but can be brought into consciousness when necessary. Answer C is an example of a nonconscious thought process which remains outside of awareness but nonetheless affects behavior.

2.   Answer C is correct. Basic concepts are units of thought that have a moderate number of instances and are easier to acquire than those that have either few or many instances. Footwear (Answer A) includes more instances and is more abstract than shoes. High heels (Answer B) is a very specific concept. Clothing (Answer D), like footwear, has more instances than shoes.

3. Answer C is correct. Propositions are defined as units of meaning that are made up of concepts and that express a unitary idea. Answer A describes cognitive schemas which are propositions that are linked together in complicated networks of knowledge, associations, beliefs, and expectations. Prototypes (Answer B) is a representative example of a concept. Answer D is the reverse of the correct information. Propositions are not composed of cognitive schemas, rather cognitive schemas are made up of propositions that are linked together.

4. Answer B is correct because propositions are units of meaning that are made up of concepts and that express a unitary idea. Answer A is incorrect because this statement represents more than just a concept. It is a unit of meaning that is made up of concepts and expresses a unitary idea. Answer C is incorrect because cognitive schemas are more complicated networks of knowledge, associations, beliefs, and expectations. Answer D is incorrect because this statement represents neither a visual, auditory nor kinesthetic mental image

5. Answer B is correct. Intuition may be an orderly nonconscious process involving two stages. In the first stage, clues in the problem automatically activate certain memories or knowledge which guides you toward a hunch or hypothesis. In the second stage your thinking becomes conscious, and you become aware of a possible solution. Answer A is incorrect because subconscious processes can be brought into consciousness when necessary. Answer C is incorrect because mindlessness refers to thinking that is conscious though it is thought without analysis. Intuition is not a type of conscious thought (Answer D) because we are not aware of the thought processes involved.

6. Answer D is correct. Subconscious processes are those that lie outside of awareness but can be brought into consciousness when necessary. Automatic routines performed "without thinking" fall into this category. Mindless actions involve conscious thought but involve acting out of habit, without stopping to analyze why or what we are doing. The other term used in all of these answers is nonconscious processes which refers to processes that remain outside of awareness but nonetheless affect behavior. Answer A includes subconscious processes which is correct but nonconscious processes which is incorrect. Answer B has the correct terms in reverse order. Answer C contains the correct answer for the second part of the question but the incorrect answer for the first part.

7. Answer D is correct. Answer B is correct because in inductive reasoning, the premise provide support for the conclusion, but the conclusion could still be false; that is, the conclusion does not follow necessarily from the premises, as it does in deductive reasoning. Answers A and D are also correct because inductive reasoning is a type of formal reasoning and uses logic.

582

8.	Answer C is correct because dialectical reasoning is a type of informal reasoning while deductive reasoning is a type of formal reasoning. Answer A is incorrect because deductive and inductive are both types of formal reasoning and are therefore in a different relationship to one another than dialectical and deductive. Answer B is incorrect because the terms are in the opposite relationship to one another than the correct answer. Answer D is incorrect because both dialectic and reflective are types of informal reasoning.

9.	Answer B is correct because reflective judgment is basically "critical thinking" or the ability to evaluate and integrate evidence. This is a decision that is too complex to rely on formal reasoning which includes inductive (Answer A) and deductive (Answer B) reasoning. Therefore Answer D, all of the above, is also incorrect.

10.	Answer A is correct. The prereflective stages assume that a correct answer exists and that it can be obtained directly through the senses. Answer B is incorrect because in the middle three quasi-reflective stages, people recognize that some things cannot be known with absolute certainty but they are not sure how to deal with these situations. In the reflective stages (Answer C) a person understands that although some things can never be known with certainty, certain judgments are more valid than others because of their coherence, their usefulness, and so on. Answer D refers to one of the stages of development in psychoanalytic theory and does not relate to this topic.

11.	Answer C is correct. A heuristic is a rule of thumb that suggests a course of action without guaranteeing an optimal solution. When people are faced with incomplete information on which to base a decision they must therefore rely on heuristics. Formal logic (Answer A) refers to deductive and inductive reasoning and are types of logic used to draw conclusions but may not be adequate for making decisions described in the questions. Answer B, inductive reasoning is incorrect for the same reasons as that given in the description of Answer A. Answer D is incorrect because a heuristic is the correct answer.

12.	Answer B is correct. The availability heuristic is the tendency to judge the probability of an event by how easy it is to think of examples or instances. Catastrophes stand out in our minds and are therefore more "available" than other kinds of negative events. In this example, earthquakes are more frightening to Allison than getting mugged because the likelihood of their occurrence is exaggerated. Loss Aversion (Answer A) refers to the bias people make when decisions are based on trying to avoid or minimize risks or losses. Cognitive dissonance (Answer C) is a state of tension that occurs when a person simultaneously holds two cognitions that are psychologically inconsistent, or holds a belief that is incongruent with the person's behavior. Confirmation bias (Answer D) occurs when people pay attention only to evidence that confirms what they want to believe.

13. Answer B is correct. Larry is likely to reduce dissonance because he free chose the class and that is one of the conditions under which people are particularly likely to try to reduce dissonance. Harry is not likely to experience dissonance (Answer A) because he knows why he took the class; he does not have to avoid the realization that he made a poor choice. Answer C is incorrect since Larry made a poor choice, he is likely to experience dissonance. Answer D is incorrect since it is unlikely that Harry will experience dissonance.

14. Answer D is correct. Gardner, in his theory of multiple intelligences, suggests that there are seven "intelligences" or domains of talent. The g factor takes the opposite point of view; that a general ability, or g factor, underlies specific abilities and talents. Answer A is incorrect because factor analysis refers to a statistical method that researchers use to to identify which basic abilities underlie performance on a test. The triarchic approach (Answer B) refers to a cognitive approach developed by Sternberg that distinguishes three aspects of intelligence: componential (which is Answer C), experiential, and contextual.

15. Answer A is correct because the psychometric approach to intelligence focuses on how well people perform on standardized mental tests. The triarchic approach (Answer B) refers to a cognitive approach to intelligence developed by Sternberg. The cognitive approach (Answer C) emphasizes the strategies people use when thinking about problems and arriving at a solution.

16. Answer B is correct. The psychometric approach to intelligence focuses on how well people perform on standardized mental tests whereas the cognitive approach emphasizes the strategies people use when thinking about problems and arriving at a solution. Answer A presents the correct terms but the relationship is in the reverse order. Answer C compares two theories that are both cognitive approaches to intelligence. Answer D compares two theories of intelligence rather than describing the two general approaches.

17. Answer D is correct. Answer A is correct since people strong in componential intelligence tend to do well on conventional mental tests. Answers B and C are correct since componential intelligence refers to the information-processing strategies that go on inside people's head when they are thinking intelligently about a problem.

18. Answer C is correct because experiential intelligence refers to how well you transfer skills to new situations. Emily is transferring her skills to a new situation. Answer A refers to information-processing strategies. Contextual intelligence (Answer B) refers to the practical application of intelligence; knowing when to adapt to an environment and when to change environments and when to fix the situation. Metacognitive (Answer D) is not one of the types of Sternberg's intelligences. Rather it refers to having knowledge of one's own cognitive processes and the ability to monitor and control those processes.

19. Answer D is correct because intelligence tests began to be administered to huge groups of people (Answer A). Americans used the tests not to bring slow learners up to the average (Answer B) but instead they were used to "track" people in school and in the armed services according to their presumed "natural ability" (Answer C).

20. Answer C is correct. Critics complained that tests developed between World War I and the 1960s favored city children over rural ones, middle-class children over poor ones, and white children over minority children. They said that the tests did not measure the kinds of knowledge and skills that are intelligent in a minority neighborhood or in the hills of Appalachia. Answer A and B represent other criticisms of the use of IQ tests but not the one represented in this question. Prior to 1937, girls scored higher than boys at every age, so in the 1937 revision of the Stanford-Binet test, Terman deleted the items on which boys had done poorly thereby eliminating sex differences (Answer D).

21. Answer B is correct. The domains of intelligence identified by Gardner are relatively independent, and each may even have its own neural structures. People with brain damage often lose one of the seven without losing their competence in the others. Sternberg's theory (Answer A) does not describe separate, independent domains of intelligence. The text does not describe a theory of intelligence advanced by Terman (Answer C), but rather the longest-running psychological study of the top 1 percent of the distribution of IQ scores. Because Gardner's theory is the correct answer, Answer D is incorrect.

22. Answer C is correct. Actors, athletes, and dancers use bodily-kinesthetic intelligence while insight into oneself and others requires the use of emotional intelligence. Answers A, B, and D refer to others of Garner's domains of intelligence with the exception of D which uses the term interpersonal intelligence. Interpersonal abilities are related to the domain of emotional intelligence.

23. Answer C is correct. Various research studies have identified motivation as a crucial factor in success. There is no evidence that low contextual intelligence (Answer A), poor practical intelligence (Answer B) or mild brain damage (Answer D) would explain why someone with a very high IQ would continue to perform below his ability in school.

24. Answer D is correct. Stevenson and his colleagues found that the following differences were present between Asians and Americans: Americans believed that certain abilities were innate whereas the Asians emphasized working hard (Answer A), American parents had far lower standards for their children's performance (Answer B), American students had more conflicting demands on their time than the Asian students (Answer D).

25. Answer C is correct because displacement refers to the aspect of language that permits communication about objects and events that are not present here and now--that are displaced in time or space. Meaningfulness (Answer A) refers to the use of consistent combination of sounds or gestures into meaningful units such as world or signs. Productivity (Answer B) refers to a set of grammatical rules that allow the expression and comprehension of an infinite number of novel utterances. Creativity (Answer D) is not one of the criteria for human language.

ANSWER KEY - PRACTICE TEST 3 - SHORT ANSWER

1. mental
2. concept
3. basic
4. proposition; cognitive schema
5. subconscious
6. nonconscious
7. must; is probably
8. formal; algorithm
9. informal reasoning
10. reflective
11. quasi-reflective
12. mental sets
13. availability heuristic
14. dissonance
15. achievement; aptitude
16. psychometric approach; cognitive approach
17. biased; culture
18. general; multiple
19. triarchic; contextual
20. componential, experiential, contextual
21. multiple
22. motivation; cultural attitudes
23. lower
24. displacement; productivity
25. anthropomorphism

ANSWER KEY - PRACTICE TEST 4 - TRUE/FALSE

1. F	2. T	3. T	4. F	5. F
6. F	7. T	8. F	9. F	10. T
11. T	12. T	13. F	14. F	15. F
16. T	17. F	18. F	19. F	20. F
21. F	22. T	23. T	24. F	25. F

ANSWER KEY - PRACTICE TEST 5 - ESSAY

1.   A.   Coat   B.   Horse
       C.   Dog   D.   Uncle

2.   A.   The ship's position must be deduced. The position of the North Star and the formula are two premises that, once known, will allow the conclusion to be determined with certainty.
       B.   Scientists of all types rely on inductive reasoning. Enough cases must be collected before a conclusion can be drawn.
       C.   The overall process is dialectical reasoning, which is likely to incorporate inductive and deductive reasoning. It will be necessary to assess potential outcomes, risks, losses and appropriate considerations.
       D.   Again, the overall process is dialectical reasoning, which will probably incorporate inductive and deductive reasoning.

3.   A.   Exaggerating the improbable
       B.   Cognitive dissonance and justification of effort
       C.   Confirmation bias

4.   A.   Sternberg's componential intelligence; Gardner's logical-mathematical intelligence
       B.   Sternberg's contextual intelligence; Gardner's interpersonal intelligence
       C.   Sternberg's experiential intelligence; Gardner's interpersonal intelligence and intrapersonal intelligence

5. A. Evidence supporting cognitive abilities in nonhumans:
    1. Evidence on herons, sea otters and assassin bugs related to their food gathering habits reflects behaviors that appear intelligent.
    2. Some chimpanzees use objects as rudimentary tools, and there is evidence for some summing abilities and the use of numerals to label quantities.
    3. Some primates demonstrate the ability to use some aspects of language like: learning signs from sign language, understanding words and some sentences, using signs to converse with each other, ability to manipulate keyboard symbols to request food without formal training, use of some simple grammatical rules.
    4. Other evidence exists from dolphins and parrots.

    B. Evidence against cognitive abilities in nonhumans:
    1. The meaning of these abilities is questioned; human meaning may be attributed to these actions.
    2. Early studies were overinterpreted and biased.
    3. It's unclear whether the use of signs and symbols were strung together without any particular order or syntax.
    4. While an animal may be "conscious," in the sense of being aware of its environment, it does not know that it knows and is unable to think about its own thoughts in the way that human beings do.

CROSSWORD PUZZLE KEY

ACROSS

1. confirmation
2. set
4. thinking
5. propositions
13. dissonance
14. reasoning
16. deductive
17. componential

DOWN

1. concept
2. experiential
5. heuristics
6. intelligence
8. prototypical
9. schemas
10. inductive
11. nonconscious
12. metacognition
14. triarchic

ANSWER KEYS FOR CHAPTER 10

ANSWER KEY - PRACTICE TEST 1- MULTIPLE CHOICE

1. A (p. 351)	2. D (pp. 351-352)	3. C (p. 357)	4. B (p. 359)
5. C (p. 359)	6. C (p. 359)	7. D (pp. 361-363)	8. D (p. 359)
9. C (p. 361)	10. B (pp. 360-361)	11. A (p. 361)	12. B (pp. 361-363)
13. C (p. 363)	14. A (p. 364)	15. C (p. 364)	16. C (pp. 364-365)
17. C (p. 366)	18. C (p. 366)	19. B (pp. 367-368)	20. A (pp. 369-371)
21. D (pp. 372-373)	22. B (p. 378)	23. D (pp. 376-381)	24. D (pp. 382-383)
25. C (pp. 383-385)			

ANSWER KEY - PRACTICE TEST 2 - MULTIPLE CHOICE

1. D	2. A	3. D	4. B
5. C	6. D	7. A	8. C
9. C	10. D	11. C	12. D
13. D	14. D	15. A	16. C
17. B	18. B	19. A	20. D
21. C	22. C	23. D	24. A
25. B			

ANNOTATED ANSWER KEY - PRACTICE TEST 2

1. Answer D is correct. Laboratory research shows that false memories can be confused with real memories and false memories can be as stable over time as true ones. While witnesses may not lie to cover memory errors (Answer A), they may unintentionally reconstruct memories to fill in the gaps in memory. Reconstructed memories may contain some aspects of truth but they are constructed and not remembered (Answer B). The text does not discuss the relationship between reconstructed testimony and outcomes on lie detector tests (Answer C).

2. Answer D is correct. Memories are unintentionally reconstructed to cover memory deficits. The text gives an example with the patient H.M. Answers A, B, and C are not cited as reasons people unintentionally reconstruct memories.

3. Answer D is correct. Recognition and recall are the two methods for measuring explicit memory (conscious recollection). Recall is the ability to retrieve and reproduce information encountered earlier. Essay and fill-in-the-blank exams require recall. Recognition involves the ability to identify information you have previously observed, read, or heard about. True-false and multiple-choice tests call for recognition. Answer A mismatches multiple choice with recall and uses relearning as the second term. Relearning requires you to relearn information or a task that you learned earlier. If you fail to recall some or all of the material, yet you master it more quickly the second time, you must be remembering something from the first experience. Answer B contains the correct terms but in the wrong order. Answer C correctly matches recall with essay, but incorrectly lists priming as the term related to recall that is analogous to multiple choice. Priming is a method that is used to identify implicit memories.

4. Answer B is correct. Relearning (Answer A) requires you to relearn information or a task that you learned earlier. If you fail to recall some or all of the material yet you master it more quickly the second time, you must be remembering something from the first experience. Explicit memory (Answer C) is conscious memory and recall and recognition are the two methods used to measure explicit memory. The question describes the method of priming. Priming (Answer D), the method used for measuring implicit memory, is described in the question.

5. Answer C is correct. Information-processing models of memory suggest that remembering begins with the conversion of information to a form that the brain can process and store. One of the ways we convert information is to integrate it with what we already know or believe, incorporating it into an existing web of knowledge called a cognitive schema. The parallel distributed processing model (Answer A) suggests that knowledge is represented not as propositions but as connections among thousands of interacting processing units, distributed in a vast network and all operating in parallel. This model is considered a connectionist model, therefore Answer B is also incorrect. Implicit, the term used in Answer D, refers to a type of memory, not a model of memory.

6. Answer D is correct. Answers A, B, and C all describe aspects of the parallel distributed processing model.

7. Answer A is correct. The parallel distributed processing model suggests that knowledge is represented as connections among thousands of interacting processing units, all operating in parallel. It reverses the notion that the human brain can be modeled after a computer. This model suggests that the brain is much more complex than a computer (Answer B). Answers C and D give incorrect information about the brain.

8. Answer C is correct. According to the three-box model, pattern recognition, the preliminary identification of a stimulus on the basis of information already contained in long-term memory, occurs during the transfer of information from sensory memory to short-term memory. Pattern recognition does not occur during storage of information in short-term memory (Answer A). It occurs before the transfer of information from short-term memory to long-term memory, therefore Answers C and D are incorrect.

9. Answer C is correct. Short-term memory retains information for up to about 30 seconds. Answer A gives too short a time period, while Answers B and D give too long a period.

10. Answer D is correct. Maintenance rehearsal (Answer A) involves the rote repetition of the material and is fine for keeping information in STM. Deep processing (Answer B) is a strategy for prolonging retention and refers to the processing of meaning. Elaborative rehearsal (Answer C) is a strategy more likely to lead to long-term retention. It involves associating new items of information with material that has already been stored or with other new facts.

11. Answer C is correct. Short-term memory has a limited capacity and information only passes through there briefly (like a loading dock). The capacity of long-term memory seems to have no practical limits and information can remain there for the long-term (like a huge warehouse). Answers A, B, and D all present terms that are not analogous.

12. Answer D is correct. Deep processing (Answer A) prolongs retention and involves the processing of meaning. Chunking (Answer B) involves grouping small bits of information into larger units which increases the amount of information that can be contained in STM, and therefore, passed on to LTM. Elaborative rehearsal (Answer C) involves forming associations between new material and that which has already been stored. All three of these methods helps transfer information from STM to LTM.

13. Answer D is correct. Because long-term memory contains so much information, the contents is indexed by semantic categories, the sound of a word, familiarity, relevance, or association. Information in sensory memory is short-lived (Answers A and C). Visual images, or icons, remain for a maximum of half a second and auditory images, or echoes, remain for a slightly longer time. The storage of information in STM is not discussed in the text (Answer B).

14. Answer D is correct. Operant conditioning involves the process by which a response becomes more or less likely to occur, depending on the consequences. Declarative memories (Answer A) are memories of "knowing that," and they are usually assumed to be explicit or conscious (Answer C). Knowing that a particular consequence follows a certain response influences the likelihood a response will reoccur. Therefore operant conditioning depends on declarative memory. Semantic memory (Answer B) is one of the two types of declarative memory. Semantic memories include facts, rules, and concepts.

15. Answer A is correct. Semantic memories are internal representations of the world, independent of any particular context. Episodic memories are internal representations of personally experienced events. Both are types of declarative memories, which involve "knowing that" and are explicit. Procedural memories (Answer C), memories of knowing how, are sometimes considered implicit (Answer B) because they do not require much conscious processing. The primacy effect (Answer D) refers to the way information on a list is retained and is not closely related to semantic and episodic memories.

16. Answer C is correct. At the time of recall, the last few items are still sitting in short-term memory. The first few items on a list, not the last few as suggested by Answer A, are remembered well because they have the best chance of getting into long-term memory. Short-term memory was relatively empty at the time the first few items on a list are entered, not when the last few items as suggested in Answer B. When the last few items are being entered, short-term memory is full but that information gets dumped as the recent information is entered. Because Answers A and B are incorrect, Answer D is also incorrect.

17. Answer B is correct. Under some conditions, the last items on a list are well remembered even when the test is delayed past the time when short-term memory has presumably been "emptied" and filled with other information. The recency effect occurs even when, according to the three-box model, it should not. The question does not describe the primacy effect (Answer A) which occurs when recall is best for items at the beginning of a list. The question does not mention the use of strategies for extending recall in STM (Answer C). Information remains in sensory memory for only several seconds or less, therefore the question is not referring to sensory memory (Answer D).

18. Answer B is correct. Elaborative rehearsal involves associating new items of information with material that has already been stored or with other new facts and it increases long-term retention. Answers A and C refer to the rote repetition of material and are fine for keeping information in STM, not for getting information into LTM. Therefore, Answer D is incorrect as well.

19. Answer A is correct. In short-term memory, changes occur within neurons that temporarily alter their ability to release neurotransmitters. In long-term memory, changes occur that involve permanent structural changes in the brain. Answer B provides the correct answers in the opposite order. During short-term memory tasks, areas in the frontal lobes of the brain are especially active, while in the formation of long-term declarative memories, the hippocampus and adjacent parts of the temporal lobe cortex play a critical role. Answer C provides different information and is therefore, incorrect. Answer D indicates that long-term potentiation is associated with short-term memory and changes in the neurons are associated with long-term memory. Long-term potentiation, which is an increase in the strength of synaptic responsiveness, is associated with long-term memory while changes in the neuron's ability to release neurotransmitters is associated with short-term memory.

20. Answer D is correct. Long-term potentiation which is a long-lasting increase in the strength of synaptic responsiveness (Answers A and C), is associated with the formation of long-term memories (Answer B).

21. Answer C is correct. Proactive interference is a type of forgetting in which old information may interfere with the ability to remember new information. Retroactive interference (Answer A) refers to forgetting because new information interferes with the ability to remember old information. Motivated forgetting (Answer B) is an explanation of forgetting that suggests people might be motivated to forget events for many reasons, including embarrassment, guilt, shock, and a desire to protect one's pride. The decay theory (Answer D) holds that memory traces fade with time if they are not "accessed" now and then.

22. Answer C is correct. When we need to remember, we rely on retrieval cues. Cues that were present at the time you learned a new fact are apt to be especially useful as retrieval aids. That may explain why remembering is often easier when you are in the same physical environment as you were when an event occurred. In this question, the study environment can serve as a retrieval cue for information you are trying to remember on the test. Your mental or physical state may also act as a retrieval cue, evoking a state-dependent memory (Answer A). Elaborated rehearsal (Answer B) involves associating new items of information with material that has already been stored or with other new facts and it increases long-term retention. Deja vu (Answer D) refers to the false sense of having been in exactly the same situation before. The experience of deja vu is likely related to a match between present and past retrieval cues.

23. Answer D is correct. The explanations given in Answers A, B, and C are all described in the text as possible reasons for childhood amnesia.

24. Answer A is correct. Because people often find childhood amnesia difficult to accept, some people claim to remember events from the second or even the first year of life. These memories are merely reconstructions based on photographs, family stories, and imagination. Early memories such as those described by Jocelyn are more likely to be the incorporation of other information into her memories than lies or intentional deception. If they are lies or intentional construction, they are clearly not memories (Answers B and D). There is no evidence that certain people have early memory capacity (Answer C).

25. Answer B is correct. Gerbner suggests that we compose narratives to make sense of our lives and, in turn, the narratives can shape our lives. This statement is not about human creativity (Answer A), self-deception (Answer C) or innate story-telling motivations (Answer D). It is about trying to make sense of our lives and the effects doing so.

ANSWER KEY - PRACTICE TEST 3 - SHORT ANSWER

1. reconstructive
2. source
3. stable
4. suggestive
5. recall; recognition
6. explicit
7. implicit; priming
8. information processing
9. encode; store; retrieve
10. sensory; short-term
11. parallel distributed processing
12. chunks
13. semantic
14. network
15. semantic; episodic; declarative
16. serial position
17. maintenance; elaborative
18. mnemonics
19. potentiation; consolidation
20. epinephrine
21. decay
22. retroactive; proactive
23. retrieval; cue-dependent
24. state-dependent
25. amnesia

ANSWER KEY - PRACTICE TEST 4 - TRUE/FALSE

1. T	2. F	3. T	4. F	5. F
6. T	7. T	8. T	9. F	10. T
11. T	12. F	13. T	14. F	15. T
16. F	17. F	18. F	19. T	20. T
21. F	22. F	23. T	24. F	25. T

ANSWER KEY - PRACTICE TEST 5 - ESSAY

1. To be remembered, material first must be encoded into the form in which it is to be retained. Storage takes place in various areas of the brain, which appears to correspond to structural changes in the brain. Retrieval is the process by which stored material is located for current use.

2. Information entering through the senses is briefly held in sensory memory, where preliminary sorting and encoding take place. It is then transferred to short-term storage, where it is rehearsed. Finally, as a result of deep processing or elaborative rehearsal, it is forwarded to long-term storage, where it is indexed and organized to become part of the network of more permanent material.

3. A.   Procedural memory
    B.   Episodic memory
    C.   Semantic memory

4. Memory processes are subject to distortion in recall. Selection pressures bias information within sensory memory. Short-term memory simplifies, condenses and even adds meaning as information is being processed. In long-term storage, information is organized and indexed within the pre-existing framework, allowing memories to become intermixed. As information is retrieved, distortion can result from interferences and reasoning involved in reconstructing the event.

5. A. According to decay theory, virtually all the details should be forgotten because of the long time interval involved. The only memories remaining should be those used from time to time as the person grew older.

    B. The absence of retrieval cues is often a source of forgetting. The example suggests that the mental image created by the description of the homeroom was a cue that released a set of associated memories.

    C. Some emotionally unpleasant situations may be forgotten more rapidly and may be harder to recall than other situations. For the sake of emotional comfort, Henry may be motivated to forget situations associated with personal distress.

6. Interference arises as memory incorporates similar material in succession. Assuming there is greatest similarity between Italian and Spanish, these should be kept as separate as possible, as well as overlearned and frequently reviewed. Breaks would also help as you go from one topic of study to another. A sequence like Italian, math, English, history and Spanish would be better than Spanish, Italian, English, math and history.

CROSSWORD PUZZLE KEY

ACROSS

1. memory
3. semantic
5. recognition
6. cues
8. storage
9. recall
11. narratives
14. short-term
16. amnesia
17. episodic
18. primacy
19. proactive

DOWN

1. mnemonics
2. reconstruction
3. sensory
4. consolidation
5. retrieval
7. deep
10. long-term
12. retroactive
13. procedural
15. decay

ANSWER KEYS FOR CHAPTER 11

ANSWER KEY - PRACTICE TEST 1 - MULTIPLE CHOICE

1. D (p. 385)	2. A (p. 385)	3. B (p. 385)	4. C (p. 386)
5. A (p. 387)	6. C (p. 388)	7. D (p. 388)	8. D (pp. 388-389)
9. C (p. 390)	10. B (pp. 390)	11. A (p. 389)	12. B (p. 390)
13. D (p. 390)	14. A (p. 390)	15. A (p. 391)	16. D (pp. 390-391)
17. B (pp. 394-395)	18. B (p. 394)	19. C (p. 396)	20. D (pp. 399-400)
21. C (p. 402)	22. D (pp. 402-403)	23. A (p. 402)	24. B (p. 406)
25. D (pp. 406-410)			

ANSWER KEY - PRACTICE TEST 2 - MULTIPLE CHOICE

1. A	2. B	3. D	4. C
5. D	6. D	7. D	8. C
9. D	10. B	11. C	12. B
13. B	14. A	15. C	16. B
17. C	18. C	19. B	20. D
21. D	22. D	23. C	24. C
25. C			
25. C			

ANNOTATED ANSWER KEY - PRACTICE TEST 2

1. Answer A is correct because this example includes the three influences on the full experience of emotions: physiological changes in the face and body (Terri's heart races and she smiles), cognitive processes such as interpretations of events (she interprets the situation as a positive one), and cultural influences that shape the experience and expression of emotions (it is expected that she is to receive the award publicly, to control her nervousness and to smile). Answers B and D are incorrect because they leave out all the physiological responses like racing heart. Answer C is incorrect because it leaves out the cognitive and cultural influences described in the question.

2. Answer B is correct. Darwin argued that facial expressions evolved in order that humans might tell at a glance the difference between a friendly and hostile stranger. Knowing this difference had a survival value. Modern psychologists have supported Darwin's evolutionary explanation by confirming that certain emotional expressions are recognized the world over. Answer A is incorrect since facial expressions are not discussed in terms of primary or secondary functions. Answer C is incorrect since two-factor refers to a theory of emotion and does not have to do with the consequences of recognizing whether strangers are friendly or hostile. Answer D is incorrect since neurocultural refers to Ekman's theory of how we recognize facial expressions.

3. Answer D is correct. Answers A, B, and C are all conclusions of Ekman's cross-cultural studies on facial expressions.

4. Answer C is correct because some researchers argue that facial expressions may or may not correspond with our internal emotional states. Also because we can use facial expressions to lie about our feelings as well as to reflect them, Answers A, B, and D are incorrect. We cannot necessarily tell what someone is feeling based on their facial expressions.

5. Answer D is correct. The role of facial feedback refers to the idea that facial muscles send messages to the brain about the basic emotion being expressed and therefore facial expressions can influence emotions. The two-factor theory (Answer A) refers to Schachter and Singer's theory that emotion depends on two factors: physiological arousal and the interpretation of that arousal. The neurocultural theory (Answer B) suggests that there are two factors involved in facial expression: a neurophysiological one and a cultural one. Neither of these theories explains why someone's mood would improved as a result of smiling. The idea that there are primary or universal emotions (Answer C) would not account for an improvement in mood that is related to continued smiling.

6. Answer D is correct. The right hemisphere is especially important for processing and expressing emotional information such as, the ability understand jokes and emotions portrayed in films and stories. Therefore Answers B, C, and D are all incorrect.

7. Answer D is correct. Pathways in the limbic system (Answer A) prompt the amygdala (Answer C) to respond to incoming sensory information, which may then be "overridden" by a more accurate appraisal from the cerebral cortex (Answer B).

8. Answer C is correct. The two cerebral hemispheres play different roles in the experience of positive and negative emotions. Regions of the left hemisphere are specialized for processing such positive emotions as happiness, whereas certain regions of the right hemisphere are specialized for such negative emotions as fear and sadness. Answer A contains the terms in the reverse order. Answer B contains terms that are both related to positive emotions while Answer D contains terms that are both related to negative emotions.

9. Answer D is correct. Epinephrine (Answer A) and norepinephrine (Answer C) activate the sympathetic division of the autonomic nervous system and thus produce a state of arousal. The adrenal glands (Answer B) produce epinephrine and norepinephrine in response to many challenges in the environment.

10. Answer B is correct. Though some emotions do produce common reactions that mobilize the body to cope with the environment, they have chemical as well as anatomical differences. Answer A is incorrect because in one series of experiments the emotions of fear, disgust, anger, sadness, surprise, and happiness was each associated with a somewhat different pattern of autonomic activity. Anger and surprise are not considered the same emotion (Answer C). Though they involve distinct patterns of autonomic activity, they both involve the autonomic nervous system, so Answer D is incorrect.

11. Answer C is correct. The two-factor theory says that while bodily changes are necessary to experience an emotion, they are not enough. You must also interpret, explain, and label that arousal as an emotion or you won't feel a true emotion. Answer A is incorrect since it states that you will not feel a need to explain the changes in your body. Since the two-factor theory states that the interpretation of bodily changes is necessary to feel a true emotion, Answer B is incorrect. Answer D is incorrect because, according to this theory, your emotional response will depend on your interpretation of the arousal.

12. Answer B is correct. Most people assume that success on a project brings happiness, and failure brings unhappiness. In fact, people's emotions depend on how they explain their success and failure as demonstrated by a series on experiments with students. Students' emotions were more closely associated with their explanations than with the outcome of the test. Therefore, Answer A is incorrect. The perceptions of others (Answer C) and past experiences with success or failure (Answer D) were not discussed in relation to this study.

13.   Answer B is correct.   Most researchers regard polygraph tests as invalid because no physiological patterns of responses are specific to lying.   There are no reports about the frequency of breakage (Answer A) or corruption associated with their use (Answer D). While they may let the guilty go free, they may also find the innocent guilty so Answer C is incorrect.

14.   Answer A is correct. Cognitive appraisals, or explanations of events, are an essential part of the experience of emotion.   No research is cited regarding the influence on emotions of a person's participation in events (Answer B), control over (Answer C) or disagreement with events (Answer D).

15.   Answer C is correct because anger often occurs in association with shame. Studies show that guilt (Answer A) is not related to anger.   Regret (Answer B) is not discussed in relation to anger. Answer D is incorrect because research does show that there is a link between shame and anger.

16.   Answer B is correct. Shame is related to anger, resentment, and blame, but guilt is not. Therefore, Answers A, C. and D are incorrect. In the case of guilt, people think they can try to fix their bad behavior.

17.   Answer C is correct. Studies suggest that people can learn how their thinking affects their emotions and change their thinking accordingly. This, in turn, can modify their emotions. Cognitive therapy (Chapter 17) is based on this assumption. Therefore Answers A, B, and D are incorrect.

18.   Answer C is correct. The terms used in this question represent emotions described only in particular cultures.   Secondary emotions are culture-specific.   Primary emotions (Answer A) refers to emotions that are experienced universally and the emotions described in the question are not those experienced universally. Emotion work (Answer B) refers to acting out an emotion we don't really feel. Prototypes (Answer D) of emotions are those basic emotions that people everywhere consider the core examples of the category "emotion."   Because the terms in this question are culture specific, they are not prototypes.

19. Answer B is correct. Primary emotions are thought to be experienced universally and therefore they do not differ in each culture (Answer A). Though they are experienced universally, they do not result in similar behaviors in different cultures (Answer C). Cultures have different display rules that govern how and when emotions may be expressed. Primary emotions are not thought to be blends of secondary emotions (Answer D).

20. Answer D is correct. Culture can affect what people feel emotional about (Answer A), how emotions are expressed (Answer B) and the meaning of expressions of emotions (Answer C).

21. Answer D is correct. "Being emotional" refers to an internal emotional state (Answer A), nonverbal expressions (Answer B), and the display of an emotion (Answer C).

22. Answer D is correct. Critics of the universalist argument maintain that the effort to find biological universals in emotion masks the profound influence of culture on every aspect of emotional experience (Answer B), starting with which feelings a culture considers "basic" (Answer A). Many people disagree on which emotions are really primary (Answer C).

23. Answer C is correct because emotion work refers to acting out an emotion we don't really feel, or trying to create the right emotion for the occasion. Employees are expected to be cooperative and cheerful and comply with their bosses demands. Answers A, B, and D are all examples of emotional expressions that are inconsistent with cultural expectations.

24. Answer C is correct. There is little evidence that, around the world, one sex feels emotions more often than the other. Therefore, Answer A is incorrect. Answer B is incorrect because women report a greater tendency to talk about their emotions--especially emotions that reveal vulnerability and helplessness, such as fear, sadness, loneliness, shame, and guilt. Answer D is incorrect because less powerful people learn to read the powerful person's signals, usually for self-protection.

25. Answer C is correct. Riessman found that while the men in her study claimed they felt sad only "some or a little of the time" (the opposite of Answers A and B) and that they felt depressed or lonely "none of the time", they expressed grief in ways that are acceptably masculine: "frantic work," heavy drinking, driving too fast, singing sentimental songs. Men did not report staying in bed or talking about their unhappiness with friends and family (Answer D).

ANSWER KEY - PRACTICE TEST 3 - SHORT ANSWER

1. face
2. basic
3. neurocultural
4. facial feedback
5. amygdala; cerebral cortex
6. left; right
7. sympathetic (or autonomic); epinephrine, norepinephrine
8. patterns
9. physiological; cognitive
10. attributions
11. appraisals
12. shame; guilt
13. cognitions; emotions
14. primary; secondary
15. prototypes
16. display rules
17. work
18. nonverbal
19. cultures
20. contagion
21. no
22. provocation; sensitive
23. perceptions
24. power
25. express

ANSWER KEY - PRACTICE TEST 4 - TRUE/FALSE

1. F	2. T	3. F	4. T	5. F
6. T	7. F	8. F	9. F	10. T
11. T	12. F	13. F	14. T	15. F
16. F	17. T	18. F	19. F	20. F
21. T	22. T	23. F	24. F	25. T

ANSWER KEY - PRACTICE TEST 5 - ESSAY

1.   A.   The facial-feedback hypothesis assumes that emotion and facial expression are intimately interconnected. Distinct facial expressions not only identify emotions but contribute to them as well. By posing the face, performers may actually engender emotions in themselves.

       B.   They indicate that outward expressions can be masked or even faked. More importantly, they indicate that learning is important in the expression of emotion.

       C.   Emotion work might be defined as the ability to intentionally alter facial expression and body language to simulate a chosen emotion.

       D.   For Darwin, facial expression was biologically wired because of its adaptive communication value. Because the face rather than the body is the focal point of social interaction, body expressions need not be similarly wired.

2.   A.   An increase in epinephrine and norepinephrine is brought about by the adrenal glands and under the control of the autonomic nervous system. Involvement of the amygdala, limbic system and cortex contribute to this arousal response.

       B.   The patient is functioning according to the display rules for men, which dictate that men should not feel fear or anxiety. The nurse is doing the emotion work associated with the role of a nurse. Nurses are supposed to be comforting and pleasant to patients.

       C.   Cerebral cortex

3.   These results are consistent with the idea that it is our interpretation of events that is instrumental in the experiencing of emotion rather than the event. The students' reactions are based on their explanations and interpretations of why they got those grades. Larry studied hard and expected a better grade. His depressive reaction may have to do with the fact that since he studied and did not do better, he may see himself as stupid, which is an internal and stable interpretation. Curly studied a little bit for the test so he felt relieved that he got a "C". The grade has no bearing on his view of himself. He did not expect to fail, but did not really expect a better grade. Moe did not study at all so he interpreted the grade as very lucky. The grade did not influence his view of himself, but rather he interpreted it as due to external luck.

4. A. Display rules govern the recipients of gifts.
   B. Emotion work involves acting out emotions not truly felt.
   C. The facial expression of anger is universally recognizable. Moreover, the husband's familiarity with Mary should make any idiosyncratic expressive features easily identifiable.
   D. The emotion work is implied by gender roles.
   E. She has a combination of lower status, high familiarity, sexual similarity and gender.
   F. All of the reactions do.

CROSSWORD PUZZLE KEY

ACROSS

3. facial-feedback
5. emotion
6. body
7. display
10. primary
11. cognitions
12. polygraph

DOWN

1. epinephrine
2. secondary
4. norepinephrine
8. amygdala
9. two-factor

ANSWER KEYS FOR CHAPTER 12

ANSWER KEY - PRACTICE TEST 1 - MULTIPLE CHOICE

1. C (p. 421)	2. B (p. 421)	3. C (p. 421)	4. D (p. 422)
5. A (p. 422)	6. C (pp. 422-423)	7. A (p. 422)	8. C (p. 426)
9. B (p. 426-428)	10. C (pp. 427-428)	11. D (p. 433)	12. D (p. 433)
13. A (p. 435)	14. C (p. 436)	15. B (p. 436)	16. C (p. 436)
17. B (p. 437)	18. D (p. 440)	19. D (pp. 438-439)	20. D (pp. 441-444)
21. B (p. 448)	22. B (pp. 442-443)	23. A (p. 443)	24. A (p. 449)
25. B (p. 451)			

ANSWER KEY - PRACTICE TEST 2 - MULTIPLE CHOICE

1. C	2. B	3. A	4. B
5. D	6. B	7. D	8. B
9. D	10. C	11. C	12. B
13. B	14. B	15. C	16. C
17. C	18. B	19. D	20. A
21. A	22. B	23. C	24. A
25. D			

ANNOTATED ANSWER KEY - PRACTICE TEST 2

1.	Answer C is correct. Motivation refers to an inferred process within a person or animal that causes that organism to move toward a goal or away from an unpleasant situation. The example in this question describes the movement away from one situation and toward another. Answers A, B and D refer to drive theory which, for many decades, dominated the study of motivation. Drive theory emphasized biological needs resulting from states of physical deprivation, such as a lack of food or water (Answers A and B). Such needs create a physiological drive that motivates an organism to satisfy the need (Answer D). The behavior described in this question does not include physiological drives. Since we have only a few primary, unlearned drives, it soon became apparent that drive theory could not account for the complexity and variety of human emotions.

2.	Answer B is correct. Affiliation, attachment, love, and work are considered social motives. They are learned (therefore Answers A, C, and D are all incorrect), some in childhood, some in later life.

3.   Answer A is correct. The need for affiliation refers to the motive to be with others, to make friends, to cooperate, to love. This questions describes two people with different needs to be with others. Attachment needs (Answer B) refers to the need for the deep emotional tie to, and sense of almost physical connection with, a loved one. The questions does not describe Jerry's or Harry's attachment needs. Contact comfort (Answer C) refers to the need for touching. The question does not address this. The text describes several love styles (Answer D), but neither Jerry's nor Harry's style of loving is described.

4.   Answer B is correct. Margaret and Harry Harlow first demonstrated the primate need for touching, or contact comfort. Psychologists concluded that one of the purposes of infant attachment is contact comfort. Based on these studies, we would expect Lucia to be most likely to go to her dad when she is upset. Therefore, Answers A, C, and D are incorrect.

5.   Answer D is correct. The Harlow studies demonstrated the need for contact and Answers A, B, and C all describe accurate examples of the importance of touching.

6.   Answer B is correct. Ainsworth identified three attachment types in children. Anxious or ambivalent children may cry to be picked up and then demand to be put down, or they may behave as if they are angry with the mother and resist her efforts to comfort them. Children with an avoidant attachment style (Answer A) did not care if their mothers left the room and made little effort to seek contact with her on her return. Children with a secure attachment style (Answer C) cried if their parent left the room and welcomed her back upon her return. Ainsworth did not use the category of "psychological problems" to describe the subjects in her study.

7.   Answer D is correct. Temperament, stressful events, and family circumstances may all have an influence on attachment styles.

8.   Answer B is correct. Eros, according to Lee's theory of styles of loving, is romantic, passionate love. All the remaining answer options belong to Lee's theory. Pragma (Answer A) refers to logical, pragmatic love. Ludus (Answer C) refers to game-playing love and storge (Answer D) refers to affectionate, friendly love.

9.   Answer D is correct. Pragma refers to logical, pragmatic love according to Lee's theory of styles of loving. Ludus (Answer A) refers to game-playing love. Storge (Answer B) refers to affectionate, friendly love and agape (Answer C) refers to unselfish love.

10. Answer C is correct. In Lee's terms, pragmatic and storgic lovers are likely to be securely attached and those with secure attachments aren't jealous, nervous, or worried about being abandoned. A combination of avoidant-avoidant love styles (Answer A) would probably not occur since avoidant people distrust and avoid all intimate attachments. A ludic-ludic combination (Answer B) would be likely to result in game-playing by both partners. An avoidant female-anxious male combination (Answer D) would be likely to result in a relationship in which the female was continually backing away and the male was jealous and anxious about rejection.

11. Answer C is correct. Many kinds of studies have implicated the role of testosterone in sexual motivation: studies of men who have been chemically castrated; of men who have abnormally low testosterone levels; of women who are taking androgens after having their ovaries removed; and of women who kept diaries of their sexual activity while also having their hormone levels measured. The studies described focus on the biology of desire. Cognitive interpretations (Answer A) and cultural scripts (Answer B) have an influence on sexual behavior but are studied in different ways. Therefore, Answer D is also incorrect.

12. Answer B is correct. Kinsey pioneered the idea that males and females are alike in their basic anatomy and physiology. Masters and Johnson confirmed that male and female arousal and orgasms are remarkably similar. Answer A is incorrect because Masters and Johnson confirmed that all orgasms are physiologically the same, regardless of the source of stimulation. Answer C is incorrect because one of the criticisms of Masters and Johnson is that they did not examine how sexual response might vary among individuals according to age, experience, and culture. Answer D is incorrect because research has found that people's subjective experience of orgasm does not always correlate strongly with their physiological responses (the opposite of Answer D).

13. Answer B is correct. In one survey of college students, 63 percent of the men reported having had unwanted intercourse because of peer pressure, inexperience, a desire for popularity, and a fear of seeming homosexual or "unmasculine." Women said they "gave in" because it was easier than having an argument; because they didn't want to lose the relationship; because they felt obligated, or because the partner made them feel guilty or inhibited. Answers A, C, and D present combinations that are associated with the other gender.

14. Answer B is correct. What many women experience as coercion is not seen as such by many men. The explanation is one of interpretation of behavior rather than an inferred psychological process such as denial (Answer A). There is no evidence to support the idea that women overexaggerate these experiences (Answer C) and that idea perpetuates a stereotype about sexual coercion. Answer D refers to a belief that is sometimes used to justify sexual coercion and could be part of the gender difference in the perception of coercion.

15. Answer C is correct. Researchers found that sexually aggressive males are characterized by hostile masculinity (being insecure, defensive, and hostile toward women, and wishing to dominate women) and by a preference for promiscuous, impersonal sex. Psychiatric disorders (Answer A) is not discussed as a predictor of men who rape. In most cases the rapist is known to the victim. They may have dated once or a few times; they may have been friends; they may even be married. Rape is not just a matter of sexual desire (Answer B), but by its very nature, it implies hostility and a devaluing of the victim (not an adoration of women as stated in Answer D).

16. Answer C is correct. Cultural scripts describe the larger culture's requirements for proper sexual behavior. Interpersonal scripts (Answer A) refers to the rules of behavior that a couple develops in the course of their relationship. Intrapsychic scripts (Answer B) are the scenarios for ideal or fantasized sexual behavior that develop out of a person's unique history. Social scripts (Answer D) is not a term used in the text.

17. Answer C is correct. Human beings learn from experience and culture what they are supposed to do with their sexual desires and how they are expected to behave sexually. Therefore, since the two students are from different cultures, they would not necessarily agree that kissing is enjoyable (Answers A and B), nor would they agree that they should not kiss and that they should wait for a long time.

18. Answer B is correct. Biological explanations of sexual orientation cannot explain the complexity and variation in sexual identity. Felicia's behavior does not rule out psychological explanations (Answer A), cultural explanations (Answer B), or the notion that sexual orientation is a choice (Answer D).

19. Answer D is correct. None of the answer options has been supported by research. At present, the most reasonable conclusion may be that sexual identity and behavior involve an interaction of biology, culture, experiences, and opportunities; and, most of all, that the route to sexual identity for one person may not be the same for another.

20. Answer A is correct. If you are fairly certain of success, you will work much harder to reach your goal than if you are fairly certain of failure. Material success (Answer B) can motivate some people, but it must be one of their values. Performance goals (Answer C) refer to goals that are centered on how well one is performing. People who are motivated by performance goals stop trying to improve when they do poorly.

21. Answer A is correct. A person's motivation to work include expectations, values, goals, and the need for achievement whereas certain aspects of the work environment such as, working conditions and opportunity, can influence a person's motivation. Answer B gives the correct phrases but in the reverse order. Expectations, values, goals and the need for achievement are internal forces while working conditions and opportunity are external forces. This is the opposite of Answer C. Answer D is incorrect since Answer A is correct.

22. Answer B is correct. Many women and members of minority groups encounter a "glass ceiling" in management--a barrier to promotion that is so subtle as to be transparent, yet strong enough to prevent advancement. Many people believe that women are underrepresented in leadership positions because of something about women--their style of managing is different than men (Answer A), they have lower self-esteem and feelings of competence than men (Answer D), or they have less commitment to the job than men (Answer C). None of these popular beliefs has been supported by research.

23. Answer C is correct. McClelland's research with the Thematic Apperception Test found that people with high achievement motivation told stories about becoming rich and famous and clobbering the opposition. They did not tell stories about pleasing others (Answer A), about pursuing social goals (Answer B) nor about having a great adventure (Answer D).

24. Answer A is correct. You would like to avoid going to the dentist but you would also like to avoid having your teeth fall out (two things you would like to avoid or avoidance-avoidance). You want to go out with Dan AND Stan (to things you would like to do or approach-approach). You would like to travel this summer (approach) but you do not want to miss your friends (avoidance). Answers B, C, and D label some or all of the conflicts incorrectly.

25. Answer D is correct. People can choose higher needs over lower ones (Answer A) and develop their own hierarchies (Answer B). People may also have many needs simultaneously (Answer C).

ANSWER KEY - PRACTICE TEST 3 - SHORT ANSWER

1. toward; away
2. drives
3. affiliation
4. terry-cloth; contact comfort
5. Ainsworth; strange situation
6. avoidant
7. mothers; temperament
8. agape; storge; ludus
9. possessive
10. triangle; passion; commitment
11. commitment
12. Attachment
13. express
14. economic
15. testosterone
16. similar
17. partner approval; peer approval
18. misperceptions
19. dominance
20. sexual
21. cultural norms
22. industrial/organizational
23. value
24. power-achievement
25. opportunities

ANSWER KEY - PRACTICE TEST 4 - TRUE/FALSE

1. F	2. F	3. T	4. F	5. T
6. F	7. F	8. T	9. T	10. T
11. T	12. T	13. T	14. F	15. F
16. F	17. F	18. T	19. F	20. F
21. T	22. T	23. T	24. F	25. T

ANSWER KEY - PRACTICE TEST 5 - ESSAY

1. We cannot be certain what motivates any given behavior. Each behavior described may be activated by a variety of different motives. Below are some possible explanations.
    a. Calling her friend shows need for affiliation.
    b. Visiting her boyfriend demonstrates the motivation for love.
    c. Doing extra credit assignments and an extra work project could reflect need for achievement, performance goals or learning goals.

2. Ludus: "Want to play hide and seek? Come find me for fun and excitement."
    Eros: "For passion, romance and intensity; I'm looking for the love of my life."
    Storge: "Looking for a soul-mate, friend, lover, companion to walk through life with."
    Mania: "Looking for someone made for me; intense, emotional, inseparable."
    Pragma: "Looking for a non-smoker, who likes to travel and listen to jazz. NO children."
    Agape: "Let me spoil you. I want to be there for you and be your main support."

3. <u>Information that supports homosexuality as a choice and refutes the biological argument</u>:
    a. The fluidity of women's experiences
    b. There are flaws in the biological evidence
        *Methodological problems in the findings on brain differences
        *The majority of homosexuals do not have a close gay relative
    c. Psychological theories have not been well-supported

    <u>Information that supports the biological information and refutes the choice position</u>:
    a. Research findings that women with a history of prenatal exposure to estrogen are more likely to become bisexual or lesbian
    b. Research findings on differences in brain structures of homosexual and heterosexual men
    c. Studies that show a moderate heritability

    <u>Political implications include</u>: If homosexuality is biological, then it is a fact of nature and not a choice, and therefore, people should not be prejudiced. Those who are prejudiced against homosexuals suggest that the biological evidence says that it is a "defect" and should be eradicated or "cured." Those who say it is a choice, say it can be "unchosen."

4. A.   Multiple approach-avoidance conflict
      B.   Avoidance-avoidance conflict
      C.   Approach-approach conflict
      D.   Approach-avoidance conflict

CROSSWORD PUZZLE ANSWER KEY

ACROSS		DOWN	
2.	secure	1.	Maslow
3.	motivation	4.	attachment
7.	avoidant	5.	companionate
9.	hormone	6.	value
11.	approach	8.	pragma
14.	achievement	10.	eros
15.	mastery	13.	anxious

ANSWER KEYS FOR CHAPTER 13

ANSWER KEY - PRACTICE TEST 1 - MULTIPLE CHOICE

1. C (p. 457)	2. A (p. 459)	3. C (p. 459)	4. B (p. 459)
5. C (p. 460)	6. D (p. 464)	7. A (p. 464)	8. D (p. 465)
9. C (p. 4668	10. A (p. 468)	11. C (pp. 467-468)	12. D (pp. 470-471)
13. A (p. 476)	14. A (pp. 476-477)	15. C (p. 477)	16. A (p. 478)
17. C (p. 479)	18. C (p. 4798	19. D (p. 480)	20. B (p. 481)
21. C (p. 482)	22. C (pp. 485-486)	23. A (pp. 487-488)	24. A (p. 487)
25. B (p. 489)			

ANSWER KEY - PRACTICE TEST 2 - MULTIPLE CHOICE

1. B	2. C	3. B	4. C
5. D	6. C	7. C	8. D
9. B	10. C	11. C	12. C
13. D	14. B	15. A	16. B
17. B	18. D	19. D	20. D
21. C	22. A	23. C	24. D
25. D			

ANNOTATED ANSWER KEY - PRACTICE TEST 2

1. Answer B is correct. Personality is defined as a distinctive and stable pattern of behavior, thoughts, motives, and emotions that characterizes an individual over time. Consideration and warmth are behaviors and emotions that characterize Ruth most of the time. Answer A is incorrect because mood is not the same thing as personality. Moods are more changeable than personality. Answer C is incorrect because Ron's behavior is neither consistent nor stable. He is shy in one setting and outgoing in another. Answer D is incorrect because it states that Rene was funny today which is not a stable pattern.

2. Answer C is correct. Central traits, according to Allport's theory, reflect a characteristic way of behavior, dealing with others, and reacting to new situations. The question does not describe a cardinal trait (Answer A) because cardinal traits are of overwhelming importance to an individual and influence almost everything the person does. Since Rudolph's suspiciousness doesn't seem to influence his work or friendships, it is not a central trait. Answer B is not correct since secondary traits are more changeable aspects of personality like preferences, habits, or casual opinions. Rudolph's suspiciousness is stable and not changeable, so it is not a secondary trait. Answer D (introversion) is an example of a trait rather than a type of trait.

3. Answer B is correct. The traits used to describe Joe match the big five. The big five include introversion versus extroversion (Joe is described as sociable which relates to extroversion), emotional stability versus neuroticism (Joe is described as positive which matches emotional stability), agreeableness (which matches Joe's trait of being good-natured), conscientiousness (Joe is responsible), and openness to experience (Joe is imaginative which is an aspect of openness to experience). Answer A is incorrect because the traits associated with Cattell include humor, intelligence, creativity, leadership, and emotional disorder and Joe is not described in terms of these traits. Answer C is incorrect because these would not be cardinal traits as defined by Allport's theory. Cardinal traits are of overwhelming importance to an individual and influence almost everything the person does. No particular traits are discussed as having been identified by factor analysis (Answer D).

4. Answer C is correct. Petra's characteristics relate to the big five trait of neuroticism. Longitudinal studies have found that the big five traits remain stable year after year. Therefore, Answers A and B which suggest she will or is likely to change, are incorrect. There is not evidence to suggest that the traits will increase in strength (Answer D).

5. Answer D is correct. Temperaments are relatively stable, characteristic styles of responding to the environment that appear in infancy or early childhood and have some genetic basis. The person described in this question has been content since childhood, while the sister has always been difficult. These are stable, characteristic ways of responding that appeared in infancy. Personality (Answer A) refers to stable patterns of behavior, thoughts, motives, and emotions that characterize an individual over time. This description suggests that personality appears over time and is not necessarily evident in infancy. Traits (Answer B) refers to characteristics that describe the person across many situations. Traits are the characteristics that comprise personality and temperament. Motives (Answer C) are inferred processes within a person or animal that causes that organism to move toward a goal or away from an unpleasant situation.

6. Answer C is correct. Heritability refers to the percent of variance in a trait that is attributable to genetic differences within a group of people. Answers A, B, and C are incorrect because heritability estimates do not give information about a particular individual, about most people, or about differences between groups. Heritability tells you only about the percent of variance of a given trait within a single group.

7. Answer C is correct because research on the environmental contribution to personality differences comes from nonshared experiences. Answer C is the only nonshared experience listed. Answers A, B, and D are all shared experiences.

8.   Answer D is correct. Heritability of traits diminishes over time (Answer A), the influence of the environment increases over time (Answer B), and for some traits, experiences at certain periods in life become particularly influential (Answer C).

9.   Answer B is correct. Social-cognitive theorists view traits as behaviors that are influenced by a particular situation, and by the beliefs and expectations of the individual. Accordingly, Christian could behave differently in another situation if he had different beliefs and expectations. Answer C is incorrect because social-cognitive theorists look to environmental influences and not to genes as the basis for behaviors. Answer A is incorrect since central traits are not part of the social-cognitive perspective, they are part of Allport's trait theory. Since Answer B is correct, Answer D cannot be correct.

10. Answer C is correct. According to cognitive social-cognitive theorists, personality is self-regulated--shaped by our thoughts, values, emotions, and goals. The behavioral approach (Answer A) suggests that personality is learned through classical and operant conditioning. Trait theories (Answer B) have tried to identify the many individual traits that make up personality. The humanistic approach (Answer D) takes the view that people have the free will to work toward self-acceptance and self-actualization.

11. Answer C is correct. Locus of control refers to people's beliefs about whether or not the results of their actions are under their own control. People who have an external locus of control tend to believe they are victims of luck, fate, or other people. People who have an internal locus of control (Answer A) tend to believe they are responsible for what happens to them. Observational learning (Answer B) refers to a school of cognitive social-learning in which people can learn a new behavior from observing a model. Self-handicapping is a strategy in which people place obstacles in the path of their own success. If they fail, they can blame the failure on the handicap instead of a lack of ability.

12. Answer C is correct. Researchers tend to explore one influence on learning at a time. In real life, though, people are surrounded by hundreds of interacting influences which makes if difficult to show that any one thing actually is having an influence. The description of the research in the question is testable (Answer A) and is falsifiable (Answer B) and it is not based on the retrospective memories of subjects (Answer C).

13. Answer D is correct. Psychodynamic theories share five general elements. One of these elements is the assumption that adult behavior and ongoing problems are determined primarily by experiences in early childhood. Answer A is an idea from the cognitive perspective. Answer B focuses on current events and psychodynamic theories focus on the past. Answer C refers to aspects from the humanist perspective.

14. Answer B is correct. Someone who is too controlled by the superego is rigid, moralistic, and bossy. The superego represents morality, the rules of parents and society, and the power of authority. The defense mechanism of displacement occurs when people direct their emotions toward things, animals, or other people that are not the real object of their feelings. The question does not describe an example of displacement. Answer C is incorrect because the ego is the referee between the needs of instinct and the demands of society. The ego represents "reason and good sense" according to Freud. Freud talks about the results of having too weak an ego, but not too strong an ego. Answer D is incorrect because Answer B is correct.

15. Answer A is correct. The id operates according to the pleasure principle, seeking to reduce tension, avoid pain, and obtain pleasure ("let's get a pizza"). The ego obeys the reality principle, putting a rein on the id's desire for pleasure ("if you don't study, you will fail"). The superego represents morality, the rules of parents and society, and the power of authority ("you owe it to your parents to get good grades"). Answers B, C, and D present the terms in the incorrect order.

16. Answer B is correct. Projection occurs when one's own unacceptable or threatening feelings are repressed and then attributed to someone else (Les's own sexual impulses are unacceptable, so he attributes them to others). Displacement (Answer A) occurs when people direct their emotions toward things, animals, or other people that are not the real object of their feelings (a boy is forbidden to express anger at his father, so he "takes it out" on his younger brother). Reaction formation (Answer C) occurs when a feeling that produces unconscious anxiety is transformed into its opposite in consciousness (a woman who is afraid to admit that she doesn't love her husband may cling to him). Denial (Answer D) occurs when people refuse to admit that something unpleasant is happening or that they are experiencing a "forbidden" emotion (some people deny they are angry).

17. Answer B is correct. Sublimation occurs when unacceptable "instincts" of the id are blocked from direct expression and are displaced onto a substitute that is socially acceptable (Johnny's aggression is displaced onto an acceptable substitute, football). Regression (Answer A) occurs when a person reverts to a previous phase of psychic development. Reaction formation (Answer C) occurs when a feeling that produces unconscious anxiety is transformed into its opposite in consciousness. Projection (Answer D) occurs when one's own unacceptable or threatening feelings are repressed and then attributed to someone else.

18. Answer D is correct. The Oedipal complex (Answer A) occurs during the phallic stage which lasts roughly from age 3 to 5, therefore Max has gone through that developmental stage. According to Freud, by about ages 5 or 6, when the Oedipus complex is resolved, the child's personality patterns are formed (Answer B). The superego emerges as a result of the resolution of the Oedipus complex (Answer C). Since Answers A, B, and C are all true, Answer D is correct.

19. Answer D is correct. Horney introduced the idea of womb envy while Jung developed the idea of the archetype. Answer A is incorrect because penis envy was introduced by Freud and not Jung. Answer B is incorrect because the concepts correspond to the opposite theorist. Answer C is incorrect since anima and animus are Jungian archetypes. Anima represents the feminine archetype in men and animus represents the masculine archetype in women.

20. Answer D is correct. The collective unconscious, according to Jung, contains the universal memories and history of humankind. Archetypes occur in myths, art, and folklore in cultures all over the work and therefore, support the idea that a shared collective unconscious exists. Penis envy (Answer A) occurs, according to Freud, when girls, upon discovering male anatomy, panic because they had only a puny clitoris instead of a stately penis. Both Jung and Adler believed in the strength of the ego (Answer B), but this belief is not related to the idea of archetypes. Psychosocial stages (Answer C) is part of Freudian theory, but it is not related to the idea of archetypes.

21. Answer C is correct. A theory that is impossible to disconfirm in principle is not a scientific theory and violates the principle of falsifiability (Julia's agreement AND disagreement both support Dr. Sigmund's interpretation, therefore, it cannot be found false). Many psychodynamic ideas about unconscious motivations are, in fact, impossible to confirm or disprove. Answer A refers to the fact that Freud and most of his followers generalized from a very few individuals, often patients in therapy, to all human beings. This question does not describe that problem. Answer B refers to the fact that most psychodynamic theorists have worked backward, creating theories based on themes in adults' recollections. Since memory is often inaccurate and is influenced by current events, this represents a problem with psychodynamic theories, though not the one described in the question. Retrospective analysis has another problem: It creates an illusion of causality between events or the belief that if A came before B, then A must have caused B. This is not the problem in the question.

22. Answer A is correct. In object-relation's view, if boys are to develop a masculine identity, they must break away from the mother. Therefore, a man's identity is more insecure than a woman's identity, because it is based on <u>not</u> being like a woman. Object-relations school does not suggest that male's superegos are too strong (Answer B) nor that they have great difficulty resolving the anal stage (Answer C), therefore Answer D is also incorrect.

23. Answer C is correct. This questions describes a study in which the subjects are asked to remember information about their early childhoods. Most psychodynamic theorists have worked backward, creating theories based on themes in adults' recollections which can be inaccurate. Violating the principle of falsifiability (Answer A) occurs when a theory is impossible to disconfirm. The study described in this question does not include this problem. A prospective study (Answer B) is one which makes predictions about future events based on examining subjects' behavior now (rather than collecting recollections from the past). Answer D, that people are seen as too malleable, is a criticism of behavioral theories not psychodynamic theories.

24. Answer D is correct because humanistic theories, unlike behavioral and psychodynamic theories, focus on a person's sense of self (Answer A) and positive aspects of human nature (Answer B). The humanists also believe that human beings have free will (Answer C) whereas both psychodynamic and behavioral theories see human beings as determined.

25. Answer D is correct. Roger's theory states that to become a fully functioning person, one's self (one's conscious view of oneself) must be congruent with the organism (the sum of all one's experiences) (Answer A) and to have received unconditional positive regard (love and support without strings attached) (Answer B). If one is raised with conditional regard, then one will suppress or deny feelings (Answer C) that are unacceptable to those they love and the result is incongruence which produces low self-regard.

ANSWER KEY - PRACTICE TEST 3 - SHORT ANSWER

1. behavior; thoughts
2. objective; projective
3. MMPI
4. Allport; central; secondary
5. agreeableness; conscientiousness
6. inhibited
7. heritability
8. nonshared
9. Social-cognitive; perceptions
10. self-efficacy
11. expectations; self-fulfilling
12. internal
13. Reciprocal determinism
14. collectivist
15. polychronic
16. Psychodynamic
17. id; realities; superego
18. defense mechanisms
19. sublimation
20. Horney; Thompson
21. collective; archetypes
22. representation
23. Rorschach; reliable (or valid)
24. falsifiability
25. self-actualized; functioning; unconditional positive

ANSWER KEY - PRACTICE TEST 4 - TRUE/FALSE

1. F	2. T	3. F	4. F	5. F
6. T	7. T	8. F	9. F	10. T
11. T	12. T	13. F	14. F	15. F
16. T	17. F	18. T	19. F	20. T
21. F	22. T	23. T	24. F	25. T

1. A.   Cognitive social learning approach
    B.   Trait approach
    C.   Psychodynamic approach
    D.   Humanistic approach

2. A.   According to the reality principle, the ego would seek to prepare for the test.
    B.   The id seeks pleasure and immediate gratification, according to the pleasure principle.
    C.   The id seeks pleasure and is not concerned with the consequences of reality.
    D.   The ego is appraising reality.
    E.   The internalized parental values of the superego are discouraging him from cheating.
    F.   The ego is defending against threats from the superego.
    G.   Violations of the superego produce guilt.

3. A.   Reaction formation   D.   Denial
    B.   Projection   E.   Regression
    C.   Repression   F.   Displacement

4. A.   Phallic stage   C.   Phallic stage
    B.   Oral stage   D.   Anal stage

5. A.   Adler
    B.   Jung
    C.   Horney
    D.   Object-relations school

6. The behavioral school:
    Classical and operant conditioning are the central processes of the behavioral school. Parents are therefore viewed in terms of the way they associate stimuli and reinforce responses for the child. Parental impact is related to the consistency of their procedures and is limited by the conditioning that takes place outside their sphere of influence.

    The cognitive social learning school:
    Observational learning, self-regulation and interpretation and perception of events are central processes. Parents are therefore seen as role models and sources of information about values, expectations and perceptions. They can influence a child's perceptions about his or her locus of control and self-efficacy.

7.	Abraham Maslow:
Self-actualization was a basic need for Maslow. However, its achievement depended on gratifying even more fundamental needs, such as physiological drives and social needs.

Rollo May:
May believes that alienation, loneliness and helplessness are basic components of human existence. The person strives to overcome these through effective choices.

Carl Rogers:
According to Rogers, self-actualization and full functioning are related to the presence of unconditional positive regard. However, most children and adults live in situations in which they receive conditional positive regard.

8.	A.	Low levels of neuroticism, high levels of extroversion and agreeableness
	B.	High levels of conscientiousness, and probably agreeableness, and a low level of openness to experience
	C.	High levels of neuroticism and openness to experience, but a low level of extroversion

CROSSWORD PUZZLE KEY

ACROSS		**DOWN**	
1.	personality	1.	psychoanalysis
7.	Cattell	2.	repression
9.	ego	3.	archetypes
10.	projective	4.	trait
11.	Freud	5.	humanistic
13.	superego	6.	collective
14.	internal	8.	temperaments
16.	Oedipus	12.	intrapsychic
17.	identification	15.	Horney
18.	denial		

ANSWER KEYS FOR CHAPTER 14

ANSWER KEY - PRACTICE TEST 1 - MULTIPLE CHOICE

1. C (pp. 498-499) 2. A (p. 499) 3. D (pp. 499-500) 4. B (p. 500)
5. A (p. 501) 6. A (p. 501) 7. D (pp. 506-508) 8. A (p. 505)
9. C (p. 507) 10. D (pp. 508-510) 11. C (p. 504) 12. B (p. 505)
13. C (p. 513) 14. A (pp. 514-515) 15. D (p. 516) 16. C (p. 511)
17. C (p. 511) 18. A (pp. 511-512) 19. D (p. 522) 20. A (p. 520)
21. A (p. 518) 22. A (p. 522) 23. C (p. 524) 24. C (pp. 525-526)
25. A (pp. 537-538)

ANSWER KEY - PRACTICE TEST 2 - MULTIPLE CHOICE

1. B 2. D 3. D 4. B
5. A 6. A 7. C 8. A
9. D 10. C 11. D 12. A
13. C 14. C 15. A 16. B
17. B 18. B 19. B 20. C
21. B 22. D 23. B 24. C
25. A

ANNOTATED ANSWER KEY - PRACTICE TEST 2

1. Answer B is correct. Testosterone is secreted by the rudimentary testes in embryos that are genetically male during the fourth to eighth week of pregnancy (the embryonic stage). Adrenalin is a hormone but it is not one of the sex hormones, therefore Answer A is incorrect. Since sex differentiation occurs during the embryonic and not the fetal stage of prenatal development, Answer C is incorrect. Answer D is incorrect because it lists the wrong hormone and the wrong stage.

2. Answer D is correct. Cigarette smoking during pregnancy increases the likelihood of miscarriage (Answer A), premature birth (Answer B), hyperactivity in later childhood (Answer C) as well as other problems.

3. Answer D is correct. Having more than two drinks of alcohol a day significantly increases the risk of a baby having fetal alcohol syndrome (Answer A). Drugs can be harmful to the fetus whether they are illicit drugs or commonly used substances (Answers A and B).

4. Answer B is correct. Newborns can see, hear, touch, smell, and taste. They are far from being passive and inert (Answer A). They can discriminate their mother or other primary caregiver on the basis of smell, sight, or sound almost immediately (Answer C). Newborns can distinguish contrasts, shadows, and edges (Answer D).

5. Answer A is correct. Synchrony refers to the adjustment of one person's nonverbal behavior to coordinate with another's. Newborns synchronize their behavior and attention to adult speech but not to other sounds. Parents too coordinate their movements and rhythms with those of their baby. Answer B is incorrect since synchrony occurs in newborns and does not appear to be dependent on visual development. Newborns do not synchronize their behavior and attention to other sounds, therefore Answer C is incorrect. Since synchronization occurs in newborns, Answer D is incorrect.

6. Answer A is correct. Assimilation is fitting new information into present systems of knowledge and beliefs or into mental schemas. This terms refers to a process described in Piaget's theory of cognitive development. Conservation (Answer B), which develops during the concrete operations stage of development, is the ability to recognize that physical properties do not change when their forms or appearances change. Accommodation (Answer C) is what you do when, as a result of new information, you must change or modify your existing schemas. Butch did not have to modify the existing schema of "birdie" therefore, Answer C is incorrect. An operation (Answer D) refers to mental abilities that allow children to understand abstract principles or cause and effect. Neither abstract principles nor cause and effect are used in this question.

7. Answer C is correct because in this example, Butch needed to modify his existing schema, which is accommodation. Butch tried unsuccessfully to use assimilation (Answer A) to fit the new information into existing schemas. Schemas (Answer B) refer to categories of things and people. While both birdie and butterfly are schemas, the question describes the adaptation of new observations and experiences into existing schemas. An operation (Answer D) refers to mental abilities that allow children to understand abstract principles or cause and effect. Neither abstract principles nor cause and effect are used in this question.

8. Answer A is correct. Representational thought refers to the capacity for using mental imagery and other symbolic systems. Birdie and butterfly represent certain objects to Butch which reflect the use of representational thought. Formal operations (Answer B) refers to the ability to use abstract reasoning. Butch is not demonstrating that in this example. Egocentrism (Answer C) refers to the inability to take another person's point of view and it is not described in this question. The ability to use concrete operations (Answer D) occurs at about ages 6 or 7. Since Butch is still learning early language skills he cannot be at this stage of cognitive development, according to Piaget.

9.   Answer D is correct. All answers present challenges to Piaget's theory. That babies look longer at a ball if it seems to roll through a solid barrier (Answer A) suggests that children can understand more than Piaget gave them credit for. Preschoolers are not as egocentric as Piaget thought since when 4-year-olds play with 2-year-olds they modify and simplify their speech so the younger child will understand (Answer B). By age 4 or 5 children have developed a theory of mind (Answer C), a theory about how their own and other people's minds work and how people are affected by their beliefs and feelings.

10.   Answer C is correct. By 4 to 6 months, babies can recognize their own names and other words that regularly get spoken with emotion, such as "mommy" and "daddy." Children begin to develop a repertoire of symbolic gestures at about 11 months of age, so Answer A is incorrect. Telegraphic speech occurs between the ages of 18 months and 2 years therefore, Answers B and D are incorrect.

11.   Answer D is correct. In the first months of life, babies are highly responsive to the pitch, intensity, and sound of language. They are responsive to emotions in the voice before they respond to facial expressions. They do not recognize their own names, words that are spoken regularly like "mommy" and "daddy" or the key sounds of their native language until they are about 4 to 6 months old, so Answers A, B, and C are incorrect.

12.   Answer A is correct. The behavior described in the question refers to gender socialization. Gender socialization is the psychological process by which boys and girls learn what it means to be masculine or feminine, including the abilities, interests, personality traits, actions, and self-concepts that their culture says are appropriate for males and females. Fixations in the oral stage (Answer B) refer to stages of development according to Freudian theory. Freudian explanations are not given in the text to explain our beliefs about gender. Gender identity (Answer C) refers to a fundamental sense of maleness or femaleness that exists regardless of what one wears or does. A person can have a strong gender identity and not be sex typed. Since Answers B and C are incorrect, Answer D is also incorrect.

13.   Answer C is correct. By the age of 4 or 5 children develop a secure gender identity, a fundamental sense of maleness or femaleness that exists regardless of what one wears or does. Before gender identity is established children may not realize that gender is fixed and does not change. Since this is a normal part of the gender development process, it would be incorrect to say that Jill has a psychological problem (Answer A) or that it has significance regarding her sexual orientation (Answer B). This statement does not provide information about Jill's gender socialization (Answer D).

14. Answer C is correct. Cognitive approaches to gender suggest that as children mature, they develop a gender schema; they begin to divide people into categories of male and female. The schemas expand to include characteristics that are considered male and female. Children between the ages of 4 and 7 expand the categories to include characteristics described in this question. This question does not tell us anything about a child's gender identity (Answer A) which is the child's own sense of maleness or femaleness. No evidence is cited that the distinctions described in the question are a result of reinforcement (Answer B) or biological factors (Answer D).

15. Answer A is correct. Adults will respond to the same baby differently based solely on how the infant is dressed. Even when children are behaving the same way, adults respond to children differently, therefore Answers B, C, and D are incorrect.

16. Answer B is correct. Kohlberg's theory is one of moral reasoning rather than one of moral behavior (Answer C) and he determined a person's moral stage by their answers to hypothetical moral dilemmas. He did not use direct questions as in Answer A, nor tests of moral feelings (Answer D).

17. Answer B is correct. While parents cannot make inhibited children into extroverts (Answer A), they can help them become more sociable and less frightened of new situations. Answer C is incorrect because children, like adults, are oriented to their peers. Since Answers A and C are incorrect, Answer D must be incorrect.

18. Answer B is correct. Authoritarian parents exercise too much power and give too little nurturance. Children of these parents tend to be less socially skilled than other children, have lower self-esteem, and do more poorly in school. Authoritative parents travel a middle road, knowing when and how to discipline their children. They set high, but reasonable expectations and give their children emotional support. Their children tend to have good self-control, high self-esteem, and high self-efficacy. Answer C is incorrect because it reverses the correct terms. Answers A and D include permissive parents. This is incorrect because permissive parents exercise too little control. Their children are likely to be impulsive, immature, irresponsible, and academically unmotivated.

19.   Answer B is correct. While early-maturing boys generally have a more positive view of their bodies, and their relatively greater size and strength gives them a boost in sports and the prestige that being a good athlete brings, they are also more likely to smoke, drink, use drugs, and break the law than later-maturing boys. Therefore, Answers A and C are incorrect. Generally, they have less self-control and emotional stability (therefore Answer D is incorrect).

20.   Answer C is correct. At puberty boys have a higher level of androgens than girls do, and girls have a higher level of estrogens than boys do (which is why Answer B is incorrect). Until puberty, both boys and girls produce roughly the same amount of male hormones (androgens) and female hormones (estrogens) (that is why Answer A is incorrect). Answer D describes the maturity pattern for girls, not for boys. For boys, the average adolescent growth spurt starts at about age 12 and ends at about age 18.

21.   Answer B is correct. Only about 10 percent of all women have unusually sever physical symptoms (therefore, Answer D is incorrect). The negative view of menopause as a "syndrome" that causes depression and other emotional reactions was based on women who had an early menopause following hysterectomy or who have had a lifetime history of depression (therefore, Answer A is incorrect). Only 3 percent reported regret at having reached menopause (Answer C). The vast majority had no serious physical symptoms and did not suffer from depression.

22.   Answer D is correct because Answers A, B, and C all cite stereotypes about aging that are changing. The definition of "old" has gotten older (Answer A), aging has been separated from illness (Answer B), the biology of aging has been separated from its psychology, and the benefits of aging have been recognized (Answer C).

23.   Answer B is correct. Fluid intelligence is the capacity for deductive reasoning and the ability to use new information to solve problems and it is relatively independent of education and experience. It reflects an inherited predisposition, and like other biological capacities, it declines in later years. Therefore Answer A is incorrect. Answers C and D both describe crystallized intelligence which depends heavily on culture, education, and experience, and tends to remain stable or even improve over the life span.

24.   Answer C is correct. The crisis of young adulthood, according to Erikson's theory is intimacy versus isolation. Heather must learn to share herself with another and learn to make commitments. No matter how successful you are in work, you are not complete until you are capable of intimacy. Identity crisis (Answer A) describes what Erikson considered to be the primary conflict of adolescence. Generativity versus stagnation (Answer B) is the crisis of middle age. Competence versus inferiority (Answer D) is the crisis for school-age children.

25.   Answer A is correct. Studies that follow people from childhood to adulthood do not confirm the widespread belief that childhood traumas always have specific and inescapable effects. Although more children of abusive parents become abusive as adults than do children of nonviolent parents, the majority of them do not. Therefore, Answer B is incorrect. Answer C implies that to avoid becoming an abusive parent, she would need counseling and since most children of abusive parents do not become abusive, this is not necessarily true. Resilience (Answer D) has to do with the ability of children of violent, neglectful, or alcoholic parents to recover from painful or traumatic childhoods.

ANSWER KEY - PRACTICE TEST 3 - SHORT ANSWER

1.   socialization
2.   germinal; embryonic
3.   placenta; x-rays; drugs
4.   synchrony
5.   "parentese"
6.   eleven; symbolic
7.   Piaget
8.   schema; assimilation
9.   object permanence
10.   egocentrism; preoperational
11.   concrete operations
12.   underestimated; overestimated
13.   conventional
14.   typing
15.   schema
16.   socialization
17.   assertion; aggressiveness
18.   authoritarian; authoritative
19.   temperament; peer groups; culture
20.   androgens
21.   menarche; menopause
22.   individuate
23.   separatists; acculturation
24.   eight; crisis
25.   Fluid; declines; Crystallized; stable

ANSWER KEY - PRACTICE TEST 4 - TRUE/FALSE

1. T	2. F	3. T	4. F	5. T
6. F	7. T	8. F	9. T	10. T
11. T	12. T	13. T	14. F	15. T
16. T	17. F	18. T	19. F	20. T
21. F	22. F	23. F	24. T	25. T

ANSWER KEY - PRACTICE TEST 5 - ESSAY

1.   A.   Fetal abnormalities and deformities
       B.   There is an increased likelihood of miscarriage, premature birth, abnormal fetal heartbeat and underweight babies; and after the child's birth, there are increased rates of sickness and Sudden Infant Death Syndrome; in later childhood, hyperactivity and difficulties in school.
       C.   Fetal alcohol syndrome
       D.   Effects vary with specific drugs; extreme caution must be exercised, even with prescribed and over-the-counter drugs.

2.   A.   Newborns should have the following reflexes: rooting, sucking, swallowing, Moro, Babinski, grasp, stepping. They should follow a moving light with their eyes and turn toward a familiar sound. They should be able to distinguish contrasts, shadows and edges, and be able to discriminate their primary caregiver.
       B.   Newborns are sociable from birth and show a preference for the human face. They can distinguish their primary caregiver by smell, sight or sound almost immediately. They establish synchrony with the primary caregiver very early.

3.   A.   The child is in the preoperational stage and is demonstrating egocentric thinking.
       B.   The child is incorrectly trying to use assimilation; she should use accommodation.
       C.   The younger child is in the preoperational stage and lacks the ability to conserve; the older child is in the concrete operations stage.
       D.   Johnny is in the sensory-motor stage and has developed object permanence.

4.   At 4 months old: Jennie would cry and coo and respond to high-pitched and more varied verbalizations in which the intonation is exaggerated. She can recognize her own name.
At 10 months old: She would be increasingly familiar with the sound structure of her native language. She might be making babbling sounds such as "ba-ba" or "goo-goo".
At 14 months old: She could begin using gestures.
At 23 months old: She would use telegraphic speech because she is not yet able to use article and auxiliary words. She would probably say, "Apple table."

5.   A.   Authoritative parenting
       B.   Authoritarian parenting
       C.   Permissive parenting

6.   A.   Conventional morality
       B.   Conventional morality
       C.   Postconventional morality
       D.   Postconventional morality
       E.   Preconventional morality

7.   A.   The biological changes for Ron include: Development of primary and secondary sex characteristics - hormone production in the testes produce sperm, males now have higher androgen levels than girls, nocturnal emissions, the growth of the testes, scrotum and penis, deepened voice, facial, chest and pubic hair. Later he will experience a growth spurt.

              The biological changes for Rita include: Development of primary and secondary sex characteristics - hormones stimulate the ovaries, which release eggs and mark the beginning of menstruation or menarche. She now has higher levels of estrogens than males. She develops breasts and pubic hair and has a growth spurt that occurs earlier than in males.

       B.   Both will be dealing with issues related to identity, but they will not necessarily experience emotional turmoil. They will begin to learn the rules of adult sexuality, morality, work and family. They will try to develop their own standards and values. They will begin to individuate from their parents.

KEY FOR CROSSWORD PUZZLE

ACROSS		DOWN	
1.	development	2.	egocentric
9.	germinal	4.	maturation
14.	accommodation	5.	fetal
16.	Piaget	7.	synchrony
17.	representational	8.	puberty
18.	conservation	10.	induction
19.	authoritarian	11.	assimilation
		12.	menarche
		15.	operations

ANSWER KEYS FOR CHAPTER 15

ANSWER KEY - PRACTICE TEST 1 - MULTIPLE CHOICE

1. A (p. 546)	2. D (p. 548)	3. C (p. 550)	4. D (p. 550)
5. A (pp. 550-551)	6. D (p. 549)	7. C (p. 504)	8. A (p. 552)
9. A (p. 557)	10. C (p. 553)	11. D (pp. 552-553)	12. B (p. 555)
13. C (p. 554)	14. B (p. 556)	15. C (pp. 557-558)	16. C (p. 557)
17. C (p. 559)	18. D (p. 559)	19. C (pp. 562-563)	20. A (p. 563)
21. B (pp. 561-563)	22. D (pp. 563-564)	23. D (p. 565)	24. D (pp. 566-567)
25. D (pp. 569-570)			

ANSWER KEY - PRACTICE TEST 2 - MULTIPLE CHOICE

1. C	2. A	3. A	4. D
5. D	6. A	7. C	8. D
9. D	10. A	11. C	12. C
13. C	14. A	15. D	16. B
17. A	18. D	19. A	20. C
21. B	22. C	23. D	24. A
25. D			

ANNOTATED ANSWER KEY - PRACTICE TEST 2

1. Answer C is correct. During the resistance phase, the body's physiological responses are in high gear--a response to the original stressor--but this very mechanism makes the body more susceptible to other stressors. During the alarm phase (Answer A) the organism mobilizes to meet the threat with a package of biological responses that allow the person or animal to escape from danger. The exhaustion phase (Answer B) occurs if the stressor persists. Over time, the body's resources may be overwhelmed. There is no activation stage (Answer D) in Selye's model.

2. Answer A is correct. One approach to studying individual vulnerability to stress focuses on psychological factors, such as personality traits, perceptions, and emotions. An event that is stressful for one person may be challenging for another. For this reason, we could not say that all students will find finals week stressful (Answer B) or that the stress will result in the stress response described by Selye (Answer D). While the amount of effort could be a factor (Answer C), psychological responses and coping skills are identified in the text as important factors.

3. Answer A is correct. White blood cells of the immune system are designed to recognize foreign substances, such as flu, viruses, and bacteria and then destroy or deactivate them. Answer B is incorrect because although brain chemicals are involved, they do not transform the foreign substance. Answer A is incorrect since an antigen is another term for a foreign substance. Red blood cells (Answer D) are not discussed in the context of responding to foreign substances.

4. Answer D is correct. Jerry is at higher risk for getting sick (Answer A) because prolonged stress depletes the body of energy (Answer B). But it is also true that how he responds to this stress depends on psychological characteristics and his coping skills (Answer C).

5. Answer D is correct. Health psychology (Answer A), psychoneuroimmunology (Answer B), and psychosomatic medicine (Answer C) are all terms used in the text for disciplines that examine the link between stress and illness.

6. Answer A is correct. Psychologists once thought that daily hassles increased the risk of illness, but now we know that they do not pose much threat to health. This makes Answers A and B are incorrect because they state that the hassle described in the question can increase the risk of illness and heart disease. Finally, there is no research to support the idea that such hassles decrease the risk of illness (Answer D).

7. Answer C is correct. Health psychologists now define stress to include qualities of the individual (such as how the person perceives the stressor) and whether the individual feels able to cope with the stressor. Answer A describes Selye's narrow definition of stress. Answer B includes only part of the correct description and Answer D is not part of the current definition.

8. Answer D is correct. One unhealthy chronic stressor is loud noise, which impairs the ability to think and work even when people believe they have adjusted to it. Children in noisy schools, such as those near airports, tend to have higher blood pressure (Answer A) and other elevated physiological responses, be more distractable, have poorer long-term memory (Answer B), and have more difficulty with puzzles, reading (Answer C), and math than do children in quieter schools.

9. Answer D is correct. Crowds are detrimental to health and intellectual performance not when you <u>are</u> crowded but when you <u>feel</u> crowded or trapped. Therefore, Answers A, B, and C are less relevant to the negative affects of crowding than a person's perception of being crowded.

10. Answer A is correct. The most serious threat to health occurs when stress becomes interminable and uncontrollable--when people feel caught in a situation they can't escape. While crowding (Answer A), traffic jams (Answer B), and deadlines (Answer D) may all be stressful, a chronic and uncontrollable stressor is a more serious threat to health.

11. Answer C is correct. The evidence on the relationship between illness and depression is conflicting. The long-term health implications of chronic depression are still unknown. Therefore, Answers A, B, and D are incorrect.

12. Answer C is correct. Research on Type A behavior found that hostility is the characteristic that is dangerous to health. A longitudinal study found that men who were chronically angry and resentful and who had a hostile attitude toward others were five times as likely as non hostile men to get coronary heart disease. Among the men described in this question, Don has the characteristics of hostility. The characteristics of the men described in Answers A, B, and D are not thought to be predictive of heart disease.

13. Answer C is correct. Never being angry, fearful, or anxious is characteristic of suppressors, or those who are emotionally inhibited. Suppressors are at greater risk of becoming ill than people who can acknowledge their fears, and once they contract a serious disease, suppressors may even die sooner. The relationship between depression and illness is conflicting, so Answer A is incorrect. Type A behavior pattern itself is not a risk factor in heart disease, so Answer B is incorrect. Type A behavior is dangerous when hostility is present. No evidence is cited that Type B personalities are at greater risk of serious illness, so Answer D is incorrect.

14. Answer A is correct. Pessimists explain negative events as internal, stable, and global. Answer A follows that pattern. The explanation in Answer B does characterizes the problem as an external one. Answer C gives a temporary (rather than stable) explanation for a problem. Answer D provides an optimist response to a problem.

15. Answer D is correct. Maria is exhibiting internal locus of control (Answer A) which can help to reduce pain, improve adjustment to surgery and illness, and speed up recovery from some diseases. She is also exhibiting optimism (Answer B) in the belief that she can influence the outcome. Finally, she is demonstrating self-efficacy (Answer C) or the belief that she is basically in charge of her own life and well-being and that she can take steps to improve her health.

16.   Answer B is correct. Eastern cultures emphasize secondary control, a type of control in which people try to accommodate to reality by changing their own aspirations or desires: If you have a problem, learn to live with it or act in spite of it. Primary control (Answer A) reflects the Western approach and is a type of control in which people try to influence existing reality by changing other people, events or circumstances. Locus of control (Answer C) refers to your general expectation of whether you can control the things that happen to you. External locus of control (Answer D) refers to the expectations of people who think they are the victims of circumstances.

17.   Answer A is correct. In one study, the only aspect of control that was related to health was self-efficacy: the belief that you are basically in charge of your own life and well-being, and that if you become sick you can take steps to improve your health. The statement in Answer A reflects self-efficacy and an internal locus of control. The statement in Answer B reflects self-blame, an unrealistic kind of control which is not related to health. The statement in Answer C represents the belief that all disease can be prevented by doing the right thing, another type of unrealistic control. Answer D represents secondary control, the effort to accommodate to reality.

18.   Answer D is correct. Answer D represents a combination of emotion-focused and problem-focused coping. Emotion-focused coping is normal for a period of time after any personal tragedy or trauma. Eventually, though, most people become ready to move beyond their emotional state and concentrate on the problem itself. Answer A represents only problem-focused coping and does not deal with the emotions. Answer B represents only dealing with emotions and does not get to dealing with the problem. Answer C represents avoidance or denial and reflects no expectation of control.

19.   Answer A is correct. When successful copers are sick or in a difficult situation, they often compare themselves to others who are (they feel) less fortunate. This is not an example of vigilance (Answer B) or the "tell me everything" approach, nor an example of the use of humor (Answer C) or avoidance (Answer D).

20.   Answer C is correct. Rethinking the problem includes the following strategies: reappraisal, social comparison, vigilance versus avoidance, and humor. Solving the problem (Answer A) involves the use of problem-focused coping and is not described in this question. Living with the problem (Answer B) involves the implementation of stress-reduction strategies like relaxation, massage, exercise, looking outward, and developing healthy habits. Vigilance (Answer D) is an example of coping that involves rethinking the problem.

21. Answer B is correct. For a period of time after any tragedy or trauma, it is normal to give in to emotions. In this stage, people often need to talk about the event in order to come to terms with it. Eventually though, most people are ready to move on and focus on the problem itself. Because it can be useful to express feelings initially after a trauma, Answer A is incorrect. Since over time, problem-focused strategies are associated with better adjustment than are emotion-focused ones, Answer C is incorrect. No research is cited that shows different personality styles respond better to emotion-focused or problem-focused coping, therefore Answer D is incorrect.

22. Answer C is correct. Reducing bodily arousal as a coping strategy involves the using techniques such as relaxation, massage, and exercise. Amanda is doing these things. Solving and reappraising the problem (Answers A and B) are different categories of coping techniques. Making social comparisons (Answer D) is a strategy that involves rethinking the problem.

23. Answer D is correct. Social supports are helpful because they are sources of attachment and connection (Answer A), which everyone needs throughout life. As with other factors that are related to health, social support may produce its benefits because of its effects on the immune system (Answer B). Friends can also help evaluate problems and plan a course of action (Answer C). Therefore, Answer D is correct.

24. Answer D is correct. Though social supports provide many benefits, other people are not always helpful. Friends can be sources of conflict, may be unsupportive, say something stupid or block efforts to change bad habits (Answer A). Carl's invitations to go drinking were not an example of an attempt to reduce the effects of stress (Answer B). Healing through helping refers to efforts to look outside oneself and help other people. Carl's behavior is not an attempt to heal himself through helping Anne, therefore Answer C is incorrect. A person with an external locus of control (Answer D) believes that he or she is a victim of circumstances. This question does not provide any information about Carl or Anne's locus of control.

25. Answer D is correct. Social support (Answer A), health habits (Answer B), feelings of control (Answer C) are all important to good health.

ANSWER KEY - PRACTICE TEST 3 - SHORT ANSWER

1. Health
2. Selye; alarm; resistance; exhaustion
3. widowed
4. worse; higher
5. psychosomatic
6. antigen; immune
7. psychoneuroimmunology
8. immune
9. hostility
10. emotional inhibition
11. optimistic; illusions
12. control
13. primary; secondary
14. coping
15. contact comfort; exercise
16. Emotion-focused; problem-focused
17. Reappraising
18. compare
19. reduce; cause
20. psychological
21. vulnerability; inhibition; coping
22. sixty-five percent
23. "pop-health"
24. either-or
25. emotional; bacteria

ANSWER KEY - PRACTICE TEST 4 - TRUE/FALSE

1. F	2. T	3. F	4. F	5. T
6. F	7. F	8. F	9. T	10. T
11. F	12. T	13. T	14. T	15. F
16. F	17. T	18. T	19. T	20. T
21. F	22. T	23. T	24. T	25. T

ANSWER KEY - PRACTICE TEST 5 - ESSAY

1.   A.   Air traffic controllers are likely to face a higher degree of daily irritation and uncontrollable events than fishermen.

       B.   Type A people, particularly if they have antagonistic hostility and experience greater stress.

       C.   Those with an external locus of control are less likely to feel they can predict and control their environments, and prediction and control reduce stress.

       D.   Generally, those with social networks experience buffers to stress.

       E.   Pessimistic explanatory styles result in the perception that the stressor is unchangeable, therefore these people will feel less control over the stress.

2.   A.   The alarm phase will be the most prominent as the person is being captured. Bodily resources will be mobilized as the person attempts to fight or flee.

       B.   Resistance will coincide with early captivity. Its duration is related to the victim's capacity to manage potentially overwhelming events. Signs of arousal will be prominent and bodily preparedness is the rule. Biologically, use of energy resources will be above normal. Psychologically, the victim is actively fighting the situation.

       C.   The timing of exhaustion depends on individual characteristics, such as coping styles. Biologically, it is signaled by bodily fatigue and susceptibility to illness. Psychologically, the person shows signs of giving up and wearing down.

3.   A.   Prolonged stress is capable of suppressing the disease and infection fighting cells of the immune system. As this happens, bodily defenses are impaired and susceptibility to symptoms increases.

       B.   Though the evidence is mixed, it is possible that the depression is contributing to his illness by affecting the immune system. It is also possible, however, that his continuous illness is contributing to the depression. It may be that poor health habits are causing both or that an entirely different thing is causing both. Finally, the depression and the illnesses could be mutually influencing each other.

       C.   David must examine his personality for antagonistic hostility; his personal style of evaluating and managing changes, daily hassles, and problems; the quality and quantity of his social relationships and interest; and everyday habits relating to rest exercise, and diet.

4.   A.   Margaret is rethinking the problem and using some denial.

       B.   The situation is being directly attacked with a problem-focused strategy.

       C.   Frank is reappraising the problem using social comparisons.

       D.   Tony is using an emotion-focused strategy.

       E.   Joan is trying to live with the problem.

CROSSWORD PUZZLE ANSWER KEY

ACROSS

4.   Selye
6.   control
8.   hostility
11.   resistance
13.   humor
14.   primary

DOWN

1.   poverty
2.   secondary
3.   health
5.   exhaustion
6.   coping
7.   relaxation
9.   pessimism
10.   supports
11.   reappraisal
12.   suppressors
13.   hassles

ANSWER KEYS FOR CHAPTER 16

ANSWER KEY - PRACTICE TEST 1 - MULTIPLE CHOICE

1. B (pp. 576-577) 2. A (pp. 576-577) 3. B (pp. 576) 4. A (p. 577)
5. B (pp. 579-580) 6. B (p. 582) 7. D (p. 584) 8. C (p. 584)
9. D (p. 586) 10. B (p. 586) 11. A (p. 587) 12. C (p. 588)
13. B (p. 591) 14. B (p. 592) 15. D (p. 593) 16. A (p. 595)
17. A (p. 596) 18. C (p. 599) 19. D (pp. 599-600) 20. A (p. 603
21. A (p. 606) 22. D (p. 606) 23. A (p. 609) 24. D (pp. 608-609)
25. C (p. 610)

ANSWER KEY - PRACTICE TEST 2 - MULTIPLE CHOICE

1. A 2. C 3. B 4. C
5. D 6. C 7. B 8. C
9. C 10. D 11. B 12. D
13. A 14. C 15. B 16. D
17. B 18. A 19. D 20. A
21. D 22. A 23. A 24. C
25. D

ANNOTATED ANSWER KEY - PRACTICE TEST 2

1. Answer A is correct. The behavior described in this question is maladaptive for the individual. Impaired judgment (Answer B) and lack of self-control (Answer D) relates to the legal definition of mental disorder and rests primarily on whether a person is aware of the consequences of his or her actions and can control his or her behavior. Violation of cultural standards (Answer C) involves a violation of a group standards and cultural rules.

2. Answer C is correct. Clinicians are encouraged to evaluate clients according to five axes. The third axis is medical conditions that are relevant to the disorder. The primary clinical problem (Answer A) is the first axis. Ingrained aspects of the client's personality (Answer B) is the second axis. Social and environmental problems that can make the disorder worse (Answer D) is the forth axis and the fifth axis is a global assessment of the client's overall level of functioning.

3. Answer B is correct. Rosenhan's famous study demonstrated how once a person has been given a diagnosis, as were the subjects in his study, other people begin to see that person primarily in terms of the label. The label becomes a self-fulfilling prophecy. An example of confusing serious mental disorders with normal problems (Answer A) is the diagnosis of "caffeine-induced sleep disorder." An example of the danger of overdiagnosis (Answer C) is the increase in the diagnosis of ADHD. The illusion of objectivity (Answer D) is demonstrated by the addition or removal of several diagnostic categories from the DSM by a vote.

4. Answer C is correct. The compilers of the DSM keep adding everyday problems to the manual. This confounds serious mental disorders with normal problems in living. Answers A, B, and D are all criticisms of the DSM but not the one represented by the inclusion of Disorder of Written Expression and Caffeine-Induced Sleep Disorder.

5. Answer D is correct. DSM advocates argue that Answers A, B, and C are all valid.

6. Answer C is correct. People who have a social phobia have a persistent, irrational fear of situations in which they will be observed by others. An antisocial personality disorder (Answer A) is a type of personality disorder in which people lack empathy, shame, remorse, or sorrow. They have no conscience. A generalized anxiety disorder (Answer B) is continuous, uncontrollable anxiety or worry that occurs more days than not in a six-month period and is not brought on by physical causes such as disease, drugs, or drinking too much coffee. Agoraphobia (Answer D) is the fear of being alone in a public place from which escape might be difficult or help unavailable.

7. Answer B is correct. Agoraphobia is the fear of being alone in a public place from which escape might be difficult or help unavailable. A social phobia (Answer A) is a persistent, irrational fear of situations in which they will be observed by others. Obsessive-compulsive disorder (Answer C) is characterized by recurrent, persistent, unwished-for thoughts or images and repetitive, ritualized, stereotyped behaviors that the person feels must be carried out to avoid disaster. Acute stress disorder (Answer D) consists of emotional symptoms that are common in people who have suffered traumatic experiences such as war, rape, other assaults, and natural disasters.

8. Answer C is correct. People who suffer from compulsions feel they have no control over them but if they try to refrain from engaging in the behavior, they feel mounting anxiety that is relieved only by giving in to the compulsion. Feelings of depression (Answer A) are not part of the obsessive-compulsive disorder. Obsessive-compulsive disorder is an anxiety disorder whereas depression is a mood disorder. A phobia (Answer B) is an unrealistic fear of a specific situation, activity, or thing. Answer D is incorrect because a correct answer is given.

9. Answer C is correct. Depression is accompanied by physical changes. The depressed person may stop eating or overeat, have difficulty falling asleep or sleeping through the night, lose sexual desire, have trouble concentrating, and feel tired all the time. A phobia (Answer A) is an unrealistic fear of a specific situation, activity, or thing. Mania (Answer B) is an abnormally high state of exhilaration. The symptoms are the opposite of those in depression. Panic disorder (Answer D) is an anxiety disorder in which a person has recurring attacks of intense fear or panic, with feelings of impending doom or death.

10. Answer D is correct. Symptoms of mania (Answer A) are the opposite of those of depression. Instead of feeling unambitious, hopeless, and powerless, the manic person feels full of ambitions, plans, and power. Most manic episodes are a sign of bipolar disorder (Answer B), in which depression alternates with mania. Bipolar disorder is one of the mood disorders (Answer C).

11. Answer B is correct. Drugs that increase the levels of serotonin and norepinephrine sometimes alleviate symptoms of depression and are called "antidepressants." They do not affect dopamine levels (Answers A and D). They do not decrease levels of serotonin and norepinephrine (Answer C).

12. Answer D is correct. According to the social view of depression, reasons that women are more likely than men to suffer from depression is that women are more likely to have experienced childhood sexual abuse and other forms of violence (Answer A), to lack fulfilling jobs or family relations (Answer B), and to be primary caretakers (Answer C). Mothers are especially vulnerable to depression: The more children they have, the more likely women are to become depressed.

13. Answer A is correct. Cognitive explanations propose that depression results from particular habits of thinking and interpreting events. The theory evolved into the idea that some depression results from having a hopeless and pessimistic explanatory style. Social explanations (Answer B) include such variables as jobs, family relations, a history of violence, and social-economic conditions. Attachment explanations emphasize the importance to well-being of affiliation and attachment. Biological explanations (Answer D) account for depression in terms of genetics and brain chemistry.

14. Answer C is correct. Paranoid personality disorder is characterized by a pervasive, unfounded suspiciousness and mistrust of other people, irrational jealousy, secretiveness, and doubt about the loyalty of others. Narcissistic personality disorder is characterized by an exaggerated sense of self-importance and self-absorption. Answer A diagnosis Bob correctly but identifies Babs as an antisocial personality disorder. Antisocial personality disorder is characterized by the lack of empathy, the ability to take another person's perspective, lack of shame, guilt or the ability to feel remorse or sorrow for immoral actions. Answers B and D provide the correct diagnosis for Babs but not for Bob.

15. Answer B is correct. When people with antisocial personality disorder are caught in a lie or crime, they may seem sincerely sorry and promise to make amends, but it is all an act. They are unlikely to become nervous (Answer A), angry (Answer C) or upset (Answer D). They can lie, charm, seduce, and manipulate others.

16. Answer D is correct. One theory maintains that people who are antisocial, hyperactive, addicted, or impulsive have a common inherited disorder. These conditions all involve problems in behavioral inhibition--the ability to control responses to frustration or to inhibit a pleasurable action that may have unpleasant repercussions. Answer A is incorrect because antisocial, hyperactive, addicted, and impulsive qualities do not all fit types of personality disorders, though they may be accounted for by other disorders. They do not share the same behaviors (Answer B) or explanatory styles (Answer D).

17. Answer B is correct. Several routes lead to the development of antisocial personality disorder: Having a genetic disposition toward impulsivity, addiction, or hyperactivity, which leads to rule breaking and crime; being neglected or rejected by parents; having brain damage as a result of birth complications or being beaten in childhood; and living in a culture or environment that rewards and fosters certain antisocial traits. These are not associated with mood disorders (Answer A) or dissociative disorders (Answer D) nor are they considered foundations for any mental disorder (Answer C).

18. Answer A is correct. Psychogenic amnesia occurs when a person "forgets" only information that is threatening to the self. A person in a fugue state not only forgets his or her identity, but gives up customary habits and wanders far from home. Answer B is incorrect because while people with psychogenic amnesia might forget a trauma, the central feature of psychogenic fugue is forgetting one's identity and habits and this feature is not included in Answer B. Forgetting one's name (Answer C) is not a central feature of psychogenic amnesia and forgetting specific incidents is not a symptom of fugue. The amount of time one forgets (Answer D) is not the defining characteristic of these two disorders.

19.   Answer D is correct. Those who believe that dissociative identity disorder is a real disorder have used changes in physiological patterns (Answer A) that occur when the person manifests different personalities. Answer B, the media, has also played a major role in fostering the DID diagnosis. Finally, clinicians may actually be creating the disorder through the power of suggestion (Answer C).

20.   Answer A is correct. The DSM-IV definition of substance abuse is "a maladaptive pattern of substance use leading to clinically significant impairment or distress." Symptoms of such impairment include the failure to fulfill role obligations at work, home, or school; use of the drug in hazardous situations; recurrent arrests for drug use; and persistent conflicts with others about use of the drug or caused by the drug. Michael demonstrates most of these. Answer B is incorrect because Michael's drinking has gone beyond problem drinking. While Michael probably has developed tolerance (Answer C), that is not described in the question. While most researchers and the public accept the biological model of addiction, not all agree with the concept that alcoholism is a disease (Answer D).

21.   Answer A is correct. Because having biological relatives who are alcoholic contributes to a person's risk of becoming alcoholic, proponents of the biological model believe that alcoholism involves an inherited predisposition. Genes may also affect a person's level of response to alcohol, which is an independent risk factor in becoming an alcoholic. Answers B and C are used to refute the biological model and to support the learning model. Answer D is incorrect because there is considerable research that supports the biological model.

22.   Answer A is correct. Positive symptoms of schizophrenia refer to symptoms that involve an exaggeration or distortion of normal thinking processes and behavior such as bizarre delusions, hallucinations, disorganized, incoherent speech, or grossly disorganized and inappropriate behavior. Elizabeth is exhibiting many of these symptoms. Negative symptoms (Answer B) involve the loss of former traits and abilities and are more subtle. They include loss of motivation; poverty of speech; emotional flatness (Answer D) such as unresponsive facial expressions, poor eye contact, and diminished emotionality. Catatonic symptoms (Answer D) include rigid postures and motionlessness.

23.   Answer A is correct. Bad parenting is no longer considered to be a contributing factor to the development of schizophrenia while Answers B, C, and D all increase the likelihood of its occurrence.

24. Answer C is correct. The vulnerability-stress model is an interactive theory. In this view, genes or brain damage alone will not inevitably produce schizophrenia, and a vulnerable person who lives in a good environment may never show full-fledged signs of it. Combinations of risk factors increase the likelihood of schizophrenia. Gary has both the vulnerability and stressful environmental factors. Harry (Answer A) has only the vulnerability factors while Jerry (Answer B) has only the stressful environment risk. According to this model, we can identify those at higher risk, so Answer D is incorrect.

25. Answer D is correct. Some individuals with schizophrenia (but not all of them) have decreased brain weight (Answer A), a decrease in the volume of the temporal lobe or limbic regions, reduced numbers of neurons in specific layers of the prefrontal cortex (Answer B), or enlarged ventricles (Answer C).

ANSWER KEY - PRACTICE TEST 3 - SHORT ANSWER

1. cultural
2. Diagnostic and Statistical Manual of Mental Disorders (DSM-IV)
3. overdiagnosis
4. Generalized
5. post-traumatic stress disorder
6. interpret
7. social phobia
8. agoraphobia
9. Obsessions; compulsions; anxiety
10. behavioral, cognitive
11. Depression
12. attachment
13. stability; lack of control
14. personality
15. inhibition
16. vulnerability-stress; stresses
17. amnesia; fugue
18. common; clinicians
19. sociocognitive
20. biochemistry
21. learning
22. psychosis
23. delusions; hallucinations
24. genetic; prenatal
25. virus

ANSWER KEY - PRACTICE TEST 4 - TRUE/FALSE

1. F	2. F	3. T	4. F	5. T
6. T	7. T	8. F	9. F	10. F
11. T	12. T	13. F	14. T	15. F
16. F	17. T	18. F	19. T	20. F
21. T	22. F	23. F	24. T	25. T

ANSWER KEY - PRACTICE TEST 4 - ESSAY

1. A. This definition considers the violation of norms and standards to be abnormal. Jason violates norms governing social interaction, appearance and good taste.
    B. Maladaptive behavior is behavior that results in disharmony and distress. Jason is behaving disruptively toward others.
    C. This definition relies on signs of distress. Jason is apparently seeking forgiveness based on some internal experience of guilt or distress.
    D. Jason does not seem to be able to distinguish between acceptable and unacceptable behavior, or, if he makes this distinction, he is unable to control himself.

2. A. Included
    B. Excluded
    C. Excluded
    D. Included
    E. Included
    Explanation: The DSM-IV classifies disorders on five axes: primary diagnosis, ingrained aspects of personality, relevant medical conditions, current stressors and overall level of functioning. The included items reflect those axes and the others do not.

3. A. Abnormal: panic attack
    B. Abnormal: obsessive-compulsive disorder
    C. Normal
    D. Abnormal: phobia
    E. Abnormal: post traumatic stress disorder

4.   A.   Mood disorders involve emotional, behavioral, cognitive and physical symptoms.

        B.   In bipolar disorder, mania alternates with depression.

        C.   Antidepressant drugs raise the levels of the neurotransmitters, serotonin and norepinephrine.

        D.   There is no change.

        E.   Negative thinking seems to be both a result and a cause of depression.

        F.   Repeated failure can be a source of learned helplessness, a characteristic related to depression.

5.   A.   Josephine has delusions. The fact that she believes that airplanes dirty the streets and sidewalks by dripping oil, that pilots have a power called "telectic penetration" and that she is being used as a radar are all examples of delusions.

        B.   Josephine is experiencing hallucinations. She hears the pilots talking to her about her location.

        C.   Josephine is demonstrating incoherent associations, including "telectic penetration," her latitude and longitude, and airplanes.

        D.   Josephine's behavior is inappropriate in that she withdraws and is unable to speak.

        E.   From the description, it is unclear if Josephine is exhibiting emotional flatness.

CROSSWORD PUZZLE ANSWER KEY

ACROSS		DOWN	
2.	mood	1.	social
4.	depression	3.	bipolar
5.	anxiety	5.	agoraphobia
6.	dissociative	7.	abuse
9.	mania	8.	maladaptive
12.	disease	10.	amnesia
13.	psychosis	11.	antisocial
14.	schizophrenia		
15.	attachment		
16.	hopelessness		

ANSWER KEYS FOR CHAPTER 17

ANSWER KEY - PRACTICE TEST 1 - MULTIPLE CHOICE

1. A (p. 618)   2. A (pp. 618-619)   3. D (pp. 619-620) 4. C (p. 619)
5. D (pp. 620-621) 6. A (p. 622)   7. B (p. 623)   8. D (p. 620)
9. B (p. 624)   10. A (p. 624)   11. C (p. 626)   12. D (pp. 625-626)
13. C (p. 625)   14. A (p. 627)   15. B (p. 628)   16. C (pp. 624-625)
17. C (pp. 643-644) 18. A (p. 6353   19. D (p. 636)   20. C (p. 636)
21. B (p. 639)   22. A (p. 639)   23. D (pp. 640-641) 24. B (p. 641)
25. B (p. 646)

ANSWER KEY - PRACTICE TEST 2 - MULTIPLE CHOICE

1. C   2. D   3. A   4. B
5. D   6. A   7. C   8. C
9. D   10. C   11. A   12. C
13. C   14. C   15. C   16. B
17. A   18. B   19. D   20. A
21. D   22. C   23. A   24. D
25. D

ANNOTATED ANSWER KEY - PRACTICE TEST 2

1. Answer C is correct. Antidepressant drugs are used primarily in the treatment of depression, anxiety, phobias, and obsessive-compulsive disorder. Answers A and B are incorrect because even though tranquilizers may help an anxious person temporarily feel calmer, they are not considered the treatment of choice over a long period of time. Answer D is incorrect because lithium is used for bipolar disorder.

2. Answer D is correct. Antipsychotic drugs can have potentially dangerous effects including a neurological disorder called tardive dyskinesia (Answer A). For some patients, they remove or lessen the most dramatic symptoms, but they usually cannot restore normal thought patterns or relationships (Answer B). They allow many people to be released from hospitals, but often these individuals cannot care for themselves (Answer C).

3. Answer A is correct. Monoamine oxidase inhibitors and tricyclic drugs are antidepressants that elevate the level of norepinephrine and serotonin. "Minor" tranquilizers, such as Valium or Xanax , are classified as depressants and are often prescribed by physicians for patients who complain of anxiety (Answer B). A special category of drug, a salt called lithium carbonate, is often successful in helping people who suffer from bipolar disorder (Answer C). Antipsychotic drugs, or major tranquilizers, include chlorpromazine, haloperidol, clozapine, and risperidone are prescribed for a psychosis (Answer D).

4. Answer B is correct. Tricyclic drugs are a category of antidepressants. Neuroleptics (Answer A), lithium (Answer C), and tranquilizers (Answer D) are not antidepressants. Neuroleptics are used for psychosis, lithium is used for bipolar disorder, and tranquilizers are used for anxiety.

5. Answer D is correct. New drugs often promise quick and effective cures. Yet the placebo effect ensures that some people will respond positively to new drugs just because of the enthusiasm surrounding them. After a while, when placebo effects decline, many drugs turn out to be neither as effective as promised nor as widely applicable (Answer A). Another important research limitation on drug testing is that new drugs are often tested on only a few hundred people for only a few weeks--even when the drug is one that patients might take for many years (Answer B). The challenge with drugs is to find the "therapeutic window," the amount that is enough but not too much (Answer C),

6. Answer A is correct. ECT is most effective with suicidally depressed people, for whom there is a risk in waiting until antidepressants or psychotherapy can take effect. ECT is not used for anxiety (Answer B) nor for people with moderate depression (Answer C). ECT is a controversial procedure that has made a dramatic return, therefore Answer D is incorrect.

7. Answer C is correct. Individuals who take antidepressants without learning how to cope have higher relapse rates than those who receive some other type of help. Answers A and B are incorrect because while medication alone might provide short-term relief, to decrease the likelihood of relapse, a person should learn ways to improve their coping while taking medication. Answer D is incorrect because the question does not provide enough information to determine which treatment approach is best for Stan.

8. Answer C is correct. In psychoanalysis and some other psychodynamic therapies, the client lies on a couch and uses free association to say whatever comes to mind. The purpose is to explore the unconscious dynamics of personality. Transference is another technique (different from the one described in the question) of psychodynamic psychotherapies, therefore Answer A is incorrect. Flooding is a technique that is part of behavioral approaches (Answer B), but it is not the technique described in the question. While transference is a technique of psychodynamic psychotherapies (Answer D), it is not the one described in the question. Transference involves the patient's transfer of emotional elements of his or her inner life outward onto the analyst.

9. Answer D is correct. Freud believed that intensive probing of the past and of the mind would produce insight--the patient's moment of truth (Answer A), the awareness of the reason for his or her symptoms and anguish. With insight and emotional release, the symptoms would disappear (Answer B) and this is the key to therapeutic gains in psychodynamic approaches (Answer C).

10. Answer C is correct. Systematic desensitization is a behavioral approach using a step-by-step process of "desensitizing" a client to a feared object or experience. It combines relaxation training with a systematic hierarchy of stimuli leading gradually to the one that is most feared. Answer A is incorrect because the technique described in the question is not a cognitive technique and it is not part of rational emotive therapy. The technique is not a humanistic technique (Answer B), nor is it flooding (which is a behavioral technique). Answer D is correct that the approach described in the question is a behavioral technique, but it is systematic desensitization and not flooding.

11. Answer A is correct. Cognitive therapies aim to help clients identify the beliefs and expectations that might be unnecessarily prolonging their unhappiness. The aim of humanistic approaches is to help people feel better about themselves. Answers B and C are incorrect because cognitive approaches focus more on thinking than on behaviors. Behavioral approaches focus on behaviors. In addition, humanistic therapies do not necessarily focus on changing families (family therapies focus on this) and on insight into the past (psychodynamic therapies focus on this). Answer D correctly identifies that cognitive approaches focus on thoughts, but it incorrectly matches humanistic approaches with and emphasis on skills. Behavioral approaches teach new skills.

12. Answer C is correct since cognitive approaches focus on our thoughts and developing rational responses to them. Answer A would be an approach taken by a psychodynamic therapist. Answer B represents a behavioral approach to procrastination. Answer D describes a humanistic approach.

13. Answer C is correct since Dr. Smith is borrowing a method from here, an idea from there, and avoiding strong allegiances to one theory or school of thought. Dr. Smith is using methods from the behavioral (Answer A), cognitive (Answer B), and humanistic (Answer D) approaches.

14. Answer C is correct. The clubhouse model is a comprehensive program to help schizophrenics function in the everyday world. It provides rehabilitation counseling, job and skills training, and a support network. It is not a self-help group (Answer A) since professionals are involved and it provides more than just group work. This model also provides more than just behavioral training (Answer B). Answer D is incorrect since ongoing depth psychotherapy is generally not used for people with schizophrenia and so it is not part of this approach.

15. Answer C is correct. Participants in self-help groups say that the primary benefits they get are the awareness that they are not alone, encouragement when they are feeling down, and help in feeling better about themselves. Although self-help groups can be immensely therapeutic, they are not the same as psychotherapy that focuses on specific problems and they are not designed to help people with serious psychological difficulties (Answers A and B). Since a correct answer is given, Answer D is incorrect.

16. Answer B is correct. Many psychotherapists assume that measuring psychotherapy is a futile task. Most believe that clinical experience is more valuable than research. But scientific psychologists are concerned that when therapists fail to keep up with empirical findings in the field--about the most beneficial methods for particular problems, about ineffective or potentially harmful techniques, and about basic research on topics relevant to their practice, their clients may pay the price. This is called the scientist-practitioner gap. Answer A is incorrect because this debate is not among scientists and paraprofessionals. Answers C and D are incorrect because the terms used are very similar and refer to people on the same side of the issue.

17. Answer A is correct. People who receive almost any professional treatment improve more than people who do not get help. Answer B is incorrect because the people who do the best in psychotherapy have less serious problems and are motivated to improve. Answer C is incorrect because while it is true that in some cases psychotherapy is harmful, it has not been found that it is harmful in 30 percent of all cases. Psychotherapy is not helpful in all types of psychological problems (Answer D). For example, traditional "talk" therapies are not effective for most schizophrenics.

18.   Answer B is correct. Successful therapy depends, among other things, on the bond between the client and therapist which is called the therapeutic alliance. In a good therapeutic alliance, both parties respect and understand one another, feel reaffirmed, and work toward a common goal. This is more important than providing information (Answer D). Establishing a successful therapeutic alliance does not mean that the therapist and client must be the same race, gender, sexual orientation, or religion (Answer A). Therapists whose efforts are most successful tend to be empathic, expressive, and actively invested in the interaction with the client--as opposed to being an "impartial," detached observer in the manner of Freud (Answer C).

19.   Answer D is correct. Clients who are likely to do well in psychotherapy have a strong sense of self, are motivated, have family support and a personal style of dealing actively with problems. No research has been cited that found the characteristics in Answers A, B, and C to be associated with positive outcomes in therapy.

20.   Answer A is correct. Cognitive therapy's greatest success has been in the treatment of mood disorders, especially depression. Answer B is incorrect since other approaches (behavioral family interventions) have been found useful for people with schizophrenia. Psychodynamic and humanistic approaches are best for self-exploration (Answer C). Since Answers B and C are incorrect, Answer D must also be incorrect.

21.   Answer D is correct because exposure therapy (Answer A) and flooding (Answer B) are both types of behavior therapy (Answer C) used for agoraphobia.

22.   Answer C is correct. Cognitive-behavior therapies (Answers A and B) are designed for specific identifiable problems, but sometimes people seek therapy for less clearly defined reasons--they may wish to introspect about their feelings and lives, find solace and courage or explore moral issues. Psychodynamic and existential approaches may be well suited for such individuals. Solution focused therapy (Answer D) is a type of family therapy and focuses on helping clients specify and achieve their goals.

23.   Answer A is correct. Some therapists so zealously believe in the prevalence of certain problems that they inadvertently induce the client to produce the symptoms they are looking for. It is also the mechanism by which people create pseudomemories--constructed fantasies shaped by the suggestions and expectations of the therapist. It is not harmful for clients and therapists to disagree sometimes (Answer B) nor is it expected that clients can receive immediate appointments (Answer C). Since Answers B and C are not considered harmful, Answer D is incorrect.

24. Answer D is correct. Under no circumstances is it acceptable for a therapist to engage in sexual relations or other intimate behaviors with a client. Answers A, B, and C are all incorrect.

25. Answer D is correct. Psychotherapy can help you make decisions and clarify your values and goals. It can teach you new skills and ways of thinking. It can help you get along better with your family and break out of repetitive, destructive family patterns. It can get you through bad times when no one seems to care or understand.

ANSWER KEY - PRACTICE TEST 3 - SHORT ANSWER

1. schizophrenia; psychoses
2. tardive dyskinesia
3. antidepressant
4. Lithium carbonate
5. relapse
6. prefrontal lobotomy
7. electroconvulsive therapy
8. psychodynamic; free association
9. transference
10. systematic desensitization
11. exposure (or flooding)
12. evidence; interpretations
13. emotive behavior
14. client-centered
15. Family
16. research
17. coercive
18. empathy; genuineness
19. cognitive; anxiety
20. behavioral
21. coercion
22. multiple personality disorder
23. Self-help
24. Community; Rehabilitation
25. evidence

ANSWER KEY - PRACTICE TEST 4 - TRUE/FALSE

1. F	2. F	3. T	4. T	5. T
6. T	7. F	8. F	9. T	10. T
11. F	12. T	13. T	14. F	15. T
16. T	17. F	18. F	19. F	20. F
21. F	22. T	23. F	24. T	25. T

ANSWER KEY - PRACTICE TEST 5 - ESSAY

1. Medical treatments feature drugs and other forms of organic intervention. Drugs are very useful for psychotic disorders, and, in combination with psychotherapy, they are useful for other disorders, including: major depression, bipolar disorder, some anxiety disorders.

    Psychotherapies attempt to change thinking, emotional and behavioral processes. They're designed to help clients think about their lives in new ways in order to find solutions to the problems that plague them. They have been shown to be very useful with mood disorders, anxiety disorders, eating disorders, chronic fatigue syndrome.

    Community services tend to be problem-oriented and offer counseling, support groups, and skills training. They can be useful for those with mental or physical disabilities, including schizophrenia.

2. A. Anxiety disorders: minor tranquilizers
    B. Mood disorders: antidepressants
    C. Psychotic disorders: antipsychotics

    Drug treatments are limited by the complications of side effects and finding the right dosage. They may not be effective for everyone or may work effectively only in the short-term. Often there is little research on the effects of long-term usage. Moreover, drugs relieve symptoms and do nothing to help people learn new coping skills.

3. Psychodynamic therapies strive for insight into the unconscious processes that produce a problem. With insight and emotional release, symptoms should disappear. The goal of treatment is not to solve an individual's immediate problem, since it is only the tip of the iceberg. Techniques include free association and transference. Psychoanalysis was the original model proposed by Freud in which a patient was seen multiple times in a week for many years.

Cognitive therapy aims to correct distorted, unrealistic thoughts, beliefs and expectations. Techniques vary but revolve around examining negative thoughts, formulating reasonable responses and using realistic perspectives.

Behavior therapy attempts to eliminate maladaptive responses and behavior patterns. Techniques are based on learning principles and include systematic desensitization, aversive conditioning, flooding and operant strategies.

Humanistic therapy is designed to increase self-esteem, positive feelings and self-actualization. Approaches include client-centered therapy and existential therapy. Client-centered therapy utilizes unconditional positive regard, empathy and genuineness.

Family therapy aims to correct the forces in the family that are contributing to the expression of a problem. The family may be analyzed from a multigenerational standpoint, using a genogram, or as a social system.

The shared features include: support factors, which allow the client to feel secure and safe; learning factors, which allow the client to see and experience his or her problems in a new light and think about how to solve them; and action factors, which allow the client to reduce fears, take risks and make necessary changes.

4.   Client features: commitment to therapy, willingness to work on their problems, and expectations of success; cooperativeness with suggested interventions and positive feelings during the therapy session.

Therapist features: empathy, warmth, genuineness and imagination; make clients feel respected, accepted, and understood; expressive and actively invested in the interaction with the client.

Therapeutic alliance: a relationship in which both parties respect and understand one another, feel reaffirmed and work toward a common goal.

5.   Coercion by the therapist to accept the therapist's advice, sexual intimacies, or other unethical behavior. Bias on the part of a therapist who doesn't understand the client because of the client's gender, race, religion, sexual orientation, or ethnic group. Therapist-induced disorders can be harmful. When a therapist so zealously believes in the prevalence of certain problems that they induce the client to produce the symptoms they are looking for.

CROSSWORD PUZZLE KEY

ACROSS

1. desensitization
7. placebo
8. lithium
12. group
13. alliance
14. family
15. psychosurgery
16. psychotherapy

DOWN

1. dyskinesia
2. narrative
3. tricyclic
4. unconditional
5. transference
6. existential
7. psychoanalysis
9. humanistic
10. aversive
11. flooding

ANSWER KEYS FOR APPENDIX A

ANSWER KEY - PRACTICE TEST 1 - MULTIPLE CHOICE

1. C (p.A-1)	2. A (p.A-2)	3. D (p.A-4)	4. A (pp. A-3,4)
5. B (p.A-4)	6. D (p.A-5)	7. C (p.A-6)	8. A (p.A-7)
9. C (p.A-8)	10. B (A-8)		

ANSWER KEY - PRACTICE TEST 2 - MULTIPLE CHOICE

1. B	2. C	3. A	4. D
5. B	6. A	7. B	8. B
9. C	10. D		

ANNOTATED ANSWER KEY - PRACTICE TEST 2

1. Answer B is correct. A frequency distribution shows how often each possible score actually occurred in a set of scores. A normal curve (Answer A) shows a pattern of a distribution of scores that when plotted in a frequency polygon, has a symmetrical, bell-shaped form. A frequency polygon (Answer C) is a line graph. A histogram (Answer D) is a bar graph. Since Dr. Starr did not graph the scores, Answers B, C, and D are all incorrect.

2. Answer C is correct because a histogram is a bar graph and a polygon is a line graph. Null and alternative (Answer B) refer to two types of hypotheses. Histograms and polygons are types of graphs, therefore Answer B is incorrect. Answer C describes the opposite relationship to that given in the question. Answer D describes two types of curves, rather than two types of graphs.

3. Answer A is correct since the mode is the score that occurs most often. Seventy-seven is the only score that occurs more than once in this distribution of scores. Therefore Answers B, C, and D are incorrect.

4. Answer D is correct. The median is the midpoint in a set of scores ordered from highest to lowest. In any set of scores, the same number of scores falls above the median as below it. Therefore, Answers A, B, and C are incorrect.

5. Answer B is correct. The range is the simplest measure of variability and is found by subtracting the lowest score from the highest one. Therefore Answers A, C, and D are incorrect.

6.   Answer A is correct. Deviation scores for numbers above the mean will be positive, those for numbers below the mean will be negative, and the positive scores will exactly balance the negative ones. In other words, the sum of the deviation scores will be zero. That is a problem, since the next step in our calculation is to add. The solution is to square all the deviation scores. This step gets rid of negative values. The mean of the deviation scores (Answer B) is not used nor is the square root of the deviation scores (Answer C). Therefore, Answer D is also incorrect.

7.   Answer B is correct. To compute a z-score, you subtract the mean of a distribution from the raw score and divide by the standard deviation. Therefore 8 (raw score) minus 10 (mean) is -2, which is then divided by 2 to equal -1. Therefore Answers A, C, and D are incorrect.

8.   Answer B is correct. The direction of a curve's skewness is determined by the position of the long tail, not by the position of the bulge. Since there are more low scores, the bulge would be on the left and since there are few high scores, the "tail" would be longer on the right. When the "tail" of the curve is longer on the right than on the left, as it would be in this example, the curve is said to be positively skewed. This would not be a normal curve (Answer A) since it would not be symmetrical and bell-shaped. The curve would not be bimodal (Answer C) since there are not two high points as there would be on a bimodal curve. Answer D is incorrect since a negatively skewed curve would result with the opposite set of scores; many high scores (causing a bulge on the right) and few low scores (causing a tail on the left).

9.   Answer C is correct since the null hypothesis expresses the possibility that the experimental manipulations will have no effect on the subjects' behavior. If the experimental manipulations had no effect, then any differences between experimental and control groups must be due to chance fluctuations. Both standard deviations (Answer A) and skew (Answer B) are used to describe a set of scores. Once descriptive statistics have described the effects of the experimental manipulations, then inferential statistics are used to determine whether any differences between the experimental and control groups are true differences (Answer D) or they have occurred by chance. If the null hypothesis is true, then we know the differences are not true ones and they must have occurred by chance.

10.   Answer D is true. If experimental results are found to be statistically significant, it does suggest that the results are unlikely to have occurred by chance alone (Answer A). However, some cautions are in order. Statistical significance does not mean that results are necessarily psychologically interesting or important (Answer B) and a large sample increases the likelihood of reliable results (Answer C).

ANSWER KEY - PRACTICE TEST 3 - SHORT ANSWER

1. frequency
2. polygon
3. mean; mode
4. central
5. range; deviation; mean
6. percentages; z-scores
7. normal
8. negative
9. null
10. statistically

ANSWER KEY - PRACTICE TEST 4 - TRUE/FALSE

1. F	2. T	3. F	4. T	5. F
6. T	7. T	8. F	9. F	10. F

ANSWER KEY - PRACTICE TEST 4 - ESSAY

1.   A.   These descriptive statistics are measures of central tendency and describe data by a single, representative number.
   B.   These descriptive statistics measure variability and reflect the spread of obtained scores.
   C.   These statistical pictures are used to organize data in terms of an overall visual summary.
   D.   These transformations are used when scores are put in a standardized format for easier comparisons.

2.   A.   This statement is justified because the mean and mode are equal in a normal distribution.
   B.   This statement is unjustified because the normal distribution is symmetrical, with either side of the mean mirror-imaging the other.
   C.   This statement is justified because less than 16 percent of the population get a score about one standard deviation from the mean.
   D.   This statement is unjustified because this curve is likely to be skewed to the right given that basketball players are chosen for their height.

3.   A.   The null hypothesis is rejected whenever results are statistically significant.

   B.   Statistical significance occurs when differences between the experimental and control groups are very unlikely to be caused by chance or random errors.

ANSWER KEY FOR CROSSWORD PUZZLE

ACROSS		DOWN	
2.	frequency	1.	graph
5.	histogram	3.	polygon
8.	skewed	4.	distribution
9.	normal	6.	range
10.	median	7.	mean
13.	curve	10.	mode
15.	significant	11.	deviation
17.	null	12.	alternative
18.	percentile	14.	hypothesis
		16.	z-score

I WANT TO HEAR FROM **YOU!!**

To write the most helpful study guide possible, I need your reactions and ideas about this study guide. What did you like best and least. What would you like to have more or less of? How could it have been more helpful. **Please** jot down your suggestions, cut out this page, fold and tape or staple it and mail it to me.

Many thanks!!

Tina Stern, Ph.D.

****

1. Do you feel this study guide helped your grade in the course? If so, how? What was your grade in the course?

2. What did you like best about the study guide?

3. What did you like least about the study guide?

4. What would you add to, subtract from, or change about the study guide?

5. Please write any other comments, suggestions, or criticisms about the study guide.

OVER

Tina Stern, Ph.D.
Georgia Perimeter College
2101 Womack Rd.
Dunwoody, Georgia 30338